Franz Delitzsch, James Martin

Biblical Commentary on the Prophecies of Isaiah

Vol. I

Franz Delitzsch, James Martin

Biblical Commentary on the Prophecies of Isaiah
Vol. I

ISBN/EAN: 9783743399174

Manufactured in Europe, USA, Canada, Australia, Japa

Cover: Foto ©Lupo / pixelio.de

Manufactured and distributed by brebook publishing software (www.brebook.com)

Franz Delitzsch, James Martin

Biblical Commentary on the Prophecies of Isaiah

BIBLICAL COMMENTARY

ON

THE PROPHECIES OF ISAIAH.

BY

FRANZ DELITZSCH, D.D.,
PROFESSOR OF THEOLOGY.

Translated from the German,
BY
THE REV. JAMES MARTIN, B. A.

VOL. I.

EDINBURGH:
T. & T. CLARK, 38, GEORGE STREET.
MDCCCLXXXIV.

TABLE OF CONTENTS.

                              PAGE

INTRODUCTION TO THE PROPHETICAL BOOKS OF THE OLD TESTAMENT, .   1

THE PROPHECIES OF ISAIAH.

INTRODUCTION.

Time of the Prophet,	31
Arrangement of the Collection,	53
The Critical Questions,	56
Exposition in its existing state,	63

EXPOSITION.

FIRST HALF OF THE COLLECTION (CHAP. I.–XXXIX.).

I. PROPHECIES RELATING TO THE ONWARD COURSE OF THE GREAT MASS OF THE PEOPLE TOWARDS HARDENING OF HEART (CHAP. I.–VI.):

Opening Address concerning the Ways of Jehovah with His Ungrateful and Rebellious Nation (Chap. i. 2 sqq.),	73
The Way of general Judgment; or the Course of Israel from False Glory to the True (Chap. ii.–iv.),	110
Judgment of Devastation upon the Vineyard of Jehovah (Chap v.),	159
The Prophet's Account of his own divine Mission (Chap. vi.),	188

II. CONSOLATION OF IMMANUEL IN THE MIDST OF THE ASSYRIAN
OPPRESSIONS (CHAP. VII.-XII.):

Divine Sign of the Virgin's wondrous Son (Chap. vii.), . 206

Two Omens of the Immediate Future (Chap. viii. 1-4), . 228

Esoteric Addresses (Chap. viii. 5-xii.):

A. Consolation of Immanuel in the coming Darkness (Chap. viii. 5-ix. 6), ... 231

B. Jehovah's outstretched Hand (Chap. ix. 7-x. 4), . . 255

C. Destruction of the imperial Kingdom of the World, and Rise of the Kingdom of Jehovah in His Anointed (Chap. x. 5-xii.), ... 264

III. COLLECTION OF ORACLES CONCERNING THE HEATHEN (CHAP. XIII.-XXIII.):

Oracle concerning the Chaldeans, the Heirs of the Assyrians (Chap. xiii. 1-xiv. 27), ... 294

The Oracle concerning Philistia (Chap. xiv. 28-32), . . 317

The Oracle concerning Moab (Chap. xv. xvi.), . . . 321

The Oracle concerning Damascus and Israel (Chap. xvii.), . 339

Ethiopia's Submission to Jehovah (Chap. xviii.), . . 347

The Oracle concerning Egypt (Chap. xix.), . . . 354

Symbol of the Fall of Egypt and Ethiopia, and its Interpretation (Chap. xx.), ... 370

The Oracles concerning the Desert of the Sea (Babylon) (Chap. xxi. 1-10), ... 376

The Oracle concerning the Silence of Death (Edom) (Chap. xxi. 11, 12), ... 383

The Oracle in the Evening (against Arabia) (Chap. xxi. 13-17), 386

The Oracle concerning the Valley of Vision (Jerusalem) (Chap. xxii. 1-14), ... 389

Against Shebna the Steward (Chap. xxii. 15-25), . . 398

The Oracle concerning Tyre (Chap. xxiii.), . . . 404

IV. FINALE OF THE GREAT CATASTROPHE (CHAP. XXIV.-XXVII.), . 421

The Judgment upon the Earth (Chap. xxiv.), . . . 424

PAGE

The Fourfold Melodious Echo (Chap. xxv. xxvi.) :
  A. First Echo: Salvation of the Nations after the Fall of the
     imperial City (Chap. xxv. 1-8), .   .   .   436
  B. Second Echo: The Humiliation of Moab (Chap. xxv. 9-12),   441
  C. Third Echo : Israel brought back, or raised from the Dead
     (Chap. xxvi.), ...   443
  D. The Fourth Echo : The Fruit-bearing Vineyard under the
     Protection of Jehovah (Chap. xxvii. 2-6), .   .   455
Jehovah's chastising and saving Course towards Israel (Chap.
  xxvii. 7-13), ...   457

INTRODUCTION

TO THE

PROPHETICAL BOOKS OF THE OLD TESTAMENT.

THE prophetical histories are followed in the Old Testament canon by the prophetical books of prediction. The two together form the middle portion of the threefold canon, under the common name of נְבִיאִים. On account of their relative position in the canon, the former are also described as נְבִיאִים הָרִאשֹׁנִים, the first prophets, and the latter הָאַחֲרוֹנִים, the last prophets. In the Masora this central portion is sometimes designated as אִשְׁלְמָתָא, possibly because it exhibits a complete and homogeneous whole. The first prophets are in that case distinguished from the last, as אִשְׁלמתא קדמיתא and אשלמתא תנינא.

The *thorah* is indeed also a prophetical work, since Moses, the mediator through whom the law was revealed, was for that very reason a prophet without an equal (Deut. xxxiv. 10); and even the final codification of the great historical law-book possessed a prophetical character (Ezra ix. 11). But it would not have been right to include the *thorah* (Pentateuch) in that portion of the canon which is designated as "the prophets" (*nebiim*), inasmuch as, although similar in character, it is not similar in rank to the other prophetical books. It stands by itself as perfectly unique—the original record which regulated on all sides the being and life of Israel as the chosen nation, and to which all other prophecy in Israel stood in a derivative relation. And this applies not to prophecy alone, but to all the later writings. The *thorah* was not only the type of the prophetic histories, but of the non-prophetic, the priestly, political, and popular histories also. The former followed the Jehovistic or Deuteronomic type, the latter the Elohistic. The *thorah* unites the prophetical and (so to speak) hagiographical styles of historical composition in a manner which is peculiar to itself, and not to be met with in any of the works included among the נביאים ראשנים.

Those who imagine that it is only because of their later origin, that the historical works which are found among the hagiographa have not found their appropriate place among the " first prophets," have evidently no idea whatever of this diversity in the style of historical writing. Ezra—whom we have good reason for regarding as the author of the larger " book of the Kings," which the chronicler refers to under the title of " the story of the book of the Kings" (*midrash sepher hammelacim*, 2 Chron. xxiv. 27), a compilation relating to the history of Israel, to which he had appended the history of the time of the restoration as the concluding part—is never called a prophet (*nabi*), and in fact was not one. The chronicler—who not only had before him our book of Samuel, which has been so arbitrarily divided into two parts, and our book of Kings, which has been just as arbitrarily divided in the same manner, but used as his principal authority the book of Ezra just referred to, and who worked out from this the compendium of history which lies before us, concluding with the memorabilia of Ezra, which we possess in a distinct form as the book of Ezra—also asserts no claim to be a prophet, and, judging from the liturgico-historical purpose of his work, is more likely to have been a priest. Nehemiah, from whose memorabilia our book of Nehemiah is an extract arranged in conformity with the book of Ezra, was, as we well know, not a prophet, but a *Tirsâta*,[1] *i.e.* a royal Persian governor, and at the same time an Israelitish patriot, whose prayerful heart was set upon the welfare of his people, and who had performed good service in connection with the restoration of Jerusalem by the erection of buildings and the introduction of reforms. The book of Esther, with its religious features kept as they are in the background,

---

[1] The title *Tirshatha* is probably to be explained according to the Armenian *tir-sât*, " lord of the kingdom or province." *Shatha* is another form of the terminations to such names of towns as Artaxata (= Artasata, for *sât* is equivalent to the Persian *khsatra*), Samosata, etc.

is as far removed as possible from the prophetic style of historical composition: it differs indeed from this quite as much as the feast of purim—that Jewish carnival—differs from the feast of passover, the Israelitish Christmas. It does appear surprising, however, that the book of Ruth should stand among the hagiographa. This little book is so similar in character to the concluding portion of the book of Judges (ch. xvii.-xxi.), that it might be placed between Judges and Samuel. And in all probability it did stand there originally, but for liturgical reasons it was added to the so-called five *megilloth* (festal rolls), which follow one another in our editions, so to speak, according to the calendar of feasts of the ecclesiastical year: for the Song of Solomon is the lesson for the eighth day of the feast of passover; Ruth, that of the second day of the feast of *Shabuoth* (pentecost); Kinoth (Lamentations), that of the ninth Abib; Koheleth (Ecclesiastes), that of the third day of the feast of tabernacles; and Esther, that of the feast of purim, which fell in the middle of Adar.

This is also the simplest answer to the question why the Lamentations of Jeremiah are not placed among the prophetic writings, and appended, as we should expect, to the collection of Jeremiah's prophecies. The Psalms are placed first among the hagiographa—although David might be called a prophet (Acts ii. 30), and Asaph is designated "the seer"—for the simple reason that they do not belong to the literature of prophecy, but to that of the *shir Jehovah*, *i.e.* the sacred (liturgical) lyric poetry. Their prophetic contents rest entirely upon a lyric ground, whereas it is the very reverse with the Lamentations of Jeremiah, the lyric contents of which, though less prophetic in themselves, presuppose throughout the official position and teaching of Jeremiah the prophet. The canonical *nebiim* or prophets embrace only the writings of such persons as were called to proclaim the word of God publicly, whether in writing or by word of mouth; not like the priests, according to definite modes prescribed by the law, but in a free unfettered manner, by virtue of a special gift and calling. The word *nabi* is to be regarded, as we may judge from its Arabic flexion, not as a passive, but as an active form; in fact, as an emphatic form of the active participle, denoting the proclaimer, publisher, speaker, namely, of God and of His secrets. The oldest use of the word (*vid.* Gen. xx. 7, cf. xviii. 17-19, and Ps. cv. 15), which was revived by the chronicler, is incomparably less restricted in its meaning than the later use. But when used to designate the middle portion of the Old Testament canon, although the word is not so limited as in Amos vii. 14, where it signifies a man who has passed through a school of the prophets and been trained in intercourse with other prophets, and has made prophetic teaching from the very first the exclusive profession of his life; yet it is employed in a sense connected with the organization of the theocratic life, as the title given to those who stood forward as public teachers by virtue of a divine call and divine revelations, and who therefore not only possessed the gift (*charisma*) of prophecy, but performed the duties of a prophet both in preaching and writing, and held an office to which, at least on Ephraimitish soil, the institution of schools of the prophets gave the distinct stamp of a separate order. This will serve to explain the fact that the book of Daniel was not placed among the *nebiim*. Daniel himself was not a prophet in this sense. Not only was the mode in which the divine revelations were made to him a different one from the prevailing ἐπίπνοια προφητική, as Julius Africanus observes in his writing to Origen concerning Susanna, but he did not hold the office of a prophet; and for this reason even the Talmud (*b. Megilla* 3a), when speaking of the relation in which the prophets after the captivity stood to him, says, "They stood above him, for they were prophets; but he was not a prophet." "A distinction must be drawn," as Witsius has said, "between the *gift of prophecy*, which was bestowed even upon private persons, and consisted in the revelation of secret things, and the *prophetic office*, which was an extraordinary function in the church, committed to certain persons who were set apart by a special call from God."[1]

The reason, therefore, why all the historical and prophetic books which are to be found among the hagiographa (*cethubim*, which the son of Sirach speaks of in his prologue as "other books of our fathers," and "the rest of the books") were excluded from the second or middle part of the Old Testament canon called *nebiim*, rested upon a primary distinction between writings that were strictly prophetic and writings that were

[1] See my article on Daniel in Herzog's *Cyclopædia*.

not so,—a distinction which existed in the domain of history as well as in that of prophecy. Thus the historical books from Joshua to Kings, and the prophetical books from Isaiah to Malachi, were separated, as works written by men whose vocation in life was that of a prophet and therefore works of a prophetical character, from such books as Chronicles and Daniel, which were written indeed under the influence of the Holy Spirit, but not in the exercise of a prophetical calling received through a prophetical impulse of the Spirit of God. The two different kinds of historical composition are also perfectly unmistakeable. Each of them has its own peculiar history. The best designation for the non-prophetical, taking into account its history and remains, would be the rational or annalistic. Of course it is quite possible for a prophetical history like the book of Kings, or an annalistic history like that of Chronicles, to embrace within itself certain ingredients which really belong to the other historical style; but when we have once discovered the characteristics of the two styles, it is almost always possible to single out at once, and with perfect certainty, those ingredients which are foreign to the peculiar character of the work in which they are found, and have simply been made subservient to the writer's plan. It is very necessary, therefore, that we should look more minutely at the two styles of historical writing, for the simple reason that the literature of the books of prophecy gradually arose out of the literature of the prophetical books of history, and so eventually attained to an independent standing, though they never became entirely separate and distinct, as we may see from the book of Isaiah itself, which is interwoven with many fragments of prophetico-historical writing.

The oldest type of non-prophetic historical writing is to be found, as we have already observed, in the priestly Elohistic style which characterizes one portion of the Pentateuch, as distinguished from the Jehovistic or Deuteronomic style of the other. These two types are continued in the book of Joshua; and taken as a whole, the Jehovistic, Deuteronomic type is to be seen in those sections which relate to the history of the conquest; the priestly, Elohistic, in those which refer to the division of the land. At the same time, they are coloured in many other ways; and there is nothing to favour the idea that the book of Joshua ought to be combined with the Pentateuch, so as to form a hexateuchical whole. The stamp of prophetic history is impressed upon the book of Judges at the very outset by the introduction, which shows that the history of the judges is to be regarded as a mirror of the saving government of God; whilst the concluding portion, like the book of Ruth, is occupied with Bethlehemitish narratives that point to the Davidic kingdom, the kingdom of promise, which formed the direct sphere of prophecy. The body of the book is founded, indeed, upon oral and even written forms of the *saga* of the judges; but not without the intervention of a more complete work, from which only extracts are given, and in which the prophetic pencil of a man like Samuel had combined into one organic whole the histories of the judges not only to the time of Samson, but to the entire overthrow of the Philistian oppression. That the books of Samuel are a prophetico-historical work, is expressly attested by a passage in the Chronicles, of which we shall speak more fully presently; but in the passages relating to the conflicts with the four Philistian children of the giants (2 Sam. xxi. 15 sqq. = 1 Chron. xx. 4 sqq.), and to the Davidic *gibborim*, *i.e.* the heroes who stood nearest to him (2 Sam. xxiii. 8 sqq. = 1 Chron. xi. 11 sqq.), they contain at least two remnants of popular or national historical writing, in which we discern a certain liking for the repetition of the same opening and concluding words, which have all the ring of a refrain, and give to the writing very much of the character of an epic or popular ode, suggesting, as Eisenlohr has said, the legend of Roland and Artus, or the Spanish Cid. We find more of these remains in the Chronicles—such, for example, as the list of those who attached themselves to David in Ziklag, and, in fact, during the greater part of Saul's persecutions. It commences thus : " And these are they that came to David to Ziklag, whilst still hard pressed on the part of Saul the son of Kish; and they belong to the heroes, those ready to help in war, armed with bows, both with the right hand and the left hand using stones and arrows by means of the bow." Some of these fragments may have fallen singly and unwrought into the hands of the later historians; but so far as they are tabulated, the chronicler leaves us in no doubt as to the place where they were chiefly to be found. After giving a census of the Levites from thirty years old and upwards, in 1 Chron. xxiii. 2-24a, he adds, in ver. 24b and the following verses, in a fragmentary manner, that David, taking into account the fact that the hard work of past times had no longer to be performed, lowered the age for commencing official service to twenty, "for in the last words of David (*dibre David ha-acheronim*) the descendants of Levi are numbered from the twentieth year of their age." He refers here to the last part of the history of David's life in the "book of the kings of Israel" (*sepher malce Israel*), which lay before him; and from what other work such lists as these had been taken into this his main source, we may learn from 1 Chron. xxvii. 24, where he follows up the list of the tribe-princes of Israel with this remark with reference to a general census which David had intended to take: "Joab the son of Zeruiah began to number, but he did not finish it; and there arose a bursting forth of wrath upon Israel in consequence, and this numbering was not placed in the numbering (במספר, read בספר, 'in the book') of the chronicles (*dibre hayyamim*) of David." Consequently the annals or chronicles of David contained such tabular notices as these, having the character of popular or national historical composition; and they were copied from these annals into the great king's-book, which lay before the chronicler.

The official annals commenced with David, and led to those histories of the kingdom from which the authors of the books of Kings and Chronicles for the most part drew their materials, even if they did not do so directly. Saul's government consisted chiefly in military supremacy, and the unity of the kingdom as renewed by him did not embrace much more than the simple elements of a military constitution. But under David there grew up a reciprocal relation between the throne and the people, of the most comprehensive character; and the multiplication of government offices followed, as a matter of course, from the thorough organization of the kingdom. We find David, as head of the kingdom, asserting his official supremacy on all hands, even in relation to religious affairs, and meet with several entirely new posts that were created by him. Among these was the office of *mazcir* (*recorder* in Eng. ver.: Tr.), *i.e.* as the LXX. have often rendered it, ὑπομνηματόγραφος or (in 2 Sam. viii. 16) ἐπὶ τῶν ὑπομνημάτων (Jerome: *a commentariis*, a thoroughly Roman translation). The Targums give a similar rendering, עַל־דִּכְרָנַיָּא מְמַנָּא, the keeper of the memorabilia (*i.e.* of the "book of records" or annals, 2 Chron. xxxiv. 8, cf. Ezra iv. 15, Esther vi. 1). The *mazeir* had to keep the annals of the kingdom; and his office was a different one from that of the *sopher*, or chancellor. The *sopher* (*scribe* in Eng. ver.: TR.) had to draw up the public documents; the *mazeir* had to keep them, and incorporate them in the connected history of the nation. Both of these offices are met with throughout the whole of the East, both ancient and modern, even to the remotest parts of Asia.[1] It is very evident that the office in question was created by David, from the fact that allusions to the annals commence with the chronicles (*dibre hayyamim*) of David (1 Chron. xxvii. 24), and are continued in the *sepher dibre Shelomoh* (a contraction for *sepher dibre hayyamim Shelomoh*, "book of the chronicles of Solomon," 1 Kings xi. 41). The references are then carried on in Judah to the end of the reign of Jehoiakim, and in Israel to the end of the reign of Pekah. Under David, and also under Solomon, the office of national annalist was filled by Jehoshaphat ben-Ahilûd. The fact that, with the exception of the annals of David and Solomon, the references are always made to annals of the "kings of Judah" and "kings of Israel," admits of a very simple explanation. If we regard the national annals as a complete and independent work, they naturally divide themselves into four parts, of which the first two treated of the history of the kingdom in its unity; the last two, viz. the annals of the kings of Judah and Israel, of the history of the divided kingdom. The original archives, no doubt, perished when Jerusalem was laid in ashes by the Chaldeans. But copies were taken from them and preserved, and the histories of the reigns of David and Solomon in the historical books which have come down to us, and are peculiarly rich in annalistic

[1] The office of national annalist among the ancient Persians (see Brissonius, *De regno Persarum*, i. § 229), and that of *wakôjinuwis*, or historian, which still exists at the Persian court, are perfectly similar in character. The Chinese have had their national historians from the time of the Emperor *Wu-ti* of the Han dynasty (in the second century after Christ), and the annals of each dynasty are published on its extinction. The same institution existed in the kingdom of Barma, where the annals of every king were written after his death.

materials, show very clearly that copies of the annals of David and Solomon were taken and distributed with special diligence, and that they were probably circulated in a separate form, as was the case with some of the decades of Livy.

Richard Simon supposed the *écrivains publics* to be prophets; and upon this hypothesis he founded an exploded view as to the origin of the Old Testament writings. Even in more recent times the annals have occasionally been regarded as prophetic histories, in which case the distinction between prophetic and annalistic histories would unquestionably fall to the ground. But the arguments adduced in support of this do not prove what is intended. In the *first* place, appeal is made to the statements of the chronicler himself, with regard to certain prophetic elements in the work which constituted his principal source, viz. the great king's-book; and it is taken for granted that this great king's-book contained the combined annals of the kings of Judah and Israel. But (*a*) the chronicler speaks of his principal source under varying names as a book of the kings, and on one occasion as *dibre*, *i.e. res gestæ* or *historiæ*, of the kings of Israel (2 Chron. xxxiii. 18), but never as the annals of the kings of Israel or Judah: he even refers to it once as *midrash sepher hammelacim* (*commentarius libri regum*), and consequently as an expository and more elaborate edition either of our canonical book of Kings, or else (a point which we will leave undecided) of an earlier book generally. (*b*) In this *midrash* the history of the kings was undoubtedly illustrated by numerous comprehensive prophetico-historical portions: but the chronicler says expressly, on several occasions, that these were ingredients incorporated into it (2 Chron. xx. 34, xxxii. 32); so that no conclusion can be drawn from them with regard to the prophetic authorship of his principal source, and still less as to that of the annals. We do not, in saying this, dispute for a moment the fact, that there were prophetic elements to be found among the documents admitted into the annals, and not merely such as related to levitical and military affairs, or others of a similar kind; nor do we deny that the interposition of great prophets in the history of the times would be there mentioned and described. There are, in fact, distinct indications of this, of which we shall find occasion to speak more fully by and by. But it would be the greatest literary blunder that could be made, to imagine that the accounts of Elijah and Elisha, for example, which have all the stamp of their Ephraimitish and prophetic authorship upon the forefront, could possibly have been taken from the annals; more especially as Joram the king of Israel, in whose reign Elisha lived, is the only king of the northern kingdom in connection with whose reign there is no reference to the annals at all. The kind of documents, which were principally received into the annals and incorporated into the connected history, may be inferred from such examples as 2 Chron. xxxv. 4, where the division of the Levites into classes is taken from "the writing of David" and "the writing of Solomon :" whether we suppose that the documents in question were designated royal writings, because they were drawn up by royal command and had received the king's approval; or that the sections of the annals, in which they were contained, were really based upon documents written with the king's own hand (*vid.* 1 Chron. xxviii. 11–19). When we bear in mind that the account given by the chronicler of the arrangements made by David with reference to priests and Levites rests upon the annals as their ultimate source, we have, at any rate, in 2 Chron. xxxv. 4 a confirmation of the national, and so to speak, regal character of the year-books in question. A *second* argument employed to prove that the annals were prophetic histories, is the fact that otherwise they would not have been written in a theocratic spirit, especially in the kingdom of Israel. But (1) their official or state origin is evident, from the fact that they break off just where the duties of the prophets as historiographs really began. For fourteen of the references to the annals in our book of Kings, from Rehoboam and Jeroboam onwards, are to be found in the history of the kings of Judah (it being only in the case of Ahaziah, Amaziah, and Jehoahaz that the references are wanting), and seventeen in the history of the kings of Israel (the reference failing in the case of Joram alone); whilst in both lines the annals do not reach to the last king in each kingdom, but only to Jehoiakim and Pekah, from which we may conclude that the writing of annals was interrupted with the approaching overthrow of the two kingdoms. Now, if (*b*) we examine the thirty-one references carefully, we shall find that sixteen of them merely affirm that the rest of the acts of the king in question, what he did, are written in the annals (1 Kings xiv. 29; 2 Kings viii. 23, xii. 20, xv. 6, 36, xvi. 19, xxi. 25, xxiii. 28, xxiv. 5; 1 Kings xv. 31, xvi. 14; 2 Kings i. 18, xv. 11, 21, 26, 31). In the case of four Israelitish kings, it is simply stated in addition to this, that their *geburah* (might, heroism, *i.e.* their bravery in war) is written in the annals (1 Kings xvi. 5, 27; 2 Kings x. 34, xiii. 8). But in the accounts of the following kings we find more precise statements as to what was to be read in the annals concerning them, viz.: Abijam carried on war with Jeroboam, as might be read in them (1 Kings xv. 7); in the case of Asa they contained an account of "his heroism, and all that he did, and the cities which he built" (1 Kings xv. 23); in that of Jehoshaphat—"the heroic acts that he performed, and what wars he carried on" (1 Kings xxii. 46); in that of Hezekiah—"all his heroism, and how he made the pool, and the aqueduct, and brought the water into the city" (2 Kings xx. 20); in that of Manasseh—"all that he did, and his sin in which he sinned" (2 Kings xxi. 17); in that of Jeroboam—"what wars he waged, and how he reigned" (1 Kings xiv. 19); in that of Zimri—"his conspiracy that he set on foot" (1 Kings xvi. 20); in that of Ahab—"all that he did, and the ivory house which he erected, and all the towns that he built" (1 Kings xxii. 39); in that of Joash—"his heroism, how he fought with Amaziah king of Judah" (2 Kings xiii. 12, xiv. 15); in that of Jeroboam II.—"his heroism, how he warred, and how he recovered Damascus and Hamath to Judah in Israel" (2 Kings xiv. 28); and in that of Shallum—"his conspiracy which he made" (2 Kings xv. 15). These references furnish a very obvious proof, that the annalistic history was not written in a prophetico-pragmatical form; though there is no necessity on that account to assume, that in either of the two kingdoms it stooped to courtly flattery, or became the mere tool of dynastic selfishness, or of designs at variance with the theocracy. It simply registered outward occurrences, entering into the details of new buildings, and still more into those of wars and warlike deeds; it had its roots in the spirit of the nation, and moved in the sphere of the national life and its institutions; in comparison with the prophetic histories, it was more external than ideal,—more purely historical than didactic, —more of the nature of a chronicle than written with any special bias or intention: in short, it was more distinctly connected with political than with sacred history.

From the time of Samuel, with whom the prophetic period in the history of the legally constituted Israel strictly speaking commenced (Acts iii. 24), the prophets as a body displayed great literary activity in the department of historical composition. This is evident from the numerous references made by the author of the Chronicles to original historical writings by prophetic authors. At the close of the history of David he refers to the *dibre* (Eng. ver. "book") of Samuel the seer, Nathan the prophet, and Gad the seer; at the close of the history of Solomon (2 Chron. ix. 29), to *dibre* (Eng. ver. "book") of Nathan the prophet, *nebuoth* (Eng. ver. "the prophecy") of Ahijah the Shilonite, and *chazoth* (visions) of Ye'di (Ye'do; Eng. ver. Iddo) the seer; in the case of Rehoboam (2 Chron. xii. 15), to *dibre* of Shemaiah the prophet and 'Iddo the seer; in that of Abijah (2 Chron. xiii. 22), to the *midrash* (Eng. ver. "story") of the prophet 'Iddo; in that of Jehoshaphat (2 Chron. xx. 34), to *dibre* of Jehu ben Hanani, which were included in the book of the kings of Israel; in that of Uzziah (2 Chron. xxvi. 22), to a complete history of that king, which had been composed by Isaiah ben Amoz; in that of Hezekiah (2 Chron. xxxii. 32), to a *chazon* (Eng. ver. "vision") of Isaiah, which was to be found in the book of the kings of Judah and Israel; and in that of Manasseh (2 Chron. xxxiii. 19), to *dibre* of Hosai. The question might be raised, indeed, whether the *dibre* referred to in these passages are not to be understood—as in 1 Chron. xxiii. 27, for example—as signifying the historical account of such and such a person; but the following are sufficient proofs that the chronicler used the expression in the sense of historical accounts written by the persons named. In the first place, we may see from 2 Chron. xxvi. 22 how customary it was for him to think of prophets as historians of particular epochs of the history of the kings; secondly, even in other passages in which the name of a prophet is connected with *dibre*,—such, for example, as 2 Chron. xxix. 30, xxxiii. 18,—the former is the genitive of the subject or author, not of the object; thirdly, in the citations given above, *dibre* is used interchangeably with על־דברי, which requires still more decidedly that it should be understood as denoting authorship: and fourthly, this is placed beyond all doubt by the alternation of *midrash Iddo* (2 Chron. xiii. 22) with *dibre Iddo* (2 Chron. xii. 15). At the same time, it is evident that these accounts, which are called by prophets' names, were not lying before the chronicler in the form of separate writings in addition to the work which constituted his principal source, from the fact that, with the exception of 2 Chron. xxxiii. 18, 19, he never quotes the two together. They were incorporated into the *midrash sepher hammelakim* ("the story of the book of the kings," Eng. ver.), which lay before him (2 Chron. xxiv. 27), though not without showing their prophetic origin in distinction from the annalistic sources of the work in question; and inasmuch as it is inconceivable that the authors of our canonical books of Samuel and Kings should have made no use of these prophetic records, the question is allowable, whether it is still possible for critical analysis to trace them out either in whole or in part, with the same certainty with which it can be affirmed that the list of officers which is employed as a boundary-stone in 2 Sam. xx. 23–26, and the general survey of Solomon's ministers and court in 1 Kings iv. 2–19, together with the account of the daily provision for the royal kitchen in 1 Kings iv. 22, 23, and the number of stalls for the king's horses in 1 Kings iv. 26, 27, and others of a similar kind, were taken from the annals.

This is not the place in which to enter more minutely into such an analysis. It is quite sufficient for our purpose to have exhibited, in the citations we have made from the Chronicles, the stirring activity of the prophets as historians from the time of Samuel onwards; although this is evident enough, even without citations, from the many prophetico-historical extracts from the writings of the prophets which we find in the book of Kings. Both authors draw either directly or indirectly from annalistic and prophetic sources. But when we look at the respective authors, and their mode of rounding off and working up the historical materials, the book of Kings and the Chronicles exhibit of themselves, at least as a whole, the two different kinds of historical composition; for the book of Kings is a thoroughly prophetic book, the Chronicles a priestly one. The author of the book of Kings formed his style upon the model of Deuteronomy and the prophetic writings; whilst the chronicler so thoroughly imitated the older *dibre-hayyamim* style, that it is often impossible to distinguish his own style from that of the sources which came either directly or indirectly to his hand; and consequently his work contains a strange admixture of very ancient and very modern forms. The observation inserted in 2 Kings xvii. 7 sqq. shows clearly enough in what spirit and with what intention the writer of the book of Kings composed his work. Like the author of the book of Judges, who wrote in a kindred spirit (see Judg. ii. 11 sqq.), he wished to show, in his history of the kings, how the Israel of the two kingdoms sank lower and lower both inwardly and outwardly till it had fallen into the depths of captivity, in consequence of its contempt of the word of God as spoken by the prophets, and still more because of the radical evil of idolatry; but how Judah, with its Davidic government, was not left without hope of rescue from the abyss, provided it would not shut its heart against such prophetic preaching as was to be found in its own past history. The chronicler, on the other hand, whose love to the divinely chosen monarchy and priesthood of the tribes of Judah and Levi is obvious enough, from the annalistic survey with which he prefaces his work, commences with the mournful end of Saul, and wastes no words upon the path of sorrow through which David reached the throne, but passes at once to the joyful beginning of his reign, which he sets before us in the popular, warlike, priestly style of the annals. He then relates the history of Judah and Jerusalem under the rule of the house of David, almost without reference to the history of the northern kingdom, and describes it with especial completeness wherever he has occasion to extol the interest shown by the king in the temple and worship of God, and his co-operation with the Levites and priests. The author of the book of Kings shows us in *prophecy* the spirit which pervaded the history, and the divine power which moulded it. The chronicler exhibits in the *monarchy and priesthood* the two chambers of its beating heart. In the former we see storm after storm gather in the sky that envelopes the history, according to the attitude of the nation and its kings towards the word of God; with the latter the history is ever encircled by the cloudless sky of the divine institutions. The writer of the Chronicles dwells with peculiar preference, and a certain partiality, upon the brighter portions of the history; whereas, with the author of the book of Kings, the law of retribution which prevails in the historical materials requires that at least an equal prominence should be given to the darker side. In short, the history of the book of Kings is more inward, divine, theocratic in its character; that of the Chronicles more outward, human, and popular. The author of the book of Kings writes with a prophet's pen; the chronicler with the pen of an annalist.

Nevertheless, they both of them afford us a deep insight into the laboratory of the two modes of writing history; and the historical productions of both are rich in words of the prophets, which merit a closer inspection, since they are to be regarded, together with the prophetico-historical writings quoted, as preludes and side-pieces to the prophetic literature, properly so called, which gradually established itself in more or less independence, and to which the *nebiim acharonim* (the last prophets) belong. The book of Kings contains the following words and sayings of prophets: (1) Ahijah of Shilo to Jeroboam (1 Kings xi. 29-39); (2) Shemaiah to Rehoboam (1 Kings xii. 22-24); (3) a man of God to the altar of Jeroboam (1 Kings xiii. 1, 2); (4) Ahijah to the wife of Jeroboam (1 Kings xiv. 5-16); (5) Jehu ben Hanani to Baasha (1 Kings xvi. 1-4); (6) a prophet to Ahab king of Israel (1 Kings xx. 13, 14, 22, 28); (7) a pupil of the prophets to Ahab (1 Kings xx. 35 sqq.); (8) Elijah to Ahab (1 Kings xxi. 17-26); (9) Micha ben Yimla to the two kings Ahab and Jehoshaphat (1 Kings xxii. 14 sqq.); (10) Elisha to Jehoram and Jehoshaphat (2 Kings iii. 11 sqq.); (11) a pupil of Elisha to Jehu (2 Kings ix. 1-10); (12) a *massa* concerning the house of Ahab (2 Kings ix. 25, 26); (13) Jehovah to Jehu (2 Kings x. 30); (14) Jonah to Jeroboam II. (indirectly; 2 Kings xiv. 25-27); (15) leading message of the prophets (2 Kings xvii. 13); (16) Isaiah's words to Hezekiah (2 Kings xix. xx.); (17) threat on account of Manasseh (2 Kings xxi. 10-15); (18) Huldah to Josiah (2 Kings xxii. 14 sqq.); (19) threat of Jehovah concerning Judah (2 Kings xxiii. 27). Of all these prophetic words and sayings, Nos. 2, 9, and 18 are the only ones that are given by the chronicler (2 Chron. xi. 2-4, xviii., and xxxiv.), partly because he confined himself to the history of the kings of Judah, and partly because he wrote with the intention of supplementing our book of Kings, which was no doubt lying before him. On the other hand, we find the following words of prophets in the Chronicles, which are wanting in the book of Kings: (1) words of Shemaiah in the war between Rehoboam and Shishak (2 Chron. xii. 7, 8); (2) Azariah ben Oded before Asa (2 Chron. xv. 1-7); (3) Hanani to Asa (2 Chron. xvi. 7-9); (4) Jahaziel the Asaphite in the national assembly (2 Chron. xx. 14-17); (5) Eliezer ben Dodavahu to Jehoshaphat (2 Chron. xx. 37); (6) letter of Elijah to Jehoram (2 Chron. xxi. 12-15); (7) Zechariah ben Jehoiada in the time of Joash (2 Chron. xxiv. 20); (8) a man of God to Amaziah (2 Chron. xxv. 7-9); (9) a prophet to Amaziah (2 Chron. xxv. 15, 16); (10) Oded to Pekah (2 Chron. xxviii. 9-11). To extend the range of our observation still further, we may add, (1) the address of the *maleach Jehovah* in Bochim (Judg. ii. 1-5); (2) the address of a prophet (*ish nabi*) to Israel, in Judg. vi. 8-10; (3) that of a man of God to Eli (1 Sam. ii. 27 sqq.); (4) Jehovah to Samuel concerning Eli's house (1 Sam. iii. 11-14); (5) Samuel to Israel before the battle at Ebenezer (1 Sam. vii. 3); (6) Samuel to Saul in Gilgal (1 Sam. xiii. 13, 14); (7) Samuel to Saul after the victory over Amalek (1 Sam. xv.); (8) Nathan to David concerning his wish to build the temple (2 Sam. vii.); (9) Nathan to David after his adultery (2 Sam. xii.); (10) Gad to David after the numbering of the people (2 Sam. xxiv.).

If we take a general survey of these prophetic words and sayings, and compare them with one another, there can be no doubt that some of them have come down to us in their original form; such, for example, as the address of the man of God to Eli, in the first book of Samuel, and the words of Samuel to Saul after the victory over Amalek. This is guaranteed by their distinct peculiarity, their elevated tone, and the manifest difference between them and the ordinary style of the historian who relates them. In the case of others, at least, all that is essential in their form has been preserved; as, for example, in the addresses of Nathan to David: this is evident from the echoes that we find of them in the subsequent history. Among the sayings that have been handed down *verbatim* by the author of the book of Kings, we may include those of Isaiah, whose originality several things combine to sustain,—viz. the *massa* in 2 Kings ix. 25, 26, the construction of which is peculiar and primitive; together with a few other brief prophetic words, possibly in all that is essential the words of Huldah: for it is only in the mouth of Huldah (2 Kings xxii. 19; 2 Chron. xxxiv. 27) and Isaiah (2 Kings xix. 33), and in the *massa* referred to, that we meet with the prophetic "saith the Lord" (נְאֻם יְהוָֹה), which we also find in 1 Sam. ii. 30, with other marks of originality, whilst its great antiquity is attested by Gen. xxii. 16, the Davidic Psalms, and 2 Sam. xxiii. 1. In some of these sayings the historian is not at all concerned to give them in their original words: they are simply prophetic voices generally, which were heard at a particular time, and the leading tones of which he desires to preserve,—such, for example, as Judg. vi. 8-10, 2 Kings xvii. 13, xxi. 10-15. Reproductions of prophetic witnesses in so general a form as this naturally bear the stamp of the writer who reproduces them. In the books of Judges and Kings, for example, they show clearly the Deuteronomic training of their last editors. But we can go still further, and maintain generally, that the prophecies in the books of Samuel, Kings, and Chronicles contain marked traces of the historian's own hand, as well as of the sources from which they were indirectly drawn. Such sayings as are common to the two books (Chronicles and Kings) are almost word for word the same in the former as in the latter; but the rest have all a marked peculiarity, and a totally different physiognomy. The sayings in the book of Kings almost invariably begin with "Thus saith the Lord," or "Thus saith the Lord God of Israel" (also Judg. vi. 8, and 2 Kings xix. 20, before the message of Isaiah); and nothing is more frequent in them than the explanatory phrase יַעַן אֲשֶׁר, and such Deuteronomic expressions as הבעים, החטיא, ביד נתן, and others; to which we may add a fondness for similes introduced with "as" (*e.g.* 1 Kings xiv. 10, 15; 2 Kings xxi. 13). The thought of Jehovah's *choosing* occurs in the same words in 1 Kings xi. 36 and 2 Kings xxiii. 27; and the expression, "that David may have a light alway," in 1 Kings xi. 36, is exclusively confined to the Deuteronomic author of the work (*vid.* 1 Kings xv. 4, 2 Kings viii. 19, cf. 2 Chron. xxi. 7). The words, "I exalted thee from among the people, and made thee prince over my people Israel," are not only to be found in the second address of Ahijah in 1 Kings xiv. 7, but, with slight alteration, in the address of Jehu in ch. xvi. 2. The words, "Him that dieth in the city shall the dogs eat, and him that dieth in the field shall the fowls of the air eat," are found in the same form in Ahijah's second address (1 Kings xiv. 11), in Jehu's address (ch. xvi. 4), and in that of Elijah to Ahab (ch. xxi. 24). The threat, "I will cut off all that pisseth against the wall, that is shut up and that is free in Israel, and will sweep behind the house of Jeroboam," is found, with trifling variations, in Ahijah's second address (1 Kings xiv. 10), in Elijah's address to Ahab (ch. xxi. 21), and in Elisha's address to Jehu (2 Kings ix. 8); whilst it is evident from 1 Kings xvi. 11 and 2 Kings xiv. 26, that the form of the threat is just in the style of the Deuteronomic historian. There can be no question, therefore, that nearly all these prophetic sayings, so far as a common impress can exist at all, are of one type, and that the common bond which encircles them is no other than the prophetic subjectivity of the Deuteronomic historian. A similar conclusion may be drawn with regard to the prophetic sayings contained in the Chronicles. They also bear so decidedly the evident marks of the chronicler's own work, that Caspari himself, in his work upon the Syro-Ephraimitish war, is obliged to admit that the prophetic address in 2 Chron. xv. 2-7, which is apparently the most original of all, recalls the peculiar style of the chronicler. At the same time, in the case of the chronicler, whose principal source of information must have resembled his own work in spirit and style (as we are warranted in assuming by the book of Ezra especially), it is not so easy to determine how far his own freedom of treatment extended as it is in the case of the author of the book of Kings, who appears to have found the greater part of the sayings given in mere outline in the annals, and in taking them thence, to have reproduced them freely, in the consciousness of his own unity of spirit with the older prophets.

If these sayings had been handed down to us in their original form, we should possess in them a remarkably important source of information with regard to the historical development of the prophetic ideas and modes of expression. We should then know for certain that Isaiah's favourite phrase,

" for the Lord hath spoken it," was first employed by Ahijah (1 Kings xiv. 11); that when Joel prophesied " in Jerusalem shall be deliverance " (Joel ii. 32), he had already been preceded by Shemaiah (2 Chron. xii. 7); that Hosea (in ch. iii. 4, 5, cf. v. 15) took up the declaration of Azariah ben Oded, " And many days will Israel continue without the God of truth, and without a teaching priest, and without law; but when it turneth in its trouble," etc. (2 Chron. xv. 3, 4, where, as the parallel proves, the preterites of ver. 4 are to be interpreted according to the prophetic context); that in Jer. xxxi. 16, " for thy work shall be rewarded," we have the echo of another word of the same Azariah; that in the words spoken by Hanani in 2 Chron. xvi. 9, " The eyes of the Lord run to and fro throughout the whole earth," he was the precursor of Zechariah (ch. iv. 10); and other instances of a similar kind. But, with the influence which was evidently exerted upon the sayings quoted by the subjective peculiarities of the two historians (compare, for example, 2 Chron. xv. 2 with xiii. 4 and 1 Chron. xxviii. 9; 2 Chron. xii. 5 with xxiv. 20; also ver. 7 with 2 Chron. xxxiv. 21, and the parallel 2 Kings xxii. 13; and 2 Chron. xv. 5, " In those times," with Dan. xi. 14), and with the difficulty of tracing the original elements in these sayings (it is quite possible, for example, that the thought of a light remaining to David, 1 Kings xv. 4, 2 Kings viii. 19, was really uttered first of all by Ahijah, 1 Kings xi. 36), it is only a very cautious and sparing use that can be made of them for this purpose. It is quite possible, since Deuteronomy is the real prophet's book, as compared with the other books of the Pentateuch, that the prophets of the earlier regal times took pleasure in employing Deuteronomic expressions; but it cannot be decided whether such expressions as " put my name there," in 1 Kings xi. 36, and " root up Israel," etc., in 1 Kings xiv. 15, received their Deuteronomic form (cf. Deut. xii. 5, 21, xiv. 24, xxix. 27) from the prophet himself, or from the author of the book of Kings (cf. 1 Kings ix. 3, and the parallel passages, 2 Chron. vii. 20, ix. 7, 2 Kings xxi. 7, 8). At the same time, quite enough of the original has been retained in the prophecies of these earlier prophets, to enable us to discern in them the types and precursors of the later ones. Shemaiah, with his threat and its subsequent modification in the case of Asa, calls to mind

Micah and his words to Hezekiah, in Jer. xxvi. 17 sqq. The attitude of Hanani towards Asa, when he had appealed to Aram for help, is just the same as that which Isaiah assumed towards Ahaz; and there is also a close analogy in the consequences of the two events. Hosea and Amos prophesy against "the high places of Aven" (Hos. x. 8), and "the altars of Bethel" (Amos iii. 14, ix. 1), like the man of God in Bethel. When Amos leaves his home in consequence of a divine call (ch. vii. 15) and goes to Bethel, the headquarters of the image-worship of the Israelites, to prophesy against the idolatrous kingdom; is there not a repetition in this of the account of the prophet in 1 Kings xiii.? And when Hanani is cast into prison on account of his denunciation of Asa; is not this a prelude, as it were, to the subsequent fate of Micah ben-Imlah (1 Kings xxii.) and Jeremiah (Jer. xxxii.)? And so, again, Ahijah's confirmation and symbolical representation of what he predicted, by the rending in pieces of a new garment (the symbol of the kingdom in its unity and strength), has its analoga in the history of the earlier prophets (1 Sam. xv. 26-29) as well as in that of the latest (*e.g.* Jer. xxii.). It is only such signs (*mophethim*), as that by which the prophet who came out of Judah into Bethel confirmed his prophecy, that disappear entirely from the later history, although Isaiah does not think it beneath him to offer Ahaz a sign, either in the depth or in the height above, in attestation of his prophetic testimony.

There was no essential difference, however, between the prophets of the earlier and those of the later times; and the unity of spirit which linked together the prophets of the two kingdoms from the very first, notwithstanding the inevitable diversity in their labours in consequence of the different circumstances in which they were placed, continued all through. Still we do meet with differences. The earlier prophets are uniformly occupied with the internal affairs of the kingdom, and do not bring within their range the history of other nations, with which that of Israel was so intimately interwoven. Their prophecies are directed exclusively to the kings and people of the two kingdoms, and not to any foreign nation at all, either to those immediately adjoining, or what we certainly might expect, to Egypt and Aram. The Messianic element still remains in a somewhat obscure chrysalis state; and the poetry of thoughts and words, which grew up afterwards as the result of prophetic inspiration, only just manifests itself in certain striking figures of speech. It is indeed true, as we have already seen, that it is hardly possible to pronounce a decided opinion respecting the delivery of these earlier prophets; but from a sufficiently reliable and general impression, we may trace this distinction between the prophecy which prevailed till about the reign of Joash and that of the later times, that the former was for the most part prophecy in irresistible actions, the latter prophecy in convincing words. As G. Baur has observed; in the case of the older prophets it is only as the modest attendants of mighty outward acts, that we meet with words at all concerned to produce clear inward conviction. For this very reason, they could hardly produce prophetic writings in the strict sense of the word. But from the time of Samuel downwards, the prophets had made the theocratic and pragmatic treatment of the history of their own times a part of the regular duties of their calling. The cloistral, though by no means quietistic, retirement of their lives in the schools of the prophets, was very favourable to this literary occupation, more especially in the northern kingdom, and secured for it unquestioned liberty. We may see, however, from 2 Chron. xx. 34, that the prophets of Judah also occupied themselves with writing history; for the prophet Jehu was a Judæan, and, as we may infer from 2 Chron. xix. 1–3, had his home in Jerusalem.

The literature of the prophetic writings, strictly so called, commenced in the time of Jehoram king of Judah with a fugitive writing against Edom; if, as we think we have proved elsewhere, the vision of OBADIAH was occasioned by the calamity described in 2 Chron. xxi. 16, 17, to which Joel and Amos also refer. He was followed by JOEL, who had Obadiah's prophecy before him, since he introduces into the wider and more comprehensive range of his announcement, not only Obadiah's prophetic matter, but Obadiah's prophetic words. We may also see from Joel's writings how the prophetic literature, in the stricter sense, sprang out of prophetical histories; for Joel himself relates the result of the penitential worship, which was occasioned by his appeal, in a historical statement in ch. ii. 18, 19 a, through which the two halves of his writings are linked together. The time when he prophesied can be distinctly proved to have been the first half of the reign of Joash king of Judah. Obadiah and Joel were both of them contemporaries of Elisha. Elisha himself did not write anything, but the schools under his superintendence not only produced prophetic deeds, but prophetic writings also; and it is a characteristic circumstance, that the writings which bear the name of JONAH, whom an ancient Haggada describes as one of the sons of the prophets belonging to Elisha's school, belong far less to the prophetic literature in the strict sense of the term than to the prophetical histories, and in fact to the historical writings of prophets. At what period it was that Jonah's mission to Nineveh took place, may be gathered to some extent from 2 Kings xiv. 25, where Jonah ben-Amittai, the prophet of Gath ha-Hepher, in the territory of Zebulun, is said to have predicted the restoration of the kingdom of Israel to its promised boundaries,—a prediction which was fulfilled in Jeroboam ben-Joash, the third in succession from Jehu, and therefore was uttered at the commencement of the reign of Jeroboam II., if not under Joash himself. The mission to Nineveh may possibly belong to a somewhat earlier period than this prediction, namely, to the time of the older Assyrian kingdom, which was fast approaching its dissolution. Eusebius is probably correct in making Sardanapalus the last ruler of the old kingdom of Ninos, who was overcome by Arbaces the Mede, a contemporary of Jeroboam II. A glance at the book of AMOS, on the other hand, will show us that, at the time when he prophesied, a new Asshur was arising, and had already made considerable conquests. The date given in Amos i. 1, "two years before the earthquake," does not afford us any clue. But if Amos prophesied "in the days of Uzziah king of Judah, and Jeroboam ben-Joash king of Israel;" assuming that Jeroboam II. reigned forty-one years, commencing with the fifteenth year of Amaziah (2 Kings xiv. 23), and therefore was contemporary with Amaziah for fourteen years and with Uzziah for twenty-seven, it must have been in the last twenty-seven years of Jeroboam's reign that Amos prophesied. At the time when his ministry began, the kingdom of Israel was at the summit of its greatness in consequence of the successes of Jeroboam, and the kingdom of Judah still continued in the depression into which it had fallen in the time of Amaziah; and to both of them he foretells a common fate at the hands of Asshur, which is indicated clearly enough, although not mentioned by name. The commencement of the ministry of HOSEA coincides at the most with the close of that of Amos. The symbolical portion (ch. i.-iii.), with which his book commences, brings us to the five last years of Jeroboam's reign; and the prophetic addresses which follow are not at variance with the statement in ch. i. 1, which is by a later hand, and according to which he still continued to prophesy even under Hezekiah, and therefore until the fall of Samaria, which occurred in the sixth year of Hezekiah's reign. Hosea, the Ephraimitish Jeremiah, was followed by ISAIAH, who received his call, if ch. vi. contains the account of his prophetic consecration, in the last year of Uzziah's reign, and therefore twenty-five years after the death of Jeroboam II., and continued his labours at least till the second half of Hezekiah's reign, possibly to the commencement of that of Manasseh. His younger contemporary was MICAH of Moresheth, whose first appearance took place, according to ch. i. 1, within the reign of Jotham, and whose book must have been written, according to the heading "concerning Samaria and Jerusalem," before the fall of Samaria, in the sixth year of Hezekiah's reign (with which the account in Jer. xxvi. 17 sqq. also agrees); so that his labours began and ended within the incomparably longer period of Isaiah's ministry. This also applies to NAHUM, whose "burden of Nineveh" closes the prophetic writings of the Assyrian age. He prophesied after the defeat of Sennacherib, when the power of Asshur was broken, and also the yoke upon Judah's neck (ch. i. 13), provided, that is to say, that Asshur did not recover itself again. HABAKKUK is linked on to Nahum. He was the last prophet of Isaiah's type in the book of twelve prophets, and began to foretell a new era of judgment, namely the Chaldean. He prophesied in the time of Josiah, before Zephaniah and Jeremiah, and possibly even as early as the time of Manasseh. With ZEPHANIAH the line of prophets of Jeremiah's type begins. He resembles Jeremiah in his reproductive, and, as it were, mosaic use of the words of the older prophets. As JEREMIAH was called, according to Jer. i. 2, in the thirteenth year of Josiah's reign, his ministry commenced before that of

Zephaniah, since we are compelled by internal grounds to assign the prophecies of the latter to the period subsequent to the eighteenth year of Josiah's reign. Jeremiah's labours in Judæa, and eventually in Egypt, extended over a period of more than forty years. He gave, as a warrant of the threats contained in his last prophetic address in ch. xliv., the approaching fall of Pharaoh Hophra, who lost his throne and life in the year 570 B.C., upon the very spot where his great-grandfather Psammetichus had obtained forcible possession of the throne of Egypt a century before. Contemporaneous with Jeremiah was EZEKIEL, who, though not personally acquainted with him, so far as we know, laboured in the very same spirit as he among the exiles of Judah. According to ch. i. 1, 2, the year of his call was the thirtieth year, viz. of the era of Nabopolassar, which was really the fifth year after the captivity of Jehoiachin, B.C. 595. The latest date given in connection with his ministry (ch. xxix. 17) is the seven-and-twentieth year of the captivity, which was the sixteenth year from the destruction of Jerusalem, the time between Nebuchadnezzar's raising of the siege of Tyre and his expedition against Egypt. We are aware, therefore, of twenty-two years of active life on the part of this prophet, who may have been older when called than Jeremiah, who was youthful still. Jeremiah and Ezekiel were the two great prophets who spread their praying hands over Jerusalem as a shield as long as they possibly could, and when the catastrophe was inevitable, saved it even in its fall. Their prophecies bridged over the great chasm of the captivity (though not without the co-operation of the "book of consolation," Isa. xl.-lxvi., which was unsealed in the time of exile), and prepared the way for the restoration of the national community when the captivity was over. Into this community HAGGAI infused a new spirit in the second year of Darius Hystaspis, through his prediction of the glory which awaited the newly-built temple and the house of David, that was raised to honour once more in the person of Zerubbabel. ZECHARIAH began to prophesy only two months later. His last prophetic address belongs to the third year of Darius Hystaspis, the year after the edict requiring that the building of the temple should be continued. The predictions of the second part of his book (ch. ix.-xiv.) were hardly delivered publicly: they are throughout eschatological and apocalyptical, and take earlier situations and prophetic words as emblems of the last days. Prophecy was now silent for a long time. At length the last prophetic voice of the old covenant was heard in MAL'ACHI. His book coincides with the condition of things which Nehemiah found on his second sojourn in Jerusalem under Darius Notus; and his peculiar calling in connection with the sacred history was to predict, that the messenger who was appointed to precede the coming of Jehovah would soon appear,—namely, Elijah the Tishbite,—and that he, the forerunner, a pioneer, would then be followed by the Lord Himself, as "the Angel of the covenant," *i.e.* the Messenger or Mediator of a new covenant.

This general survey will show very clearly that the arrangement of the *nebiim acharonim* (last prophets) in the canon is not a strictly chronological one. The three "major" prophets, who are so called on account of the comparative size of their books of prophecy, are placed together; and the twelve "minor" prophets are also grouped together, so as to form one book (*monobiblos*, as Melito calls it), on account of the smaller extent of their prophetic books (*propter parvitatem colligati*, as b. Bathra says). To this the name of "the twelve," or "the twelve-prophet-book," was given (*vid.* Wisd. xlix. 10; Josephus, *c. Apion*, i. 8; cf. Eusebius, *h. e.* iii. 10). In the collection itself, on the other hand, the chronological order has so far been regarded, that the whole is divisible into three groups, representing three periods of prophetic literature, viz. prophets of the Assyrian period (Hosea to Nahum), prophets of the Chaldean period (Habakkuk and Zephaniah), and prophets after the captivity (Haggai to Malachi). And there is also an obvious desire to pair off as far as possible a prophet of the kingdom of Israel with one of the kingdom of Judah, viz. Hosea and Joel; Amos and Obadiah; Jonah and Micah; Nahum and Habakkuk (for the Elkosh of Nahum, if not the town on the eastern bank of the Tigris near to Mosul, was at any rate, according to Eusebius and Jerome, a Galilean town). *Hosea* is placed first, not because the opening word *techillath* made this book a very suitable one with which to begin the collection; still less because Hosea was the first to be called of the four prophets, Hosea and Isaiah, Amos and Micah, as *b. Bathra* affirms; but for the very same reason for which the

Epistle to the Romans is placed first among the Pauline epistles, viz. because his book is the largest in the collection,—a point of view which comes out still more prominently in the Septuagint, where Hosea, Amos, Micah, Joel, and Obadiah follow one another, the first with fourteen chapters, the second with nine, the third with seven, the fourth with three, and the last with one, and then a new series commences with Jonah. But the reason why *Joel* is placed next to Hosea in the Hebrew canon, may possibly be found in the contrast which exists between the lamentations of the former on account of the all-parching heat and the all-consuming swarms of insects, and the dewy, verdant, and flowery imagery with which the book of Hosea closes. *Amos* then follows Joel, because he not only takes up again his denunciations of judgment, but opens with one of the utterances with which Joel closes (ch. iv. 16): "Jehovah will roar out of Zion, and utter His voice from Jerusalem." Then follows *Obadiah*, on account of the reciprocal relation between Obad. 19 and Amos ix. 12. And *Jonah* is linked on to Obadiah: for Obadiah begins thus, "We have heard tidings from Jehovah, and a messenger is sent among the nations;" and Jonah was such a messenger. Such grounds as these, the further study of which we must leave to the introduction to the book of the twelve prophets, also had their influence upon the pairing of the prophets of Judah with those of Israel. The fact that Zephaniah follows Habakkuk may be accounted for from a similar ground, which coincides in this case with the chronological order; for a catchword in Zephaniah's prophecy, "Hold thy peace at the presence of Jehovah" (i. 7), is taken from Hab. ii. 20. The prophets after the captivity (called in the Talmud *nebiim ha-acharonim*, the last prophets), which necessarily followed one another in the order determined by the date and contents of their books, bring the whole to a close.

The so-called greater prophets are attached in the Hebrew canon to the book of Kings; and in both the Hebrew and Alexandrian canons *Isaiah* stands at the head. Isaiah, Jeremiah, Ezekiel—this is the order in which they follow one another in our editions, in accordance with the time of their respective labours. In German and French codices, we occasionally meet with a different arrangement, viz. Kings, Jeremiah, Ezekiel, Isaiah. This is the order given in the Talmud, *b. Bathra*, 14*b*. The principle upon which it is founded is the kindred nature of the contents, which also helped to determine the order of the twelve. Jeremiah follows the book of Kings, because nearly all his predictions group themselves around the Chaldean catastrophe, with which the book of Kings closes; and Isaiah follows Ezekiel, whose book closes in a consolatory strain, because that of Isaiah is, as the Talmud says, nothing but consolation. But the other arrangement, adopted in the Masora and MSS. of the Spanish class, has prevailed over this talmudic order, which has been appealed to, though without any good ground, by the opponents of the authenticity of Isa. xl.–lxvi. as supporting their conclusions.[1]

[1] Isaiah was regarded as the consolatory prophet pre-eminently, and more especially on account of ch. xl.–lxvi., so that, according to *b. Berachoth*, 57*b*, whoever saw Isaiah in a dream might look for consolation; and, according to the Midrash on the Lamentations, Isaiah had previously rectified all the evils that Jeremiah foretold.

THE PROPHECIES OF ISAIAH.

Qui sancto Isaiæ inspirasti ut scriberet, inspira quæso mihi ut quod scripsit intelligam, quia jam inspirasti ut credam; nisi enim crediderimus, non intelligemus.—AELREDUS († 1166).

INTRODUCTION.

(MORE ESPECIALLY TO THE FIRST PART. CHAP. I.-XXXIX.)[1]

TIME OF THE PROPHET.

THE first prerequisite to a clear understanding and full appreciation of the prophecies of Isaiah, is a knowledge of his time, and of the different periods of his ministry. The *first* period was in the reigns of Uzziah (B.C. 811–759) and Jotham (759–743). The precise starting-point depends upon the view we take of ch. vi. But, in any case, Isaiah commenced his ministry towards the close of Uzziah's reign, and laboured on throughout the sixteen years of the reign of Jotham. The first twenty-seven of the fifty-two years that Uzziah reigned run parallel to the last twenty-seven of the forty-one that Jeroboam II. reigned (B.C. 825–784). Under Joash, and his son Jeroboam II., the kingdom of Israel passed through a period of outward glory, which surpassed, both in character and duration, any that it had reached before; and this was also the case with the kingdom of Judah under Uzziah and his son Jotham. As the glory of the one kingdom faded away, that of the other increased. The bloom of the northern kingdom was destroyed and surpassed by that of the southern. But outward splendour contained within itself the fatal germ of decay and ruin in the one case as much as in the other; for prosperity degenerated into luxury, and the worship of Jehovah became stiffened into idolatry. It was in this last and longest time of Judah's prosperity that Isaiah

[1] See my article on Isaiah in the *Bible Cyclopædia*, edited by Professor Fairbairn.

arose, with the mournful vocation to preach repentance without success, and consequently to have to announce the judgment of hardening and devastation, of the ban and of banishment. The *second* period of his ministry extended from the commencement of the reign of Ahaz to that of the reign of Hezekiah. Within these sixteen years three events occurred, which combined to bring about a new and calamitous turn in the history of Judah. In the place of the worship of Jehovah, which had been maintained with outward regularity and legal precision under Uzziah and Jotham; as soon as Ahaz ascended the throne, open idolatry was introduced of the most abominable description and in very various forms. The hostilities which began while Jotham was living, were perpetuated by Pekah the king of Israel and Rezin the king of Damascene Syria; and in the Syro-Ephraimitish war, an attack was made upon Jerusalem, with the avowed intention of bringing the Davidic rule to an end. Ahaz appealed to Tiglath-pileser, the king of Assyria, to help him out of these troubles. He thus made flesh his arm, and so entangled the nation of Jehovah with the kingdom of the world, that from that time forward it never truly recovered its independence again. The kingdom of the world was the heathen state in its Nimrodic form. Its perpetual aim was to extend its boundaries by constant accretions, till it had grown into a world-embracing colossus; and in order to accomplish this, it was ever passing beyond its natural boundaries, and coming down like an avalanche upon foreign nations, not merely for self-defence or revenge, but for the purpose of conquest also. Assyria and Rome were the first and last links in that chain of oppression by the kingdom of the world, which ran through the history of Israel. Thus Isaiah, standing as he did on the very threshold of this new and all-important turn in the history of his country, and surveying it with his telescopic glance, was, so to speak, the universal prophet of Israel. The *third* period of his ministry extended from the accession of Hezekiah to the fifteenth year of his reign. Under Hezekiah the nation rose, almost at the same pace at which it had previously declined under Ahaz. He forsook the ways of his idolatrous father, and restored the worship of Jehovah. The mass of the people, indeed, remained inwardly unchanged, but Judah had once more an upright king, who hearkened to the word of the prophet by his side,—two pillars of the state, and men mighty in prayer (2 Chron. xxxii. 20). When the attempt was afterwards made to break away from the Assyrian yoke, so far as the leading men and the great mass of the people were concerned, this was an act of unbelief originating merely in the same confident expectation of help from Egypt which had occasioned the destruction of the northern kingdom in the sixth year of Hezekiah's reign; but on the part of Hezekiah it was an act of faith and confident reliance upon Jehovah (2 Kings xviii. 7). Consequently, when Sennacherib, the successor of Shalmaneser, marched against Jerusalem, conquering and devastating the land as he advanced, and Egypt failed to send the promised help, the carnal defiance of the leaders and of the great mass of the people brought its own punishment. But Jehovah averted the worst extremity, by destroying the kernel of the Assyrian army in a single night; so that, as in the Syro-Ephraimitish war, Jerusalem itself was never actually besieged. Thus the faith of the king, and of the better portion of the nation, which rested upon the word of promise, had its reward. There was still a divine power in the state, which preserved it from destruction. The coming judgment, which nothing indeed could now avert, according to ch. vi., was arrested for a time, just when the last destructive blow would naturally have been expected. It was in this miraculous rescue, which Isaiah predicted, and for which he prepared the way, that the public ministry of the prophet culminated. Isaiah was the Amos of the kingdom of Judah, having the same fearful vocation to foresee and to declare the fact, that for Israel as a people and kingdom the time of forgiveness had gone by. But he was not also the Hosea of the southern kingdom; for it was not Isaiah, but Jeremiah, who received the solemn call to accompany the disastrous fate of the kingdom of Judah with the knell of prophetic denunciations. Jeremiah was the Hosea of the kingdom of Judah. To Isaiah was given the commission, which was refused to his successor Jeremiah,—namely, to press back once more, through the might of his prophetic word, coming as it did out of the depths of the strong spirit of faith, the dark night which threatened to swallow up his people at the time of the Assyrian judgment. After the fifteenth year of Hezekiah's reign, he took no further part in public affairs; but he lived till the commencement of Manasseh's reign, when, according to a credible tradition, to which there is an evident allusion in Heb. xi. 37 ("they were sawn asunder"),[1] he fell a victim to the heathenism which became once more supreme in the land.

To this sketch of the times and ministry of the prophet we will add a review of the scriptural account of the four kings, under whom he laboured according to ch. i. 1; since nothing is more essential, as a preparation for the study of his book, than a minute acquaintance with these sections of the books of Kings and Chronicles.

I. HISTORICAL ACCOUNT OF UZZIAH-JOTHAM.—The account of *Uzziah* given in the book of Kings (2 Kings xv. 1–7, to which we may add xiv. 21, 22), like that of Jeroboam II., is not so full as we should have expected. After the murder of Amaziah, the people of Judah, as related in ch. xiv. 21, 22, raised to the throne his son Azariah, probably not his firstborn, who was then sixteen years old. It was he who built the Edomitish seaport town of Elath (for navigation and commerce), and made it a permanent possession of Judah (as in the time of Solomon). This notice is introduced, as a kind of appendix, at the close of Amaziah's life and quite out of its chronological position, because the conquest of Elath was the crowning point of the subjugation of Edom by Amaziah, and not, as Thenius supposes, because it was Azariah's first feat of arms, by which, immediately after his accession, he satisfied the expectations with which the army had made him king. For the victories gained by this king over Edom and the other neighbouring nations cannot have been obtained at the time when Amos prophesied, which was about the tenth year of Uzziah's reign. The attack made by Amaziah upon the kingdom of Israel, had brought the kingdom of Judah into a state of dependence upon the former, and almost of total ruin, from which it only recovered gradually, like a house that had fallen into decay. The chronicler, following the text of the book of Kings, has introduced the notice concerning Elath in the same place (2 Chron. xxvi. 1, 2 : it is written *Eloth*, as in 1 Kings

---

[1] According to *b. Jebamoth*, 49b, it was found in a roll containing the history of a Jerusalem family; and according to *Sanhedrin*, 103b, in the Targum on 2 Kings xxi. 16.

ix. 26, and the Septuagint at 2 Kings xiv. 22). He calls the king *Uzziahu;* and it is only in the table of the kings of Judah, in 1 Chron. iii. 12, that he gives the name as *Azariah.* The author of the book of Kings, according to our Hebrew text, calls him sometimes *Azariah* or *Azariahu,* sometimes *Uzziah* or *Uzziahu;* the Septuagint always gives the name as *Azarias.* The occurrence of the two names in both of the historical books is an indubitable proof that they are genuine. Azariah was the original name: out of this Uzziah was gradually formed by a significant elision; and as the prophetical books, from Isa. i. 1 to Zech. xiv. 5, clearly show, the latter was the name most commonly used.

Azariah, as we learn from the section in the book of Kings relating to the reign of this monarch (2 Kings xv. 1–7), ascended the throne in the twenty-seventh year of Jeroboam's reign, that is to say, in the fifteenth year of his sole government, the twenty-seventh from the time when he shared the government with his father Joash, as we may gather from 2 Kings xiii. 13. The youthful sovereign, who was only sixteen years of age, was the son of Amaziah by a native of Jerusalem, and reigned fifty-two years. He did what was pleasing in the sight of God, like his father Amaziah; *i.e.* although he did not come up to the standard of David, he was one of the better kings. He fostered the worship of Jehovah, as prescribed in the law: nevertheless he left the high places (*bamoth*) standing; and while he was reigning, the people maintained in all its force the custom of sacrificing and burning incense upon the heights. He was punished by God with leprosy, which compelled him to live in a sick-house (*chophshuth* = *chophshith*: sickness) till the day of his death, whilst his son Jotham was over the palace, and conducted the affairs of government. He was buried in the city of David, and Jotham followed him on the throne. This is all that the author of the book of Kings tells us concerning Azariah: for the rest, he refers to the annals of the kings of Judah. The section in the Chronicles relating to Uzziah (2 Chron. xxvi.) is much more copious: the writer had our book of Kings before him, as ch. xxvi. 3, 4, 21, clearly proves, and completed the defective notices from the source which he chiefly employed,—namely, the much more elaborate *midrash.*

Uzziah, he says, was zealous in seeking Elohim in the days

of Zechariah, who had understanding in divine visions; and in the days when he sought Jehovah, God made him to prosper. Thus the prophet Zechariah, as a faithful pastor and counsellor, stood in the same relation to him in which Jehoiada the high priest had stood to Joash, Uzziah's grandfather. The chronicler then enumerates singly the divine blessings which Uzziah enjoyed. *First*, his *victories* over the surrounding nations (passing over the victory over Edom, which had been already mentioned), viz.: (1) he went forth and warred against the Philistines, and brake down the wall of Gath, and the wall of Jabneh, and the wall of Ashdod, and built towns *b'ashdod* and *b'phelistim* (*i.e.* in the conquered territory of Ashdod, and in Philistia generally); (2) God not only gave him victory over the Philistines, but also over the Arabians who dwelt in Gur-Baal (an unknown place, which neither the LXX. nor the Targumists could explain), and the Mehunim, probably a tribe of Arabia Petræa; (3) the Ammonites gave him presents in token of allegiance, and his name was honoured even as far as Egypt, to such an extent did his power grow. *Secondly*, his *buildings*: he built towers (fortifications) above the corner gate, and above the valley gate, and above the *Mikzoa*, and fortified these (the weakest) portions of Jerusalem: he also built towers in the desert (probably in the desert between Beersheba and Gaza, to protect either the land, or the flocks and herds that were pasturing there); and dug many cisterns, for he had large flocks and herds both in the *shephelah* (the western portion of Southern Palestine) and in the *mishor* (the extensive pasture-land of the tribe territory of Reuben on the other side of the Jordan): he had also husbandmen and vine-dressers on the mountains, and in the fruitful fields, for he was a lover of agriculture. *Thirdly*, his well-organized *troops*: he had an army of fighting men which consisted—according to a calculation made by Jeiel the scribe, and Maaseiah, the officer under the superintendence of Hananiah, one of the royal princes—of 2600 heads of families, who had 307,500 men under their command, "that made war with mighty power to help the king against the enemy." Uzziah furnished these, according to all the divisions of the army, with shields, and spears, and helmets, and coats of mail, and bows, even with slinging-stones. He also had ingenious slinging-machines (*balistae*) made in Jerusalem, to fix upon the towers and ramparts, for the purpose of shooting arrows and large stones. His name resounded far abroad, for he had marvellous success, so that he became very powerful.

Up to this point the chronicler has depicted the brighter side of Uzziah's reign. His prosperous deeds and enterprises are all grouped together, so that it is doubtful whether the history within these several groups follows the chronological order or not. The light thrown upon the history of the times by the group of victories gained by Uzziah, would be worth twice as much if the chronological order were strictly observed. But even if we might assume that the victory over the Philistines preceded the victory over the Arabians of Gur-Baal and the Mehunim, and this again the subjugation of Ammon, it would still be very uncertain what position the expedition against Edom—which was noticed by anticipation at the close of Amaziah's life—occupied in relation to the other wars, and at what part of Uzziah's reign the several wars occurred. All that can be affirmed is, that they preceded the closing years of his life, when the blessing of God was withdrawn from him.

The chronicler relates still further, in ch. xxvi. 16, that as Uzziah became stronger and stronger, he fell into pride of heart, which led him to perform a ruinous act. He sinned against Jehovah his God, by forcing his way into the holy place of the temple, to burn incense upon the altar of incense, from the proud notion that royalty involved the rights of the priesthood, and that the priests were only the delegates and representatives of the king. Then Azariah the high priest, and eighty other priests, brave men, hurried after him, and went up to him, and said, "This does not belong to thee, Uzziah, to burn incense to Jehovah; but to the priests, the sons of Aaron, who are consecrated to burn incense: go out of the sanctuary, for thou sinnest; and this is not for thine honour with Jehovah Elohim!" Then Uzziah was wroth, as he held the censer in his hand; and while he was so enraged against the priests, leprosy broke out upon his forehead in the sight of the priests, in the house of Jehovah, at the altar of incense. When Azariah the high priest and the rest of the priests turned to him, behold, he was leprous in his forehead; and they brought him hurriedly away from thence,—in fact, he himself hasted to go out,—for Jehovah had smitten him. After having thus explained the circumstances which led to the king's leprosy, the chronicler follows once more the text of the book of Kings, —where the leprosy itself is also mentioned,—and states that the king remained a leper until the day of his death, and lived in a sick-house, without ever being able to visit the temple again. But instead of the statement in the book of Kings, that he was buried in the city of David, the chronicler affirms more particularly that he was not placed in the king's sepulchre; but, inasmuch as he was leprous, and would therefore have defiled it, was buried in the field near the sepulchre. But before introducing this conclusion to the history of Uzziah's reign, and instead of referring to the annals of the kings of Judah, as the author of the book of Kings has done, or making such citations as we generally find, the author simply states, that "the rest of the acts of Uzziah, first and last, did Isaiah the prophet, the son of Amoz, write."

It cannot possibly be either the prophecies of Isaiah of the time of Uzziah, or a certain historical portion of the original book of Isaiah's predictions, to which reference is here made; for in that case we should expect the same notice at the close of the account of Jotham's reign, or, at any rate, at the close of that of Ahaz (cf. ch. xxvii. 7 and xxviii. 26). It is also inconceivable that Isaiah's book of predictions should have contained either a prophetical or historical account of the first acts of Uzziah, since Isaiah was later than Amos, later even than Hosea; and his public ministry did not commence till the close of his reign,—in fact, not till the year of his death. Consequently the chronicler must refer to some historical work distinct from "the visions of Isaiah." Just as he mentions two historical works within the first epoch of the divided kingdom, viz. Shemaiah's and Iddo's,—the former of which referred more especially to the entire history of Rehoboam, and the latter to the history of Abijah,—and then again, in the second epoch, an historical work by Jehu ben Hanani, which contained a complete history of Jehoshaphat from the beginning to the end; so here, in the third epoch, he speaks of Isaiah ben Amoz, the greatest Judæan prophet of this epoch, as the author of a special history of Uzziah, which was not incorporated in his "visions" like the history of Hezekiah (cf. ch. xxxii. 32), but formed an independent work. Besides this prophetical history of Uzziah, there was also an annalistic history, as 2 Kings xv. 6 clearly shows; and it is quite possible that the annals of Uzziah were finished when Isaiah commenced his work, and that they were made use of by him. For the leading purpose of the prophetical histories was to exhibit the inward and divine connection between the several outward events, which the annals simply registered. The historical writings of a prophet were only the other side of his more purely prophetic work. In the light of the Spirit of God, the former looked deep into the past, the latter into the present. Both of them had to do with the ways of divine justice and grace, and set forth past and present, alike in view of the true goal, in which these two ways coincide.

Jotham succeeded Uzziah, after having acted as regent, or rather as viceroy, for several years (2 Kings xv. 32–38). He ascended the throne in the second year of Pekah king of Israel, in the twenty-fifth year of his age, and reigned for sixteen years in a manner which pleased God, though he still tolerated the worship upon high places, as his father had done. He built the upper gate of the temple. The author has no sooner written this than he refers to the annals, simply adding, before concluding with the usual formula concerning his burial in the city of David, that in those days, *i.e.* towards the close of Jotham's reign, the hostilities of Rezin of Damascus and Pekah of Israel commenced, as a judgment from God upon Judah. The chronicler, however, makes several valuable additions to the text of the book of Kings, which he has copied word for word down to the notice concerning the commencement of the Syro-Ephraimitish hostilities (*vid.* 2 Chron. xxvii.). We do not include in this the statement that Jotham did not force his way into the holy place in the temple: this is simply intended as a limitation of the assertion made by the author of the book of Kings as to the moral equality of Jotham and Uzziah, and in favour of the former. The words, "the people continued in their destructive course," also contain nothing new, but are simply the shorter expression used in the Chronicles to indicate the continuance of the worship of the high places during Jotham's reign. But there is something new in what the chronicler appends to the remark concerning the building of the upper gate of the temple, which is very bold and abrupt as it stands in the book of Kings, viz., "on the wall of the Ophel he built much (*i.e.* he fortified this southern spur of the temple hill still more strongly), and put towns on the mountains of Judah, and erected castles and towers in the forests (for watch-towers and defences against hostile attacks). He also fought with the king of the Ammonites; and when conquered, they were obliged to give him that year and the two following a hundred talents of silver, ten thousand cors of wheat, and the same quantity of barley. Jotham grew stronger and stronger, because he strove to walk before Jehovah his God." The chronicler breaks off with this general statement, and refers, for the other memorabilia of Jotham, and all his wars and enter-prises, to the book of the Kings of Israel and Judah.

This is what the two historical books relate concerning the royal pair—Uzziah-Jotham—under whom the kingdom of Judah enjoyed once more a period of great prosperity and power,— "the greatest since the disruption, with the exception of that of Jehoshaphat; the longest during the whole period of its existence, the last before its overthrow" (Caspari). The sources from which the two historical accounts were derived were the annals: they were taken directly from them by the author of the book of Kings, indirectly by the chronicler. No traces can be dis-covered of the work written by Isaiah concerning Uzziah, although it may possibly be employed in the *midrash* of the chronicler. There is an important supplement to the account given by the chronicler in the casual remark made in 1 Chron. v. 17, to the effect that Jotham had a census taken of the tribe of Gad, which was settled on the other side of the Jordan. We see from this, that in proportion as the northern kingdom sank down from the eminence to which it had attained under Jeroboam II., the supremacy of Judah over the land to the east of the Jordan was renewed. But we may see from Amos, that it was only gradually that the kingdom of Judah revived under Uzziah, and that at first, like the wall of Jerusalem, which was partially broken down by Joash, it presented the aspect of a house full of fissures, and towards Israel in a very shaky condition; also that the Ephraimitish ox- (or calf-) wor-ship of Jehovah was carried on at Beersheba, and therefore upon Judæan soil, and that Judah did not keep itself free from the idolatry which it had inherited from the fathers (Amos ii.

4, 5). Again, assuming that Amos commenced his ministry at about the tenth year of Uzziah's reign, we may learn at least so much from him with regard to Uzziah's victories over Edom, Philistia, and Ammon, that they were not gained till after the tenth year of his reign. Hosea, on the other hand, whose ministry commenced at the very earliest when that of Amos was drawing to a close, and probably not till the last five years of Jeroboam's reign, bears witness to, and like Amos condemns, the participation in the Ephraimitish worship, into which Judah had been drawn under Uzziah-Jotham. But with him Beersheba is not referred to any more as an Israelitish seat of worship (ch. iv. 15); Israel does not interfere any longer with the soil of Judah, as in the time of Amos, since Judah has again become a powerful and well-fortified kingdom (ch. viii. 14, cf. i. 7). But, at the same time, it has become full of carnal trust and manifold apostasy from Jehovah (ch. v. 10, xii. 1); so that, although receiving at first a miraculous deliverance from God (ch. i. 7), it is ripening for the same destruction as Israel (ch. vi. 11).

This survey of the kingdom of Judah in the time of Uzziah-Jotham by the Israelitish prophet, we shall find repeated in Isaiah; for the same spirit animates and determines the verdicts of the prophets of both kingdoms.

II. HISTORICAL ACCOUNT OF AHAZ AND THE SYRO-EPHRAIMITISH WAR.—The account of Ahaz, given in the book of Kings and in the Chronicles (2 Kings xvi., 2 Chron. xxviii.), may be divided into three parts: viz., first, the general characteristics; secondly, the account of the Syro-Ephraimitish war; and thirdly, the desecration of the temple by Ahaz, more especially by setting up an altar made after the model of that at Damascus.[1] (1.) 2 Kings xvi. 1-4. Ahaz ascended the throne in the seventeenth year of Pekah. He was then twenty years old (or twenty-five according to the LXX. at 2 Chron. xxviii. 1, which is much more probable, as he would otherwise have had a son, Hezekiah, in the tenth year of his age), and he reigned sixteen years. He did not please God as his forefather David had done, but took the way of the kings of Israel, and

[1] On the temple at Damascus, whose altar Ahaz imitated, see the *Commentary on the Book of Job*.

even made his son pass through the fire (*i.e.* burnt him in
honour of Moloch), according to the abominations of the (Canaanitish) people whom Jehovah had driven out before Israel;
and he offered sacrifice and burnt incense upon the high places,
and upon the hills, and under every green tree. The Deuteronomic colouring of this passage is very obvious. The corresponding passage in the Chronicles is 2 Chron. xxviii. 1-4,
where the additional fact is mentioned, that he even made
molten images for Baalim, and burnt incense in the valley of
Hinnom, and burnt his children in the fire ("*his children*,"
a generic plural like "the kings" in ver. 16, and "the sons" in
2 Chron. xxiv. 25: "*burnt*," וַיַּבְעֵר, unless the reading וַיַּעֲבֵר be
adopted, as it has been by the LXX., "he caused to pass
through.") (2.) 2 Kings xvi. 5-9. Then (in the time of this
idolatrous king Ahaz) the following well-known and memorable
event occurred: Rezin the king of Aram, and Pekah the son
of Remaliah king of Israel, went up against Jerusalem to war,
and besieged Ahaz, "but could not overcome him," *i.e.*, as we
may gather from Isa. vii. 1, they were not able to get possession of Jerusalem, which was the real object of their expedition
"At that time" (the author of the book of Kings proceeds to
observe), viz. at the time of this Syro-Epraimitish war, Rezin
king of Aram brought Elath to Aram (*i.e.* wrested again from
the kingdom of Judah the seaport town which Uzziah had
recovered a short time before), and drove the Judæans out of
Elath (*sic*); and Aramæans came to Elath and settled there
unto this day. Thenius, who starts with the needless assumption that the conquest of Elath took place subsequently to the
futile attempt to take Jerusalem, gives the preference to the
reading of the Keri, "and Edomites (*Edomina*) came to Elath,"
and would therefore correct *l'aram* (to Aram) into *l'edom* (to
Edom). "Rezin," he says, "destroyed the work of Uzziah,
and gave Edom its liberty again, in the hope that at some
future time he might have the support of Edom, and so operate
against Judah with greater success." But, in answer to this,
it may be affirmed that such obscure forms as אֲרוֹמִים for אֲרַמִּים
are peculiar to this account, and that the words do not denote
the restoration of a settlement, but mention the settlement as
a new and remarkable fact. I therefore adopt Caspari's conclusion, that the Syrian king transplanted a Syrian colony of

traders to Elath, to secure the command of the maritime trade with all its attendant advantages; and this colony held its ground there for some time after the destruction of the Damascene kingdom, as the expression "to this day," found in the earlier source of the author of the book of Kings, clearly implies.

But if the conquest of Elath fell within the period of the Syro-Ephraimitish war, which commenced towards the end of Jotham's reign, and probably originated in the bitter feelings occasioned by the almost total loss to Judah of the country on the east of the Jordan, and which assumed the form of a direct attack upon Jerusalem itself soon after Ahaz ascended the throne; the question arises, How was it that this design of the two allied kings upon Jerusalem was not successful? The explanation is given in the account contained in the book of Kings (vers. 7-9): "Ahaz sent messengers to Tiglath-pělezer (sic) the king of Asshur, to say to him, I am thy servant, and thy son; come up, and save me out of the hand of Aram, and out of the hand of the king of Israel, who have risen up against me. And Ahaz took the silver and the gold that was found in the house of Jehovah, and in the treasures of the palace, and sent it for a present to the king of Asshur. The king hearkened to his petition; and went against Damascus, and took it, and carried the inhabitants into captivity to Kir, and slew Rezin." And what did Tiglath-pileser do with Pekah? The author of the book of Kings has already related, in the section referring to Pekah (2 Kings xv. 29), that he punished him by taking away the whole of the country to the east of the Jordan, and a large part of the territory on this side towards the north, and carried the inhabitants captive to Assyria. This section must be supplied here,—an example of the great liberty which the historians allowed themselves in the selection and arrangement of their materials. The anticipation in ver. 5 is also quite in accordance with their usual style: the author first of all states that the expedition against Jerusalem was an unsuccessful one, and then afterwards proceeds to mention the reason for the failure,—namely, the appeal of Ahaz to Assyria for help. For I also agree with Caspari in this, that the Syrians and Ephraimites were unable to take Jerusalem, because the tidings reached them, that Tiglath-pileser had been appealed to by Ahaz and was coming against them; and they were consequently obliged to raise the siege and make a speedy retreat.

The account in the Chronicles (2 Chron. xxviii. 5-21) furnishes us with full and extensive details, with which to supplement the very condensed notice in the book of Kings. When we compare the two accounts, the question arises, whether they refer to two different expeditions (and if so, which of the two refers to the first expedition and which to the second), or whether they both relate to the same expedition. Let us picture to ourselves first of all the facts as given by the chronicler. "Jehovah, his God," he says of Ahaz, "delivered him into the hand of the king of Aram, and they (the Aramæans) smote him, and carried off from him a great crowd of captives, whom they brought to Damascus; and he was also given into the hand of the king of Israel, who inflicted upon him a terrible defeat." This very clearly implies, as Caspari has shown, that although the two kings set the conquest of Jerusalem before them as a common end at which to aim, and eventually united for the attainment of this end, yet for a time they acted separately. We are not told here in what direction Rezin's army went. But we know from 2 Kings xvi. 6 that it marched to Idumæa, which it could easily reach from Damascus by going through the territory of his ally, —namely, the country of the two tribes and a half. The chronicler merely describes the simultaneous invasion of Judæa by Pekah, but he does this with all the greater fulness.

"Pekah the son of Remaliah slew in Judah a hundred and twenty thousand in one day, all valiant men, because they forsook Jehovah, the God of their fathers. Zichri, an Ephraimitish hero, slew Ma'asejahu the king's son, and Azrikam the governor of the palace, and Elkanah, the second in rank to the king. And the Israelites carried away captive of their brethren two hundred thousand women, boys, and girls, and took away much spoil from them, and brought this booty to Samaria." As the Jewish army numbered at that time three hundred thousand men (2 Chron. xxv. 5, xxvi. 13), and the war was carried on with the greatest animosity, these numbers need not be regarded as either spurious or exaggerated. Moreover, the numbers, which the chronicler found in the sources he employed, merely contained the estimate of the enormous losses sustained, as generally adopted at that time on the side of Judah itself.

This bloody catastrophe was followed by a very fine and touching occurrence. A prophet of Jehovah, named Oded (a contemporary of Hosea, and a man of kindred spirit), went out before the army as it came back to Samaria, and charged the victors to release the captives of their brother nation, which had been terribly punished in God's wrath, and by so doing to avert the wrath of God which threatened them as well. Four noble Ephraimitish heads of tribes, whose names the chronicler has preserved, supported the admonition of the prophet. The army then placed the prisoners and the booty at the disposal of the princes and the assembled people: "And these four memorable men rose up, and took the prisoners, and all their naked ones they covered with the booty, and clothed and shod them, and gave them to eat and drink, and anointed them, and conducted as many of them as were cripples upon asses, and brought them to Jericho the palm-city, to the neighbourhood of their brethren, and returned to Samaria." Nothing but the rudest scepticism could ever seek to cast a slur upon this touching episode, the truth of which is so conspicuous. There is nothing strange in the fact that so horrible a massacre should be followed by a strong manifestation of the fraternal love, which had been forcibly suppressed, but was now rekindled by the prophet's words. We find an older fellow-piece to this in the prevention of a fratricidal war by Shemaiah, as described in 1 Kings xii. 22–24.

Now, when the chronicler proceeds to observe in ver. 16, that "at that time Ahaz turned for help to the royal house of Assyria" (*malce asshur*), in all probability this took place at the time when he had sustained two severe defeats, one at the hands of Pekah to the north of Jerusalem; and another from Rezin in Idumæa. The two battles belong to the period before the siege of Jerusalem, and the appeal for help from Assyria falls between the battles and the siege. The chronicler then mentions other judgments which fell upon the king in his estrangement from God, viz.: (1) "Moreover the Edomites came, smote Judah, and carried away captives;" possibly while the Syro-Ephraimitish war was still going on, after they had welcomed Rezin as their deliverer, had shaken off the Jewish yoke, and had supported the Syrian king against Judah in their own land; (2) the Philistines invaded the low land (*shephelah*) and the south land (*negeb*) of Judah, and took several towns, six of which the chronicler mentions by name, and settled in them; for "Jehovah humbled Judah because of Ahaz the king of *Israel* (an epithet with several sarcastic allusions), for he acted without restraint in Judah, and most wickedly against Jehovah." The breaking away of the Philistines from the Jewish dominion took place, according to Caspari, in the time of the Syro-Ephraimitish war. The position of ver. 18 in the section reaching from ver. 5 to ver. 21 (viz. ver. 18, invasion of the Philistines; ver. 17, that of the Edomites) renders this certainly very probable, though it is not conclusive, as Caspari himself admits.

In vers. 20, 21, the chronicler adds an appendix to the previous list of punishments: Tiglath-Pilnezer (*sic*) the king of Asshur came upon him, and oppressed him instead of strengthening him; for Ahaz had plundered both temple and palace, and given the treasures to the king of Asshur, without receiving any proper help in return. Thenius disputes the rendering, "He strengthened him not" (cf. Ezek. xxx. 21); but Caspari has shown that it is quite in accordance with the facts of the case. Tiglath-pileser did not bring Ahaz any true help; for what he proceeded to do against Syria and Israel was not taken in hand in the interests of Ahaz, but to extend his own imperial dominion. He did not assist Ahaz to bring either the Edomites or the Philistines into subjection again, to say nothing of compensating him for his losses with either Syrian or Ephraimitish territory. Nor was it only that he did not truly help him: he really oppressed him, by making him a tributary vassal instead of a free and independent prince,—a relation to Asshur which, according to many evident signs, was the direct consequence of his appeal for help, and which was established, at any rate, at the very commencement of Hezekiah's reign. Under what circumstances this took place we cannot tell; but it is very probable that, after the victories over Rezin and Pekah, a second sum of money was demanded by Tiglath-pileser, and then from that time forward a yearly tribute. The expression used by the chronicler—" he came upon him"—seems, in fact, to mean that he gave emphasis to this demand by sending a detachment of his army; even if we cannot take it, as Caspari does, in a rhetorical rather than a purely historical sense, viz. as signifying that, "although Tiglath-pileser came, as Ahaz desired, his coming was not such as Ahaz desired, a coming to help and benefit, but rather to oppress and injure."

(3.) The *third* part of the two historical accounts describes the pernicious influence which the alliance with Tiglath-pileser exerted upon Ahaz, who was already too much inclined to idolatry (2 Kings xvi. 10–18). After Tiglath-pileser had marched against the ruler of Damascus, and delivered Ahaz from the more dangerous of his two adversaries (and possibly from both of them), Ahaz went to Damascus to present his thanks in person. There he saw the altar (which was renowned as a work of art), and sent an exact model to Uriah the high priest, who had an altar constructed like it by the time that the king returned. As soon as Ahaz came back he went up to this altar and offered sacrifice, thus officiating as priest himself (probably as a thanksgiving for the deliverance he had received). The brazen altar (of Solomon), which Uriah had moved farther forward to the front of the temple building, he put farther back again, placing it close to the north side of the new one (that the old one might not appear to have the slightest preference over the new), and commanded the high priest to perform the sacrificial service in future upon the new great altar; adding, at the same time, "And (as for) the brazen altar, I will consider (what shall be done with it)." "And king Ahaz," it is stated still further, "broke out the borders of the stools, and took away the basons; and the sea he took down from the oxen that bare it, and set it upon a stone pedestal (that took the place of the oxen). And the covered sabbath-hall which had been built in the temple, and the outer king's entrance, *he removed* into the temple of Jehovah before the king of Assyria." Thenius explains this as meaning "he altered them" (taking away the valuable ornaments from both), that he might be able to take with him to Damascus the necessary presents for the king of Asshur. Ewald's explanation, however, is better than this, and more in accordance with the expression "before," viz. "in order that he might be able to secure the continued favour of the dreaded Assyrian king, by continually sending him fresh presents." But הסב does not mean to alter, and בית ה׳ = בבית ה would be an unmeaning addition in the wrong place, which would only obscure the sense. If the great alterations mentioned in ver. 17 were made for the purpose of sending presents to the king of Assyria with or from the things that were removed, those described in ver. 18 were certainly made from fear of the king; and, what appears most probable to me, not to remove the two splendid erections from the sight of the Assyrians, nor to prevent their being used in the event of an Assyrian occupation of Jerusalem, but in order that his relation to the great king of Assyria might not be disturbed by his appearing as a zealous worshipper of Jehovah. They were changes made from fear of man and servility, and were quite in keeping with the hypocritical, insincere, and ignoble character of Ahaz. The parallel passage in the Chronicles is 2 Chron. xxviii. 22–25. "In the time of his distress," says the chronicler in his reflective and rhetorical style, "he sinned still more grievously against Jehovah: he, king Ahaz. He sacrificed to the gods of Damascus, who had smitten him. For the gods of the kings of Aram, he said, helped them; I will sacrifice to them, that they may also help me. And they brought him and all Israel to ruin. And Ahaz collected together the vessels of the house of God, and cut them in pieces, and shut the doors of the house of Jehovah, and made himself altars in every corner of Jerusalem. And in every town of Judah he erected high places to burn incense to other gods, and stirred up the displeasure of Jehovah the God of his fathers." Thenius regards this passage as an exaggerated paraphrase of the parallel passage in the book of Kings, and as resting upon a false interpretation of the latter. But the chronicler does not affirm that Ahaz dedicated the new altar to the gods of Damascus, but rather that in the time of the Syro-Ephraimitish war he attempted to secure for himself the same success in war as the Syrians had obtained, by worshipping their gods. The words of Ahaz, which are reported by him, preclude any other interpretation. He there states—what by no means contradicts the book of Kings—that Ahaz laid violent hands upon the furniture of the temple. All the rest—namely, the allusion to his shutting the temple-gates, and erecting altars and high places on every hand—is a completion of the account in the book of Kings, the historical character of which it is impossible to dispute, if we bear in mind that the Syro-Ephraimitish war took place at the commencement of the reign of Ahaz, who was only sixteen years old at the time.

The author of the book of Kings closes the history of the reign of Ahaz with a reference to the annals of the kings of Judah, and with the remark that he was buried in the city of David (2 Kings xvi. 19, 20). The chronicler refers to the book of the kings of Judah and Israel, and observes that he was indeed buried in the city (LXX. "in the city of David"), but not in the king's sepulchre (2 Chron. xxviii. 26, 27). The source employed by the chronicler was his *midrash* of the entire history of the kings; from which he made extracts, with the intention of completing the text of our book of Kings, to which he appended his work. His style was formed after that of the annals, whilst that of the author of the book of Kings is formed after Deuteronomy. But from what source did the author of the book of Kings make his extracts? The section relating to Ahaz has some things quite peculiar to itself, as compared with the rest of the book, viz. a liking for obscure forms, such as *Eloth* (ver. 6), *hakkomim* (ver. 7), *Dummesek* (ver. 10), and *Aromim* (ver. 6); the name *Tiglath-peleser*;[1] מכף instead of מיר, which is customary elsewhere; the rare and more colloquial term *jehudim* (Jews); the inaccurate construction את־המסנרות המכונות (ver. 17); and the verb בַּקֵּר (to consider, ver. 15), which does not occur anywhere else. These peculiarities may be satisfactorily explained on the assumption that the author employed the national annals; and that, as these annals had been gradually composed by the successive writings of many different persons, whilst there was an essential uniformity in the mode in which the history was written, there was also of necessity a great variety in the style of composition. But is the similarity between 2 Kings xvi. 5 and Isa. vii. 1 reconcilable with this annalistic origin? The resemblance in question certainly cannot be explained, as *Thenius* supposes, from the fact that

[1] This mode of spelling the name, also the one adopted by the chronicler (*Tiglath-pilnezer*), are both incorrect. *Pal* is the Assyrian for *son*, and according to Oppert (*Expédition Scientifique en Mésopotamie*), the whole name would read thus: *Tiglath-palli-sihar, i.e.* reverence to the son of the zodiac (the Assyrian Hercules).

Isa. vii. 1 was also taken from the national annals; but rather on the ground assigned by Caspari,—namely, that the author of the Chronicles had not only the national annals before him, but also the book of Isaiah's prophecies, to which he directs his readers' attention by commencing the history of the Syro-Ephraimitish war in the words of the portion relating to Ahaz. The design of the two allies, as we know from the further contents of Isa. i., was nothing less than to get possession of Jerusalem, to overthrow the Davidic government there, and establish in its stead, in the person of a certain ben-Ṭāb'ēl ("son of Tabeal," Isa. vii. 6), a newly created dynasty, that would be under subjection to themselves. The failure of this intention is the thought that is briefly indicated in 2 Kings xvi. 5 and Isa. vii. 1.

III. HISTORICAL ACCOUNT OF HEZEKIAH, *more especially of the first six years of his reign.*—The account given of Hezekiah in the book of Kings is a far more meagre one than we should expect to find, when we have taken out the large section relating to the period of the Assyrian catastrophe (2 Kings xviii. 13–xx. 19), which is also found in the book of Isaiah, and which will come under review in the commentary on Isa. xxxvi.-xxxix. All that is then left to the author of the book of Kings is ch. xviii. 1–12 and xx. 20, 21; and in these two paragraphs, which enclose the section of Isaiah, there are only a few annalistic elements worked up in Deuteronomical style. Hezekiah began to reign in the third year of Hosea king of Israel. He was twenty-five years old when he came to the throne, and reigned twenty-nine years. He was a king after the model of David. He removed the high places, broke in pieces the statues, cut down the Asheroth, and pounded the serpent, which had been preserved from the time of Moses, and had become an object of idolatrous worship. In his confidence in Jehovah he was unequalled by any of his followers or predecessors. The allusion here is to that faith of his, by which he broke away from the tyranny of Asshur, and also recovered his supremacy over the Philistines. We have no means of deciding in what years of Hezekiah's reign these two events—the revolt from Asshur, and the defeat of the Philistines—occurred. The author proceeds directly afterwards, with a studious repetition of what he has already stated in ch. xvii. in the history of Hosea's reign,[1] to describe Shalmanassar's expedition against Israel in the fourth year of Hezekiah's reign (the seventh of Hosea's), and the fall of Samaria, which took place, after a siege of three years, in the sixth year of Hezekiah's reign, and the ninth of Hosea's. But as Shalmanassar made no attack upon Judah at the time when he put an end to the kingdom of Israel, the revolt of Hezekiah cannot have taken place till afterwards. But with regard to the victory over the Philistines, there is nothing in the book of Kings to help us even to a negative conclusion. In ch. xx. 20, 21, the author brings his history rapidly to a close, and merely refers such as may desire to know more concerning Hezekiah, especially concerning his victories and aqueducts, to the annals of the kings of Judah.

The chronicler merely gives an extract from the section of Isaiah ; but he is all the more elaborate in the rest. All that he relates in 2 Chron. xxix. 2-xxxi. is a historical commentary upon the good testimony given to king Hezekiah in the book of Kings (2 Kings xviii. 3), which the chronicler places at the head of his own text in ch. xxix. 2. Even in the month Nisan of the first year of his reign, Hezekiah re-opened the gates of the temple, had it purified from the defilement consequent upon idolatry, and appointed a re-consecration of the purified temple, accompanied with sacrifice, music, and psalms (ch. xxix. 3 sqq.). Hezekiah is introduced here (a fact of importance in relation to Isa. xxxviii.) as the restorer of "the song of the Lord" (*Shir Jehovah*), *i.e.* of liturgical singing. The Levitical and priestly music, as introduced and organized by David, Gad, and Nathan, was heard again, and Jehovah was praised once

---

[1] The *Chabor nehar Gozan* (Eng. ver.: Habor *by* the river of Gozan), which is mentioned in both passages among the districts to which the Israelitish exiles were taken, is no doubt the *Châbûr*, which flows into the Tigris from the east above Mosul, and of which it is stated in *Merâsid ed. Juynboll*, that " it comes from the mountains of the land of *Zauzân*," a district of outer Armenia lying towards the Tigris, which is described by Edrisi in Jaubert's translation, Pt. ii. p. 330. Another river, on the banks of which Ezekiel's colony of exiles lived, is the Chebar, which flows from the north-east into the Euphrates, and the source of which is in the Mesopotamian town of *Râs-el-'ain*, a place celebrated through the marvellous springs of this Chaboras, the praises of which have often been sung.

more in the words of David the king and Asaph the seer. The chronicler then relates in ch. xxx. how Hezekiah appointed a solemn passover in the second month, to which even inhabitants of the northern kingdom, who might be still in the land, were formally and urgently invited. It was an after-passover, which was permitted by the law, as the priests had been busy with the purification of the temple in the first month, and therefore had been rendered unclean themselves: moreover, there would not have been sufficient time for summoning the people to Jerusalem. The northern tribes as a whole refused the invitation in the most scornful manner, but certain individuals accepted it with penitent hearts. It was a feast of joy, such as had not been known since the time of Solomon (this statement is not at variance with 2 Kings xxiii. 22), affording, as it did, once more a representation and assurance of that national unity which had been rent in twain ever since the time of Rehoboam. Caspari has entered into a lengthened investigation as to the particular year of Hezekiah's reign in which this passover was held. He agrees with Keil, that it took place after the fall of Samaria and the deportation of the people by Shalmanassar; but he does not feel quite certain of his conclusion. The question itself, however, is one that ought not to be raised at all, if we think the chronicler a trustworthy authority. He places this passover most unquestionably in the second month of the first year of Hezekiah's reign; and there is no difficulty occasioned by this, unless we regard what Tiglath-pileser had done to Israel as of less importance than it actually was. The population that was left behind was really nothing more than a remnant; and, moreover, the chronicler draws an evident contrast between tribes and individuals, so that he was conscious enough that there were still whole tribes of the northern kingdom who were settled in their own homes. He then states in ch. xxxi. 1, that the inhabitants of the towns of Judah (whom he calls "all Israel," because a number of emigrant Israelites had settled there) went forth, under the influence of the enthusiasm consequent upon the passover they had celebrated, and broke in pieces the things used in idolatrous worship throughout both kingdoms; and in ch. xxxi. 2 sqq., that Hezekiah restored the institutions of divine worship that had been discontinued, particularly those relating to the incomes of the priests and Levites. Everything else that he mentions in ch. xxxii. 1–26, 31, belongs to a later period than the fourteenth year of Hezekiah's reign; and so far as it differs from the section in Isaiah, which is repeated in the book of Kings, it is a valuable supplement, more especially with reference to Isa. xxii. 8–11 (which relates to precautions taken in the prospect of the approaching Assyrian siege). But the account of Hezekiah's wealth in ch. xxxii. 27–29 extends over the whole of his reign. The notice respecting the diversion of the upper Gihon (ch. xxxii. 30) reaches rather into the period of the return after the Assyrian catastrophe, than into the period before it; but nothing can be positively affirmed.

Having thus obtained the requisite acquaintance with the historical accounts which bear throughout upon the book of Isaiah, so far as it has for its starting-point and object the history of the prophet's own times, we will now turn to the book itself, for the purpose of acquiring such an insight into its general plan as is necessary to enable us to make a proper division of our own work of exposition.

ARRANGEMENT OF THE COLLECTION.

We may safely enter upon our investigation with the preconceived opinion that the collection before us was edited by the prophet himself. For, with the exception of the book of Jonah, which belongs to the prophetico-historical writings rather than to the literature of prediction, or the prophetical writings in the ordinary acceptation of the term, all the canonical books of prophecy were written and arranged by the prophets whose names they bear. The most important to our purpose is the analogy of the larger books of Jeremiah and Ezekiel. No one denies that Ezekiel prepared his work for publication exactly as it lies before us now; and Jeremiah informs us himself, that he collected and published his prophecies on two separate occasions. Both collections are arranged according to the two different points of view of the subject-matter and the order of time, which are interwoven the one with the other. And this is also the case with the collection of Isaiah's prophecies. As a whole, it is arranged chronologically. The dates given in ch. vi. 1, vii. 1, xiv. 28, xx. 1;

xxxvi. 1, are so many points in a progressive line. The three principal divisions also form a chronological series. For ch. i.–vi. set forth the ministry of Isaiah under Uzziah-Jotham; ch. vii.–xxxix., his ministry under Ahaz and Hezekiah down to the fifteenth year of the reign of the latter; whilst ch. xl.–lxvi., assuming their authenticity, were the latest productions of the deepest inner-life, and were committed directly to writing. In the central part, the Ahaz group (ch. vii.–xii.) also precedes the Hezekiah group (ch. xiii.–xxxix.) chronologically. But the order of time is interrupted in several places by an arrangement of the subject-matter, which was of greater importance to the prophet. The address in ch. i. is not the oldest, but is placed at the head as an introduction to the whole. The consecration of the prophet (ch. vi.), which ought to stand at the beginning of the Uzziah-Jotham group, if it relates to his original consecration to his office, is placed at the end, where it looks both backwards and forwards, as a prophecy that was in course of fulfilment. The Ahaz group, which follows next (ch. vii.–xii.), is complete in itself, and, as it were, from one casting. And in the Hezekiah group (ch. xiii.–xxxix.) the chronological order is frequently interrupted again. The prophecies against the nations (ch. xiv. 24–xxii.), which belong to the Assyrian period, have a *massa* upon Babel, the city of the world's power, for their opening piece (ch. xiii.–xiv. 23); a *massa* upon Tyre, the city of the world's commerce, which was to be destroyed by the Chaldeans, for their *finale* (ch. xxiii.); and a shorter *massa* upon Babel, for a party-wall dividing the cycle into two halves (ch. xxi. 1–10); and all the prophecies upon the nations run into a grand apocalyptic epilogue (ch. xxiv.–xxvii.), like rivers into a sea. The first part of the Hezekiah group, the contents of which are pre-eminently ethnic (ch. xiii.–xxvii.), are interwoven with passages which may not have been composed till after the fifteenth year of Hezekiah's reign. The grand epilogue (ch. xxxiv. xxxv.), in which the second portion of the Hezekiah group dies away, is also another such passage. This second part is occupied chiefly with the fate of Judah, the judgment inflicted upon Judah by the imperial power of Assyria, and the deliverance which awaited it (ch. xxvii.–xxxiii.). This prediction closes with a declaration, in ch. xxxiv. xxxv., on the one hand, of the judgment of God upon the world of

Israel's foes; and on the other hand, of the redemption of Israel itself. This passage, which was composed after the fifteenth year of Hezekiah's reign, is followed by the historical portions (ch. xxxvi.-xxxix.), which enclose in a historical frame the predictions of Isaiah delivered when the Assyrian catastrophe was close at hand, and furnish us with the key to the interpretation not only of ch. vii.-xxxv., but of ch. xl.-lxvi. also.

Taking the book of Isaiah, therefore, as a whole, in the form in which it lies before us, it may be divided into two halves, viz. ch. i. to xxxix., and ch. xl. to lxvi. The former consists of seven parts, the latter of three. The first half may be called the *Assyrian*, as the goal to which it points is the downfall of Asshur; the second the *Babylonian*, as its goal is the deliverance from Babel. The first half, however, is not purely Assyrian; but there are Babylonian pieces introduced among the Assyrian, and such others, as a rule, as break apocalyptically through the limited horizon of the latter. The following are the seven divisions in the first half. (1.) *Prophecies founded upon the growing obduracy of the great mass of the people* (ch. ii.-vi.). (2.) *The consolation of Immanuel under the Assyrian oppressions* (ch. vii.-xii.). These two form a syzygy, which concludes with a psalm of the redeemed (ch. xii.), the echo, in the last days, of the song at the Red Sea. The whole is divided by the consecration of the prophet (ch. vi.), which looks backwards and forwards with threatenings and promises. It is introduced by a summary prologue (ch. i.), in which the prophet, standing midway between Moses and Jesus the Christ, commences in the style of the great Mosaic ode. (3.) *Predictions of the judgment and salvation of the heathen*, which belong, for the most part, to the time of the Assyrian judgment, though they are enclosed and divided by Babylonian portions. For, as we have already observed, an oracle concerning Babel, the city of the world-power, forms the introduction (ch. xiii.-xiv. 23), an oracle concerning Tyre, the city of the world's commerce, which was to receive its mortal wound from the Chaldeans, the conclusion (ch. xxiii.); and a second oracle on the desert by the sea, *i.e.* Babel, the centre (ch. xxi. 1-10). (4.) To this so thoughtfully arranged collection of predictions concerning the nations outside the Israelitish pale, there is attached a grand apocalyptic *prophecy of the judgment of the world and the last things* (ch. xxiv.-xxvii.), which gives it a background that fades away into eternity, and forms with it a second syzygy. (5.) From these eschatological distances the prophet returns to the realities of the present and of the immediate future, and describes *the revolt from Asshur, and its consequences* (ch. xxviii.-xxxiii.). The central point of this group is the prophecy of the precious corner-stone laid in Zion. (6.) This is also paired off by the prophet with a far-reaching eschatological prediction of *revenge and redemption* for the church (ch. xxxiv. xxxv.), in which we already hear, as in a prelude, the keynote of ch. xl.-lxvi. (7.) After these three syzygies we are carried back, in the first two historical accounts of ch. xxxvi.-xxxix., into the Assyrian times, whilst the other two show us in the distance the future entanglement with Babylon, which was commencing already. These four accounts are arranged without regard to the chronological order, so that one half looks backwards and the other forwards, and thus the two halves of the book are clasped together. The prophecy in ch. xxxix. 5-7 stands between these two halves like a sign-post, with the inscription "To Babylon" upon it. It is thither that the further course of Israel's history tends. There, from this time forward, is Isaiah buried in spirit with his people. And there, in ch. xl.-lxvi., he proclaims to the Babylonian exiles their approaching deliverance. The trilogical arrangement of this book of consolation has been scarcely disputed by any one, since it was first pointed out by Rückert in his *Translation and Exposition of Hebrew Prophets* (1831). It is divided into three sections, each containing three times three addresses, with a kind of refrain at the close.

THE CRITICAL QUESTIONS.

The collection of Isaiah's prophecies is thus a complete work, most carefully and skilfully arranged. It is thoroughly worthy of the prophet. Nevertheless, we should be unable to attribute it to him in its present form, (1) if it were impossible that ch. xiii.-xiv. 23, xxi. 1-10, xxiii., xxiv.-xxvii., xxxiv., xxxv., could have been composed by Isaiah, and (2) if the historical accounts in ch. xxxvi.-xxxix., which are also to be found in 2 Kings xviii.

13-xx. 19, have been copied from the book of Kings, or even directly from the national annals. For if the prophecies in question be taken away, the beautiful whole unquestionably falls into a confused *quodlibet*, more especially the book against the nations; and if ch. xxxvi.-xxxix. were not written directly by Isaiah, the two halves of the collection would be left without a clasp to bind them together. It would be irregular to think of deciding the critical questions bearing upon this point now, instead of taking them up in connection with our exegetical inquiries. At the same time, we will put the reader in possession at once of the more general points, which cause us to dissent from the conclusions of the modern critics, who regard the book of Isaiah as an anthology composed of the productions of different authors.

The critical treatment of Isaiah commenced as follows:—It began with the *second part*. Koppe first of all expressed some doubts as to the genuineness of ch. l. Döderlein then gave utterance to a decided suspicion as to the genuineness of the whole; and Justi, followed by Eichhorn, Paulus, and Bertholdt, raised this suspicion into firm assurance that the whole was spurious. The result thus obtained could not possibly continue without reaction upon the first part. Rosenmüller, who was always very dependent upon his predecessors, was the first to question whether the oracle against Babylon in ch. xiii.-xiv. 23 was really Isaiah's, as the heading affirms; and to his great relief, Justi and Paulus undertook the defence of his position. Further progress was now made. With the first oracle against Babylon in ch. xiii.-xiv. 23, the second, in ch. xxi. 1-10, was also condemned; and Rosenmüller was justly astonished when Gesenius dropped the former, but maintained that the arguments with regard to the latter were inconclusive. There still remained the oracle against Tyre in ch. xxiii., which might either be left as Isaiah's, or attributed to a younger unknown prophet, according to the assumption that it predicted the destruction of Tyre by Assyrians or by Chaldeans. Eichhorn, followed by Rosenmüller, decided that it was not genuine. But Gesenius understood by the destroyers the Assyrians; and as the prophecy consequently did not extend beyond Isaiah's horizon, he defended its authenticity. Thus the Babylonian series was set aside, or at any rate pronounced thoroughly suspicious. But the keen eyes of the critics made still further discoveries. Eichhorn found a play upon words in the cycle of predictions in ch. xxiv.–xxvii., which was unworthy of Isaiah. Gesenius detected an allegorical announcement of the fall of Babylon. Consequently they both condemned these three chapters; and it had its effect, for Ewald transferred them to the time of Cambyses. Still shorter work was made with the cycle of predictions in ch. xxxiv. xxxv., on account of its relation to the second part. Rosenmüller pronounced it, without reserve, "a song composed in the time of the Babylonian captivity, when it was approaching its termination." This is the true account of the origin of the criticism upon Isaiah. It was in the swaddling-clothes of rationalism that it attained its maturity. Its first attempts were very juvenile. The names of its founders have been almost forgotten. It was Gesenius, Hitzig, and Ewald, who first raised it to the eminence of a science.

If we take our stand upon this eminence, we find that the book of Isaiah contains prophecies by Isaiah himself, and also prophecies by persons who were either directly or indirectly his disciples. The New Testament passages in which the second half of the book of Isaiah is cited as Isaiah's, are no proof to the contrary, since Ps. ii., for example, which has no heading at all, is cited in Acts iv. 25 as David's, merely because it is contained in the Davidic Psalter, and no critic would ever feel that he was bound by that. But many objections present themselves to such a conclusion. In the first place, nothing of the kind can be pointed out in any of the other canonical books of prophecy, except indeed the book of Zechariah, in which ch. ix.–xiv. is said to stand in precisely the same position as Isa. xl.–lxvi., according to Hitzig, Ewald, and others; with this difference, however, that Isa. xl.–lxvi. is attributed to a later prophet than Isaiah, whereas Zech. ix.–xiv. is attributed to one or two prophets before the time of Zechariah. But even De Wette, who maintained, in the first three editions of his *Introduction to the Old Testament*, that Zech. ix.–xiv. was written before the captivity, altered his views in the fourth edition; and Köhler has lately confirmed the unity of the book of Zechariah after an unbiassed investigation. It is Zechariah himself who prophesies of the last times in ch. ix.–xiv., in images drawn from the past, and possibly with the introduction of earlier oracles. It remains, therefore, that not a single book of prophecy is open to any such doubts as to the unity of its authorship; and Hitzig admits that even the book of Jeremiah, although interpolated, does not contain spurious sections. Nevertheless, it is quite possible that something extraordinary might have taken place in connection with the book of Isaiah. But there are grave objections even to such an assumption as this in the face of existing facts. For example, it would be a marvellous occurrence in the history of chances, for such a number of predictions of this particular kind to have been preserved,—all of them bearing so evidently the marks of Isaiah's style, that for two thousand years they have been confounded with his own prophecies. It would be equally marvellous that the historians should know nothing at all about the authors of these prophecies; and thirdly, it would be very strange that the names of these particular prophets should have shared the common fate of being forgotten, although they must all have lived nearer to the compiler's own times than the old model prophet, whose style they imitated. It is true that these difficulties are not conclusive proofs to the contrary; but, at any rate, they are so much to the credit of the traditional authorship of the prophecies attacked. On the other hand, the weight of this tradition is not properly appreciated by opponents. Wilful contempt of external testimony, and frivolity in the treatment of historical data, have been from the very first the fundamental evils apparent in the manner in which modern critics have handled the questions relating to Isaiah. These critics approach everything that is traditional with the presumption that it is false; and whoever would make a scientific impression upon them, must first of all declare right fearlessly his absolute superiority to the authority of tradition. Now tradition is certainly not infallible. No more are the internal grounds of the so-called higher criticism, especially in the questions relating to Isaiah. And in the case before us, the external testimony is greatly strengthened by the relation in which Zephaniah and Jeremiah, the two most reproductive prophets, stand not only to ch. xl.–lxvi., but also to the suspected sections of the first half. They had these prophecies in their possession, since they evidently copy them and incorporate passages taken from them into their own prophecies; a fact which Caspari has most conclusively demonstrated, but which not one of the negative critics has ventured to look fairly in the face, or to set aside by counter-proofs of equal force. Moreover, although the suspected prophecies do indeed contain some things for which vouchers cannot be obtained from the rest of the book, yet the marks which are distinctly characteristic of Isaiah outweigh by far these peculiarities, which have been picked out with such care; and even in the prophecies referred to, it is Isaiah's spirit which animates the whole, Isaiah's heart which beats, and Isaiah's fiery tongue which speaks in both the substance and the form. Again, the type of the suspected prophecies—which, if they are genuine, belong to the prophet's latest days—is not thoroughly opposed to the type of the rest; on the contrary, those prophecies which are acknowledged to be genuine, present many a point of contact with this; and even the transfigured form and richer eschatological contents of the disputed prophecies have their preludes there. There is nothing strange in this great variety of ideas and forms, especially in Isaiah, who is confessedly the most universal of all the prophets, even if we only look at those portions which are admitted to be genuine, and who varies his style in so masterly a way to suit the demands of his materials, his attitude, and his purpose. One might suppose that these three counter-proofs, which can be followed up even to the most minute details, would have some weight; but for Hitzig, Ewald, and many others, they have absolutely none. Why not? These critics think it impossible that the worldwide empire of Babel, and its subsequent transition to Medes and Persians, should have been foreseen by Isaiah in the time of Hezekiah. Hitzig affirms in the plainest terms, that the very same *caligo futuri* covered the eyes of the Old Testament prophets generally, as that to which the human race was condemned during the time that the oracle at Delphi was standing. Ewald speaks of the prophets in incomparably higher terms; but even to him the prophetic state was nothing more than a blazing up of the natural spark which lies slumbering in every man, more especially in Ewald himself. These two *coryphæi* of the modern critical school find themselves hemmed in between the two foregone conclusions, "There is no true prophecy," and "There is no true miracle." They call their criticism free; but when examined more closely, it is in a vice. In this vice it has two magical formularies, with which it fortifies itself against any impression from historical testimony. It either turns the prophecies into merely retrospective glances (*vaticinia post eventum*), as it does the account of miracles into *sagas* and myths; or it places the events predicted so close to the prophet's own time, that there was no need of inspiration, but only of combination, to make the foresight possible. This is all that it can do. Now we could do more than this. We could pronounce all the disputed prophecies the production of other authors than Isaiah, without coming into contact with any dogmatical assumptions: we could even boast, as in the critical analysis of the historical books, of the extent to which the history of literature was enriched through this analysis of the book of Isaiah. And if we seem to despise these riches, we simply yield to the irresistible force of external and internal evidence. This applies even to ch. xxxvi.–xxxix. For whilst it is true that the text of the book of Kings is the better of the two, yet, as we shall be able to prove, the true relation is this, that the author of the book of Kings did not obtain the parallel section (2 Kings xviii. 13—xx. 19) from any other source than the book of Isaiah. We have similar evidence in 2 Kings xxiv. 18 sqq. and xxv., as compared with Jer. lii., that the text of a passage may sometimes be preserved in greater purity in a secondary work than in the original work from which it was taken. It was Isaiah's prophetico-historical pen which committed to writing the accounts in ch. xxxvi.–xxxix. The prophet not only wrote a special history of Uzziah, according to 2 Chron. xxvi. 22, but he also incorporated historical notices of Isaiah in his "vision" (2 Chron. xxxii. 32). We reserve the fuller demonstration of all this. For whilst, on the one hand, we consider ourselves warranted in rejecting those tendencies of modern criticism, to which naturalistic views of the world have dictated at the very outset full-blown negative results, and we do so on the ground of supernatural facts of personal experience; on the other hand, we are very far from wishing to dispute the well-founded rights of criticism as such. For centuries, yea, for thousands of years, no objection was raised as to the Davidic origin of a psalm headed " a psalm *of David*," to say nothing of a prophecy of Isaiah; and therefore no such objection was refuted. Apart from the whims of a few individuals,[1] which left no traces behind them, it was universally assumed by both Jewish and Christian writers down to the last century, that all the canonical books of the Old Testament had the Holy Ghost as their one *auctor primarius*, and for their immediate authors the men by whose names they are called. But when the church in the time of the Reformation began to test and sift what had been handed down; when the rapid progress that was made in classical and oriental philology compelled the students of the Scriptures to make larger if not higher demands upon themselves; when their studies were directed to the linguistic, historical, archæological, æsthetic—in short, the human—side of the Scriptures, and the attempt was made to comprehend the several aspects presented by sacred literature in their progressive development and relation to one another,—Christian science put forth many branches that had never been anticipated till then; and biblical criticism sprang up, which from that time forward has been not only an inalienable, but a welcome and even necessary, member in the theological science of the church. That school of criticism, indeed, which will not rest till all miracles and prophecies, which cannot be set aside exegetically, have been eliminated critically, must be regarded by the church as self-condemned; but the labour of a spiritual criticism, and one truly free in spirit, will not only be tolerated, because "the spiritual man discerneth all things" (1 Cor. ii. 15), but will be even fostered, and not looked upon as suspicious, although its results should seem objectionable to minds that are weakly strung, and stand in a false and fettered attitude in relation to the Scriptures. For it will be no more offended that the word of God should appear in the form of a servant, than that Christ Himself should do so; and, moreover, criticism not only brings any blemishes in the Scriptures to the light, but affords an ever-deepening insight into its hidden glory. It makes the sacred writings, as they lie before us, live again; it takes us into its very laboratory; and without it we cannot possibly obtain a knowledge of the historical production of the biblical books.

[1] *E.g.* that of Abenezra, who regarded king Jehoiakim, who was set free in the thirty-seventh year of his Babylonian captivity, as the author of Isa. xl.-lx.

EXPOSITION IN ITS EXISTING STATE.

It was at the time of the Reformation also that historico-grammatical exposition first originated with a distinct consciousness of the task that it had to perform. It was then that the first attempt was made, under the influence of the revival of classical studies, and with the help of a knowledge of the language obtained from Jewish teachers, to find out the one true meaning of the Scriptures, and an end was put to the tedious jugglery of *multiplex Scripturæ sensus*. But very little was accomplished in the time of the Reformation for the prophecies of Isaiah.

Calvin's *Commentarii* answer the expectations with which we take them up; but Luther's *Scholia* are nothing but college notes, of the most meagre description. The productions of Grotius, which are generally valuable, are insignificant in Isaiah, and, indeed, throughout the prophets. He mixes up things sacred and profane, and, because unable to follow prophecy in its flight, cuts off its wings. Aug. Varenius of Rostock wrote the most learned commentary of all those composed by writers of the orthodox Lutheran school, and one that even now is not to be despised; but though learned, it is too great a medley, and written without discipline of mind. Campegius Vitringa († 1722) threw all the labours of his predecessors into the shade, and none even of his successors approach him in spirit, keenness, and scholarship. His *Commentary on Isaiah* is still incomparably the greatest of all the exegetical works upon the Old Testament. The weakest thing in the Commentary is the allegorical exposition, which is appended to the grammatical and historical one. In this the temperate pupil of the Cocceian school is dependent upon what was then the prevalent style of commentary in Holland, where there was an utter absence of all appreciation of the "complex-apotelesmatical" character of prophecy, whilst the most minute allusions were traced in the prophets to events connected with the history of both the world and the church. The shady sides of the Commentary are generally the first to present themselves to the reader's eye; but the longer he continues to use it, the more highly does he learn to value it. There is deep research everywhere, but nowhere a luxuriance of dry and dead scholarship. The author's heart is in his work. He sometimes halts in his toilsome path of inquiry, and gives vent to loud, rapturous exclamations. But the rapture is very different from that of the Lord Bishop Robert Lowth, who never gets below the surface, who alters the Masoretic text at his pleasure, and goes no further than an æsthetic admiration of the form.

The modern age of exegesis commenced with that destructive theology of the latter half of the eighteenth century, which pulled down without being able to build. But even this demolition was not without good result. The negative of anything divine and eternal in the Scriptures secured a fuller recognition of its human and temporal side, bringing out the charms of its poetry, and, what was of still greater importance, the concrete reality of its history. Rosenmüller's *Scholia* are a careful, lucid, and elegant compilation, founded for the most part upon Vitringa, and praiseworthy not only for the judicious character of the selection made, but also for the true earnestness which is displayed, and the entire absence of all frivolity. The decidedly rationalistic Commentary of Gesenius is more independent in its verbal exegesis; displays great care in its historical expositions; and is peculiarly distinguished for its pleasing and transparent style, for the survey which it gives of the whole of the literature bearing upon Isaiah, and the thoroughness with which the author avails himself of all the new sources of grammatical and historical knowledge that have been opened since the days of Vitringa. Hitzig's Commentary is his best work in our opinion, excelling as it does in exactness and in the sharpness and originality of its grammatical criticisms, as well as in delicate tact in the discovery of the train of thought and in thoroughness and precision in the exposition of well-pondered results; but it is also disfigured by rash pseudo-critical caprice, and by a studiously profane spirit, utterly unaffected by the spirit of prophecy. Hendewerk's Commentary is often very weak in philological and historical exposition. The style of description is broad, but the eye of the disciple of Herbart is too dim to distinguish Israelitish prophecy from heathen poetry, and the politics of Isaiah from those of Demosthenes. Nevertheless, we cannot fail to observe the thoughtful diligence displayed, and the anxious desire to point out the germs of eternal truths, although the author is fettered even in this by his philosophical standpoint. Ewald's natural penetration is universally recognised, as well as the noble enthusiasm with which he dives into the contents of the prophetical books, in which he finds an eternal presence. His earnest endeavours to obtain deep views are to a certain extent rewarded. But there is something irritating in the self-sufficiency with which he ignores nearly all his predecessors, the dictatorial assumption of his criticism, his false and often nebulous pathos, and his unqualified identification of his own opinions with truth itself. He is a perfect master in the characteristics of the prophets, but his translations of them are stiff, and hardly to any one's taste. Umbreit's *Practical Commentary on Isaiah* is a useful and stimulating production, exhibiting a deep æsthetic and religious sensibility to the glory of the prophetic word, which manifests itself in lofty poetic language, heaping image upon image, and, as it were, never coming down from the cothurnus. Knobel's prose is the very opposite extreme. The precision and thoroughness of this scholar, the third edition of whose *Commentary on Isaiah* was one of his last works (he died 25th May 1863), deserve the most grateful acknowledgment, whether from a philological or an archæological point of view; but his peculiar triviality, which amounts almost to an affectation, seems to shut his eyes to the deeper meaning of the work, whilst his excessive tendency to "historize" (*historisiren, i.e.* to give a purely historical interpretation to everything) makes him blind even to the poetry of the form. Drechsler's Commentary was a great advance in the exposition of Isaiah. He was only able to carry it out himself as far as ch. xxvii.; but it was completed by Delitzsch and H. A. Hahn of Greifswald († 1st Dec. 1861), with the use of Drechsler's notes, though they contained very little that was of any service in relation to ch. xl.-lxvi. This was, comparatively speaking, the best commentary upon Isaiah that had appeared since the time of Vitringa, more especially the portion on ch. xiii.-xxvii. Its peculiar excellency is not to be found in the exposition of single sentences, which is unsatisfactory, on account of the comminuting, glossatorial style of its exegesis, and, although diligent and thorough enough, is unequal and by no means productive, more especially from a grammatical point of view; but in the spiritual and spirited grasp of the whole, the deep insight which it exhibits into the character and ideas of the prophet and of prophecy, its vigorous penetration into the very heart of the plan and substance of the whole book. In the meantime (1850), there had appeared the Commentary written by the catholic Professor Peter Schegg, which follows the Vulgate, although with as little slavishness as possible, and contains many good points, especially the remarks relating to the history of translation. At the same time there also appeared the Commentary of Ernst Meier, the Tübingen orientalist, which did not get beyond the first half. If ever any one was specially called to throw fresh light upon the book of Isaiah, it was C. P. Caspari of Christiania; but all that has yet appeared of his Norwegian Commentary only reaches to the end of ch. v. Its further progress has been hindered partly by the exhaustive thoroughness at which he aimed, and the almost infinite labour which it involved, and partly by the fact that the Grundtvig controversy involved him in the necessity of pursuing the most extensive studies in ecclesiastical history. In the meantime, he has so far expanded his treatise *om Serapherne* (on the Seraphim), that it may be regarded as a commentary on Isa. vi.; and rich materials for the prophetic sayings which follow may be found in his contributions to the introduction to the book of Isaiah, and to the history of Isaiah's own times, which appeared as a second volume of our biblico-theological and apologetico-critical *Studien* (1848), his *Programme* on the Syro-Ephraimitish war (1849), and his comprehensive and by no means obsolete article, entitled, "Jeremiah a witness to the genuineness of Isa. xxxiv., and therefore also to that of Isa. xl.-lxvi., xiii.-xiv. 23, and xxi. 1-10," which appeared in the *Zeitschrift für d. ges. luth. Theologie u. Kirche* (1843), together with an excursus on the relation of Zephaniah to the disputed prophecies of Isaiah.

We shall reserve those works which treat more particularly of the second part of the book of Isaiah for our special introduction to that part. But there are two other distinguished commentaries that we must mention here, both of them by Jewish scholars: viz. that of M. L. Malbim (Krotoshin 1849), which is chiefly occupied with the precise ideas conveyed by synonymous words and groups of words; and that of S. D. Luzzatto of Padua,—a stimulating work, entitled *Profeta Isaia volgarizzato e commentato ad uso degli Israeliti*, which aims throughout at independence, but of which only five parts have yet appeared.

EXPOSITION.

IN passing to our exposition of the book, the first thing which strikes us is its traditional title — *Yeshaiah* (Isaiah). In the book itself, and throughout the Old Testament Scriptures, the prophet is called *Yeshayahu;* and the shorter form is found in the latest books as the name of other persons. It was a common thing in the very earliest times for the shorter forms of such names to be used interchangeably with the longer; but in later times the shorter was the only form employed, and for this reason it was the one adopted in the traditional title. The name is a compound one, and signifies "Jehovah's salvation." The prophet was conscious that it was not merely by accident that he bore this name; for יֵשַׁע (he shall save) and יְשׁוּעָה (salvation) are among his favourite words. It may be said, in fact, that he lived and moved altogether in the coming salvation, which was to proceed from Jehovah, and would be realized hereafter, when Jehovah should come at last to His people as He had never come before. This salvation was the goal of the sacred history (*Heilsgeschichte,* literally, history of salvation); and *Jehovah* was the peculiar name of God in relation to that history. It denotes "the existing one," not however "the always existing," *i.e.* eternal, as Bunsen and the Jewish translators render it, but "existing evermore," *i.e.* filling all history, and displaying His glory therein in grace and truth. The ultimate goal of this historical process, in which God was ever ruling as the absolutely free One, according to His own self-assertion in Ex. iii. 14, was true and essential *salvation,* proceeding outwards from Israel, and eventually embracing all mankind. In the name of the prophet the tetragrammaton יהוה is contracted into יו

(יה) by the dropping of the second ה. We may easily see from this contraction that the name of God was pronounced with an *a* sound, so that it was either called *Yahveh*, or rather *Yahaveh*, or else *Yahvāh*, or rather *Yahavāh*. According to Theodoret, it was pronounced 'Ιαβε (*Yahaveh*) by the Samaritans; and it is written in the same way in the list of the names of the Deity given in Epiphanius. That the *ah* sound was also a customary pronunciation, may not only be gathered from such names as Jimnah, Jimrah, Jishvah, Jishpah (compare Jithlah, the name of a place), but is also expressly attested by the ancient variations, *Jao, Jeuo, Jo* (Jer. xxiii. 6, LXX.), on the one hand, and on the other hand by the mode of spelling adopted by Origen (*Jaoia*) and Theodoret (*Aia*, not only in *quæst. in Ex.* § 15, but also in *Fab. hæret.* v. 4: "*Aia* signifies the existing one; it was pronounced thus by Hebrews, but the Samaritans call it Jabaì, overlooking the force of the word"). The dull-sounding long *a* could be expressed by *omega* quite as well as by *alpha*. Isidor follows these and similar testimonies, and says (*Orig.* vii. 7), " The tetragrammaton consisted of *ia* written twice (*ia, ia*), and with this reduplication it constituted the unutterable and glorious name of God." The Arabic form adopted by the Samaritans leaves it uncertain whether it is to be pronounced *Yahve* or *Yahva*. They wrote to Job Ludolf (in the *Epistola Samaritana Sichemitarum tertia*, published by Bruns, 1781), in opposition to the statement of Theodoret, that they pronounced the last syllable with *damma;* that is to say, they pronounced the name *Yahavoh* (*Yahvoh*), which was the form in which it was written in the last century by Velthusen, and also by Muffi in his *Disegno di lezioni e di ricerche sulla lingua Ebraica* (Pavia, 1792). The pronunciation *Jehovah* (*Yehovah*) arose out of a combination of the *keri* and the *chethib*, and has only become current since the time of the Reformation. Genebrard denounces it in his *Commentary upon the Psalms* with the utmost vehemence, in opposition to Beza, as an intolerable innovation. " Ungodly violators of what is most ancient," he says, " profaning and transforming the unutterable name of God, would read JOVA or JEHOVA,—a new, barbarous, fictitious, and irreligious word, that savours strongly of the Jove of the heathen." Nevertheless this *Jehova* (*Jova*) forced its way into general adoption, and we shall therefore retain it, notwithstanding the fact that the *o* sound is decidedly wrong. To return, then: the prophet's name signifies " Jehovah's salvation." In the Septuagint it is always written 'Ησαΐας, with a strong aspirate; in the Vulgate it is written *Isaias*, and sometimes *Esaias*.

In turning from the outward to the inward title, which is contained in the book itself, there are two things to be observed at the outset: (1.) The division of the verses indicated by *soph pasuk* is an arrangement for which the way was prepared as early as the time of the Talmud, and which was firmly established in the Masoretic schools; and consequently it reaches as far back as the extreme limits of the middle ages—differing in this respect from the division of verses in the New Testament. The arrangement of the chapters, however, with the indications of the separate sections of the prophetic collection, is of no worth to us, simply because it is not older than the thirteenth century. According to some authorities, it originated with Stephen Langton, Archbishop of Canterbury († 1227); whilst others attribute it to Cardinal Hugo of St Caro († 1262). It is only since the fifteenth century that it has been actually adopted in the text. (2.) The small ring or star at the commencement points to the footnote, which affirms that Isa. i. 1-28 (where we find the same sign again) was the *haphtarah*, or concluding *pericope*, taken from the prophets, which was read on the same Sabbath as the *parashah* from the Pentateuch, in Deut. i. 1 sqq. It was, as we shall afterwards see, a very thoughtful principle of selection which led to the combination of precisely these two lessons.

Title of the collection, as given in ver. 1: " *Seeing of Yesha'yahu, son of Amoz, which he saw over Judah and Jerusalem in the days of 'Uzziyahu, Jotham, Ahaz,* and *Yehizkiyahu, the kings of Judah.*" Isaiah is called the " *son of Amoz.*" There is no force in the old Jewish doctrine (*b. Megilla* 15a), which was known to the fathers, that whenever the name of a prophet's father is given, it is a proof that the father was also a prophet. And we are just as incredulous about another old tradition, to the effect that Amoz was the brother of Amaziah, the father and predecessor of Uzziah (*b. Sota* 10*b*). There is some significance in this tradition, however, even if it is not true. There is something royal in the nature and bearing of Isaiah throughout. He speaks to kings as if he himself were a king. He confronts with majesty the magnates of the nation and of the imperial power. In his peculiar style, he occupies the same place among the prophets as Solomon among the kings. Under all circumstances, and in whatever state of mind, he is completely master of his materials—simple, yet majestic in his style—elevated, yet without affectation—and beautiful, though unadorned. But this regal character had its roots somewhere else than in the blood. All that can be affirmed with certainty is, that Isaiah was a native of Jerusalem; for notwithstanding his manifold prophetic missions, we never find him outside Jerusalem. There he lived with his wife and children, and, as we may infer from ch. xxii. 1, and the mode of his intercourse with king Hezekiah, down in the lower city. And there he laboured under the four kings named in ver. 1, viz. Uzziah (who reigned 52 years, 811–759), Jotham (16 years, 759–743), Ahaz (16 years, 743–728), and Hezekiah (29 years, 728–699). The four kings are enumerated without a *Vav cop.;* there is the same *asyndeton enumerativum* as in the titles to the books of Hosea and Micah. Hezekiah is there called *Yehizkiyah*, the form being almost the same as ours, with the simple elision of the concluding sound. The chronicler evidently preferred the fullest form, at the commencement as well as the termination. Roorda imagines that the chronicler derived this ill-shaped form from the three titles, where it is a copyist's error for וְחִזְקִיָּהוּ or וְחִזְקִיָּה; but the estimable grammarian has overlooked the fact that the same form is found in Jer. xv. 4 and 2 Kings xx. 10, where no such error of the pen can have occurred. Moreover, it is not an ill-shaped form, if, instead of deriving it from the *piel,* as Roorda does, we derive it from the *kal* of the verb ("strong is Jehovah," an imperfect noun with a connecting *i,* which is frequently met with in proper names from verbal roots, such as *Jesimiēl* from *sim,* 1 Chron. iv. 36: *vid.* Olshausen, § 277, p. 621). Under these four kings Isaiah laboured, or, as it is expressed in ver. 1, saw the sight which is committed to writing in the book before us. Of all the many Hebrew synonyms for seeing, חָזָה (cf. *cernere,* κρίνειν, and the Sanscrit and Persian *kar,* which is founded upon the radical notion of cutting and separating) is the standing general expression used to denote prophetic perception, whether the form in which the divine revelation was made to the prophet was in vision or by word.

In either case he *saw* it, because he distinguished this divine revelation from his own conceptions and thoughts by means of that inner sense, which is designated by the name of the noblest of all the five external senses. From this verb *chazah* there came both the abstract *chazon*, seeing, and the more concrete *chizzayon*, a sight (*visum*), which is a stronger form of *chizyon* (from *chazai* = *chazah*). The noun *chazon* is indeed used to denote a particular sight (comp. Isa. xxix. 7 with Job xx. 8, xxxiii. 15), inasmuch as it consists in seeing (*visio*); but here in the title of the book of Isaiah the abstract meaning passes over into the collective idea of the sight or vision in all its extent, *i.e.* the sum and substance of all that was seen. It is a great mistake, therefore, for any one to argue from the use of the word *chazon* (vision), that ver. 1*a* was originally nothing more than the heading to the first prophecy, and that it was only by the addition of ver. 1*b* that it received the stamp of a general title to the whole book. There is no force in the argument. Moreover, the chronicler knew the book of Isaiah by this title (2 Chron. xxxii. 32); and the titles of other books of prophecy, such as Hosea, Amos, Micah, and Zephaniah, are very similar. A more plausible argument in favour of the twofold origin of ver. 1 has been lately repeated by Schegg and Meier, namely, that whilst "*Judah and Jerusalem*" are appropriate enough as defining the object of the first prophecy, the range is too limited to apply to all the prophecies that follow; since their object is not merely Judah, including Jerusalem, but they are also directed against foreign nations, and at ch. vii. the king of Israel, including Samaria, also comes within the horizon of the prophet's vision. And in the title to the book of Micah, both kingdoms are distinctly named. But it was necessary there, inasmuch as Micah commences at once with the approaching overthrow of Samaria. Here the designation is a central one. Even, according to the well-known maxims *a potiori*, and *a proximo, fit denominatio*, it would not be unsuitable; but Judah and Jerusalem are really and essentially the sole object of the prophet's vision. For within the largest circle of the imperial powers there lies the smaller one of the neighbouring nations; and in this again, the still more limited one of all Israel, including Samaria; and within this the still smaller one of the kingdom of Judah. And all these circles together form the circumference of Jerusalem, since the entire history of the world, so far as its inmost pragmatism and its ultimate goal were concerned, was the history of the church of God, which had for its peculiar site the city of the temple of Jehovah, and of the kingdom of promise. The expression "*concerning Judah and Jerusalem*" is therefore perfectly applicable to the whole book, in which all that the prophet sees is seen from Judah-Jerusalem as a centre, and seen for the sake and in the interests of both. The title in ver. 1 may pass without hesitation as the heading written by the prophet's own hand. This is admitted not only by Caspari (*Micah*, pp. 90–93), but also by Hitzig and Knobel. By if ver. 1 contains the title to the whole book, where is the heading to the first prophecy? Are we to take אֲשֶׁר as a nominative instead of an accusative (*qui* instead of *quam, sc. visionem*), as Luzzatto does? This is a very easy way of escaping from the difficulty, and stamping ver. 1 as the heading to the first prophetic words in ch. i.; but it is unnatural, as חזון אשר חזה, according to Ges. (§ 138, note 1), is the customary form in Hebrew of connecting the verb with its own substantive. The real answer is simple enough. The first prophetic address is left intentionally without a heading, just because it is the prologue to all the rest; and the second prophetic address has a heading in ch. ii. 1, although it really does not need one, for the purpose of bringing out more sharply the true character of the first as the prologue to the whole.

FIRST HALF OF THE COLLECTION.

CHAP. I.-XXXIX.

PART I.

PROPHECIES RELATING TO THE ONWARD COURSE OF THE GREAT MASS OF THE PEOPLE TOWARDS HARDENING OF HEART (CHAP. I.–VI.).

OPENING ADDRESS CONCERNING THE WAYS OF JEHOVAH WITH HIS UNGRATEFUL AND REBELLIOUS NATION.—CHAP. I. 2 SQQ.

THE difficult question as to the historical and chronological standpoint of this overture to all the following addresses, can only be brought fully out when the exposition is concluded. But there is one thing which we may learn even from a cursory inspection: namely, that the prophet was standing at the eventful boundary line between two distinct halves in the history of Israel. The people had not been brought to reflection and repentance either by the riches of the divine goodness, which they had enjoyed in the time of Uzziah-Jotham, the copy of the times of David and Solomon, or by the chastisements of divine wrath, by which wound after wound was inflicted. The divine methods of education were exhausted, and all that now remained for Jehovah to do was to let the nation in its existing state be dissolved in fire, and to create a new one from the remnant of gold that stood the fiery test. At this time, so pregnant with storms, the prophets were more active than at any other period. Amos appeared about the tenth year of Uzziah's reign, the twenty-fifth of Jeroboam II.; Micah prophesied from the time of Jotham till the fall of Samaria, in the sixth year of Hezekiah's reign ; but most prominent of all was Isaiah, the prophet *par excellence,* standing as he did midway between Moses and Christ.

In the consciousness of his exalted position in relation to the history of salvation, he commences his opening address in Deuteronomic style. Modern critics are of opinion, indeed, that Deuteronomy was not composed till the time of Josiah, or at any rate not earlier than Manasseh; and even Kahnis adduces this as a firmly established fact (see his *Dogmatik,* i. 277). But if this be the case, how comes it to pass, not only that Micah (ch. vi. 8) points back to a saying in Deut. x. 12, but that all the post-Mosaic prophecy, even the very earliest of all, is tinged with a Deuteronomic colouring. This surely confirms the self-attestation of the authorship of Moses, which is declared most distinctly in ch. xxxi. 9. Deuteronomy was most peculiarly Moses' own law-book—his last will, as it were : it was also the oldest national book of Israel, and therefore the basis of all intercourse between the prophets and the nation. There is one portion of this peculiarly Mosaic *thorah,* however, which stands not only in a more truly primary relation to the prophecy of succeeding ages than any of the rest, but in a normative relation also. We refer to Moses' dying song, which has recently been expounded by Volck and Camphausen, and is called *shirath haazinu* (song of " Give ear"), from the opening words in ch. xxxii. This song is a compendious outline or draft, and also the common key to all prophecy, and bears the same fundamental relation to it as the Decalogue to all other laws, and the Lord's Prayer to all other prayers. The lawgiver summed up the whole of the prophetic contents of his last words (ch. xxvii.-xxviii. xxix.-xxx.), and threw them into the form of a song, that they might be perpetuated in the memories and mouths of the people. This song sets before the nation its entire history to the end of time. That history divides itself into four great periods : the creation and rise of Israel ; the ingratitude and apostasy of Israel ; the consequent surrender of Israel to the power of the heathen ; and finally, the restoration of Israel, sifted, but not destroyed, and the unanimity of all nations in the praise of Jehovah, who reveals Himself both in judgment and in mercy. This fourfold character is not only verified in every part of the history of Israel, but is also the seal of that history as a whole, even to its remotest end, in New Testament times. In every age, therefore, this song has presented to Israel a mirror of its existing condition and future fate. And it was the task of the prophets to hold up this mirror to the people of their own times. This is what Isaiah does. He begins his prophetic address in the same form in which Moses begins his song. The opening words of Moses are: " Give ear, O ye heavens, and I will speak; and let the earth hear the words of my mouth" (Deut. xxxii. 1). In what sense he invoked the heaven and the earth, he tells us himself in Deut. xxxi. 28, 29. He foresaw in spirit the future apostasy of Israel, and called heaven and earth, which would outlive his earthly life, that was now drawing to a close, as witnesses of what he had to say to his people, with such a prospect before them. Isaiah commences in the same way (ch. i. 2*a*), simply transposing the two parallel verbs " hear" and " give ear :" "*Hear, O heavens, and give ear, O earth; for Jehovah speaketh !*" The reason for the appeal is couched in very general terms : they were to hear, because Jehovah was speaking. What Jehovah said coincided essentially with the words of Jehovah, which are introduced in Deut. xxxii. 20 with the expression " And He said." What it was stated there that Jehovah would one day have to say in His wrath, He now said through the prophet, whose existing *present* corresponded to the coming *future* of the Mosaic ode. The time had now arrived for heaven and earth, which are always existing, and always the same, and which had accompanied Israel's history thus far in all places and at all times, to fulfil their duty as witnesses, according to the word of the lawgiver. And this was just the special, true, and ultimate sense in which they were called upon by the prophet, as they had previously been by Moses, to " hear." They had been present, and had taken part, when Jehovah gave the *thorah* to His people : the heavens, according to Deut. iv. 36, as the place from which the voice of God came forth; and the earth, as the scene of His great fire. They were solemnly invoked when Jehovah gave His people the choice between blessing and cursing, life and death (Deut. xxx. 19, iv. 26). And so now they are called upon to hear and join in bearing witness to all that Jehovah, their Creator, and the God of Israel, had to say, and the complaints that He had to make: "*I have brought up children, and raised them high, and they have fallen away from me*" (ver. 2b). Israel is referred to; but Israel is not specially named. On the contrary, the historical facts are generalized almost into a parable, in order that the appalling condition of things which is crying to heaven may be made all the more apparent. Israel was Jehovah's son (Ex. iv. 22, 23). All the members of the nation were His children (Deut. xiv. 1, xxxii. 20). Jehovah was Israel's father, by whom it had been begotten (Deut. xxxii. 6, 18). The existence of Israel as a nation was secured indeed, like that of all other nations, by natural reproduction, and not by spiritual regeneration. But the primary ground of Israel's origin was the supernatural and mighty word of promise given to Abraham, in Gen. xvii. 15, 16; and it was by a series of manifestations of miraculous power and displays of divine grace, that the development of Israel, which dated from that starting-point, was brought up to the position it had reached at the time of the exodus from Egypt. It was in this sense that Israel had been begotten by Jehovah. And this relation between Jehovah and Israel, as His children, had now, at the time when Jehovah was speaking through the mouth of Isaiah, a long and gracious past behind it, viz. the period of Israel's childhood in Egypt; the period of its youth in the desert; and a period of growing manhood from Joshua to Samuel: so that Jehovah could say, "I have brought up children, and raised them high." The *piel* (*giddel*) used here signifies "to make great;" and when applied to children, as it is here and in other passages, such as 2 Kings x. 6, it means to bring up, to make great, so far as natural growth is concerned. The *pilel* (*romem*), which corresponds to the *piel* in the so-called *verbis cavis*, and which is also used in ch. xxiii. 4 and Ezek. xxxi. 4 as the parallel to *giddel*, signifies to lift up, and is used in a " dignified (dignitative) sense," with reference to the position of eminence, to which, step by step, a wise and loving father advances a child. The two verses depict the state of Israel in the times of David and Solomon, as one of mature manhood and proud exaltation, which had to a certain extent returned under Uzziah and Jotham. But how base had been the return which it had made for all that it had received from God: "*And they have fallen away from me.*" We should have expected an adversative particle here; but instead of that, we have merely a *Vav cop.*, which is used energetically, as in ch. vi. 7 (cf. Hos. vii. 13). Two things which ought never to be coupled—Israel's filial relation to Jehovah, and Israel's base rebellion against Jehovah—had been realized in their most contradictory forms. The radical meaning of the verb is to break away, or break loose; and the object against which the act is directed is construed with *Beth*. The idea is that of dissolving connection with a person with violence and self-will; here it relates to that inward severance from God, and renunciation of Him, which preceded all outward acts of sin, and which not only had idolatry for its full and outward manifestation, but was truly idolatry in all its forms. From the time that Solomon gave himself up to the worship of idols, at the close of his reign, down to the days of Isaiah, idolatry had never entirely or permanently ceased to exist, even in public. In two different reformations the attempt had been made to suppress it, viz. in the one commenced by Asa and concluded by Jehoshaphat; and in the one carried out by Joash, during the lifetime of the high priest Jehoiada, his tutor and deliverer. But the first was not successful in suppressing it altogether; and what Joash removed, returned with double abominations as soon as Jehoiada was dead. Consequently the words, "They have rebelled against me," which sum up all the ingratitude of Israel in one word, and trace it to its root, apply to the whole history of Israel, from its culminating point under David and Solomon, down to the prophet's own time.

Ver. 3. Jehovah then complains that the rebellion with which His children have rewarded Him is not only inhuman, but even worse than that of the brutes : "*An ox knoweth its owner, and an ass its master's crib : Israel doth not know, my people doth not consider.*" An ox has a certain knowledge of its buyer and owner, to whom it willingly submits; and an ass has at least a knowledge of the crib of its master (the noun for "master" is in the plural : this is not to be understood in a numerical, but in an amplifying sense, "the authority over it," as in Ex. xxi. 29: *vid.* Ges. § 108, 2, *b*, and Dietrich's *Heb. Gram.* p. 45), *i.e.* it knows that it is its master who fills its crib or manger with fodder (*evus*, the crib, from *avas*, to feed, is radically associated witn φάτνη, vulgar πάθνη, Dor. and Lac. πάτνη, and is applied in the Talmud to the large common porringer used by labourers).[1] Israel had no such knowledge, neither instinctive and direct, nor acquired by reflection (*hithbonan*, the reflective conjugation, with a pausal change of the *ê* into a long *a*, according to Ges. § 54, note). The expressions "doth not know" and "doth not consider" must not be taken here in an objectless sense,—as, for example, in ch. lvi. 10 and Ps. lxxxii. 5,—viz. as signifying they were destitute of all knowledge and reflection; but the object is to be supplied from what goes before: they knew not, and did not consider what answered in their case to the owner and to the crib which the master fills,"—namely, that they were the children and possession of Jehovah, and that their existence and prosperity were dependent upon the grace of Jehovah alone. The parallel, with its striking contrasts, is self-drawn, like that in Jer. viii. 7, where animals are referred to again, and is clearly indicated in the words "Israel" and "my people." Those who were so far surpassed in knowledge and perception even by animals, and so thoroughly put to shame by them, were not merely a nation, like any other nation on the earth, but were "Israel," descendants of Jacob, the wrestler with God, who wrestled down the wrath of God, and wrestled out a blessing for himself and his descendants; and "my people," the nation which Jehovah had chosen out of all other nations to be the nation of His possession, and His own peculiar government. This nation, bearing as it did the God-given title of a hero of faith and prayer, this favourite nation of Jehovah, had let itself down far below the level of the brutes. This is the complaint which the exalted speaker pours out in vers. 2 and 3 before heaven and earth. The words of God, together with the introduction, consist of two tetrastichs, the measure and rhythm of which are determined by the meaning of the words and the emotion of the speaker. There is nothing strained in it at all. Prophecy lives and moves amidst the thoughts of God, which prevail above the evil reality: and for that very reason, as a reflection of the glory

---

[1] *Nedarim* iv. 4 *jer. Demai* viii. The stable is called *rephcth*. Even in *jer. Shebuoth* viii. 1, where cattle are spoken of as standing *b'evus*, the word signifies a crib or manger, not a stable. Luzzatto tries to prove that *evus* signifies a threshing-floor, and indeed an enclosed place, in distinction from *geren*; but he is mistaken.

of God, which is the ideal of beauty (Ps. l. 1), it is through and through poetical. That of Isaiah is especially so. There was no art of oratory practised in Israel, which Isaiah did not master, and which did not serve as the vehicle of the word of God, after it had taken shape in the prophet's mind.

With ver. 4 there commences a totally different rhythm. The words of Jehovah are ended. The piercing lamentation of the deeply grieved Father is also the severest accusation. The cause of God, however, is to the prophet the cause of a friend, who feels an injury done to his friend quite as much as if it were done to himself (ch. v. 1). The lamentation of God, therefore, is changed now into violent scolding and threatening on the part of the prophet; and in accordance with the deep wrathful pain with which he is moved, his words pour out with violent rapidity, like flash after flash, in climactic clauses having no outward connection, and each consisting of only two or three words.—Ver. 4. " *Woe upon the sinful nation, the guilt-laden people, the miscreant race, the children acting corruptly! They have forsaken Jehovah, blasphemed Israel's Holy One, turned away backwards.*" The distinction sometimes drawn between *hoi* (with *He*) and *oi* (with *Aleph*)—as equivalent to oh! and woe!—cannot be sustained. *Hoi* is an exclamation of pain, with certain doubtful exceptions; and in the case before us it is not so much a denunciation of woe (*væ genti*, as the Vulgate renders it), as a lamentation (*væ gentem*) filled with wrath. The epithets which follow point indirectly to that which Israel ought to have been, according to the choice and determination of God, and plainly declare what it had become through its own choice and ungodly self-determination. (1.) According to the choice and determination of God, Israel was to be a holy nation (*goi kadosh*, Ex. xix. 6); but it was a sinful nation—*gens peccatrix*, as it is correctly rendered by the Vulgate. חֹטֵא is not a participle here, but rather a participial adjective in the sense of what was habitual. It is the singular in common use for the plural חַטָּאִים, sinners, the singular of which was not used. Holy and Sinful are glaring contrasts: for *kadosh*, so far as its radical notion is concerned (assuming, that is to say, that this is to be found in *kad* and not in *dosh*: see *Psalter*, i. 588, 9), signifies that which is separated from what is common, unclean, or sinful, and raised above it. The alliteration in *hoi goi* implies that the nation, as sinful, was a nation of woe. (2.) In the *thorah* Israel was called not only "a holy nation," but also "the people of Jehovah" (Num. xvii. 6, Eng. ver. xvi. 41), the people chosen and blessed of Jehovah; but now it had become "a people heavy with iniquity." Instead of the most natural expression, a people bearing heavy sins; the sin, or iniquity, *i.e.* the weight carried, is attributed to the people themselves upon whom the weight rested, according to the common figurative idea, that whoever carries a heavy burden is so much heavier himself (cf. *gravis oneribus*, Cicero). עָוֹן (sin regarded as crookedness and perversity, whereas חָטָא suggests the idea of going astray and missing the way) is the word commonly used wherever the writer intends to describe sin in the mass (*e.g.* ch. xxxiii. 24; Gen. xv. 16, xix. 15), including the guilt occasioned by it. The people of Jehovah had grown into a people heavily laden with guilt. So crushed, so altered into the very opposite, had Israel's true nature become. It is with deliberate intention that we have rendered גּוֹי a nation (*Nation*), and עַם a people (*Volk*): for, according to Malbim's correct definition of the distinction between the two, the former is used to denote the mass, as linked together by common descent, language, and country; the latter the people as bound together by unity of government (see, for example, Ps. cv. 13). Consequently we always read of the people of the Lord, not the nation of the Lord; and there are only two instances in which *goi* is attached to a suffix relating to the ruler, and then it relates to Jehovah alone (Zeph. ii. 9; Ps. cvi. 5). (3.) Israel bore elsewhere the honourable title of the seed of the patriarch (ch. xli. 8, xlv. 19; cf. Gen. xxi. 12); but in reality it was a seed of evil-doers (miscreants). This does not mean that it was descended from evil-doers; but the genitive is used in the sense of a direct apposition to *zera* (seed), as in ch. lxv. 23 (cf. ch. lxi. 9, vi. 13, and Ges. § 116, 5), and the meaning is a seed which consists of evil-doers, and therefore is apparently descended from evil-doers instead of from patriarchs. This last thought is not implied in the genitive, but in the idea of "seed;" which is always a compact unit, having one origin, and bearing the character of its origin in itself. The rendering brood of evil-doers, however it may accord with the sense, would be inaccurate; for "seed of evil-doers" is just the same as "house of evil-doers" in ch. xxxi. 2. The singular of the noun מְרֵעִים is מֵרֵעַ, with the usual sharpening in the case of gutturals in the verbs ע״ע, מֵרַע with *patach*, מֵרָע with *kametz* in pause (ch. ix. 16, which see),—a noun derived from the *hiphil* participle. (4.) Those who were of Israel were "children of Jehovah" through the act of God (Deut. xiv. 1); but in their own acts they were "children acting destructively" (*bânim mashchithim*), so that what the *thorah* feared and predicted had now occurred (Deut. iv. 16, 25, xxxi. 29). In all these passages we find the *hiphil*, and in the parallel passage of the great song (Deut. xxxii. 5) the *piel*—both of them conjugations which contain within themselves the object of the action indicated (Ges. § 53, 2): to do what is destructive, *i.e.* so to act as to become destructive to one's self and to others. It is evident from ver. 2*b*, that the term children is to be understood as indicating their relation to Jehovah (cf. ch. xxx. 1, 9). The four interjectional clauses are followed by three declaratory clauses, which describe Israel's apostasy as total in every respect, and complete the mournful seven. There was apostasy in heart: "They have forsaken Jehovah." There was apostasy in words: "They blaspheme the Holy One of Israel." The verb literally means to sting, then to mock or treat scornfully; the use of it to denote blasphemy is antiquated Mosaic (Deut. xxxi. 20; Num. xiv. 11, 23, xvi. 30). It is with intention that God is designated here as "the Holy One of Israel,"—a name which constitutes the keynote of all Isaiah's prophecy (see at ch. vi. 3). It was sin to mock at anything holy; it was a double sin to mock at God, the Holy One; but it was a threefold sin for Israel to mock at God the Holy One, who had set Himself to be the sanctifier of Israel, and required that as He was Israel's sanctification, He should also be sanctified by Israel according to His holiness (Lev. xix. 2, etc.). And lastly, there was also apostasy in action: "they have turned away backwards;" or, as the Vulgate renders it, *abalienati sunt.* נָזוֹר is the reflective of זוּר, related to נָזַר and סוּר, for which it is the word commonly used in the Targum. The *niphal*, which is only met with here, indicates the deliberate character of their estrangement from God; and the expression is rendered still more emphatic by the introduction of the word "backwards" (*achor*, which is used emphatically in the place of מֵאַחֲרָיו). In all their actions they ought to have followed Jehovah; but they had turned their backs upon Him, and taken the way selected by themselves.—Ver. 5. In this verse a disputed question arises as to the words עַל־מֶה (מֶה, the shorter, sharper form of מָה, which is common even before non-gutturals, Ges. § 32, 1): viz. whether they mean "wherefore," as the LXX., Targums, Vulgate, and most of the early versions render them, or "upon what," *i.e.* upon which part of the body, as others, including Schröring, suppose. Luzzatto maintains that the latter rendering is spiritless, more especially because there is nothing in the fact that a limb has been struck already to prevent its being struck again; but such objections as these can only arise in connection with a purely literal interpretation of the passage. If we adopted this rendering, the real meaning would be, that there was no judgment whatever that had not already fallen upon Israel on account of its apostasy, so that it was not far from utter destruction. We agree, however, with Caspari in deciding in favour of the meaning "to what" (to what end). For in all the other passages in which the expression occurs (fourteen times in all), it is used in this sense, and once even with the verb *hiccâh*, to smite (Num. xxii. 32), whilst it is only in ver. 6 that the idea of the people as one body is introduced; whereas the question "upon what" would require that the reader or hearer should presuppose it here. But in adopting the rendering "whereto," or to what end, we do not understand it, as Malbim does, in the sense of *cui bono*, with the underlying thought, "It would be ineffectual, as all the previous smiting has proved;" for this thought never comes out in a direct expression, as we should expect, but rather—according to the analogy of the questions with *lamah* in Ezek. xviii. 31, Jer. xliv. 7—in the sense of *qua de causa*, with the underlying thought, "There would be only an infatuated pleasure in your own destruction."—Ver. 5*a* we therefore render thus: "*Why would ye be perpetually smitten, multiplying rebellion?*" עוֹד (with *tiphchah*, a stronger disjunctive than *tebir*) belongs to תֻּכּוּ; see the same form of accentuation in Ezek. xix. 9. They are not two distinct interrogative clauses ("why would ye be smitten afresh? why do ye add revolt?"—Luzzatto), but the second clause is subordinate to the first (without there being any necessity to supply *chi*, "*because*," as Gesenius supposes), an adverbial minor clause defining the main clause more precisely; at all events this is the logical connection, as in ch. v. 11 (cf. Ps. lxii. 4, "delighting in lies," and Ps. iv. 3, "loving vanity"): LXX. "adding iniquity." *Sârâh* (rebellion) is a deviation from truth and rectitude; and here, as in many other instances, it denotes apostasy from Jehovah, who is the absolutely Good, and absolute goodness. There is a still further dispute whether the next words should be rendered "every head" and "every heart," or "the whole head" and "the whole heart." In prose the latter would be impossible, as the two nouns are written without the article; but in the poetic style of the prophets the article may be omitted after *col*, when used in the sense of "the whole" (*e.g.* ch. ix. 12: with *whole* mouth, *i.e.* with full mouth). Nevertheless *col*, without the article following, never signifies "the whole" when it occurs several times in succession, as in ch. xv. 2 and Ezek. vii. 17, 18. We must therefore render ver. 5*b*, "*Every head is diseased, and every heart is sick.*" The *Lamed* in *locholi* indicates the state into which a thing has come: every head in a state of disease (Ewald, § 217, *d*: *locholi* without the article, as in 2 Chron. xxi. 18). The prophet asks his fellow-countrymen why they are so foolish as to heap apostasy upon apostasy, and so continue to call down the judgments of God, which have already fallen upon them blow after blow. Has it reached such a height with them, that among all the many heads and hearts there is not one head which is not in a diseased state, not one heart which is not thoroughly ill? (*davvai* an emphatic form of *daveh*.) Head and heart are mentioned as the noblest parts of the outer and inner man. Outwardly and inwardly every individual in the nation had already been smitten by the wrath of God, so that they had had enough, and might have been brought to reflection.

This description of the total misery of every individual in the nation is followed by a representation of the whole nation as one miserably diseased body. Ver. 6. "*From the sole of the foot even to the head there is nothing sound in it: cuts, and stripes, and festering wounds; they have not been pressed out, nor bound up, nor has there been any soothing with oil.*" The body of the nation, to which the expression "*in it*" applies (*i.e.* the nation as a whole), was covered with wounds of different kinds: and no means whatever had been applied to heal these many, various wounds, which lay all together, close to one another, and one upon the other, covering the whole body. Cuts (from פָּצַע, to cut) are wounds that have cut into the flesh—sword-cuts, for example. These need binding up, in order that the gaping wound may close again. Stripes (*chabbûrâh*, from *châbar*, to stripe), swollen stripes, or weals, as if from a cut with a whip, or a blow with a fist: these require softening with oil, that the coagulated blood or swelling may disperse. Festering wounds, *maccâh teriyâh*, from *târâh*, to be fresh (a different word from the talmudic word *t're*, *Chullin* 45b, to thrust violently, so as to shake): these need pressing, for the purpose of cleansing them, so as to facilitate their healing. Thus the three predicates manifest an approximation to a *chiasm* (the crossing of the members); but this retrospective relation is not thoroughly carried out. The predicates are written in the plural, on account of the collective subject. The clause וְלֹא רֻכְּכָה בַּשָּׁמֶן, which refers to חבורה (stripes), so far as the sense is concerned (olive-oil, like all *oleosa*, being a dispersing medium), is to be taken as neuter, since this is the only way of explaining the change in the number: "And no softening has been effected with oil." *Zoru* we might suppose to be a *pual*, especially on account of the other *puals* near: it is not so, however, for the simple reason that, according to the accentuation (viz. with two *pashtahs*, the first of which gives the tone, as in *tohu*, Gen. i. 2, so that it must be pronounced *zóru*), it has the tone upon the penultimate, for which it would be impossible to discover any reason, if it were derived from *zârâh*. For the assumption that the tone is drawn back to prepare the way for the strong tone of the next verb (*chubbáshu*) is arbitrary, as the influence of the pause, though it sometimes reaches the last word but one, never extends to the last but two. Moreover, according to the usage of speech, *zorâh* signifies to be dispersed, not to be pressed out; whereas *zur* and *zârar* are commonly used in the sense of pressing together and squeezing out. Consequently *zoru* is either the *kal* of an intransitive *zor* in the middle voice (like *boshu*), or, what is more probable—as *zoru*, the middle voice in Ps. lviii. 4, has a different meaning (*ahalienati sunt*: cf. ver. 4)—the *kal* of *zârar* (= Arab. *constringere*), which is here conjugated as an intransitive (cf. Job xxiv. 24, *rommu*, and Gen. xlix. 23, where *robbu* is used in an active sense). The surgical treatment so needed by the nation was a figurative representation of the pastoral addresses of the prophets, which had been delivered indeed, but, inasmuch as their salutary effects were dependent upon the penitential sorrow of the people, might as well have never been delivered at all. The people had despised the merciful, compassionate kindness of their God. They had no liking for the radical cure which the prophets had offered to effect. All the more pitiable, therefore, was the condition of the body, which was sick within, and diseased from head to foot. The prophet is speaking here of the existing state of things. He affirms that it is all over with the nation; and this is the ground and object of his reproachful lamentations. Consequently, when he passes in the next verse from figurative language to literal, we may presume that he is still speaking of his own times. It is Isaiah's custom to act in this manner as his own expositor (compare ver. 22 with ver. 23). The body thus inwardly and outwardly diseased, was, strictly speaking, the people and the land in their fearful condition at that time. This is described more particularly in ver. 7, which commences with the most general view, and returns to it again at the close. Ver. 7. " *Your land . . a desert; your cities . . burned with fire; your field . . foreigners consuming it before your eyes, and a desert like overthrowing by strangers.*" Caspari has pointed out, in his *Introduction to the Book of Isaiah* (p. 204), how nearly every word corresponds to the curses threatened in Lev. xxvi. and Deut. xxviii. (xxix.); Mic. vi. 13–16 and Jer. v. 15 sqq. stand in the very same relation to these sections of the Pentateuch. From the time of Isaiah downwards, the state of Israel was a perfect realization of the curses of the law. The prophet intentionally employs the words of the law to describe his own times; he designates the enemy, who devastated the land, reduced its towers to ashes, and took possession of its crops, by the simple term *zarim*, foreigners or barbarians (a word which would have the very same meaning if it were really the reduplication of the Aramæan *bar;* compare the Syriac *baróye*, a foreigner), without mentioning their particular nationality.

He abstracts himself from the definite historical present, in order that he may point out all the more emphatically how thoroughly it bears the character of the fore-ordained curse. The most emphatic indication of this was to be found in the fact, which the clause at the close of ver. 7 palindromically affirms, that a desolation had been brought about "like the overthrow of foreigners." The repetition of a catchword like *zarim* (foreigners) at the close of the verse in this emphatic manner, is a figure of speech, called *epanaphora*, peculiar to the two halves of our collection. The question arises, however, whether *zarim* is to be regarded as the genitive of the subject, as Caspari, Knobel, and others suppose, "such an overthrow as is commonly produced by barbarians" (cf. 2 Sam. x. 3, where the verb occurs), or as the genitive of the subject, "such an overthrow as comes upon barbarians." As *mahpechâh* (overthrow) is used in other places in which it occurs to denote the destruction of Sodom, Gomorrah, etc., according to the primary passage, Deut. xxix. 22, and Isaiah had evidently also this catastrophe in his mind, as ver. 8 clearly shows; we decide in favour of the conclusion that *zârim* is the genitive of the object (cf. Amos iv. 11). The force of the comparison is also more obvious, if we understand the words in this sense. The desolation which had fallen upon the land of the people of God resembled that thorough desolation (*subversio*) with which God visited the nations outside the covenant, who, like the people of the Pentapolis, were swept from off the earth without leaving a trace behind. But although there was similarity, there was not sameness, as vers. 8, 9 distinctly affirm. Jerusalem itself was still preserved; but in how pitiable a condition! There can be no doubt that *bath-Zion* ("daughter of Zion," Eng. ver.) in ver. 8 signifies Jerusalem. The genitive in this case is a genitive of apposition: "daughter Zion," not "daughter of Zion" (cf. ch. xxxvii. 22: see Ges. § 116, 5). Zion itself is represented as a daughter, *i.e.* as a woman. The expression applied primarily to the *community* dwelling around the fortress of Zion, to which the individual inhabitants stood in the same relation as children to a mother, inasmuch as the community sees its members for the time being come into existence and grow: they are born within her, and, as it were, born and brought up by her. It was then applied secondarily to the *city itself*, with or without the inhabitants (cf. Jer. xlvi. 19, xlviii. 18; Zech. ii. 11). In this instance the latter are included, as ver. 9 clearly shows. This is precisely the point in the first two comparisons. Ver. 8*a*. "*And the daughter of Zion remains like a hut in a vineyard; like a hammock in a cucumber field.*" The vineyard and cucumber field (*mikshah*, from *kisshu*, a cucumber, *cucumis*, not a gourd, *cucurbita;* at least not the true round gourd, whose Hebrew name, *dalaath*, does not occur in the Old Testament) are pictured by the prophet in their condition before the harvest (not after, as the Targums render it), when it is necessary that they should be watched. The point of comparison therefore is, that in the vineyard and cucumber field not a human being is to be seen in any direction; and there is nothing but the cottage and the night barrack or hammock (cf. Job xxvii. 18) to show that there are any human beings there at all. So did Jerusalem stand in the midst of desolation, reaching far and wide, — a sign, however, that the land was not entirely depopulated. But what is the meaning of the third point of comparison? Hitzig renders it, "like a watch-tower;" Knobel, "like a guard-city." But the noun neither means a tower nor a castle (although the latter would be quite possible, according to the primary meaning, *cingere*); and *nezurâh* does not mean "watch" or "guard." On the other hand, the comparison indicated (like, or as) does not suit what would seem the most natural rendering, viz. "like a guarded city," *i.e.* a city shielded from danger. Moreover, it is inadmissible to take the first two *Caphs* in the sense of *sicut* (as) and the third in the sense of *sic* (so); since, although this correlative is common in clauses indicating identity, it is not so in sentences which institute a simple comparison. We therefore adopt the rendering, ver. 8*b*, "*As a besieged city,*" deriving *nezurâh* not from *zur*, niphal *nâzor* (never used), as Luzzatto does, but from *nâzar*, which signifies to observe with keen eye, either with a good intention, or, as in Job vii. 20, for a hostile purpose. It may therefore be employed, like the synonyms in 2 Sam. xi. 16 and Jer. v. 6, to denote the reconnoitring of a city. Jerusalem was not actually blockaded at the time when the prophet uttered his predictions; but it was like a blockaded city. In the case of such a city there is a desolate space, completely cleared of human beings, left between it and the blockading army, in the centre of which the city itself stands solitary and still, shut up to itself. The citizens do not venture out; the enemy does not come within the circle that immediately surrounds the city, for fear of the shots of the citizens; and everything within this circle is destroyed, either by the citizens themselves, to prevent the enemy from finding anything useful, or else by the enemy, who cut down the trees. Thus, with all the joy that might be felt at the preservation of Jerusalem, it presented but a gloomy appearance. It was, as it were, in a state of siege. A proof that this is the way in which the passage is to be explained, may be found in Jer. iv. 16, 17, where the actual storming of Jerusalem is foretold, and the enemy is called *nozerim*, probably with reference to the simile before us.

For the present, however, Jerusalem was saved from this extremity.—Ver. 9. The omnipotence of God had mercifully preserved it: "*Unless Jehovah of hosts had left us a little of what had escaped, we had become like Sodom, we were like Gomorrah.*" *Sarid* (which is rendered inaccurately σπέρμα in the Sept.; cf. Rom. ix. 29) was used, even in the early Mosaic usage of the language, to signify that which escaped the general destruction (Deut. ii. 34, etc.); and כִּמְעָט (which might very well be connected with the verbs which follow: "we were very nearly within a little like Sodom," etc.) is to be taken in connection with *sarid*, as the pausal form clearly shows: "a remnant which was but a mere trifle" (on this use of the word, see ch. xvi. 14; 2 Chron. xii. 7; Prov. x. 20; Ps. cv. 12). *Jehovah Zebaoth* stands first, for the sake of emphasis. It would have been all over with Israel long ago, if it had not been for the compassion of God (*vid.* Hos. xi. 8). And because it was the omnipotence of God, which set the will of His compassion in motion, He is called *Jehovah Zebaoth*, Jehovah (the God) of the heavenly hosts,—an expression in which *Zebaoth* is a dependent genitive, and not, as Luzzatto supposes, an independent name of God as the Absolute, embracing within itself all the powers of nature. The prophet says "us" and "we." He himself was an inhabitant of Jerusalem; and even if he had not been so, he was nevertheless an Israelite. He therefore associates himself with his people, like Jeremiah in Lam. iii. 22. He had had to experience the anger of God along with the rest; and so, on the other hand, he also celebrates the mighty compassion of God, which he had experienced in common with them. But for this compassion, the people of God would have become like Sodom, from which only four human beings escaped: it would have resembled Gomorrah, which was absolutely annihilated. (On the perfects in the protasis and apodosis, see Ges. § 126, 5.)

The prophet's address has here reached a resting-place. The fact that it is divided at this point into two separate sections, is indicated in the text by the space left between vers. 9 and 10. This mode of marking larger or smaller sections, either by leaving spaces or by breaking off the line, is older than the vowel points and accents, and rests upon a tradition of the highest antiquity (Hupfeld, *Gram.* p. 86 sqq.). The space is called *pizka;* the section indicated by such a space, a closed *parashah* (*sethumah*); and the section indicated by breaking off the line, an open *parashah* (*pethuchah*). The prophet stops as soon as he has affirmed, that nothing but the mercy of God has warded off from Israel the utter destruction which it so well deserved. He catches in spirit the remonstrances of his hearers. They would probably declare that the accusations which the prophet had brought against them were utterly groundless, and appeal to their scrupulous observance of the law of God. In reply to this self-vindication which he reads in the hearts of the accused, the prophet launches forth the accusations of God. In vers. 10, 11, he commences thus: "*Hear the word of Jehovah, ye Sodom judges; give ear to the law of our God, O Gomorrah nation! What is the multitude of your slain-offerings to me? saith Jehovah. I am satiated with whole offerings of rams, and the fat of stalled calves; and blood of bullocks and sheep and he-goats I do not like.*" The second start in the prophet's address commences, like the first, with "hear" and "give ear." The summons to hear is addressed in this instance (as in the case of Isaiah's contemporary Micah, ch. iii.) to the *kezinim* (from *kâzâh, decidere,* from which comes the Arabic *el-Kadi,* the judge, with the substantive termination *in*: see *Jeshurun,* p. 212 ss.), *i.e.* to the men of decisive authority, the rulers in the broadest sense, and to the people subject to them. It was through the mercy of God that Jerusalem was in existence still, for Jerusalem was "spiritually Sodom," as the Revelation (xi. 8) distinctly affirms of Jerusalem, with evident allusion to this passage of Isaiah. Pride, lust of the flesh, and unmerciful conduct, were the leading sins of Sodom, according to Ezek. xvi. 49; and of these, the rulers of Jerusalem, and the crowd that was subject to them and worthy of them, were equally guilty now. But they fancied that they could not possibly stand in such evil repute with God, inasmuch as they rendered outward satisfaction to the law. The prophet therefore called upon them to hear the law of the God of Israel, which he would announce to them: for the prophet was the appointed interpreter of the law, and prophecy the spirit of the law, and the prophetic institution the constant living presence of the true essence of the law bearing its own witness in Israel. "To what purpose is the multitude of your sacrifices unto me? saith Jehovah." The prophet intentionally uses the word יֹאמַר, not אָמַר: this was the incessant appeal of God in relation to the spiritless, formal worship offered by the hypocritical, ceremonial righteousness of Israel (the future denoting continuous action, which is ever at the same time both present and future). The multitude of *zebâchim*, *i.e.* animal sacrifices, had no worth at all to Him. As the whole worship is summed up here in one single act, *zebâchim* appears to denote the *shelamim*, peace-offerings (or better still, communion offerings), with which a meal was associated, after the style of a sacrificial festival, and Jehovah gave the worshipper a share in the sacrifice offered. It is better, however, to take *zebachim* as the general name for all the bleeding sacrifices, which are then subdivided into *'oloth* and *cheleb*, as consisting partly of whole offerings, or offerings the whole of which was placed upon the altar, though in separate pieces, and entirely consumed, and partly of those sacrifices in which only the fat was consumed upon the altar, namely the sin-offerings, trespass-offerings, and pre-eminently the *shelâmim* offerings. Of the sacrificial animals mentioned, the bullocks (*pârim*) and fed beasts (*meri'im*, fattened calves) are species of oxen (*bakar*); and the lambs (*cebâshim*) and he-goats (*atturim*, young he-goats, as distinguished from *se'ir*, the old long-haired he-goat, the animal used as a sin-offering), together with the ram (*ayil*, the customary whole offering of the high priest, of the tribe prince, and of the nation generally on all the high feast days), were species of the flock. The blood of these sacrificial animals—such, for example, as the young oxen, sheep, and he-goats—was thrown all round the altar in the case of the whole offering, the peace-offering, and the trespass-offering; in that of the sin-offering it was smeared upon the horns of the altar, poured out at the foot of the altar, and in some instances sprinkled upon the walls of the altar, or against the vessels of the inner sanctuary. Of such offerings as these Jehovah was weary, and He wanted no more (the two perfects denote that which long has been and still is: Ges. § 126, 3); in fact, He never had desired anything of the kind. Jeremiah says this with regard to the sacrifices (ch. vii. 22); Isaiah also applies it to visits to the temple: Ver. 12. *"When ye come to appear before my face, who hath required this at your hand, to tread my courts?"* לֵרָאוֹת is a contracted infinitive *niphal* for לְהֵרָאוֹת (compare the *hiphil* forms contracted in the same manner in ch. iii. 8, xxiii. 11). This is the standing expression for the appearance of all male Israelites in the temple at the three high festivals, as prescribed by the law, and then for visits to the temple generally (cf. Ps. xlii. 3, lxxxiv. 8). *"My face"* (*panai*): according to Ewald, § 279, *c*, this is used with the passive to designate the subject ("to be seen by the face of God"); but why not rather take it as an adverbial accusative, "in the face of," or "in front of," as it is used interchangeably with the prepositions לְ, אֵת, and אֶל? It is possible that לֵרָאוֹת is pointed as it is here, and in Ex. xxxiv. 24 and Deut. xxxi. 11, instead of לִרְאוֹת,—like יְרָאוּ for יִרְאוּ, in Ex. xxiii. 15, xxxiv. 20,—for the purpose of avoiding an expression which might be so easily misunderstood as denoting a sight of God with the bodily eye. But the *niphal* is firmly established in Ex. xxiii. 17, xxxiv. 23, and 1 Sam. i. 22; and in the Mishnah and Talmud the terms רְאִיָּה and רָאיֹן are applied without hesitation to appearance before God at the principal feasts. They visited the temple diligently enough indeed, but who had required *this* at their hand, *i.e.* required them to do this? Jehovah certainly had not. *"To tread my courts"* is in apposition to *this*, which it more clearly defines. Jehovah did not want them to appear before His face, *i.e.* He did not wish for this spiritless and undevotional tramping thither, this mere *opus operatum*, which might as well have been omitted, since it only wore out the floor.—Ver. 13*a*. Because they had not performed what Jehovah commanded as He commanded it, He expressly forbids them to continue it. "*Continue not to bring lying meat-offering; abomination incense is it to me.*" *Minchah* (the meat-offering) was the vegetable offering, as distinguished from *zebach*, the animal sacrifice. It is called a "lying meat-offering," as being a hypocritical dead work, behind which there was none of the feeling which it appeared to express. In the second clause the Sept., Vulg., Gesenius, and others adopt the rendering "incense—an abomination is it to me," *ketoreth* being taken as the name of the daily burning of incense upon the golden altar in the holy place (Ex. xxx. 8). But neither in Ps. cxli. 2, where prayer is offered by one who is not a priest, nor in the passage before us, where the reference is not to the priesthood, but to the people and to their deeds, is this continual incense to be thought of. Moreover, it is much more natural to regard the word *ketoreth* not as a bold absolute case, but, according to the conjunctive *darga* with which it is marked, as constructive rather; and this is perfectly allowable. The meat-offering is called "incense" (*ketoreth*) with reference to the so-called *azcarah, i.e.* that portion which the priest burned upon the altar, to bring the grateful offerer into remembrance before God (called "burning the memorial," *hiktir azcârâh*, in Lev. ii. 2). As a general rule, this was accompanied with incense (ch. lxvi. 3), the whole of which was placed upon the altar, and not merely a small portion of it. The meat-offering, with its sweet-smelling savour, was merely the form, which served as an outward expression of the thanksgiving for God's blessing, or the longing for His blessing, which really ascended in prayer. But in their case the form had no such meaning. It was nothing but the form, with which they thought they had satisfied God; and therefore it was an abomination to Him.

Ver. 13*b*. God was just as little pleased with their punctilious observance of the feasts: "*New-moon and Sabbath, calling of festal meetings . . . I cannot bear ungodliness and a festal crowd.*" The first objective notions, which are logically governed by "I cannot bear" (לֹא־אוּכַל: literally, a future *hophal*—I am unable, incapable, viz. to bear, which may be supplied, according to Ps. ci. 5, Jer. xliv. 22, Prov. xxx. 21), become *absolute cases* here, on account of another grammatical object presenting itself in the last two nouns:

"ungodliness and a festal crowd." As for new-moon and Sabbath (the latter always signifies the weekly Sabbath when construed with *chodesh*),—and, in fact, the calling of meetings of the whole congregation on the weekly Sabbath and high festivals, which was a simple duty according to Lev. xxiii.,— Jehovah could not endure festivals associated with wickedness. עֲצָרָה (from עָצַר, to press, or crowd thickly together) is synonymous with מִקְרָא, so far as its immediate signification is concerned, as Jer. ix. 1 clearly shows, just as πανήγυρις is synonymous with ἐκκλησία. אָוֶן (from אָן, to breathe) is moral worthlessness, regarded as an utter absence of all that has true essence and worth in the sight of God. The prophet intentionally joins these two nouns together. A densely crowded festal meeting, combined with inward emptiness and barrenness on the part of those who were assembled together, was a contradiction which God could not endure.

Ver. 14. He gives a still stronger expression to His repugnance: "*Your new-moons and your festive seasons my soul hateth; they have become a burden to me; I am weary of bearing them.*" As the soul (*nephesh*) of a man, regarded as the band which unites together bodily and spiritual life, though it is not the actual principle of self-consciousness, is yet the place in which he draws, as it were, the circle of self-consciousness, so as to comprehend the whole essence of His being in the single thought of " I ;" so, according to a description taken from godlike man, the "soul" (*nephesh*) of God, as the expression "my soul" indicates, is the centre of His being, regarded as encircled and pervaded (personated) by self-consciousness; and therefore, whatever the soul of God hates (*vid.* Jer. xv. 1) or loves (ch. xlii. 1), is hated or loved in the inmost depths and to the utmost bounds of His being (*Psychol.* p. 218). Thus He hated each and all of the festivals that were kept in Jerusalem, whether the beginnings of the month, or the high feast-days (*moadim*, in which, according to Lev. xxiii., the Sabbath was also included) observed in the course of the month. For a long time past they had become a burden and annoyance to Him: His long-suffering was weary of such worship. "*To bear*" (נָשָׂא, in Isaiah, even in ch. xviii. 3, for שְׂאֵת or שְׂאָה, and here for לָשֵׂאת: Ewald, § 285, c) has for its object the seasons of worship already mentioned.

Ver. 15. Their self-righteousness, so far as it rested upon sacrifices and festal observances, was now put to shame, and the last inward bulwark of the sham holy nation was destroyed: "*And if ye stretch out your hands, I hide my eyes from you; if ye make ever so much praying, I do not hear: your hands are full of blood.*" Their praying was also an abomination to God. Prayer is something common to man: it is the interpreter of religious feeling, which intervenes and mediates between God and man;[1] it is the true spiritual sacrifice. The law contains no command to pray, and, with the exception of Deut. xxvi., no form of prayer. Praying is so natural to man as man, that there was no necessity for any precept to enforce this, the fundamental expression of the true relation to God. The prophet therefore comes to prayer last of all, so as to trace back their sham-holiness, which was corrupt even to this the last foundation, to its real nothingness. "Spread out," *parash*, or *pi. pēresh*, to stretch out; used with *cappaim* to denote swimming in ch. xxv. 11. It is written here before a strong suffix, as in many other passages, *e.g.* ch. lii. 12, with the inflection *i* instead of *e*. This was the gesture of a man in prayer, who spread out his hands, and when spread out, stretched them towards heaven, or to the most holy place in the temple, and indeed (as if with the feeling of emptiness and need, and with a desire to receive divine gifts) held up the hollow or palm of his hand (*cappaim*: cf. *tendere palmas*, *e.g.* Virg. Aen. xii. 196, *tenditque ad sidera palmas*). However much they might stand or lie before Him in the attitude of prayer, Jehovah hid His eyes, *i.e.* His omniscience knew nothing of it; and even though they might pray loud and

---

[1] The primary idea of *hithpallel* and *tephillah* is not to be obtained from Deut. ix. 18 and Ezra x. 1, as Dietrich and Fürst suppose, who make *hithpallel* equivalent to *hithnappel*, to throw one's self down; but from 1 Sam. ii. 25, "If a man sin against a man, the authorities right him" (וּפִלְלוֹ אֱלֹהִים: it is quite a mistake to maintain that *Elohim* cannot have this meaning), *i.e.* they can set right the relation which he has disturbed. "But if one sin against Jehovah, who shall mediate for him (מִי יִתְפַּלֶּל־לוֹ, *quis intercedat pro eo*)?" We may see from this that prayer is regarded as mediation, which sets right and establishes fellowship; and *hithpallel* signifies to make one's self a healer of divisions, or to settle for one's self, to strive after a settlement (*sibi, pro se, intercedere*: cf. Job xix. 16, *hithchannen, sibi propitium facere*; xiii. 27, *hithchakkah, sibi insculpere*, like the Arabic *ichtattu*, to bound off for one's self).

long (*gam chi, etiamsi* : compare the simple *chi*, Jer. xiv. 12), He was, as it were, deaf to it all. We should expect *chi* here to introduce the explanation ; but the more excited the speaker, the shorter and more unconnected his words. The plural *damim* always denotes human blood as the result of some unnatural act, and then the bloody deed and the bloodguiltiness itself. The plural number neither refers to the quantity nor to the separate drops, but is the plural of production, which Dietrich has so elaborately discussed in his *Abhandlung*, p. 40.[1] The terrible *damim* stands very emphatically before the governing verb, pointing to many murderous acts that had been committed, and deeds of violence akin to murder. Not, indeed, that we are to understand the words as meaning that there was really blood upon their hands when they stretched them out in prayer; but before God, from whom no outward show can hide the true nature of things, however clean they might have washed themselves, they still dripped with blood. The expostulations of the people against the divine accusations have thus been negatively set forth and met in vers. 11-15: Jehovah could not endure their work-righteous worship, which was thus defiled with unrighteous works, even to murder itself. The divine accusation is now positively established in vers. 16, 17, by the contrast drawn between the true righteousness of which the accused were destitute, and the false righteousness of which they boasted. The crushing charge is here changed into an admonitory appeal; and the love which is hidden behind the wrath, and would gladly break through, already begins to disclose itself. There are eight admonitions. The first three point to the removal of evil; the other five to the performance of what is good.

Ver. 16. The first three run thus: "*Wash, clean yourselves; put away the badness of your doings from the range of my eyes; cease to do evil.*" This is not only an advance from figurative language to the most literal, but there is also an advance in what is said. The first admonition requires, primarily and above all, purification from the sins committed, by means

[1] As *chittah* signified corn standing in the field, and *chittim* corn threshed and brought to the market, so *damim* was not blood when flowing through the veins, but when it had flowed out,—in other words, when it had been violently shed. (For the Talmudic misinterpretation of the true state of the case, see my *Genesis*, p. 626.)

of forgiveness sought for and obtained. *Wash: rachatzu*, from *rachatz*, in the frequent middle sense of washing one's self. *Clean yourselves: hizzaccu*, with the tone upon the last syllable, is not the *niphal* of *zâkak*, as the first plur. imper. *niph.* of such verbs has generally and naturally the tone upon the penultimate (see ch. lii. 11; Num. xvii. 10), but the *hithpael* of *zacah* for *hizdaccu*, with the preformative *Tav* resolved into the first radical letter, as is very common in the *hithpael* (Ges. § 54, 2, *b*). According to the difference between the two synonyms (to wash one's self, to clean one's self), the former must be understood as referring to the one great act of repentance on the part of a man who is turning to God, the latter to the daily repentance of one who has so turned. The second admonition requires them to place themselves in the light of the divine countenance, and put away the evil of their doings, which was intolerable to pure eyes (Hab. i. 13). They were to wrestle against the wickedness to which their actual sin had grown, until at length it entirely disappeared. *Neged*, according to its radical meaning, signifies prominence (compare the Arabic *négd*, high land which is visible at a great distance), conspicuousness, so that *minneged* is really equivalent to *ex apparentia*.

Ver. 17. Five admonitions relating to the practice of what is good: " *Learn to do good, attend to judgment, set the oppressor right, do justice to the orphan, conduct the cause of the widow.*" The first admonition lays the foundation for the rest. They were to learn to do good,—a difficult art, in which a man does not become proficient merely by good intentions. " Learn to do good : " *hetib* is the object to *limdu* (learn), regarded as an accusative; the inf. abs. הָרֵעַ in ver. 16 takes the place of the object in just the same manner. The division of this primary admonition into four minor ones relating to the administration of justice, may be explained from the circumstance that no other prophet directs so keen an eye upon the state and its judicial proceedings as Isaiah has done. He differs in this respect from his younger contemporary Micah, whose prophecies are generally more ethical in their nature, whilst those of Isaiah have a political character throughout. Hence the admonitions: " Give diligent attention to judgment " (*dârash*, to devote one's self to a thing with zeal and assiduity); and " bring the oppressor to the right way." This is the true rendering, as *châmotz* (from *châmatz,* to be sharp in flavour, glaring in appearance, violent and impetuous in character) cannot well mean "the oppressed," or the man who is deprived of his rights, as most of the early translators have rendered it, since this form of the noun, especially with an immutable *kametz* like בְּגוֹדָה בָּגוֹד (cf. נְקֻדָּה נָקֹד), is not used in a passive, but in an active or attributive sense (Ewald, § 152, *b* : *vid.* at Ps. cxxxvii. 8) : it has therefore the same meaning as *chometz* in Ps. lxxi. 4, and *âshok* in Jer. xxii. 3, which is similar in its form. But if *châmotz* signifies the oppressive, reckless, churlish man, אַשֵּׁר cannot mean to make happy, or to congratulate, or to set up, or, as in the talmudic rendering, to strengthen (Luzzatto : *rianimate chi è oppresso*) ; but, as it is also to be rendered in ch. iii. 12, ix. 15, to lead to the straight road, or to cause a person to keep the straight course. In the case before us, where the oppressor is spoken of, it means to direct him to the way of justice, to keep him in bounds by severe punishment and discipline.[1] In the same way we find in other passages, such as ch. xi. 4 and Ps. lxxii. 4, severe conduct towards oppressors mentioned in connection with just treatment of the poor. There follow two admonitions relating to widows and orphans. Widows and orphans, as well as foreigners, were the *protégés* of God and His law, standing under His especial guardianship and care (see, for example, Ex. xxii. 22 (21), cf. 21 (20). "*Do justice to the orphan*" (*shâphat*, as in Deut. xxv. 1, is a contracted expression for *shâphat mishpat*) : for if there is not even a settlement or verdict in their cause, this is the most crying injustice of all, as neither the form nor the appearance of justice is preserved. "*Conduct the cause of the widows :* " רִיב with an accusative, as in ch. li. 22, the only other passage in which it occurs, is a contracted form for רִיב רִיב. Thus all the grounds of self-defence, which existed in the hearts of the accused, are both negatively and positively overthrown. They

---

[1] The *Talmud* varies in its explanation of *chamoz:* in one instance it is applied to a judge who lets his sentence be thoroughly leavened before pronouncing it ; in another the *chamuz* is said to signify a person robbed and injured, in opposition to *chomez* (*b. Sanhedrin* 35a). It is an instructive fact in relation to the idea suggested by the word, that, according to *Joma* 39*b*, a man who had not only taken possession of his own inheritance, but had seized upon another person's also, bore the nickname of *ben chimzon* as long as he lived.

are thundered down and put to shame. The law (*thorah*), announced in ver. 10, has been preached to them. The prophet has cast away the husks of their dead works, and brought out the moral kernel of the law in its universal application.

The first leading division of the address is brought to a close, and ver. 18 contains the turning-point between the two parts into which it is divided. Hitherto Jehovah has spoken to His people in wrath. But His love began to move even in the admonitions in vers. 16, 17. And now this love, which desired not Israel's destruction, but Israel's inward and outward salvation, breaks fully through. Ver. 18. "*O come, and let us reason together, saith Jehovah. If your sins come forth like scarlet cloth, they shall become white as snow; if they are red as crimson, they shall come forth like wool!*" Jehovah here challenges Israel to a formal trial: *nocach* is thus used in a reciprocal sense, and with the same meaning as *nishpat* in ch. xliii. 26 (Ges. § 51, 2). In such a trial Israel must lose, for Israel's self-righteousness rests upon sham righteousness; and this sham righteousness, when rightly examined, is but unrighteousness dripping with blood. It is taken for granted that this must be the result of the investigation. Israel is therefore worthy of death. Yet Jehovah will not treat Israel according to His retributive justice, but according to His free compassion. He will remit the punishment, and not only regard the sin as not existing, but change it into its very opposite. The reddest possible sin shall become, through His mercy, the purest white. On the two *hiphils* here applied to colour, see Ges. § 53, 2; though he gives the meaning incorrectly, viz. "to take a colour," whereas the words signify rather to emit a colour: not *colorem accipere*, but *colorem dare*. *Shâni*, bright red (the plural *shânim*, as in Prov. xxxi. 21, signifies materials dyed with *shâni*), and *tolâ*, warm colour, are simply different names for the same colour, viz. the crimson obtained from the cochineal insect, *color coccineus*. The representation of the work of grace promised by God as a change from red to white, is founded upon the symbolism of colours, quite as much as when the saints in the Revelation (ch. xix. 8) are described as clothed in white raiment, whilst the clothing of Babylon is purple and scarlet (ch. xvii. 4). Red is the colour of fire, and therefore of life: the blood is red because life is a fiery process. For this reason the heifer, from which the ashes of purification were obtained for those who had been defiled through contact with the dead, was to be red; and the sprinkling-brush, with which the unclean were sprinkled, was to be tied round with a band of scarlet wool. But red as contrasted with white, the colour of light (Matt. xvii. 2), is the colour of selfish, covetous, passionate life, which is self-seeking in its nature, which goes out of itself only to destroy, and drives about with wild tempestuous violence: it is therefore the colour of wrath and sin. It is generally supposed that Isaiah speaks of red as the colour of sin, because sin ends in murder; and this is not really wrong, though it is too restricted. Sin is called red, inasmuch as it is a burning heat which consumes a man, and when it breaks forth consumes his fellow-man as well. According to the biblical view, throughout, sin stands in the same relation to what is well-pleasing to God, and wrath in the same relation to love or grace, as fire to light; and therefore as red to white, or black to white, for red and black are colours which border upon one another. In the Song of Solomon (ch. vii. 5), the black locks of Shulamith are described as being " like purple," and Homer applies the same epithet to the dark waves of the sea. But the ground of this relation lies deeper still. Red is the colour of fire, which flashes out of darkness and returns to it again; whereas white without any admixture of darkness represents the pure, absolute triumph of light. It is a deeply significant symbol of the act of justification. Jehovah offers to Israel an *actio forensis*, out of which it shall come forth justified by grace, although it has merited death on account of its sins. The righteousness, white as snow and wool, with which Israel comes forth, is a gift conferred upon it out of pure compassion, without being conditional upon any legal performance whatever.

But after the restoration of Israel *in integrum* by this act of grace, the rest would unquestionably depend upon the conduct of Israel itself. According to Israel's own decision would Jehovah determine Israel's future. Vers. 19, 20. "*If ye then shall willingly hear, ye shall eat the good of the land; if ye shall obstinately rebel, ye shall be eaten by the sword: for the mouth of Jehovah hath spoken it.*" After their justification, both blessing and cursing lay once more before the justified, as they had both been long before proclaimed by the law (compare ver. 19*b* with Deut. xxviii. 3 sqq., Lev. xxvi. 3 sqq., and ver. 20*b* with the threat of vengeance with the sword in Lev. xxvi. 25). The promise of eating, *i.e.* of the full enjoyment of domestic blessings, and therefore of settled, peaceful rest at home, is placed in contrast with the curse of being eaten with the sword. *Chereb* (the sword) is the accusative of the instrument, as in Ps. xvii. 13, 14; but this adverbial construction without either genitive, adjective, or suffix, as in Ex. xxx. 20, is very rarely met with (Ges. § 138, Anm. 3); and in the passage before us it is a bold construction which the prophet allows himself, instead of saying, חֶרֶב הָאֲכַלְכֶם, for the sake of the *paronomasia* (Böttcher, *Collectanea*, p. 161). In the conditional clauses the two futures are followed by two preterites (compare Lev. xxvi. 21, which is more in conformity with our western mode of expression), inasmuch as obeying and rebelling are both of them consequences of an act of will: if ye shall be willing, and in consequence of this obey; if ye shall refuse, and rebel against Jehovah. They are therefore, strictly speaking, *perfecta consecutiva*. According to the ancient mode of writing, the passage vers. 18-20 formed a separate *parashah* by themselves, viz. a *sethumah*, or *parashah* indicated by spaces left within the line. The *piskah* after ver. 20 corresponds to a long pause in the mind of the speaker.—Will Israel tread the saving path of forgiveness thus opened before it, and go on to renewed obedience; and will it be possible for it to be brought back by this path? Individuals possibly may, but not the whole. The divine appeal therefore changes now into a mournful complaint. So peaceful a solution as this of the discord between Jehovah and His children was not to be hoped for. Jerusalem was far too depraved.

Ver. 21. "*How is she become a harlot, the faithful citadel! she, full of right, lodged in righteousness, and now—murderers.*" It is the keynote of an elegy (*kinah*) which is sounded here. אֵיכָה, and but rarely אֵיךְ, which is an abbreviated form, is expressive of complaint and amazement. This longer form, like a long-drawn sigh, is a characteristic of the *kinah*. The *kinoth* (Lamentations) of Jeremiah commence with it, and receive their title from it; whereas the shorter form is indicative of scornful complaining, and is characteristic of the *mashól* (*e.g.* ch. xiv. 4, 12; Mic. ii. 4). From this word, which gives the keynote, the rest all follows, soft, full, monotonous, long drawn out and slow, just in the style of an elegy. We may see clearly enough that forms like מְלֵאֲתִי for מְלֵאָה, softened by lengthening, were adapted to elegiac compositions, from the first verse of the Lamentations of Jeremiah, where three of these forms occur. Jerusalem had previously been a faithful city, *i.e.* one stedfastly adhering to the covenant of Jehovah with her (*vid.* Ps. lxxviii. 37).[1] This covenant was a marriage covenant. And she had broken it, and had thereby become a *zonâh* (harlot),—a prophetic view, the germs of which had already been given in the Pentateuch, where the worship of idols on the part of Israel is called whoring after them (Deut. xxxi. 16; Ex. xxxiv. 15, 16; in all, seven times). It was not, however, merely gross outward idolatry which made the church of God a "harlot," but infidelity of heart, in whatever form it might express itself; so that Jesus described the people of His own time as an "adulterous generation," notwithstanding the pharisaical strictness with which the worship of Jehovah was then observed. For, as the verse before us indicates, this marriage relation was founded upon *right* and *righteousness* in the broadest sense: *mishpat*, "right," *i.e.* a realization of right answering to the will of God as positively declared; and *tzedek*, "righteousness," *i.e.* a righteous state moulded by that will, or a righteous course of conduct regulated according to it (somewhat different, therefore, from the more qualitative *tzedâkâh*). Jerusalem was once full of such right; and righteousness was not merely there in the form of a hastily passing guest, but had come down from above to take up her permanent abode in Jerusalem: she tarried there day and night as if it were her home. The prophet had in his mind the times of David and Solomon, and also more especially the time of Jehoshaphat (about one hundred and fifty years before Isaiah's appearance), who restored the administration of justice, which had fallen into neglect since the

---

[1] We have translated the word *kiryah* "*citadel*" (*Burg*), instead of "city;" but *Burg* also became the name of the town which sprang up around the citadel, and the persons living in and around the *Burg* or citadel were called *burgenses*, "burghers." Jerusalem, which was also called Zion, might be called, with quite as much right, a citadel (*Burg*), as a city.

closing years of Solomon's reign and the time of Rehoboam and Abijah, to which Asa's reformation had not extended, and re-organized it entirely in the spirit of the law. It is possible also that Jehoiada, the high priest in the time of Joash, may have revived the institutions of Jehoshaphat, so far as they had fallen into disuse under his three godless successors; but even in the second half of the reign of Joash, the administration of justice fell into the same disgraceful state, at least as compared with the times of David, Solomon, and Jehoshaphat, as that in which Isaiah found it. The glaring contrast between the present and the past is indicated by the expression "*and now.*" In all the correct MSS. and editions, *mishpat* is not accented with *zakeph*, but with *rebia;* and *bâh*, which ought to have *zakeph*, is accented with *tiphchah*, on account of the brevity of the following clause. In this way the statement as to the past condition is sufficiently distinguished from that relating to the present.[1] Formerly righteousness, now "*murderers*" (*merazzechim*), and indeed, as distinguished from *rozechim*, murderers by profession, who formed a band, like king Ahab and his son (2 Kings vi. 32). The contrast was as glaring as possible, since murder is the direct opposite, the most crying violation, of righteousness.

The complaint now turns from the city generally to the authorities, and first of all figuratively. Ver. 22. "*Thy silver has become dross, thy drink mutilated with water.*" It is upon this passage that the figurative language of Jer. vi. 27 sqq. and Ezek. xxii. 18–22 is founded. *Silver* is here a figurative representation of the princes and lords, with special reference to the nobility of character naturally associated with nobility of birth and rank; for silver—refined silver—is an image of all that is noble and pure, light in all its purity being reflected by it (Bähr, *Symbolik*, i. 284). The princes and lords had once possessed all the virtues which the Latins called unitedly *candor* animi, viz. the virtues of magnanimity, affability, im-

---

[1] It is well known that *rebia* has less force as a disjunctive than *tiphchah*, and that *zakeph* is stronger than either. With regard to the law, according to which *bâh* has *rebia* instead of *zakeph*, see Bär, *Thorath Emeth*, p. 70. To the copies enumerated by Luzzatto, as having the correct accentuation (including Brescia 1494, and Venice, by J. B. Chayim, 1526), we may add Plantin (1582), Buxtorf (1618), Nissel (1662), and many others (cf. Dachselt's *Biblia accentuata*, which is not yet out of date).

partiality, and superiority to bribes. This silver had now become *l'sigim*, dross, or base metal separated (thrown off) from silver in the process of refining (*sig*, pl. *sigim*, *siggim* from *sug*, *recedere*, refuse left in smelting, or dross: cf. Prov. xxv. 4, xxvi. 23). A second figure compares the leading men of the older Jeruselem to good wine, such as drinkers like. The word employed here (*sobe*) must have been used in this sense by the more cultivated classes in Isaiah's time (cf. Nahum i. 10). This pure, strong, and costly wine was now adulterated with water (*lit. castratum*, according to Pliny's expression in the *Natural History*: compare the Horatian phrase, *jugulare Falernum*), and therefore its strength and odour were weakened, and its worth was diminished. The present was nothing but the dross and shadow of the past.

In ver. 23 the prophet says this without a figure: "*Thy rulers are rebellious, and companions of thieves; every one loveth presents, and hunteth after payment; the orphan they right not, and the cause of the widow has no access to them.*" In two words the prophet depicts the contemptible baseness of the national rulers (*sârim*). He describes first of all their baseness in relation to God, with the alliterative *sorerim*: rebellious, refractory; and then, in relation to men, *companions of thieves*, inasmuch as they allowed themselves to be bribed by presents of stolen goods to acts of injustice towards those who had been robbed. They not only willingly accepted such bribes, and that not merely a few of them, but every individual belonging to the rank of princes (*cullo*, equivalent to *haccol*, the whole: every one *loveth* gifts); but they went eagerly in pursuit of them (*rodeph*). It was not *peace* (*shâlom*) that they hunted after (Ps. xxxiv. 16), but *shalmonim*, things that would pacify their avarice; not what was good, but compensation for their partiality.—This was the existing state of Jerusalem, and therefore it would hardly be likely to take the way of mercy opened before it in ver. 18; consequently Jehovah would avail himself of other means of setting it right:—

Ver. 24. "*Therefore, saying of the Lord, of Jehovah of hosts, of the Strong One of Israel: Ah! I will relieve myself on mine adversaries, and will avenge myself upon mine enemies.*" Salvation through judgment was the only means of improvement and preservation left to the congregation, which called itself by the name of Jerusalem. Jehovah would therefore afford satisfaction to His holiness, and administer a judicial sifting to Jerusalem. There is no other passage in Isaiah in which we meet with such a crowding together of different names of God as we do here (compare ch. xix. 4, iii. 1, x. 16, 33, iii. 15). With three names, descriptive of the irresistible omnipotence of God, the irrevocable decree of a sifting judgment is sealed. The word נְאֻם, which is used here instead of אָמַר and points back to a verb נָאַם, related to נָהַם and הָמָה, corresponds to the deep, earnest pathos of the words. These verbs, which are imitations of sounds, all denote a dull hollow groaning. The word used here, therefore, signifies that which is spoken with significant secrecy and solemn softness. It is never written absolutely, but is always followed by the subject who speaks (saying of Jehovah it is, *i.e.* Jehovah says). We meet with it first of all in Gen. xxii. 16. In the prophetic writings it occurs in Obadiah and Joel, but most frequently in Jeremiah and Ezekiel. It is generally written at the close of the sentence, or parenthetically in the middle; very rarely at the commencement, as it is here and in 1 Sam. ii. 30 and Ps. cx. 1. The "*saying*" commences with *hoi* (*ah!*), the painfulness of pity being mingled with the determined outbreak of wrath. By the side of the niphal *nikkam min* (to be revenged upon a person) we find the niphal *nicham* (lit. to console one's self). The two words are derived from kindred roots. The latter is conjugated with *ĕ* in the preformative syllable, the former with *i*, according to the older system of vowel-pointing adopted in the East.[1] Jehovah would procure Himself relief from His enemies by letting out upon them the wrath with which He had hitherto been burdened (Ezek. v. 13). He now calls the masses of Jerusalem by their right name.

Ver. 25 states clearly in what the revenge consisted with which Jehovah was inwardly burdened (*innakmah*, a cohortative with the *ah*, indicating internal oppression): "*And I will bring my hand over thee, and will smelt out thy dross as with*

---

[1] The so-called Assyrian mode of pointing, which was entirely supplanted, with the exception of a few relics, by the Tiberian mode which now lies before us, has no *seghol* (see *DMZ.* xviii. 322). According to Luzzatto (*Proleg.* p. 200), they wrote *ektol* instead of *iktol*, to avoid confounding it with יִקְטֹל, which was pronounced *iktol*, and not *yiktol*.

alkali, and will clear away all thy lead." As long as God leaves a person's actions or sufferings alone, His hand, *i.e.* His acting, is at rest. Bringing the hand over a person signifies a movement of the hand, which has been hitherto at rest, either for the purpose of inflicting judicial punishment upon the person named (Amos i. 8; Jer. vi. 9; Ezek. xxxviii. 12; Ps. lxxxi. 15), or else, though this is seldom the case, for the purpose of saving him (Zech. xiii. 7). The reference here is to the divine treatment of Jerusalem, in which punishment and salvation were combined—punishment as the means, salvation as the end. The interposition of Jehovah was, as it were, a smelting, which would sweep away, not indeed Jerusalem itself, but the ungodly in Jerusalem. They are compared to dross, or (as the verb seems to imply) to ore mixed with dross, and, inasmuch as lead is thrown off in the smelting of silver, to such ingredients of lead as Jehovah would speedily and thoroughly remove, "*like alkali*," *i.e.* "as if with alkali" (*cabbor, comparatio decurtata*, for *c'babbor*: for this mode of dropping *Beth* after *Caph*, compare ch. ix. 3, Lev. xxii. 13, and many other passages). By *bedilim* (from *bâdal*, to separate) we are to understand the several pieces of *stannum* or lead[1] in which the silver is contained, and which are separated by smelting, all the baser metals being distinguished from the purer kinds by the fact that they are combustible (*i.e.* can be oxidized). Both *bor*, or potash (an alkali obtained from land-plants), and *nether*, natron (*i.e.* soda, or natron obtained from the ashes of marine plants, which is also met with in many mineral waters), have been employed from the very earliest times to accelerate the process of smelting, for the purpose of separating a metal from its ore.

[1] *Plumbum nigrum*, says Pliny, *h. n.* xxiv. 16, is sometimes found alone, and sometimes mixed with silver: *ejus qui primus fluit in fornacibus liquor, stannum appellatur*. The reference here is to the lead separated from the ore in the process of obtaining pure silver. In the form of powder this dross is called *bedil*, and the pieces *bedilim;* whereas *ophereth* is the name of solid lead, obtained by simply melting down from ore which does not contain silver. The fact that *bedil* is also apparently used as a name for tin, may be explained in the same way as the homonymy of iron and basalt (com. on Job xxviii. 2), and of the oak and terebinth. The two metals are called by the same name on account of their having a certain outward resemblance, viz. in softness, pliability, colour, and specific gravity.

Ver. 26. As the threat couched in the previous figure does not point to the destruction, but simply to the smelting of Jerusalem, there is nothing strange in the fact that in ver. 26 it should pass over into a pure promise; the meltingly soft and yearningly mournful termination of the clauses with *ayich*, the keynote of the later songs of Zion, being still continued. "*And I will bring back thy judges as in the olden time, and thy counsellors as in the beginning; afterwards thou wilt be called city of righteousness, faithful citadel.*" The threat itself was, indeed, relatively a promise, inasmuch as whatever could stand the fire would survive the judgment; and the distinct object of this was to bring back Jerusalem to the purer metal of its own true nature. But when that had been accomplished, still more would follow. The indestructible kernel that remained would be crystallized, since Jerusalem would receive back from Jehovah the judges and counsellors which it had had in the olden flourishing times of the monarchy, ever since it had become the city of David and of the temple; not, indeed, the very same persons, but persons quite equal to them in excellence. Under such God-given leaders Jerusalem would become what it had once been, and what it ought to be. The names applied to the city indicate the impression produced by the manifestation of its true nature. The second name is written without the article, as in fact the word *kiryah* (city), with its massive, definite sound, always is in Isaiah. Thus did Jehovah announce the way which it had been irrevocably determined that He would take with Israel, as the only way to salvation. Moreover, this was the fundamental principle of the government of God, the law of Israel's history.

Ver. 27 presents it in a brief and concise form: "*Sion will be redeemed through judgment, and her returning ones through righteousness.*" *Mishpat* and *tzedâkâh* are used elsewhere for divine gifts (ch. xxxiii. 5, xxviii. 6), for such conduct as is pleasing to God (ch. i. 21, xxxii. 16), and for royal Messianic virtues (ch. ix. 6, xi. 3-5, xvi. 5, xxxii. 1). Here, however, where we are helped by the context, they are to be interpreted according to such parallel passages as ch. iv. 4, v. 16, xxviii. 17, as signifying God's right and righteousness in their primarily judicious self-fulfilment. A judgment, on the part of God the righteous One, would be the means by which Zion itself, so far as it had remained faithful to Jehovah, and those who were converted in the midst of the judgment, would be redeemed,—a judgment upon sinners and sin, by which the power that had held in bondage the divine nature of Zion, so far as it still continued to exist, would be broken, and in consequence of which those who turned to Jehovah would be incorporated into His true church. Whilst, therefore, God was revealing Himself in His punitive righteousness; He was working out a righteousness which would be bestowed as a gift of grace upon those who escaped the former. The notion of "righteousness" is now following a New Testament track. In front it has the fire of the law; behind, the love of the gospel. Love is concealed behind the wrath, like the sun behind the thunder-clouds. Zion, so far as it truly is or is becoming Zion, is redeemed, and none but the ungodly are destroyed. But, as is added in the next verse, the latter takes place without mercy.

Ver. 28. "*And breaking up of the rebellious and sinners together; and those who forsake Jehovah will perish.*" The judicial side of the approaching act of redemption is here expressed in a way that all can understand. The exclamatory substantive clause in the first half of the verse is explained by a declaratory verbal clause in the second. The "*rebellious*" were those who had both inwardly and outwardly broken away from Jehovah; "*sinners*," those who were living in open sins; and "*those who forsake Jehovah*," such as had become estranged from God in either of these ways.

Ver. 29 declares how God's judgment of destruction would fall upon all of these. The verse is introduced with an explanatory "for" (*chi*): "*For they become ashamed of the terebinths, in which ye had your delight; and ye must blush for the gardens, in which ye took pleasure.*" The terebinths and gardens (the second word with the article, as in Hab. iii. 8, first *binharim*, then *banneharim*) are not referred to as objects of luxury, as Hitzig and Drechsler assume, but as unlawful places of worship and objects of worship (see Deut. xvi. 21). They are both of them frequently mentioned by the prophets in this sense (ch. lvii. 5, lxv. 3, lxvi. 17): *châmar* and *bâchar* are also the words commonly applied to an arbitrary choice of false gods (ch. xliv. 9, xli. 24, lxvi. 3), and *bosh min* is the general phrase used to denote the shame which falls upon idolaters, when the worthlessness of their idols becomes conspicuous through their impotence. On the difference between *bosh* and *châpher*, see the comm. on Ps. xxxv. 4.[1] The word *elim* is erroneously translated "idols" in the Septuagint and other ancient versions. The feeling which led to this, however, was a correct one, since the places of worship really stand for the idols worshipped in those places.[2] The excited state of the prophet at the close of his prophecy is evinced by his abrupt leap from an exclamation to a direct address (Ges. § 137, Anm. 3).

Ver. 30. He still continues in the same excitement, piling a second explanatory sentence upon the first, and commencing this also with "*for*" (*chi*); and then, carried away by the association of ideas, he takes terebinths and gardens as the future figures of the idolatrous people themselves. "*For ye shall become like a terebinth with withered leaves, and like a garden that hath no water.*" Their prosperity is destroyed, so that they resemble a terebinth withered as to its leaves, which in other cases are always green (*nobeleth 'aleah*, a genitive connection according to Ges. § 112, 2). Their sources of help

---

[1] It is perfectly certain that *châpher* (*Arab. chafira*, as distinguished from *châphar, hafara*, to dig) signifies to blush, *erubescere*; but the combination of *bosh* and *yâbash* (*bâda*), which would give *albescere* or *expallescere* (to turn white or pale) as the primary idea of *bosh*, has not only the Arabic use of *bayyada* and *ibyadda* (to rejoice, be made glad) against it, but above all the dialectic *bechath, bahita* (*bahuta*), which, when taken in connection with *bethath* (*batta*), points rather to the primary idea of being cut off (*abscindi*: cf. *spes abscissa*). See Lane's *Arabic-English Lexicon*, i. 263.

[2] With regard to the derivation, *êlim*, whether used in the sense of strong men, or gods, or rams, or terebinths, is still but one word, derived from *il* or *ûl*, so that in all three senses it may be written either with or without Yod. Nevertheless *elim* in the sense of "rams" only occurs without Yod in Job xlii. 8. In the sense of "gods" it is always written without Yod; in that of "strong men" with Yod. In the singular the name of the terebinth is always written *elah* without Yod; in the plural, however, it is written either with or without. But this no more presupposes a singular *êl* (*ayil*) in common use, than *bêtzim* presupposes a singular *bêts* (*bayits*); still the word *êl* with Yod does occur once, viz. in Gen. xiv. 6. *Allâh* and *allôn*, an oak, also spring from the same root, namely *âlal* = *il*; just as in Arabic both *il* and *ill* are used for *êl* (God); and *âl* and *ill*, in the sense of relationship, point to a similar change in the form of the root.

are dried up, so that they are like a garden without water, and therefore waste. In this withered state terebinths and gardens, to which the idolatrous are compared, are easily set on fire. All that is wanted is a spark to kindle them, when they are immediately in flames.

Ver. 31 shows in a third figure where this spark was to come from: "*And the rich man becomes tow, and his work the spark; and they will both burn together, and no one extinguishes them.*" The form *poalo* suggests at first a participial meaning (its maker), but הֶחָסֹן would be a very unusual epithet to apply to an idol. Moreover, the figure itself would be a distorted one, since the natural order would be, that the idol would be the thing that kindled the fire, and the man the object to be set on fire, and not the reverse. We therefore follow the LXX., Targ., and Vulg., with Gesenius and other more recent grammarians, and adopt the rendering "his work" (*opus ejus*). The forms פָּעֳלוֹ and פָּעְלוֹ (cf. ch. lii. 14 and Jer. xxii. 13) are two equally admissible changes of the ground-form פָּעֳלוֹ (פָּעְלוֹ). As ver. 29 refers to idolatrous worship, *poalo* (his work) is an idol, a god made by human hands (cf. ch. ii. 8, xxxvii. 19, etc.). The prosperous idolater, who could give gold and silver for idolatrous images out of the abundance of his possessions (*châson* is to be interpreted in accordance with ch. xxxiii. 6), becomes *tow* (talm. "the refuse of flax:" the radical meaning is to shake out, viz. in combing), and the idol the *spark* which sets this mass of fibre in flames, so that they are both irretrievably consumed. For the fire of judgment, by which sinners are devoured, need not come from without. Sin carries the fire of indignation within itself. And an idol is, as it were, an idolater's sin embodied and exposed to the light of day.

The date of the composition of this first prophecy is a puzzle. Caspari thoroughly investigated every imaginary possibility, and at last adopted the conclusion that it dates from the time of Uzziah, inasmuch as vers. 7–9 do not relate to an actual, but merely to an ideal, present. But notwithstanding all the acuteness with which Caspari has worked out his view, it still remains a very forced one. The oftener we return to the reading of this prophetic address, the stronger is our impression that vers. 7–9 contain a description of the state of things which really existed at the time when the words were spoken. There were actually two devastations of the land of Judah which occurred during the ministry of Isaiah, and in which Jerusalem was only spared by the miraculous interposition of Jehovah: one under Ahaz in the year of the Syro-Ephraimitish war; the other under Hezekiah, when the Assyrian forces laid the land waste but were scattered at last in their attack upon Jerusalem. The year of the Syro-Ephraimitish war is supported by Gesenius, Rosenmüller (who expresses a different opinion in every one of the three editions of his *Scholia*), Maurer, Movers, Knobel, Hävernick, and others; the time of the Assyrian oppression by Hitzig, Umbreit, Drechsler, and Luzzatto. Now, whichever of these views we may adopt, there will still remain, as a test of its admissibility, the difficult question, How did this prophecy come to stand at the head of the book, if it belonged to the time of Uzziah-Jotham? This question, upon which the solution of the difficulty depends, can only be settled when we come to ch. vi. Till then, the date of the composition of ch. i. must be left undecided. It is enough for the present to know, that, according to the accounts given in the books of Kings and Chronicles, there were two occasions when the situation of Jerusalem resembled the one described in the present chapter.

THE WAY OF GENERAL JUDGMENT; OR THE COURSE OF ISRAEL FROM FALSE GLORY TO THE TRUE.—CHAP. II.–IV.

The limits of this address are very obvious. The end of ch. iv. connects itself with the beginning of ch. ii., so as to form a circle. After various alternations of admonition, reproach, and threatening, the prophet reaches at last the object of the promise with which he started. Chap. v., on the other hand, commences afresh with a parable. It forms an independent address, although it is included, along with the previous chapters, under the heading in ch. ii. 1: "*The word which Isaiah the son of Amoz saw over Judah and Jerusalem.*" Chap. ii.-v. may have existed under this heading before the whole collection arose. It was then adopted in this form into the general collection, so as to mark the transition from the prologue to the body of the book. The prophet describes what he here says concerning Judah and Jerusalem as "*the word which he saw.*" When men speak to one another, the words are not seen, but heard. But when God spoke to the prophet, it was in a supersensuous way, and the prophet saw it. The mind indeed has no more eyes than ears; but a mind qualified to perceive what is supersensuous is altogether eye.

The manner in which Isaiah commences this second address is altogether unparalleled. There is no other example of a prophecy beginning with וְהָיָה. And it is very easy to discover the reason why. The *præt. consecutivum v'hâyâh* derives the force of a future from the context alone; whereas the *fut. consecutivum vay'hi* (with which historical books and sections very generally commence) is shown to be an aorist by its simple form. Moreover, the *Vav* in the *fut. consecut.* has almost entirely lost its copulative character; in the *præt. consec.*, on the other hand, it retains it with all the greater force. The prophet therefore commences with "and"; and it is from what follows, not from what goes before, that we learn that *hayah* is used in a future sense. But this is not the only strange thing. It is also an unparalleled occurrence, for a prophetic address, which runs as this does through all the different phases of the prophetic discourses generally (viz. exhortation, reproof, threatening, and promise), to commence with a promise. We are in a condition, however, to explain the cause of this remarkable phenomenon with certainty, and not merely to resort to conjecture. Vers. 2–4 do not contain Isaiah's own words, but the words of another prophet taken out of their connection. We find them again in Mic. iv. 1–4; and whether Isaiah took them from Micah, or whether both Isaiah and Micah took them from some common source, in either case they were not originally Isaiah's.[1]

---

[1] The historical statement in Jer. xxvi. 18, from which we learn that it was in the days of Hezekiah that Micah uttered the threat contained in Mic. iii. 12 (of which the promises in Mic. iv. 1–4 and Isa. ii. 2–4 are the direct antithesis), apparently precludes the idea that Isaiah borrowed from Micah, whilst the opposite is altogether inadmissible, for reasons assigned above. Ewald and Hitzig have therefore come to the conclusion, quite independently of each other, that both Micah and Isaiah repeated the words of a third and earlier prophet, most probably of *Joel*. And the passage in question has really very much in common with the book of Joel, viz. the idea of the melting down of ploughshares and pruning-hooks (Joel iii. 10), the combination of *râb* (many) and *âtsum* (strong), of *gephen* (vine) and *te'enah* (fig-tree), as compared with Mic. iv. 4; also the attesting formula, " For Jehovah hath spoken it" (*chi Jehovah dibber:* Joel iii. (iv.) 8),

Nor was it even intended that they should appear to be his. Isaiah has not fused them into the general flow of his own prophecy, as the prophets usually do with the predictions of their predecessors. He does not reproduce them, but, as we may observe from the abrupt commencement, he quotes them. It is true, this hardly seems to tally with the heading, which describes what follows as the word of Jehovah which Isaiah saw. But the discrepancy is only an apparent one. It was the spirit of prophecy, which called to Isaiah's remembrance a prophetic saying that had already been uttered, and made it the starting-point of the thoughts which followed in Isaiah's mind. The borrowed promise is not introduced for its own sake, but is simply a self-explaining introduction to the exhortations and threatenings which follow, and through which the prophet works his way to a conclusion of his own, that is closely intertwined with the borrowed commencement.

Ver. 2. The subject of the borrowed prophecy is Israel's future glory: "*And it cometh to pass at the end of the days, the mountain of the house of Jehovah will be set at the top of the mountains, and exalted over hills; and all nations pour unto it.*"

which is not found in Micah, whereas it is very common in Isaiah,—a fact which makes the sign itself a very feeble one (cf. 1 Kings xiv. 11, also Ob. 18). Hitzig, indeed, maintains that it is only by restoring this passage that the prophetic writings of Joel receive their proper rounding off and an appropriate termination; but although swords and spears beaten into ploughshares and pruning-hooks form a good antithesis to ploughshares and pruning-hooks beaten into swords and spears (Joel iv. 10), the coming of great and mighty nations to Mount Zion after the previous judgment of extermination would be too unprepared or much too abrupt a phenomenon. On the other hand, we cannot admit the force of the arguments adduced either by E. Meier (*Joel*, p. 195) or by Knobel and G. Baur (*Amos*, p. 29) against the authorship of Joel, which rest upon a misapprehension of the meaning of Joel's prophecies, which the former regards as too full of storm and battle, the latter as too exclusive and one-sided, for Joel to be the author of the passage in question. At the same time, we would call attention to the fact, that the promises in Micah form the obverse side to the previous threatenings of judgment, so that there is a presumption of their originality; also that the passage contains as many traces of Micah's style (see above at ver. 3) as we could expect to find in these three verses; and, as we shall show at the conclusion of this cycle of predictions (ch. i.-vi.), that the historical fact mentioned in Jer. xxvi. 18 may be reconciled in the simplest possible manner with the assumption that Isaiah borrowed these words of promise from Micah. (See Caspari, *Micha*, p. 444 sqq.)

The expression "the last days" (*acharith hayyamim*, "the end of the days"), which does not occur anywhere else in Isaiah, is always used in an eschatological sense. It never refers to the course of history immediately following the time being, but invariably indicates the furthest point in the history of this life — the point which lies on the outermost limits of the speaker's horizon. This horizon was a very fluctuating one. The history of prophecy is just the history of its gradual extension, and of the filling up of the intermediate space. In Jacob's blessing (Gen. xlix.) the conquest of the land stood in the foreground of the *acharith* or last days, and the perspective was regulated accordingly. But here in Isaiah the *acharith* contained no such mixing together of events belonging to the more immediate and the most distant future. It was therefore the last time in its most literal and purest sense, commencing with the beginning of the New Testament æon, and terminating at its close (compare Heb. i. 1, 1 Pet. i. 20, with 1 Cor. xv. and the Revelation). The prophet here predicted that the mountain which bore the temple of Jehovah, and therefore was already in dignity the most exalted of all mountains, would one day tower in actual height above all the high places of the earth. The basaltic mountains of Bashan, which rose up in bold peaks and columns, might now look down with scorn and contempt upon the small limestone hill which Jehovah had chosen (Ps. lxviii. 16, 17); but this was an incongruity which the last times would remove, by making the outward correspond to the inward, the appearance to the reality and the intrinsic worth. That this is the prophet's meaning is confirmed by Ezek. xl. 2, where the temple mountain looks gigantic to the prophet, and also by Zech. xiv. 10, where all Jerusalem is described as towering above the country round about, which would one day become a plain. The question how this can possibly take place in time, since it presupposes a complete subversion of the whole of the existing order of the earth's surface, is easily answered. The prophet saw the new Jerusalem of the last days on this side, and the new Jerusalem of the new earth on the other (Rev. xxi. 10), blended as it were together, and did not distinguish the one from the other. But whilst we thus avoid all unwarrantable spiritualizing, it still remains a question what meaning the prophet attached to the word *b'rosh* ("*at the top*"). Did he mean that Moriah would one day stand *upon the top* of the mountains that surrounded it (as in Ps. lxxii. 16), or that it would stand *at their head* (as in 1 Kings xxi. 9, 12, Amos vi. 7, Jer. xxxi. 7)? The former is Hofmann's view, as given in his *Weissagung und Erfüllung*, ii. 217: "he did not indeed mean that the mountains would be piled up one upon the other, and the temple mountain upon the top, but that the temple mountain would appear to float upon the summit of the others." But as the expression "*will be set*" (*nacon*) does not favour this apparently romantic exaltation, and *b'rosh* occurs more frequently in the sense of "*at the head*" than in that of "*on the top*," I decide for my own part in favour of the second view, though I agree so far with Hofmann, that it is not merely an exaltation of the temple mountain in the estimation of the nations that is predicted, but a physical and external elevation also. And when thus outwardly exalted, the divinely chosen mountain would become the rendezvous and centre of unity for all nations. They would all "flow unto it" (*nâhar*, a denom. verb, from *nâhâr*, a river, as in Jer. li. 44, xxxi. 12). It is the temple of Jehovah which, being thus rendered visible to nations afar off, exerts such magnetic attraction, and with such success. Just as at a former period men had been separated and estranged from one another in the plain of Shinar, and thus different nations had first arisen; so would the nations at a future period assemble together on the mountain of the house of Jehovah, and there, as members of one family, live together in amity again. And as Babel (*confusion*, as its name signifies) was the place whence the stream of nations poured into all the world; so would Jerusalem (the *city of peace*) become the place into which the stream of nations would empty itself, and where all would be reunited once more. At the present time there was only one people, viz. Israel, which made pilgrimages to Zion on the great festivals, but it would be very different then.

Ver. 3. "*And peoples in multitude go and say, Come, let us go up to the mountain of Jehovah, to the house of the God of Jacob; let Him instruct us out of His ways, and we will walk in His paths.*" This is their signal for starting, and their song by the way (cf. Zech. viii. 21, 22). What urges them on is the desire for salvation. Desire for salvation expresses itself in the name they give to the point towards which they are travelling: they call Moriah "the mountain of Jehovah," and the temple upon it "the house of the God of Jacob." Through frequent use, *Israel* had become the popular name for the people of God; but the name they employ is the choicer name *Jacob*, which is the name of affection in the mouth of Micah, of whose style we are also reminded by the expression "many peoples" (*ammim rabbim*). Desire for salvation expresses itself in the object of their journey; they wish Jehovah to teach them "*out of His ways*,"—a rich source of instruction with which they desire to be gradually entrusted. The preposition *min* (out of, or from) is not partitive here, but refers, as in Ps. xciv. 12, to the source of instruction. The "ways of Jehovah" are the ways which God Himself takes, and by which men are led by Him—the revealed ordinances of His will and action. Desire for salvation also expresses itself in the resolution with which they set out: they not only wish to learn, but are resolved to act according to what they learn. "*We will walk in His paths:*" the hortative is used here, as it frequently is (*e.g.* Gen. xxvii. 4, *vid.* Ges. § 128, 1, *c*), to express either the subjective intention or subjective conclusion. The words supposed to be spoken by the multitude of heathen going up to Zion terminate here. The prophet then adds the reason and object of this holy pilgrimage of the nations: "*For instruction will go out from Zion, and the word of Jehovah from Jerusalem.*" The principal emphasis is upon the expressions "from Zion" and "from Jerusalem." It is a triumphant utterance of the sentiment that "salvation is of the Jews" (John iv. 22). From Zion-Jerusalem there would go forth *thorah*, *i.e.* instruction as to the questions which man has to put to God, and *debar Jehovah*, the word of Jehovah, which created the world at first, and by which it is spiritually created anew. Whatever promotes the true prosperity of the nations, comes from Zion-Jerusalem. There the nations assemble together; they take it thence to their own homes, and thus Zion-Jerusalem becomes the fountain of universal good. For from the time that Jehovah made choice of Zion, the holiness of Sinai was transferred to Zion (Ps. lxviii. 17), which now presented the same aspect as Sinai had formerly done, when God invested it with holiness by appearing there in the midst of myriads of angels. What had been commenced at Sinai for Israel, would be completed at Zion for all the world. This was fulfilled on that day of Pentecost, when the disciples, the first-fruits of the church of Christ, proclaimed the *thorah* of Zion, *i.e.* the gospel, in the languages of all the world. It was fulfilled, as Theodoret observes, in the fact that the word of the gospel, rising from Jerusalem "as from a fountain," flowed through the whole of the known world. But these fulfilments were only preludes to a conclusion which is still to be looked for in the future. For what is promised in the following verse is still altogether unfulfilled.

Ver. 4. "*And He will judge between the nations, and deliver justice to many peoples; and they forge their swords into coulters, and their spears into pruning-hooks: nation lifts not up the sword against nation, neither do they exercise themselves in war any more.*" Since the nations betake themselves in this manner as pupils to the God of revelation and the word of His revelation, He becomes the supreme judge and umpire among them. If any dispute arise, it is no longer settled by the compulsory force of war, but by the word of God, to which all bow with willing submission. With such power as this in the peace-sustaining word of God (Zech. ix. 10), there is no more need for weapons of iron: they are turned into the instruments of peaceful employment, into *ittim* (probably a synonym for *ethim* in 1 Sam. xiii. 21), plough-knives or coulters, which cut the furrows for the ploughshare to turn up; and *mazmeroth*, bills or pruning-hooks, with which vines are pruned to increase their fruit-bearing power. There is also no more need for military practice, for there is no use in exercising one's self in what cannot be applied. It is useless, and men dislike it. There is peace, not an armed peace, but a full, true, God-given and blessed peace. What even a Kant regarded as possible is now realized, and that not by the so-called Christian powers, but by the power of God, who favours the object for which an Elihu Burritt enthusiastically longs, rather than the politics of the Christian powers. It is in war that the power of the beast culminates in the history of the world. This beast will then be destroyed. The true humanity which sin has choked up will gain the mastery, and the world's history will keep Sabbath. And may we not indulge the hope, on the ground of such prophetic words as these, that the history of the world will not terminate without having kept a Sabbath? Shall we correct Isaiah, according to Quenstedt, lest we should become chiliasts? "The humanitarian ideas of Christendom," says a thoughtful Jewish scholar, "have their roots in the Pentateuch, and more especially in Deuteronomy. But in the prophets, particularly in Isaiah, they reach a height which will probably not be attained and fully realized by the modern world for centuries to come." Yet they will be realized. What the prophetic words appropriated by Isaiah here affirm, is a moral postulate, the goal of sacred history, the predicted counsel of God.

Isaiah presents himself to his contemporaries with this older prophecy of the exalted and world-wide calling of the people of Jehovah, holds it up before them as a mirror, and exclaims in ver. 5, "*O house of Jacob, come, let us walk in the light of Jehovah.*" This exhortation is formed under the influence of the context, from which vers. 2-4 are taken, as we may see from Mic. iv. 5, and also of the quotation itself. The use of the term *Jacob* instead of *Israel* is not indeed altogether strange to Isaiah (ch. viii. 17, x. 20, 21, xxix. 23), but he prefers the use of *Israel* (compare ch. i. 24 with Gen. xlix. 24). With the words "O house of Jacob" he now turns to his people, whom so glorious a future awaits, because Jehovah has made it the scene of His manifested presence and grace, and summons it to walk in the light of such a God, to whom all nations will press at the end of the days. The summons, "Come, let us walk," is the echo of ver. 3, "Come, let us go;" and as Hitzig observes, "Isaiah endeavours, like Paul in Rom. xi. 14, to stir up his countrymen to a noble jealousy, by setting before them the example of the heathen." The "light of Jehovah" (*'or Jehovah*, in which the echo of *v'yorenu* in ver. 3 is hardly accidental; cf. Prov. vi. 23) is the knowledge of Jehovah Himself, as furnished by means of positive revelation, His manifested love. It was now high time to walk in the light of Jehovah, *i.e.* to turn this knowledge into life, and reciprocate this love; and it was especially necessary to exhort Israel to this, now that Jehovah had given up His people, just because in their perverseness they had done the very opposite. This mournful declaration, which the prophet was obliged to make in order to explain his warning cry, he changes into the form of a prayerful sigh. Ver. 6. "*For Thou hast rejected Thy people, the house of Jacob; for they are filled with things from the east, and are conjurors like the Philistines; and with the children of foreigners they go hand in hand.*" Here again we have "*for*" (*chi*) twice in succession; the first giving the reason for the warning cry, the second vindicating the reason assigned. The words are addressed to Jehovah, not to the people. Saad., Gecatilia, and Rashi adopt the rendering, "Thou hast given up thy nationality;" and this rendering is supported by J. D. Michaelis, Hitzig, and Luzzatto. But the word means "people," not "nationality;" and the rendering is inadmissible, and would never have been thought of were it not that there was apparently something strange in so sudden an introduction of an address to God. But in ch. ii. 9, ix. 2, and other passages, the prophecy takes the form of a prayer. And *nâtash* (cast off) with *âm* (people) for its object recals such passages as Ps. xciv. 14 and 1 Sam. xii. 22. Jehovah had put away His people, *i.e.* rejected them, and left them to themselves, for the following reasons: (1.) Because they were "full from the east" (*mikkedem*: *min* denotes the source from which a person draws and fills himself, Jer. li. 34, Ezek. xxxii. 6), *i.e.* full of eastern manners and customs, more especially of idolatrous practices. By "the east" (*kedem*) we are to understand Arabia as far as the peninsula of Sinai, and also the Aramæan lands of the Euphrates. Under Uzziah and Jotham, whose sway extended to Elath, the seaport town of the Elanitic Gulf, the influence of the south-east predominated; but under Ahaz and Hezekiah, on account of their relations to Asshur, Aram, and Babylon, that of the north-east. The conjecture of Gesenius, that we should read *mikkesem*, *i.e.* of soothsaying, is a very natural one; but it obliterates without any necessity the name of the region from which Judah's imitative propensities received their impulse and materials. (2.) They were *onenim* (= *meonenim*, Mic. v. 11, from the *poel onen*: 2 Kings xxi. 6), probably "*cloud-gatherers*" or "*storm-raisers*,"[1] like the Philis-

---

[1] There is no force in the explanation "concealing," *i.e.* practising secret arts; for the meaning "cover" or "conceal" is arbitrarily transferred to the verb *onen*, from *gânan* and *cânan*, which are supposed to be cognate roots. As a denominative of *ânân*, the cloud, however (on this name for

tines (the people conquered by Uzziah, and then again by Hezekiah), among whom witchcraft was carried on in guilds, whilst a celebrated oracle of Baal-Zebub existed at Ekron. (3.) And they make common cause with children of foreigners. This is the explanation adopted by Gesenius, Knobel, and others. *Sâphak* with *cappaim* signifies *to clap hands* (Job xxvii. 23). The *hiphil* followed by *Beth* is only used here in the sense of *striking hands with a person*. Luzzatto explains it as meaning, " They find satisfaction in the children of foreigners; it is only through them that they are contented;" but this is contrary to the usage of the language, according to which *hispik* in post-biblical Hebrew signifies either *suppeditare* or (like *saphak* in 1 Kings xx. 10) *sufficere*. Jerome renders it *pueris alienis adhæserunt;* but *yalde nâc'rim* does not mean *pueri alieni*, boys hired for licentious purposes, but the "sons of strangers" generally (ch. lx. 10, lxi. 5), with a strong emphasis upon their unsanctified birth, the heathenism inherited from their mother's womb. With heathen by birth, the prophet would say, the people of Jehovah made common cause.

In vers. 7, 8 he describes still further how the land of the people of Jehovah, in consequence of all this (on the future consec. see Ges. § 129, 2, *a*), was crammed full of objects of luxury, of self-confidence, of estrangement from God: "*And their land is filled with silver and gold, and there is no end of their treasures; and their land is filled with horses, and there is no end of their chariots. And their land is filled with— idols; the work of their own hands they worship, that which their*

the clouds, see at ch. iv. 5), *onen* might mean "he gathered auguries from the clouds." Or if we take *onen* as a synonym of *innen* in Gen. ix. 14, it would mean "to raise storms," which would give the rendering νεφοδιῶκται, *tempestarii*, storm-raisers. The derivation of *onen* from עין, in the sense of the Arabic *'âna* (impf. *ya 'tnu*), as it were to ogle, *oculo maligno petere et fascinare*, founders on *annen*, the word used in the Targums, which cannot possibly be traced to עין. From a purely philological standpoint, however, there is still another explanation possible. From the idea of *coming to meet* we get the transitive meaning to hold back, shut in, or hinder, particularly to hold back a horse by the reins (*'inân*), or when applied to sexual relations, *'unna (unnina, u'inna) 'an el-mar'ati*, "he is prevented (by magic) from approaching his wife." Beside the Arabic *'innîn* and *ma'nûn* (to render sexually impotent by witchcraft), we find the Syriac *'anono* used in the same sense.

own fingers have made." The glory of Solomon, which revived under Uzziah's fifty-two years' reign, and was sustained through Jotham's reign of sixteen years, carried with it the curse of the law; for the law of the king, in Deut. xvii. 14 sqq., prohibited the multiplying of horses, and also the accumulation of gold and silver. Standing armies, and stores of national treasures, like everything else which ministers to carnal self-reliance, were opposed to the spirit of the theocracy. Nevertheless Judæa was immeasurably full of such seductions to apostasy; and not of those alone, but also of things which plainly revealed it, viz. of *elilim*, idols (the same word is used in Lev. xix. 4, xxvi. 1, from *elil*, vain or worthless; it is therefore equivalent to "not-gods"). They worshipped the work of "their own" hands, what "their own" fingers had made: two distributive singulars, as in ch. v. 23, the hands and fingers of every individual (*vid.* Mic. v. 12, 13, where the idols are classified). The condition of the land, therefore, was not only opposed to the law of the king, but at variance with the decalogue also. The existing glory was the most offensive caricature of the glory promised to the nation; for the people, whose God was one day to become the desire and salvation of all nations, had exchanged Him for the idols of the nations, and was vying with them in the appropriation of heathen religion and customs.

It was a state ripe for judgment, from which, therefore, the prophet could at once proceed, without any further preparation, to the proclamation of judgment itself. Ver. 9. "*Thus, then, men are bowed down, and lords are brought low; and forgive them—no, that Thou wilt not.*" The consecutive futures depict the judgment, as one which would follow by inward necessity from the worldly and ungodly glory of the existing state of things. The future is frequently used in this way (for example, in ch. ix. 7 sqq.). It was a judgment by which small and great, *i.e.* the people in all its classes, were brought down from their false eminence. "*Men*" and "*lords*" (*âdâm* and *ish*, as in ch. v. 15, Ps. xlix. 3, and Prov. viii. 4, and like ἄνθρωπος and ἀνήρ in the Attic dialect), *i.e.* men who were lost in the crowd, and men who rose above it,—all of them the judgment would throw down to the ground, and that without mercy (Rev. vi. 15). The prophet expresses the conviction (*al* as in 2 Kings vi. 27), that on this occasion God neither could nor would take away the sin by forgiving it. There was nothing left for them, therefore, but to carry out the command of the prophet in ver. 10: "*Creep into the rock, and bury thyself in the dust, before the terrible look of Jehovah, and before the glory of His majesty.*" The glorious nation would hide itself most ignominiously, when the only true glory of Jehovah, which had been rejected by it, was manifested in judgment. They would conceal themselves in holes of the rocks, as if before a hostile army (Judg. vi. 2; 1 Sam. xiii. 6, xiv. 11), and bury themselves with their faces in the sand, as if before the fatal simoom of the desert, that they might not have to bear this intolerable sight. And when Jehovah manifested Himself in this way in the fiery glance of judgment, the result summed up in ver. 11 must follow: "*The people's eyes of haughtiness are humbled, and the pride of their lords is bowed down; and Jehovah, He only, stands exalted in that day.*" The result of the process of judgment is expressed in perfects: *nisgab* is the third *pers. præt.*, not the participle: Jehovah "is exalted," *i.e.* shows Himself as exalted, whilst the haughty conduct of the people is brought down (*shâphel* is a verb, not an adjective; it is construed in the singular by attraction, and either refers to *âdâm*, man or people: Ges. § 148, 1; or what is more probable, to the logical unity of the compound notion which is taken as subject, the *constr. ad synesin s. sensum*: Thiersch, § 118), and the pride of the lords is bowed down (*shach* = *shâchach*, Job ix. 13). The first strophe of the proclamation of judgment appended to the prophetic saying in vers. 2–4 is here brought to a close. The second strophe reaches to ver. 17, where ver. 11 is repeated as a concluding verse.

The expression "*that day*" suggests the inquiry, What day is referred to? The prophet answers this question in the second strophe. Ver. 12. "*For Jehovah of hosts hath a day over everything towering and lofty, and over everything exalted; and it becomes low.*" "*Jehovah hath a day*" (*yom layehovah*), lit. there is to Jehovah a day, which already exists as a finished divine thought in that wisdom by which the course of history is guided (ch. xxxvii. 26, cf. xxii. 11), the secret of which He revealed to the prophets, who from the time of Obadiah and Joel downwards proclaimed that day with one uniform watchword. But when the time appointed for that day should arrive, it would pass out of the secret of eternity into the history of time,—a day of world-wide judgment, which would pass, through the omnipotence with which Jehovah rules over the higher as well as lower spheres of the whole creation, upon all worldly glory, and it would be brought low (*shaphel*). The current accentuation of ver. 12*b* is wrong; correct MSS. have על with *mercha*, כל־נשׂא with *tifcha*. The word *v'shâphel* (third pers. præt. with the root-vowel *ê*) acquires the force of a future, although no grammatical future precedes it, from the future character of the day itself: "and it will sink down" (Ges. § 126, 4).

The prophet then proceeds to enumerate all the high things upon which that day would fall, arranging them two and two, and binding them in pairs by a double correlative *Vav*. The day of Jehovah comes, as the first two pairs affirm, upon everything lofty in nature. Vers. 13, 14. "*As upon all the cedars of Lebanon, the lofty and exalted, so upon all the oaks of Bashan. As upon all mountains, the lofty ones, so upon all hills the exalted ones.*" But wherefore upon all this majestic beauty of nature? Is all this merely figurative? Knobel regards it as merely a figurative description of the grand buildings of the time of Uzziah and Jotham, in the erection of which wood had been used from Lebanon as well as from Bashan, on the western slopes of which the old shady oaks (*sindiân* and *ballût*) are flourishing still.[1] But the idea that trees can be used to signify the houses built with the wood obtained from them, is one that cannot be sustained from ch. ix. 9 (10), where the reference is not to houses built of sycamore and cedar wood, but to trunks of trees of the kind mentioned; nor even from Nahum ii. 4 (3), where *habberoshim* refers to the fir lances which are brandished about in haughty thirst for battle. So again mountains and hills cannot denote the castles and fortifications built upon them, more especially as these are expressly mentioned in ver. 15 in the most literal terms. In order to understand the prophet, we must bear in mind what the Scriptures invariably assume, from their first chapter to the very close, namely, that the totality of nature is bound up with man in one common history; that man and the totality of nature are inseparably connected together as

---

[1] On the meaning of the name of this region, *Bashan* (*Basanitis*), see *Job*, vol. ii. pp. 398–400, Eng. Tr.

centre and circumference; that this circumference is affected by the sin which proceeds from man, as well as by the anger or the mercy which proceeds from God to man; that the judgments of God, as the history of the nations proves, involve in fellow-suffering even that part of the creation which is not free; and that this participation in the "corruption" (*phthora*) and "glory" (*doxa*) of humanity will come out with peculiar distinctness and force at the close of the world's history, in a manner corresponding to the commencement; and lastly, that the world in its present condition needs a *palingenesia*, or regeneration, quite as much as the corporeal nature of man, before it can become an object of good pleasure on the part of God. We cannot be surprised, therefore, that, in accordance with this fundamental view of the Scriptures, when the judgment of God fell upon Israel, it should also be described as going down to the land of Israel, and as overthrowing not only the false glory of the nation itself, but everything glorious in the surrounding nature, which had been made to minister to its national pride and love of show, and to which its sin adhered in many different ways. What the prophet foretold began to be fulfilled even in the Assyrian wars. The cedar woods of Lebanon were unsparingly destroyed; the heights and valleys of the land were trodden down and laid waste; and, in the period of the great empires which commenced with Tiglath-pileser, the Holy Land was reduced to a shadow of its former promised beauty.

The glory of nature is followed by what is lofty and glorious in the world of men, such as magnificent fortifications, grand commercial buildings, and treasures which minister to the lust of the eye. Vers. 15, 16. "*As upon every high tower, so upon every fortified wall. As upon all ships of Tarshish, so upon all works of curiosity.*" It was by erecting fortifications for offence and defence, both lofty and steep (*bâzur*, præruptus, from *bâzar*, abrumpere, secernere), that Uzziah and Jotham especially endeavoured to serve Jerusalem and the land at large. The chronicler relates, with reference to Uzziah, in 2 Chron. xxvi., that he built strong towers above "the corner-gate, the valley-gate, and the southern point of the cheese-makers' hollow," and fortified these places, which had probably been till that time the weakest points in Jerusalem; also that he built towers in the desert (probably in the desert between

Beersheba and Gaza, to increase the safety of the land, and the numerous flocks which were pastured in the *shephelah*, *i.e* the western portion of southern Palestine). With regard to Jotham, it is related in both the book of Kings (2 Kings xv. 32 sqq.) and the Chronicles, that he built the upper gate of the temple; and in the Chronicles (2 Chron. xxvii.) that he fortified the 'Ofel, *i.e.* the southern spur of the temple hill, still more strongly, and built cities on the mountains of Judah, and erected castles and towers in the forests (to watch for hostile attacks and ward them off). Hezekiah also distinguished himself by building enterprises of this kind (2 Chron. xxxii. 27–30). But the allusion to the ships of Tarshish takes us to the times of Uzziah and Jotham, and not to those of Hezekiah (as Ps. xlviii. 7 does to the time of Jehoshaphat); for the seaport town of Elath, which was recovered by Uzziah, was lost again to the kingdom of Judah during the reign of Ahaz. Jewish ships sailed from this Elath (Ailath) through the Red Sea and round the coast of Africa to the harbour of Tartessus, the ancient Phœnician emporium of the maritime region watered by the Bætis (Guadalquivir), which abounded in silver, and then returned through the Pillars of Hercules (the Straits of Gibraltar: *vid.* Duncker, *Gesch.* i. 312-315). It was to these Tartessus vessels that the expression "ships of Tarshish" primarily referred, though it was afterwards probably applied to mercantile ships in general. The following expression, "works of curiosity" (*sechiyyoth hachemdah*), is taken in far too restricted a sense by those who limit it, as the LXX. have done, to the ships already spoken of, or understand it, as Gesenius does, as referring to beautiful flags. Jerome's rendering is correct: "*et super omne quod visu pulcrum est*" (and upon everything beautiful to look at); *seciyyâh*, from *sâcâh*, to look (see *Job*, p. 468), is sight generally. The reference therefore is to all kinds of works of art, whether in sculpture or paintings (*mascith* is used of both), which delighted the observer by their imposing, tasteful appearance. Possibly, however, there is a more especial reference to curiosities of art and nature, which were brought by the trading vessels from foreign lands.

Ver. 17 closes the second strophe of the proclamation of judgment appended to the earlier prophetic word: "*And the haughtiness of the people is bowed down, and the pride of the lords brought low; and Jehovah, He alone, stands exalted on that day.*" The closing refrain only varies a little from ver. 11. The subjects of the verbs are transposed. With a feminine noun denoting a thing, it is almost a rule that the predicate shall be placed before it in masculine (Ges. § 147, *a*).

The closing refrain of the next two strophes is based upon the concluding clause of ver. 10. The proclamation of judgment turns now to the *elilim*, which, as being at the root of all the evil, occupied the lowest place in the things of which the land was full (vers. 7, 8). In a short verse of one clause consisting of only three words, their future is declared as it were with a lightning-flash. Ver. 18. "*And the idols utterly pass away.*" The translation shows the shortness of the verse, but not the significant *synallage numeri*. The idols are one and all a mass of nothingness, which will be reduced to absolute annihilation: they will vanish *câlil*, *i.e.* either "they will utterly perish" (*funditus peribunt*), or, as *câlil* is not used adverbially in any other passage, "they will all perish" (*tota peribunt*, Judg. xx. 40)—their images, their worship, even their names and their memory (Zech. xiii. 2).

What the idolaters themselves will do when Jehovah has so completely deprived their idols of all their divinity, is then described in ver. 19: "*And they will creep into caves in the rocks, and cellars in the earth, before the terrible look of Jehovah, and before the glory of His majesty, when He ariseth to put the earth in terror.*" *Meârâh* is a natural cave, and *mechillah* a subterraneous excavation: this is apparently the distinction between the two synonyms. "*To put the earth in terror:*" *laarotz hâ-aretz*, a significant paronomasia, which can be reproduced in Latin, thus: *ut terreat terram*. Thus the judgment would fall upon the earth without any limitation, upon men universally (compare the word *hâ-âdâm* in ver. 20, which is scarcely ever applied to a single individual (Josh. xiv. 15), excepting, of course, the first man, but generally to men, or to the human race) and upon the totality of nature as interwoven in the history of man—one complete whole, in which sin, and therefore wrath, had gained the upper hand. When Jehovah rose up, *i.e.* stood up from His heavenly throne, to reveal the glory manifested in heaven, and turn its judicial fiery side towards the sinful earth, the earth would receive such a shock as would throw it into a state resembling the chaos of the beginning. We may see very clearly from Rev. vi. 15, where this description is borrowed, that the prophet is here describing the last judgment, although from a national point of view and bounded by a national horizon.

Ver. 20 forms the commencement to the fourth strophe: "*In that day will a man cast away his idols of gold and his idols of silver, which they made for him to worship, to the moles and to the bats.*" The traditional text separates *lachpor peroth* into two words,[1] though without its being possible to discover what they are supposed to mean. The reason for the separation was simply the fact that *plurilitera* were at one time altogether misunderstood and regarded as *composita*: for other *plurilitera*, written as two words, compare ch. lxi. 1, Hos. iv. 18, Jer. xlvi. 20. The prophet certainly pronounced the word *lachparpâroth* (Ewald, § 157, *c*); and *chapharpârâh* is apparently a *mole* (lit. thrower up of the soil), *talpa*, as it is rendered by Jerome and interpreted by Rashi. Gesenius and Knobel, however, have raised this objection, that the mole is never found in *houses*. But are we necessarily to assume that they would throw their idols into lumber-rooms, and not hide them in holes and crevices out of doors? The mole, the shrewmouse, and the bat, whose name (*atalleph*) is regarded by Schultens as a compound word (*atal-eph*, night-bird), are generically related, according to both ancient and modern naturalists. Bats are to birds what moles are to the smaller beasts of prey (*vid*. Levysohn, *Zoologie des Talmud*, p. 102). The LXX. combine with these two words *Uhishtachavoth* (to worship). Malbim and Luzzatto adopt this rendering, and understand the words to mean that they would sink down to the most absurd descriptions of animal worship. But the

[1] Abulwalid Parchon and others regard the double word as the singular of a substantive, applied to a particular bird (possibly a woodpecker), as a pecker of fruit (*peroth*). Kimchi would rather take *lachpor* as an infinitive (as in Josh. ii. 2), to dig pits; and compares with it the talmudic word *pēr*, a pit or grave. No one adopts the rendering "into mouse-holes," simply because *pērah*, a mouse (from an Arabic word *fa'ara*, to dig, or root up), was not a Hebrew word at all, but was adopted at a later period from the Arabic (hence the Hebræo-Arabic *purah*, a mousetrap).

accentuation, which does not divide the verse at עשׂו־לו, as we should expect if this were the meaning, is based upon the correct interpretation. The idolaters, convinced of the worthlessness of their idols through the judicial interposition of God, and enraged at the disastrous manner in which they had been deceived, would throw away with curses the images of gold and silver which artists' hands had made according to their instructions, and hide them in the holes of bats and in molehills, to conceal them from the eyes of the Judge, and then take refuge there themselves after ridding themselves of this useless and damnable burden.

Ver. 21. "*To creep into the cavities of the stone-blocks, and into the clefts of the rocks, before the terrible look of Jehovah, and before the glory of His majesty, when He arises to put the earth in terror.*" Thus ends the fourth strophe of this "*dies iræ, dies illa,*" which is appended to the earlier prophetic word. But there follows, as an *epiphonem*, this *nota bene* in ver. 22: *Oh, then, let man go, in whose nose is a breath; for what is he estimated at?* The Septuagint leaves this verse out altogether. But was it so utterly unintelligible then? Jerome adopted a false pointing, and has therefore given this marvellous rendering: *excelsus* (*bâmâh!*) *reputatus est ipse,* by which Luther was apparently misled. But if we look backwards and forwards, it is impossible to mistake the meaning of the verse, which must be regarded not only as the resultant of what precedes it, but also as the transition to what follows. It is preceded by the prediction of the utter demolition of everything which ministers to the pride and vain confidence of men; and in ch. iii. 1 sqq. the same prediction is resumed, with a more special reference to the Jewish state, from which Jehovah is about to take away every prop, so that it shall utterly collapse. Accordingly the prophet exhorts, in ver. 22, to a renunciation of trust in man, and everything belonging to him, just as in Ps. cxviii. 8, 9, cxlvi. 3, and Jer. xvii. 5. The construction is as general as that of a gnome. The *dat. commodi* לכם (Ges. § 154, 3, *e*) renders the exhortation both friendly and urgent: from regard to yourselves, for your own good, for your own salvation, desist from man, *i.e.* from your confidence in him, in whose nose (*in cujus naso,* the singular, as in Job xxvii. 3; whereas the plural is used in Gen. ii. 7 in the same sense, *in nares ejus,* "into his nostrils ") is a breath, a breath of life, which God gave to him, and can take back as soon as He will (Job xxxiv. 14; Ps. civ. 29). Upon the breath, which passes out and in through his nose, his whole earthly existence is suspended; and this, when once lost, is gone for ever (Job vii. 7). It is upon this breath, therefore, that all the confidence placed in man must rest,—a bad soil and foundation! Under these conditions, and with this liability to perish in a moment, the worth of man as a ground of confidence is really nothing. This thought is expressed here in the form of a question: At (for) what is he estimated, or to be estimated? The passive participle *nechshâb* combines with the idea of the actual (*æstimatus*) that of the necessary (*æstimandus*), and also of the possible or suitable (*æstimabilis*); and that all the more because the Semitic languages have no special forms for the latter notions. The *Beth* is *Beth pretii*, corresponding to the Latin genitive (*quanti*) or ablative (*quanto*),—a modification of the *Beth instrumenti*, the price being regarded as the medium of exchange or purchase: " at what is he estimated," not with what is he compared, which would be expressed by *'eth* (ch. liii. 12; compare μετά, Luke xxii. 37) or *'im* (Ps. lxxxviii. 5). The word is בַּמֶּה, not בָּמָה, because this looser form is only found in cases where a relative clause follows (*eo quod*, Eccles. iii. 22), and not *bammâh*, because this termination with *â* is used exclusively where the next word begins with *Aleph*, or where it is a pausal word (as in 1 Kings xxii. 21); in every other case we have *bammeh*. The question introduced with this *quanto* (*quanti*), " at what," cannot be answered by any positive definition of value. The worth of man, regarded in himself, and altogether apart from God, is really nothing.

The proclamation of judgment pauses at this *porisma*, but only for the purpose of gathering fresh strength. The prophet has foretold in four strophes the judgment of God upon every exalted thing in the *kosmos* that has fallen away from communion with God, just as Amos commences his book with a round of judgments, which are uttered in seven strophes of uniform scope, bursting like seven thunder-claps upon the nations of the existing stage of history. The seventh stroke falls upon Judah, over which the thunderstorm rests after finding such abundant booty. And in the same manner Isaiah, in the instance before us, reduces the universal proclamation of judgment to one more especially affecting Judah and Jerusalem. The current of the address breaks through the bounds of the strophe; and the exhortation in ch. ii. 22 not to trust in man, the reason for which is assigned in what precedes, also forms a transition from the universal proclamation of judgment to the more special one in ch. iii. 1, where the prophet assigns a fresh ground for the exhortation :—

Ch. iii. 1. "*For, behold, the Lord, Jehovah of hosts, takes away from Jerusalem and from Judah supporter and means of support, every support of bread and every support of water.*" The divine name given here, "The Lord, Jehovah of hosts," with which Isaiah everywhere introduces the judicial acts of God (cf. ch. i. 24, x. 16, 33, xix. 4), is a proof that the proclamation of judgment commences afresh here. Trusting in man was the crying sin, more especially of the times of Uzziah-Jotham. The glory of the kingdom at that time carried the wrath of Jehovah within it. The outbreak of that wrath commenced in the time of Ahaz; and even under Hezekiah it was merely suspended, not changed. Isaiah foretells this outbreak of wrath. He describes how Jehovah will lay the Jewish state in ruins, by taking away the main supports of its existence and growth. "Supporter and means of support" (*mash'en* and *mash'enah*) express, first of all, the general idea. The two nouns, which are only the masculine and feminine forms of one and the same word (compare Mic. ii. 4, Nahum ii. 11, and the examples from the Syriac and Arabic in Ewald, § 172, *c*), serve to complete the generalization: *fulcra omne genus* (props of every kind, *omnigena*). They are both technical terms, denoting the prop which a person uses to support anything, whilst *mish'an* signifies that which yields support; so that the three correspond somewhat to the Latin *fulcrum, fultura, fulcimen.* Of the various means of support, bread and wine are mentioned first, not in a figurative sense, but as the two indispensable conditions and the lowest basis of human life. Life is supported by bread and water: it walks, as it were, upon the crutch of bread, so that "breaking the staff of bread" (Lev. xxvi. 26; Ezek. iv. 16, v. 16, xiv. 13; Ps. cv. 16) is equivalent to physical destruction. The destruction of the Jewish state would accordingly be commenced by a removal on the part of Jehovah of all the support afforded by bread and water, *i.e.* all the stores of both. And this was literally fulfilled, for both in the Chaldean and Roman times Jerusalem perished in the midst of just such terrible famines as are threatened in the curses in Lev. xxvi., and more especially in Deut. xxviii.; and in both cases the inhabitants were reduced to such extremities, that women devoured their own children (Lam. ii. 20; Josephus, *Wars of Jews*, vi. 3, 3, 4). It is very unjust, therefore, on the part of modern critics, such as Hitzig, Knobel, and Meier, to pronounce ver. 1*b* a gloss, and, in fact, a false one. Gesenius and Umbreit retracted this suspicion. The construction of the verse is just the same as that of ch. xxv. 6; and it is Isaiah's custom to explain his own figures, as we have already observed when comparing ch. i. 7 sqq. and i. 23 with what preceded them. " Every support of bread and every support of water" are not to be regarded in this case as an explanation of the general idea introduced before, "supporters and means of support," but simply as the commencement of the detailed expansion of the idea. For the enumeration of the supports which Jehovah would take away is continued in the next two verses.

Vers. 2, 3. "*Hero and man of war, judge and prophet, and soothsayer and elder; captains of fifty, and the highly distinguished, and counsellors, and masters in art, and those skilled in muttering.*" As the state had grown into a military state under Uzziah-Jotham, the prophet commences in both verses with military officers, viz. the *gibbor*, *i.e.* commanders whose bravery had been already tried; the "*man of war*" (*ish milchâmâh*), *i.e.* private soldiers who had been equipped and well trained (see Ezek. xxxix. 20); and the " captain of fifty" (*sar chamisshim*), leaders of the smallest divisions of the army, consisting of only fifty men (*pentekontarchos*, 2 Kings i. 9, etc.). The prominent members of the state are all mixed up together : " *the judge*" (*shophet*), *i.e.* the officers appointed by the government to administer justice ; " *the elder*" (*zâkēn*), *i.e.* the heads of families and the senators appointed by the town corporations ; the " *counsellor*" (*yōetz*), those nearest to the king; the " *highly distinguished*" (*nesu panim*), lit. those whose personal appearance (*panim*) was accepted, *i.e.* welcome and regarded with honour (Saad.· *wa'gih*, from *wa'gh*, the face or appearance), that is to say, persons of influence, not only on account of their office, but also on account of wealth, age, goodness, etc.; "*masters in art*" (*chacam charâshim* : LXX. σοφὸς ἀρχιτέκτων), or, as Jerome has very well rendered it, *in artibus mechanicis exercitatus easque callide tractans* (persons well versed in mechanical arts, and carrying them out with skill). In the Chaldean captivities skilled artisans are particularly mentioned as having been carried away (2 Kings xxiv. 14 sqq.; Jer. xxiv. 1, xxix. 2); so that there can be no doubt whatever that *charâshim* (from *cheresh*) is to be understood as signifying *mechanical* and not *magical* arts, as Gesenius, Hitzig, and Meier suppose, and therefore that *chacam charâshim* does not mean "wizards," as Ewald renders it (*chărâshim* is a different word from *chârâshim*, *fabri*, from *chârâsh*, although in 1 Chron. iv. 14, cf. Neh. xi. 35, the word is regularly pointed חָרָשִׁים even in this personal sense). Moreover, the rendering "wizards" produces tautology, inasmuch as masters of the black art are cited as *nebon lachash*, "skilled in muttering." *Lachash* is the whispering or muttering of magical formulas; it is related both radically and in meaning to *nachash*, enchantment (Arabic *nachs*, misfortune); it is derived from *lâchash*, *sibilare*, to hiss (a kindred word to *nâchash*; hence *nâchâsh*, a serpent). Beside this, the masters of the black art are also represented as *kosem*, which, in accordance with the radical idea of making fast, swearing, conjuring, denoted a soothsayer following heathen superstitions, as distinguished from the *nabi*, or false Jehovah prophet (we find this as early as Deut. xviii. 10, 14).[1] These came next to bread

---

[1] According to the primary meaning of the whole *thema*, which is one of hardness, rigidity, firmness, *aksama* (*hi.* of *kâsam*) signifies, strictly speaking, to *make sure*, *i.e.* to *swear*, either by swearing to the truth and certainty of a thing, or by making a person swear that he will do or not do a certain thing, by laying as it were a *kasam* upon him. The *kal*, on the other hand (*kasama*), gets its meaning to divide from the turn given to the radical idea in the substantive *kism*, which signifies, according to the original lexicographers, something fixed (= *nasib*), definite, *i.e.* a definite portion. There is just the same association of ideas in '*azama* as in *aksama*, namely, literally to be firm or make firm, *i.e.* to direct one's will firmly towards an object or place; also to direct one's will firmly towards a person, to adjure him to do a thing or not to do it; sometimes with a softer meaning, to urge or invite a person to anything, at other times to recite conjuring formulas (*'azâim*).

and water, and were in a higher grade the props of the state. They are mixed together in this manner without regular order, because the powerful and splendid state was really a *quodlibet* of things Jewish and heathen; and when the wrath of Jehovah broke out, the godless glory would soon become a mass of confusion.

Ver. 4. Thus robbed of its support, and torn out of its proper groove, the kingdom of Judah would fall a prey to the most shameless despotism: "*And I give them boys for princes, and caprices shall rule over them.*" The revived "Solomonian" glory is followed, as before, by the times of Rehoboam. The king is not expressly named. This was intentional. He had sunk into the mere shadow of a king: it was not he who ruled, but the aristocratic party that surrounded him, who led him about in leading strings as *unum inter pares*. Now, if it is a misfortune in most cases for a king to be a child (*na'ar*, Eccles. x. 16), the misfortune is twice as great when the princes or magnates who surround and advise him are youngsters (*ne'ârim*, *i.e.* young lords) in a bad sense. It produces a government of *taalulim*. None of the nouns in this form have a personal signification. According to the primary meaning of the verbal stem, the word might signify childishnesses, equivalent to little children (the abstract for the concrete, like τὰ παιδικά, *amasius*), as Ewald supposes; or puppets, *fantocci*, poltroons, or men without heart or brain, as Luzzatto maintains. But the latter has no support in the general usage of the language, and the verb *yimshelu* (shall rule) does not necessarily require a personal subject (cf. Ps. xix. 14, ciii. 19). The word *taalulim* is formed from the reflective verb *hithallel*, which means to meddle, to gratify one's self, to indulge one's caprice. Accordingly *taalulim* itself might be rendered *vexatione*s (ch. lxvi. 4). Jerome, who translates the word *effeminati*, appears to have thought of התעלל in an erotic sense. The Sept. rendering, ἐμπαῖκται, is better, though ἐμπαίγματα would be more exact. When used, as the word is here, along with *ne'arim*, it signifies outbursts of youthful caprice, which do injury to others, whether in joke or earnest. Neither law nor justice would rule, but the very opposite of justice: a course of conduct which would make subjects, like slaves, the helpless victims at one time of their lust (Judg. xix. 25), and at another of their cruelty.

They would be governed by lawless and bloodstained caprice, of the most despotic character and varied forms. And the people would resemble their rulers: their passions would be let loose, and all restraints of modesty and decorum be snapt asunder.

Ver. 5. "*And the people oppress one another, one this and another that; the boy breaks out violently upon the old man, and the despised upon the honoured.*" *Niggas* is a reciprocal *niphal*, as the clause depicting the reciprocity clearly shows (cf. *nilcham*, ch. xix. 2); *nagas* followed by *Beth* means to treat as a tyrant or taskmaster (ch. ix. 3). The commonest selfishness would then stifle every nobler motive; one would become the tyrant of another, and ill-mannered insolence would take the place of that reverence, which is due to the old and esteemed from boys and those who are below them in position, whether we regard the law of nature, the Mosaic law (Lev. xix. 32), or the common custom of society. *Nikleh* (from *kâlâh*, the synonym of הקל, ch. viii. 23, xxiii. 9; cf. ch. xvi. 14, *kal*, to be light or insignificant) was a term used to denote whoever belonged to the lowest stratum of society (1 Sam. xviii. 23). It was the opposite of *nicbâd* (from *cabed*, to be heavy or of great importance). The Septuagint rendering, ὁ ἄτιμος πρὸς τὸν ἔντιμον is a very good one (as the Semitic languages have no such antithetical formations with ἀ στερητικόν). With such contempt of the distinctions arising from age and position, the state would very soon become a scene of the wildest confusion.

At length there would be no authorities left; even the desire to rule would die out: for despotism is sure to be followed by mob-rule, and mob-rule by anarchy in the most literal sense. The distress would become so great, that whoever had a coat (cloak), so as to be able to clothe himself at all decently, would be asked to undertake the government. Vers. 6, 7. "*When a man shall take hold of his brother in his father's house, Thou hast a coat, thou shalt be our ruler, and take this ruin under thy hand; he will cry out in that day, I do not want to be a surgeon; there is neither bread nor coat in my house: ye cannot make me the ruler of the people.*" "*His father's house*"—this is not an unmeaning trait in the picture of misery. The population would have become so thin and dispirited through hunger, that with a little energy it would be possible to decide within the narrow circle of a family who should be ruler, and to give effect to the decision. "In his father's house:" *Beth âbiv* is an *acc. loci.* The father's house is the place where brother meets with brother; and one breaks out with the urgent petition contained in the words, which follow without the introductory "saying" (cf. ch. xiv. 8, 16, and xxii. 16, xxxiii. 14). לְכָה for לְךָ with *He otians*, a form rarely met with (*vid.* Gen. xxvii. 37). תִּהְיֶה, which would be written תְּהִי before the predicate, is jussive in meaning, though not in form. "*This ruin:*" *macshelah* is used in Zeph. i. 3 for that which occasions a person's fall; here it signifies what has been overthrown; and as *câshal* itself, which means not only to stumble, trip, or slide, but also to fall in consequence of some force applied from without, is not used in connection with falling buildings, it must be introduced here with an allusion to the prosopopœia which follows in ver. 8. The man who was distinguished above all others, or at any rate above many others, by the fact that he could still dress himself decently (even if it were only in a blouse), should be made supreme ruler or dictator (cf. *kâtzin*, Judg. xi. 6); and the state which lay so miserably in ruins should be under his hand, *i.e.* his direction, protection, and care (2 Kings viii. 20; Gen. xli. 35, cf. ch. xvi. 9, where the plural is used instead of the ordinary singular *yâd*). The apodosis to the protasis introduced with *chi* as a particle of time (*when*) commences in ver. 7. The answer given by the brother to the earnest petition is introduced with "*he will raise* (viz. his voice, ch. xxiv. 14) *in that day, saying.*" It is given in this circumstantial manner because it is a solemn protest. He does not want to be a *chobêsh, i.e.* a *binder,* namely of the broken arms, and bones, and ribs of the ruined state (ch. xxx. 26, i. 6, lxi. 1). The expression *ehyeh* implies that he does not like it, because he is conscious of his inability. He has not confidence enough in himself, and the assumption that he has a coat is a false one: he not only has no coat at home (we must remember that the conversation is supposed to take place in his father's house), but he has not any bread; so that it is utterly impossible for a naked, starving man like him to do what is suggested ("in my house," *ubebethi* with a *Vav* of causal connection: Ges. 155, 1, *c*).

The prophet then proceeds, in vers. 8–12, to describe this deep, tragical misery as a just retribution. Ver. 8. "*For Jerusalem* is ruined and Judah fallen; because their tongue and their doings (are) *against Jehovah, to defy the eyes of His glory.*" *Jerusalem* as a city is feminine, according to the usual personification; *Judah* as a people is regarded as masculine.[1] The two preterites *câsh'lâh* and *nâphal* express the general fact, which occasioned such scenes of misery as the one just described. The second clause, beginning with "because" (*chi*), is a substantative clause, and attributes the coming judgment not to future sin, but to sin already existing. "*Against Jehovah:*" אֶל is used to denote a hostile attitude, as in ch. ii. 4, Gen. iv. 8, Num. xxxii. 14, Josh. x. 6. The capital and the land are against Jehovah both in word and deed, "to defy the eyes of His glory" (*lamroth 'ēnē chebodo*). עֲנֵי is equivalent to עֵינֵי; and *lamroth* is a syncopated *hiphil*, as in ch. xxiii. 11, and like the *niphal* in ch. i. 12: we find the same form of the same word in Ps. lxxviii. 17. The kal *mârâh*, which is also frequently construed with the accusative, signifies to thrust away in a refractory manner; the hiphil *himrâh*, to treat refractorily, literally to set one's self rigidly in opposition, *obniti; mar, stringere,* to draw tightly, with which unquestionably the meaning bitter as an astringent is connected, though it does not follow that *mârâh, himrâh,* and *hemar* (Ex. xxiii. 21) can be rendered παραπικραίνειν, as they have been in the Septuagint, since the idea of opposing, resisting, fighting in opposition, is implied in all these roots, with distinct reference to the primary meaning. The *Lamed* is a shorter expression instead of לְמַעַן, which is the term generally employed in such circumstances (Amos ii. 7; Jer. vii. 18, xxxii. 29). But what does the prophet mean by "the eyes of His glory?" Knobel's assertion, that *châbod* is used here for the religious glory, *i.e.* the holiness of God, is a very strange one, since the *châbod* of God is invariably the fiery, bright *doxa* which reveals Him as the Holy One. But his remark does not meet the question, inasmuch as it does not settle the point in dispute, whether the expression "the eyes of His glory" implies that the glory itself has eyes, or the glory is a quality of the eyes. The construction is certainly not a different one from "the arm of His glory" in ch. lii. 10, so

---

[1] As a rule, the name of a people (apart from the personification of the people as *beth*, a house) is only used as a feminine, when the name of the land stands for the nation itself (see Gesenius, *Lehrbegr.* p. 469).

that it is to be taken as an attribute. But this suggests the further question, what does the prophet mean by the glory-eyes or glorious eyes of Jehovah? If we were to say the eyes of Jehovah are His knowledge of the world, it would be impossible to understand how they could be called holy, still less how they could be called glorious. This abstract explanation of the anthropomorphisms cannot be sustained. The state of the case is rather the following. The glory (*chabod*) of God is that eternal and glorious *morphe* which His holy nature assumes, and which men must picture to themselves anthropomorphically, because they cannot imagine anything superior to the human form. In this glorious form Jehovah looks upon His people with eyes of glory. His pure but yet jealous love, His holy love which breaks out in wrath against all who meet it with hatred instead of with love, is reflected therein.

But Israel, instead of walking in the consciousness of being a constant and favourite object of these majestic, earnestly admonishing eyes, was diligently engaged in bidding them defiance both in word and deed, not even hiding its sin from fear of them, but exposing them to view in the most shameless manner.—Ver. 9. "*The look of their faces testifies against them, and their sin they make known like Sodom, without concealing it: woe to their soul! for they do themselves harm.*" In any case, the prophet refers to the impudence with which their enmity against God was shamelessly stamped upon their faces, without even the self-condemnation which leads in other cases to a diligent concealment of the sin. But we cannot follow Luzzatto and Jos. Kimchi, who take *haccárath* as used directly for *azzuth* (impudence), inasmuch as the Arabic *hakara* (*hakir'a*), to which Kimchi appeals, signifies to be astonished and to stare (see at Job xix. 3). And in this case there would be nothing strange in the substantive form, which would be a *piel* formation like חַטָּאָה בַּלֵּהָה. But it may be a *hiphil* formation (Ewald, § 156, *a*); and this is incomparably the more probable of the two, as *hiccir panim* is a very common phrase. It signifies to look earnestly, keenly, or inquiringly in the face of a person, to fix the eye upon him; and, when used of a judge, to take the part of a person, by favouring him unjustly (Deut. i. 17, xvi. 19). But this latter idea, viz. "their acceptance of the person, or partiality" (according to Prov. xxiv. 23, xxviii. 21), is inadmissible here, for the simple reason that the passage refers to the whole nation, and not particularly to the judges. "The look of their faces" (*haccârath p'nêhem*) is to be understood in an objective sense, viz. the appearance (τὸ εἶδος, Luke ix. 29), like the *agnitio* of Jerome, *id quo se agnoscendum dat vultus eorum.* This was probably the expression commonly employed in Hebrew for what we designate by a very inappropriate foreign word, viz. physiognomy, *i.e.* the expression of the face which reveals the state of the mind. This expression of their countenance testified against them (*anah b'*, as in ch. lix. 12), for it was the disturbed and distorted image of their sin, which not only could not be hidden, but did not even wish to be; in a word, of their *azzuth* (Eccles. viii. 1). And it did not even rest with this open though silent display: they spoke openly of their sin (*higgid* in its simplest meaning, *palam facere*, from *nâgad*, *nagáda*, to be open, evident) without making any secret of it, like the Sodomites, who publicly proclaimed their fleshly lusts (Gen. xix.). Jerusalem was spiritually Sodom, as the prophet called it in ch. i. 10. By such barefaced sinning they did themselves harm (*gâmal, lit.* to finish, then to carry out, to show practically[1]).

The prophet's meaning is evident enough. But inasmuch as it is the curse of sin to distort the knowledge of what is most obvious and self-evident, and even to take it entirely away, the prophet dwells still longer upon the fact that all sinning is self-destruction and self-murder, placing this general truth against its opposite in a palillogical Johannic way, and calling out to his contemporaries in vers. 10, 11: "*Say of the righteous, that it is well with him; for they will enjoy the fruit of their doings. Woe to the wicked! it is ill; for what his hands have wrought will be done to him.*" We cannot adopt the rendering "Praise the righteous," proposed by Vitringa and other modern commentators; for although *âmar* is sometimes construed with the accusative of the object (Ps. xl. 11, cxlv. 6, 11), it never means to praise, but to declare (even in Ps. xl. 11). We have here what was noticed from Gen. i. 4 onwards,—namely, the

---

[1] It may now be accepted as an established fact, that the verb *gâmal* is connected with the Arabic *'gamala*, to collect together, *'gamula*, to be perfect, *kamala*, *kamula id.*, and *gâmar*, to finish (see Hupfeld on Ps. vii. 5, and Fürst, *Heb. Lex.*).

obvious antiptôsis or antiphonêsis in the verbs רָאָה (cf. ch. xxii. 9, Ex. ii. 2), יָדַע (1 Kings v. 17), and אָמַר (like λέγειν, John ix. 9) : *dicite justum quod bonum = dicite justum esse bonum* (Ewald, § 336, *b*). The object of sight, knowledge, or speech, is first of all mentioned in the most general manner; then follows the qualification, or more precise definition. טוֹב, and in ver. 11 רָע (רַע without the pause), might both of them be the third pers. pret. of the verbs, employed in a neuter sense: the former signifying, it is well, viz. with him (as in Deut. v. 30, Jer. xxii. 15, 16); the latter, it is bad (as in Ps. cvi. 32). But it is evident from Jer. xliv. 17 that טוֹב הוּא and רַע הוּא may be used in the sense of καλῶς (κακῶς) ἔχει, and that the two expressions are here thought of in this way, so that there is no לוֹ to be supplied in either case. The form of the first favours this; and in the second the accentuation fluctuates between אוֹי *tiphchah* לְרֹשׁע *munach*, and the former with *merka*, the latter *tiphchah*. At the same time, the latter mode of accentuation, which is favourable to the personal rendering of רַע, is supported by editions of some worth, such as Brescia 1494, Pesaro 1516, Venice 1515, 1521, and is justly preferred by Luzzatto and Bär. The summary assertions, The righteous is well, the wicked ill, are both sustained by their eventual fate, in the light of which the previous misfortune of the righteous appears as good fortune, and the previous good fortune of the wicked as misfortune. With an allusion to this great difference in their eventual fate, the word " say," which belongs to both clauses, summons to an acknowledgment of the good fortune of the one and the misfortune of the other. O that Judah and Jerusalem would acknowledge this to their own salvation before it was too late! For the state of the poor nation was already miserable enough, and very near to destruction.

Ver. 12. "*My people, its oppressors are boys, and women rule over it; my people, thy leaders are misleaders, who swallow up the way of thy paths.*" It is not probable that *me'olel* signifies maltreaters or triflers, by the side of the parallel *náshim;* moreover, the idea of despotic treatment is already contained in *nogesaiv*. We expect to find children where there are women. And this is one meaning of *me'olel*. It does not mean a suckling, however, as Ewald supposes (§ 160, *a*), more especially as it occurs in connection with *yonek* (Jer. xliv. 7; Lam. ii. 11), and

therefore cannot have precisely the same meaning; but, like
עוֹלֵל and עוֹלָל (the former of which may be contracted from
meolēl), it refers to the boy as playful and wanton (lascivum,
protervum). Böttcher renders it correctly, pueri, lusores, though
meolēl is not in itself a collective form, as he supposes; but the
singular is used collectively, or perhaps better still, the predicate is intended to apply to every individual included in the
plural notion of the subject (compare ch. xvi. 8, xx. 4, and Ges.
§ 146, 4): the oppressors of the people, every one without
exception, were (even though advanced in years) mere boys or
youths in their mode of thinking and acting, and made all
subject to them the football of their capricious humour. Here
again the person of the king is allowed to fall into the background. But the female rule, referred to afterwards, points
us to the court. And this must really have been the case when
Ahaz, a young rake, came to the throne at the age of twenty
(according to the LXX. twenty-five), possibly towards the close
of the reign of Jotham. With the deepest anguish the prophet
repeats the expression " my people," as he passes in his address
to his people from the rulers to the preachers: for the *meas-
sherim* or leaders are prophets (Mic. iii. 5); but what prophets!
Instead of leading the people in a straight path, they lead them
astray (ch. ix. 15, cf. 2 Kings xxi. 9). This they did, as we
may gather from the history of this crowd of prophets, either
by acting in subservience to the ungodly interests of the court
with dynastic or demagogical servility, or by flattering the
worst desires of the people. Thus the way of the path of the
people, *i.e.* the highway or road by whose ramifying paths the
people were to reach the appointed goal, had been swallowed
up by them, *i.e.* taken away from the sight and feet of the
people, so that they could not find it and walk therein (cf. ch.
xxv. 7, 8, where the verb is used in another connection). What
is swallowed up is invisible, has disappeared, without a trace
being left behind. The same idea is applied in Job xxxix. 27
to a galloping horse, which is said to swallow the road, inasmuch
as it leaves piece after piece behind it in its rapid course. It
is stated here with regard to the prophets, that they swallow up
the road appointed by Jehovah, as the one in which His people
were to walk, just as a criminal swallows a piece of paper which
bears witness against him, and so hides it in his own stomach,

Thus the way of salvation pointed out by the law was no longer to be either heard of or seen. The prophets, who ought to have preached it, said *mum, mum*, and kept it swallowed. It had completely perished, as it were, in the erroneous preaching of the false prophets.

This was how it stood. There was but little to be expected from the exhortations of the prophet; so that he had to come back again and again to the proclamation of judgment. The judgment of the world comes again before his mind.—Ver. 13. "*Jehovah has appeared to plead, and stands up to judge the nations.*" When Jehovah, weary with His long-suffering, rises up from His heavenly throne, this is described as "standing up" (*kum*, ch. ii. 19, 21, xxxiii. 10); and when He assumes the judgment-seat in the sight of all the world, this is called "sitting down" (*yashab*, Ps. ix. 5, Joel iv. 12); when, having come down from heaven (Mic. i. 2 sqq.), He comes forward as accuser, this is called "standing" (*nizzab* or *amad*, Ps. lxxxii. 1 : *amad* is coming forward and standing, as the opposite of sitting; *nizzab*, standing, with the subordinate idea of being firm, resolute, ready). This pleading (*ribh*, Jer. xxv. 31) is also judging (*din*), because His accusation, which is incontrovertible, contains the sentence in itself; and His sentence, which executes itself irresistibly, is of itself the infliction of punishment. Thus does he stand in the midst of the nations at once accuser, judge, and executioner (Ps. vii. 8). But among the nations it is more especially against Israel that He contends; and in Israel it is more especially against the leaders of the poor misguided and neglected people that He sets Himself.

Vers. 14, 15. "*Jehovah will proceed to judgment with the elders of His people, and its princes. And ye, ye have eaten up the vineyard; prey of the suffering is in your houses. What mean ye that ye crush my people, and grind the face of the suffering? Thus saith the Lord Jehovah of hosts.*" The words of God Himself commence with "*and ye*" (*v'attem*). The sentence to which this (*et vos = at vos*) is the antithesis is wanting, just as in Ps. ii. 6, where the words of God commence with "and I" (*va'ani, et ego = ast ego*). The tacit clause may easily be supplied, viz. I have set you over my vineyard, but ye have consumed the vineyard. The only question is, whether the sentence is to be regarded as suppressed by Jehovah Himself, or by the prophet. Most certainly by Jehovah Himself. The majesty with which He appeared before the rulers of His people was, even without words, a practical and undeniable proof that their majesty was only a shadow of His, and their office His trust. But their office consisted in the fact that Jehovah had committed His people to their care. The vineyard of Jehovah was His people—a self-evident figure, which the prophet dresses up in the form of a parable in ch. v. Jehovah had appointed them as gardeners and keepers of this vineyard, but they themselves have become the very beasts that they ought to have warded off. בָּעֵר is applied to the beasts which completely devour the blades of a corn-field or the grapes of a vineyard (Ex. xxii. 4). This change was perfectly obvious. The possessions stolen from their unhappy countrymen, which were still in their houses, were the tangible proof of their plundering of the vineyard. "The suffering:" 'ani (*depressus*, the crushed) is introduced as explanatory of *haccerem*, the prey, because depression and misery were the ordinary fate of the congregation which God called His vineyard. It was *ecclesia pressa*, but woe to the oppressors! In the question "what mean ye?" (*mallâcem*) the madness and wickedness of their deeds are implied. מָה and לָכֶם are fused into one word here, as if it were a prefix (as in Ex. iv. 2, Ezek. viii. 6, Mal. i. 13; *vid.* Ges. § 20, 2). The *keri* helps to make it clear by resolving the *chethibh*. The word *mallâcem* ought, strictly speaking, to be followed by *chi*: "What is there to you *that* ye crush my people?" as in ch. xxii. 1, 16; but the words rush forwards (as in Jonah i. 6), because they are an explosion of wrath. For this reason the expressions relating to the behaviour of the rulers are the strongest that can possibly be employed. דִּכָּא (crush) is also to be met with in Prov. xxii. 22; but "grind the face" (*tâchan p'ne*) is a strong metaphor without a parallel. The former signifies "to pound," the latter "to grind," as the millstone grinds the corn. They grind the faces of those who are already bowed down, thrusting them back with such unmerciful severity, that they stand as it were annihilated, and their faces become as white as flour, or as the Germans would say, cheese-white, chalk-white, as pale as death, from oppression and despair. Thus the language supplied to a certain extent appropriate figures, with which to describe the conduct of the rulers of Israel; but it contained no words that could exhaust the immeasurable wickedness of their conduct: hence the magnitude of their sin is set before them in the form of a question, "What is to you?" *i.e.* What indescribable wickedness is this which you are committing? The prophet hears this said by Jehovah, the majestic Judge, whom he here describes as *Adonai Elohim Zebaoth* (according to the Masoretic pointing). This triplex name of God, which we find in the prophetic books, viz. frequently in Amos and also in Jer. ii. 19, occurs for the first time in the Elohistic Psalm, Ps. lxix. 7. This scene of judgment is indeed depicted throughout in the colours of the Psalms, and more especially recals the (Elohistic) Psalm of Asaph (Ps. lxxxii.).

But notwithstanding the dramatic vividness with which the prophet pictures to himself this scene of judgment, he is obliged to break off at the very beginning of his description, because another word of Jehovah comes upon him. This applies to the women of Jerusalem, whose authority, at the time when Isaiah prophesied, was no less influential than that of their husbands who had forgotten their calling.—Vers. 16, 17. "*Jehovah hath spoken: Because the daughters of Zion are haughty, and walk about with extended throat, and blinking with the eyes, walk about with tripping gait, and tinkle with their foot-ornaments: the Lord of all makes the crown of the daughters of Zion scabbed, and Jehovah will uncover their shame.*" Their inward pride (*gâbah*, as in Ezek. xvi. 50; cf. Zeph. iii. 11) shows itself outwardly. They walk with extended throat, *i.e.* bending the neck back, trying to make themselves taller than they are, because they think themselves so great. The *keri* substitutes the more usual form, נטויות; but Isaiah in all probability intentionally made use of the rarer and ruder form *netuvoth*, since such a form really existed (1 Sam. xxv. 18), as well as the singular *nâtu* for *nâtui* (Job xv. 22, xli. 25: Ges. § 75, Anm. 5). They also went winking the eyes (*mesakkeroth*, for which we frequently find the erratum *meshakkeroth*), *i.e.* casting voluptuous and amatory glances with affected innocence (νεύματα ὀφθαλμῶν, LXX). "*Winking:*" *sâkar* is not used in the sense of *fucare* (Targ. *b. Sabbath* 62*b*, *Joma* 9*b*, Luther),—which is all the more inappropriate, because blackening the eyelids with powder of antimony was regarded in the East of the Old Testament as indispensable to female beauty,—but in the sense of *nictare* (LXX., Vulg., Syr., *syn. remaz*, cf. *sekar*, Syr. to squint; Targ. = *shâzaph*, Job xx. 9). Compare also the talmudic saying: God did not create woman out of Adam's ear, that she might be no eavesdropper (*tsaithânith*), nor out of Adam's eye, that she might be no winker (*sakrânith*).[1] The third was, that they walked *incedendo et trepidando*. The second inf. abs. is in this case, as in most others, the one which gives the distinct tone, whilst the other serves to keep before the eye the occurrence indicated in its finite verb (Ges. § 131, 3). They walk about tripping (*táphoph*, a wide-spread onomato-poetic word), *i.e.* taking short steps, just putting the heel of one foot against the toe of the other (as the Talmud explains it). Luther renders it, "they walk along and waggle" (*schwänzen, i.e. clunibus agitatis*). The rendering is suitable, but incorrect. They could only take short steps, because of the chains by which the costly foot-rings (*achâsim*) worn above their ankles were connected together. These chains, which were probably ornamented with bells, as is sometimes the case now in the East, they used to tinkle as they walked: they made an ankle-tinkling with their feet, setting their feet down in such a manner that these ankle-rings knocked against each other. The writing *beraglēhem* (masc.) for *beraglēhen* (fem.) is probably not an unintentional *synallage gen.*: they were not modest *virgines*, but cold, masculine *viragines*, so that they themselves were a *synallage generis*. Nevertheless they tripped along. Tripping is a child's step. Although well versed in sin and old in years, the women of Jerusalem tried to maintain a youthful, childlike appearance. They therefore tripped along with short, childish steps. The women of the Mohammedan East still take pleasure in such coquettish tinklings, although they are forbidden by the Koran, just as the women of Jerusalem did in the days of Isaiah. The attractive influence of natural charms, especially

---

[1] Also *b. Sota* 47*b*: "Since women have multiplied with extended necks and winking eyes, the number of cases has also multiplied in which it has been necessary to resort to the curse water (Num. v. 18)." In fact, this increased to such an extent, that Johanan ben Zakkai, the pupil of Hillel, abolished the ordeal (divine-verdict) of the Sota (the woman suspected of adultery) altogether. The people of his time were altogether an adulterous generation.

when heightened by luxurious art, is very great; but the prophet is blind to all this splendour, and seeing nothing but the corruption within, foretells to these rich and distinguished women a foul and by no means æsthetic fate. The Sovereign Ruler of all would smite the crown of their head, from which long hair was now flowing, with scab (*v'sippach*, a progressive preterite with *Vav apodosis*, a denom. verb from *sappachath*, the scurf which adheres to the skin: see at Hab. ii. 15); and Jehovah would uncover their nakedness, by giving them up to violation and abuse at the hands of coarse and barbarous foes,—the greatest possible disgrace in the eyes of a woman, who covers herself as carefully as she can in the presence of any stranger (ch. xlvii. 3; Nahum iii. 5; Jer. xiii. 22; Ezek. xvi. 37).

The prophet then proceeds to describe still further how the Lord would take away the whole of their toilet as plunder. Vers. 18–23. "*On that day the Lord will put away the show of the ankle-clasps, and of the head-bands, and of the crescents; the ear-rings, and the arm-chains, and the light veils; the diadems, and the stepping-chains, and the girdles, and the smelling-bottles, and the amulets; the finger-rings, and the nose-rings; the gala-dresses, and the sleeve-frocks, and the wrappers, and the pockets; the hand-mirrors, and the Sindu-cloths, and the turbans, and the gauze mantles.*" The fullest explanation of all these articles of female attire is to be found in N. W. Schröder's work, entitled *Commentarius de vestitu mulierum Hebræarum ad Jes.* iii. 16–24, Lugd. Batav. 1745 (a quarto volume), and in that of Ant. Theod. Hartmann, consisting of three octavo volumes, and entitled *Die Hebräerin am Putztische und als Braut* (The Jewess at the Toilet-table, and as Bride, 1809–10); to which we may also add, Saalschütz, *Archæologie*, ch. iii., where he treats of the dresses of men and women. It was not usually Isaiah's custom to enter into such minute particulars. Of all the prophets, Ezekiel was the one most addicted to this, as we may see, for example, from Ezek. xvi. And even in other prophecies against the women we find nothing of the kind again (ch. xxxii. 9 sqq.; Amos iv. 1 sqq.). But in this instance, the enumeration of the female ornaments is connected with that of the state props in ch. iii. 1–3, and that of the lofty and exalted in ch. ii. 13–16, so as to form a trilogy, and has its own special explanation in that boundless love of ornament which had become prevalent in the time of Uzziah-Jotham. It was the prophet's intention to produce a ludicrous, but yet serious impression, as to the immeasurable luxury which really existed; and in the prophetic address, his design throughout is to bring out the glaring contrast between the titanic, massive, worldly glory, in all its varied forms, and that true, spiritual, and majestically simple glory, whose reality is manifested from within outwards. In fact, the theme of the whole address is the way of universal judgment leading on from the false glory to the true. The general idea of *tiphereth* (show: rendered "bravery" in Eng. ver.) which stands at the head and includes the whole, points to the contrast presented by a totally different *tiphereth* which follows in ch. iv. 2. In explaining each particular word, we must be content with what is most necessary, and comparatively the most certain. "*Ankle-clasps*" (*acâsim*): these were rings of gold, silver, or ivory, worn round the ankles; hence the denom. verb (*icces*) in ver. 16, to make a tinkling sound with these rings. "*Head-bands*," or "*frontlets*" (*shebisim*, from *shâbas* = *shâbatz*: *plectere*), were plaited bands of gold or silver thread worn below the hair-net, and reaching from one ear to the other. There is some force, however, in the explanation which has been very commonly adopted since the time of Schröder, namely, that they were sun-like balls (= *shemisim*), which were worn as ornaments round the neck, from the Arabic *'sumeisa* (*'subeisa*), a little sun. The "*crescents*" (*saharonim*) were little pendants of this kind, fastened round the neck and hanging down upon the breast (in Judg. viii. 21 we meet with them as ornaments hung round the camels' necks). Such ornaments are still worn by Arabian girls, who generally have several different kinds of them; the *hilâl*, or new moon, being a symbol of increasing good fortune, and as such the most approved charm against the evil eye. "*Ear-rings*" (*netiphoth*, ear-drops): we meet with these in Judg. viii. 26, as an ornament worn by Midianitish kings. Hence the Arabic *munattafe*, a woman adorned with ear-rings. "*Arm-chains:*" *sheroth*, from *shârar*, to twist. According to the Targum, these were chains worn upon the arm, or spangles upon the wrist, answering to the spangles upon the ankles. "*Fluttering veils*" (*re'âloth*, from *râ'al*, to hang loose): these were more expensive than the ordinary veils worn by girls, which were called *tza'iph*. "*Diadems*" (*pe'erim*) are only mentioned in other parts of the Scriptures as being worn by men (*e.g.* by priests, bridegrooms, or persons of high rank). "*Stepping-chains:*" *tze'ádoth*, from *tze'ádah*, a step; hence the chain worn to shorten and give elegance to the step. "*Girdles:*" *kisshurim*, from *káshar* (*cingere*), dress girdles, such as were worn by brides upon their wedding-day (compare Jer. ii. 32 with Isa. xlix. 18); the word is erroneously rendered hair-pins (*kalmasmezayyah*) in the Targum. "*Smelling-bottles:*" *botte hannephesh*, holders of scent (*nephesh*, the breath of an aroma). "*Amulets:*" *lechashim* (from *láchash*, to work by incantations), gems or metal plates with an inscription upon them, which were worn as a protection as well as an ornament. "*Finger-rings:*" *tabbá'oth*, from *tába*, to impress or seal, signet-rings worn upon the finger, corresponding to the *chothâm* worn by men upon the breast suspended by a cord. "*Nose-rings*" (*nizmē hâaph*) were fastened in the central division of the nose, and hung down over the mouth: they have been ornaments in common use in the East from the time of the patriarchs (Gen. xxiv. 22) down to the present day. "*Gala-dresses*" (*machalá-tsoth*) are dresses not usually worn, but taken off when at home. "*Sleeve-frocks*" (*ma'atâphâh*): the second tunic, worn above the ordinary one, the Roman *stola*. "*Wrappers*" (*mitpâchoth*, from *táphach*, *expandere*), broad cloths wrapped round the body, such as Ruth wore when she crept in to Boaz in her best attire (Ruth iii. 15). "*Pockets*" (*charitim*) were for holding money (2 Kings v. 23), which was generally carried by men in the girdle, or in a purse (*cis*). "*Hand-mirrors*" (*gilyonim*): the Septuagint renders this διαφανῆ Λακωνικὰ, *sc.* ἱμάτια, Lacedæmonian gauze or transparent dresses, which showed the nakedness rather than concealed it (from *gâlâh*, *retegere*); but the better rendering is mirrors with handles, polished metal plates (from *gâlâh*, *polire*), as *gillâyon* is used elsewhere to signify a smooth table. "*Sindu-cloths*" (*sedinim*), veils or coverings of the finest linen, viz. of Sindu or Hindu cloth (σινδύνες),—*Sindu*, the land of Indus, being the earlier name of India.[1] "*Turbans*" (*tseniphoth*, from *tsânaph*, *convolvere*), the head-dress composed

---

[1] The Mishna (*Kelim* xxiv. 13) mentions three different *sedinin*: night dresses, curtains, and embroidery. The *sindon* is frequently referred to as a covering wrapped round the person; and in *b. Menachoth* 41a, it is stated that the *sindon* is the summer dress, the *sarbal* (cloak) the winter dress, which may help to explain Mark xiv. 51, 52.

of twisted cloths of different colours. "*Gauze mantles*" (*redidim*, from *râdad, extendere, tenuem facere*), delicate veil-like mantles thrown over the rest of the clothes. Stockings and handkerchiefs are not mentioned: the former were first introduced into Hither Asia from Media long after Isaiah's time, and a Jerusalem lady no more thought of using the latter than a Grecian or Roman lady did. Even the veil (*burko*) now commonly worn, which conceals the whole of the face with the exception of the eyes, did not form part of the attire of an Israelitish woman in the olden time.[1] The prophet enumerates twenty-one different ornaments: three sevens of a very bad kind, especially for the husbands of these state-dolls. There is no particular order observed in the enumeration, either from head to foot, or from the inner to the outer clothing; but they are arranged as much *ad libitum* as the dress itself.

When Jehovah took away all this glory, with which the women of Jerusalem were adorned, they would be turned into wretched-looking prisoners, disfigured by ill-treatment and dirt.—Ver. 24. "*And instead of balmy scent there will be mouldiness, and instead of the sash a rope, and instead of artistic ringlets a baldness, and instead of the dress-cloak a frock of sackcloth, branding instead of beauty.*" *Mouldiness*, or *mother* (*mak*, as in ch. v. 24, the dust of things that have moulded away), with which they would be covered, and which they would be obliged to breathe, would take the place of the *bosem, i.e.* the scent of the balsam shrub (*bâsâm*), and of sweet-scented pomade in general; and *nikpâh* that of the beautifully embroidered girdle (Prov. xxxi. 24). The meaning of this word is neither "a wound," as the Targums and Talmud render it, nor "rags," as given by Knobel, ed. 1 (from *nâkaph, percutere, perforare*), but the *rope* thrown over them as prisoners (from *kâphâh*=*kâvâh, contorquere:* LXX., Vulg., Syr.).[2] *Baldness* takes the place of

[1] Rashi, however, makes a different statement (*Sabbath* 65a), viz. that "Israelitish women in Arabia go out with veils which conceal the face, and those in Media with their mantles fastened about the mouth."

[2] Credner (*Joel*, p. 147) renders the word "tatters," from *nâkaph*, to rub in pieces; but the word has no such meaning, whereas the meaning *vulnus*, lit. *percussio*, is admissible (see at Job xix. 26), but does not suit the antithesis. Luzzatto connects it with *n'kaph*, to bind (from which the *makkeph* derives its name), and understands it as referring to the dressing applied to wounds, to lint into which the girdle was torn. The

artistic ringlets (מַעֲשֵׂה מִקְשֶׁה, not מַעֲשֶׂה, so that it is in apposition: cf. ch. xxx. 20; Ges. § 113; Ewald, § 287, *b*). The reference is not to golden ornaments for the head, as the Sept. rendering gives it, although *miksheh* is used elsewhere to signify embossed or carved work in metal or wood; but here we are evidently to understand by the "artificial twists" either curls made with the curling-tongs, or the hair plaited and twisted up in knots, which they would be obliged to cut off in accordance with the mourning customs (ch. xv. 2, xxii. 12), or which would fall off in consequence of grief. *A frock of sackcloth* (*machagoreth sak*), *i.e.* a smock of coarse haircloth worn next to the skin, such as Layard found depicted upon a bas-relief at Kouyunjik, would take the place of the *pethigil*, *i.e.* the *dress-cloak* (either from *páthag*, to be wide or full, with the substantive termination *îl*, or else composed of *pethi*, breadth, and *gil*, festive rejoicing); and *branding* the place of *beauty*. Branding ($ci = cevi$, from *cávâh*, καίειν), the mark burnt upon the forehead by their conquerors: *ci* is a substantive,[1] not a particle, as the Targum and others render it, and as the *makkeph* might make it appear. There is something very effective in the inverted order of the words in the last clause of the five. In this five-fold reverse would shame and mourning take the place of proud, voluptuous rejoicing.

The prophet now passes over to a direct address to Jerusalem itself, since the "daughters of Zion" are the daughter of Zion in her present degenerate condition. The daughter of Zion

most plausible derivation is from *káphâh*, which is really employed in post-biblical usage to signify not only to congeal and wrinkle, but also to thicken (*Sabbath* 21*a*, *l'hakpoth:* "Make the wick thicker, that it may burn the brighter"). It is probably radically akin to the Arabic *nukbe* (explained in Lamachzari as equivalent to the Persian *miján-bend*, a girdle), which is apparently used to denote the coarse girdle worn by peasants or by Arab women of the wandering tribes, resembling a rope of goat's hair, as distinguished from the artistic and costly girdle worn by women of the upper classes in the towns.

[1] It is so understood in *b. Sabbath* 62*b*, with an allusion to the proverb, "The end of beauty is burning" (viz. inflammation). In Arabia, the application of the *cey* with a red-hot iron (*mikwâh*) plays a very important part in the medical treatment of both man and beast. You meet with many men who have been burned not only on their legs and arms, but in their faces as well, and, as a rule, the finest horses are disfigured by the *cey*.—WETZSTEIN.

loses her sons, and consequently the daughters of Zion their husbands.—Ver. 25. "*Thy men will fall by the sword, and thy might in war.*" The plural *methim* (the singular of which only occurs in the form *methu*, with the connecting vowel *û* as a component part of the proper names) is used as a prose word in the Pentateuch; but in the later literature it is a poetic archaism. "*Thy might*" is used interchangeably with "thy men," the possessors of the might being really intended, like *robur* and *robora* in Latin (compare Jer. xlix. 35).

What the prophet here foretells to the daughter of Zion he sees in ver. 26 fulfilled upon her: "*Then will her gates lament and mourn, and desolate is she, sits down upon the ground.*" The gates, where the husbands of the daughters of Zion, who have now fallen in war, used at one time to gather together in such numbers, are turned into a state of desolation, in which they may, as it were, be heard complaining, and seen to mourn (ch. xiv. 31; Jer. xiv. 2; Lam. i. 4); and the daughter of Zion herself is utterly vacated, thoroughly emptied, completely deprived of all her former population; and in this state of the most mournful widowhood or orphanage, brought down from her lofty seat (ch. xlvii. 1) and princely glory (Jer. xiii. 18), she sits down upon the ground, just as Judæa is represented as doing upon Roman medals that were struck after the destruction of Jerusalem, where she is introduced as a woman thoroughly broken down, and sitting under a palm-tree in an attitude of despair, with a warrior standing in front of her, the inscription upon the medal being *Judæa capta*, or *devicta*. The Septuagint rendering is quite in accordance with the sense, viz. καὶ καταλειφθήσῃ μόνη καὶ εἰς τὴν γῆν ἐδαφισθήσῃ (cf. Luke xix. 44), except that וְשֵׁבָה is not the second person, but the third, and נִקָּתָה the third pers. pret. *niph.* for נִקְּתָה,—a pausal form which is frequently met with in connection with the smaller distinctive accents, such as *silluk* and *athnach* (here it occurs with *tiphchah*, as, for example, in Amos iii. 8). The clause "sits down upon the ground" is appended ἀσυνδέτως;—a frequent construction in cases where one of two verbs defines the other in a manner which is generally expressed adverbially (*vid.* 1 Chron. xiii. 2, and the inverted order of the words in Jer. iv. 5; cf. xii. 6): Zion sits upon the earth in a state of utter depopulation.

When war shall thus unsparingly have swept away the men of Zion, a most unnatural effect will ensue, namely, that women will go in search of husbands, and not men in search of wives.—Ch. iv. 1. "*And seven women lay hold of one man in that day, saying, We will eat our own bread, and wear our own clothes; only let thy name be named upon us, take away our reproach.*" The division of the chapters is a wrong one here, as this verse is the closing verse of the prophecy against the women, and the closing portion of the whole address does not begin till ch. iv. 2. The present pride of the daughters of Zion, every one of whom now thought herself the greatest as the wife of such and such a man, and for whom many men were now the suitors, would end in this unnatural self-humiliation, that seven of them would offer themselves to the same man, the first man who presented himself, and even renounce the ordinary legal claim upon their husband for clothing and food (Ex. xxi. 10). It would be quite sufficient for them to be allowed to bear his name ("let thy name be named *upon* us:" the name is put upon the thing named, as giving it its distinctness and character), if he would only take away their reproach (namely, the reproach of being unmarried, ch. liv. 4, as in Gen. xxx. 23, of being childless) by letting them be called his wives. The number *seven* (seven women to one man) may be explained on the ground that there is a bad seven as well as a holy one (*e.g.* Matt. xii. 45).

In ch. iv. 1 the threat denounced against the women of Jerusalem is brought to a close. It is the side-piece to the threat denounced against the national rulers. And these two scenes of judgment were only parts of the general judgment about to fall upon Jerusalem and Judah, as a state or national community. And this again was merely a portion, viz. the central group of the picture of a far more comprehensive judgment, which was about to fall upon everything lofty and exalted on the earth. Jerusalem, therefore, stands here as the centre and focus of the great judgment-day. It was in Jerusalem that the ungodly glory which was ripe for judgment was concentrated; and it was in Jerusalem also that the light of the true and final glory would concentrate itself. To this promise, with which the address returns to its starting-point, the prophet now passes on without any further introduction.

In fact it needed no introduction, for the judgment in itself was the medium of salvation. When Jerusalem was judged, it would be sifted; and by being sifted, it would be rescued, pardoned, glorified. The prophet proceeds in this sense to speak of what would happen in that day, and describes the one great day of God at the end of time (not a day of four-and-twenty hours any more than the seven days of creation were), according to its general character, as opening with judgment, but issuing in salvation.—Ver. 2. "*In that day will the sprout of Jehovah become an ornament and glory, and the fruit of the land pride and splendour for the redeemed of Israel.*" The four epithets of glory, which are here grouped in pairs, strengthen our expectation, that now that the mass of Israel has been swept away, together with the objects of its worthless pride, we shall find a description of what will become an object of well-grounded pride to the "escaped of Israel," *i.e.* to the remnant that has survived the judgment, and been saved from destruction. But with this interpretation of the promise it is impossible that it can be the church of the future itself, which is here called the "*sprout of Jehovah*" and "*fruit of the land,*" as Luzzatto and Malbim suppose; and equally impossible, with such an antithesis between what is promised and what is abolished, that the "sprout of Jehovah" and "fruit of the earth" should signify the harvest blessings bestowed by Jehovah, or the rich produce of the land. For although the expression *zemach Jehovah* (sprout of Jehovah) may unquestionably be used to signify this, as in Gen. ii. 9 and Ps. civ. 14 (cf. Isa. lxi. 11), and fruitfulness of the land is a standing accompaniment of the eschatological promises (*e.g.* ch. xxx. 23 sqq., compare the conclusion of Joel and Amos), and it was also foretold that the fruitful fields of Israel would become a glory in the sight of the nations (Ezek. xxxiv. 29; Mal. iii. 12; cf. Joel ii. 17); yet this earthly, material good, of which, moreover, there was no lack in the time of Uzziah and Jotham, was altogether unsuitable to set forth such a contrast as would surpass and outshine the worldly glory existing before. But even granting what Hofmann adduces in support of this view,—namely, that the natural God-given blessings of the field do form a fitting antithesis to the studied works of art of which men had hitherto been proud,—there is still truth in the remark of Rosenmüller, that "the magnificence of the whole passage is at variance with such an interpretation." Only compare ch. xxviii. 5, where Jehovah Himself is described in the same manner, as the glory and ornament of the remnant of Israel. But if the "sprout of Jehovah" is neither the redeemed remnant itself, nor the fruit of the field, it must be the name of the Messiah. And it is in this sense that it has been understood by the Targum, and by such modern commentators as Rosenmüller, Hengstenberg, Steudel, Umbreit, Caspari, Drechsler, and others. The great King of the future is called *zemach*, ἀνατολή in the sense of Heb. vii. 14, viz. as a shoot springing out of the human, Davidic, earthly soil,—a shoot which Jehovah had planted in the earth, and would cause to break through and spring forth as the pride of His congregation, which was waiting for this heavenly child. It is He again who is designated in the parallel clause as the "*fruit of the land*" (or lit. fruit of the earth), as being the fruit which the land of Israel, and consequently the earth itself, would produce, just as in Ezek. xvii. 5 Zedekiah is called a "seed of the earth." The reasons already adduced to show that "the sprout of Jehovah" cannot refer to the blessings of the field, apply with equal force to "the fruit of the earth." This also relates to the Messiah Himself, regarded as the fruit in which all the growth and bloom of this earthly history would eventually reach its promised and divinely appointed conclusion. The use of this double epithet to denote "the coming One" can only be accounted for, without anticipating the New Testament standpoint,[1] from the desire to depict His double-sided origin. He would come, on the one hand, from *Jehovah;* but, on the other hand, from *the earth*, inasmuch as He would spring from Israel. We have here the passage, on the basis of which *zemach* (the sprout or "Branch")

---

[1] From a New Testament point of view we might say that the "sprout of Jehovah" or "fruit of the earth" was the grain of wheat which redeeming love sowed in the earth on Good Friday; the grain of wheat which began to break through the ground and grow towards heaven on Easter Sunday; the grain of wheat whose golden blade ascended heavenwards on Ascension Day; the grain of wheat whose myriad-fold ear bent down to the earth on the day of Pentecost, and poured out the grains, from which the holy church not only was born, but still continues to be born. But such thoughts as these lie outside the historico-grammatical meaning.

was adopted by Jeremiah (ch. xxiii. 5 and xxxiii. 15) and Zechariah (ch. iii. 8, vi. 12) as a proper name for the Messiah, and upon which Matthew, by combining this proper name *zemach* (sprout) with *nezer* (ch. xi. 1, cf. liii. 2), rests his affirmation, that according to the Old Testament prophecies the future Messiah was to be called a Nazarene. It is undoubtedly strange that this epithet should be introduced so entirely without preparation even by Isaiah, who coined it first. In fact, the whole passage relating to the Messiah stands quite alone in this cycle of prophecies in ch. i.–vi. But the book of Isaiah is a complete and connected work. What the prophet indicates merely in outline here, he carries out more fully in the cycle of prophecies which follows in ch. vii.–xii.; and there the enigma, which he leaves as an enigma in the passage before us, receives the fullest solution. Without dwelling any further upon the *man* of the future, described in this enigmatically symbolical way, the prophet hurries on to a more precise description of the *church* of the future.—Ver. 3. "*And it will come to pass, whoever is left in Zion and remains in Jerusalem, holy will he be called, all who are written down for life in Jerusalem.*" The leading emphasis of the whole verse rests upon *kadosh* (holy). Whereas formerly in Jerusalem persons had been distinguished according to their rank and condition, without any regard to their moral worth (ch. iii. 1–3, 10, 11; cf. ch. xxxii. 5); so the name *kadosh* (holy) would now be the one chief name of honour, and would be given to every individual, inasmuch as the national calling of Israel would now be realized in the persons of all (Ex. xix. 6, etc.). Consequently the expression "*he shall be called*" is not exactly equivalent to "he shall be," but rather presupposes the latter, as in ch. i. 26, lxi. 6, lxii. 4. The term *kadosh* denotes that which is withdrawn from the world, or separated from it. The church of the saints or holy ones, which now inhabits Jerusalem, is what has been left from the smelting: and their holiness is the result of washing. הַנּוֹתָר is interchanged with הַנִּשְׁאָר. The latter, as Papenheim has shown in his Hebrew synonyms, involves the idea of intention, viz. "that which has been left behind;" the former merely expresses the fact, viz. that which remains. The character of this "remnant of grace," and the number of members of which it would consist, are shown in the apposition contained in ver. 3*b*. This apposition means something more than those who are entered as living in Jerusalem, *i.e.* the population of Jerusalem as entered in the city register (Hofmann); for the verb with *Lamed* does not mean merely to enter as a certain thing, but (like the same verb with the accusative in Jer. xxii. 30) to enter as intended for a certain purpose. The expression לַחַיִּים may either be taken as a noun, viz. " to life" (Dan. xii. 2), or as an adjective, " to the living" (a meaning which is quite as tenable; cf. Ps. lxix. 29, 1 Sam. xxv. 29). In either case the notion of predestination is implied, and the assumption of the existence of a divine " book of life" (Ex. xxxii. 32, 33; Dan. xii. 1; cf. Ps. cxxxix. 16); so that the idea is the same as that of Acts xiii. 48: " As many as were ordained to eternal life." The reference here is to persons who were entered in the book of God, on account of the good kernel of faith within them, as those who should become partakers of the life in the new Jerusalem, and should therefore be spared in the midst of the judgment of sifting in accordance with this divine purpose of grace. For it was only through the judgment setting this kernel of faith at liberty, that such a holy community as is described in the protasis which comes afterwards, as in Ps. lxiii. 6, 7, could possibly arise.

Ver. 4. " *When the Lord shall have washed away the filth of the daughters of Zion, and shall have purged away the bloodguiltinesses of Jerusalem from the midst thereof, by the spirit of judgment and by the spirit of sifting.*" " *When,*" followed by a preterite (equivalent to a *fut. exact.* as in ch. xxiv. 13; Ges. § 126, 5), introduces the circumstance, whose previous occurrence would be the condition of all the rest. The force of the future *yádiach* (" shall have purged") is regulated by that of the preterite *ráchatz*, as in ch. vi. 11; for although, when regarded simply by itself, as in ch. x. 12, the future tense may suggest the idea of a future perfect, it cannot have the force of such a future. The double purification answers to the two scenes of judgment described in ch. iii. The filth of the daughters of Zion is the moral pollution hidden under their vain and coquettish finery; and the murderous deeds of Jerusalem are the acts of judicial murder committed by its rulers upon the poor and innocent. This filth and these spots of blood the Sovereign Ruler washes and purges away (see 2 Chron. iv. 6), by causing His spirit or His breath to burst in upon all the inhabitants of Jerusalem, both male and female. This breath is called " the spirit of judgment," because it punishes evil; and " the spirit of sifting," inasmuch as it sweeps or cleans it away. בָּעֵר is to be explained, as in ch. vi. 13, in accordance with Deut. xiii. 6 (5, Eng. Ver.; " put the evil away") and other passages, such especially as ch. xix. 13, xxi. 9. The rendering given in the Septuagint and Vulgate, viz. " in the spirit of burning," is founded upon the radical meaning of the verb, which signifies literally to burn up, and hence to clear away or destroy (see *Job*, vol. ii. p. 180, Eng. Tr.). Nevertheless, " burning" in connection with judgment is not definite enough, since every manifestation of divine judgment is a manifestation of fire; but it is not every judgment that has connected with it what is here implied,—namely, the salutary object of burning away, or, in other words, of winnowing. The " spirit" is in both instances the Spirit of God which pervades the world, not only generating and sustaining life, but also at times destroying and sifting (ch. xxx. 27, 28), as it does in the case before us, in which the imperishable glory described in ver. 5 is so prepared.

Ver. 5. "*And Jehovah creates over every spot of Mount Zion, and over its festal assemblies, a cloud by day, and smoke, and the shining of flaming fire by night: for over all the glory comes a canopy.*" Just as Jehovah guided and shielded Israel in the days of the redemption from Egypt in a smoke-cloud by day and a fire-cloud by night, which either moved in front like a pillar, or floated above them as a roof (Num. xiv. 14, etc.), the perpetuation of His presence at Sinai (Ex. xix. 9, 16 sqq.); so would Jehovah in like manner shield the Israel of the final redemption, which would no longer need the pillar of cloud since its wanderings would be over, but only the cloudy covering; and such a covering Jehovah would create, as the *præt. consec.* וּבָרָא (" and He creates") distinctly affirms. The verb *bârâh* always denotes a divine and miraculous production, having its commencement in time; for even the natural is also supernatural in its first institution by God. In the case before us, however, the reference is to a fresh manifestation of His gracious presence, exalted above the present course of nature. This manifestation would consist by day in "a cloud," and as the *hendiadys* "cloud and smoke" (*i.e.* cloud in form and smoke in substance) distinctly affirms, a smoke-cloud, not a watery cloud, like those which ordinarily cover the sky; and by night in a fiery splendour, not merely a lingering fiery splendour like that of the evening sky, but, as the words clearly indicate, a flaming brightness (*lehâbâh*), and therefore real and living fire. The purpose of the cloud would not only be to overshadow, but also to serve as a wall of defence against opposing influences;[1] and the fire would not only give light, but by flaming and flashing would ward off hostile powers. But, above all, the cloud and fire were intended as signs of the nearness of God, and His satisfaction. In the most glorious times of the temple a smoke-cloud of this kind filled the Holy of holies; and there was only one occasion— namely, at the dedication of Solomon's temple—on which it filled the whole building (1 Kings viii. 10); but now the cloud, the smoke of which, moreover, would be turned at night into flaming fire, would extend over every spot (*mâcōn*, a more poetical word for *mâkōm*) of Mount Zion, and over the festal assemblies thereon. The whole mountain would thus become a Holy of holies. It would be holy not only as being the dwelling-place of Jehovah, but as the gathering-place of a community of saints. "*Her assemblies*" (*mikrâehâ*) points back to Zion, and is a plural written defectively (at least in our editions[2]),—as, for example, in Jer. xix. 8. There is no necessity to take this noun in the sense of "meeting halls" (a meaning which it never has anywhere else), as Gesenius, Ewald, Hitzig, and others have done, since it may also signify "the meetings," though not in an abstract, but in a concrete sense (*ecclesiæ*).[3] The explanatory clause, "*for over all the*

---

[1] The cloud derived its name, *'ânân*, not from the idea of covering, but from that of coming to meet one. The clouds come towards the man who gazes at them, inserting themselves between him and the sky, and thus forcing themselves upon his notice instead of the sky; hence the visible outer side of the vault of heaven is also called *'anan* (plur. *a'nân*), just as the same word is used to denote the outermost portion of the branches or foliage of a tree which is the first to strike the eye (in contradistinction to the inner portions, which are not so easily seen, even if visible at all).

[2] Such codices and ancient editions as Soncino (1488), Brescia (1494), and many others, have the word with the *yod* of the plural.

[3] It is doubtful whether the form מִפְעָל (מִפְעָל) is ever strictly a *nomen*

glory (comes) *a canopy*," admits of several interpretations. Dr Schegg and others take it in the general sense: "for defence and covering are coming for all that is glorious." Now, even if this thought were not so jejune as it is, the word *chuppáh* would not be the word used to denote covering for the sake of protection; it signifies rather covering for the sake of beautifying and honouring that which is covered. *Chuppáh* is the name still given by the Jews to the wedding canopy, *i.e.* a canopy supported on four poles and carried by four boys, under which the bride and bridegroom receive the nuptial blessing,— a meaning which is apparently more appropriate, even in Ps. xix. 6 and Joel ii. 16, than the ordinary explanation *thalamus* or *torus*. Such a canopy would float above Mount Zion in the form of a cloud of smoke and blaze of fire. (There is no necessity to take *chuppáh* as a third pers. *pual*, since תִּהְיֶה, which follows immediately afterwards in ver. 6, may easily be supplied in thought.) The only question is whether *col-cábod* signifies "every kind of glory," or according to Ps. xxxix. 6, xlv. 14, "pure glory" (Hofmann, *Stud. u. Krit.* 1847, pp. 936-38). The thought that Jerusalem would now be "all glory," as its inhabitants were all holiness, and therefore that this shield would be spread out over pure glory, is one that thoroughly commends itself. But we nevertheless prefer the former, as more in accordance with the substantive clause. The glory which Zion would now possess would be exposed to no further injury: Jehovah would acknowledge it by signs of His gracious presence; for henceforth there would be nothing glorious in Zion, over which there would not be a canopy spread in the manner described, shading and yet enlightening, hiding, defending, and adorning it.

Thus would Zion be a secure retreat from all adversities and disasters. Ver. 6. "*And it will be a booth for shade by day from the heat of the sun, and for a refuge and covert from storm and from rain.*" The subject to "*will be*" is not the miraculous roofing; for *ánán* (cloud) is masculine, and the verb feminine, and there would be no sense in saying that a *chuppáh* or canopy would be a *succáh* or booth. Either, therefore, the

actionis kal (Ges. § 84, 14). Its meaning seems rather to be always concrete, even in Arabic, where *menám* signifies a sleeping-place, sleeping-time, or a dream, but never sleep, or sleeping (like *sine*, Heb. *shenáh*, or *naum*, Heb. *núm*).

verb contains the subject in itself, and the meaning is, "There will be a booth" (the verb *hâyâh* being used in a pregnant sense, as in ch. xv. 6, xxiii. 13); or else Zion (ver. 5) is the subject. We prefer the latter. Zion or Jerusalem would be a booth, that is to say, as the parallel clause affirms, a place of security and concealment (*mistor*, which only occurs here, is used on account of the alliteration with *machseh* in the place of *sether*, which the prophet more usually employs, viz. in ch. xxviii. 17, xxxii. 2). "*By day*" (*yōmâm*, which is construed with לְצֵל in the construct state, cf. Ezek. xxx. 16) is left intentionally without any "*by night*" to answer to it in the parallel clause, because reference is made to a place of safety and concealment for all times, whether by day or night. Heat, storm, and rain are mentioned as examples to denote the most manifold dangers; but it is a singular fact that rain, which is a blessing so earnestly desired in the time of *chōreb*, i.e. of drought and burning heat, should also be included. At the present day, when rain falls in Jerusalem, the whole city dances with delight. Nevertheless rain, i.e. the rain which falls from the clouds, is not paradisaical; and its effects are by no means unfrequently destructive. According to the archives of Genesis, rain from the clouds took the place of dew for the first time at the flood, when it fell in a continuous and destructive form. The Jerusalem of the last time will be paradise restored; and there men will be no longer exposed to destructive changes of weather. In this prediction the close of the prophetic discourse is linked on to the commencement. This mountain of Zion, roofed over with a cloud of smoke by day and the shining of a flaming fire by night, is no other than the mountain of the house of Jehovah, which was to be exalted above all the mountains, and to which the nations would make their pilgrimage; and this Jerusalem, so holy within, and all glorious without, is no other than the place from which the word of Jehovah was one day to go forth into all the world. But what Jerusalem is this? Is it the Jerusalem of the time of final glory awaiting the people of God in this life, as described in Rev. xi. (for, notwithstanding all that a spiritualistic and rationalistic anti-chiliasm may say, the prophetic words of both Old and New Testament warrant us in expecting such a time of glory in this life); or is it the Jerusalem of the new heaven and new earth described in Rev.

xx. 21? The true answer is, "Both in one." The prophet's real intention was to depict the holy city in its final and imperishable state after the last judgment. But to his view, the state beyond and the closing state here were blended together, so that the glorified Jerusalem of earth and the glorified Jerusalem of heaven appeared as if fused into one. It was a distinguishing characteristic of the Old Testament, to represent the closing scene on this side the grave, and the eternal state beyond, as a continuous line, having its commencement here. The New Testament first drew the cross line which divides time from eternity. It is true, indeed, as the closing chapters of the Apocalypse show, that even the New Testament prophecies continue to some extent to depict the state beyond in figures drawn from the present world; with this difference, however, that when the line had once been drawn, the demand was made, of which there was no consciousness in the Old Testament, that the figures taken from this life should be understood as relating to the life beyond, and that eternal realities should be separated from their temporal forms.

JUDGMENT OF DEVASTATION UPON THE VINEYARD OF JEHOVAH.—CHAP. V.

Closing Words of the First Cycle of Prophecies.

The foregoing prophecy has run through all the different phases of prophetic exhortation by the time that we reach the close of ch. iv.; and its leading thought, viz. the overthrow of the false glory of Israel, and the perfect establishment of true glory through the medium of judgment, has been so fully worked out, that ch. v. cannot possibly be regarded either as a continuation or as an appendix to that address. Unquestionably there are many points in which ch. v. refers back to ch. ii.-iv. The parable of the vineyard in ch. v. 1-7 grows, as it were, out of ch. iii. 14; and in ch. v. 15 we have a repetition of the *refrain* in ch. ii. 9, varied in a similar manner to ch. ii. 17. But these and other points of contact with ch. ii.-iv., whilst they indicate a tolerable similarity in date, by no means prove the absence of independence in ch. v. The historical circumstances of the two addresses are the same; and the range of thought is therefore closely related. But the leading idea which is carried out in ch. v. is a totally different one. The basis of the address is a parable representing Israel as the vineyard of Jehovah, which, contrary to all expectation, had produced bad fruit, and therefore was given up to devastation. What kind of bad fruit it produced is described in a six-fold "woe;" and what kind of devastation was to follow is indicated in the dark nocturnal conclusion to the whole address, which is entirely without a promise.

The prophet commenced his first address in ch. i. like another Moses; the second, which covered no less ground, he opened with the text of an earlier prophecy; and now he commences the third like a musician, addressing both himself and his hearers with enticing words. Ver. 1a. "*Arise, I will sing of my beloved, a song of my dearest touching his vineyard.*" The fugitive rhythm, the musical euphony, the charming assonances in this appeal, it is impossible to reproduce. They are perfectly inimitable. The *Lamed* in *līdīdī* is the *Lamed objecti*. The person to whom the song referred, to whom it applied, of whom it treated, was the singer's own beloved. It was a song of his dearest one (not his cousin, *patruelis*, as Luther renders it in imitation of the Vulgate, for the meaning of *dōd* is determined by *yādid*, beloved) touching his vineyard. The *Lamed* in *l'carmo* is also *Lamed objecti*. The song of the beloved is really a song concerning the vineyard of the beloved; and this song is a song of the beloved himself, not a song written about him, or attributed to him, but such a song as he himself had sung, and still had to sing. The prophet, by beginning in this manner, was surrounded (either in spirit or in outward reality) by a crowd of people from Jerusalem and Judah. The song is a short one, and runs thus in vers. 1b, 2: "*My beloved had a vineyard on a fatly nourished mountain-horn, and dug it up and cleared it of stones, and planted it with noble vines, and built a tower in it, and also hewed out a wine-press therein; and hoped that it would bring forth grapes, and it brought forth wild grapes.*" The vineyard was situated upon a *keren, i.e.* upon a prominent mountain peak projecting like a horn, and therefore open to the sun on all sides; for, as Virgil says in the *Georgics*, "*apertos Bacchus amat colles.*" This mountain horn was *ben-shemen*, a child of fatness: the fatness was innate, it belonged to it by nature (*shemen* is used, as in ch. xxviii. 1, to denote the fertility of a nutritive loamy soil). And the owner of the vineyard spared no attention or trouble. The plough could not be used, from the steepness of the mountain slope: he therefore dug it up, that is to say, he turned up the soil which was to be made into a vineyard with a hoe (*izzēk*, to hoe; Arab. *mi'zak, mi'zaka*); and as he found it choked up with stones and boulders, he got rid of this rubbish by throwing it out (*sikkēl*, a privative *piel, lapidibus purgare*, then *operam consumere in lapides, sc. ejiciendos*, to stone, or clear of stones: Ges. § 52, 2). After the soil had been prepared he planted it with *sorek, i.e.* the finest kind of eastern vine, bearing small grapes of a bluish-red, with pips hardly perceptible to the tongue. The name is derived from its colour (compare the Arabic *zerka*, red wine). To protect and adorn the vineyard which had been so richly planted, he built a tower in the midst of it. The expression "*and also*" calls especial attention to the fact that he hewed out a wine-trough therein (*yekeb*, the trough into which the must or juice pressed from the grapes in the wine-press flows, *lacus* as distinguished from *torcular*); that is to say, in order that the trough might be all the more fixed and durable, he constructed it in a rocky portion of the ground (*châtsēb bo* instead of *châtsab bo*, with *a* and the accent drawn back, because a *Beth* was thereby easily rendered inaudible, so that *châtsēb* is not a participial adjective, as Böttcher supposes). This was a difficult task, as the expression "and also" indicates; and for that very reason it was an evidence of the most confident expectation. But how bitterly was this deceived! The vineyard produced no such fruit, as might have been expected from a *sorek* plantation; it brought forth no '*anâbim* whatever, *i.e.* no such grapes as a cultivated vine should bear, but only *b'ushim*, or wild grapes. Luther first of all adopted the rendering *wild grapes*, and then altered it to harsh or sour grapes. But it comes to the same thing. The difference between a wild vine and a good vine is only qualitative. The *vitis vinifera*, like all cultivated plants, is assigned to the care of man, under which it improves; whereas in its wild state it remains behind its true intention (see *Genesis*, § 622). Consequently the word *b'ushim* (from *bâ'ash*, to be bad, or smell bad) denotes not only the grapes of the wild vine, which are naturally small and harsh (Rashi, *lambruches, i.e.* grapes of the *labrusca*, which is used now, however, as the botanical name of a vine that is American in its origin), but also grapes of a good stock, which have either been spoiled or have failed to ripen.[1] These were the grapes which the vineyard produced, such as you might indeed have expected from a wild vine, but not from carefully cultivated vines of the very choicest kind.

The song of the beloved who was so sorely deceived terminates here. The prophet recited it, not his beloved himself; but as they were both of one heart and one soul, the prophet proceeds thus in vers. 3 and 4: "*And now, O inhabitants of Jerusalem and men of Judah, judge, I pray you, between me and my vineyard! What could have been done more to my vineyard that I have not done in it? Wherefore did I hope that it would bring forth grapes, and it brought forth wild grapes?*" The fact that the prophet speaks as if he were the beloved himself, shows at once who the beloved must be. The beloved of the prophet and the lover of the prophet (*yâdid* and *dōd*) were Jehovah, with whom he was so united by a *unio mystica* exalted above all earthly love, that, like the angel of Jehovah in the early histories, he could speak as if he were Jehovah Himself (see especially Zech. ii. 12-15). To any one with spiritual intuition, therefore, the parabolical meaning and object of the song would be at once apparent; and even the inhabitants of Jerusalem and the men of Judah (*yōshēb* and *īsh* are used collectively, as in ch. viii. 14, ix. 8, xxii. 21, cf. xx. 6) were not so stupefied by sin, that they could not perceive to what the prophet was leading. It was for them to decide where the guilt of this unnatural issue lay—that is to say, of this thorough contradiction between the "doing" of the vineyard and the "doing" of the Lord; that instead of the grapes he hoped for, it brought forth wild grapes. (On the expression "what could have been done," *quid faciendum est, mah-la'asoth,*

---

[1] In the Jerusalem Talmud such grapes are called *ūbshin*, the letters being transposed; and in the Mishnah (*Ma'aseroth* i. 2, *Zebi'ith* iv. 8) הַבְאִישׁ is the standing word applied to grapes that are only half ripe (see Löwy's *Leshon Chachamim*, or *Wörterbuch des talmudischen Hebräisch*, Prag 1845). With reference to the wild grape (τὸ ἀγριόκλημα), a writer, describing the useful plants of Greece, says, "Its fruit (τὰ ἀγριοστάφυλα) consists of very small berries, not much larger than bilberries, with a harsh flavour."

see at Hab. i. 17, Ges. § 132, Anm. 1.) Instead of לָמָה (לָמָּה) we have the more suitable term מַדּוּעַ, the latter being used in relation to the actual cause (*causa efficiens*), the former in relation to the object (*causa finalis*). The parallel to the second part, viz. ch. 1. 2, resembles the passage before us, not only in the use of this particular word, but also in the fact that there, as well as here, it relates to both clauses, and more especially to the latter of the two. We find the same paratactic construction in connection with other conjunctions (cf. ch. xii. 1, lxv. 12). They were called upon to decide and answer as to this *what* and *wherefore;* but they were silent, just because they could clearly see that they would have to condemn themselves (as David condemned himself in connection with Nathan's parable, 2 Sam. xii. 5). The Lord of the vineyard, therefore, begins to speak. He, its accuser, will now also be its judge.—Ver. 5. "*Now then, I will tell you what I will do at once to my vineyard: take away its hedge, and it shall be for grazing; pull down its wall, and it shall be for treading down.*" Before "*now then*" (*v'attâh*) we must imagine a pause, as in ch. iii. 14. The Lord of the vineyard breaks the silence of the umpires, which indicates their consciousness of guilt. They shall hear from Him what He will do at once to His vineyard (*Lamed* in *l'carmi*, as, for example, in Deut. xi. 6). "*I will do:*" *ani 'ōseh*, *fut. instans*, equivalent to *facturus sum* (Ges. § 134, 2, *b*). In the *inf. abs.* which follow He opens up what He will do. On this explanatory use of the *inf. abs.*, see ch. xx. 2, lviii. 6, 7. In such cases as these it takes the place of the object, as in other cases of the subject, but always in an abrupt manner (Ges. § 131, 1). He would take away the *mesucah, i.e.* the green thorny hedge (Prov. xv. 19; Hos. ii. 8) with which the vineyard was enclosed, and would pull down the *gârēd, i.e.* the low stone wall (Num. xxii. 24; Prov. xxiv. 31), which had been surrounded by the hedge of thorn-bushes to make a better defence, as well as for the protection of the wall itself, more especially against being undermined; so that the vineyard would be given up to grazing and treading down (LXX. καταπάτημα), *i.e.* would become an open way and gathering-place for man and beast.

This puts an end to the unthankful vineyard, and indeed a hopeless one. Ver. 6. "*And I will put an end to it: it shall not be pruned nor digged, and it shall break out in thorns and thistles; and I will command the clouds to rain no rain over it.*" "*Put an end:*" *bâthâh* (= *battâh*: Ges. § 67, Anm. 11) signifies, according to the primary meaning of *bâthath* (בּוּח, בְּחַת, see at ch. i. 29), viz. *abscindere*, either *abscissum* = *locus abscissus* or *præruptus* (ch. vii. 19), or *abscissio* = *deletio*. The latter is the meaning here, where *shīth bâthâh* is a refined expression for the more usual עָשָׂה כָלָה, both being construed with the accusative of the thing which is brought to an end. Further pruning and hoeing would do it no good, but only lead to further disappointment: it was the will of the Lord, therefore, that the deceitful vineyard should shoot up in thorns and thistles ('*âlâh* is applied to the soil, as in ch. xxxiv. 13 and Prov. xxiv. 31 ; *shâmir vâshaith*, thorns and thistles, are in the accusative, according to Ges. § 138, 1, Anm. 2 ; and both the words themselves, and also their combination, are exclusively and peculiarly Isaiah's).[1] In order that it might remain a wilderness, the clouds would also receive commandment from the Lord not to rain upon it. There can be no longer any doubt who the Lord of the vineyard is. He is Lord of the clouds, and therefore the Lord of heaven and earth. It is He who is the prophet's beloved and dearest one. The song which opened in so minstrel-like and harmless a tone, has now become painfully severe and terribly repulsive. The husk of the parable, which has already been broken through, now falls completely off (cf. Matt. xxii. 13, xxv. 30). What it sets forth in symbol is really true. This truth the prophet establishes by an open declaration.—Ver. 7. "*For the vineyard of Jehovah of hosts is the house of Israel, and the men of Judah are the plantation of His delight: He waited for justice, and behold grasping ; for righteousness, and behold a shriek.*" The meaning is not that the Lord of the vineyard would not let any more rain fall upon it, because this Lord was Jehovah (which is not affirmed in fact in the words commencing with "for," *ci*), but

---

[1] Cassel associates *shâmir* as the name of a plant (*saxifraga*) with σμύρις, and *shaith* with *sentis*, ἄκανθα ; but the name *shâmir* is not at all applicable to those small delicate plants, which are called *saxifraga* (stone-breakers) on account of their growing out of clefts in the rock, and so appearing to have split the rock itself. Both *shâmir vâshaith* and *kōts v'dardar*, in Gen. iii. 18, seem rather to point to certain kinds of *rhamnus*, together with different kinds of thistles. The more arid and waste the ground is, the more does it abound, where not altogether without vegetation, in thorny, prickly, stunted productions.

a more general one. This was how the case stood with the vineyard; for all Israel, and especially the people of Judah, were this vineyard, which had so bitterly deceived the expectations of its Lord, and indeed "the vineyard of Jehovah of hosts," and therefore of the omnipotent God, whom even the clouds would serve when He came forth to punish. The expression "for" (ci) is not only intended to vindicate the truth of the last statement, but the truth of the whole simile, including this: it is an explanatory "for" (*ci explic.*), which opens the *epimythion*. "The vineyard of the Lord of hosts" (*cerem Jehovah Zebaoth*) is the predicate. "The house of Israel" (*beth Yisrâel*) was the whole nation, which is also represented in other passages under the same figure of a vineyard (ch. xxvii. 2 sqq.; Ps. lxxx., etc.). But as Isaiah was prophet in Judah, he applies the figure more particularly to Judah, which was called Jehovah's favourite plantation, inasmuch as it was the seat of the divine sanctuary and of the Davidic kingdom. This makes it easy enough to interpret the different parts of the simile employed. The fat mountain-horn was Canaan, flowing with milk and honey (Ex. xv. 17); the digging of the vineyard, and clearing it of stones, was the clearing of Canaan from its former heathen inhabitants (Ps. xliv. 3); the sorek-vines were the holy priests and prophets and kings of Israel of the earlier and better times (Jer. ii. 21); the defensive and ornamental tower in the midst of the vineyard was Jerusalem as the royal city, with Zion the royal fortress (Mic. iv. 8); the winepress-trough was the temple, where, according to Ps. xxxvi. 9 (8), the wine of heavenly pleasures flowed in streams, and from which, according to Ps. xlii. and many other passages, the thirst of the soul might all be quenched. The grazing and treading down are explained in Jer. v. 10 and xii. 10. The bitter deception experienced by Jehovah is expressed in a play upon two words, indicating the surprising change of the desired result into the very opposite. The explanation which Gesenius, Caspari, Knobel, and others give of *mispâch*, viz. bloodshed, does not commend itself; for even if it must be admitted that *sâphach* occurs once or twice in the "Arabizing" book of Job (ch. xxx. 7, xiv. 19) in the sense of pouring out, this verbal root is strange to the Hebrew (and the Aramæan). Moreover, *mispâch* in any case would only mean pouring or shedding, and not bloodshed; and although the latter would certainly be possible by the side of the Arabic *saffâch, saffâk* (shedder of blood), yet it would be such an ellipsis as cannot be shown anywhere else in Hebrew usage. On the other hand, the rendering "leprosy" does not yield any appropriate sense, as *mispachath* (*sappachath*) is never generalized anywhere else into the single idea of "dirt" (Luzzatto: *sozzura*), nor does it appear as an ethical notion. We therefore prefer to connect it with a meaning unquestionably belonging to the verb ספח (see *kal*, 1 Sam. iii. 36; *niphal*, xiv. 1; *hithpael*, 1 Sam. xxvi. 19), which is derived in יָסַף, אָסַף, סוּף, from the primary notion "to sweep," *spec.* to sweep towards, sweep in, or sweep away. Hence we regard *mispach* as denoting the forcible appropriation of another man's property; certainly a suitable antithesis to *mishpât*. The prophet describes, in full-toned figures, how the expected noble grapes had turned into wild grapes, with nothing more than an outward resemblance. The introduction to the prophecy closes here.

The prophecy itself follows next, a seven-fold discourse composed of the six-fold woe contained in vers. 8–23, and the announcement of punishment in which it terminates. In this six-fold woe the prophet describes the bad fruits one by one. In confirmation of our rendering of *mispâch*, the first woe relates to covetousness and avarice as the root of all evil.—Ver. 8. "*Woe unto them that join house to house, who lay field to field, till there is no more room, and ye alone are dwelling in the midst of the land.*" The participle is continued in the finite verb, as in ver. 23, ch. x. 1; the regular syntactic construction in cases of this kind (Ges. § 134, Anm. 2). The preterites after "till" (there are two such preterites, for *'ephes* is an intensified אִין enclosing the verbal idea) correspond to future perfects: "They, the insatiable, would not rest till, after every smaller piece of landed property had been swallowed by them, the whole land had come into their possession, and no one beside themselves was settled in the land" (Job xxii. 8). Such covetousness was all the more reprehensible, because the law of Israel had provided so very stringently and carefully, that as far as possible there should be an equal distribution of the soil, and that hereditary family property should be inalienable. All landed property that had been alienated reverted to the family every fiftieth year, or year of jubilee; so that alienation simply had reference to the usufruct of the land till that time. It was only in the case of houses in towns that the right of redemption was restricted to one year, at least according to a later statute. How badly the law of the year of jubilee had been observed, may be gathered from Jer. xxxiv., where we learn that the law as to the manumission of Hebrew slaves in the sabbatical year had fallen entirely into neglect. Isaiah's contemporary, Micah, makes just the same complaint as Isaiah himself (*vid.* Mic. ii. 2). And the denunciation of punishment is made by him in very similar terms to those which we find here in vers. 9, 10 : "*Into mine ears Jehovah of hosts: Of a truth many houses shall become a wilderness, great and beautiful ones deserted. For ten yokes of vineyard will yield one pailful, and a quarter of seed-corn will produce a bushel.*" We may see from ch. xxii. 14 in what sense the prophet wrote the substantive clause, "Into mine ears," or more literally, "In mine ears [is] Jehovah Zebaoth," viz. He is here revealing Himself to me. In the pointing, בְּאָזְנָי is written with *tiphchah* as a pausal form, to indicate to the reader that the boldness of the expression is to be softened down by the assumption of an ellipsis. In Hebrew, "to say into the ears" did not mean to "speak softly and secretly," as Gen. xxiii. 10, 16, Job xxxiii. 8, and other passages, clearly show ; but to speak in a distinct and intelligible manner, which precludes the possibility of any misunderstanding. The prophet, indeed, had not Jehovah standing locally beside him ; nevertheless, he had Him objectively over against his own personality, and was well able to distinguish very clearly the thoughts and words of his own personality, from the words of Jehovah which arose audibly within him. These words informed him what would be the fate of the rich and insatiable landowners. "Of a truth :" אִם־לֹא (if not) introduces an oath of an affirmative character (the complete formula is *chai ani 'im-lo'*, "as I live if not"), just as *'im* (if) alone introduces a negative oath (*e.g.* Num. xiv. 23). The force of the expression *'im-lo'* extends not only to *rabbim*, as the false accentuation with *gershayim* (doublegeresh) would make it appear, but to the whole of the following sentence, as it is correctly accentuated with *rebia* in the Venetian (1521) and other early editions. A universal desolation would ensue: *rabbim* (many) does not mean less than all; but the houses (*bâttim*, as the word should be pronounced, notwithstanding

Ewald's objection to Köhler's remarks on Zech. xiv. 2; cf. *Job*, ii. 31) constituted altogether a very large number (compare the use of the word "many" in ch. ii. 3, Matt. xx. 28, etc.). מֵאֵין is a double, and therefore an absolute, negation (so that there is not, no inhabitant, *i.e.* not any inhabitant at all). Ver. 10, which commences with *ci*, explains how such a desolation of the houses would be brought about: failure of crops produces famine, and this is followed by depopulation. "*Ten zimdē* (with *dagesh lene*, Ewald) *of vineyard*" are either ten pieces of the size that a man could plough in one day with a *yoke* of oxen, or possibly ten portions of *yoke*-like espaliers of vines, *i.e.* of vines trained on cross laths (the *vina jugata* of Varro), which is the explanation adopted by Biesenthal. But if we compare 1 Sam. xiv. 14, the former is to be preferred, although the links are wanting which would enable us to prove that the early Israelites had one and the same system of land measure as the Romans;[1] nevertheless فدان (in Hauran) is precisely similar, and this word signifies primarily a *yoke* of oxen, and then a *yoke* (*jugerum*) regarded as a measure of land. Ten days' work would only yield a single *bath*. This liquid measure, which was first introduced in the time of the kings, corresponded to the *ephah* in dry measure (Ezek. xlv. 11). According to Josephus (*Ant.* viii. 2, 9), it was equal to seventy-two Roman *sextarii*, *i.e.* a little more than thirty-three Berlin quarts; but in the time of Isaiah it was probably smaller. The *homer*, a dry measure, generally

---

[1] On the *jugerum*, see Hultsch, *Griechische und römische Metrologie*, 1862. The Greek *plethron*, which was smaller by two and a half, corresponded to some extent to this; also the Homeric *tetraguon*, which cannot be more precisely defined (according to Eustathius, it was a piece of land which a skilful labourer could plough in one day). According to Herod. ii. 168, in the Egyptian square-measure an ἄρουρα was equal to 150 cubits square. The Palestinian, according to the tables of Julian the Ashkalonite, was the plethron. "The plethron," he says, "was ten perches, or fifteen fathoms. or thirty paces, sixty cubits, ninety feet" (for the entire text, see L. F. v. Fennersberg's *Untersuchungen über alte Langen-, Feld-, und Wegemaasse*, 1859). Fennersberg's conclusion is, that the *tzemed* was a plethron, equal in length to ten perches of nine feet each. But the meaning of the word *tzemed* is of more importance in helping to determine the measure referred to, than the tables of long measure of the architect of Ashkalon, which have been preserved in the imperial collection of laws of Constantine Harmenopulos, and which probably belong to a much later period.

called a *cor* after the time of the kings, was equal to ten Attic *medimnoi*;[1] a *medimnos* being (according to Josephus, *Ant.* xv. 9, 2) about 15-16ths of a Berlin bushel, and therefore a little more than fifteen pecks. Even if this quantity of corn should be sown, they would not reap more than an *ephah*. The harvest, therefore, would only yield the tenth part of the sowing, since an *ephah* was the tenth part of a *homer*, or three *seahs*, the usual minimum for one baking (*vid.* Matt. xiii. 33). It is, of course, impossible to give the relative measures exactly in our translation.

The second woe, for which the curse about to fall upon vinedressing (ver. 10a) prepared the way by the simple association of ideas, is directed against the debauchees, who in their carnal security carried on their excesses even in the daylight. Ver. 11. " *Woe unto them that rise up early in the morning to run after strong drink; who continue till late at night with wine inflaming them!* " *Boker* (from *bâkar, bakara*, to slit, to tear up, or split) is the break of day; and *nesheph* (from *nâshaph*, to blow) the cool of the evening, including the night (ch. xxi. 4, lix. 10); *'ichēr*, to continue till late, as in Prov. xxiii. 30 : the construct state before words with a preposition, as in ch. ix. 2, xxviii. 9, and many other passages (Ges. § 116, 1). *Shēcâr*, in connection with *yayin*, is the general name for every other kind of strong drink, more especially for wines made artificially from fruit, honey, raisins, dates, etc., including barley-wine (οἶνος κρίθινος) or beer (ἐκ κριθῶν μέθυ in Æschylus, also called βρῦτον βρυτόν, ζῦθος ζύθος, and by many other names), a beverage known in Egypt, which was half a wine country and half a beer country, from as far back as the time of the Pharaohs. The form *shēcâr* is composed, like עֵנָב (with the fore-tone *tsere*), from *shâcar*, to intoxicate; according to the Arabic, literally to close by stopping up, *i.e.* to stupefy.[2] The clauses after the two participles are circum-

---

[1] Or rather 7½ Attic *medimnoi* = 10 Attic *metretoi* = 45 Roman *modia* (see Böckh, *Metrologische Untersuchungen*, p. 259).

[2] It is a question, therefore, whether the name of sugar is related to it or not. The Arabic *sakar* corresponds to the Hebrew *shecâr;* but sugar is called *sukkar*, Pers. *'sakkar, 'sakar*, no doubt equivalent to σάκχαρι (Arrian in *Periplus*, μέλι τὸ καλάμινον τὸ λεγόμενον σάκχαρι), *saccharum*, an Indian word, which is pronounced *çarkarâ* in Sanscrit and *sakkara* in Prakrit, and signifies " forming broken pieces," *i.e.* sugar in grains or small lumps

stantial clauses (Ewald, § 341, b), indicating the circumstances under which they ran out so early, and sat till long after dark: they hunted after mead, they heated themselves with wine, namely, to drown the consciousness of their deeds of darkness.

Ver. 12 describes how they go on in their blindness with music and carousing: "*And guitar and harp, kettle-drum, and flute, and wine, is their feast; but they regard not the work of Jehovah, and see not the purpose of His hands.*" "*Their feast*" is so and so (מִשְׁתֵּיהֶם is only a plural in appearance; it is really a singular, as in Dan. i. 10, 16, and many other passages, with the *Yod* of the primary form, מִשְׁתֶּה = מִשְׁתֵּי, softened: see the remarks on עָלֶה at ch. i. 30, and עֲשִׂיָה at ch. xxii. 11); that is to say, their feast consisted or was composed of exciting music and wine. Knobel construes it, "and there are guitar, etc., and wine is their drink;" but a divided sentence of this kind is very tame; and the other expression, based upon the general principle, "The whole is its parts," is thoroughly Semitic (see Fleischer's *Abhandlungen über einige Arten der Nominalapposition in den Sitzungsberichten der sächs. Gesellschaft der Wissenschaft*, 1862). *Cinnor* (guitar) is a general name for such instruments as have their strings drawn (upon a bridge) over a sounding board; and *nebel* (the harp and lyre) a general name for instruments with their strings hung freely, so as to be played with both hands at the same time. *Toph* (Arab. *duff*) is a general name for the tambourin, the drum, and the kettle-drum; *chalil* (lit. that which is bored through) a general name for the flute and double flute. In this tumult and riot they had no thought or eye for the work of Jehovah and the purpose of His hands. This is the phrase used to express the idea of the eternal counsel of God (ch. xxxvii. 26), which leads to salvation by the circuitous paths of judgment (ch. x. 12, xxviii. 21, xxix. 23), so far as that counsel is embodied in

(brown sugar). The art of boiling sugar from the cane was an Indian invention (see Lassen, *Indische Alterthumskunde*, i. 269 sqq.). The early Egyptian name for beer is *hek* (Brugsch, *Recueil*, p. 118); the demotic and hieratic name *henk*, the Coptic *henke*. The word ζῦθος (ζύθος) is also old Egyptian. In the *Book of the Dead* (79, 8) the deceased says, "I have taken sacrificial cakes from the table, I have drunk *seth-t* in the evening." Moses Stuart wrote an *Essay upon the Wines and Strong Drinks of the Ancient Hebrews*, which was published in London (1831), with a preface by J. Pye Smith.

history, as moulded by the invisible interposition of God. In their joy and glory they had no sense for what was the most glorious of all, viz. the moving and working of God in history; so that they could not even discern the judgment which was in course of preparation at that very time.

Therefore judgment would overtake them in this blind, dull, and stupid animal condition. Ver. 13. "*Therefore my people go into banishment without knowing; and their glory will become starving men, and their tumult men dried up with thirst.*" As the word "*therefore*" (*lâcēn*, as in ch. i. 24) introduces the threat of punishment, *gâlâh* (go into captivity) is a prophetic preterite. Israel would go into exile, and that "without knowing" (*mibb'li-da'ath*). The meaning of this expression cannot be "from want of knowledge," since the *min* which is fused into one word with *b'li* is not causal, but negative, and *mibb'li*, as a preposition, always signifies "without" (*absque*). But are we to render it "without knowing it" (as in Hos. iv. 6, where *hadda'ath* has the article), or "unawares?" There is no necessity for any dispute on this point, since the two renderings are fundamentally one and the same. The knowledge, of which ver. 12 pronounces them destitute, was more especially a knowledge of the judgment of God that was hanging over them; so that, as the captivity would come upon them without knowledge, it would necessarily come upon them unawares. "*Their glory*" (*cebôdô*) and "*their tumult*" (*hamono*) are therefore to be understood, as the predicates show, as collective nouns used in a personal sense, the former signifying the more select portion of the nation (cf. Mic. i. 15), the latter the mass of the people, who were living in rioting and tumult. The former would become "*men of famine*" (*mĕthē rââb*: מְתֵי, like אַנְשֵׁי in other places, viz. 2 Sam. xix. 29, or בְּנֵי, 1 Sam. xxvi. 16); the latter "*men dried up with thirst*" (*tsichēh tsâmâh*: the same number as the subject). There is no necessity to read מֵתֵי (dead men) instead of מְתֵי, as the LXX. and Vulgate do, or מְזֵי (מְזֵה) according to Deut. xxxii. 24, as Hitzig, Ewald, Böttcher, and others propose (compare, on the contrary, Gen. xxxiv. 30 and Job xi. 11). The adjective *tzicheh* (*hapax leg.*) is formed like *chirēsh*, *cēheh*, and other adjectives which indicate defects: in such formations from verbs *Lamed-He*, instead of *e* we have an *æ* that has grown out of *ay* (Olshausen, § 182, *b*). The rich gluttons would starve, and the tippling crowd would die with thirst.

The threat of punishment commences again with "therefore;" it has not yet satisfied itself, and therefore grasps deeper still. Ver. 14. "*Therefore the under-world opens its jaws wide, and stretches open its mouth immeasurably wide; and the glory of Jerusalem descends, and its tumult, and noise, and those who rejoice within it.*" The verbs which follow *lâcēn* (therefore) are prophetic preterites, as in ver. 13. The feminine suffixes attached to what the lower world swallows up do not refer to *sheol* (though this is construed more frequently, no doubt, as a feminine than as a masculine, as it is in Job xxvi. 6), but, as expressed in the translation, to Jerusalem itself, which is also necessarily required by the last clause, "those who rejoice within it." The withdrawal of the tone from וְעָלֵז to the penultimate (cf. *châphētz* in Ps. xviii. 20, xxii. 9) is intentionally omitted, to cause the rolling and swallowing up to be heard as it were. A mouth is ascribed to the under-world, also a *nephesh*, *i.e.* a greedy soul, in which sense *nephesh* is then applied metonymically sometimes to a thirst for blood (Ps. xxvii. 12), and sometimes to simple greediness (ch. lvi. 11), and even, as in the present passage and Hab. ii. 5, to the throat or swallow which the soul opens "without measure," when its craving knows no bounds (*Psychol.* p. 204). It has become a common thing now to drop entirely the notion which formerly prevailed, that the noun *sheol* was derived from the verb *shâal* in the sense in which it was generally employed, viz. to ask or demand; but Caspari, who has revived it again, is certainly so far correct, that the derivation of the word which the prophet had in his mind was this and no other. The word *sheol* (an infinitive form, like *pekōd*) signified primarily the irresistible and inexorable demand made upon every earthly thing; and then secondarily, in a local sense, the place of the abode of shades, to which everything on the surface of the earth is summoned; or essentially the divinely appointed curse which demands and swallows up everything upon the earth. We simply maintain, however, that the word *sheol*, as generally used, was associated in thought with *shâal*, to ask or demand. Originally, no doubt, it may have been derived from the primary and more material idea of the verb שָׁאַל, possibly from the meaning "to be hollow," which is also assumed to be the primary meaning of שְׁאוֹל.[1] At any rate, this derivation answers to the view that generally prevailed in ancient times. According to the prevalent idea, Hades was in the interior of the earth. And there was nothing really absurd in this, since it is quite within the power and freedom of the omnipresent God to manifest Himself wherever and however He may please. As He reveals Himself above the earth, *i.e.* in heaven, among blessed spirits in the light of His love; so did He reveal Himself underneath the earth, viz. in Sheôl, in the darkness and fire of His wrath. And with the exception of Enoch and Elijah, with their marvellous departure from this life, the way of every mortal ended there, until the time when Jesus Christ, having first paid the λύτρον, *i.e.* having shed His blood, which covers our guilt and turns the wrath of God into love, descended into Hades and ascended into heaven, and from that time forth has changed the death of all believers from a descent into Hades into an ascension to heaven. But even under the Old Testament the believer may have known, that whoever hid himself on this side the grave in Jehovah the living One, would retain his eternal germ of life even in Sheôl in the midst of the shades, and would taste the love of God even in the midst of wrath. It was this postulate of faith which lay at the foundation of the fact, that even under the Old Testament the broader and more comprehensive idea of Sheôl began to be contracted into

[1] The meaning "to be hollow" is not very firmly established, however; as the primary meaning of שְׁאוֹל, and the analogy sometimes adduced of hell = hollow (*Hölle* = *Höhle*), is a deceptive one, as *Hölle* (hell), to which Luther always gives the more correct form *Helle*, does not mean a hollow, but a hidden place (or a place which renders invisible: from *hëln*, to conceal), Lat. *celans* (see Jütting, *Bibl. Wörterbuch*, 1864, pp. 85, 86). It is much more probable that the meaning of *sheôl* is not the hollow place, but the depression or depth, from שָׁאַל, which corresponds precisely to the Greek χαλᾶν so far as its primary meaning is concerned (compare the talmudic *shilshêl*, to let down; *shilshul*, sinking or depression, *Erubin* 83b; *shul*, the foundation, *fundus*): see Hupfeld on Ps. vi. 6. Luzzatto on this passage also explains *sheol* as signifying depth, and compares the talmudic *hishchîl*=*hëshîl*, to let down (or, according to others, to draw up,—two meanings which may easily be combined in the same word, starting from its radical idea, which indicates in general a loosening of the previous connection). Fürst has also given up the meaning *cavitas*, a hollow, and endeavours to find a more correct explanation of the primary signification of *shâ'ul* (see at ch. xl. 12).

the more limited notion of hell (see *Psychol.* p. 415). This is the case in the passage before us, where Isaiah predicts of everything of which Jerusalem was proud, and in which it revelled, including the persons who rejoiced in these things, a descent into Hades; just as the Korahite author of Ps. xlix. wrote (ver. 14) that the beauty of the wicked would be given up to Hades to be consumed, without having hereafter any place in the upper world, when the upright should have dominion over them in the morning. Hades even here is almost equivalent to the New Testament *gehenna*.

The prophet now repeats a thought which formed one of the refrains of the second prophetic address (ch. ii. 9, 11, cf. ver. 17). It acquires here a still deeper sense, from the context in which it stands. Vers. 15, 16. "*Then are mean men bowed down, and lords humbled, and the eyes of lofty men are humbled. And Jehovah of hosts shows Himself exalted in judgment, and God the Holy One sanctifies Himself in righteousness.*" That which had exalted itself from earth to heaven, would be cast down earthwards into hell. The consecutive futures depict the coming events, which are here represented as historically present, as the direct sequel of what is also represented as present in ver. 14: Hades opens, and then both low and lofty in Jerusalem sink down, and the soaring eyes now wander about in horrible depths. God, who is both exalted and holy in Himself, demanded that as the exalted One He should be exalted, and that as the Holy One He should be sanctified. But Jerusalem had not done that; He would therefore prove Himself the exalted One by the execution of justice, and sanctify Himself (*nikdash* is to be rendered as a reflective verb, according to Ezek. xxxvi. 23, xxxviii. 23) by the manifestation of righteousness, in consequence of which the people of Jerusalem would have to give Him glory against their will, as forming part of "the things under the earth" (Phil. ii. 10). Jerusalem has been swallowed up twice in this manner by Hades; once in the Chaldean war, and again in the Roman. But the invisible background of these outward events was the fact, that it had already fallen under the power of hell. And now, even in a more literal sense, ancient Jerusalem, like the company of Korah (Num. xvi. 30, 33), has gone underground. Just as Babylon and Nineveh, the ruins of which are dug out of the inexhaustible mine of their far-stretching foundation and soil, have sunk beneath the ground; so do men walk about in modern Jerusalem over the ancient Jerusalem, which lies buried beneath; and many an enigma of topography will remain an enigma until ancient Jerusalem has been dug out of the earth again.

And when we consider that the Holy Land is at the present time an extensive pasture-ground for Arab shepherds, and that the modern Jerusalem which has arisen from the dust is a Mohammedan city, we may see in this also a literal fulfilment of ver. 17: "*And lambs feed as upon their pasture, and nomad shepherds eat the waste places of the fat ones.*" There is no necessity to supply an object to the verb וְרָעוּ, as Knobel and others assume, viz. the waste lands mentioned in the second clause; nor is *cedâbrâm* to be taken as the object, as Caspari supposes; but the place referred to is determined by the context: in the place where Jerusalem is sunken, there lambs feed after the manner of their own pasture-ground, *i.e.* just as if they were in their old accustomed pasture (*dober*, as in Mic. ii. 12, from *dâbăr*, to drive). The lambs intended are those of the *gârim* mentioned in the second clause. The *gârim* themselves are men leading an unsettled, nomad, or pilgrim life; as distinguished from *gērim, strangers* visiting, or even settled at a place. The LXX. have ἄρνες, so that they must have read either *cârim* or *gedâim*, which Ewald, Knobel, and others adopt. But one feature of the prophecy, which is sustained by the historical fulfilment, is thereby obliterated. *Chârboth mēchim* are the lands of those that were formerly marrowy, *i.e.* fat and strutting about in their fulness; which lands had now become waste places. Knobel's statement, that *ácăl* is out of place in connection with *gârim*, is overthrown by ch. i. 7, to which he himself refers, though he makes he-goats the subject instead of men. The second woe closes with ver. 17. It is the longest of all. This also serves to confirm the fact that luxury was the leading vice of Judah in the time of Uzziah-Jotham, as it was that of Israel under Jeroboam II. (see Amos vi., where the same threat is held out).

The third woe is directed against the supposed strong-minded men, who called down the judgment of God by presumptuous sins and wicked words Ver. 18. "*Woe unto them that draw crime with cords of lying, and sin as with the rope of the waggon.*" Knobel and most other commentators take *mâshak* in the sense of *attrahere* (to draw towards one's self) : " They draw towards them sinful deeds with cords of lying palliation, and the cart-rope of the most daring presumption;" and cite, as parallel examples, Job xl. 25 and Hos. xi. 4. But as *mâshak* is also used in Deut. xxi. 3 in the sense of drawing in a yoke, that is to say, drawing a plough or chariot; and as the waggon or cart (*agâlâh*, the word commonly used for a transport-waggon, as distinguished from *mercâbâh*, the state carriage or war chariot : see *Genesis*, pp. 562–3) is expressly mentioned here, the figure employed is certainly the same as that which underlies the New Testament ἑτεροζυγεῖν ("unequally yoked," 2 Cor. vi. 14). Iniquity was the burden which they drew after them with cords of lying (*shâv'h*: see at Ps. xxvi. 4 and Job xv. 31), *i.e.* "want of character or religion;" and sin was the waggon to which they were harnessed as if with a thick cart-rope (Hofmann, Drechsler, and Caspari; see Ewald, § 221, *a*). Iniquity and sin are mentioned here as carrying with them their own punishment. The definite הֶעָוֹן (crime or misdeed) is generic, and the indefinite חַטָּאָה qualitative and massive. There is a bitter sarcasm involved in the bold figure employed. They were proud of their unbelief; but this unbelief was like a halter with which, like beasts of burden, they were harnessed to sin, and therefore to the punishment of sin, which they went on drawing further and further, in utter ignorance of the waggon behind them.

Ver. 19 shows very clearly that the prophet referred to the free-thinkers of his time, the persons who are called fools (*nabal*) and scorners (*lētz*) in the Psalms and Proverbs. " *Who say, Let Him hasten, accelerate His work, that we may see; and let the counsel of the Holy One of Israel draw near and come, that we may experience it.*" They doubted whether the day of Jehovah would ever come (Ezek. xii. 22 ; Jer. v. 12, 13), and went so far in their unbelief as to call out for what they could not and would not believe, and desired it to come that they might see it with their own eyes and experience it for themselves (Jer. xvii. 15 ; it is different in Amos v. 18 and Mal. ii. 17–iii. 1, where this desire does not arise from scorn and defiance, but from impatience and weakness of faith). As the two verbs denoting haste are used both transitively and intransitively (*vid.* Judg. xx. 37, to hasten or make haste), we might render the passage " let His work make haste," as Hitzig, Ewald, Umbreit, and Drechsler do; but we prefer the rendering adopted by Gesenius, Caspari, and Knobel, on the basis of ch. lx. 22, and take the verb as transitive, and Jehovah as the subject. The forms *yâchishâh* and *taboâh* are, with Ps. xx. 4 and Job xi. 17, probably the only examples of the expression of a wish in the third person, strengthened by the *âh*, which indicates a summons or appeal; for Ezek. xxiii. 20, which Gesenius cites (§ 48, 3), and Job xxii. 21, to which Knobel refers, have no connection with this, as in both passages the *âh* is the feminine termination, and not hortative (*vid. Job*, i. p. 187 note, and i. p. 441). The fact that the free-thinkers called God "the Holy One of Israel," whereas they scoffed at His intended final and practical attestation of Himself as the Holy One, may be explained from ch. xxx. 11 : they took this name of God from the lips of the prophet himself, so that their scorn affected both God and His prophet at the same time.

Ver. 20. The fourth woe: " *Woe to those who call evil good, and good evil; who give out darkness for light, and light for darkness; who give out bitter for sweet, and sweet for bitter.*" The previous woe had reference to those who made the facts of sacred history the butt of their naturalistic doubt and ridicule, especially so far as they were the subject of prophecy. This fourth woe relates to those who adopted a code of morals that completely overturned the first principles of ethics, and was utterly opposed to the law of God; for evil, darkness, and bitter, with their respective antitheses, represent moral principles that are essentially related (Matt. vi. 23; Jas. iii. 11). Evil, as hostile to God, is dark in its nature, and therefore loves darkness, and is exposed to the punitive power of darkness. And although it may be sweet to the material taste, it is nevertheless bitter, inasmuch as it produces abhorrence and disgust in the godlike nature of man, and, after a brief period of self-deception, is turned into the bitter woe of fatal results. Darkness and light, bitter and sweet, therefore, are not tautological metaphors for evil and good; but epithets applied to evil and good according to their essential principles, and their necessary and internal effects.

Ver. 21. The fifth woe: " *Woe unto them that are wise in*

their own eyes, and prudent in their own sight." The third woe had reference to the unbelieving naturalists, the opponents of prophecy (*nebuâh*) ; the fourth to the moralists, who threw all into confusion ; and to this there is appended, by a very natural association of ideas, the woe denounced upon those whom want of humility rendered inaccessible to that wisdom which went hand in hand with prophecy, and the true foundation of which was the fear of Jehovah (Prov. i. 7 ; Job xxviii. 28 ; Eccles. xii. 13). "Be not wise in thine own eyes," is a fundamental rule of this wisdom (Prov. iii. 7). It was upon this wisdom that that prophetic policy rested, whose warnings, as we read in ch. xxviii. 9, 10, they so scornfully rejected. The next woe, which has reference to the administration of justice in the state, shows very clearly that in this woe the prophet had more especially the want of theocratic wisdom in relation to the affairs of state in his mind.

Vers. 22, 23. The sixth woe : *" Woe to those who are heroes to drink wine, and brave men to mix strong drink ; who acquit criminals for a bribe, and take away from every one the righteousness of the righteous."* We see from ver. 23 that the drinkers in ver. 22 are unjust judges. The threat denounced against these is Isaiah's universal *ceterum censeo;* and accordingly it forms, in this instance also, the substance of his sixth and last woe. They are *heroes;* not, however, in avenging wrong, but in drinking wine ; they are men of renown, though not for deciding between guilt and innocence, but for mixing up the ingredients of strong artistic wines. For the terms applied to such mixed wines, see Ps. lxxv. 9, Prov. xxiii. 30, Song of Sol. vii. 3. It must be borne in mind, however, that what is here called *shecâr* was not, properly speaking, wine, but an artificial mixture, like date wine and cider. For such things as these they were noteworthy and strong ; whereas they judged unjustly, and took bribes that they might consume the reward of their injustice in drink and debauchery (ch. xxviii. 7, 8 ; Prov. xxxi. 5). *"For reward:"* ĕkĕb (Arab. *'ukb;* different from âkēb, a heel, = *'akib*) is an adverbial accusative, "in recompense," or "for pay." *"From him"* (*mimmennu*) is distributive, and refers back to *tsaddikim* (the righteous) ; as, for example, in Hos. iv. 8.

In the three exclamations in vers. 18-21, Jehovah rested

contented with the simple undeveloped "woe" (*hoi*). On the other hand, the first two utterances respecting the covetous and the debauchees were expanded into an elaborate denunciation of punishment. But now that the prophet has come to the unjust judges, the denunciation of punishment bursts out with such violence, that a return to the simple exclamation of "woe" is not to be thought of. To the two "therefores" in vers. 13, 14, a third is now added in ver. 24: "*Therefore, as the tongue of fire devours stubble, and hay sinks together in the flame, their root will become like mould, and their blossom fly up like dust; for they have despised the law of Jehovah of hosts, and scornfully rejected the proclamation of the Holy One of Israel.*" The persons primarily intended are those described in vers. 22, 23, but with a further extension of the range of vision to Judah and Jerusalem, the vineyard of which they are the bad fruit. The sinners are compared to a plant which moulders into dust both above and below, *i.e.* altogether (cf. Mal. iii. 19, and the expression, "Let there be to him neither root below nor branch above," in the inscription upon the sarcophagus of the Phœnician king *Es'mun-'azar*). Their root moulders in the earth, and their blossom (*perach*, as in ch. xviii. 5) turns to fine dust, which the wind carries away. And this change in root and blossom takes place suddenly, as if through the force of fire. In the expression *ce'ecol kash leshon 'ēsh* ("as the tongue of fire devours stubble"), which consists of four short words with three sibilant letters, we hear, as it were, the hissing of the flame. When the infinitive construct is connected with both subject and object, the subject generally stands first, as in ch. lxiv. 1; but here the object is placed first, as in ch. xx. 1 (Ges. § 133, 3; Ewald, § 307). In the second clause, the infinitive construct passes over into the finite verb, just as in the similarly constructed passage in ch. lxiv. 1. As *yirpeh* has the intransitive meaning *collabi*, to sink together, or collapse; either *lehâbâh* must be an *acc. loci*, or *chashash lehâbâh* the construct state, signifying flame-hay, *i.e.* hay destined to the flame, or ascending in flame.[1] As the reason

---

[1] In Arabic also, *chashish* signifies hay; but in common usage (at least in Syriac) it is applied not to dried grass, but to green grass or barley: hence the expression *yachush* there is green fodder. Here, however, in Isaiah, *.hashash* is equivalent to *chashish yâbis*, and this is its true etymological meaning (see the Lexicons). But *kash* is still used in Syro-Arabic, to

for the sudden dissolution of the plantation of Judah, instead of certain definite sins being mentioned, the sin of all sins is given at once, namely, the rejection of the word of God with the heart (*mâ'as*), and in word and deed (*ni'ēts*). The double *'ēth* (with *yethib* immediately before *pashta*, as in eleven passages in all; see Heidenheim's *Mispetê hate'amim*, p. 20) and *v'ēth* (with *tebir*) give prominence to the object; and the interchange of Jehovah of hosts with the Holy One of Israel makes the sin appear all the greater on account of the exaltation and holiness of God, who revealed Himself in this word, and indeed had manifested Himself to Israel as His own peculiar people. The prophet no sooner mentions the great sin of Judah, than the announcement of punishment receives, as it were, fresh fuel, and bursts out again.—Ver. 25. "*Therefore is the wrath of Jehovah kindled against His people, and He stretches His hand over them, and smites them; then the hills tremble, and their carcases become like sweepings in the midst of the streets. For all this His anger is not appeased, and His hand is stretched out still.*" We may see from these last words, which are repeated as a refrain in the cycle of prophecies relating to the time of Ahaz (ch. ix. 11, 16, x. 4), that the prophet had before his mind a distinct and complete judgment upon Judah, belonging to the immediate future. It was certainly a coming judgment, not one already past; for the verbs after "therefore" (*'al-cēn*), like those after the three previous *lâcēn*, are all prophetic preterites. It is impossible, therefore, to take the words "and the hills tremble" as referring to the earthquake in the time of Uzziah (Amos i. 1; Zech. xiv. 5). This judgment, which was closer at hand, would consist in the fact that Jehovah would stretch out His hand in His wrath over His people (or, as it is expressed elsewhere, would swing His hand: Luther, "wave His hand," *i.e.* move it to and fro; *vid.* ch. xi. 15, xix. 16, xxx. 30, 32), and bring it down upon Judah with one stroke, the violence of which would be felt not only by men, but by surrounding nature as well. What kind of stroke this would be, was to be inferred from the circumstance that the corpses would lie unburied

signify not stubble, but wheat that has been cut and is not yet threshed; whereas the radical word itself signifies to be dry, and *châshash* consequently is used for mown grass, and *kash* for the dry halm of wheat, whether as stubble left standing in the ground, or as straw (*vid. Job*, ii. 377).

in the streets, like common street-sweepings. The reading חַצּוֹת must be rejected. Early editors read the word much more correctly חֻצוֹת; Buxtorf (1618) even adopts the reading הַחוּצוֹת, which has the Masoretic pointing in Num. xxii. 39 in its favour. It is very natural to connect *cassuchâh* with the Arabic *kusâcha* (sweepings; see at ch. xxxiii. 12): but *kusâcha* is the common form for waste or rubbish of this kind (*e.g. kulâme*, nail-cuttings), whereas *cassuach* is a form which, like the forms *faōl* (*e.g. châmōts*) and *faûl* (compare the Arabic *fâsûs*, a wind-maker, or wind-bag, *i.e.* a boaster), has always an intensive, active (*e.g. channun*), or circumstantial signification (like *shaccul*), but is never found in a passive sense. The *Caph* is consequently to be taken as a particle of comparison (followed, as is generally the case, with a definite article); and *sûchâh* is to be derived from *sûach* (= *verrere*, to sweep). The reference, therefore, is not to a pestilence (which is designated, as a stroke from God, not by *hiccâh*, but by *nâgaph*), but to the slaughter of battle; and if we look at the other terrible judgment threatened in vers. 26 sqq., which was to proceed from the imperial power, there can be no doubt that the spirit of prophecy here points to the massacre that took place in Judah in connection with the Syro-Ephraimitish war (see 2 Chron. xxviii. 5, 6). The mountains may then have trembled with the marching of troops, and the din of arms, and the felling of trees, and the shout of war. At any rate, nature had to participate in what men had brought upon themselves; for, according to the creative appointment of God, nature bears the same relation to man as the body to the soul. Every stroke of divine wrath which falls upon a nation equally affects the land which has grown up, as it were, with it; and in this sense the mountains of Judah trembled at the time referred to, even though the trembling was only discernible by initiated ears. But "for all this" (*Beth*, = "notwithstanding," " in spite of," as in Job i. 22) the wrath of Jehovah, as the prophet foresaw, would not turn away, as it was accustomed to do when He was satisfied; and His hand would still remain stretched out over Judah, ready to strike again.

Jehovah finds the human instruments of His further strokes, not in Israel and the neighbouring nations, but in the people of distant lands. Ver. 26. "*And lifts up a banner to the distant nations, and hisses to it from the end of the earth; and, behold, it comes with haste swiftly.*" What the prophet here foretold began to be fulfilled in the time of Ahaz. But the prophecy, which commences with this verse, has every possible mark of the very opposite of a *vaticinium post eventum*. It is, strictly speaking, only what had already been threatened in Deut. xxviii. 49 sqq. (cf. ch. xxxii. 21 sqq.), though here it assumes a more plastic form, and is here presented for the first time to the view of the prophet as though coming out of a mist. Jehovah summons the nations afar off: *haggōyim mērāchok* signifies, as we have rendered it, the " distant nations," for *mērāchok* is virtually an adjective both here and ch. xlix. 1, just as in Jer. xxiii. 23 it is virtually a substantive. The visible working of Jehovah presents itself to the prophet in two figures. Jehovah plants a banner or standard, which, like an optical telegraph, announces to the nations at a more remote distance than the horn of battle (*shophâr*) could possibly reach, that they are to gather together to war. A " banner" (*nēs*) : *i.e.* a lofty staff with flying colours (ch. xxxiii. 23) planted upon a bare mountain-top (ch. xiii. 2). נֵשָׂא alternates with הָרִים in this favourite figure of Isaiah. The nations through whom this was primarily fulfilled were the nations of the Assyrian empire. According to the Old Testament view, these nations were regarded as far off, and dwelling at the end of the earth (ch. xxxix. 3), not only inasmuch as the Euphrates formed the boundary towards the north-east between what was geographically known and unknown to the Israelites (Ps. lxxii. 8 ; Zech. ix. 10), but also inasmuch as the prophet had in his mind a complex body of nations stretching far away into further Asia. The second figure is taken from a bee-master, who entices the bees, by hissing or whistling, to come out of their hives and settle on the ground. Thus Virgil says to the bee-master who wants to make the bees settle, " Raise a ringing, and beat the cymbals of Cybele all around" (*Georgics*, iv. 54). Thus does Jehovah entice the hosts of nations like swarms of bees (vii. 18), and they swarm together with haste and swiftness. The plural changes into the singular, because those who are approaching have all the appearance at first of a compact and indivisible mass; it is also possible that the ruling nation among the many is singled out. The thought and expression are both misty, and this is perfectly characteristic. With the word "behold" (*hinnēh*) the prophet points to them; they are approaching *mehērâh kal*, i.e. in the shortest time with swift feet, and the nearer they come to his view the more clearly he can describe them.—Ver. 27. "*There is none exhausted, and none stumbling among them: it gives itself no slumber, and no sleep; and to none is the girdle of his hips loosed; and to none is the lace of his shoes broken.*" Notwithstanding the long march, there is no *exhausted* one, obliged to separate himself and remain behind (Deut. xxv. 18; Isa. xiv. 31); no *stumbling* one (*cōshēl*), for they march on, pressing incessantly forwards, as if along a well-made road (Jer. xxxi. 9). They do not *slumber* (*nūm*), to say nothing of *sleeping* (*yâshēn*), so great is their eagerness for battle: *i.e.* they do not slumber to refresh themselves, and do not even allow themselves their ordinary night's rest. No one has the *girdle* of his armour-shirt or coat of mail, in which he stuck his sword (Neh. iv. 18), at all *loosened;* nor has a single one even the *shoe-string*, with which his sandals were fastened, *broken* (*nittak, disrumpitur*). The statement as to their want of rest forms a *climax descendens;* the other, as to the tightness and durability of their equipment, a *climax ascendens:* the two statements follow one another after the nature of a *chiasmus*.

The prophet then proceeds to describe their weapons and war-chariots. Ver. 28. "*He whose arrows are sharpened, and all his bows strung; the hoofs of his horses are counted like flint, and his wheels like the whirlwind.*" In the prophet's view they are coming nearer and nearer. For he sees that they have brought the sharpened arrows in their quivers (ch. xxii. 6); and the fact that all their bows are already *trodden* (namely, as their length was equal to a man's height, by treading upon the string with the left foot, as we may learn from Arrian's *Indica*), proves that they are near to the goal. The correct reading in Jablonsky (according to Kimchi's *Lex.* cf. *Michlal yofi*) is

קְשֻׁתֹתָיו with *dagesh dirimens*, as in Ps. xxxvii. 15 (Ges. § 20, 2, *b*).

As the custom of shoeing horses was not practised in ancient times, firm hoofs (ὅπλαι καρτεραί, according to Xenophon's *Hippikos*) were one of the most important points in a good horse. And the horses of the enemy that was now drawing near to Judah had hoofs that would be found like flint (*tzar*, only used here, equivalent to the Arabic *zirr*). Homer designates such horses *chalkopodes*, brazen-footed. And the two wheels of the war-chariots, to which they were harnessed, turned with such velocity, and overthrew everything before them with such violence, that it seemed not merely as if a whirlwind drove them forward, but as if they were the whirlwind itself (ch. lxvi. 15; Jer. iv. 13). Nahum compares them to lightning (ch. ii. 5). Thus far the prophet's description has moved on, as if by forced marches, in clauses of from two to four words each. It now changes into a heavy, stealthy pace, and then in a few clauses springs like a wild beast upon its prey.—Ver. 29. "*Roaring issues from it as from the lioness: it roars like lions, and utters a low murmur; seizes the prey, carries it off, and no one rescues.*" The futures, with the preceding שְׁאָגָה לוֹ which is equivalent to a future, hold each feature in the description fast, as if for prolonged contemplation. The lion roars when eager for prey; and such is now the war-cry of the bloodthirsty enemy, which the prophet compares to the roaring of a lion or of young lions (*cephirim*) in the fulness of their strength. (The lion is described by its poetic name, לָבִיא; this does not exactly apply to the lioness, which would rather be designated by the term לְבִיָּה.) The roar is succeeded by a low growl (*nâham, fremere*), when a lion is preparing to fall upon its prey.[1] And so the prophet hears a low and ominous murmur in the army, which is now ready for battle. But he also sees immediately afterwards how the enemy seizes its booty and carries it irrecoverably away: literally, "how he causes it to escape," *i.e.* not "lets it slip in cruel sport," as Luzzatto interprets it, but carries it to a place of safety (Mic. vi. 14). The prey referred to is Judah. It also adds to the gloomy and mysterious character of the prophecy, that the prophet never mentions Judah. In the following verse also (ver. 30) the object is still suppressed, as if the prophet could not let it pass his lips. Ver. 30. "*And it utters a deep roar over it in that day like the roaring of the sea: and it looks to the earth, and behold darkness, tribulation, and light; it becomes night over it in the clouds of heaven.*" The subject to "roars" is the mass of the enemy; and in the expressions "over it" and "it looks" (*nibbat;* the *niphal,* which is only

---

[1] In Arabic, *en-nehem* is used to signify greediness (see Ali's *Proverbs*, No. 16).

met with here, in the place of the *hiphil*) the prophet has in his mind the nation of Judah, upon which the enemy falls with the roar of the ocean—that is to say, overwhelming it like a sea. And when the people of Judah look to the earth, *i.e.* to their own land, darkness alone presents itself, and darkness which has swallowed up all the smiling and joyous aspect which it had before. And what then? The following words, *tzar vâ'ōr*, have been variously rendered, viz. "moon (= *sahar*) and sun" by the Jewish expositors, "stone and flash," *i.e.* hail and thunder-storm, by Drechsler; but such renderings as these, and others of a similar kind, are too far removed from the ordinary usage of the language. And the separation of the two words, so that the one closes a sentence and the other commences a fresh one (*e.g.* "darkness of tribulation, and the sun becomes dark"), which is adopted by Hitzig, Gesenius, Ewald, and others, is opposed to the impression made by the two monosyllables, and sustained by the pointing, that they are connected together. The simplest explanation is one which takes the word *tzar* in its ordinary sense of tribulation or oppression, and *'ōr* in its ordinary sense of light, and which connects the two words closely together. And this is the case with the rendering given above: *tzar vâ'ōr* are "tribulation and brightening up," one following the other and passing over into the other, like morning and night (ch. xxi. 12). This pair of words forms an interjectional clause, the meaning of which is, that when the predicted darkness had settled upon the land of Judah, this would not be the end; but there would still follow an alternation of anxiety and glimmerings of hope, until at last it had become altogether dark in the cloudy sky over all the land of Judah (*'ariphim*, the cloudy sky, is only met with here; it is derived from *'âraph*, to drop or trickle, hence also *'arâphel:* the suffix points back to *lâ'âretz*, *eretz* denoting sometimes the earth as a whole, and at other times the land as being part of the earth). The prophet here predicts that, before utter ruin has overtaken Judah, sundry approaches will be made towards this, within which a divine deliverance will appear again and again. Grace tries and tries again and again, until at last the measure of iniquity is full, and the time of repentance past. The history of the nation of Judah proceeded according to this law until the destruction of Jerusalem by the Romans.

The Assyrian troubles, and the miraculous light of divine help which arose in the destruction of the military power of Sennacherib, were only the foreground of this mournful but yet ever and anon hopeful course of history, which terminated in utter darkness, that has continued now for nearly two thousand years.

This closes the third prophetic address. It commences with a parable which contains the history of Israel *in nuce*, and closes with an emblem which symbolizes the gradual but yet certain accomplishment of the judicial, penal termination of the parable. This third address, therefore, is as complete in itself as the second was. The kindred allusions are to be accounted for from the sameness of the historical basis and arena. During the course of the exposition, it has become more and more evident and certain that it relates to the time of Uzziah and Jotham,—a time of peace, of strength, and wealth, but also of pride and luxury. The terrible slaughter of the Syro-Ephraimitish war, which broke out at the end of Jotham's reign, and the varied complications which king Ahaz introduced between Judah and the imperial worldly power, and which issued eventually in the destruction of the former kingdom,—those five marked epochs in the history of the kingdoms of the world, or great empires, to which the Syro-Ephraimitish war was the prelude,—were still hidden from the prophet in the womb of the future. The description of the great mass of people that was about to roll over Judah from afar is couched in such general terms, so undefined and misty, that all we can say is, that everything that was to happen to the people of God on the part of the imperial power during the five great and extended periods of judgment that were now so soon to commence (viz. the Assyrian, the Chaldean, the Persian, the Grecian, and the Roman), was here unfolding itself out of the mist of futurity, and presenting itself to the prophet's eye. Even in the time of Ahaz the character of the prophecy changed in this respect. It was then that the eventful relation, in which Israel stood to the imperial power, generally assumed its first concrete shape in the form of a distinct relation to Asshur (Assyria). And from that time forth the imperial power in the mouth of the prophet is no longer a majestic thing without a name; but although the notion of the imperial power was not yet embodied in Asshur, it was called Asshur, and Asshur stood as its representative. It also necessarily follows from this, that ch. ii.-iv. and v. belong to the times anterior to Ahaz, *i.e.* to those of Uzziah and Jotham. But several different questions suggest themselves here. If ch. ii.-iv. and v. were uttered under Uzziah and Jotham, how could Isaiah begin with a promise (ch. ii. 1-4) which is repeated word for word in Mic. iv. 1 sqq., where it is the direct antithesis to ch. iii. 12, which was uttered by Micah, according to Jer. xxvi. 18, in the time of Hezekiah? Again, if we consider the advance apparent in the predictions of judgment from the general expressions with which they commence in ch. i. to the close of ch. v., in what relation does the address in ch. i. stand to ch. ii.-iv. and v., inasmuch as vers. 7-9 are not ideal (as we felt obliged to maintain, in opposition to Caspari), but have a distinct historical reference, and therefore at any rate presuppose the Syro-Ephraimitish war? And lastly, if ch. vi. does really relate, as it apparently does, to the call of Isaiah to the prophetic office, how are we to explain the singular fact, that three prophetic addresses precede the history of his call, which ought properly to stand at the commencement of the book? Drechsler and Caspari have answered this question lately, by maintaining that ch. vi. does not contain an account of the call of Isaiah to the prophetic office, but simply of the call of the prophet, who was already installed in that office, to one particular mission. The proper heading to be adopted for ch. vi. would therefore be, "The ordination of the prophet as the preacher of the judgment of hardening;" and ch. i.-v. would contain warning reproofs addressed by the prophet to the people, who were fast ripening for this judgment of hardening (reprobation), for the purpose of calling them to repentance. The final decision was still trembling in the balance. But the call to repentance was fruitless, and Israel hardened itself. And now that the goodness of God had tried in vain to lead the people to repentance, and the long-suffering of God had been wantonly abused by the people, Jehovah Himself would harden them. Looked at in this light, ch. vi. stands in its true historical place. It contains the divine sequel to that portion of Isaiah's preaching, and of the prophetic preaching generally, by which it had been preceded. But true as it is that the whole of the central portion of Israel's history, which lay midway between the commencement and the close, was divided in half by the contents of ch. vi., and that the distinctive importance of Isaiah as a prophet arose especially from the fact that he stood upon the boundary between these two historic halves; there are serious objections which present themselves to such an explanation of ch. vi. It is possible, indeed, that this distinctive importance may have been given to Isaiah's official position at his very first call. And what Umbreit says — namely, that ch. vi. must make the impression upon every unprejudiced mind, that it relates to the prophet's inaugural vision — cannot really be denied. But the position in which ch. vi. stands in the book itself must necessarily produce a contrary impression, unless it can be accounted for in some other way. Nevertheless the impression still remains (just as at ch. i. 7-9), and recurs again and again. We will therefore proceed to ch. vi. without attempting to efface it. It is possible that we may discover some other satisfactory explanation of the enigmatical position of ch. vi. in relation to what precedes.

THE PROPHET'S ACCOUNT OF HIS OWN DIVINE MISSION.—CHAP. VI.

The time of the occurrence here described, viz. "*the year that king Uzziah (Uzîyahu) died,*" was of importance to the prophet. The statement itself, in the naked form in which it is here introduced, is much more emphatic than if it commenced with "it came to pass" (*vay'hi;* cf. Ex. xvi. 6, Prov. xxiv. 17). It was the year of Uzziah's death, not the first year of Jotham's reign; that is to say, Uzziah was still reigning, although his death was near at hand. If this is the sense in which the words are to be understood, then, even if the chapter before us contains an account of Isaiah's first call, the heading to ch. i., which dates the ministry of the prophet from the time of Uzziah, is quite correct, inasmuch as, although his public ministry under Uzziah was very short, this is properly to be included, not only on account of its own importance, but as inaugurating a new era (*lit.* "an epoch-making beginning"). But is it not stated in 2 Chron. xxvi. 22, that Isaiah wrote a historical work embracing the whole of Uzziah's reign? Unquestionably; but it by no means follows from this, that he commenced his ministry long before the death of Uzziah. If Isaiah received his call in the year that Uzziah died, this historical work contained a retrospective view of the life and times of Uzziah, the close of which coincided with the call of the prophetic author, which made a deep incision into the history of Israel. Uzziah reigned fifty-two years (809–758 B.C.). This lengthened period was just the same to the kingdom of Judah as the shorter age of Solomon to that of all Israel, viz. a time of vigorous and prosperous peace, in which the nation was completely overwhelmed with manifestations of divine love. But the riches of divine goodness had no more influence upon it, than the troubles through which it had passed before. And now the eventful change took place in the relation between Israel and Jehovah, of which Isaiah was chosen to be the instrument before and above all other prophets. The year in which all this occurred was the year of Uzziah's death. It was in this year that Israel as a people was given up to hardness of heart, and as a kingdom and country to devastation and annihilation by the imperial power of the world. How significant a fact, as Jerome observes in connection with this passage, that the year of Uzziah's death should be the year in which Romulus was born; and that it was only a short time after the death of Uzziah (viz. 754 B.C. according to Varro's chronology) that Rome itself was founded! The national glory of Israel died out with king Uzziah, and has never revived to this day.

In that year, says the prophet, "*I saw the Lord of all sitting upon a high and exalted throne, and His borders filling the temple.*" Isaiah *saw*, and that not when asleep and dreaming; but God gave him, when awake, an insight into the invisible world, by opening an inner sense for the supersensuous, whilst the action of the outer senses was suspended, and by condensing the supersensuous into a sensuous form, on account of the composite nature of man and the limits of his present state. This was the mode of revelation peculiar to an ecstatic vision (ἐν ἐκστάσει, Eng. ver. "in a trance," or ἐν πνεύματι, "in the spirit"). Isaiah is here carried up into heaven; for although in other instances it was undoubtedly the earthly temple which was presented to a prophet's view in an ecstatic vision (Amos ix. 1; Ezek. viii. 3, x. 4, 5; cf. Acts xxii. 17), yet here, as the description which follows clearly proves, the "*high and exalted throne*"[1] is the *heavenly antitype* of the earthly throne which was formed by the ark of the covenant; and the "*temple*" (*hēcâl*: lit. a spacious hall, the name given to the temple as the palace of God the King) is the temple in heaven, as in Ps. xi. 4, xviii. 7, xxix. 9, and many other passages. There the prophet sees the Sovereign Ruler, or, as we prefer to render the noun, which is formed from '*âdan* = *dūn*, "*the Lord of all*" (*All-herrn*, sovereign or absolute Lord), seated upon the throne, and in human form (Ezek. i. 26), as is proved by the robe with a train, whose flowing ends or borders (*fimbriœ: shūlim*, as in Ex. xxviii. 33, 34) filled the hall. The Sept., Targum, Vulgate, etc., have dropped the figure of the robe and train, as too anthropomorphic. But John, in his Gospel, is bold enough to say that it was Jesus whose glory Isaiah saw (John xii. 41). And truly so, for the incarnation of God is the truth embodied in all the scriptural anthropomorphisms, and the name of Jesus is the manifested mystery of the name Jehovah. The heavenly temple is that super-terrestrial place, which Jehovah transforms into heaven and a temple, by manifesting Himself there to angels and saints. But whilst He manifests His glory there, He is obliged also to veil it, because created beings are unable to bear it. But that which veils His glory is no less splendid, than that portion of it which is revealed. And this was the truth embodied for Isaiah in the long robe and train. He saw the Lord, and what more he saw was the all-filling robe of the indescribable One. As far as the eye of the seer could look at first, the ground was covered by this splendid robe. There was consequently no room for any one to stand. And the vision of the seraphim is in accordance with this. Ver. 2. "*Above it stood seraphim: each one had six wings; with two he covered his face, and with two he covered his feet, and with two he did fly.*" We must not render מִמַּעַל לוֹ "near him;" for although עַל or מֵעַל is applied to a person standing near or over against another who is sitting down (Ex. xviii. 13; Jer. xxxvi. 21; compare 2 Chron. xxvi. 19, where the latter is used

---

[1] It is to this, and not to '*Adonâi*, as the Targum and apparently the accents imply, that the words "high and exalted" refer.

to signify " over against" the altar of incense), and is used in this sense to denote the attitude of spirits (Job i. 6; 1 Kings xxii. 19; Zech. vi. 5), and even of men (Zech. iv. 14), in relation to God when seated on His throne, in which case it cannot possibly be employed in the sense of " towering above;" yet מִמַּעַל לוֹ, the strongest expression for *supra*, cannot be employed in any other than a literal sense here; for which reason Rashi and the Targums understand it as signifying "above in the attitude of service," and the accentuation apparently, though erroneously, implies this (Luzzatto). What Isaiah meant by this standing above, may be inferred from the use which the seraphim are said to have made of their wings. The imperfects do not describe what they were accustomed to do (Böttcher and others), but what the seer saw them do: with two of their six wings he saw them fly. Thus they stood flying, *i.e.* they hovered or soared (cf. Num. xiv. 14), as both the earth and stars are said to stand, although suspended in space (Job xxvi. 7). The seraphim would not indeed tower above the head of Him that sat upon the throne, but they hovered above the robe belonging to Him with which the hall was filled, sustained by two extended wings, and covering their faces with two other wings in their awe at the divine glory (Targ. *ne videant*), and their feet with two others, in their consciousness of the depth at which the creature stands below the Holiest of all (Targ. *ne videantur*), just as the cherubim are described as veiling their bodies in Ezek. i. 11. This is the only passage in the Scriptures in which the seraphim are mentioned. According to the orthodox view, which originated with Dionysius the Areopagite, they stand at the head of the nine choirs of angels, the first rank consisting of *seraphim, cherubim*, and *throni*. And this is not without support, if we compare the cherubim mentioned in Ezekiel, which carried the chariot of the divine throne; whereas here the seraphim are said to surround the seat on which the Lord was enthroned. In any case, the seraphim and cherubim were heavenly beings of different kinds; and there is no weight in the attempts made by Hendewerk and Stickel to prove that they are one and the same. And certainly the name *seraphim* does not signify merely spirits as such, but even, if not the highest of all, yet a distinct order from the rest; for the Scriptures really teach that there are gradations in rank in the hierarchy of heaven. Nor were they mere symbols or fanciful images, as Hävernick imagines, but real spiritual beings, who visibly appeared to the prophet, and that in a form corresponding to their own supersensuous being, and to the design of the whole transaction. Whilst these seraphim hovered above on both sides of Him that sat upon the throne, and therefore formed two opposite choirs, each ranged in a semicircle, they presented antiphonal worship to Him that sat upon the throne.

Ver. 3. "*And one cried to the other, and said, Holy, holy, holy is Jehovah of hosts: filling the whole earth is His glory.*" The meaning is not that they all lifted up their voice in concert at one and the same time (just as in Ps. xlii. 8 *el* is not used in this sense, viz. as equivalent to *c'neged*), but that there was a continuous and unbroken antiphonal song. One set commenced, and the others responded, either repeating the "*Holy, holy, holy,*" or following with "*filling the whole earth is His glory.*" Isaiah heard this antiphonal or "hypophonal" song of the seraphim, not merely that he might know that the uninterrupted worship of God was their blessed employment, but because it was with this doxology as with the doxologies of the Apocalypse, it had a certain historical significance in common with the whole scene. God is in Himself the *Holy One* (*kâdōsh*), *i.e.* the separate One, beyond or above the world, true light, spotless purity, the perfect One. His *glory* (*câbod*) is His manifested holiness, as Oetinger and Bengel express it, just as, on the other hand, His holiness is His veiled or hidden glory. The design of all the work of God is that His holiness should become universally manifest, or, what is the same thing, that His glory should become the fulness of the whole earth (ch. xi. 9; Num. xiv. 21; Hab. ii. 14). This design of the work of God stands before God as eternally present; and the seraphim also have it ever before them in its ultimate completion, as the theme of their song of praise. But Isaiah was a man living in the very midst of the history that was moving on towards this goal; and the cry of the seraphim, in the precise form in which it reached him, showed him to what it would eventually come on earth, whilst the heavenly shapes that were made visible to him helped him to understand the nature of that divine glory with which the earth was to be filled. The whole of the book of Isaiah contains traces of the impression made by this ecstatic vision. The favourite name of God in the mouth of the prophet, viz. "the Holy One of Israel" (*kedosh Yisrael*), is the echo of this seraphic *sanctus*; and the fact that this name already occurs with such marked preference on the part of the prophet in the addresses contained in ch. i. 2-iv. 5, supports the view that Isaiah is here describing his own first call. All the prophecies of Isaiah carry this name of God as their stamp. It occurs twenty-nine times (including ch. x. 17, xliii. 15, xlix. 7), viz. twelve times in ch. i.-xxxix., and seventeen times in ch. xl.-lxvi. As Luzzatto has well observed, "the prophet, as if with a presentiment that the authenticity of the second part of his book would be disputed, has stamped both parts with this name of God, 'the Holy One of Israel,' as if with his own seal." The only other passages in which the word occurs, are three times in the Psalms (Ps. lxxi. 22, lxxviii. 41, lxxxix. 19), and twice in Jeremiah (Jer. l. 29, li. 5), and that not without an allusion to Isaiah. It forms an essential part of Isaiah's distinctive prophetic signature. And here we are standing at the source from which it sprang. But did this thrice-holy refer to the triune God? Knobel contents himself with saying that the threefold repetition of the word "holy" serves to give it the greater emphasis. No doubt men are accustomed to say three times what they wish to say in an exhaustive and satisfying manner; for three is the number of expanded unity, of satisfied and satisfying development, of the key-note extended into the chord. But why is this? The Pythagoreans said that numbers were the first principle of all things; but the Scriptures, according to which God created the world in twice three days by ten mighty words, and completed it in seven days, teach us that God is the first principle of all numbers. The fact that three is the number of developed and yet self-contained unity, has its ultimate ground in the circumstance that it is the number of the trinitarian process; and consequently the trilogy (*trisagion*) of the seraphim (like that of the cherubim in Rev. iv. 8), whether Isaiah was aware of it or no, really pointed in the distinct consciousness of the spirits themselves to the triune God.

When Isaiah heard this, he stood entranced at the farthest possible distance from Him that sat upon the throne, namely, under the door of the heavenly palace or temple. What he still further felt and saw, he proceeds to relate in ver. 4: "*And the foundations of the thresholds shook with the voice of them that cried; and the house became full of smoke.*" By '*ammoth hassippim*, the LXX., Vulgate, Syriac, and others understand the posts of the lintels, the supporting beams of the *superliminaria*, which closed the doorway at the top. But as *saph* is only used in other places to signify the threshold and porch (*limen* and *vestibulum*), '*ammoth hassippim* must be understood here in the (perfectly appropriate) sense of "the foundations of the thresholds" ('*ammâh*, which bears the same relation to אֵם, mother, as *matrix* to *mater*, is used to denote the receptive basis into which the door-steps with their plugs were inserted, like the talmudic *ammetâh derēchayyâh*, the frame or box of the hand-mill (*Berachoth* 18*b*), and *ammath megērah*, the wood-work which runs along the back of the saw and keeps it firmly extended (*Kelim* 21, 3); compare the "*Schraubenmutter*," literally screw-*mother*, or female screw, which receives and holds the cylindrical screw). Every time that the choir of seraphim (הַקֹּרֵא: compare such collective singulars as *hâ'oreb*, the ambush, in Josh. viii. 19; *hechâlutz*, the men of war, in Josh. vi. 7, etc.) began their song, the support of the threshold of the porch in which Isaiah was standing trembled. The building was seized with reverential awe throughout its whole extent, and in its deepest foundations: for in the blessed state beyond, nothing stands immoveable or unsusceptible in relation to the spirits there; but all things form, as it were, the *accidentia* of their free personality, yielding to their impressions, and voluntarily following them in all their emotions. The house was also "*filled with smoke.*" Many compare this with the similar occurrence in connection with the dedication of Solomon's temple (1 Kings viii. 10); but Drechsler is correct in stating that the two cases are not parallel, for there God simply attested His own presence by the cloud of smoke behind which He concealed Himself, whereas here there was no need of any such self-attestation. Moreover, in this instance God does not dwell in the cloud and thick darkness, whilst the smoke is represented as the effect of the songs of praise in which the seraphim have joined, and not of the presence of God. The smoke arose from the altar of incense mentioned in ver. 6. But when Drechsler says that it was the prayers of *saints* (as in Rev. v. 8, viii. 3, 4), which ascended to the Lord in the smoke, this is a thought which is quite out of place here. The smoke was the immediate consequence of the seraphs' song of praise.

This begins to throw a light upon the name *seraphim*, which may help us to decipher it. The name cannot possibly be connected with *sâráph*, a snake (Sanscr. *sarpa*, Lat. *serpens*); and to trace the word to a verb *sâraph* in the sense of the Arabic *'sarafa* (*'sarufa*), to tower high, to be exalted, or highly honoured (as Gesenius, Hengstenberg, Hofmann, and others have done), yields a sense which does not very strongly commend itself. On the other hand, to follow Knobel, who reads *shârâthim* (worshippers of God), and thus presents the Lexicon with a new word, and to pronounce the word *seraphim* a copyist's error, would be a rash concession to the heaven-storming omnipotence which is supposed to reside in the ink of a German scholar. It is hardly admissible, however, to interpret the name as signifying directly spirits of light or fire, since the true meaning of *sâraph* is not *urere* (to burn), but *comburere* (to set on fire or burn up). Umbreit endeavours to do justice to this transitive meaning by adopting the explanation " fiery beings," by which all earthly corruption is opposed and destroyed. The vision itself, however, appears to point to a much more distinctive and special meaning in the name, which only occurs in this passage of Isaiah. We shall have more to say upon this point presently.

The seer, who was at first overwhelmed and intoxicated by the majestic sight, now recovers his self-consciousness. Ver. 5. " *Then said I, Woe to me! for I am lost; for I am a man of unclean lips, and I am dwelling among a people of unclean lips: for mine eyes have seen the King, Jehovah of hosts.*" That a man cannot see God without dying is true in itself, and was an Old Testament conviction throughout (Ex. xxxiii. 20, etc.). He must die, because the holiness of God is to the sinner a consuming fire (ch. xxxiii. 14); and the infinite distance between the creature and the Creator is sufficient of itself to produce a prostrating effect, which even the seraphim could not resist without veiling their faces. Isaiah therefore regarded himself as lost (*nidmêthi*, like ὄλωλα, *perii*, a preterite denoting the fact which, although not outwardly completed, is yet effected so far as a man's own consciousness is concerned), and all the more because he himself was of unclean lips, and he was also a member of a nation of unclean lips. The unholiness of his own person was doubled, in consequence of the closeness of the natural connection, by the unholiness of the nation to which he belonged. He designates this unholiness as uncleanness of lips, because he found himself transported into the midst of choirs of beings who were praising the Lord with pure lips; and he calls the King *Jehovah*, because, although he had not seen Jehovah face to face, he had seen the throne, and the all-filling robe, and the seraphim who surrounded and did homage to Him that sat upon the throne; and therefore, as he had seen the heavenly King in His revealed majesty, he describes the scene according to the impression that he had received. But to stand here in front of Jehovah of hosts, the exalted King, to whom everything does homage, and to be obliged to remain mute in the consciousness of deep uncleanness, excited within him the annihilating anguish of self-condemnation. And this is expressed in the confession made by the contrite seer.

This confession was followed by the forgiveness of his sins, of which he received an attestation through a heavenly sacrament, and which was conveyed to him through the medium of a seraphic absolution. Vers. 6, 7. "*And one of the seraphim flew to me with a red-hot coal in his hand, which he had taken with the tongs from the altar. And he touched my mouth with it, and said, Behold, this hath touched thy lips, and thine iniquity is taken away; and so thy sin is expiated.*" One of the beings hovering round the Lord (there were, therefore, a large and indefinite number) flew to the altar of incense,—the heavenly original of the altar of incense in the earthly temple, which was reckoned as belonging to the Most Holy Place,—and took from this altar a *ritzpâh, i.e.* either a red-hot stone (Vulg. *calculum*, Ar. *radfe* or *radafe*), or, according to the prevailing tradition, a red-hot coal (*vid. râtzĕph = râshaph*, to scatter sparks, sparkle, or glow: syn. *gacheleth*), and that with a pair of tongs, because even a seraph's hand cannot touch the vessels consecrated to God, or the sacrifices that belong to Him. With this red-hot coal he flew to Isaiah, and having touched his mouth with it, *i.e.* that member of his body of whose uncleanness he had more especially complained (cf. Jer. i. 9, where the prophet's mouth is touched by Jehovah's hand, and made eloquent in consequence), he assured him of the forgiveness of his sins, which coincided with the application of this sacramental sign. The *Vav* connects together what is affirmed by *nâga‘* (hath touched) and *sâr* (a taker away) as being simultaneous; the *zeh* (this) points as a neuter to the red-hot coal. The future *tecuppâr* is a future consec., separated by *Vav* conversive for the purpose of bringing the subject into greater prominence; as it is practically impossible that the removal of guilt should be thought of as immediate and momentary, and the expiation as occurring gradually. The fact that the guilt was taken away was the very proof that the expiation was complete. *Cipper*, with the "sin" in the accusative, or governed by עַל, signifies to cover it up, extinguish, or destroy it (for the primary meaning, *vid.* ch. xxviii. 18), so that it has no existence in relation to the penal justice of God. All sinful uncleanness was burned away from the prophet's mouth. The seraph, therefore, did here what his name denotes: he burned up or burned away (*comburit*). He did this, however, not by virtue of his own fiery nature, but by means of the divine fire which he had taken from the heavenly altar. As the smoke which filled the house came from the altar, and arose in consequence of the adoration offered to the Lord by the seraphim, not only must the incense-offering upon the altar and this adoration be closely connected; but the fire, which revealed itself in the smoke and consumed the incense-offering, and which must necessarily have been divine because of its expiatory power, was an effect of the love of God with which He reciprocated the offerings of the seraphim. A fiery look from God, and that a fiery look of pure love as the seraphim were sinless, had kindled the sacrifice. Now, if the fact that a seraph absolved the seer by means of this fire of love is to be taken as an illustrative example of the historical calling of the seraphim, they were the vehicles and media of the fire of divine love, just as the cherubim in Ezekiel are vehicles and media of the fire of divine wrath. For just as, in the case before us, a seraph takes the fire of love from the altar; so there, in Ezek. x. 6, 7, a cherub takes the fire of wrath from the throne-chariot. Consequently the cherubim appear as the vehicles and media of the wrath which destroys sinners, or rather of the divine *doxa*, with its fiery side turned towards the world; and the seraphim as the vehicles and media of the love which destroys sin, or of the same divine *doxa* with its light side towards the world.[1]

When Isaiah had been thus absolved, the true object of the heavenly scene was made apparent. Ver. 8. " *Then I heard the voice of the Lord, saying, Whom shall I send, and who will go for us? Then I said, Behold me here; send me!*" The plural "for us" (*lânu*) is not to be accounted for on the ground that, in a case of reflection or self-consultation, the subject also stands as the object in antithesis to itself (as Hitzig supposes); nor is it a *pluralis majestatis*, as Knobel maintains; nor is the original abstract signification of the plural hinted at, as Meier thinks. The plural is no doubt used here with reference to the seraphim, who formed, together with the Lord, one deliberative council (*sōd kedoshim*, Ps. lxxxix. 8), as in 1 Kings xxii. 19–22, Dan. iv. 14, etc.; just as, from their very nature as "sons of God" (*b'nē Hâ-elohim*), they made one family with God their Creator (*vid.* Eph. iii. 15), all linked so closely together that they themselves could be called Elohim, like God their Creator, just as in 1 Cor. xii. 12 the church of believers is called *Christos*, like Christ its head. The task for which the right man was sought was not merely *divine*, but heavenly in the broadest sense : for it is not only a matter in which God Himself is interested, that the earth should become full of the glory of God, but this is also an object of solicitude to the spirits that minister unto Him. Isaiah, whose anxiety to serve the Lord was no longer suppressed by the consciousness of his own sinfulness, no sooner heard the voice of the Lord, than he exclaimed, in holy self-consciousness, " Behold me here; send me." It is by no means a probable thing, that he had already acted as a messenger of God, or held the office of prophet. For if the joy, with which he offered himself here as the messenger of God, was the direct consequence of the forgiveness of sins, of which he had received the seal; the consciousness of his own personal sinfulness, and his membership in a sinful nation, would certainly have prevented him hitherto from coming forward to denounce

---

[1] Seraphic love is the expression used in the language of the church to denote the *ne plus ultra* of holy love in the creature. The Syriac fathers regarded the burning coal as the symbol of the incarnate Son of God, who is often designated in poetry as the "live or burning coal" (*kemurto denuro*): *DMZ.* 1860, pp. 679, 681.

judgment upon that nation. And as the prophetic office as such rested upon an extraordinary call from God, it may fairly be assumed, that when Isaiah relates so extraordinary a call as this, he is describing the sealing of his prophetic office, and therefore his own first call.

This is confirmed by the words in which his commission is expressed, and the substance of the message.—Vers. 9, 10. "*He said, Go, and tell this people, Hear on, and understand not; and look on, but perceive not. Make ye the heart of this people greasy, and their ears heavy, and their eyes sticky; that they may not see with their eyes, and hear with their ears, and their heart understand, and they be converted, and one heal them.*" "*This people*" points back to the people of unclean lips, among whom Isaiah had complained of dwelling, and whom the Lord would not call "my people." It was to go to this people and preach to them, and therefore to be the prophet of this people, that he was called. But how mournful does the divine commission sound! It was the terrible opposite of that seraphic mission, which the prophet had experienced in himself. The seraph had absolved Isaiah by the burning coal, that he as prophet might not absolve, but harden his people by his word. They were to hear and see, and that continually as the *gerundives* imply (Ges. § 131, 3, *b*; Ewald, § 280, *b*), by having the prophet's preaching *actu directo* constantly before them; but not to their salvation. The two prohibitory expressions, "understand not" and "perceive not," show what the result of the prophet's preaching was to be, according to the judicial will of God. And the imperatives in ver. 10 are not to be understood as simply instructing the prophet to tell the people what God had determined to do; for the fact that "prophets are often said to do what they announce as about to happen," in proof of which Jer. i. 10 is sometimes quoted (cf. Jer. xxxi. 28; Hos. vi. 5; Ezek. xliii. 3), has its truth not in a rhetorical figure, but in the very nature of the divine word. The prophet was the organ of the word of God, and the word of God was the expression of the will of God, and the will of God is a divine act that has not yet become historical. For this reason a prophet might very well be said to perform what he announced as about to happen: God was the *causa efficiens principalis*, the word was the *causa media*, and the prophet the *causa ministerialis*. This is the force of the three imperatives; they are three figurative expressions of the idea of hardening. The first, *hishmin*, signifies to make fat (*pinguem*), *i.e.* without susceptibility or feeling for the operations of divine grace (Ps. cxix. 70); the second, *hicbīd*, to make heavy, more especially heavy or dull of hearing (ch. lix. 1); the third, הֵשַׁע or הָשַׁע (whence the imperative הָשַׁע or הָשַׁע), to smear thickly, or paste over, *i.e.* to put upon a person what is usually the result of weak eyes, which become firmly closed by the hardening of the adhesive substance secreted in the night. The three future clauses, with "lest" (*pen*), point back to these three imperatives in inverse order: their spiritual sight, spiritual hearing, and spiritual feeling were to be taken away, their eyes becoming blind, and their ears deaf, and their hearts being covered over with the grease of insensibility. Under the influence of these futures the two preterites שָׁב וְרָפָא לוֹ affirm what might have been the result if this hardening had not taken place, but what would never take place now. The expression רָפָא ל is used in every other instance in a transitive sense, "to heal a person or a disease," and never in the sense of becoming well or being healed; but in the present instance it acquires a passive sense from the so-called impersonal construction (Ges. § 137, 3), "and one heal it," *i.e.* "and it be healed:" and it is in accordance with this sense that it is paraphrased in Mark iv. 12, whereas in the three other passages in which the words are quoted in the New Testament (viz. Matthew, John, and Acts) the Septuagint rendering is adopted, "and I should heal them" (God Himself being taken as the subject). The commission which the prophet received, reads as though it were quite irreconcilable with the fact that God, as the Good, can only will what is good. But our earlier doctrinarians have suggested the true solution, when they affirm that God does not harden men *positive aut effective*, since His true will and direct work are man's salvation, but *occasionaliter et eventualiter*, since the offers and displays of salvation which man receives necessarily serve to fill up the measure of his sins, and *judicialiter* so far as it is the judicial will of God, that what was originally ordained for man's salvation should result after all in judgment, in the case of any man upon whom grace has ceased to work, because all its ways and means have been completely exhausted. It is not only the loving will of God which is good, but also the wrathful will into which His loving will changes, when determinately and obstinately resisted. There is a self-hardening in evil, which renders a man thoroughly incorrigible, and which, regarded as the fruit of his moral behaviour, is no less a judicial punishment inflicted by God, than self-induced guilt on the part of man. The two are bound up in one another, inasmuch as sin from its very nature bears its own punishment, which consists in the wrath of God excited by sin. For just as in all the good that men do, the active principle is the love of God; so in all the harm that they do, the active principle is the wrath of God. An evil act in itself is the result of self-determination proceeding from a man's own will; but evil, regarded as the mischief in which evil acting quickly issues, is the result of the inherent wrath of God, which is the obverse of His inherent love; and when a man hardens himself in evil, it is the inward working of God's peremptory wrath. To this wrath Israel had delivered itself up through its continued obstinacy in sinning. And consequently the Lord now proceeded to shut the door of repentance against His people. Nevertheless He directed the prophet to preach repentance, because the judgment of hardness suspended over the people as a whole did not preclude the possibility of the salvation of individuals.

Isaiah heard with sighing, and yet with obedience, in what the mission to which he had so cheerfully offered himself was to consist. Ver. 11a. "*Then said I, Lord, how long?*" He inquired how long this service of hardening and this state of hardness were to continue,—a question forced from him by his sympathy with the nation to which he himself belonged (cf. Ex. xxxii. 9–14), and one which was warranted by the certainty that God, who is ever true to His promises, could not cast off Israel as a people for ever. The answer follows in vers. 11*b*–13 : "*Until towns are wasted without inhabitant, and houses are without man, and the ground shall be laid waste, a wilderness, and Jehovah shall put men far away, and there shall be many forsaken places within the land. And is there still a tenth therein, this also again is given up to destruction, like the terebinth and like the oak, of which, when they are felled, only a root-stump remains : such a root-stump is a holy seed.*" The answer is intentionally commenced, not with עַד־פִּי, but with עַד אֲשֶׁר אִם

(the expression only occurs again in Gen. xxviii. 15 and Num. xxxii. 17), which, even without dropping the conditional force of אִם, signified that the hardening judgment would only come to an end when the condition had been fulfilled, that towns, houses, and the soil of the land of Israel and its environs had been made desolate, in fact, utterly and universally desolate, as the three definitions (without inhabitant, without man, wilderness) affirm. The expression *richak* (put far away) is a general and enigmatical description of exile or captivity (cf. Joel iv. 6, Jer. xxvii. 10); the literal term *gâlâh* has been already used in ch. v. 13. Instead of a national term being used, we find here simply the general expression "*men*" (*ethhâ-'âdâm*; the consequence of depopulation, viz. the entire absence of men, being expressed in connection with the depopulation itself. The participial noun *hâ'azubâh* (the forsaken) is a collective term for places once full of life, that had afterwards died out and fallen into ruins (ch. xvii. 2, 9). This judgment would be followed by a second, which would expose the still remaining tenth of the nation to a sifting. וְהָיָה שָׁב, to *become again* (Ges. § 142, 3); הָיָה לְבָעֵר, not as in ch. v. 5, but as in ch. iv. 4, after Num. xxiv. 22: the feminine does not refer to the land of Israel (Luzzatto), but to the tenth. Up to the words "given up to destruction," the announcement is a threatening one; but from this point to "remains" a consolatory prospect begins to dawn; and in the last three words this brighter prospect, like a distant streak of light, bounds the horizon of the gloomy prophecy. It shall happen as with the terebinth and oak. These trees were selected as illustrations, not only because they were so near akin to evergreens, and produced a similar impression, or because there were so many associations connected with them in the olden times of Israel's history; but also because they formed such fitting symbols of Israel, on account of their peculiar facility for springing up again from the root (like the beech and nut, for example), even when they had been completely felled. As the forms *yabbesheth* (dryness), *dalleketh* (fever), *'avvereth* (blindness), *shachepheth* (consumption), are used to denote certain qualities or states, and those for the most part faulty ones (*Concord.* p. 1350); so *shalleceth* here does not refer to the act itself of felling or casting away, but rather to the condition of a tree that has been hewn or thrown down; though not to the condition of the trunk as it lies prostrate upon the ground, but to that of the root, which is still left in the earth. Of this tree, that had been deprived of its trunk and crown, there was still a *mazzebeth* (a kindred form of *mazzebâh*), *i.e.* a root-stump (*truncus*) fast in the ground. The tree was not yet entirely destroyed; the root-stump could shoot out and put forth branches again. And this would take place: the root-stump of the oak or terebinth, which was a symbol of Israel, was "a holy seed." The root-stump was the remnant that had survived the judgment, and this remnant would become a seed, out of which a new Israel would spring up after the old had been destroyed. Thus in a few weighty words is the way sketched out, which God would henceforth take with His people. The passage contains an outline of the history of Israel to the end of time. Israel as a nation was indestructible, by virtue of the promise of God; but the mass of the people were doomed to destruction through the judicial sentence of God, and only a remnant, which would be converted, would perpetuate the nationality of Israel, and inherit the glorious future. This law of a blessing sunk in the depths of the curse actually inflicted, still prevails in the history of the Jews. The way of salvation is open to all. Individuals find it, and give us a presentiment of what might be and is to be; but the great mass are hopelessly lost, and only when they have been swept away will a holy seed, saved by the covenant-keeping God, grow up into a new and holy Israel, which, according to ch. xxvii. 6, will fill the earth with its fruits, or, as the apostle expresses it in Rom. xi. 12, become "the riches of the Gentiles."

Now, if the impression which we have received from ch. vi. is not a false one,—namely, that the prophet is here relating his first call to the prophetic office, and not, as Seb. Schmidt observes, his call to one particular duty (*ad unum specialem actum officii*),—this impression may be easily verified, inasmuch as the addresses in ch. i.–v. will be sure to contain the elements which are here handed to the prophet by revelation, and the result of these addresses will correspond to the sentence judicially pronounced here. And the conclusion to which we have come will stand this test. For the prophet, in the very first address, after pointing out to the nation as a whole the gracious pathway of justification and sanctification, takes the turn indicated in ch. vi. 11–13, in full consciousness that all is in vain. And the theme of the second address is, that it will be only after the overthrow of the false glory of Israel that the true glory promised can possibly be realized, and that after the destruction of the great body of the people only a small remnant will live to see this realization. The parable with which the third begins, rests upon the supposition that the measure of the nation's iniquity is full; and the threatening of judgment introduced by this parable agrees substantially, and in part verbally, with the divine answer received by the prophet to his question "How long?" On every side, therefore, the opinion is confirmed, that in ch. vi. Isaiah describes his own consecration to the prophetic office. The addresses in ch. ii.–iv. and v., which belong to the times of Uzziah and Jotham, do not fall earlier than the year of Uzziah's death, from which point the whole of Jotham's sixteen years' reign lay open before them. Now, as Micah commenced his ministry in Jotham's reign, though his book was written in the form of a complete and chronologically indivisible summary, by the working up of the prophecies which he delivered under Jotham, Ahaz, and Hezekiah, and was then read or published in the time of Hezekiah, as we may infer from Jer. xxvi. 18, it is quite possible that Isaiah may have taken from Micah's own lips (though not from Micah's book) the words of promise in ch. ii. 1–4, which he certainly borrowed from some quarter. The notion that this word of promise originated with a third prophet (who must have been Joel, if he were one of the prophets known to us), is rendered very improbable by the many marks of Micah's prophetic peculiarities, and by its natural position in the context in which it there occurs (*vid.* Caspari, *Micha*, pp. 444–5).

Again, the *situation* of ch. vi. is not inexplicable. As Hävernick has observed, the prophet evidently intended to vindicate in ch. vi. the style and method of his previous prophecies, on the ground of the divine commission that he had received. But this only serves to explain the reason why Isaiah has not placed ch. vi. at the commencement of the collection, and not why he inserts it in this particular place. He has done this, no doubt, for the purpose of bringing close together the prophecy and its fulfilment; for whilst on the one hand the judgment of hardening suspended over the Jewish nation is brought distinctly out in the person of king Ahaz, on the other hand we find ourselves in the midst of the Syro-Ephraimitish war, which formed the introduction to the judgments of extermination predicted in ch. vi. 11-13. It is only the position of ch. i. which still remains in obscurity. If ch. i. 7-9 is to be understood in a historically literal sense, then ch. i. must have been composed after the dangers of the Syro-Ephraimitish war had been averted from Jerusalem, though the land of Judah was still bleeding with the open wounds which this war, designed as it was to destroy it altogether, had inflicted upon it. Ch. i. would therefore be of more recent origin than ch. ii.–v., and still more recent than the connected ch. vii.–xii. It is only the comparatively more general and indefinite character of ch. i. which seems at variance with this. But this difficulty is removed at once, if we assume that ch. i., though not indeed the first of the prophet's addresses, was yet in one sense the first, —namely, the first that was committed to writing, though not the first that he delivered, and that it was primarily intended to form the preface to the addresses and historical accounts in ch. ii.–xii., the contents of which were regulated by it. For ch. ii.–v. and vii.–xii. form two prophetic cycles, ch. i. being the portal which leads into them, and ch. vi. the band which connects them together. The prophetic cycle in ch. ii.–v. may be called the *Book of hardening*, as it is by Caspari, and ch. vii.–xii. the *Book of Immanuel*, as Chr. Aug. Crusius suggests, because in all the stages through which the proclamation in ch. vii.–xii. passes, the coming Immanuel is the banner of consolation, which it lifts up even in the midst of the judgments already breaking upon the people, in accordance with the doom pronounced upon them in ch. **vi.**

PART II.

CONSOLATION OF IMMANUEL IN THE MIDST OF THE ASSYRIAN OPPRESSIONS.—Chap. VII.–XII.

DIVINE SIGN OF THE VIRGIN'S WONDROUS SON.—CHAP. VII.

As the following prophecies could not be understood apart from the historical circumstances to which they refer, the prophet commences with a historical announcement. Ver. 1. "*It came to pass, in the days of Ahaz the son of Jotham, the son of Uzziah* (*Uziyâhu*), *king of Judah, that Rezin the king of Aramæa, and Pekah* (*Pekach*) *the son of Remaliah* (*Remalyâhu*), *king of Israel, went up toward Jerusalem to war against it, and* (*he*) *could not make war upon it.*" We have the same words, with only slight variations, in the history of the reign of Ahaz in 2 Kings xvi. 5. That the author of the book of Kings copied them from the book of Isaiah, will be very apparent when we come to examine the historical chapters (xxxvi.–xxxix.) in their relation to the parallel sections of the book of Kings. In the passage before us, the want of independence on the part of the author of the book of Kings is confirmed by the fact that he not only repeats, but also interprets, the words of Isaiah. Instead of saying, "And (he) could not make war upon it," he says, "And they besieged Ahaz, and could not make war." The singular *yâcol* (he could) of Isaiah is changed into the simpler plural, whilst the statement that the two allies could not assault or storm Jerusalem (which must be the meaning of *nilcham 'al* in the passage before us), is more clearly defined by the additional information that they did besiege Ahaz, but to no purpose (*tzur 'al*, the usual expression for *obsidione claudere*; cf. Deut. xx. 19). The statement that "they besieged Ahaz" cannot merely signify that "they attempted to besiege him," although nothing further is known about this siege. But happily we have two accounts of the Syro-Ephraimitish war (2 Kings xvi. and 2 Chron. xxviii.). The two historical books complete one another. The book of Kings relates that the invasion of Judah by the two allies commenced at the end of Jotham's reign (2 Kings xv. 37); and in addition to the statement taken from Isa. vii. 1, it also mentions that Rezin conquered the seaport town of Elath, which then belonged to the kingdom of Judah; whilst the Chronicles notice the fact that Rezin brought a number of Judæan captives to Damascus, and that Pekah conquered Ahaz in a bloody and destructive battle. Indisputable as the credibility of these events may be, it is nevertheless very difficult to connect them together, either substantially or chronologically, in a certain and reliable manner, as Caspari has attempted to do in his monograph on the Syro-Ephraimitish war (1849). We may refer here to our own manner of dovetailing the historical accounts of Ahaz and the Syro-Ephraimitish war in the introduction to the present work (p. 41 sqq.). If we could assume that יָכֹל (not יָכְלוּ) was the authentic reading, and that the failure of the attempt to take Jerusalem, which is mentioned here, was occasioned by the strength of the city itself, and not by the intervention of Assyria, —so that ver. 1*b* did not contain such an anticipation as we have supposed (p. 43), although summary anticipations of this kind were customary with biblical historians, and more especially with Isaiah,—the course of events might be arranged in the following manner, viz., that whilst Rezin was on his way to Elath, Pekah resolved to attack Jerusalem, but failed in his attempt; but that Rezin was more successful in his expedition, which was a much easier one, and after the conquest of Elath united his forces with those of his allies.

It is this which is referred to in ver. 2 : "*And it was told the house of David, Aram has settled down upon Ephraim: then his heart shook, and the heart of his people, as trees of the wood shake before the wind.*" The expression *nuach ʽal* (settled down upon) is explained in 2 Sam. xvii. 12 (cf. Judg. vii. 12) by the figurative simile, "as the dew falleth upon the ground:" there it denotes a hostile invasion, here the arrival of one army to the support of another. *Ephraim* (*feminine*, like the names of countries, and of the people that are regarded as included in their respective countries: see, on the other hand, ch. iii. 8) is used as the name of the leading tribe of Israel, to signify the whole kingdom; here it denotes the whole military force of Israel. Following the combination mentioned above, we find that the allies now prepared for a second united expedition against Jerusalem. In the meantime, Jerusalem was in the condition described in ch. i. 7–9, viz. like a besieged city, in the midst of enemies plundering and burning on every side. Elath had fallen, as Rezin's timely return clearly showed; and in the prospect of his approaching junction with the allied army, it was quite natural, from a human point of view, that the court and people of Jerusalem should tremble like aspen leaves. וַיָּנַע is a contracted *fut. kal*, ending with an *a* sound on account of the guttural, as in Ruth iv. 1 (Ges. § 72, Anm. 4); and נוֹעַ, which is generally the form of the *infin. abs.* (ch. xxiv. 20), is here, and only here, the *infin. constr.* instead of נוֹעַ (cf. *noach*, Num. xi. 25; *shob*, Josh. ii. 16; *mōt*, Ps. xxxviii. 17, etc.: *vid.* Ewald, § 238, *b*).

In this season of terror Isaiah received the following divine instructions. Ver. 3. "*Then said Jehovah to Isaiah, Go forth now to meet Ahaz, thou and Shear-jashub thy son, to the end of the aqueduct of the upper pool, to the road of the fuller's field.*" The fuller's field (*sedēh cōbēs*) was situated, as we may assume with Robinson, Schultz, and Thenius, against Williams, Krafft, etc., on the western side of the city, where there is still an "upper pool" of great antiquity (2 Chron. xxxii. 30). Near to this pool the fullers, *i.e.* the cleaners and thickeners of woollen fabrics, carried on their occupation (*cōbēs*, from *cābas*, related to *cābash*, *subigere*, which bears the same relation to *ráchatz* as πλύνειν to λούειν). Robinson and his companions saw some people washing clothes at the upper pool when they were there; and, for a considerable distance round, the surface of this favourite washing and bleaching place was covered with things spread out to bleach or dry. The road (*mesillâh*), which ran past this fuller's field, was the one which leads from the western gate to Joppa. King Ahaz was there, on the west of the city, and outside the fortifications,—engaged, no doubt, in making provision for the probable event of Jerusalem being again besieged in a still more threatening manner. Jerusalem received its water supply from the upper Gihon pool, and there, according to Jehovah's directions, Isaiah was to go with his son and meet him. The two together were, as it were, a personified blessing and curse, presenting themselves to the king for him to make his own selection. For the name *Sheâr-yáshub* (which is erroneously accentuated with *tiphchah munach* instead of *merchah tiphchah*, as in ch. x. 22), *i.e.* the remnant is converted (ch. x. 21, 22), was a kind of abbreviation of the divine answer given to the prophet in ch. vi. 11–13, and was indeed at once threatening and promising, but in such a way that the curse stood in front and the grace behind. The prophetic name of Isaiah's son was intended to drive the king to Jehovah by force, through the threatening aspect it presented; and the prophetic announcement of Isaiah himself, whose name pointed to salvation, was to allure him to Jehovah with its promising tone.

No means were left untried. Ver. 4. "*And say unto him, Take heed, and keep quiet; and let not thy heart become soft from these two smoking firebrand-stumps: at the fierce anger of Rezin, and Aram, and the son of Remaliah.*" The imperative הִשָּׁמֵר (not pointed הִשָּׁמֶר, as is the case when it is to be connected more closely with what follows, and taken in the sense of *cave ne*, or even *cave ut*) warned the king against acting for himself, in estrangement from God; and the imperative *hashkēt* exhorted him to courageous calmness, secured by confidence in God; or, as Calvin expresses it, exhorted him "to restrain himself outwardly, and keep his mind calm within." The explanation given by Jewish expositors to the word *hisshamēr*, viz. *conside super fæces tuas* (Luzzatto: *vivi riposato*), according to Jer. xlviii. 11, Zeph. i. 12, yields a sense which hardly suits the exhortation. The object of terror, at which and before which the king's heart was not to despair, is introduced first of all with *Min* and then with *Beth*, as in Jer. li. 46. The two allies are designated at once as what they were in the sight of God, who sees through the true nature and future condition. They were two tails, *i.e.* nothing but the fag-ends, of wooden pokers (*lit.* stirrers, *i.e.* fire-stirrers), which would not blaze any more, but only continue smoking. They would burn and light no more, though their smoke might make the eyes smart still. Along with Rezin, and to avoid honouring him with the title of king, Aram (Syria) is especially mentioned; whilst Pekah is called Ben-Remaliah, to recal to mind his low birth, and the absence of any promise in the case of his house.

The *ya'an 'asher* ("*because*") which follows (as in Ezek. xii. 12) does not belong to ver. 4 (as might appear from the *sethume* that comes afterwards), in the sense of "do not be afraid because," etc., but is to be understood as introducing the reason for the judicial sentence in ver. 7.—Vers. 5–7. "*Because Aram hath determined evil over thee, Ephraim and the son of Remaliah* (*Remalyahu*), *saying, We will march against Judah, and terrify it, and conquer it for ourselves, and make the son of Tâb'êl king in the midst of it: thus saith the Lord Jehovah, It will not be brought about, and will not take place.*" The inference drawn by Caspari (*Krieg*, p. 98), that at the time when Isaiah said this, Judæa was not yet beaten or conquered, is at any rate not conclusive. The promise given to Ahaz was founded upon the wicked design, with which the war had been commenced. How far the allies had already gone towards this last goal, the overthrow of the Davidic sovereignty, it does not say. But we know from 2 Kings xv. 37 that the invasion had begun before Ahaz ascended the throne; and we may see from ver. 16 of Isaiah's prophecy, that the "terrifying" (*nekîtzennah*, from *kûtz*, *tædere*, *pavere*) had actually taken place; so that the "conquering" (*hibkia'*, *i.e.* splitting, forcing of the passes and fortifications, 2 Kings xxv. 4, Ezek. xxx. 16, 2 Chron xxi. 17, xxxii. 1) must also have been a thing belonging to the past. For history says nothing about a successful resistance on the part of Judah in this war. Only Jerusalem had not yet fallen, and, as the expression "king in the midst of it" shows, it is to this that the term "Judah" especially refers; just as in ch. xxiii. 13 *Asshur* is to be understood as signifying Nineveh. There they determined to enthrone a man named *Tâb'êl* (*vid.* Ezra iv. 7; it is written *Tâb'al* here in pause, although this change does not occur in other words (*e.g. Israel*) in pause—a name resembling the Syrian name *Tab-rimmon*),[1] a man who is otherwise unknown; but it never went beyond the determination, never was even on the way towards being realized, to say nothing of being fully accomplished. The allies would not succeed in altering the course of history as it had been appointed by the Lord.— Vers. 8, 9. "*For head of Aram is Damascus, and head of*

---

[1] The Hauran inscriptions contain several such composite names formed like *Tâb'êl* with *el:* see Wetzstein, *Ausgewählte griechische und lateinische Inschriften*, pp. 343–4, 361–363). By the transformation into Tab'al, as Luzzatto says, the name is changed from *Bonus Deus* to *Bonus minime*.

Damascus Rezin, and in five-and-sixty years will Ephraim as a people be broken in pieces. And head of Ephraim is Samaria, and head of Samaria the son of Remalyahu; if ye believe not, surely ye will not remain." The attempt to remove ver. 8*b*, as a gloss at variance with the context, which is supported by Eichhorn, Gesenius, Hitzig, Knobel, and others, is a very natural one; and in that case the train of thought would simply be, that the two hostile kingdoms would continue in their former relation without the annexation of Judah. But when we look more closely, it is evident that the removal of ver. 8*b* destroys both the internal connection and the external harmony of the clauses. For just as 8*a* and 8*b* correspond, so do 9*a* and 9*b*. Ephraim, *i.e.* the kingdom of the ten tribes, which has entered into so unnatural and ungodly a covenant with idolatrous Syria, will cease to exist as a nation in the course of sixty-five years; "and ye, if ye do not believe, but make flesh your arm, will also cease to exist." Thus the two clauses answer to one another: 8*b* is a prophecy announcing Ephraim's destruction, and 9*b* a warning, threatening Judah with destruction, if it rejects the promise with unbelief. Moreover, the style of 8*b* is quite in accordance with that of Isaiah (on בְּעוֹד, see ch. xxi. 16 and xvi. 14; and on מֵעָם, "away from being a people," in the sense of "so that it shall be no longer a nation," ch. xvii. 1, xxv. 2, and Jer. xlviii. 2, 42). And the doctrinal objection, that the prophecy is too minute, and therefore taken *ex eventu*, has no force whatever, since the Old Testament prophecy furnishes an abundance of examples of the same kind (*vid.* ch. xx. 3, 4, xxxviii. 5, xvi. 14, xxi. 16; Ezek. iv. 5 sqq., xxiv. 1 sqq., etc.). The only objection that can well be raised is, that the time given in ver. 8*b* is wrong, and is not in harmony with ver. 16. Now, undoubtedly the sixty-five years do not come out if we suppose the prophecy to refer to what was done by Tiglath-pileser after the Syro-Ephraimitish war, and to what was also done to Ephraim by Shalmanassar in the sixth year of Hezekiah's reign, to which ver. 16 unquestionably refers, and more especially to the former. But there is another event still, through which the existence of Ephraim, not only as a kingdom, but also as a people, was broken up,—namely, the carrying away of the last remnant of the Ephraimitish population, and the planting of colonies from

Eastern Asia by Esarhaddon[1] on Ephraimitish soil (2 Kings xvii. 24; Ezra iv. 2). Whereas the land of Judah was left desolate after the Chaldean deportation, and a new generation grew up there, and those who were in captivity were once more enabled to return; the land of Ephraim was occupied by heathen settlers, and the few who were left behind were melted up with these into the mixed people of the Samaritans, and those in captivity were lost among the heathen. We have only to assume that what was done to Ephraim by Esarhaddon, as related in the historical books, took place in the twenty-second and twenty-third years of Manasseh (the sixth year of Esarhaddon), which is very probable, since it must have been under Esarhaddon that Manasseh was carried away to Babylon about the middle of his reign (2 Chron. xxxiii. 11); and we get exactly sixty-five years from the second year of the reign of Ahaz to the termination of Ephraim's existence as a nation (viz. Ahaz, 14; Hezekiah, 29; Manasseh, 22; in all, 65). It was then that the unconditional prediction, "Ephraim as a people will be broken in pieces," was fulfilled (*yēchath mē'âm;* this is certainly not the 3d pers. fut. *kal,* but the *niphal,* Mal. ii. 5), just as the conditional threat "ye shall not remain" was fulfilled upon Judah in the Babylonian captivity. נֶאֱמַן signifies to have a fast hold, and הֶאֱמִין to prove fast-holding. If Judah did not *hold fast* to its God, it would lose its *fast hold* by losing its country, the ground beneath its feet. We have the same play upon words in 2 Chron. xx. 20. The suggestion of Geiger is a very improbable one, viz. that the original reading was אִם לֹא תַאֲמִינוּ בִּי, but that בִּי appeared objectionable, and was altered into כִּי. Why should it be objectionable, when the words form the conclusion to a direct address of Jehovah Himself, which is introduced with all solemnity? For this כִּי, passing over from a confirmative into an affirmative sense, and employed, as it is here, to introduce the apodosis of the hypothetical clause, see 1 Sam. xiv. 39, and (in the formula כִּי עַתָּה) Gen. xxxi. 42, xliii. 10, Num. xxii. 29, 33, 1 Sam. xiv. 30: their continued existence would depend upon their faith, as this *chi* emphatically declares.

Thus spake Isaiah, and Jehovah through him, to the king

[1] The meaning of this king's name is *Assur fratrem dedit* (*Asur-ach-yiddin*): vid. Oppert, *Expedition,* t. ii. p. 354.

of Judah. Whether he replied, or what reply he made, we are not informed. He was probably silent, because he carried a secret in his heart which afforded him more consolation than the words of the prophet. The invisible help of Jehovah, and the remote prospect of the fall of Ephraim, were not enough for him. His trust was in Asshur, with whose help he would have a far greater superiority over the kingdom of Israel, than Israel had over the kingdom of Judah through the help of Damascene Syria. The pious, theocratic policy of the prophet did not come in time. He therefore let the enthusiast talk on, and had his own thoughts about the matter. Nevertheless the grace of God did not give up the unhappy son of David for lost. Vers. 10, 11. "*And Jehovah continued speaking to Ahaz as follows: Ask thee a sign of Jehovah thy God, going deep down into Hades, or high up to the height above.*" Jehovah continued: what a deep and firm consciousness of the identity of the word of Jehovah and the word of the prophet is expressed in these words! According to a very marvellous interchange of idioms (*communicatio idiomatum*) which runs through the prophetic books of the Old Testament, at one time the prophet speaks as if he were Jehovah, and at another, as in the case before us, Jehovah speaks as if He were the prophet. Ahaz was to ask for a sign from Jehovah his God. Jehovah did not scorn to call Himself the God of this son of David, who had so hardened his heart. Possibly the holy love with which the expression "*thy God*" burned, might kindle a flame in his dark heart; or possibly he might think of the covenant promises and covenant duties which the words "thy God" recalled to his mind. From this, his God, he was to ask for a sign. A *sign* ('*oth*, from '*uth*, to make an incision or dent) was something, some occurrence, or some action, which served as a pledge of the divine certainty of something else. This was secured sometimes by visible miracles performed at once (Ex. iv. 8, 9), or by appointed symbols of future events (ch. viii. 18, xx. 3); sometimes by predicted occurrences, which, whether miraculous or natural, could not possibly be foreseen by human capacities, and therefore, if they actually took place, were a proof either retrospectively of the divine causality of other events (Ex. iii. 12), or prospectively of their divine certainty (ch. xxxvii. 30; Jer.

xliv. 29, 30). The thing to be confirmed on the present occasion was what the prophet had just predicted in so definite a manner, viz. the maintenance of Judah with its monarchy, and the failure of the wicked enterprise of the two allied kingdoms. If this was to be attested to Ahaz in such a way as to demolish his unbelief, it could only be effected by a miraculous sign. And just as Hezekiah asked for a sign when Isaiah foretold his recovery, and promised him the prolongation of his life for fifteen years, and the prophet gave him the sign he asked, by causing the shadow upon the royal sun-dial to go backwards instead of forwards (ch. xxxviii.); so here Isaiah meets Ahaz with the offer of such a supernatural sign, and offers him the choice of heaven, earth, and Hades as the scene of the miracle. הַעֲמֵק and הַגְבֵּהַּ are either in the infinitive absolute or in the imperative; and שְׁאָלָה is either the imperative שְׁאַל with the *He* of challenge, which is written in this form in half pause instead of שְׁאָלָה (for the two similar forms with *pashtah* and *zakeph*, vid. Dan. ix. 19), "Only ask, going deep down, or ascending to the height," without there being any reason for reading שְׁאָלָה with the tone upon the last syllable, as Hupfeld proposes, in the sense of *profundam fac* (or *faciendo*) *precationem* (*i.e.* go deep down with thy petition); or else it is the pausal subordinate form for שְׁאֵלָה, which is quite allowable in itself (cf. *yechpâtz*, the constant form in pause for *yachpōtz*, and other examples, Gen. xliii. 14, xlix. 3, 27), and is apparently preferred here on account of its consonance with לְמָעְלָה (Ewald, § 93, 3). We follow the Targum, with the Sept., Syr., and Vulgate, in giving the preference to the latter of the two possibilities. It answers to the antithesis; and if we had the words before us without points, this would be the first to suggest itself. Accordingly the words would read, Go deep down (in thy desire) to Hades, or go high up to the height; or more probably, taking העמק and הגבה in the sense of gerundives, "Going deep down to Hades, or (אוֹ from אָוָה, like *vel* from *velle* = *si velis, malis*) going high up to the height." This offer of the prophet to perform any kind of miracle, either in the world above or in the lower world, has thrown rationalistic commentators into very great perplexity. The prophet, says Hitzig, was playing a very dangerous game here; and if Ahaz had closed with his offer, Jehovah would probably have left him in the lurch. And Meier observes, that "it can never have entered the mind of an Isaiah to perform an actual miracle:" probably because no miracles were ever performed by Göthe, to whose high poetic consecration Meier compares the consecration of the prophet as described in ch. vi. Knobel answers the question, "What kind of sign from heaven would Isaiah have given in case it had been asked for?" by saying, "Probably a very simple matter." But even granting that an extraordinary heavenly phenomenon could be a "simple matter," it was open to king Ahaz not to be so moderate in his demands upon the venturesome prophet, as Knobel with his magnanimity might possibly have been. Dazzled by the glory of the Old Testament prophecy, a rationalistic exegesis falls prostrate upon the ground; and it is with such frivolous, coarse, and common words as these that it tries to escape from its difficulties. It cannot acknowledge the miraculous power of the prophet, because it believes in no miracles at all. But Ahaz had no doubt about his miraculous power, though he would not be constrained by any miracle to renounce his own plans and believe in Jehovah. Ver. 12. "*But Ahaz replied, I dare not ask, and dare not tempt Jehovah.*" What a pious sound this has! And yet his self-hardening reached its culminating point in these well-sounding words. He hid himself hypocritically under the mask of Deut. vi. 16, to avoid being disturbed in his Assyrian policy, and was infatuated enough to designate the acceptance of what Jehovah Himself had offered as tempting God. He studiously brought down upon himself the fate denounced in ch. vi., and indeed not upon himself only, but upon all Judah as well. For after a few years the forces of Asshur would stand upon the same fuller's field (ch. xxxvi. 2) and demand the surrender of Jerusalem. In that very hour, in which Isaiah was standing before Ahaz, the fate of Jerusalem was decided for more than two thousand years.

The prophet might have ceased speaking now; but in accordance with the command in ch. vi. he was obliged to speak, even though his word should be a savour of death unto death. Ver. 13. "*And he spake, Hear ye now, O house of David! Is it too little to you to weary men, that ye weary my God also?*" "He spake." Who spake? According to ver. 10 the speaker was Jehovah; yet what follows is given as the word of the prophet. Here again it is assumed that the word of the prophet was the word of God, and that the prophet was the organ of God even when he expressly distinguished between himself and God. The words were addressed to the "house of David," *i.e.* to Ahaz, including all the members of the royal family. Ahaz himself was not yet thirty years old. The prophet could very well have borne that the members of the house of David should thus frustrate all his own faithful, zealous human efforts. But they were not content with this (on the expression *minus quam vos = quam ut vobis sufficiat*, see Num. xvi. 9, Job xv. 11): they also wearied out the long-suffering of his God, by letting Him exhaust all His means of correcting them without effect. They would not believe without seeing; and when signs were offered them to see, in order that they might believe, they would not even look. Jehovah would therefore give them, against their will, a sign of His own choosing.—Vers. 14, 15. "*Therefore the Lord, He will give you a sign: Behold, the virgin conceives, and bears a son, and calls his name Immanuel. Butter and honey will he eat, at the time that he knows to refuse the evil and choose the good.*" In its form the prophecy reminds one of Gen. xvi. 11, "Behold, thou art with child, and wilt bear a son, and call his name Ishmael." Here, however, the words are not addressed to the person about to bear the child, although Matthew gives this interpretation to the prophecy;[1] for קָרָאת is not the second person, but the third, and is synonymous with קָרְאָה (according to Ges. § 74. Anm. 1), another form which is also met with in Gen. xxxiii. 11, Lev. xxv. 21, Deut. xxxi. 29, and Ps. cxviii. 23.[2] Moreover, the condition of pregnancy, which is here designated by the participial adjective הָרָה (cf. 2 Sam. xi. 5), was not an already existing one in this instance, but (as in all probability also in Judg. xiii. 5, cf. 4) something future, as well as the act of bearing, since *hinnēh* is always used by Isaiah to introduce a future occurrence. This use of *hinneh* in Isaiah is a sufficient answer to Gesenius, Knobel, and others, who understand *hâ'almâh* as referring to the young wife of the prophet himself, who was at that very time with child. But it is

---

[1] Jerome discusses this diversity in a very impartial and intelligent manner, in his *ep. ad Pammachium de optimo genere interpretandi*.

[2] The pointing makes a distinction between קָרָאת (she calls) and קָרָאתְ, as Gen. xvi. 11 should be pointed (thou callest); and Olshausen (§ 35, *b*) is wrong in pronouncing the latter a mistake.

altogether improbable that the wife of the prophet himself should be intended. For if it were to her that he referred, he could hardly have expressed himself in a more ambiguous and unintelligible manner; and we cannot see why he should not much rather have said אִשְׁתִּי or הַנְּבִיאָה, to say nothing of the fact that there is no further allusion made to any son of the prophet of that name, and that a sign of this kind founded upon the prophet's own family affairs would have been one of a very precarious nature. And the meaning and use of the word *'almâh* are also at variance with this. For whilst *bethulâh* (from *bâthal*, related to *bâdal*, to separate, *sejungere*) signifies a maiden living in seclusion in her parents' house and still a long way from matrimony, *'almâh* (from *'âlam*, related to *châlam*, and possibly also to אָלַם, to be strong, full of vigour, or arrived at the age of puberty) is applied to one fully mature, and approaching the time of her marriage.[1] The two terms could both be applied to persons who were betrothed, and even to such as were married (Joel ii. 16; Prov. xxx. 19: see Hitzig on these passages). It is also admitted that the idea of spotless virginity was not necessarily connected with *'almâh* (as in Gen. xxiv. 43, cf. 16), since there are passages—such, for example, as Song of Sol. vi. 8 —where it can hardly be distinguished from the Arabic *surrîje*; and a person who had a very young-looking wife might be said to have an *'almah* for his wife. But it is inconceivable that in a well-considered style, and one of religious earnestness, a woman who had been long married, like the prophet's own wife, could be called *hâ'almâh* without any reserve.[2] On the other hand, the expression itself warrants the assumption that by *hâ'almâh* the prophet meant one of the *'alâmoth* of the king's harem (Luzzatto); and if we consider that the birth of the child was to take place, as the prophet foresaw, in the immediate future, his thoughts might very well have been fixed upon *Abijah* (*Abi*)

[1] On the development of the meanings of *'âlam* and *châlam*, see Ges. *Thes.*, and my *Psychol.* p. 282 (see also the commentary on Job xxxix. 4). According to Jerome, *alma* was Punic also. In Arabic and Aramæan the diminutive form *guleime*, *'alleimtah*, was the favourite one, but in Syriac *'alimto* (the ripened).

[2] A young and newly-married wife might be called *callâh* (as in Homer νύμφη = *nubilis* and *nupta*; Eng. *bride*); and even in Homer a married woman, if young, is sometimes called κουριδίη ἄλοχος, but neither κούρη nor νέηνις.

bath-Zechariah (2 Kings xviii. 2 ; 2 Chron. xxix. 1), who became the mother of king Hezekiah, to whom apparently the virtues of the mother descended, in marked contrast with the vices of his father. This is certainly possible. At the same time, it is also certain that the child who was to be born was the Messiah, and not a new Israel (Hofmann, *Schriftbeweis*, ii. 1, 87, 88); that is to say, that he was no other than that " wonderful" heir of the throne of David, whose birth is hailed with joy in ch. ix., where even commentators like Knobel are obliged to admit that the Messiah is meant. It was the Messiah whom the prophet saw here as about to be born, then again in ch. ix. as actually born, and again in ch. xi. as reigning,—an indivisible triad of consolatory images in three distinct stages, interwoven with the three stages into which the future history of the nation unfolded itself in the prophet's view. If, therefore, his eye was directed towards the Abijah mentioned, he must have regarded her as the future mother of the Messiah, and her son as the future Messiah. Now it is no doubt true, that in the course of the sacred history Messianic expectations were often associated with individuals who did not answer to them, so that the Messianic prospect was moved further into the future ; and it is not only possible, but even probable, and according to many indications an actual fact, that the believing portion of the nation did concentrate their Messianic wishes and hopes for a long time upon Hezekiah ; but even if Isaiah's prophecy may have evoked such human conjectures and expectations, through the measure of time which it laid down, it would not be a prophecy at all, if it rested upon no better foundation than this, which would be the case if Isaiah had a particular maiden of his own day in his mind at the time.

Are we to conclude, then, that the prophet did not refer to any one individual, but that the " virgin" was a personification of the house of David ? This view, which Hofmann propounded, and Stier appropriated, and which Ebrard has revived, notwithstanding the fact that Hofmann relinquished it, does not help us over the difficulty ; for we should expect in that case to find " daughter of Zion," or something of the kind, since the term " virgin" is altogether unknown in a personification of this kind, and the house of David, as the prophet knew it, was by no means worthy of such an epithet.

No other course is left, therefore, than to assume that whilst, on the one hand, the prophet meant by "the virgin" a maiden belonging to the house of David, which the Messianic character of the prophecy requires; on the other hand, he neither thought of any particular maiden, nor associated the promised conception with any human father, who could not have been any other than Ahaz. The reference is the same as in Mic. v. 3 ("she which travaileth," *yōlēdah*). The objection that *hā'almâh* (*the virgin*) cannot be a person belonging to the future, on account of the article (Hofmann, p. 86), does not affect the true explanation: it was the virgin whom the spirit of prophecy brought before the prophet's mind, and who, although he could not give her name, stood before him as singled out for an extraordinary end (compare the article in *hanna'ar* in Num. xi. 27, etc.). With what exalted dignity this mother appeared to him to be invested, is evident from the fact that it is she who gives the name to her son, and *that* the name Immanuel. This name sounds full of promise. But if we look at the expression "therefore," and the circumstance which occasioned it, the *sign* cannot have been intended as a pure or simple promise. We naturally expect, first, that it will be an extraordinary fact which the prophet foretells; and secondly, that it will be a fact with a threatening front. Now a humiliation of the house of David was indeed involved in the fact that the God of whom it would know nothing would nevertheless mould its future history, as the emphatic הוא implies, *He* (αὐτός, the Lord *Himself*), by His own impulse and unfettered choice. Moreover, this moulding of the future could not possibly be such an one as was desired, but would of necessity be as full of threatening to the unbelieving house of David as it was full of promise to the believers in Israel. And the threatening character of the "sign" is not to be sought for exclusively in ver. 15, since both the expressions "therefore" (*lâcēn*) and "behold" (*hinnēh*) place the main point of the sign in ver. 14, whilst the introduction of ver. 15 without any external connection is a clear proof that what is stated in ver. 14 is the chief thing, and not the reverse. But the only thing in ver. 14 which indicated any threatening element in the sign in question, must have been the fact that it would not be by Ahaz, or by a son of Ahaz, or by the house of David generally, which at that time had hardened itself against God, that God would save His people, but that a nameless maiden of low rank, whom God had singled out and now showed to the prophet in the mirror of His counsel, would give birth to the divine deliverer of His people in the midst of the approaching tribulations, which was a sufficient intimation that He who was to be the pledge of Judah's continuance would not arrive without the present degenerate house of David, which had brought Judah to the brink of ruin, being altogether set aside.

But the further question arises here, What constituted the extraordinary character of the fact here announced? It consisted in the fact that, according to ch. ix. 5, Immanuel Himself was to be a פֶּלֶא (wonder or wonderful). He would be God in corporeal self-manifestation, and therefore a "wonder" as being a superhuman person. We should not venture to assert this if it went beyond the line of Old Testament revelation, but the prophet asserts it himself in ch. ix. 5 (cf. ch. x. 21): his words are as clear as possible; and we must not make them obscure, to favour any preconceived notions as to the development of history. The incarnation of Deity was unquestionably a secret that was not clearly unveiled in the Old Testament, but the veil was not so thick but that some rays could pass through. Such a ray, directed by the spirit of prophecy into the mind of the prophet, was the prediction of Immanuel. But if the Messiah was to be *Immanuel* in this sense, that He would Himself be *El* (God), as the prophet expressly affirms, His birth must also of necessity be a wonderful or miraculous one. The prophet does not affirm, indeed, that the "*'almâh*," who had as yet known no man, would give birth to Immanuel without this taking place, so that he could not be born of the house of David as well as into it, but be a gift of Heaven itself; but this "*'almâh*" or virgin continued throughout an enigma in the Old Testament, stimulating "inquiry" (1 Pet. i. 10-12), and waiting for the historical solution. Thus the sign in question was, on the one hand, a mystery glaring in the most threatening manner upon the house of David; and, on the other hand, a mystery smiling with rich consolation upon the prophet and all believers, and couched in these enigmatical terms, in order that those who hardened themselves might not understand it, and that believers might increasingly long to comprehend its meaning.

In ver. 15 the threatening element of ver. 14 becomes the predominant one. It would not be so, indeed, if "butter (thickened milk) and honey" were mentioned here as the ordinary food of the tenderest age of childhood (as Gesenius, Hengstenberg, and others suppose). But the reason afterwards assigned in vers. 16, 17, teaches the very opposite. Thickened milk and honey, the food of the desert, would be the only provisions furnished by the land at the time in which the ripening youth of Immanuel would fall. חֶמְאָה (from חָמָא, to be thick) is a kind of butter which is still prepared by nomads by shaking milk in skins. It may probably include the cream, as the Arabic *semen* signifies both, but not the curds or cheese, the name of which (at least the more accurate name) is *gebīnâh*. The object to יֵדַע is expressed in vers. 15, 16 by infinitive absolutes (compare the more usual mode of expression in ch. viii. 4). The *Lamed* prefixed to the verb does not mean "until" (Ges. § 131, 1), for *Lamed* is never used as so definite an indication of the *terminus ad quem;* the meaning is either "towards the time when he understands" (Amos iv. 7, cf. Lev. xxiv. 12, "to the end that"), or about the time, at the time when he understands (ch. x. 3; Gen. viii. 11; Job xxiv. 14). This kind of food would coincide in time with his understanding, that is to say, would run parallel to it. Incapacity to distinguish between good and bad is characteristic of early childhood (Deut. i. 39, etc.), and also of old age when it relapses into childish ways (2 Sam. xix. 36). The commencement of the capacity to understand is equivalent to entering into the so-called years of discretion—the riper age of free and conscious self-determination. By the time that Immanuel reached this age, all the blessings of the land would have been so far reduced, that from a land full of luxuriant corn-fields and vineyards, it would have become a large wooded pasture-ground, supplying milk and honey, and nothing more. A thorough devastation of the land is therefore the reason for this limitation to the simplest, and, when compared with the fat of wheat and the cheering influence of wine, most meagre and miserable food. And this is the ground assigned in vers. 16, 17. Two successive and closely connected events would occasion this universal desolation.

Vers. 16, 17. "*For before the boy shall understand to refuse the evil, and choose the good, the land will be desolate, of whose two kings thou art afraid. Jehovah will bring upon thee, and upon thy people, and upon thy father's house, days such as have not come since the day when Ephraim broke away from Judah— the king of Asshur."* The land of the two kings, Syria and Israel, was first of all laid waste by the Assyrians, whom Ahaz called to his assistance. Tiglath-pileser conquered Damascus and a portion of the kingdom of Israel, and led a large part of the inhabitants of the two countries into captivity (2 Kings xv. 29, xvi. 9). Judah was then also laid waste by the Assyrians, as a punishment for having refused the help of Jehovah, and preferred the help of man. Days of adversity would come upon the royal house and people of Judah, such as (*'asher, quales*, as in Ex. x. 6) had not come upon them since the calamitous day (*l'miyyōm, inde a die*; in other places we find *l'min-hayyom*, Ex. ix. 18, Deut. iv. 32, ix. 7, etc.) of the falling away of the ten tribes. The appeal to Asshur laid the foundation for the overthrow of the kingdom of Judah, quite as much as for that of the kingdom of Israel. Ahaz became the tributary vassal of the king of Assyria in consequence; and although Hezekiah was set free from Asshur through the miraculous assistance of Jehovah, what Nebuchadnezzar afterwards performed was only the accomplishment of the frustrated attempt of Sennacherib. It is with piercing force that the words " the king of Assyria " (*'eth melek Asshur*) are introduced at the close of the two verses. The particle *'eth* is used frequently where an indefinite object is followed by the more precise and definite one (Gen. vi. 10, xxvi. 34). The point of the verse would be broken by eliminating the words as a gloss, as Knobel proposes. The very king to whom Ahaz had appealed in his terror, would bring Judah to the brink of destruction. The absence of any link of connection between vers. 16 and 17 is also very effective. The hopes raised in the mind of Ahaz by ver. 16 are suddenly turned into bitter disappointment. In the face of such catastrophes as these, Isaiah predicts the birth of Immanuel. His eating only thickened milk and honey, at a time when he knew very well what was good and what was not, would arise from the desolation of the whole of the ancient territory of the Davidic kingdom that had preceded the riper years of his youth, when he would certainly have chosen other kinds of food, if they could possibly have been found. Consequently the birth of Immanuel apparently falls between the time then present and the Assyrian calamities, and his earliest childhood appears to run parallel to the Assyrian oppression. In any case, their consequences would be still felt at the time of his riper youth. In what way the truth of the prophecy was maintained notwithstanding, we shall see presently. What follows in vers. 18–25, is only a further expansion of ver. 17. The promising side of the "sign" remains in the background, because this was not for Ahaz. When Ewald expresses the opinion that a promising strophe has fallen out after ver. 17, he completely mistakes the circumstances under which the prophet uttered these predictions. In the presence of Ahaz he must keep silence as to the promises. But he pours out with all the greater fluency his threatening of judgment.

Ver. 18. "*And it comes to pass in that day, Jehovah will hiss for the fly which is at the end of the Nile-arms of Egypt, and the bees that are in the land of Asshur; and they come and settle all of them in the valleys of the slopes, and in the clefts of the rocks, and in all the thorn-hedges, and upon all grass-plats.*" The prophet has already stated, in ch. v. 26, that Jehovah would hiss for distant nations; and now he is able to describe them by name. The Egyptian nation, with its vast and unparalleled numbers, is compared to the swarming fly; and the Assyrian nation, with its love of war and conquest, to the stinging bee which is so hard to keep off (Deut. i. 44; Ps. cxviii. 12). The emblems also correspond to the nature of the two countries: the fly to slimy Egypt with its swarms of insects (see ch. xviii. 1),[1] and the bee to the more mountainous and woody Assyria, where the keeping of bees is still one of the principal branches of trade. יְאֹר, pl. יְאֹרִים, is an Egyptian name (*yaro*, with the article *phiaro*, pl. *yarôu*) for the Nile and its several arms. The end of the Nile-arms of Egypt, from a Palestinian point of view, was the extreme corner of the land. The military force of Egypt would march out of the whole compass of the land, and meet the Assyrian force in the Holy

---

[1] Egypt abounds in gnats, etc., more especially in flies (*muscariæ*), including a species of small fly (*nemâth*), which is a great plague to men throughout all the country of the Nile (see Hartmann, *Natur-geschichtlich-medicinische Skizze der Nilländer*, 1865, pp. 204-5).

Land; and both together would cover the land in such a way that the valleys of steep precipitous heights (*nachalē habbattoth*), and clefts of the rocks (*nekikē hasselā'im*), and all the thorn-hedges (*nă'azūzīm*) and pastures (*nahalolim*, from *nihēl*, to lead to pasture), would be covered with these swarms. The fact that just such places are named, as afforded a suitable shelter and abundance of food for flies and bees, is a filling up of the figure in simple truthfulness to nature. And if we look at the historical fulfilment, it does not answer even in this respect to the actual letter of the prophecy; for in the time of Hezekiah no collision really took place between the Assyrian and Egyptian forces; and it was not till the days of Josiah that a collision took place between the Chaldean and Egyptian powers in the eventful battle fought between Pharaoh-Necho and Nebuchadnezzar at Carchemish (Circesium), which decided the fate of Judah. That the spirit of prophecy points to this eventful occurrence is evident from ver. 20, where no further allusion is made to Egypt, because of its having succumbed to the imperial power of Eastern Asia.

Ver. 20. "*In that day will the Lord shave with a razor, the thing for hire on the shore of the river, with the king of Assyria, the head and the hair of the feet; and even the beard it will take away.*" Knobel takes the hair to be a figurative representation of the produce of the land; but the only thing which at all favours the idea that the flora is ever regarded by biblical writers as the hairy covering of the soil, is the use of the term *nâzir* as the name of an uncultivated vine left to itself (Lev. xxv. 5). The nation of Judah is regarded here, as in ch. i. 6, as a man stript naked, and not only with all the hair of his head and feet shaved off (*raglaim*, a euphemism), but what was regarded as the most shameful of all, with the hair of his beard shaved off as well. To this end the Almighty would make use of a razor, which is more distinctly defined as hired on the shore of the Euphrates (*conductitia in litoribus Euphratis: nâhâr* stands here for *hannâhâr*), and still more precisely as the king of Asshur (the latter is again pronounced a gloss by Knobel and others). "*The thing for hire:*" *hasseeīrâh* might be an abstract term (hiring, *conductio*), but it may also be the feminine of *sâcīr*, which indicates an emphatic advance from the indefinite to the more definite; in the sense of "with a razor, namely, that which was standing ready to be hired in the lands on both sides of the Euphrates, the king of Assyria." In *hassecîrāh* (the thing for hire) there was involved the bitterest sarcasm for Ahaz. The sharp knife, which it had hired for the deliverance of Judah, was hired by the LORD, to shave Judah most thoroughly, and in the most disgraceful manner. Thus shaved, Judah would be a depopulated and desert land, in which men would no longer live by growing corn and vines, or by trade and commerce, but by grazing alone.—Vers. 21, 22. "*And it will come to pass in that day, that a man will keep a small cow and a couple of sheep; and it comes to pass, for the abundance of the milk they give he will eat cream: for butter and honey will every one eat that is left within the land.*" The former prosperity would be reduced to the most miserable housekeeping. One man would keep a milch cow and two head of sheep (or goats) alive with the greatest care, the strongest and finest full-grown cattle having fallen into the hands of the foe (חָיָה, like הַחִיָּה in other places: *shtē*, not *shnē*, because two female sheep or goats are meant). But this would be quite enough, for there would be only a few men left in the land; and as all the land would be pasture, the small number of animals would yield milk in abundance. Bread and wine would be unattainable. Whoever had escaped the Assyrian razor, would eat thickened milk and honey, that and nothing but that, without variation, *ad nauseam*. The reason for this would be, that the hills, which at other times were full of vines and corn-fields, would be overgrown with briers.

The prophet repeats this three times in vers. 23–25 : "*And it will come to pass in that day, every place, where a thousand vines stood at a thousand silverlings, will have become thorns and thistles. With arrows and with bows will men go, for the whole land will have become thorns and thistles. And all the hills that were accustomed to be hoed with the hoe, thou wilt not go to them for fear of thorns and thistles; and it has become a gathering-place for oxen, and a treading-place for sheep.*" The "thousand silverlings" ('*eleph ceseph, i.e.* a thousand shekels of silver) recal to mind Song of Sol. viii. 11, though there it is the value of the yearly produce, whereas here the thousand shekels are the value of a thousand vines, the sign of a peculiarly valuable piece of a vineyard. At the present time they reckon the worth

of a vineyard in Lebanon and Syria according to the value of
the separate vines, and generally take the vines at one piastre
(from 2d. to 3d.) each; just as in Germany a Johannisberg
vine is reckoned at a ducat. Every piece of ground, where
such valuable vines were standing, would have fallen a prey
to the briers. People would go there with bow and arrow,
because the whole land had become thorns and thistles (see at
ch. v. 12*a*), and therefore wild animals had made their homes
there. And thou (the prophet addresses the countryman thus)
comest not to all the hills, which were formerly cultivated in
the most careful manner; thou comest not thither to make
them arable again, because thorns and thistles deter thee from
reclaiming such a fallow. They would therefore give the oxen
freedom to rove where they would, and let sheep and goats
tread down whatever grew there. The description is intentionally thoroughly tautological and pleonastic, heavy and slow in
movement. The writer's intention is to produce the impression of a waste heath, or tedious monotony. Hence the repeti-
tions of *hâyâh* and *yihyeh*. Observe how great the variations
are in the use of the future and perfect, and how the meaning
is always determined by the context. In vers. 21, 22, the
futures have a really future sense; in ver. 23 the first and
third *yihyeh* signify "will have become" (*factus erit omnis
locus*), and the second "was" (*erat*); in ver. 24 יָבֹא means
"will come" (*veniet*), and *tihyeh* "will have become" (*facta
erit terra*); in ver. 25 we must render *yēʿâdērūn, sarciebantur*
(they used to be hoed). And in vers. 21, 22, and 23, *hâyâh* is
equivalent to *fiet* (it will become); whilst in ver. 25 it means
factum est (it has become). Looked at from a western point of
view, therefore, the future tense is sometimes a simple future,
sometimes a future perfect, and sometimes an imperfect or
synchronistic preterite; and the perfect sometimes a prophetic
preterite, sometimes an actual preterite, but in the sphere of
an ideal past, or what is the same thing, of a predicted future.

This ends Isaiah's address to king Ahaz. He does not
expressly say when Immanuel is to be born, but only what
will take place before he has reached the riper age of boyhood,
—namely, first, the devastation of Israel and Syria, and then
the devastation of Judah itself, by the Assyrians. From the
fact that the prophet says no more than this, we may see that

his spirit and his tongue were under the direction of the Spirit of God, who does not descend within the historical and temporal range of vision, without at the same time remaining exalted above it. On the other hand, however, we may see from what he says, that the prophecy has its human side as well. When Isaiah speaks of Immanuel as eating thickened milk and honey, like all who survived the Assyrian troubles in the Holy Land; he evidently looks upon and thinks of the childhood of Immanuel as connected with the time of the Assyrian calamities. And it was in such a perspective combination of events lying far apart, that the *complex* character of prophecy consisted. The reason for this complex character was a double one, viz. the human limits associated with the prophet's telescopic view of distant times, and the pedagogical wisdom of God, in accordance with which He entered into these limits instead of removing them. If, therefore, we adhere to the letter of prophecy, we may easily throw doubt upon its veracity; but if we look at the substance of the prophecy, we soon find that the complex character by no means invalidates its truth. For the things which the prophet saw in combination were essentially connected, even though chronologically separated. When, for example, in the case before us (ch. vii.–xii.), Isaiah saw Asshur only, standing out as the imperial kingdom; this was so far true, that the four imperial kingdoms from the Babylonian to the Roman were really nothing more than the full development of the commencement made in Assyria. And when he spoke of the son of the virgin (ch. vii.) as growing up in the midst of the Assyrian oppressions; this also was so far true, that Jesus was really born at a time when the Holy Land, deprived of its previous abundance, was under the dominion of the imperial power, and in a condition whose primary cause was to be traced to the unbelief of Ahaz. Moreover, He who became flesh in the fulness of time, did really lead an ideal life in the Old Testament history. He was in the midst of it in a pre-existent presence, moving on towards the covenant goal. The fact that the house and nation of David did not perish in the Assyrian calamities, was actually to be attributed, as ch. viii. presupposes, to His real though not His bodily presence. In this way the apparent discrepancy between the prophecy and the history of the fulfilment may be solved. We do not require the solution proposed by Vitringa, and recently appropriated by Haneberg,—namely, that the prophet takes the stages of the Messiah's life out of the distant future, to make them the measure of events about to take place in the immediate future; nor that of Bengel, Schegg, Schmieder, and others,—namely, that the sign consisted in an event belonging to the immediate future, which pointed typically to the birth of the true Immanuel; nor that of Hofmann, who regards the words of the prophet as an emblematical prediction of the rise of a new Israel, which would come to the possession of spiritual intelligence in the midst of troublous times, occasioned by the want of intelligence in the Israel of his own time. The prophecy, as will be more fully confirmed as we proceed, is directly Messianic; it is a divine prophecy within human limits.

TWO OMENS OF THE IMMEDIATE FUTURE.—
CHAP. VIII. 1-4.

In the midst of the Syro-Ephraimitish war, which was not yet at an end, Isaiah received instructions from God to perform a singular prophetic action. Vers. 1, 2. *" Then Jehovah said to me, Take a large slab, and write upon it with common strokes, ' In Speed Spoil, Booty hastens;' and I will take to me trustworthy witnesses, Uriyah the priest, and Zecharyahu the son of Yeberechyahu."* The slab or table (cf. ch. iii. 23, where the same word is used to signify a metal mirror) was to be large, to produce the impression of a monument; and the writing upon it was to be "a man's pen" (*cheret 'enōsh*), *i.e.* written in the vulgar, and, so to speak, popular character, consisting of inartistic strokes that could be easily read (*vid.* Rev. xiii. 18, xxi. 17). Philip d'Aquin, in his *Lexicon*, adopts the explanation, " *Enosh*-writing, *i.e.* hieroglyphic writing, so called because it was first introduced in the time of *Enosh*." Luzzatto renders it, *a lettere cubitali;* but the reading for this would be *b'cheret ammath 'ish*. The only true rendering is *stylo vulgari* (see Ges. *Thes. s.v. 'enosh*). The words to be written are introduced with *Lamed*, to indicate dedication (as in Ezek. xxxvii. 16), or the object to which the inscription was dedicated or applied, as if it read, " A table devoted to 'Spoil very quickly, booty hastens;'"

unless, indeed, *l'maher* is to be taken as a *fut. instans*, as it is by Luzzatto—after Gen. xv. 12, Josh. ii. 5, Hab. i. 17—in the sense of *acceleratura sunt spolia*, or (what the position of the words might more naturally suggest) with *maher* in a transitive sense, as in the construction הָיָה לְבָעֵר, and others, *accelerationi spolia*, *i.e.* they are ready for hastening. Most of the commentators have confused the matter here by taking the words as a proper name (Ewald, § 288, *c*), which they were not at first, though they became so afterwards. At first they were an oracular announcement of the immediate future, *accelerant spolia, festinat præda* (spoil is quick, booty hastens). *Spoil; booty;* but who would the vanquished be? Jehovah knew, and His prophet knew, although not initiated into the policy of Ahaz. But their knowledge was studiously veiled in enigmas. For the writing was not to disclose anything to the people. It was simply to serve as a public record of the fact, that the course of events was one that Jehovah had foreseen and indicated beforehand. And when what was written upon the table should afterwards take place, they would know that it was the fulfilment of what had already been written, and therefore was an event pre-determined by God. For this reason Jehovah took to Himself witnesses. There is no necessity to read וָאָעִידָה (and I had it witnessed), as Knobel and others do; nor וְהָעִידָה (and have it witnessed), as the Sept., Targum, Syriac, and Hitzig do. Jehovah said what He would do; and the prophet knew, without requiring to be told, that it was to be accomplished instrumentally through him. Uriah was no doubt the priest (Urijah), who afterwards placed himself at the service of Ahaz to gratify his heathenish desires (2 Kings xvi. 10 sqq.). Zechariah ben Yeberechyahu (Berechiah) was of course not the prophet of the times after the captivity, but possibly the Asaphite mentioned in 2 Chron. xxix. 13. He is not further known to us. In good editions, *ben* is not followed by *makkeph*, but marked with *mercha*, according to the Masora at Gen. xxx. 19. These two men were reliable witnesses, being persons of great distinction, and their testimony would weigh with the people. When the time should arrive that the history of their own times solved the riddle of this inscription, these two men were to tell the people how long ago the prophet had written that down in his prophetic capacity.

But something occurred in the meantime whereby the place of the lifeless table was taken by a more eloquent and living one. Vers. 3, 4. "*And I drew near to the prophetess; and she conceived, and bare a son: and Jehovah said to me, Call his name In-speed-spoil-booty-hastens (Maher-shalal-hash-baz): for before the boy shall know how to cry, My father, and my mother, they will carry away the riches of Damascus, and the spoil of Samaria, before the king of Asshur.*" To his son Shear-yashub, in whose name the law of the history of Israel, as revealed to the prophet on the occasion of his call (chap. vi.), viz. the restoration of only a remnant of the whole nation, had been formulated, there was now added a second son, to whom the inscription upon the table was given as a name (with a small abbreviation, and if the *Lamed* is the particle of dedication, a necessary one). He was therefore the symbol of the approaching chastisement of Syria and the kingdom of the ten tribes. Before the boy had learned to stammer out the name of father and mother, they would carry away (*yissâ'*, not the third pers. fut. *niphal*, which is *yinnâsê'*, but *kal* with a latent, indefinite subject *hannōsē'*: Ges. § 137, 3) the treasures of Damascus and the trophies (*i.e.* the spoil taken from the flying or murdered foe) of Samaria before the king of Asshur, who would therefore leave the territory of the two capitals as a conqueror. It is true that Tiglath-pileser only conquered Damascus, and not Samaria; but he took from Pekah, the king of Samaria, the land beyond the Jordan, and a portion of the land on this side. The trophies, which he took thence to Assyria, were no less the spoil of Samaria than if he had conquered Samaria itself (which Shalmanassar did twenty years afterwards). The birth of Maher-shalal took place about three-quarters of a year later than the preparation of the table (as the verb *vá'ekrab* is an aorist and not a pluperfect); and the time appointed, from the birth of the boy till the chastisement of the allied kingdoms, was about a year. Now, as the Syro-Ephraimitish war did not commence later than the first year of the reign of Ahaz, *i.e.* the year 743, and the chastisement by Tiglath-pileser occurred in the lifetime of the allies, whereas Pekah was assassinated in the year 739, the interval between the commencement of the war and the chastisement of the allies cannot have been more than three years; so that the preparation of the table must not be assigned to a much later period than the interview with Ahaz. The inscription upon the table, which was adopted as the name of the child, was not a purely consolatory prophecy, since the prophet had predicted, a short time before, that the same Asshur which devastated the two covenant lands would lay Judah waste as well. It was simply a practical proof of the omniscience and omnipotence of God, by which the history of the future was directed and controlled. The prophet had, in fact, the mournful vocation to harden. Hence the enigmatical character of his words and doings in relation to both kings and nation. Jehovah foreknew the consequences which would follow the appeal to Asshur for help, as regarded both Syria and Israel. This knowledge he committed to writing in the presence of witnesses. When this should be fulfilled, it would be all over with the rejoicing of the king and people at their self-secured deliverance.

But Isaiah was not merely within the broader circle of an incorrigible nation ripe for judgment. He did not stand alone; but was encircled by a small band of believing disciples, who wanted consolation, and were worthy of it. It was to them that the more promising obverse of the prophecy of Immanuel belonged. Mahershalal could not comfort them; for they knew that when Asshur had done with Damascus and Samaria, the troubles of Judah would not be over, but would only then be really about to commence. To be the shelter of the faithful in the terrible judicial era of the imperial power, which was then commencing, was the great purpose of the prediction of Immanuel; and to bring out and expand the consolatory character of that prophecy for the benefit of believers, was the design of the addresses which follow.

ESOTERIC ADDRESSES.—CHAP. VIII. 5–XII.

A. Consolation of Immanuel in the coming darkness.—
Chap. viii. 5–ix. 6.

The heading or introduction, "*And Jehovah proceeded still further to speak to me, as follows,*" extends to all the following addresses as far as ch. xii. They all finish with consolation. But consolation presupposes the need of consolation. Consequently, even in this instance the prophet is obliged to commence with a threatening of judgment. Vers. 6, 7. " *Forasmuch as this people despiseth the waters of Siloah that go softly, and regardeth as a delight the alliance with Rezin and the son of Remalyahu, therefore, behold! the Lord of all bringeth up upon them the waters of the river, the mighty and the great, the king of Asshur and all his military power; and he riseth over all his channels, and goeth over all his banks.*" The Siloah had its name (*Shiloach*, or, according to the reading of this passage contained in very good MSS., *Shilloach*), *ab emittendo*, either in an infinitive sense, "shooting forth," or in a participial sense, with a passive colouring, *emissus*, sent forth, spirted out (*vid.* John ix. 7; and on the variations in meaning of this substantive form, *Concord.* p. 1349, s.). Josephus places the fountain and pool of Siloah at the opening of the Tyropœon, on the south-eastern side of the ancient city, where we still find it at the present day (*vid.* Jos. *Wars of the Jews*, v. 4, 1; also Robinson, *Pal.* i. 504). The clear little brook—a pleasant sight to the eye as it issues from the ravine which runs between the south-western slope of Moriah and the south-eastern slope of Mount Zion[1] (v. Schubert, *Reise*, ii. 573)—is used here as a symbol of the Davidic monarchy enthroned upon Zion, which had the promise of God, who was enthroned upon Moriah, in contrast with the imperial or world kingdom, which is compared to the overflowing waters of the Euphrates. The reproach of despising the waters of Siloah applied to Judah as well as Ephraim: to the former because it trusted in Asshur, and despised the less tangible but more certain help which the house of David, if it were but believing, had to expect from the God of promise; to the latter, because it had entered into alliance with Aram to overthrow the house of David; and yet the house of David, although degenerate and deformed, was the divinely appointed source of that salvation, which is ever realized through quiet, secret ways. The second reproach applied more especially to Ephraim. The *'eth* is not to be taken as the sign of the accusative, for *sūs* never occurs with the accusative of the object (not even in ch. xxxv. 1), and could not well be so used. It is to

[1] It is with perfect propriety, therefore, that Jerome sometimes speaks of the *fons Siloe* as flowing *ad radices Montis Zion*, and at other times as flowing *in radicibus Montis Moria*.

be construed as a preposition in the sense of "*and* (or because) *delight* (is felt) *with* (*i.e.* in) *the alliance with Rezin and Pekah.*" (On the constructive before a preposition, see Ges. § 116, 1: *sûs 'ēth*, like *râtzâh 'im*.) Luzzatto compares, for the construction, Gen. xli. 43, *v'nâthōn;* but only the *inf. abs.* is used in this way as a continuation of the finite verb (see Ges. § 131, 4, *a*). Moreover, מָשׂוֹשׂ is not an Aramaic infinitive, but a substantive used in such a way as to retain the power of the verb (like מַפָּע in Num. x. 2, and מִסְפָּר in Num. xxiii. 10, unless, indeed, the reading here should be מִי סָפַר). The substantive clause is preferred to the verbal clause יָשִׂישׂ, for the sake of the antithetical consonance of מָשׂוֹשׂ with מֹאֵס. It is also quite in accordance with Hebrew syntax, that an address which commences with יַעַן כִּי should here lose itself in the second sentence "in the twilight," as Ewald expresses it (§ 351, *c*), of a substantive clause. Knobel and others suppose the reproof to relate to dissatisfied Judæans, who were secretly favourable to the enterprise of the two allied kings. But there is no further evidence that there were such persons; and ver. 8 is opposed to this interpretation. The overflowing of the Assyrian forces would fall first of all upon Ephraim. The threat of punishment is introduced with וְהִנֵּה, the *Vav* being the sign of sequence (Ewald, § 348, *b*). The words "the king of Asshur" are the prophet's own gloss, as in ch. vii. 17, 20.

Not till then would this overflowing reach as far as Judah, but then it would do so most certainly and incessantly. Ver. 8. "*And presses forward into Judah, overflows and pours onward, till it reaches to the neck, and the spreading out of its wings fill the breadth of thy land, Immanuel.*" The fate of Judah would be different from that of Ephraim. Ephraim would be laid completely under water by the river, *i.e.* would be utterly destroyed. And in Judah the stream, as it rushed forward, would reach the most dangerous height; but if a deliverer could be found, there was still a possibility of its being saved. Such a deliverer was Immanuel, whom the prophet sees in the light of the Spirit living through all the Assyrian calamities. The prophet appeals complainingly to him that the land, which is his land, is almost swallowed up by the world-power: the spreadings out (*muttoth*, a *hophal* noun: for similar substantive forms, see ver. 23, ch. xiv. 6, xxix. 3, and more especially Ps.

lxvi. 14) of the wings of the stream (*i.e.* of the large bodies of water pouring out on both sides from the main stream, as from the trunk, and covering the land like two broad wings) have filled the whole land. According to Norzi, *Immanuël* is to be written here as one word, as it is in ch. vii. 14; but the correct reading is '*Immânu El*, with *mercha silluk* (see note on ch. vii. 14), though it does not therefore cease to be a proper name. As Jerome observes, it is *nomen proprium, non interpretatum;* and so it is rendered in the Sept., Μεθ' ἡμῶν ὁ Θεός.

The prophet's imploring look at Immanuel does not remain unanswered. We may see this from the fact, that what was almost a silent prayer is changed at once into the *jubilate* of holy defiance.—Vers. 9, 10. "*Exasperate yourselves, O nations, and go to pieces; and see it, all who are far off in the earth! Gird yourselves, and go to pieces; gird yourselves, and go to pieces! Consult counsel, and it comes to nought; speak the word, and it is not realized: for with us is God.*" The second imperatives in ver. 9 are threatening words of authority, having a future signification, which change into futures in ver. 10 (Ges. § 130, 2): Go on exasperating yourselves (רֹעוּ with the tone upon the penultimate, and therefore not the *pual* of רָעָה, *consociari*, which is the rendering adopted in the Targum, but the *kal* of רָעַע, *malum esse;* not *vociferari*, for which רוּעַ, a different verb from the same root, is commonly employed), go on arming; ye will nevertheless fall to pieces (*chōttu*, from *châthath*, related to *câthath*, *confringi, consternari*). The prophet classes together all the nations that are warring against the people of God, pronounces upon them the sentence of destruction, and calls upon all distant lands to hear this ultimate fate of the kingdom of the world, *i.e.* of the imperial power. The world-kingdom must be wrecked on the land of Immanuel; "*for with us,*" as the watchword of believers runs, pointing to the person of the Saviour, "*with us is God.*"

There then follows in ver. 11 an explanatory clause, which seems at first sight to pass on to a totally different theme, but it really stands in the closest connection with the triumphant words of vers. 9, 10. It is Immanuel whom believers receive, constitute, and hold fast as their refuge in the approaching times of the Assyrian judgment. He is their refuge and God in Him, and not any human support whatever. This is the link of connection with vers. 11, 12 : "*For Jehovah hath spoken thus to me, overpowering me with God's hand, and instructing me not to walk in the way of this people, saying, Call ye not conspiracy all that this people calls conspiracy; and what is feared by it, fear ye not, neither think ye dreadful.*" הַיָּד, "*the hand,*" is the absolute hand, which is no sooner laid upon a man than it overpowers all perception, sensation, and thought: *chezkath hayyâd* (viz. *'âlai*, upon me, Ezek. iii. 14) therefore describes a condition in which the hand of God was put forth upon the prophet with peculiar force, as distinguished from the more usual prophetic state, the effect of a peculiarly impressive and energetic act of God. Luther is wrong in following the Syriac, and adopting the rendering, "taking me by the hand;" as *chezkath* points back to the *kal* (*invalescere*), and not to the *hiphil* (*apprehendere*). It is this circumstantial statement, which is continued in *v'yissereni* ("*and instructing me*"), and not the leading verb *'âmar* ("*he said*"); for the former is not the third pers. pret. *piel*, which would be *v'yisserani*, but the third pers. fut. *kal*, from the future form *yissōr* (Hos. x. 10, whereas the fut. *piel* is *v'yassēr*); and it is closely connected with *chezkath hayyâd*, according to the analogy of the change from the participial and infinitive construction to the finite verb (Ges. § 132, Anm. 2). With this overpowering influence, and an instructive warning against going in the way of "this people," Jehovah spake to the prophet as follows. With regard to the substance of the following warning, the explanation that has been commonly adopted since the time of Jerome, viz. *noli duorum regum timere conjurationem* (fear not the conspiracy of the two kings), is contrary to the reading of the words. The warning runs thus: The prophet, and such as were on his side, were not to call that *kesher* which the great mass of the people called *kesher* (cf. 2 Chron. xxiii. 13, "She said, Treason, Treason!" *kesher, kesher*); yet the alliance of Rezin and Pekah was really a conspiracy—a league against the house and people of David. Nor can the warning mean that believers, when they saw how the unbelieving Ahaz brought the nation into distress, were not to join in a conspiracy against the person of the king (Hofmann, Drechsler); they are not warned at all against making a conspiracy, but against joining in the popular cry when the people called out *kesher*. The true explanation has been given by Roorda, viz. that the reference is to the conspiracy, as it was called, of the prophet and his disciples (" *sermo hic est de conjuratione, quæ dicebatur prophetæ et discipulorum ejus*"). The same thing happened to Isaiah as to Amos (Amos vii. 10) and to Jeremiah. Whenever the prophets were at all zealous in their opposition to the appeal for foreign aid, they were accused and branded as standing in the service of the enemy, and conspiring for the overthrow of the kingdom. In such perversion of language as this, the honourable among them were not to join. The way of God was now a very different one from the way of that people. If the prophet and his followers opposed the alliance with Asshur, this was not a common human conspiracy against the will of the king and nation, but the inspiration of God, the true policy of Jehovah. Whoever trusted in Him had no need to be afraid of such attempts as those of Rezin and Pekah, or to look upon them as dreadful.

The object of their fear was a very different one. Vers. 13-15. "*Jehovah of hosts, sanctify Him; and let Him be your fear, and let Him be your terror. So will He become a sanctuary, but a stone of stumbling and a rock of offence (vexation) to both the houses of Israel, a snare and trap to the inhabitants of Jerusalem. And many among them shall stumble, and shall fall; and be dashed to pieces, and be snared and taken.*" The logical apodosis to ver. 13 commences with *v'hâyâh* (so shall He be). If ye actually acknowledge Jehovah the Holy One as the Holy One (*hikdîsh*, as in ch. xxix. 23), and if it is He whom ye fear, and who fills you with dread (*ma'arîtz*, used for the object of dread, as *môrah* is for the object of fear; hence "that which terrifies" in a causative sense), He will become a *mikdâsh*. The word *mikdâsh* may indeed denote the object sanctified, and so Knobel understands it here according to Num. xviii. 29; but if we adhere to the strict notion of the word, this gives an unmeaning apodosis. *Mikdâsh* generally means the sanctified place or sanctuary, with which the idea of an asylum would easily associate itself, since even among the Israelites the temple was regarded and respected as an asylum (1 Kings i. 50, ii. 28). This is the explanation which most of the commentators have adopted here; and the punctuators also took it in the same sense, when they divided the two halves of ver. 14 by *athnach* as antithetical. And *mikdâsh* is really to be taken in this sense, although it cannot be exactly rendered "asylum," since this would improperly limit the meaning of the word. The temple was not only a place of shelter, but also of grace, blessing, and peace. All who sanctified the Lord of lords He surrounded like temple walls; hid them in Himself, whilst death and tribulation reigned without, and comforted, fed, and blessed them in His own gracious fellowship. This is the true explanation of *v'hâyâh l'mikdâsh*, according to such passages as ch. iv. 5, 6, Ps. xxvii. 5, xxxi. 21. To the two houses of Israel, on the contrary, *i.e.* to the great mass of the people of both kingdoms who neither sanctified nor feared Jehovah, He would be a rock and snare. The synonyms are intentionally heaped together (cf. ch. xxviii. 13), to produce the fearful impression of death occurring in many forms, but all inevitable. The first three verbs of ver. 15 refer to the "stone" (*'eben*) and "rock" (*tzûr*); the last two to the "snare" (*pach*), and "trap" or springe (*mōkēsh*).[1] All who did not give glory to Jehovah would be dashed to pieces upon His work as upon a stone, and caught therein as in a trap. This was the burden of the divine warning, which the prophet heard for himself and for those that believed.

The words that follow in ver. 16, "*Bind up the testimony, seal the lesson in my disciples,*" appear at first sight to be a command of God to the prophet, according to such parallel passages as Dan. xii. 4, 9, Rev. xxii. 10, cf. Dan. viii. 26; but with this explanation it is impossible to do justice to the words "in my disciples" (*b'limmudâi*). The explanation given by Rosenmüller, Knobel, and others, viz. "by bringing in men divinely instructed" (*adhibitis viris piis et sapientibus*), is grammatically inadmissible. Consequently I agree with Vitringa, Drechsler, and others, in regarding ver. 16 as the prophet's own prayer to Jehovah. We *tie together* (צָרַר, imperf. צֹר = צוּר) what we wish to keep from getting separated and lost; we *seal* (*châtham*) what is to be kept secret, and only opened by a person duly qualified. And so the prophet here prays that Jehovah would take his testimony with regard to the

---

[1] Malbim observes quite correctly, that "the *pach* catches, but does not hurt; the *mokesh* catches and hurts (*e.g.* by seizing the legs or nose, Job xl. 24): the former is a simple snare (or net), the latter a springe, or snare which catches by means of a spring" (Amos iii. 5).

future, and his instruction, which was designed to prepare for this future,—that *testimony* and *thorah* which the great mass in their hardness did not understand, and in their self-hardening despised,—and lay them up well secured and well preserved, as if by band and seal, in the hearts of those who received the prophet's words with believing obedience (*limmūd*, as in ch. 1. 4, liv. 13). For it would be all over with Israel, unless a community of believers should be preserved, and all over with this community, if the word of God, which was the ground of their life, should be allowed to slip from their hearts. We have here an announcement of the grand idea, which the second part of the book of Isaiah carries out in the grandest style. It is very evident that it is the prophet himself who is speaking here, as we may see from ver. 17, where he continues to speak in the first person, though he does not begin with וַאֲנִי.

Whilst offering this prayer, and looking for its fulfilment, he waits upon Jehovah. Ver. 17. "*And I wait upon Jehovah, who hides His face before the house of Jacob, and hope for Him.*" A time of judgment had now commenced, which would still last a long time; but the word of God was the pledge of Israel's continuance in the midst of it, and of the renewal of Israel's glory afterwards. The prophet would therefore hope for the grace which was now hidden behind the wrath.

His home was the future, and to this he was subservient, even with all his house. Ver. 18. "*Behold, I and the children which Jehovah hath given me for signs and types in Israel, from Jehovah of hosts, who dwelleth upon Mount Zion.*" He presents himself to the Lord with his children, puts himself and them into His hands. They were Jehovah's gift, and that for a higher purpose than every-day family enjoyment. They subserved the purpose of signs and types in connection with the history of salvation. "*Signs and types:*" *'oth* (sign) was an omen or prognostic ($\sigma\eta\mu\epsilon\hat{\iota}o\nu$) in word and deed, which pointed to and was the pledge of something future (whether it were in itself miraculous or natural); *mopheth* was either something miraculous ($\tau\acute{\epsilon}\rho\alpha\varsigma$) pointing back to a supernatural cause, or a type ($\tau\acute{\upsilon}\pi o\varsigma$, *prodigium* = *porridigium*) which pointed beyond itself to something future and concealed, literally twisted round, *i.e.* out of the ordinary course, paradoxical, striking, standing out (Arab. *aft, ift, res mira*, $\delta\epsilon\iota\nu\acute{o}\nu$ $\tau\iota$), from אָפַת (related to הָפַךְ,

אָבָה) = מאֱפֶת, like מוֹסֵר = מאֱסָר. His children were signs and enigmatical symbols of the future, and that from Jehovah of hosts who dwelt on Zion. In accordance with His counsel (to which the עַם in מֵעִם points), He had selected these signs and types: He who could bring to pass the future, which they set forth, as surely as He was Jehovah of hosts, and who would bring it to pass as surely as He had chosen Mount Zion for the scene of His gracious presence upon earth. Shear-yashub and Mahershalal were indeed no less symbols of future wrath than of future grace; but the name of the father (*Yesha'yâhu*) was an assurance that all the future would issue from Jehovah's salvation, and end in the same. Isaiah and his children were figures and emblems of redemption, opening a way for itself through judgment. The Epistle to the Hebrews (ch. ii. 13) quotes these words as the distinct words of Jesus, because the spirit of Jesus was in Isaiah,—the spirit of Jesus, which in the midst of this holy family, bound together as it was only by the bands of "the shadow," pointed forward to that church of the New Testament which would be bound together by the bands of the true substance. Isaiah, his children, and his wife, who is called "the prophetess" (*nebi'ah*) not only because she was the wife of the prophet but because she herself possessed the gift of prophecy, and all the believing disciples gathered round this family,—these together formed the stock of the church of the Messianic future, on the foundation and soil of the existing *massa perdita* of Israel.

It is to this *ecclesiola* in *ecclesia* that the prophet's admonition is addressed. Ver. 19. "*And when they shall say to you, Inquire of the necromancers, and of the soothsayers that chirp and whisper:—Should not a people inquire of its God? for the living to the dead?*" The appeal is supposed to be made by Judæans of the existing stamp; for we know from ch. ii. 6, iii. 2, 3, that all kinds of heathen superstitions had found their way into Jerusalem, and were practised there as a trade. The persons into whose mouths the answer is put by the prophet (we may supply before ver. 19*b*, "Thus shall ye say to them;" cf. Jer. x. 11), are his own children and disciples. The circumstances of the times were very critical; and the people were applying to wizards to throw light upon the dark future. '*Ob* signified primarily the spirit of witchcraft, then the possessor of such a spirit (equivalent to *Baal ob*), more especially the necromancer. *Yidd'oni*, on the other hand, signified primarily the possessor of a prophesying or soothsaying spirit ($\pi\acute{u}\theta\omega\nu$ or $\pi\nu\epsilon\hat{u}\mu\alpha$ $\tau o\hat{u}$ $\pi\acute{u}\theta\omega\nu o\varsigma$), Syr. *yodûa'* (after the intensive form *pâ'ul* with immutable vowels), and then the soothsaying spirit itself (Lev. xx. 27), which was properly called *yiddā'ōn* (the much knowing), like $\delta\alpha\acute{\iota}\mu\omega\nu$, which, according to Plato, is equivalent to $\delta\alpha\acute{\eta}\mu\omega\nu$. These people, who are designated by the LXX., both here and elsewhere, as $\epsilon\gamma\gamma\alpha\sigma\tau\rho\acute{o}\mu\nu\theta o\iota$, *i.e.* ventriloquists, imitated the chirping of bats, which was supposed to proceed from the shades of Hades, and uttered their magical formulas in a whispering tone.[1] What an unnatural thing, for the people of Jehovah to go and inquire, not of their own God, but of such heathenish and demoniacal deceivers and victims as these (*dârash 'el*, to go and inquire of a person, ch. xi. 10, synonymous with *shâ'al b'*, 1 Sam. xxviii. 6)! What blindness, to consult the dead in the interests of the living! By "*the dead*" (*hammēthim*) we are not to understand "the idols" in this passage, as in Ps. cvi. 28, but *the departed*, as Deut. xviii. 11 (cf. 1 Sam xxviii.) clearly proves; and בְּעַד is not to be taken, either here or elsewhere, as equivalent to *tachath* ("instead of"), as Knobel supposes, but, as in Jer. xxi. 2 and other passages, as signifying "for the benefit of." Necromancy, which makes the dead the instructors of the living, is a most gloomy deception.

In opposition to such a falling away to wretched superstition, the watchword of the prophet and his supporters is this. Ver. 20. "*To the teaching of God* (*thorah*, *Gotteslehre*), *and to the*

---

[1] The Mishnah *Sanhedrin* 65a gives this definition: "*Baal 'ob* is a python, *i.e.* a soothsayer ('with a spirit of divination'), who speaks from his arm-pit; *yidd'oni*, a man who speaks with his mouth." The *baal ob*, so far as he had to do with the bones of the dead, is called in the Talmud '*obâ' temayya'*, *e.g.* the witch of Endor (*b. Sabbath* 152*b*). On the history of the etymological explanation of the word, see Böttcher, *de inferis*, § 205-217. If *'ob*, a skin or leather bottle, is a word from the same root (rendered "bellows" by the LXX. at Job xxxii. 19), as it apparently is, it may be applied to a bottle as a thing which swells or can be blown out, and to a wizard or spirit of incantation on account of his puffing and gasping. The explanation "*le revenant*," from אוֹב = Arab. *âba*, to return, has only a very weak support in the proper name אִיּוֹב = *avvâb* (the penitent, returning again and again to God: see again at ch. xxix. 4).

testimony! If they do not accord with this word, they are a people for whom no morning dawns." The summons, "to the teaching and to the testimony" (namely, to those which Jehovah gave through His prophet, ver. 17), takes the form of a watchword in time of battle (Judg. vii. 18). With this construction the following אִם־לֹא (which Knobel understands interrogatively, "Should not they speak so, who, etc.?" and Luzzatto as an oath, as in Ps. cxxxi. 2, "Surely they say such words as have no dawn in them") has, at any rate, all the presumption of a conditional signification. Whoever had not this watchword would be regarded as the enemy of Jehovah, and suffer the fate of such a man. This is, to all appearance, the meaning of the apodosis אֲשֶׁר אֵין־לוֹ שָׁחַר. Luther has given the meaning correctly, "If they do not say this, they will not have the morning dawn;" or, according to his earlier and equally good rendering, "They shall never overtake the morning light," literally, "They are those to whom no dawn arises." The use of the plural in the hypothetical protasis, and the singular in the apodosis, is an intentional and significant change. All the several individuals who did not adhere to the revelation made by Jehovah through His prophet, formed one corrupt mass, which would remain in hopeless darkness. אֲשֶׁר is used in the same sense as in ch. v. 28 and 2 Sam. ii. 4, and possibly also as in 1 Sam. xv. 20, instead of the more usual כִּי, when used in the affirmative sense which springs in both particles out of the confirmative (*namque* and *quoniam*): Truly they have no morning dawn to expect.[1]

The night of despair to which the unbelieving nation would be brought, is described in vers. 21, 22: "*And it goes about therein hard pressed and hungry: and it comes to pass, when hunger befals it, it frets itself, and curses by its king and by its God, and turns its face upward, and looks to the earth, and behold distress and darkness, benighting with anguish, and thrust out into darkness.*" The singulars attach themselves to the לֹ in ver. 19, which embraces all the unbelievers in one mass; "therein" (*bâh*) refers to the self-evident land (*'eretz*). The people would be brought to such a plight in the approaching Assyrian oppressions, that they would wander about in the

[1] Strangely enough, vers. 19 and 20 are described in *Lev. Rabba*, ch. xv., as words of the prophet Hosea incorporated in the book of Isaiah.

land pressed down by their hard fate (*niksheh*) and hungry (*râ'eb*), because all provisions would be gone and the fields and vineyards would be laid waste. As often as it experienced hunger afresh, it would work itself into a rage (*v'hithkazzaph* with *Vav apod.* and *pathach*, according to Ges. § 54, Anm.), and curse by its king and God, *i.e.* by its idol. This is the way in which we must explain the passage, in accordance with 1 Sam. xiv. 43, where *killel bēlohim* is equivalent to *killel b'shēm elohim*, and with Zeph. i. 5, where a distinction is made between an oath *layehováh*, and an oath *b'malcâm*; if we would adhere to the usage of the language, in which we never find a קלל בְּ corresponding to the Latin *execrari in aliquem* (Ges.), but on the contrary the object cursed is always expressed in the accusative. We must therefore give up Ps. v. 3 and lxviii. 25 as parallels to *b'malco* and *bēlohâiv*: they curse by the idol, which passes with them for both king and God, curse their wretched fate with this as they suppose the most effectual curse of all, without discerning in it the just punishment of their own apostasy, and humbling themselves penitentially under the almighty hand of Jehovah. Consequently all this reaction of their wrath would avail them nothing: whether they turned upwards, to see if the black sky were not clearing, or looked down to the earth, everywhere there would meet them nothing but distress and darkness, nothing but a night of anguish all around (*me'ûph zūkâh* is a kind of summary; *mā'ûph* a complete veiling, or eclipse, written with *û* instead of the more usual *ô* of this substantive form: Ewald, § 160, *a*). The judgment of God does not convert them, but only heightens their wickedness; just as in Rev. xvi. 11, 21, after the pouring out of the fifth and seventh vials of wrath, men only utter blasphemies, and do not desist from their works. After stating what the people see, whether they turn their eyes upwards or downwards, the closing participial clause of ver. 22 describes how they see themselves "thrust out into darkness" (*in caliginem propulsum*). There is no necessity to supply הוא; but out of the previous *hinnēh* it is easy to repeat *hinno* or *hinnennu* (*en ipsum*). "Into darkness:" '*ăphēlâh* (*acc. loci*) is placed emphatically at the head, as in Jer. xxiii. 12.

After the prophet has thus depicted the people as without morning dawn, he gives the reason for the assumption that a restoration of light is to be expected, although not for the existing generation. Ch. ix. 1. "*For it does not remain dark where there is now distress: in the first time He brought into disgrace the land of Zebulun and the land of Naphtali, and in the last He brings to honour the road by the sea, the other side of Jordan, the circle of the Gentiles.*" כִּי is neither to be taken as equivalent to the untranslatable ὅτι *recitativum* (Knobel), nor is there any necessity to translate it "but" or "nevertheless," and supply the clause, "it will not remain so." The reason assigned for the fact that the unbelieving people of Judah had fallen into a night without morning, is, that there was a morning coming, whose light, however, would not rise upon the land of Judah first, but upon other parts of the land. *Mū'āph* and *mūzāk* are *hophal* nouns: a state of darkness and distress. The meaning is, There is not, *i.e.* there will not remain, a state of darkness over the land (*lâh*, like *bâh* in viii. 21, refers to *'eretz*), which is now in a state of distress; but those very districts which God has hitherto caused to suffer deep humiliation He will bring to honour by and by (*hekal* = *hēkēl*, according to Ges. § 67, Anm. 3, opp. *hicbīd*, as in ch. xxiii. 9). The height of the glorification would correspond to the depth of the disgrace. We cannot adopt Knobel's rendering, "as at a former time," etc., taking עֵת as an accusative of time and כְּ as equivalent to כַּאֲשֶׁר, for כְּ is never used conjunctionally in this way (see *Psalter*, i. 301, and ii. 514); and in the examples adduced by Knobel (viz. ch. lxi. 11 and Job vii. 2), the verbal clauses after *Caph* are elliptical relative clauses. The rendering adopted by Rosenmüller and others (*sicut tempus prius vilem reddidit*, etc., "as a former time brought it into contempt") is equally wrong. And Ewald, again, is not correct in taking the *Vav* in *v'hâ-acharōn* as the *Vav* of sequence used in the place of the *cēn* of comparison. כָּעֵת הָרִאשֹׁן and הָאַחֲרוֹן are both definitions of time. The prophet intentionally indicates the time of disgrace with כְּ, because this would extend over a lengthened period, in which the same fate would occur again and again. The time of glorification, on the other hand, is indicated by the *accus. temporis*, because it would occur but once, and then continue in perpetuity and without change. It is certainly possible that the prophet may have regarded *hâ-acharōn* as the subject; but this would destroy the harmony of the antithesis. By the land or territory of Naphtali (*'artzâh*, poet. for *'eretz*, as in Job xxxiv. 13, xxxvii. 12, with a toneless *ah*) we are to understand the upper Galilee of later times, and by the land of Zebulun lower Galilee. In the antithetical parallel clause, what is meant by the two lands is distinctly specified: (1) "the road by the sea," *derek hayyâm*, the tract of land on the western shore of the sea of Chinnereth; (2) "the other side of Jordan," *'ēber hayyardēn*, the country to the east of the Jordan; (3) "the circle of the Gentiles," *gelîl haggōyim*, the northernmost border-land of Palestine, only a portion of the so-called *Galilœa* of after times. Ever since the times of the judges, all these lands had been exposed, on account of the countries that joined them, to corruption from Gentile influence and subjugation by heathen foes. The northern tribes on this side, as well as those on the other side, suffered the most in the almost incessant war between Israel and the Syrians, and afterwards between Israel and the Assyrians; and the transportation of their inhabitants, which continued under Pul, Tiglath-pileser, and Shalmanassar, amounted at last to utter depopulation (Caspari, *Beitr.* 116–118). But these countries would be the very first that would be remembered when that morning dawn of glory should break. Matthew informs us (ch. iv. 13 sqq.) in what way this was fulfilled at the commencement of the Christian times. On the ground of this prophecy of Isaiah, and not of a "somewhat mistaken exposition of it," as Renan maintains in his *Vie de Jesus* (ch. xiii.), the Messianic hopes of the Jewish nation were really directed towards Galilee.[1] It is true that, according to Jerome, *in loc.*, the Nazarenes supposed ch. ix. 1*b* to refer to the light of the gospel spread by the preaching of Paul *in terminos gentium et viam universi maris.* But "the sea" (*hayyâm*) cannot possibly be understood as referring to the Mediterranean, as Meier and Hofmann suppose, for "the way of the sea" (*derek hayyâm*) would in that case have been inhabited by the Philistines and Phœnicians; whereas the prophet's intention was evidently to mention such Israelitish provinces as had suffered the greatest affliction and degradation.

[1] The Zohar was not the first to teach that the Messiah would appear in Galilee, and that redemption would break forth from Tiberias; but this is found in the Talmud and Midrash (see *Litteratur-blatt des Orients*, 1843, Col. 776).

The range of vision is first widened in ver. 2 : " *The people that walk about in darkness see a great light; they who dwell in the land of the shadow of death, upon them a light shines.*" The range of vision is here extended; not to the Gentiles, however, but to all Israel. Salvation would not break forth till it had become utterly dark along the horizon of Israel, according to the description in ch. v. 30, *i.e.* till the land of Jehovah had become a land of the shadow of death on account of the apostasy of its inhabitants from Jehovah (*zalmâveth* is modified, after the manner of a composite noun, from *zalmûth*, according to the form *kadrûth*, and is derived from צָלַם, Æth. *salema*, Arab. *zalima*, to be dark).[1] The apostate mass of the nation is to be regarded as already swept away; for if death has cast its shadow over the land, it must be utterly desolate. In this state of things the remnant left in the land beholds a great light, which breaks through the sky that has been hitherto covered with blackness. The people, who turned their eyes upwards to no purpose, because they did so with cursing (ch. viii. 21), are now no more. It is the remnant of Israel which sees this light of spiritual and material redemption arise above its head. In what this light would consist the prophet states afterwards, when describing first the blessings and then the star of the new time.

In ver. 3 he says, in words of thanksgiving and praise: " *Thou multipliest the nation, preparest it great joy; they rejoice before Thee like the joy in harvest, as men rejoice when they share the spoil.*" " The nation " (*haggoi*) is undoubtedly Israel, reduced to a small remnant. That God would make this again into a numerous people, was a leading feature in the pictures drawn of the time of glory (ch. xxvi. 15, lxvi. 8 ; Zech. xiv. 10, 11), which would be in this respect the counterpart of that of Solomon (1 Kings iv. 20). If our explanation is the correct one so far, the only way to give an intelligible meaning

---

[1] The shadow or shade, *zēl*, Arab. *zill* (radically related to *tall* = טַל, dew), derived its name *ab obtegendo*, and according to the idea attached to it as the opposite of heat or of light, was used as a figure of a beneficent shelter (ch. xvi. 3), or of what was dark and horrible (cf. Targ. *tallâni*, a night-demon). The verb *zâlam*, in the sense of the Arabic *zalima*, bears the same relation to *zâlal* as *bâham* to *bâhâh* (*Gen.* p. 93), 'âram, to be naked, to 'ârâh (*Jeshurun*, p. 159). The noun *zelem*, however, is either formed from this *zâlam*, or else directly from *zēl*, with the substantive termination *em*.

to the *chethib* לא, taking it in a negative sense, is to render it, as Hengstenberg, Hitzig, and others have done, "Thou multipliest the nation to which Thou hadst formerly not given great joy," which must signify, *per litoten*, "the nation which Thou hadst plunged into deep sorrow." But it is unnatural to take any one of the prophetic preterites, commencing with *hicbîd* in ver. 1, in any other than a future sense. We must therefore give the preference to the *keri* לו,[1] and render it, "Thou makest of the nation a great multitude, and preparest it great joy." The pronoun *lō* is written first, as in Lev. vii. 7-9, Job xli. 4 (*keri*), probably with the emphasis assumed by Drechsler: "*to it*, in which there was not the smallest indication of such an issue as this." The verbs "multiplied" (*higdaltâ*) and "increased" (*hirbithâ*) are intentionally written together, to put the intensity of the joy on a level with the extensiveness of the multitude. This joy would be a holy joy, as the expression "before Thee" implies: the expression itself recals the sacrificial meals in the courts of the temple (Deut. xii. 7, xiv. 26). It would be a joy over blessings received, as the figure of the harvest indicates; and joy over evil averted, as the figure of dividing the spoil presupposes: for the division of booty is the business of conquerors. This second figure is not merely a figure: the people that are so joyous are really victorious and triumphant. Ver. 4. "*For the yoke of its burden and the stick of its neck, the stick of its oppressor, Thou hast broken to splinters, as in the day of Midian.*" The suffixes refer to the people (*hâ'âm*). Instead of *soblō*, from *sōbel*, we have intentionally the more musical form סֻבֳּלוֹ (with *dagesh dirimens* and *chateph kametz* under the influence of the previous *u* instead of the simple *sheva*). The rhythm of the verse is anapæstic. "*Its burden*" (*subbŏlo*) and "*its oppressor*" (*nogēs bō*) both recal to mind the Egyptian bondage (Ex. ii. 11, v. 6). The future deliverance, which the prophet here celebrates, would be the counterpart of the Egyptian. But as the whole of the great nation of Israel was then redeemed, whereas only a small remnant would participate in the final redemption, he compares it to the day of Midian, when Gideon broke the seven years' dominion of Midian, not with a great army, but with a

---

[1] On the passages in which לא *chethib* is לו *keri*, see at Ps. c. 3 and Job xiii. 15.

handful of resolute warriors, strong in the Lord (Judg. vii.). The question suggests itself here, Who is the hero, Gideon's antitype, through whom all this is to occur? The prophet does not say; but building up one clause upon another with כִּי, he gives first of all the reason for the cessation of the oppressive dominion of the imperial power,—namely, the destruction of all the military stores of the enemy.—Ver. 5. "*For every boot of those who tramp with boots in the tumult of battle, and cloak rolled in blood, shall be for burning, a food of fire.*" That which is the food of fire becomes at the same time a *serēphâh*, inasmuch as the devouring fire reduces it to ashes, and destroys its previous existence. This closing statement requires for סְאוֹן the concrete sense of a combustible thing; and this precludes such meanings as business (*Handel und Wandel*), noise, or din (= שָׁאוֹן, Jerome, Syriac, Rashi, and others). On the other hand, the meaning "military equipment," adopted by Knobel and others,—a meaning derived from a comparison of the derivatives of the Aramæan *zūn, āzan*, and the Arabic *zâna*, fut. *yezîn* (to dress or equip),—would be quite admissible; at the same time, the interchange of *Samech* and *Zain* in this word cannot be dialectically established. Jos. Kimchi has very properly referred to the Targum *sēn, mesân* (Syr. also *sáûn* with an essentially long *a*), which signifies shoe (see Bynæus, *de calceo Hebræorum*),—a word which is more Aramæan than Hebrew, and the use of which in the present connection might be explained on the ground that the prophet had in his mind the annihilation of the Assyrian forces. We should no doubt expect *sá'ûn* (*sandaloumenos*) instead of *só'ēn*; but the denom. verb *sá'ăn* might be applied to a soldier's coming up in military boots, and so signify *caligatum venire*, although the primary meaning is certainly *calceare se* (*e.g.* Eph. vi. 15, Syr.). Accordingly we should render it, "every boot of him who comes booted (*des Einherstiefelnden*) into the tumult of battle," taking the word *ra'ash*, not as Drechsler does, in the sense of the noise made by a warrior coming up proudly in his war-boots, nor with Luzzatto in the sense of the war-boot itself, for which the word is too strong, but as referring to the noise or tumult of battle (as in Jer. x. 22), in the midst of which the man comes up equipped or shod for military service. The prophet names the boot and garment with an obvious purpose. The destruction of the hostile weapons follows as a matter of course, if even the military shoes, worn by the soldiers in the enemies' ranks, and the military cloaks that were lying in *dâmim*, *i.e.* in blood violently shed upon the battle-field, were all given up to the fire.

Upon the two sentences with *ci* the prophet now builds a third. The reason for the triumph is the deliverance effected; and the reason for the deliverance, the destruction of the foe; and the reason for all the joy, all the freedom, all the peace, is the new great King.—Ver. 6. "*For unto us a child is born, unto us a son is given; and the government rests upon His shoulder: and they call His name, Wonder, Counsellor, mighty God, Eternal-Father, Prince of Peace.*" The same person whom the prophet foretold in ch. vii. as the son of the virgin who would come to maturity in troublous times, he here sees as born, and as having already taken possession of the government. There he appeared as a sign, here as a gift of grace. The prophet does not expressly say that he is a son of David in this instance any more than in ch. vii. (for the remark that has been recently made, that *yeled* is used here for "infant-prince," is absurd); but this followed as a matter of course, from the fact that he was to bear the government, with all its official rights (ch. xxii. 22) and godlike majesty (Ps. xxi. 6), upon his shoulder; for the inviolable promise of eternal sovereignty, of which the new-born infant was to be the glorious fulfilment, had been bound up with the seed of David in the course of Israel's history ever since the declaration in 2 Sam. vii. In ch. vii. it is the mother who names the child; here it is the people, or indeed any one who rejoices in him: וַיִּקְרָא, "one calls, they call, he is called," as Luther has correctly rendered it, though under the mistaken idea that the Jews had altered the original וַיִּקְרָא into וַיִּקְרָא, for the purpose of eliminating the Messianic sense of the passage. But the active verb itself has really been twisted by Jewish commentators in this way; so that Rashi, Kimchi, Malbim, and others follow the Targum, and explain the passage as meaning, "the God, who is called and is Wonder, Counsellor, the mighty God, the eternal Father, calls his name the Prince of Peace;" but this rendering evidently tears asunder things that are closely connected. And Luzzatto has justly observed, that you do not expect to find attributes of God here, but such as would be characteristic of the child. He therefore renders the passage, "God the mighty, the eternal Father, the Prince of Peace, resolves upon wonderful things," and persuades himself that this long clause is meant for the proper name of the child, just as in other cases declaratory clauses are made into proper names, *e.g.* the names of the prophet's two sons. But even granting that such a sesquipedalian name were possible, in what an unskilful manner would the name be formed, since the long-winded clause, which would necessarily have to be uttered in one breath, would resolve itself again into separate clauses, which are not only names themselves, but, contrary to all expectation, names of God! The motive which prompted Luzzatto to adopt this original interpretation is worthy of notice. He had formerly endeavoured, like other commentators, to explain the passage by taking the words from "Wonderful" to "Prince of Peace" as the name of the child; and in doing this he rendered פלא יועץ "one counselling wonderful things," thus inverting the object, and regarded "mighty God" as well as "eternal Father" as hyperbolical expressions, like the words applied to the King in Ps. xlv. 7a. But now he cannot help regarding it as absolutely impossible for a human child to be called *el gibbor*, like God Himself in ch. x. 21. So far as the relation between his novel attempt at exposition and the accentuation is concerned, it certainly does violence to this, though not to such an extent as the other specimen of exegetical legerdemain, which makes the clause from פלא to אבי־עד the subject to ויקרא. Nevertheless, in the face of the existing accentuation, we must admit that the latter is, comparatively speaking, the better of the two; for if ויקרא שמו were intended to be the introduction to the list of names which follows, שמו would not be pointed with *geresh*, but with *zakeph*. The accentuators seem also to have shrunk from taking *el gibbor* as the name of a man. They insert intermediate points, as though "eternal Father, Prince of Peace," were the name of the child, and all that precedes, from "Wonder" onwards, the name of God, who would call him by these two honourable names. But, at the very outset, it is improbable that there should be two names instead of one or more; and it is impossible to conceive for what precise reason such a periphrastic description of God should be employed in connection with the naming of this child, as is not only altogether different from Isaiah's usual custom, but altogether unparalleled in itself, especially without the definite article. The names of God should at least have been defined thus, הַיוֹעֵץ פֶּלֶא הָאֵל הַגִּבּוֹר, so as to distinguish them from the two names of the child. Even assuming, therefore, that the accentuation is meant to convey this sense, "And the wonderful Counsellor, the mighty God, calls his name Eternal-Father, Prince of Peace," as appears to be the case; we must necessarily reject it, as resting upon a misunderstanding and misinterpretation.[1] We regard the whole, from פלא onwards,—as the connection, the expression, and the syntax require,—as a dependent accusative predicate to ויקרא שמו (they call his name), which stands at the head (compare קרא, they call, it is called, in Gen. xi. 9, xvi. 14, Josh. vii. 26, and above ch. viii. 4, ישׂא, they will carry: Ges. § 137, 3). If it be urged, as an objection to the Messianic interpretation of ch. vii. 14, 15, that the Christ who appeared was not named Immanuel, but Jesus, this objec-

---

[1] The *telisha* in פלא is the smallest of all disjunctive accents; the *geresh* in שמו separates rather more strongly than this; the *pashta* in יועץ separates somewhat more than the other two, but less than the *zakeph* in גבור; and this *zakeph* is the greatest divider in the sentence. The whole sentence, therefore, distributes itself in the following manner: ‖ ויקרא שמו | פלא ‖ יועץ ‖ אל גבור ‖‖ אבי־עד | שׂר־שׁלום. All the words from ויקרא onwards are subordinate to the *zakeph* attached to גבור, which is, to all appearance, intended to have the force of an introductory colon: as, for example, in 2 Sam. xviii. 5 (in the case of לאמר in the clause ואת־אבישי לאמר). In smaller subdivisions, again, פלא (*telisha*) is connected with יועץ (*pashta*), and both together with אל גבור (*munach zakeph*). If only *sar shalom* (Prince of Peace) were intended as the name of the child, it would necessarily be accentuated in the following manner: ויקרא שמו *kadma geresh*, פלא יועץ *telisha gershayim*, אל גבור *mercha tebir*, אבי עד *tifchah*, שׂר־שׁלום *silluk*; and the principal disjunctive would stand at עד instead of גבור. But if the name of the child were intended to form a declaratory clause, commencing with פלא יועץ, "determines wonderful things," as Luzzatto assumes, we should expect to find a stronger disjunctive than *telisha* at פלא, the watchword of the whole; and above all, we should expect a *zakeph* at שמו, and not at גבור. This also applies to our (the ordinary) explanation. It does not correspond to the accentuation. The introductory words ויקרא שמו ought to have a stronger distinctive accent, in order that all which follows might stand as the name which they introduce. Francke (see *Psalter*, ii. 521) perceived this, and in his *Abyssus mysteriorum Esa* (ix. 6) he lays great stress upon the fact, that God who gives the name has Himself a threefold name.

tion is sufficiently met by the fact that He did not receive as a proper name any one of the five names by which, according to this second prophecy, He was to be called. Moreover, this objection would apply quite as strongly to the notion, which has been a very favourite one with Jewish commentators (*e.g.* Rashi, A. E. Kimchi, Abravanel, Malbim, Luzzatto, and others), and even with certain Christian commentators (such as Grotius, Gesenius, etc.), that the prophecy refers to Hezekiah, —a notion which is a disgrace to those who thereby lead both themselves and others astray. For even if the hopes held out in the prophecy were attached for a long time to Hezekiah, the mistake was but too quickly discovered; whereas the commentators in question perpetuate the mistake, by forcing it upon the prophecy itself, although the prophet, even after the deception had been outlived, not only did not suppress the prophecy, but handed it down to succeeding ages as awaiting a future and infallible fulfilment. For the words in their strict meaning point to the Messiah, whom men may for a time, with pardonable error, have hoped to find in Hezekiah, but whom, with unpardonable error, men refused to acknowledge, even when He actually appeared in Jesus. The name Jesus is the combination of all the Old Testament titles used to designate the Coming One according to His nature and His works. The names contained in ch. vii. 14 and ix. 6 are not thereby suppressed; but they have continued, from the time of Mary downwards, in the mouths of all believers. There is not one of these names under which worship and homage have not been paid to Him. But we never find them crowded together anywhere else, as we do here in Isaiah; and in this respect also our prophet proves himself the greatest of the Old Testament evangelists. The first name is פֶּלֶא, or perhaps more correctly פֶּלֶא, which is not to be taken in connection with the next word, יוֹעֵץ, though this construction might seem to commend itself in accordance with הִפְלִיא עֵצָה, in ch. xxviii. 29. This is the way in which it has been taken by the Seventy and others (thus LXX., θαυμαστὸς σύμβουλος; Theodoret, θαυμαστῶς βουλεύων). If we adopted this explanation, we might regard פלא יועץ as an inverted form for יועץ פלא: counselling wonderful things. The possibility of such an inversion is apparent from ch. xxii. 2, תְּשֻׁאוֹת מְלֵאָה, *i.e.* full of tumult. Or, following the analogy of *pere' âdâm* (a wild man) in Gen. xvi. 12, we might regard it as a genitive construction: a wonder of a counsellor; in which case the disjunctive *telishâh gedolâh* in *pele'* would have to be exchanged for a connecting *mahpach*. Both combinations have their doubtful points, and, so far as the sense is concerned, would lead us rather to expect מַפְלִיא עֵצָה; whereas there is nothing at all to prevent our taking פלא and יועץ as two separate names (not even the accentuation, which is without parallel elsewhere, so far as the combination of *pashta* with *telishah* is concerned, and therefore altogether unique). Just as the angel of Jehovah, when asked by Manoah what was his name (Judg. xiii. 18), replied פֶּלִי (פִּלְאִי), and indicated thereby his divine nature—a nature incomprehensible to mortal men; so here the God-given ruler is also *pele'*, a phenomenon lying altogether beyond human conception or natural occurrence. Not only is this or that wonderful in Him; but He Himself is throughout a wonder—παραδοξασμός, as Symmachus renders it. The second name is *yō'ētz*, counsellor, because, by virtue of the spirit of counsel which He possesses (ch. xi. 2), He can always discern and give counsel for the good of His nation. There is no need for Him to surround Himself with counsellors; but without receiving counsel at all, He counsels those that are without counsel, and is thus the end of all want of counsel to His nation as a whole. The third name, *El gibbor*, attributes divinity to Him. Not, indeed, if we render the words "Strength, Hero," as Luther does; or "Hero of Strength," as Meier has done; or "a God of a hero," as Hofmann proposes; or "Hero-God," i.e. one who fights and conquers like an invincible god, as Ewald does. But all these renderings, and others of a similar kind, founder, without needing any further refutation, on ch. x. 21, where He, to whom the remnant of Israel will turn with penitence, is called *El gibbor* (the mighty God). There is no reason why we should take *El* in this name of the Messiah in any other sense than in *Immanu-El;* not to mention the fact that *El* in Isaiah is always a name of God, and that the prophet was ever strongly conscious of the antithesis between *El* and *âdâm*, as ch. xxxi. 3 (cf. Hos. xi. 9) clearly shows. And finally, *El gibbor* was a traditional name of God, which occurs as early as Deut. x. 17, cf. Jer. xxxii. 18, Neh. ix. 32, Ps. xxiv. 8, etc. The name *gibbor* is used here as an adjective, like *shaddai* in *El shaddai*. The Messiah, then, is here designated "mighty God." Undoubtedly this appears to go beyond the limits of the Old Testament horizon; but what if it should go beyond them? It stands written once for all, just as in Jer. xxiii. 6 *Jehovah Zidkenu* (Jehovah our Righteousness) is also used as a name of the Messiah,—a Messianic name, which even the synagogue cannot set aside (*vid. Midrash Mishle* 57a, where this is adduced as one of the eight names of the Messiah). Still we must not go too far. If we look at the spirit of the prophecy, the mystery of the incarnation of God is unquestionably indicated in such statements as these. But if we look at the consciousness of the prophet himself, nothing further was involved than this, that the Messiah would be the image of God as no other man ever had been (cf. *El*, Ps. lxxxii. 1), and that He would have God dwelling within Him (cf. Jer. xxxiii. 16). Who else should lead Israel to victory over the hostile world, than God the mighty? The Messiah is the corporeal presence of this mighty God; for He is with Him, He is in Him, and in Him He is with Israel. The expression did not preclude the fact that the Messiah would be God and man in one person; but it did not penetrate to this depth, so far as the Old Testament consciousness was concerned. The fourth name springs out of the third: אֲבִי־עַד, eternal Father (not Booty Father, with which Hitzig and Knobel content themselves); for what is divine must be eternal. The title Eternal Father designates Him, however, not only as the possessor of eternity (Hengstenberg), but as the tender, faithful, and wise trainer, guardian, and provider for His people even in eternity (ch. xxii. 21). He is eternal Father, as the eternal, loving King, according to the description in Ps. lxxii. Now, if He is mighty God, and uses His divine might in eternity for the good of His people, He is also, as the fifth name affirms, *sar-shâlôm*, a Prince who removes all peace-disturbing powers, and secures peace among the nations (Zech. ix. 10),—who is, as it were, the embodiment of peace come down into the world of nations (Mic. v. 4). To exalt the government of David into an eternal rule of peace, is the end for which He is born; and moreover He proves Himself to be what He is not only called, but actually is. Ver. 7. "*To the increase of government and to peace without end, upon the throne*

*of David, and over his kingdom, to strengthen it, and to support it
through judgment and righteousness from henceforth even for
ever. The jealousy of Jehovah of hosts will fulfil this.*" לְמַרְבֵּה
(written with *Mêm clausum* in the middle of the *one* word, and,
according to Elias Levita, properly to be read לְם רַבֵּה, *iis magni-
ficando*, in accordance with this way of writing the word [1]) is
not a participle here, but a substantive after the forms מִרְאֶה,
מַעֲשֶׂה, and that not from הִרְבָּה, but from רָבָה, an infinitive noun
expressing, according to its formation, the practical result of an
action, rather than the abstract idea.[2] Ever extending dominion
and endless peace will be brought in by the sublime and lofty
King's Son, when He sits upon the throne of David and rules
over David's kingdom. He is a *semper Augustus*, *i.e.* a perpetual increaser of the kingdom; not by war, however, but
with the spiritual weapons of peace. And within He gives
to the kingdom " judgment " (*mishpât*) and " righteousness "
(*zedâkâh*), as the foundations and pillars of its durability:
mishpât, judgment or right, which He pronounces and ordains;
and righteousness, which He not only exercises Himself, but
transfers to the members of His kingdom. This new epoch of
Davidic sovereignty was still only a matter of faith and hope.
But the zeal of Jehovah was the guarantee of its realization.
The accentuation is likely to mislead here, inasmuch as it
makes it appear as though the words " from henceforth even
for ever" (*me'attâh v'ad 'ôlâm*) belonged to the closing sentence, whereas the eternal perspective which they open applies
directly to the reign of the great Son of David, and only

---

[1] When Bar-Kappara says (*b. Sanhedrin* 94a) that God designed to
make Hezekiah the Messiah and Sennacherib Gog and Magog, but that
Hezekiah was not found worthy of this, and therefore the *Mem* of *l'marbeh*
was closed, there is so far some sense in this, that the Messianic hopes
really could centre for a certain time in Hezekiah; whereas the assertion
of a certain Hillel (*ib.* 98b), that Hezekiah was actually the Messiah of
Israel, and no other was to be expected, is nothing but the perverted
fancy of an empty brain. For an instance of the opposite, see Neh. ii. 13,
הם פרוצים, on which passage the Midrash observes, " The broken walls of
Jerusalem will be closed in the day of salvation, and the government
which has been closed up to the time of the King Messiah will be opened
then."

[2] We have already observed at p. 156, that this substantive formation
had not a purely abstract meaning even at the first. Fürst has given the
correct explanation in his *Lehrgebäude der Aram. Idiome*, § 130.

indirectly to the work of the divine jealousy. "*Zeal*," or *jealousy, kin'âh*, lit. glowing fire, from קנא, Arab. *kanaa*, to be deep red (Deut. iv. 24), is one of the deepest of the Old Testament ideas, and one of the most fruitful in relation to the work of reconciliation. It is two-sided. The fire of love has for its obverse the fire of wrath. For jealousy contends for the object of its love against everything that touches either the object or the love itself.[1] Jehovah loves His nation. That He should leave it in the hands of such bad Davidic kings as Ahaz, and give it up to the imperial power of the world, would be altogether irreconcilable with this love, if continued long. But His love flares up, consumes all that is adverse, and gives to His people the true King, in whom that which was only foreshadowed in David and Solomon reaches its highest antitypical fulfilment. With the very same words, " the zeal of Jehovah of hosts," etc., Isaiah seals the promise in ch. xxxvii. 32.

B. Jehovah's outstretched hand.—Chap. ix. 7–x. 4.

The great light would not arise till the darkness had reached its deepest point. The gradual increase of this darkness is predicted in this second section of the esoteric addresses. Many difficult questions suggest themselves in connection with this section. 1. Is it directed against the northern kingdom only, or against all Israel? 2. What was the historical standpoint of the prophet himself? The majority of commentators reply

---

[1] Cf. Weber, *On the Wrath of God* (p. xxxv.). It is evident that by *kin'âh*, ζῆλος, we are to understand the energy of love following up its violated claims upon the creature, from the comparison so common in the Scriptures between the love of God to His church and connubial affection. It is the jealousy of absolute love, which seeks to be loved in return, and indeed demands undivided love, and asserts its claim to reciprocity of love wherever this claim is refused. In a word, it is the self-vindication of scornful love. But this idea includes not only jealousy seeking the recovery of what it has lost, but also jealousy that consumes what cannot be saved (Nahum i. 2; Heb. x. 27); and the Scriptures therefore deduce the wrath, by which the love resisted affirms itself, and the wrath which meets those who have resisted love in the form of absolute hostility,—in other words, the jealousy of love as well as the jealousy of hatred,—not from love and holiness as two entirely distinct sources, but from the single source of absolute holy love, which, just because it is absolute and holy, repels and excludes whatever will not suffer itself to be embraced (Josh. xxiv. 19).

that the prophet is only prophesying against Ephraim here, and that Syria and Ephraim have already been chastised by Tiglath-pileser. The former is incorrect. The prophet does indeed commence with Ephraim, but he does not stop there. The fates of both kingdoms flow into one another here, as well as in ch. viii. 5 sqq., just as they were causally connected in actual fact. And it cannot be maintained, that when the prophet uttered his predictions Ephraim had already felt the scourging of Tiglath-pileser. The prophet takes his stand at a time when judgment after judgment had fallen upon all Israel without improving it. And one of these past judgments was the scourging of Ephraim by Tiglath-pileser. How much or how little of the events which the prophet looks back upon from this ideal standpoint had already taken place, it is impossible to determine; but this is a matter of indifference so far as the prophecy is concerned. The prophet, from his ideal standing-place, had not only this or that behind him, but all that is expressed in this section by perfects and aorists (Ges. § 129, 2, *b*). And we already know from ch. ii. 9, v. 25, that he used the future conversive as the preterite of the ideal past. We therefore translate the whole in the present tense. In outward arrangement there is no section of Isaiah so symmetrical as this. In ch. v. we found one partial approach to the strophe in similarity of commencement, and another in ch. ii. in similarity of conclusion. But here ch. v. 25*b* is adapted as the *refrain* of four symmetrical strophes. We will take each strophe by itself. Strophe 1. Vers. 8-12. "*The Lord sends out a word against Jacob, and it descends into Israel. And all the people must make atonement, Ephraim and the inhabitants of Samaria, saying in pride and haughtiness of heart, 'Bricks are fallen down, and we build with square stones; sycamores are hewn down, and we put cedars in their place.' Jehovah raises Rezin's oppressors high above him, and pricks up his enemies: Aram from the east, and Philistines from the west; they devour Israel with full mouth. For all this His anger is not turned away, and His hand is stretched out still.*" The *word* (*dâbâr*) is both in nature and history the messenger of the Lord: it runs quickly through the earth (Ps. cxlvii. 15, 18), and when sent by the Lord, comes to men to destroy or to heal (Ps. cvii. 20), and never returns to its sender void (ch. lv. 10, 11). Thus does the Lord now send a word against Jacob (*Jacob,* as in ch. ii. 5); and this heavenly messenger descends into Israel (*náphal,* as in Dan. iv. 28, and like the Arabic *nazala,* which is the word usually employed to denote the communication of divine revelation), taking shelter, as it were, in the soul of the prophet. Its immediate commission is directed against Ephraim, which has been so little humbled by the calamities that have fallen upon it since the time of Jehu, that the people are boasting that they will replace bricks and sycamores (or sycamines, from *shikmin*), that wide-spread tree (1 Kings x. 27), with works of art and cedars. "*We put in their place:*" *nachaliph* is not used here as in Job xiv. 7, where it signifies to sprout again (*nova germina emittere*), but as in ch. xl. 31, xli. 1, where it is construed with חַ (strength), and signifies to renew (*novas vires assumere*). In this instance, when the object is one external to the subject, the meaning is to substitute (*substituere*), like the Arabic *achlafa,* to restore. The poorest style of building in the land is contrasted with the best; for "the sycamore is a tree which only flourishes in the plain, and there the most wretched houses are still built of bricks dried in the sun, and of knotty beams of sycamore."[1] These might have been destroyed by the war, but more durable and stately buildings would rise up in their place. Ephraim, however, would be made to feel this defiance of the judgments of God (to "know," as in Hos. ix. 7, Ezek. xxv. 14). Jehovah would give the adversaries of Rezin authority over Ephraim, and instigate his foes: *sicsēc,* as in ch. xix. 2, from *sácac,* in its primary sense of "prick," *figere,* which has nothing to do with the meanings to plait and cover, but from which we have the words שֵׂךְ, סַךְ, a thorn, nail, or plug, and which is probably related to שָׂכָה, to view, lit. to fix; hence *pilpel,* to prick up, incite, which is the rendering adopted by the Targum here and in ch. xix. 2, and by the LXX. at ch. xix. 2. There is no necessity to quote the talmudic *sicsēc,* to kindle (by friction), which is never met with in the metaphorical sense of exciting. It would be even better to take our *sicsēc* as an intensive form of *sácac,* used in the same sense as the Arabic, viz. to provide one's self with weapons, to arm; but this is probably a denominative from *sicca,* signifying offensive armour, with the idea of pricking and spearing,—a radical notion, from

[1] Rosen, *Topographisches aus Jerusalem.*

VOL. I. R

which it would be easy to get at the satisfactory meaning, to spur on or instigate. "The oppressors of *Rezin*" (*tzârē Retzîn*, a simple play upon the words, like *hoi goi* in ch. i. 4, and many others in Isaiah) are the Assyrians, whose help had been sought by Ahaz against Rezin; though perhaps not these exclusively, but possibly also the Trachonites, for example, against whom the mountain fortress *Rezîn* appears to have been erected, to protect the rich lands of eastern Hauran. In ver. 12 the range of vision stretches over all Israel. It cannot be otherwise, for the northern kingdom never suffered anything from the Philistines; whereas an invasion of Judah by the Philistines was really one of the judgments belonging to the time of Ahaz (2 Chron. xxviii. 16–19). Consequently by *Israel* here we are to understand all Israel, the two halves of which would become a rich prize to the enemy. Ephraim would be swallowed up by Aram,—namely, by those who had been subjugated by Asshur, and were now tributary to it,—and Judah would be swallowed up by the Philistines. But this strait would be very far from being the end of the punishments of God. Because Israel would not turn, the wrath of God would not turn away.

Strophe 2. Vers. 13–17. "*But the people turneth not unto Him that smiteth it, and they seek not Jehovah of hosts. Therefore Jehovah rooteth out of Israel head and tail, palm-branch and rush, in one day. Elders and highly distinguished men, this is the head; and prophets, lying teachers, this is the tail. The leaders of this people have become leaders astray, and their followers swallowed up. Therefore the Lord will not rejoice in their young men, and will have no compassion on their orphans and widows: for all together are profligate and evil-doers, and every mouth speaketh blasphemy. With all this His anger is not turned away, and His hand is stretched out still.*" As the first stage of the judgments has been followed by no true conversion to Jehovah the almighty judge, there comes a second. שׁוּב עַד (to turn unto) denotes a thorough conversion, not stopping half-way. "The smiter of it" (*hammaccēhu*), or "he who smiteth it," is Jehovah (compare, on the other hand, ch. x. 20, where Asshur is intended). The article and suffix are used together, as in ch. xxiv. 2, Prov. xvi. 4 (*vid.* Ges. § 110, 2; Caspari, *Arab. Gram.* § 472). But there was coming now a great day of punishment (in the view of the prophet, it was already past), such as Israel experienced more than once in the Assyrian oppressions, and Judah in the Chaldean, when head and tail, or, according to another proverbial expression, palm-branch and rush, would be rooted out. We might suppose that the persons referred to were the high and low; but ver. 15 makes a different application of the first double figure, by giving it a different turn from its popular sense (compare the Arabic *er-ru 'ûs w-aledhnâb* = lofty and low, in Dietrich, *Abhandlung*, p. 209). The opinion which has very widely prevailed since the time of Koppe, that this verse is a gloss, is no doubt a very natural one (see Hitzig, *Begriff der Kritik;* Ewald, *Propheten*, i. 57). But Isaiah's custom of supplying his own gloss is opposed to such a view; also Isaiah's composition in ch. iii. 3 and xxx. 20, and the relation in which this verse stands to ver. 16; and lastly, the singular character of the gloss itself, which is one of the strongest proofs that it contains the prophet's exposition of his own words. The chiefs of the nation were the head of the national body; and behind, like a wagging dog's tail, sat the false prophets with their flatteries of the people, loving, as Persius says, *blando caudam jactare popello*. The prophet drops the figure of *cippâh*, the palm-branch which forms the crown of the palm, and which derives its name from the fact that it resembles the palm of the hand (*instar palmæ manus*), and *agmôn*, the rush which grows in the marsh.[1] The allusion here is to the rulers of the nation and the dregs of the people. The basest extremity were the demagogues in the shape of prophets. For it had come to

---

[1] The noun *agam* is used in the Old Testament as well as in the Talmud to signify both a marshy place (see *Baba mesi'a* 36b, and more especially *Aboda zara* 38a, where *giloi agmah* signifies the laying bare of the marshy soil by the burning up of the reeds), and also the marsh grass (*Sabbath* 11a, "if all the *agmim* were kalams, *i.e.* writing reeds, or pens;" and *Kiddûsin* 62b, where *agam* signifies a stalk of marsh-grass or reed, a rush or bulrush, and is explained, with a reference to Isa. lviii. 5, as signifying a tender, weak stalk). The noun *agmon*, on the other hand, signifies only the stalk of the marsh-grass, or the marsh-grass itself; and in this sense it is not found in the Talmud (see *Job*, ii. 374). The verbal meaning upon which these names are founded is evident from the Arabic *mâ agim* (*magûm*), "bad water" (see at ch. xix. 10). There is no connection between this and *maugil*, literally a depression of the soil, in which water lodges for a long time, and which is only dried up in summer weather.

this, as ver. 16 affirms, that those who promised to lead by a straight road led astray, and those who suffered themselves to be led by them were as good as already swallowed up by hell (cf. ch. v. 14, iii. 12). Therefore the Sovereign Ruler would not rejoice over the young men of this nation; that is to say, He would suffer them to be smitten by their enemies, without going with them to battle, and would refuse His customary compassion even towards widows and orphans, for they were all thoroughly corrupt on every side. The alienation, obliquity, and dishonesty of their heart, are indicated by the word *chânēph* (from *chânaph*, which has in itself the indifferent radical idea of inclination; so that in Arabic, *chanîf*, as a synonym of *'âdil*,[1] has the very opposite meaning of decision in favour of what is right); the badness of their actions by מֵרַע (in half pause for מֵרַע[2] = מֵרַע, *maleficus*); the vicious infatuation of their words by *nebâlâh*. This they are, and this they continue; and consequently the wrathful hand of God is stretched out over them for the infliction of fresh strokes.

Strophe 3. Vers. 18–21. "*For the wickedness burneth up like fire: it devours thorns and thistles, and burns in the thickets of the wood; and they smoke upwards in a lofty volume of smoke. Through the wrath of Jehovah of hosts the land is turned into coal, and the nation has become like the food of fire: not one spares his brother. They hew on the right, and are hungry; and devour on the left, and are not satisfied: they devour the flesh of their own arm: Manasseh, Ephraim; and Ephraim, Manasseh: these together over Judah. With all this His anger is not turned away, and His hand is stretched out still.*" The standpoint of the prophet is at the extreme end of the course of judgment, and from that he looks back. Consequently this link of the chain is also past in his view, and hence the future conversives. The curse, which the apostasy of Israel carries within itself, now breaks fully out. Wickedness, *i.e.* the constant thirst of evil, is a fire which a man kindles in himself. And when the grace

---

[1] This is the way in which it should be written in *Job*, i. 216; *'adala* has also the indifferent meaning of return or decision.

[2] Nevertheless this reading is also met with, and according to *Masora finalis*, p. 52, col. 8, this is the correct reading (as in Prov. xvii. 4, where it is doubtful whether the meaning is a friend or a malevolent person). The question is not an unimportant one, as we may see from Olshausen, § 258, p. 581.

of God, which damps and restrains this fire, is all over, it is sure to burst forth: the wickedness bursts forth like fire (the verb is used here, as in ch. xxx. 27, with reference to the wrath of God). And this is the case with the wickedness of Israel, which now consumes first of all thorns and thistles, *i.e.* individual sinners who are the most ripe for judgment, upon whom the judgment commences, and then the thicket of the wood (*sib-che*,[1] as in ch. x. 34, from *sebac*, Gen. xxii. 13 = *sobec*), that is to say, the great mass of the people, which is woven together by bands of iniquity (*vattizzath* is not a reflective *niphal*, as in 2 Kings xxii. 13, but *kal*, to kindle into anything, *i.e.* to set it on fire). The contrast intended in the two figures is consequently not the high and low (Ewald), nor the useless and useful (Drechsler), but individuals and the whole (Vitringa). The fire, into which the wickedness bursts out, seizes individuals first of all; and then, like a forest fire, it seizes upon the nation at large in all its ranks and members, who "*whirl up* (roll up) *ascending of smoke*," *i.e.* who roll up in the form of ascending smoke (*hith'abbek*, a synonym of *hithhappēk*, Judg. vii. 13, to curl or roll). This fire of wickedness was no other than the wrath (*'ebrâh*) of God: it is God's own wrath, for all sin carries this within itself as its own self-punishment. By this fire of wrath the soil of the land is gradually but thoroughly burnt out, and the people of the land utterly consumed: עֲתַם ἀπ. λεγ. to be red-hot (LXX. συγκέκαυται, also the Targum), and to be dark or black (Arabic *'atame*, late at night), for what is burnt out becomes black. Fire and darkness are therefore correlative terms throughout the whole of the Scriptures. So far do the figures extend, in which the prophet presents the inmost essence of this stage of judgment. In its historical manifestation it consisted in the most inhuman self-destruction during an anarchical civil war. Destitute of any tender emotions, they devoured one another without being satisfied: *gâzar*, to cut, to hew (hence the Arabic for a butcher): *zero'o, his arm*, according to Jer. xix. 9,

---

[1] The *metheg* (*gaya*) in סַבְכֵי (to be pronounced *sib-che*) has simply the euphonic effect of securing a distinct enunciation to the sibilant letter (in other instances to the guttural, *vid.* '*arboth*, Num. xxxi. 12), in cases where the second syllable of the word commences with a guttural or labial letter, or with an aspirate.

equivalent to the member of his own family and tribe, who was figuratively called his arm (Arabic '*adud*: see Ges. *Thes.* p. 433), as being the natural protector and support. This interminable self-immolation, and the regicide associated with the jealousy of the different tribes, shook the northern kingdom again and again to its utter destruction. And the readiness with which the unbrotherly feelings of the northern tribes towards one another could turn into combined hostility towards Judah, was evident enough from the Syro-Ephraimitish war, the consequences of which had not passed away at the time when these prophecies were uttered. This hostility on the part of the brother kingdoms would still further increase. And the end of the judgments of wrath had not come yet.

Strophe 4. Ch. x. 1–4. "*Woe unto them that decree unrighteous decrees, and to the writers who prepare trouble; to force away the needy from demanding justice, and to rob the suffering of my people of their rightful claims, that widows may become their prey, and they plunder orphans! And what will ye do in the day of visitation, and in the storm that cometh from afar? To whom will ye flee for help? and where will ye deposit your glory? There is nothing left but to bow down under prisoners, and they fall under the slain. With all this His anger is not turned away, but His hand is stretched out still.*" This last strophe is directed against the unjust authorities and judges. The *woe* pronounced upon them is, as we have already frequently seen, Isaiah's *ceterum censeo*. *Chákak* is their decisive decree (not, however, in a denominative sense, but in the primary sense of hewing in, recording in official documents, ch. xxx. 8, Job xix. 23); and *cittēb* (*piel* only occurring here, and a perfect, according to Gesenius, § 126, 3) their official signing and writing. Their decrees are *chikekē 'aven* (an open plural, as in Judg. v. 15, for *chukkē*, after the analogy of עַמְּמִי גְלָלַי, with an absolute *chăkākīm* underlying it: Ewald, § 186–7), inasmuch as their contents were worthlessness, *i.e.* the direct opposite of morality; and what they wrote out was '*âmâl*, trouble, *i.e.* an unjust oppression of the people (compare πόνος and πονηρός).[1] Poor persons who wanted to commence legal pro-

---

[1] The current accentuation, וּמְכַתְּבִים *mercha*, עָמָל *tiphchah*, is wrong. The true accentuation would be the former with *tiphchah* (and *metheg*), the

ceedings were not even allowed to do so, and possessions to which widows and orphans had a well-founded claim were a welcome booty to them (for the diversion into the finite verb, see ch. v. 24, viii. 11, xlix. 5, lviii. 5). For all this they could not escape the judgment of God. This is announced to them in ver. 3, in the form of three distinct questions (commencing with *ûmâh, quid igitur*). The noun *pekuddah* in the *first question* always signifies simply a visitation of punishment; *sho'âh* is a confused, dull, desolate rumbling, hence confusion (*turba*), desolation: here it is described as "coming from afar," because a distant nation (Asshur) was the instrument of God's wrath. *Second question:* "Upon whom will ye throw yourselves in your search for help then" (*nūs 'al*, a *constr. prægnans*, only met with here)? *Third question:* "Where, *i.e.* in whose hand, will ye deposit your wealth in money and possessions" (*câbōd*, what is weighty in value and imposing in appearance); *'âzab* with *b'yad* (Gen. xxxix. 6), or with *Lamed* (Job xxxix. 14), to leave anything with a person as property in trust. No one would relieve them of their wealth, and hold it as a deposit; it was irrecoverably lost. To this negative answer there is appended the following *bilti*, which, when used as a preposition after a previous negation, signifies *præter;* when used as a conjunction, *nisi* (*bilti 'im*, Judg. vii. 14); and where it governs the whole sentence, as in this case, *nisi quod* (cf. Num. xi. 6; Dan. xi. 18). In the present instance, where the previous negation is to be supplied in thought, it has the force of *nil reliquum est nisi quod* (there is nothing left but). The singular verb (*câra'*) is used contemptuously, embracing all the high persons as one condensed mass; and *tachath* does not mean *æque ac* or *loco* (like, or in the place of), as Ewald (§ 217, *k*) maintains, but is used in the primary and local sense of *infra* (below). Some crouch down to find room at the feet of the prisoners, who are crowded closely together in the prison; or if we suppose the prophet to

latter with *mercha;* for '*âmâl cittēbu* is an attributive (an elliptical relative) clause. According to its etymon, '*âmâl* seems to stand by the side of μῶλος, *moles, molestus* (see Pott in *Kuhn's Zeitschrift*, ix. 202); but within the Semitic itself it stands by the side of אָמַל, to fade, *marcescere*, which coincides with the Sanscrit root *mlâ* and its cognates (see Leo Meyer *Vergleichende Grammatik*. i. 353), so that '*âmâl* is, strictly speaking, to wear out or tire out (vulg. to worry).

have a scene of transportation in his mind, they sink down under the feet of the other prisoners, in their inability to bear such hardships, whilst the rest fall in war; and as the slaughter is of long duration, not only become corpses themselves, but are covered with the corpses of the slain (cf. ch. xiv. 19). And even with this the wrath of God is not satisfied. The prophet, however, does not follow out the terrible gradation any further. Moreover, the captivity, to which this fourth strophe points, actually formed the conclusion of a distinct period.

C. Destruction of the imperial kingdom of the world, and rise of the kingdom of Jehovah in His Anointed.—Chap. x. 5.-xii.

The law of contrast prevails in prophecy, as it does also in the history of salvation. When distress is at its height, it is suddenly brought to an end, and changed into relief; and when prophecy has become as black with darkness as in the previous section, it suddenly becomes as bright and cloudless as in that which is opening now. The *hoi* (woe) pronounced upon Israel becomes a *hoi* upon Asshur. Proud Asshur, with its confidence in its own strength, after having served for a time as the goad of Jehovah's wrath, now falls a victim to that wrath itself. Its attack upon Jerusalem leads to its own overthrow; and on the ruins of the kingdom of the world there rises up the kingdom of the great and righteous Son of David, who rules in peace over His redeemed people, and the nations that rejoice in Him:—the counterpart of the redemption from Egypt, and one as rich in materials for songs of praise as the passage through the Red Sea. The Messianic prophecy, which turns its darker side towards unbelief in ch. vii., and whose promising aspect burst like a great light through the darkness in ch. viii. 5–ix. 6, is standing now upon its third and highest stage. In ch. vii. it is like a star in the night; in ch. viii. 5–ix. 6, like the morning dawn; and now the sky is perfectly cloudless, and it appears like the noonday sun. The prophet has now penetrated to the light fringe of ch. vi. The name *Shear-yashub*, having emptied itself of all the curse that it contained, is now transformed into a pure promise. And it becomes perfectly clear what the name Immanuel and the name given to Immanuel, *El gibbor* (mighty God), declared.

The remnant of Israel turns to God the mighty One; and God the mighty is henceforth with His people in the Sprout of Jesse, who has the seven Spirits of God dwelling within Himself. So far as the date of composition is concerned, the majority of the more recent commentators agree in assigning it to the time of Hezekiah, because ch. x. 9–11 presupposes the destruction of Samaria by Shalmanassar, which took place in the sixth year of Hezekiah. But it was only from the prophet's point of view that this event was already past; it had not actually taken place. The prophet had already predicted that Samaria, and with Samaria the kingdom of Israel, would succumb to the Assyrians, and had even fixed the year (ch. vii. 8 and viii. 4, 7). Why, then, should he not be able to presuppose it here as an event already past? The stamp on this section does not tally at all with that of Isaiah's prophecy in the times of Hezekiah; whereas, on the other hand, it forms so integral a link in the prophetic cycle in ch. vii.–xii., and is interwoven in so many ways with that which precedes, and of which it forms both the continuation and crown, that we have no hesitation in assigning it, with Vitringa, Caspari, and Drechsler, to the first three years of the reign of Ahaz, though without deciding whether it preceded or followed the destruction of the two allies by Tiglath-pileser. It is by no means impossible that it may have preceded it.

The prophet commences with *hoi* (woe!), which is always used as an expression of wrathful indignation to introduce the proclamation of judgment upon the person named; although, as in the present instance, this may not always follow immediately (cf. ch. i. 4, 5–9), but may be preceded by the announcement of the sin by which the judgment had been provoked. In the first place, Asshur is more particularly indicated as the chosen instrument of divine judgment upon all Israel.—Vers. 5, 6. "*Woe to Asshur, the rod of mine anger, and it is a staff in their hand, mine indignation. Against a wicked nation will I send them, and against the people of my wrath give them a charge, to spoil spoil, and to prey prey, to make it trodden down like street-mire.*" "*Mine indignation:*" *za'mi* is either a permutation of the predicative הוא, which is placed emphatically in the foreground (compare the אֱמֶת־הוּא in Jer. xiv. 22, which is also written with *makkeph*), as we have translated it, though without taking הוּא as a copula (= *est*), as Ewald does; or else הוּא בְיָדָם is written elliptically for אֲשֶׁר הוּא בְיָדָם, "the staff which they hold is mine indignation" (Ges., Rosenmüller, and others), in which case, however, we should rather expect וּמַטֶּה בְיָדָם זַעְמִי הוּא. It is quite inadmissible, however, to take *za'mi* as a separate genitive to *matteh*, and to point the latter with *zere*, as Knobel has done; a thing altogether unparalleled in the Hebrew language.[1] The futures in ver. 6 are to be taken literally; for what Asshur did to Israel in the sixth year of Hezekiah's reign, and to Judah in his fourteenth year, was still in the future at the time when Isaiah prophesied. Instead of וּלְשִׂימוֹ the *keri* has וּלְשׂוּמוֹ, the form in which the infinitive is written in other passages when connected with suffixes (see, on the other hand, 2 Sam. xiv. 7). "*Trodden down:*" *mirmas* with short *a* is the older form, which was retained along with the other form with the *a* lengthened by the tone (Ewald § 160, *c*).

Asshur was to be an instrument of divine wrath upon all Israel; but it would exalt itself, and make itself the end instead of the means. Ver. 7. "*Nevertheless he meaneth not so, neither doth his heart think so; for it is in his heart to destroy and cut off nations not a few.*" Asshur did not think so (*lo'-cēn*), *i.e.* not as he ought to think, seeing that his power over Israel was determined by Jehovah Himself. For what filled his heart was the endeavour, peculiar to the imperial power, to destroy not a few nations, *i.e.* as many nations as possible, for the purpose of extending his own dominions, and with the determination to tolerate no other independent nation, and the desire to deal with Judah as with all the rest. For Jehovah was nothing more in his esteem than one of the idols of the nations. Vers. 8-11. "*For he saith, Are not my generals all kings? Is not Calno as Carchemish, or Hamath as Arpad, or Samaria as Damascus? As my hand hath reached the kingdoms of the idols, and their graven images were more than those of Jerusalem and Samaria; shall I not, as I have done unto Samaria and her idols, do likewise to Jerusalem and her idols?*" The king of Asshur bore the title of the great king (ch. xxxvi. 4), and indeed, as we may infer from Ezek. xxvi. 7, that of the king of kings. The

---

[1] In the Arabic, such a separation does occur as a poetical licence (see De Sacy, *Gramm.* t. ii. § 270).

generals in his army he could call kings,[1] because the satraps[2] who led their several contingents were equal to kings in the extent and splendour of their government, and some of them were really conquered kings (cf. 2 Kings xxv. 28). He proudly asks whether every one of the cities named has not been as incapable as the rest, of offering a successful resistance to him. *Carchemish* is the later *Circesium* (Cercusium), at the junction of the Chaboras with the Euphrates (see above); *Calno*, the later *Ctesiphon*, on the left bank of the Tigris; *Arpad* (according to *Merâshid*, i. p. 47, in the pashalic of Chaleb, *i.e.* Aleppo) and *Hamath* (*i.e.* Epiphania) were Syrian cities, the latter on the river Orontes, still a large and wealthy place. The king of Asshur had also already conquered Samaria, at the time when the prophet introduced him as uttering these words. Jerusalem, therefore, would be unable to resist him. As he had obtained possession of idolatrous kingdoms (לְ מָצָא, to reach, as in Ps. xxi. 9; *hâ-'elîl* with the article indicating the genus), which had more idols than Jerusalem or than Samaria; so would he also overcome Jerusalem, which had just as few and just as powerless idols as Samaria had. Observe here that ver. 11 is the apodosis to ver. 10, and that the comparative clause of ver. 10 is repeated in ver. 11, for the purpose of instituting a comparison, more especially with Samaria and Jerusalem. The king of Asshur calls the gods of the nations by the simple name of idols, though the prophet does not therefore make him speak from his own Israelitish standpoint. On the contrary, the great sin of the king of Asshur consisted in the manner in which he spoke. For since he recognised no other gods than his own Assyrian national deities, he placed Jehovah among the idols of the nations, and, what ought particularly to be observed, with the other idols, whose worship had been introduced into Samaria and Jerusalem. But in this very fact there was so far consolation for the worshippers of Jehovah,

---

[1] The question is expressed in Hebrew phraseology, since *sar* in Assyrian was a superior title to that of *melek*, as we may see from inscriptions and proper names.

[2] *Satrapes* is the old Persian (arrow-headed) *khshatra* (Sanscr. *xatra*) *pâvan*, *i.e.* keeper of government. *Pâvan* (nom. *pâvâ*), which occurs in the Zendik as an independent word *pavan* (nom. *pavao*) in the sense of sentry or watchman, is probably the original of the Hebrew *pechâh* (see Spiegel, in Kohler on Mal. i. 8).

that such blasphemy of the one living God could not remain unavenged; whilst for the worshippers of idols it contained a painful lesson, since their gods really deserved nothing better than that contempt should be heaped upon them. The prophet has now described the sin of Asshur. It was ambitious self-exaltation above Jehovah, amounting even to blasphemy. And yet he was only the staff of Jehovah, who could make use of him as He would.

And when He had made use of him as He would, He would throw him away. Ver. 12. "*And it will come to pass, when the Lord shall have brought to an end all His work upon Mount Zion and upon Jerusalem, I will come to punish over the fruit of the pride of heart of the king of Asshur, and over the haughty look of his eyes.*" The "fruit" (*peri*) of the heart's pride of Asshur is his vainglorious blasphemy of Jehovah, in which his whole nature is comprehended, as the inward nature of the tree is in the fruit which hangs above in the midst of the branches: *tiph'ereth*, as in Zech. xii. 7, the self-glorification which expresses itself in the lofty look of the eyes. Several constructives are here intentionally grouped together (Ges. § 114, 1), to express the great swelling of Asshur even to bursting. But Jehovah, before whom humility is the soul of all virtue, would visit this pride with punishment, when He should have completely cut off His work, *i.e.* when He should have thoroughly completed (*bizza‘*, *absolvere*) His punitive work upon Jerusalem (*ma‘aseh*, as in ch. xxviii. 21). The prep. *Beth* is used in the same sense as in Jer. xviii. 23, *agere cum aliquo*. It is evident that *ma‘aseh* is not used to indicate the work of punishment and grace together, so that *yebazza‘* could be taken as a literal future (as Schröring and Ewald suppose), but that it denotes the work of punishment especially; and consequently *yebazza‘* is to be taken as a *futurum exactum* (cf. ch. iv. 4), as we may clearly see from the choice of this word in Lam. ii. 17 (cf. Zech. iv. 9).

When Jehovah had punished to such an extent that He could not go any further without destroying Israel,—a result which would be opposed to His mercy and truth,—His punishing would turn against the instrument of punishment, which would fall under the curse of all ungodly selfishness. Vers. 13, 14. "*For he hath said, By the strength of my hand I have done it, and by my own wisdom; for I am prudent: and I removed the bounds of the nations, and I plundered their stores, and threw down rulers*[1] *like a bull. And my hand extracted the wealth of the nations like a nest: and as men sweep up forsaken eggs, have I swept the whole earth; there was none that moved the wing, and opened the mouth, and chirped.*" The futures may be taken most safely as regulated by the preterites, and used, like German imperfects, to express that which occurs not once merely, but several times. The second of these preterites, שׁוֹשֵׂיתִי, is the only example of a *poel* of verbs ל"ה; possibly a mixed form from שָׁסַס (*poel* of שָׁסַס) and שָׁסָה (*piel* of שָׁסָה). The object to this, viz. *'athidoth* (*chethib*) or *'athudoth* (*keri*), is sometimes used in the sense of τὰ μέλλοντα; sometimes, as in this instance, in the sense of τὰ ὑπάρχοντα. According to the *keri*, the passage is to be rendered, "And I, a mighty one, threw down kings" (those sitting on thrones), *cabbir* being taken in the same sense as in Job xxxiv. 17, 24, xxxvi. 5. But the chethib *câ'abbīr* is to be preferred as more significant, and not to be rendered "as a hero" (to which the *Caph similitudinis* is so little suitable, that it would be necessary to take it, as in ch. xiii. 6, as *Caph veritatis*), but "as a bull," *'abbīr* as in Ps. lxviii. 31, xxii. 13, l. 13. A bull, as the excavations show, was an emblem of royalty among the Assyrians. In ver. 14, the more stringent *Vav conv.* is introduced before the third pers. fem. The kingdoms of the nations are compared here to birds' nests, which the Assyrian took for himself (*'âsaph*, as in Hab. ii. 5); and their possessions to single eggs. The mother bird was away, so that there was not even a sign of resistance; and in the nest itself not one of the young birds moved a wing to defend itself, or opened its beak to scare the intruder away. Seb. Schmid has interpreted it correctly, "*nulla alam movet ad defendendum aut os aperit ad terrendum.*" Thus proudly did Asshur look back upon its course of victory, and thus contemptuously did it look down upon the conquered kingdoms.

This self-exaltation was a foolish sin. Ver. 15. "*Dare the axe boast itself against him that heweth therewith, or the saw magnify itself against him that useth it? As if a staff were to swing those that lift it up, as if a stick should lift up not-wood!*" "*Not-wood*" is to be taken as one word, as in ch. xxxi. 8. A

---
[1] *Thronende*, lit. those who sat (on thrones).

stick is wood, and nothing more; in itself it is an absolutely motionless thing. A man is "*not-wood*," an incomparably higher, living being. As there must be "not-wood" to lay hold of wood, so, wherever a man performs extraordinary deeds, there is always a superhuman cause behind, viz. God Himself, who bears the same relation to the man as the man to the wood. The boasting of the Assyrian was like the bragging of an instrument, such as an axe, a saw, or a stick, against the person using it. The verb *hēnīph* is applied both to saw and stick, indicating the oscillating movements of a measured and more or less obvious character. The plural, "those that lift it up," points to the fact that by Him who lifts up the stick, Jehovah, the cause of all causes, and power of all powers, is intended.

There follows in the next verse the punishment provoked by such self-deification (cf. Hab. i. 11). Ver. 16. "*Therefore will the Lord, the Lord of hosts, send consumption against his fat men; and under Asshur's glory there burns a brand like a firebrand.*" Three epithets are here employed to designate God according to His unlimited, all-controlling omnipotence: viz. *hâ'âdōn*, which is always used by Isaiah in connection with judicial and penal manifestations of power; and *adonâi zebâoth*, a combination never met with again, similar to the one used in the Elohistic Psalms, *Elohim zebaoth* (compare, on the other hand, ch. iii. 15, x. 23, 24). Even here a large number of codices and editions (Norzi's, for example) have the reading Jehovah Zebaoth, which is customary in other cases.[1] *Râzōn* (ch. xvii. 4) is one of the diseases mentioned in the catalogue of curses in Lev. xxvi. 16 and Deut. xxviii. 22. Galloping consumption comes like a destroying angel upon the great masses of flesh seen in the well-fed Assyrian magnates: *mishmannim* is used in a personal sense, as in Ps. lxxviii. 31. And under the glory of Asshur, *i.e.* its richly equipped army (*câbōd* as in ch. viii. 7), He who makes His angels flames of fire places fire so as to cause it to pass away in flames. In accordance with Isaiah's masterly art of painting in tones, the whole passage is so expressed, that we can hear the crackling, and spluttering,

---

[1] This passage is not included in the 134 *raddâ'in* (*i.e.* "real") *adonai*, or passages in which *adonai* is written, and not merely to be read, that are enumerated by the Masora (see Bär's *Psalterium*, p. 133).

and hissing of the fire, as it seizes upon everything within its reach. This fire, whatever it may be so far as its natural and phenomenal character is concerned, is in its true essence the wrath of Jehovah.—Ver. 17. "*And the light of Israel becomes a fire, and His Holy One a flame; and it sets on fire and devours its thistles and thorns on one day.*" God is fire (Deut. ix. 3), and light (1 John i. 5); and in His own self-life the former is resolved into the latter. *Kâdōsh* (holy) is here parallel to '*ōr* (light); for the fact that God is holy, and the fact that He is pure light, are essentially one and the same thing, whether *kâdash* meant originally to be pure or to be separate. The nature of all creatures, and of the whole *cosmos*, is a mixture of light and darkness. The nature of God alone is absolute light. But light is love. In this holy light of love He has given Himself up to Israel, and taken Israel to Himself. But He has also within Him a basis of fire, which sin excites against itself, and which was about to burst forth as a flaming fire of wrath against Asshur, on account of its sins against Him and His people. Before this fire of wrath, this destructive might of His penal righteousness, the splendid forces of Asshur were nothing but a mass of thistles and a bed of thorns (written here in the reverse order peculiar to Isaiah, *shâmîr râshaith*), equally inflammable, and equally deserving to be burned. To all appearance, it was a forest and a park, but it was irrecoverably lost.—Vers. 18, 19. "*And the glory of his forest and his garden-ground will He destroy, even to soul and flesh, so that it is as when a sick man dieth. And the remnant of the trees of his forest can be numbered, and a boy could write them.*" The army of Asshur, composed as it was of many and various nations, was a forest (*ya'ar*); and, boasting as it did of the beauty of both men and armour, a garden ground (*carmel*), a human forest and park. Hence the idea of "utterly" is expressed in the proverbial "even to soul and flesh," which furnishes the occasion for a leap to the figure of the wasting away of a נֹסֵס (*hap. leg.* the consumptive man, from *nâsas*, related to *nûsh*, *'ânash*, Syr. *n'sîso*, *n'shisho*, a sick man, based upon the radical notion of melting away, cf. *mâsas*, or of reeling to and fro, cf. *mūt*, *nūt*, Arab. *nâsa, nâta*). Only a single vital spark would still glimmer in the gigantic and splendid colossus, and with this its life would threaten to become entirely extinct. Or, what is the same thing, only a few trees of the forest, such as could be easily numbered (*mispâr* as in Deut. xxxiii. 6, cf. Isa. xxi. 17), would still remain, yea, so few, that a boy would be able to count and enter them. And this really came to pass. Only a small remnant of the army that marched against Jerusalem ever escaped. With this small remnant of an all-destroying power the prophet now contrasts the remnant of Israel, which is the seed of a new power that is about to arise.—Ver. 20. "*And it will come to pass in that day, the remnant of Israel, and that which has escaped of the house of Jacob, will not continue to stay itself upon its chastiser, and will stay itself upon Jehovah, the Holy One of Israel, in truth.*" Behind the judgment upon Asshur there lies the restoration of Israel. "The chastiser" was the Assyrian. While relying upon this, Israel received strokes, because Jehovah made Israel's staff into its rod. But henceforth it would sanctify the Holy One of Israel, putting its trust in Him and not in man, and that purely and truly (*be'emeth*, "in truth"), not with fickleness and hypocrisy. Then would be fulfilled the *promise* contained in the name Shear-yashub, after the fulfilment of the *threat* that it contained.—Ver. 21. "*The remnant will turn, the remnant of Jacob, to God the mighty.*" El gibbor is God as historically manifested in the heir of David (ch. ix. 6). Whilst Hosea (iii. 5) places side by side Jehovah and the second David, Isaiah sees them as one. In New Testament phraseology, it would be "to God in Christ."

To Him the remnant of Israel would turn, but only the remnant. Vers. 22, 23. "*For if thy people were even as the sea-sand, the remnant thereof will turn: destruction is firmly determined, flowing away righteousness. For the Lord, Jehovah of hosts, completes the finishing stroke and that which is firmly determined, within the whole land.*" As the words are not preceded by any negative clause, *ci 'im* are not combined in the sense of *sed* or *nisi;* but they belong to two sentences, and signify *nam si* (for if). If the number of the Israelites were the highest that had been promised, only the remnant among them, or of them (*bō* partitive, like the French *en*), would turn, or, as the nearer definition *ad Deum* is wanting here, come back to their right position. With regard to the great mass, destruction was irrevocably determined (*ráchatz*, τέμνειν, then to resolve upon anything, ἀποτόμως, 1 Kings xx. 40); and this destruction "overflowed with righteousness," or rather "flowed on (*shōtēph,* as in ch. xxviii. 18) righteousness," *i.e.* brought forth righteousness as it flowed onwards, so that it was like a swell of the penal righteousness of God (*shâtaph,* with the accusative, according to Ges. § 138, Anm. 2). That *cillâyōn* is not used here in the sense of completion any more than in Deut. xxviii. 65, is evident from ver. 23, where *câlâh* (fem. of *câleh,* that which vanishes, then the act of vanishing, the end) is used interchangeably with it, and *necherâtzâh* indicates judgment as a thing irrevocably decided (as in ch. xxviii. 22, and borrowed from these passages in Dan. ix. 27, xi. 36). Such a judgment of extermination the almighty Judge had determined to carry fully out (*'ōseh* in the sense of a *fut. instans*) within all the land (*b'kereb,* within, not *b'thok,* in the midst of), that is to say, one that would embrace the whole land and all the people, and would destroy, if not every individual without exception, at any rate the great mass, except a very few.

In these esoteric addresses, however, it is not the prophet's intention to threaten and terrify, but to comfort and encourage. He therefore turns to that portion of the nation which needs and is susceptible of consolation, and draws this conclusion from the element of consolation contained in what has been already predicted, that they may be consoled.—Ver. 24. "*Therefore thus saith the Lord, Jehovah of hosts, My people that dwellest on Zion, be not afraid of Asshur, if it shall smite thee with the rod, and lift its stick against thee, in the manner of Egypt.*" "Therefore:" *lacēn* never occurs in Hebrew in the sense of *attamen* (Gesenius and Hitzig), and this is not the meaning here, but *propterea.* The elevating appeal is founded upon what has just before been threatened in such terrible words, but at the same time contains an element of promise in the midst of the peremptory judgment. The very words in which the people are addressed, "My people that dwelleth on Zion," are indirectly encouraging. Zion was the site of the gracious presence of God, and of that sovereignty which had been declared imperishable. Those who dwelt there, and were the people of God (the servants of God), not only according to their calling, but also according to their internal character, were also heirs of the promise; and therefore, even if the Egyptian bondage should be renewed in the Assyrian, they might be assured of this to their consolation, that the redemption of Egypt would also be renewed. "*In the manner of Egypt:*" *b'derek Mitzraim,* lit. in the way, *i.e.* the Egyptians' mode of acting; *derek* denotes the course of active procedure, and also, as in ver. 26 and Amos iv. 10, the course of passive endurance.

A still further reason is given for the elevating words, with a resumption of the grounds of consolation upon which they were founded. Vers. 25, 26. "*For yet a very little the indignation is past, and my wrath turns to destroy them: and Jehovah of hosts moves the whip over it, as He smote Midian at the rock of Oreb; and His staff stretches out over the sea, and He lifts it up in the manner of Egypt.*" The expression "a very little" (as in ch. xvi. 14, xxix. 17) does not date from the actual present, when the Assyrian oppressions had not yet begun, but from the ideal present, when they were threatening Israel with destruction. The indignation of Jehovah would then suddenly come to an end (*câlâh za'am,* borrowed in Dan. xi. 36, and to be interpreted in accordance with ch. xxvi. 20); and the wrath of Jehovah would be, or go, '*al-tablithâm.* Luzzatto recommends the following emendation of the text, וְאַפִּי עַל־תֵּבֵל יִתֹּם, "and my wrath against the world will cease," *tēbēl* being used, as in ch. xiv. 17, with reference to the *oikoumenon* as enslaved by the imperial power. But the received text gives a better train of thought, if we connect it with ver. 26. We must not be led astray, however, by the preposition '*al,* and take the words as meaning, My wrath (burneth) over the destruction inflicted by Asshur upon the people of God, or the destruction endured by the latter. It is to the destruction of the Assyrians that the wrath of Jehovah is now directed; '*al* being used, as it frequently is, to indicate the object upon which the eye is fixed, or to which the intention points (Ps. xxxii. 8, xviii. 42). With this explanation ver. 25*b* leads on to ver. 26. The destruction of Asshur is predicted here in two figures drawn from occurrences in the olden time. The almighty Judge would swing the whip over Asshur ('*orer, agitare,* as in 2 Sam. xxiii. 18), and smite it, as Midian was once smitten. The rock of Oreb is the place where the Ephraimites slew the Midianitish king 'Oreb (Judg. vii. 25). His staff would then be over the sea, *i.e.* would be stretched out, like the wonder-working staff of

Moses, over the sea of affliction, into which the Assyrians had driven Israel (*yâm*, the sea, an emblem borrowed from the type; see Kohler on Zech. x. 11, cf. Ps. lxvi. 6); and He would lift it up, commanding the waves of the sea, so that they would swallow Asshur. "In the manner of Egypt:" *b'derek Mitzraim* (according to Luzzatto in both instances, "on the way to Egypt," which restricts the Assyrian bondage in a most unhistorical manner to the time of the Egyptian campaign) signifies in ver. 24, as the Egyptians lifted it up; but here, as it was lifted up above the Egyptians. The expression is intentionally conformed to that in ver. 24: because Asshur had lifted up the rod over Israel in the Egyptian manner, Jehovah would lift it up over Asshur in the Egyptian manner also.

The yoke of the imperial power would then burst asunder. Ver. 27. "*And it will come to pass in that day, its burden will remove from thy shoulder, and its yoke from thy neck; and the yoke will be destroyed from the pressure of the fat.*" We have here two figures: in the first (*cessabit onus ejus a cervice tua*) Israel is represented as a beast of burden; in the second (*et jugum ejus a collo tuo*), as a beast of draught. And this second figure is divided again into two fields. For *yâsūr* merely affirms that the yoke, like the burden, will be taken away from Israel; but *chubbal*, that the yoke itself will snap, from the pressure of his fat strong neck against it. Knobel, who alters the text, objects to this on the ground that the yoke was a cross piece of wood, and not a collar. And no doubt the simple yoke is a cross piece of wood, which is fastened to the forehead of the ox (generally of two oxen yoked together: *jumenta = jugmenta*, like *jugum*, from *jungere*); but the derivation of the name itself, '*ol*, from '*âlal*, points to the connection of the cross piece of wood with a collar, and here the yoke is expressly described as lying round the neck (and not merely fastened against the forehead). There is no necessity, therefore, to read *chebel* (*chablo*), as Knobel proposes; *chubbal* (Arabic *chubbila*) indicates here a *corrumpi* consequent upon a *disrumpi*. (On *p'nē*, vid. Job xli. 5; and for the application of the term *mippenē* to energy manifesting itself in its effects, compare Ps. lxviii. 3 as an example.) Moreover, as Kimchi has observed, in most instances the yoke creates a wound in the fat flesh of the ox by pressure and friction; but here the very opposite occurs, and the fatness of the ox leads to the destruction of the yoke (compare the figure of grafting employed in Rom. xi. 17, to which Paul gives a turn altogether contrary to nature). Salvation, as the double turn in the second figure affirms, comes no less from within (27*b*) than from without (27*a*). It is no less a consequence of the world-conquering grace at work in Isaiah, than a miracle wrought for Israel upon their foes.

The prophet now proceeds to describe how the Assyrian army advances steadily towards Jerusalem, spreading terror on every hand, and how, when planted there like a towering forest, it falls to the ground before the irresistible might of Jehovah. Eichhorn and Hitzig pronounce this prophecy a *vaticinium post eventum*, because of its far too special character; but Knobel regards it as a prophecy, because no Assyrian king ever did take the course described; in other words, as a mere piece of imagination, as Ewald maintains. Now, no doubt the Assyrian army, when it marched against Jerusalem, came from the south-west, namely, from the road to Egypt, and not directly from the north. Sennacherib had conquered Lachish; he then encamped before Libnah, and it was thence that he advanced towards Jerusalem. But the prophet had no intention of giving a fragment out of the history of the war: all that he meant to do was to give a lively representation of the future fact, that after devastating the land of Judah, the Assyrian would attack Jerusalem. There is no necessity whatever to contend, as Drechsler does, against calling the description an ideal one. There is all the difference in the world between idea and imagination. Idea is the essential root of the real, and the reality is its historical form. This form, its essential manifestation, may be either this or that, so far as individual features are concerned, without any violation of its essential character. What the prophet here predicts has, when properly interpreted, been all literally fulfilled. The Assyrian did come from the north with the storm-steps of a conqueror, and the cities named were really exposed to the dangers and terrors of war. And this was what the prophet depicted, looking as he did from a divine eminence, and drawing from the heart of the divine counsels, and then painting the future with colours which were but the broken lights of those counsels as they existed in his own mind.

Æsthetically considered, the description is one of the most magnificent that human poetry has ever produced. Vers. 28–32. "*He comes upon Ayyath, passes through Migron; in Michmash he leaves his baggage. They go through the pass: let Geba be our quarters for the night! Ramah trembles; Gibeah of Saul flees. Scream aloud, O daughter of Gallim! Only listen, O Laysha! Poor Anathoth! Madmenah hurries away; the inhabitants of Gebim rescue. He still halts in Nob to-day; swings his hand over the mountain of the daughter of Zion, the hill of Jerusalem. Behold, the Lord, Jehovah of hosts, lops down the branches with terrific force; and those of towering growth are hewn down, and the lofty are humbled. And He fells the thickets of the forest with iron; and Lebanon, it falls by a Majestic One.*" When the Assyrian came upon Ayyath (=*Ayyah,* 1 Chron. vii. 28 (?), Neh. xi. 31, generally *hâ-'ai,* or *'Ai*), about thirty miles to the north-east of Jerusalem, he trod for the first time upon Benjaminitish territory, which was under the sway of Judæa. The name of this 'AI, which signifies "stone-heap," tallies, as Knobel observes, with the name of the *Tell el-hagar,* which is situated about three-quarters of an hour to the south-east of Beitîn, *i.e.* Bethel. But there are tombs, reservoirs, and ruins to be seen about an hour to the south-east of Beitîn; and these Robinson associates with Ai. From Ai, however, the army will not proceed towards Jerusalem by the ordinary route, viz. the great north road (or "Nablus road"); but, in order to surprise Jerusalem, it takes a different route, in which it will have to cross three deep and difficult valleys. From Ai they pass to MIGRON, the name of which has apparently been preserved in the ruins of *Burg Magrun,* situated about eight minutes' walk from Beitîn.[1] MICHMASH is still to be found in the form of a deserted village with ruins, under the name of *Muchmâs,* on the eastern side of the valley of Migron. Here they deposit their baggage (*hiphkid,* Jer. xxxvi. 20), so far as they are able to dispense with it,—either to leave it lying there, or to have it conveyed after them by an easier route. For they proceed thence through the pass of Michmash, a deep and precipitous ravine about forty-eight minutes in breadth,

---

[1] I also find the name written *Magrum* (read *Magrun*), which is probably taken from a more correct hearsay than the *Machrûn* of Robinson (ii. 127).

the present Wady Suweinit. "The pass" (*ma'bârâh*) is the defile of Michmash, with two prominent rocky cliffs, where Jonathan had his adventure with the garrison of the Philistines. One of these cliffs was called *Seneh* (1 Sam. xiv. 4), a name which suggests *es-Suweinit*. Through this defile they pass, encouraging one another, as they proceed along the difficult march, by the prospect of passing the night in Geba, which is close at hand. It is still disputed whether this Geba is the same place as the following Gibeah of Saul or not. There is at the present time a village called Geba' below *Muchmâs*, situated upon an eminence. The almost universal opinion now is, that this is not Gibeah of Saul, but that the latter is to be seen in the prominent *Tell* (*Tuleil*) *el-Fûl*, which is situated farther south. This is possibly correct.[1] For there can be no doubt that this mountain, the name of which signifies "Bean-hill," would be a very strong position, and one very suitable for Gibeah of Saul; and the supposition that there were two places in Benjamin named *Geba*, *Gibeah*, or *Gibeath*, is favoured at any rate by Josh. xviii. 21-28, where *Geba* and *Gibeath* are distinguished from one another. And this mountain, which is situated to the south of *er-Râm*—that is to say, between the ancient Ramah and Anathoth—tallies very well with the route of the Assyrian as here described; whilst it is very improbable that Isaiah has designated the very same place first of all *Geba*, and then (for what reason no one can tell) Gibeah of Saul. We therefore adopt the view, that the Assyrian army took up its quarters for the night at Geba, which still bears this name, spreading terror in all directions, both east and west, and still more towards the south. Starting in the morning from the deep valley between Michmash and Geba, they pass on one side of Rama (the present *er-Râm*), situated half an hour to the west of Geba, which trembles as it sees them go by; and the inhabitants of Gibeath of Saul, upon the "Bean-hill," a height that commands the whole of the surrounding country, take to flight when they pass by. Every halting-place on their route brings them nearer to Jerusalem.

[1] This is supported by Robinson in his *Later Biblical Researches in Palestine* (1857), by Valentiner (pastor at Jerusalem), and by Keil in the *Commentary on Joshua, Judges*, etc. (pp. 188-9), where all the more recent writings on this topographical question are given.

The prophet goes in spirit through it all. It is so objectively real to him, that it produces the utmost anxiety and pain. The cities and villages of the district are lost. He appeals to the daughter, *i.e.* the population, of GALLIM, to raise a far-sounding yell of lamentation with their voice (Ges. § 138, 1, Anm. 3), and calls out in deep sympathy to LAYSHA, which was close by (on the two places, both of which have vanished now, see 1 Sam. xxv. 44 and Judg. xviii. 29), " only listen," the enemy is coming nearer and nearer ; and then for ANATHOTH (*'Anâtâ*, still to be seen about an hour and a quarter to the north of Jerusalem) he utters this lamentation (taking the name as an omen of its fate) : O poor Anathoth ! There is no necessity for any alteration of the text; *'aniyyâh* is an appeal, or rather an exclamation, as in ch. liv. 11 ; and *'anâthoth* follows, according to the same verbal order as in ch. xxiii. 12, unless indeed we take it at once as an adjective written before the noun,—an arrangement of the words which may possibly have been admissible in such interjectional sentences. The catastrophe so much to be dreaded by Jerusalem draws nearer and nearer. MADMENAH (dung-hill, see *Job*, ii. 152) flees in anxious haste : the inhabitants of GEBIM (water-pits) carry off their possessions (העיזו, from עוז, to flee, related to *chush*, hence to carry off in flight, to bring in haste to a place of security, Ex. ix. 19, cf. Jer. iv. 6, vi. 1 ; synonymous with *hēnîs*, Ex. ix. 20, Judg. vi. 11 ; different from *'âzaz*, to be firm, strong, defiant, from which *mâ'oz*, a fortress, is derived,—in distinction from the Arabic *ma'âdh*, a place of refuge : comp. ch. xxx. 2, to flee to Pharaoh's shelter). There are no traces left of either place. The passage is generally understood as implying that the army rested another day in Nob. But this would be altogether at variance with the design—to take Jerusalem by surprise by the suddenness of the destructive blow. We therefore render it, " Even to-day he will halt in Nob" (*in eo est ut subsistat*, Ges. § 132, Anm. 1),—namely, to gather up fresh strength there in front of the city which was doomed to destruction, and to arrange the plan of attack. The supposition that NOB was the village of *el-'Isawiye*, which is still inhabited, and lies to the south-west of Anâta, fifty-five minutes to the north of Jerusalem, is at variance with the situation, as correctly described by Jerome, when he says : " *Stans in oppidulo Nob et procul urbem conspiciens Jerusalem.*"

A far more appropriate situation is to be found in the hill which rises to the north of Jerusalem, and which is called *Sadr*, from its breast-like projection or roundness,—a name which is related in meaning to *nob*, *nâb*, to rise (see *Gen.* p. 635). From this eminence the way leads down into the valley of Kidron; and as you descend, the city spreads out before you at a very little distance off. It may have been here, in the prophet's view, that the Assyrians halted.[1] It was not long, however (as the *yenōphĕph* which follows ἀσυνδέτως implies), before his hand was drawn out to strike (ch. xi. 15, xix. 16), and swing over the mountain of the daughter of Zion (ch. xvi. 1), over the city of the holy hill. But what would Jehovah do, who was the only One who could save His threatened dwelling-place in the face of such an army? As far as ver. 32a, the prophet's address moved on at a hurried, stormy pace; it then halted, and seemed, as it were, panting with anxiety; it now breaks forth in a dactylic movement, like a long rolling thunder. The hostile army stands in front of Jerusalem, like a broad dense forest. But it is soon manifest that Jerusalem has a God who cannot be defied with impunity, and who will not leave His city in the lurch at the decisive moment, like the gods of Carchemish and Calno. Jehovah is the Lord, the God of both spiritual and starry hosts. He smites down the branches of this forest of an army: *sē'ēph* is a so-called *piel privativum*, to lop (lit. to take the branches in hand; cf. *sikkēl*, ch. v. 2); and *pu'rah* = *pe'urah* (in Ezekiel *pō'rah*) is used like the Latin *frons*, to include both branches and foliage,—in other words, the leafy branches as the ornament of the tree, or the branches as adorned with leaves. The instrument He employs is *ma'arâtzâh*, his terrifying and crushing power (compare the verb in ch. ii. 19, 21). And even the lofty trunks of the forest thus cleared of branches and leaves do not remain; they lie hewn down, and the lofty ones must fall. It is just the same with the trunks, *i.e.* the leaders, as with the branches and the foliage, *i.e.* with

---

[1] This is the opinion of Valentiner, who also regards the march of the Assyrians as an "execution-march" in two columns, one of which took the road through the difficult ground to the east, whilst the other inflicted punishment upon the places that stood near the road. The text does not require this, however, but describes a march, which spread alarm both right and left as it went along.

the great crowded masses. The whole of the forest thicket (as in ch. ix. 17) he hews down (*nikkaph*, third pers. *piel*, though it may also be *niphal*); and Lebanon, *i.e.* the army of Asshur which is now standing opposite to Mount Zion, like Lebanon with its forest of cedars, falls down through a Majestic One (*'addīr*), *i.e.* through Jehovah (ch. xxxiii. 21, cf. Ps. lxxvi. 5, xciii. 4). In the account of the fulfilment (ch. xxxvii. 36) it is the angel of the Lord (*mal'ach Jehovah*), who is represented as destroying the hundred and eighty-five thousand in the Assyrian camp in a single night. The angel of Jehovah is not a messenger of God sent from afar, but the chosen organ of the ever-present divine power.

This is the fate of the imperial power of the world. When the axe is laid to it, it falls without hope. But in Israel spring is returning. Ch. xi. 1. "*And there cometh forth a twig out of the stump of Jesse, and a shoot from its roots bringeth forth fruit.*" The world-power resembles the cedar-forest of Lebanon; the house of David, on the other hand, because of its apostasy, is like the stump of a felled tree (*geza'*, *truncus*, from *gâza'*, *truncare*), like a root without stem, branches, or crown. The world-kingdom, at the height of its power, presents the most striking contrast to Israel and the house of David in the uttermost depth announced in ch. vi. *fin.*, mutilated and reduced to the lowliness of its Bethlehemitish origin. But whereas the Lebanon of the imperial power is thrown down, to remain prostrate; the house of David renews its youth. And whilst the former has no sooner reached the summit of its glory, than it is suddenly cast down; the latter, having been reduced to the utmost danger of destruction, is suddenly exalted. What Pliny says of certain trees, "*inarescunt rursusque adolescunt, senescunt quidem, sed e radicibus repullulant,*" is fulfilled in the tree of Davidic royalty, that has its roots in Jesse (for the figure itself, see F. v. Lasaulx, *Philosophie der Geschichte*, pp. 117–119). Out of the stumps of Jesse, *i.e.* out of the remnant of the chosen royal family which has sunk down to the insignificance of the house from which it sprang, there comes forth a twig (*choter*), which promises to supply the place of the trunk and crown; and down below, in the roots covered with earth, and only rising a little above it, there shows itself a *nētzer*, *i.e.* a fresh green shoot (from *nâtzēr*, to shine or blossom). In the historical account of the fulfilment, even the ring of the words of the prophecy is noticed: the *nētzer*, at first so humble and insignificant, was a poor despised *Nazarene* (Matt. ii. 23). But the expression *yiphreh* shows at once that it will not stop at this lowliness of origin. The shoot will bring forth fruit (*pârâh*, different in meaning, and possibly[1] also in root, from *pârach*, to blossom and bud). In the humble beginning there lies a power which will carry it up to a great height by a steady and certain process (Ezek. xvii. 22, 23). The twig which is shooting up on the ground will become a tree, and this tree will have a crown laden with fruit. Consequently the state of humiliation will be followed by one of exaltation and perfection.

Jehovah acknowledges Him, and consecrates and equips Him for His great work with the seven spirits. Ver. 2. "*And the Spirit of Jehovah descends upon Him, spirit of wisdom and understanding, spirit of counsel and might, spirit of knowledge and fear of Jehovah.*" "The Spirit of Jehovah" (*ruach Yehovah*) is the Divine Spirit, as the communicative vehicle of the whole creative fulness of divine powers. Then follow the six spirits, comprehended by the *ruach Yehovah* in three pairs, of which the first relates to the intellectual life, the second to the practical life, and the third to the direct relation to God. For *chocmâh* (wisdom) is the power of discerning the nature of things through the appearance, and *bīnâh* (understanding) the power of discerning the differences of things in their appearance; the former is σοφία, the latter διάκρισις or σύνεσις. "Counsel" ('*etzâh*) is the gift of forming right conclusions, and "might" (*geburâh*) the ability to carry them out with energy. "The knowledge of Jehovah" (*da'ath Yehovah*) is knowledge founded upon the fellowship of love; and "the fear of Jehovah" (*yir'ath Yehovâh*), fear absorbed in reverence. There are seven spirits, which are enumerated in order from the highest downwards; since the spirit of the fear of Jehovah is

---

[1] We say possibly, for the Indo-Germanic root *bhar*, to bear (Sanscr. *bharâmi* = φέρω, *fero*, cf. *ferax*, *fertilis*), which Gesenius takes as determining the radical meaning of *pârach*, cannot be traced with any certainty in the Semitic. Nevertheless *peri* and *perach* bear the same relation to one another, in the ordinary usage of the language, as fruit and blossom: the former is so called, as that which has broken through (cf. *pĕtĕr*) the latter, as that which has broken up, or budded.

the basis of the whole (Prov. i. 7; Job xxviii. 28; Ps. cxi. 10), and the Spirit of Jehovah is the heart of all. It corresponds to the shaft of the seven-lighted candlestick, and the three pair of arms that proceeded from it. In these seven forms the Holy Spirit descended upon the second David for a permanent possession, as is affirmed in the *perf. consec.* וְנָחָה (with the tone upon the ultimate, on account of the following guttural, to prevent its being pronounced unintelligibly;[1] *nuach* like καταβαίνειν καὶ μένειν, John i. 32, 33). The seven torches before the throne of God (Rev. iv. 5, cf. i. 4) burn and give light in His soul. The seven spirits are His seven eyes (Rev. v. 6).

And His regal conduct is regulated by this His thoroughly spiritual nature. Ver. 3. "*And fear of Jehovah is fragrance to Him; and He judges not according to outward sight, neither does He pass sentence according to outward hearing.*" We must not render it: His smelling is the smelling of the fear of God, *i.e.* the penetration of it with a keen judicial insight (as Hengstenberg and Umbreit understand it); for *hērīach* with the preposition *Beth* has not merely the signification to smell (as when followed by an accusative, Job xxxix. 25), but to smell with satisfaction (like רָאָה בְ, to see with satisfaction), Ex. xxx. 38, Lev. xxvi. 31, Amos v. 21. The fear of God is that which He smells with satisfaction; it is *rēach nīchoach* to Him. Meier's objection, that fear of God is not a thing that can be smelt, and therefore that *hērīach* must signify to breathe, is a trivial one. Just as the outward man has five senses for the material world, the inner man has also a sensorium for the spiritual world, which discerns different things in different ways. Thus the second David scents the fear of God, and only the fear of God, as a pleasant fragrance; for the fear of God is a sacrifice of adoration continually ascending to God. His favour or displeasure does not depend upon brilliant or repulsive external

---

[1] This moving forward of the tone to the last syllable is also found before *Ayin* in Gen. xxvi. 10, and very commonly with *kūmâh*, and verbs of a similar kind; also before Elohim and Jehovah, to be read *Adonai*, and before the half-guttural *resh*, Ps. xliii. 1, cxix. 154, but nowhere on any other ground than the orthophonic rather than euphonic one mentioned above; compare also וְסָרָה in ver. 13, with וְסָרוּ (with ה following) in Ex. viii. 7.

qualities; He does not judge according to outward appearances, but according to the relation of the heart to His God.

This is the standard according to which He will judge when saving, and judge when punishing. Vers. 4, 5. "*And judges the poor with righteousness, and passes sentence with equity for the humble in the land; and smites the earth with the rod of His mouth, and with the breath of His lips He slays the wicked. And righteousness is the girdle of His loins, and faithfulness the girdle of His hips.*" The main feature in ver. 4 is to be seen in the objective ideas. He will do justice to the *dallim*, the weak and helpless, by adopting an incorruptibly righteous course towards their oppressors, and decide with straightforwardness for the humble or meek of the land: 'ânâv, like 'ânî, from 'ânâh, to bend, the latter denoting a person bowed down by misfortune, the former a person inwardly bowed down, *i.e.* free from all self-conceit (*hōcīach l'*, as in Job xvi. 21). The poor and humble, or meek, are the peculiar objects of His royal care; just as it was really to them that the first beatitudes of the Sermon on the Mount applied. But "the earth" and "the wicked" (the latter is not to be understood collectively, but, as in several passages in the Old Testament, viz. Ps. lxviii. 22, cx. 6, Hab. iii. 13, 14, as pointing forward prophetically to an eschatological person, in whom hostility towards Jehovah and His Anointed culminates most satanically) will experience the full force of His penal righteousness. The very word of His mouth is a rod which shatters in pieces (Ps. ii. 9; Rev. i. 16); and the breath of His lips is sufficient to destroy, without standing in need of any further means (2 Thess. ii. 8). As the girdle upon the hips (*mothnaim*, LXX. τὴν ὀσφύν), and in front upon the loins (*chălâtzaim*, LXX. τὰς πλευράς), fastens the clothes together, so all the qualities and active powers of His person have for their band *tzedâkâh*, which follows the inviolable norm of the divine will, and *hâ'emūnâh*, which holds immovably to the course divinely appointed, according to promise (ch. xxv. 1). Special prominence is given by the article to 'emūnâh; He is the faithful and true witness (Rev. i. 5, iii. 14). Consequently with Him there commences a new epoch, in which the Son of David and His righteousness acquire a world-subduing force, and find their home in a humanity that has sprung, like Himself, out of deep humiliation.

The fruit of righteousness is peace, which now reigns in humanity under the rule of the Prince of Peace, and even in the animal world, with nothing whatever to disturb it. Vers. 6–9. "*And the wolf dwells with the lamb, and the leopard lies down with the kid; and calf and lion and stalled ox together: a little boy drives them. And cow and bear go to the pasture; their young ones lie down together: and the lion eats chopped straw like the ox. And the suckling plays by the hole of the adder, and the weaned child stretches its hand to the pupil of the basilisk-viper. They will not hurt nor destroy in all my holy mountain: for the land is filled with knowledge of Jehovah, like the waters covering the sea.*" The fathers, and such commentators as Luther, Calvin, and Vitringa, have taken all these figures from the animal world as symbolical. Modern rationalists, on the other hand, understand them literally, but regard the whole as a beautiful dream and wish. It is a prophecy, however, the realization of which is to be expected on this side of the boundary between time and eternity, and, as Paul has shown in Rom. viii., is an integral link in the predestined course of the history of salvation (Hengstenberg, Umbreit, Hofmann, Drechsler). There now reign among irrational creatures, from the greatest to the least,—even among such as are invisible,—fierce conflicts and bloodthirstiness of the most savage kind. But when the Son of David enters upon the full possession of His royal inheritance, the peace of paradise will be renewed, and all that is true in the popular legends of a golden age be realized and confirmed. This is what the prophet depicts in such lovely colours. The wolf and lamb, those two hereditary foes, will be perfectly reconciled then. The leopard will let the teazing kid lie down beside it. The lion, between the calf and stalled ox, neither seizes upon its weaker neighbour, nor longs for the fatter one. Cow and bear graze together, whilst their young ones lie side by side in the pasture. The lion no longer thirsts for blood, but contents itself, like the ox, with chopped straw. The suckling pursues its sport (*pilpel* of שעע, *mulcere*) by the adder's hole, and the child just weaned stretches out its hand boldly and fearlessly to *me'ûrath tziph'ōni*. It is evident from Jer. viii. 17 that *tziph'ōni* is the name of a species of snake. According to Aquila and the Vulgate, it is *basiliskos, serpens regulus*, possibly from *tzaph*, to pipe or hiss (Ges., Fürst); for Isidorus, in his *Origg.* xii. 4, says, *Sibilus idem est qui et regulus; sibilo enim occidit, antequam mordeat vel exurat.* For the *hapax leg. hâdâh,* the meaning *dirigere, tendere,* is established by the Arabic; but there is all the more uncertainty about the meaning of the *hap. leg.* מְאוּרָה. According to the parallel חֻר, it seems to signify the hollow (Syr., Vulg., LXX., κοίτη): whether from אוּר = עוּר, from which comes מְעָרָה; or from אוֹר, the light-hole (like מָאוֹר, which occurs in the Mishna, *Ohaloth* xiii. 1) or opening where a cavern opens to the light of day. It is probable, however, that *me'ûrâh* refers to something that exerts an attractive influence upon the child, either the "blending of colours" (Saad. renders *tziph'oni, errakas',* the motley snake), or better still, the "pupil of the eye" (Targum), taking the word as a feminine of *mâ'ôr,* the light of the eye (*b. Erubin* 55*b* = the power of vision). The look of a snake, more especially of the basilisk (not merely the basilisk-lizard, but also the basilisk-viper), was supposed to have a paralyzing and bewitching influence; but now the snake will lose this pernicious power (ch. lxv. 25), and the basilisk become so tame and harmless, as to let children handle its sparkling eyes as if they were jewels. All this, as we should say with Luthardt and Hofmann (*Schriftbeweis,* ii. 2, 567), is only colouring which the hand of the prophet employs, for the purpose of painting the peace of that glorified state which surpasses all possibility of description; and it is unquestionably necessary to take the thought of the promise in a spiritual sense, without adhering literally to the medium employed in expressing it. But, on the other hand, we must guard against treating the description itself as merely a drapery thrown around the actual object; whereas it is rather the refraction of the object in the mind of the prophet himself, and therefore a manifestation of the true nature of that which he actually saw. But are the animals to be taken as the subject in ver. 9 also? The subject that most naturally suggests itself is undoubtedly the animals, of which a few that are alarming and destructive to men have been mentioned just before. And the fact that they really are thought of as the subject, is confirmed by ch. lxv. 25, where ch. xi. 6-9*a* is repeated in a compendious form. The idea that יָרֵעוּ requires men as the subject, is refuted by the common חַיָּה רָעָה (compare the parallel promise in Ezek. xxxiv. 25, which rests upon Hos.

ii. 20). That the term *yashchithu* can be applied to animals, is evident from Jer. ii. 30, and may be assumed as a matter of course. But if the animals are the subject, *har kodshi* (my holy mountain) is not Zion-Moriah, upon which wild beasts never made their home in historical times; but, as the generalizing *col* (all) clearly shows, the whole of the holy mountain-land of Israel: *har kodshi* has just this meaning in ch. lvii. 13 (cf. Ps. lxxviii. 54, Ex. xv. 17). The fact that peace prevails in the animal world, and also peace between man and beast, is then attributed to the universal prevalence of the knowledge of God, in consequence of which that destructive hostility between the animal world and man, by which estrangement and apostasy from God were so often punished (2 Kings xvii. 25; Ezek. xiv. 15, etc.: see also ch. vii. 24), have entirely come to an end. The meaning of "the earth" is also determined by that of "all my holy mountain." The *land of Israel*, the dominion of the Son of David in the more restricted sense, will be from this time forward the paradisaical centre, as it were, of the whole earth,—a prelude of its future state of perfect and universal glorification (ch. vi. 3, "all the earth"). It has now become full of "the knowledge of Jehovah," *i.e.* of that experimental knowledge which consists in the fellowship of love (דֵּעָה, like לֵדָה, is a secondary form of דַּעַת, the more common infinitive or verbal noun from ידע: Ges. § 133, 1), like the waters which cover the sea, *i.e.* the bottom of the sea (compare Hab. ii. 14, where *lâda'ath* is a virtual accusative, full of that which is to be known). "*Cover:*" *cissâh l'* (like *sâcac l'*, Ps. xci. 4), signifies to afford a covering to another; the *Lamed* is frequently introduced with a participle (in Arabic regularly) as a sign of the object (Ewald, § 292, *e*), and the omission of the article in the case of *mecassim* is a natural consequence of the inverted order of the words.

The prophet has now described, in vers. 1–5, the righteous conduct of the Son of David, and in vers. 6–9 the peace which prevails under His government, and extends even to the animal world, and which is consequent upon the living knowledge of God that has now become universal, that is to say, of the spiritual transformation of the people subject to His sway,—an allusion full of enigmas, but one which is more clearly expounded in the following verse, both in its direct contents and also in all that it presupposes. Ver. 10. "*And it will come to pass in that day: the root-sprout of Jesse, which stands as a banner of the peoples, for it will nations ask, and its place of rest is glory.*" The first question which is disposed of here, has reference to the apparent restriction thus far of all the blessings of this peaceful rule to Israel and the land of Israel. This restriction, as we now learn, is not for its own sake, but is simply the means of an unlimited extension of this fulness of blessing. The proud tree of the Davidic sovereignty is hewn down, and nothing is left except the root. The new David is *shoresh Yishai* (the root-sprout of Jesse), and therefore in a certain sense the root itself, because the latter would long ago have perished if it had not borne within itself from the very commencement Him who was now about to issue from it. But when He who had been concealed in the root of Jesse as its sap and strength should have become the rejuvenated root of Jesse itself (cf. Rev. xxii. 16), He would be exalted from this lowly beginning *l'nēs 'ammim*, into a banner summoning the nations to assemble, and uniting them around itself. Thus visible to all the world, He would attract the attention of the heathen to Himself, and they would turn to Him with zeal, and His *menuchâh*, *i.e.* the place where He had settled down to live and reign (for the word in this local sense, compare Num. x. 33 and Ps. cxxxii. 8, 14), would be glory, *i.e.* the dwelling-place and palace of a king whose light shines over all, who has all beneath His rule, and who gathers all nations around Himself. The Vulgate renders it "*et sepulcrum ejus gloriosum*" (a leading passage for encouraging pilgrimages), but the passion is here entirely swallowed up by the splendour of the figure of royalty; and *menuchah* is no more the place of rest in the grave than *nēs* is the cross, although undoubtedly the cross has become the banner in the actual fulfilment, which divides the *parousia* of Christ into a first and second coming.

A second question also concerns Israel. The nation out of which and for which this king will primarily arise, will before that time be scattered far away from its native land, in accordance with the revelation in ch. vi. How, then, will it be possible for Him to reign in the midst of it?—Vers. 11, 12. "*And it will come to pass in that day, the Lord will stretch out His hand again a second time to redeem the remnant of His people that shall* be left, out of Asshur, and out of Egypt, and out of Pathros, and out of Ethiopia, and out of 'Elam, and out of Shinar, and out of Hamath, and out of the islands of the sea. And he raises a banner for the nations, and fetches home the outcasts of Israel; and the dispersed of Judah will He assemble from the four borders of the earth." Asshur and Egypt stand here in front, and side by side, as the two great powers of the time of Isaiah (cf. ch. vii. 18-20). As appendices to Egypt, we have (1) *Pathros*, hierogl. *to-rēs*, and with the article *petorēs*, the southland, *i.e.* Upper Egypt, so that Mizraim in the stricter sense is Lower Egypt (see, on the other hand, Jer. xliv. 15); and (2) *Cush*, the land which lies still farther south than Upper Egypt on both sides of the Arabian Gulf; and as appendices to Asshur, (1) *'Elam, i.e.* Elymais, in southern Media, to the east of the Tigris; and (2) *Shinar*, the plain to the south of the junction of the Euphrates and Tigris. Then follow the Syrian *Hamath* at the northern foot of the Lebanon; and lastly, " *the islands of the sea,*" *i.e.* the islands and coast-land of the Mediterranean, together with the whole of the insular continent of Europe. There was no such *diaspora* of Israel at the time when the prophet uttered this prediction, nor indeed even after the dissolution of the northern kingdom; so that the specification is not historical, but prophetic. The redemption which the prophet here foretells is a second, to be followed by no third; consequently the banishment out of which Israel is redeemed is the ultimate form of that which is threatened in ch. vi. 12 (cf. Deut. xxx. 1 sqq.). It is the second redemption, the counterpart of the Egyptian. He will then stretch out His hand again (*yōsiph*, supply *lishloach*); and as He once delivered Israel out of Egypt, so will He now redeem it—purchase it back (*kânâh*, opp. *mâcar*) out of all the countries named. The *min* attached to the names of the countries is to be construed with *liknōth*. Observe how, in the prophet's view, the conversion of the heathen becomes the means of the redemption of Israel. The course which the history of salvation has taken since the first coming of Christ, and which it will continue to take to the end, as described by Paul in the Epistle to the Romans, is distinctly indicated by the prophet. At the word of Jehovah the heathen will set His people free, and even escort them (ch. xlix. 22, lxii. 10); and thus He will gather again (*'âsaph*, with reference to the one gathering point;

kibbētz, with reference to the dispersion of those who are to be gathered together) from the utmost ends of the four quarters of the globe, " the outcasts of the kingdom of Israel, and the dispersed of the kingdom of Judah" (*nidchē Yisráel ūnephutzōth Yehūdáh: nidchē = niddechē*, with the *dagesh* dropped before the following guttural[1]), both men and women.

But this calls to mind the present rent in the unity of the nation; and the third question very naturally arises, whether this rent will continue. The answer to this is given in ver. 13: " *And the jealousy of Ephraim is removed, and the adversaries of Judah are cut off; Ephraim will not show jealousy towards Judah, and Judah will not oppose Ephraim.*" As the suffix and genitive after *tzōrēr* are objective in every other instance (*e.g.* Amos v. 12), *tzor‛rē Yehudáh* must mean, not those members of Judah who are hostile to Ephraim, as Ewald, Knobel, and others suppose, but those members of Ephraim who are hostile to Judah, as Umbreit and Schegg expound it. In ver. 13*a* the prophet has chiefly in his mind the old feeling of enmity cherished by the northern tribes, more especially those of Joseph, towards the tribe of Judah, which issued eventually in the division of the kingdom. It is only in ver. 13*b* that he predicts the termination of the hostility of Judah towards Ephraim. The people, when thus brought home again, would form one fraternally united nation, whilst all who broke the peace of this unity would be exposed to the immediate judgment of God (*yiccárēthu*, will be cut off).

A fourth question has reference to the relation between this Israel of the future and the surrounding nations, such as the warlike Philistines, the predatory nomad tribes of the East, the unbrotherly Edomites, the boasting Moabites, and the cruel Ammonites. Will they not disturb and weaken the new Israel, as they did the old? Ver. 14. " *And they fly upon the shoulder of the Philistines seawards; unitedly they plunder the sons of the East: they seize upon Edom and Moab, and the sons of Ammon are subject to them.*" *Cáthēph* (shoulder) was the peculiar name of the coast-land of Philistia which sloped off towards the sea (Josh. xv. 11); but here it is used with an

---

[1] The same occurs in תִּקְחוּ, שָׁלְחוּ, מָלְאוּ, וַיִּקְנְאוּ, וַיִּשְׂאוּ, וַיִּסְעוּ. In every case the *dagesh* has fallen out because of the following guttural (Luzzatto, *Gramm.* § 180).

implied allusion to this, to signify the shoulder of the Philistian nation ($b^e cátheph = b^e c\check{e}th\check{e}ph$; for the cause see at ch. v. 2), upon which Israel plunges down like an eagle from the height of its mountain-land. The "object of the stretching out of their hand" is equivalent to the object of their grasp. And whenever any one of the surrounding nations mentioned should attack Israel, the whole people would make common cause, and act together. How does this warlike prospect square, however, with the previous promise of paradisaical peace, and the end of all warfare which this promise presupposes (cf. ch. ii. 4)? This is a contradiction, the solution of which is to be found in the fact that we have only figures here, and figures drawn from the existing relations and warlike engagements of the nation, in which the prophet pictures that supremacy of the future united Israel over surrounding nations, which is to be maintained by spiritual weapons.

He dwells still longer upon the miracles in which the antitypical redemption will resemble the typical one. Vers. 15, 16. *"And Jehovah pronounces the ban upon the sea-tongue of Egypt, and swings His hand over the Euphrates in the glow of His breath, and smites it into seven brooks, and makes it so that men go through in shoes. And there will be a road for the remnant of His people that shall be left, out of Asshur, as it was for Israel in the day of its departure out of the land of Egypt."* The two countries of the *diaspora* mentioned first are Asshur and Egypt. And Jehovah makes a way by His miraculous power for those who are returning out of both and across both. The sea-tongue of Egypt, which runs between Egypt and Arabia, *i.e.* the Red Sea (*sinus Heroopolitanus*, according to another figure), He smites with the ban (*hecherim*, corresponding in meaning to the pouring out of the vial of wrath in Rev. xvi. 12,—a stronger term than $gá'ar$, *e.g.* Ps. cvi. 9); and the consequence of this is, that it affords a dry passage to those who are coming back (though without there being any necessity to read *hecherīb*, or to follow Meier and Knobel, who combine *hecherīm* with *chárūm*, Lev. xxi. 18, in the precarious sense of splitting). And in order that the dividing of Jordan may have its antitype also, Jehovah swings His hand over the Euphrates, to smite, breathing upon it at the same time with burning breath, so that it is split up into seven shallow brooks, through which men can walk in sandals. בַּעְיָם stands, according to the law of sound, for בְּעָיָם; and the ἅπ. λεγ. עַיָם (with a fixed *kametz*), from עום = חום, חמם, to glow, signifies a glowing heat,—a meaning which is also so thoroughly supported by the two Arabic verbs *med. Ye* عام and غام (*inf. 'aim, gaim,* internal heat, burning thirst, also violent anger), that there is no need whatever for the conjecture of Luzzatto and Gesenius, בְּעָצְמוֹ. The early translators (*e.g.* LXX. πνεύματι βιαίῳ, Syr. *b'uchdono,* with a display of might) merely give conjectural renderings of the word, which had become obsolete before their time; Saadia, however, renders it with etymological correctness *suchûn,* from *sachana,* to be hot, or set on fire. Thus, by changing the Euphrates in the (parching) heat of His breath into seven shallow wadys, Jehovah makes a free course for His people who come out of Asshur, etc. This was the idea which presented itself to the prophet in just this shape, though it by no means followed that it must necessarily embody itself in history in this particular form.

As Israel, when redeemed from Egypt beyond the Red Sea, sang songs of praise, so also will the Israel of the second redemption, when brought, in a no less miraculous manner, across the Red Sea and the Euphrates. Ch. xii. 1, 2. "*And in that day thou wilt say, I thank Thee, O Jehovah, that Thou wast angry with me:* | *Thine anger is turned away, and Thou hast comforted me.* | *Behold, the God of my salvation;* | *I trust, and am not afraid:* | *for Jah Jehovah is my pride and song,* | *and He became my salvation.*" The words are addressed to the people of the future in the people of the prophet's own time. They give thanks for the wrath experienced, inasmuch as it was followed by all the richer consolation. The formation of the sentence after כִּי is paratactic; the principal tone falls upon 1*b*, where *yâshōb* is written poetically for *vayyâshob* (cf. Deut. xxxii. 8, 18; Ps. xviii. 12; Hos. vi. 1). We hear the notes of Ps. xc. 13, xxvii. 1, resounding here; whilst ver. 2*b* is the echo of Ex. xv. 2 (on which Ps. cxviii. 14 is also founded). עָזִּי (to be read *'ozzi,* and therefore also written עֻזִּי) is another form of עֻזִּי, and is used here to signify the proud self-consciousness associated with the possession of power: pride, and the expression of it, viz. boasting. *Zimrath* is equivalent in sense, and probably also in form, to *zimráthi*, just as in Syriac *z'mori* (my song) is regularly pronounced *z'mōr*, with the *i* of the suffix dropped (see Hupfeld on Ps. xvi. 6). It is also possible, however, that it may be only an expansion of the primary form *zimrath* = *zimráh*, and therefore that *zimrath* is only synonymous with *zimráthi*, as *chēphetz* in 2 Sam. xxiii. 5 is with *chephtzi*. One thing peculiar to this echo of Ex. xv. 2 is the doubling of the *Jah* in *Jáh Jehōváh*, which answers to the surpassing of the type by the antitype.

Ver. 3, again, contains a prophetic promise, which points back to the commencement of ver. 1 : "*And with rapture ye will draw water out of the wells of salvation.*" Just as Israel was miraculously supplied with water in the desert, so will the God of salvation, who has become your salvation, open many and manifold sources of salvation for you (מַעַיְנֵי as it is pointed here, instead of מַעְיְנֵי[1]), from which ye may draw with and according to your heart's delight. This water of salvation, then, forms both the material for, and instigation to, new songs of praise; and vers. 4-6 therefore continue in the strain of a psalm : "*And ye will say in that day, Praise Jehovah, proclaim His name, | make known His doings among the nations, | boast that His name is exalted. | Harp to Jehovah; for He has displayed majesty: | let this be known in all lands. | Shout and be jubilant, O inhabitant of Zion: | for great is the Holy One of Israel in the midst of thee.*" The first song of six lines is here followed by a second of seven lines : a prophetic word of promise, inserted between them, separates the one from the other. This second also commences with the well-known tones of a psalm (compare especially Ps. cv. 1, 1 Chron. xvi. 8). The phrase, "Call upon the name of Jehovah," signifies, Make the name of Jehovah the medium of invocation (Ges. § 138, Anm. 3*), *i.e* invoke it, or, as here, call it out. *Gē'ūth* is high, towering dignity ; here it is used of God, as in ch. xxvi. 10, with *'āsāh:* to prove it practically, just as with *lābēsh* in Ps. xciii. 1, to show one's self openly therein. Instead of the *Chethib meyudda'ath* in ver. 5,

---

[1] The root is the same as, for example, in יַעַלְיֻ (they rejoice) and יַעֲלֻ; here, however, it is more striking, because the singular is written מַעְיָן, and not מַעְיָן. At the same time, it is evident that the connecting sound *ay* was rather preferred than avoided, as Ewald maintains,—as we may see, for example, from the repeated *aychi* in Ps. ciii.

the *keri* substitutes the *hophal* form *mūda‘ath*, probably because *meyuddā‘*, according to the standing usage of speech, denotes one well known, or intimate; the passive of the *hophal* is certainly the more suitable. According to the preceding appeals, the words are to be understood as expressing a desire, that the glorious self-attestation of the God of salvation might be brought to the consciousness of the whole of the inhabitants of the earth, *i.e.* of all mankind. When God redeems His people, He has the salvation of all the nations in view. It is the knowledge of the Holy One of Israel, made known through the word of proclamation, that brings salvation to them all. How well may the church on Zion rejoice, to have such a God dwelling in the midst of it! He is great as the giver of promises, and great in fulfilling them; great in grace, and great in judgment; great in all His saving acts which spread from Israel to all mankind. Thus does this second psalm of the redeemed nation close, and with it the book of Immanuel.

PART III.

COLLECTION OF ORACLES CONCERNING THE HEATHEN.—
CHAP. XIII.–XXIII.

ORACLE CONCERNING THE CHALDEANS, THE HEIRS OF THE ASSYRIANS.—CHAP. XIII. 1–XIV. 27.

JUST as in Jeremiah (ch. xlvi.-li.) and Ezekiel (ch. xxv.-xxxii.), so also in Isaiah, the oracles concerning the heathen are all placed together. In this respect the arrangement of the three great books of prophecy is perfectly homogeneous. In Jeremiah these oracles, apart from the prelude in ch. xxv., form the concluding portion of the book. In Ezekiel they fill up that space of time, when Jerusalem at home was lying at her last gasp and the prophet was sitting speechless by the Chaboras. And here, in Isaiah, they compensate us for the interruption which the oral labours of the prophet appear to have sustained in the closing years of the reign of Ahaz. Moreover, this was their most suitable position, at the end of the cycle of Messianic prophecies in ch. vii.-xii.; for the great consolatory thought of the prophecy of Immanuel, that all kingdoms are to become the kingdoms of God and His Christ, is here expanded. And as the prophecy of Immanuel was delivered on the threshold of the times of the great empires, so as to cover the whole of that period with its consolation, the oracles concerning the heathen nations and kingdoms are inseparably connected with that prophecy, which forms the ground and end, the unity and substance, of them all.

The heading in ch. xiii. 1, "*Oracle concerning Babel, which Isaiah the son of Amoz did see,*" shows that ch. xiii. forms the commencement of another part of the whole book. *Massâh* (from נָשָׂא, *efferre*, then *effari*, Ex. xx. 7) signifies, as we may see from 2 Kings ix. 25, *effatum*, the verdict or oracle, more especially the verdict of God, and generally, perhaps always, the judicial sentence of God,[1] though without introducing the idea of *onus* (burden), which is the rendering adopted by the Targum, Syriac, Vulgate, and Luther, notwithstanding the fact that, according to Jer. xxiii. 33 sqq., it was the scoffers who associated this idea with the word. In a book which could throughout be traced to Isaiah, there could be no necessity for it to be particularly stated, that it was to Isaiah that the oracle was revealed, of which Babel was the object. We may therefore see from this, that the prophecy relating to Babylon was originally complete in itself, and was intended to be issued in that form. But when the whole book was compiled, these headings were retained as signal-posts of the separate portions of which it was composed. Moreover, in the case before us, the retention of the heading may be regarded as a providential arrangement. For if this "oracle of Babel" lay before us in a separate form, and without the name of Isaiah, we should not dare to attribute it to him, for the simple reason that the overthrow of the Chaldean empire is here distinctly announced, and that at a time when the Assyrian empire was still standing. For this reason the majority of critics, from the time of Rosenmüller and Justi downwards, have regarded the spuriousness of the pro-

---

[1] In Zech. xii. 1 sqq. the promise has, at any rate, a dark side. In Lam. ii. 14 there is no necessity to think of promises in connection with the *mas'oth*; and Prov. xxx. 1 and xxxi. 1 cannot help us to determine the prophetic use of the word.

phecy as an established fact. But the evidence which can be adduced in support of the testimony contained in the heading is far too strong for it to be set aside : viz. (1) the descriptive style as well as the whole stamp of the prophecy, which resembles the undisputed prophecies of Isaiah in a greater variety of points than any passage that can be selected from any other prophet. We will show this briefly, but yet amply, and as far as the nature of an exposition allows, against Knobel and others who maintain the opposite. And (2) the dependent relation of Zephaniah and Jeremiah,—a relation which the generally admitted muse-like character of the former, and the imitative character of the latter, render it impossible to invert. Both prophets show that they are acquainted with this prophecy of Isaiah, as indeed they are with all those prophecies which are set down as spurious. Stähelin, in his work on the Messianic prophecies (Excursus iv.), has endeavoured to make out that the derivative passages in question are the original passages; but *stat pro ratione voluntas*. Now, as the testimony of the heading is sustained by such evidence as this, the one argument adduced on the other side, that the prophecy has no historical footing in the circumstances of Isaiah's times, cannot prove anything at all. No doubt all prophecy rested upon an existing historical basis. But we must not expect to be able to point this out in the case of every single prophecy. In the time of Hezekiah, as ch. xxxix. clearly shows (compare Mic. iv. 10), Isaiah had become spiritually certain of this, that the power by which the final judgment would be inflicted upon Judah would not be Asshur, but *Babel, i.e.* an empire which would have for its centre that Babylon, which was already the second capital of the Assyrian empire and the seat of kings who, though dependent then, were striving hard for independence; in other words, a Chaldean empire. Towards the end of his course Isaiah was full of this prophetic thought; and from it he rose higher and higher to the consoling discovery that Jehovah would avenge His people upon Babel, and redeem them from Babel, just as surely as from Asshur. The fact that so far-reaching an insight was granted to him into the counsels of God, was not merely founded on his own personality, but rested chiefly on the position which he occupied in the midst of the first beginnings of the age of great empires. Consequently, according to the law of the creative intensity of all divinely effected beginnings, he surveyed the whole of this long period as a universal prophet, outstripped all his successors down to the time of Daniel, and left to succeeding ages not only such prophecies as those we have already read, which had their basis in the history of his own times and the historical fulfilment of which was not sealed up, but such far distant and sealed prophecies as those which immediately follow. For since Isaiah did not appear in public again after the fifteenth year of Hezekiah, the future, as his book clearly shows, was from that time forth his true home. Just as the apostle says of the New Testament believer, that he must separate himself from the world, and walk in heaven, so the Old Testament prophet separated himself from the present of his own nation, and lived and moved in its future alone.

The prophet hears a call to war. From whom it issues, and to whom or against whom it is directed, still remains a secret; but this only adds to the intensity. Ver. 2. "*On woodless mountain lift ye up a banner, call to them with loud sounding voice, shake the hand, that they may enter into gates of princes!*" The summons is urgent: hence a threefold signal, viz. the banner-staff planted on a mountain "made bald" (*nishpeh*, from which comes *sh^ephi*, which only occurs in Isaiah and Jeremiah), the voice raised high, and the shaking of the hand, denoting a violent beckoning,—all three being favourite signs with Isaiah. The destination of this army is to enter into a city of princes (*n^edībīm*, freemen, nobles, princes, Ps. cvii. 40, cf. Ps. cxiii. 8), namely, to enter as conquerors; for it is not the princes who invite them, but Jehovah.—Ver. 3. "*I, I have summoned my sanctified ones, also called my heroes to my wrath, my proudly rejoicing ones.*" "To my wrath" is to be explained in accordance with ch. x. 5. To execute His wrath He had summoned His "sanctified ones" (*m^ekuddāshim*), *i.e.* according to Jer. xxii. 7 (compare Jer. li. 27, 28), those who had already been solemnly consecrated by Him to go into the battle, and had called the heroes whom He had taken into His service, and who were His instruments in this respect, that they rejoiced with the pride of men intoxicated with victory (*vid.* Zeph. i. 7, cf. iii. 11). עליז is a word peculiarly Isaiah's; and the combination עליזי גאותי is so unusual, that we could hardly expect to find it employed by two authors who stood in no relation whatever to one another.

The command of Jehovah is quickly executed. The great army is already coming down from the mountains. Vers. 4, 5. "*Hark, a rumbling on the mountains after the manner of a great people; hark, a rumbling of kingdoms of nations met together! Jehovah of hosts musters an army, those that have come out of a distant land, from the end of the heaven: Jehovah and His instruments of wrath, to destroy the whole earth.*" Kōl commences an interjectional sentence, and thus becomes almost an interjection itself (compare ch. lii. 8, lxvi. 6, and on Gen. iv. 10). There is rumbling on the mountains (ch. xvii. 12, 13), for there are the peoples of Eran, and in front the Medes inhabiting the mountainous north-western portion of Eran, who come across the lofty *Shahu* (*Zagros*), and the ranges that lie behind it towards the Tigris, and descend upon the lowlands of Babylon; and not only the peoples of Eran, but the peoples of the mountainous north of Asia generally (Jer. li. 27),—an army under the guidance of Jehovah, the God of the hosts of spirits and stars, whose wrath it will execute over the whole earth, *i.e.* upon the world-empire; for the fall of Babel is a judgment, and accompanied with judgments upon all the tribes under Babylonian rule.

Then all sink into anxious and fearful trembling. Vers. 6–8. "*Howl; for the day of Jehovah is near; like a destructive force from the Almighty it comes. Therefore all arms hang loosely down, and every human heart melts away. And they are troubled: they fall into cramps and pangs; like a woman in labour they twist themselves: one stares at the other; their faces are faces of flame.*" The command הֵילִילוּ (not written defectively, הֵלִלוּ) is followed by the reason for such a command, viz. "the day of Jehovah is near," the watchword of prophecy from the time of Joel downwards. The *Caph* in *c'shod* is the so-called *Caph veritatis*, or more correctly, the *Caph* of comparison between the individual and its genus. It is destruction by one who possesses unlimited power to destroy (*shōd*, from *shâdad*, from which we have *shaddai*, after the form *chaggai*, the festive one, from *châgag*). In this play upon the words, Isaiah also repeats certain words of Joel (ch. i. 15). Then the hands hang down from despondency and helplessness, and the heart, the seat of life, melts (ch. xix. 1) in the heat of anguish. Universal consternation ensues. This is expressed by the word *v'nibhâlu*, which stands in half pause; the word has *shalsheleth* followed by *psik* (*pasek*), an accent which only occurs in seven passages in the twenty-one prose books of the Old Testament, and always with this dividing stroke after it.[1] Observe also the following *fut. paragogica*, which add considerably to the energy of the description by their anapæstic rhythm. The men (*subj.*) lay hold of cramps and pangs (as in Job xviii. 20, xxi. 6), the force of the events compelling them to enter into such a condition. Their faces are faces of flames. Knobel understands this as referring to their turning pale, which is a piece of exegetical jugglery. At the same time, it does not suggest mere redness, nor a convulsive movement; but just as a flame alternates between light and darkness, so their faces become alternately flushed and pale, as the blood ebbs and flows, as it were, being at one time driven with force into their faces, and then again driven back to the heart, so as to leave deadly paleness, in consequence of their anguish and terror.

The day of Jehovah's wrath is coming,—a starless night—a nightlike, sunless day. Vers. 9, 10. "*Behold, the day of Jehovah cometh, a cruel one, and wrath and fierce anger, to turn the earth into a wilderness: and its sinners He destroys out of it. For the stars of heaven, and its Orions, will not let their light shine: the sun darkens itself at its rising, and the moon does not let its light shine.*" The day of Jehovah cometh as one cruelly severe ('*aczâri*, an *adj. rel.* from '*aczâr*, *chosh*, *kosh*, to be dry, hard, unfeeling), as purely an overflowing of inward excitement, and as burning anger; *lâsūm* is carried on by the finite verb, according to a well-known alteration of style (= *ûl^ehashmîd*). It is not indeed the general judgment which the prophet is depicting here, but a certain historical catastrophe falling upon the nations, which draws the whole world into sympathetic suffering. '*Eretz*, therefore (inasmuch as the notions of land generally, and some particular land or portion of the earth, are blended together,—a very elastic term, with vanishing boundaries), is not merely the land of Babylon here, as Knobel supposes, but *the earth*. Ver. 10 shows in what way the day of Jehovah is a day of wrath. Even nature clothes itself in the colour of

[1] For the seven passages, see Ewald, *Lehrbuch* (ed. 7), p. 224.

wrath, which is the very opposite to light. The heavenly lights above the earth go out; the moon does not shine; and the sun, which is about to rise, alters its mind. "*The Orions*" are Orion itself and other constellations like it, just as the morning stars in Job xxxviii. 7 are Hesperus and other similar stars. It is more probable that the term *cesîl* is used for Orion in the sense of "the fool" (= foolhardy),[1] according to the older translators (LXX. ὁ Ὠρίων, Targum *nephilehon* from *nephila'*, Syr. *gaboro*, Arab. *gebbâr*, the giant), than that it refers to *Suhêl*, *i.e. Canopus* (see the notes on Job ix. 9, xxxviii. 31), although the Arabic *suhêl* does occur as a generic name for stars of surpassing splendour (see at Job xxxviii. 7). The comprehensive term employed is similar to the figure of speech met with in Arabic (called *taglîb*, *i.e.* the preponderance of the *pars potior*), in such expressions as "the two late evenings" for the evening and late evening, "the two Omars" for Omar and Abubekr, though the resemblance is still greater to the Latin *Scipiones*, *i.e.* men of Scipio's greatness. Even the Orions, *i.e.* those stars which are at other times the most conspicuous, withhold their light; for when God is angry, the principle of anger is set in motion even in the natural world, and primarily in the stars that were created "for signs" (compare Gen. i. 14 with Jer. x. 2).

The prophet now hears again the voice of Jehovah revealing to him what His purpose is,—namely, a visitation punishing the wicked, humbling the proud, and depopulating the countries. Vers. 11, 12. "*And I visit the evil upon the world, and upon sinners their guilt, and sink into silence the pomp of the proud; and the boasting of tyrants I throw to the ground. I make men more precious than fine gold, and people than a jewel of Ophir.*" The verb *pâkad* is construed, as in Jer. xxiii. 2, with the accusative of the thing punished, and with עַל of the person punished. Instead of *'eretz* we have here *tēbel*, which is always used like a proper name (never with the article), to denote the earth in its

---

[1] When R. Samuel of Nehardea, the astronomer, says in his *b. Berachoth* 58*b*, "If it were not for the heat of the *cesîl*, the world would perish from the cold of the Scorpion, and *vice versa*,"—he means by the *cesîl* Orion; and the true meaning of the passage is, that the constellations of Orion and the Scorpion, one of which appears in the hot season, and the other in the cold, preserve the temperature in equilibrium.

entire circumference. We have also *'ărītzīm* instead of *nedĭbīm:* the latter signifies merely princes, and it is only occasionally that it has the subordinate sense of despots; the former signifies men naturally cruel, or tyrants (it occurs very frequently in Isaiah). Everything here breathes the spirit of Isaiah both in thought and form. "The lofty is thrown down:" this is one of the leading themes of Isaiah's proclamation; and the fact that the judgment will only leave a remnant is a fundamental thought of his, which also runs through the oracles concerning the heathen (ch. xvi. 14, xxi. 17, xxiv. 6), and is depicted by the prophet in various ways (ch. x. 16–19, xvii. 4–6, xxiv. 13, xxx. 17). There it is expressed under the figure that men become as scarce as the finest kinds of gold. Word-painting is Isaiah's delight and strength. *'Ophir*, which resembles *'okir* in sound, was the gold country of India, that lay nearest to the Phœnicians, the coast-land of *Abhira* on the northern shore of the *Runn* (*Irina*), *i.e.* the salt lake to the east of the mouths of the Indus (see at Gen. x. 29 and Job xxii. 24; and for the Egypticized *Souphir* of the LXX., Job xxviii. 16).

Thus does the wrath of God prevail among men, casting down and destroying; and the natural world above and below cannot fail to take part in it. Ver. 13. "*Therefore I shake the heavens, and the earth trembles away from its place, because of the wrath of Jehovah of hosts, and because of the day of His fierce anger.*" The two *Beths* have a causative meaning (cf. ch. ix. 18). They correspond to *'al-cēn* (therefore), of which they supply the explanation. Because the wrath of God falls upon men, every creature which is not the direct object of the judgment must become a medium in the infliction of it. We have here the thought of ver. 9*a* repeated as a kind of refrain (in a similar manner to ch. v. 25). Then follow the several disasters. The first is flight.—Ver. 14. "*And it comes to pass as with a gazelle which is scared, and as with a flock without gatherers: they turn every one to his people, and they flee every one to his land.*" The neuter *v'hâyâh* affirms that it will then be as described in the simile and the interpretation which follows. Babylon was the market for the world in central Asia, and therefore a *rendezvous* for the most diverse nations (Jer. l. 16, cf. li. 9, 44)— for a πάμμικτος ὄχλος, as Æschylus says in his *Persæ*, v. 52. This great and motley mass of foreigners would now be scattered in the wildest flight, on the fall of the imperial city. The second disaster is violent death.—Ver. 15. "*Every one that is found is pierced through, and every one that is caught falls by the sword.*" By "every one that is *found,*" we understand those that are taken in the city by the invading conquerors; and by "every one that is *caught,*" those that are overtaken in their flight (*sâphâh, abripere,* ch. vii. 20). All are put to the sword. —The third and fourth disasters are plunder and ravage. Ver. 16. "*And their infants are dashed to pieces before their eyes, their houses plundered, and their wives ravished.*" Instead of *tisshâgalnâh,* the *keri* has the euphemistic term *tisshâcabnâh* (*concubitum patientur*), a passive which never occurs in the Old Testament text itself. The *keri* readings *shuccabt* in Jer. iii. 2, and *yishcâbennâh* in Deut. xxviii. 30, also do violence to the language, which required שׁכב עִם and אֶת (the latter as a preposition in Gen. xix. 34) for the sake of euphemism; or rather they introduce a later (talmudic) usage of speech into the Scriptures (see Geiger, *Urschrift,* pp. 407–8). The prophet himself intentionally selects the base term *shâgal,* though, as the queen's name *Shegal* shows, it must have been regarded in northern Palestine and Aramæan as by no means a disreputable word. In this and other passages of the prophecy Knobel scents a fanaticism which is altogether strange to Isaiah.

With ver. 17 the prophecy takes a fresh turn, in which the veil that has hitherto obscured it is completely broken through. We now learn the name of the conquerors. "*Behold, I rouse up the Medes over them, who do not regard silver, and take no pleasure in gold.*" It was the Medes (Darius Medus=Cyaxares II.) who put an end to the Babylonian kingdom in combination with the Persians (Cyrus). The Persians are mentioned for the first time in the Old Testament by Ezekiel and Daniel. Consequently *Mâdai* (by the side of which Elam is mentioned in ch. xxi. 2) appears to have been a general term applied to the Arian populations of Eran from the most important ruling tribe. Until nearly the end of Hezekiah's reign, the Medes lived scattered about over different districts, and in hamlets (or villages) united together by a constitutional organization. After they had broken away from the Assyrians (714 B.C.) they placed themselves in 709–8 B.C. under one common king, namely Deyoces, probably for the purpose of upholding their national independence ; or, to speak more correctly, under a common *monarch*, for even the chiefs of the villages were called kings.[1] It is in this sense that Jeremiah speaks of "kings of Madai;" at any rate, this is a much more probable supposition than that he refers to monarchs in a generic sense. But the kings of Media, *i.e.* the rulers of the several villages, are mentioned in Jer. xxv. 25 among those who will have to drink the intoxicating cup which Jehovah is about to give to the nations through Nebuchadnezzar. So that their expedition against Babylon is an act of revenge for the disgrace of bondage that has been inflicted upon them. Their disregarding silver and gold is not intended to describe them as a rude, uncultivated people: the prophet simply means that they are impelled by a spirit of revenge, and do not come for the purpose of gathering booty. Revenge drives them on to forgetfulness of all morality, and humanity also.—Ver. 18. "*And bows dash down young men ; and they have no compassion on the fruit of the womb : their eye has no pity on children.*" The *bows* do not stand for the bowmen (see ch. xxi. 17), but the bows of the latter dash the young men to the ground by means of the arrows shot from them. They did not spare the fruit of the womb, since they ripped up the bodies of those that were with child (2 Kings viii. 12, xv. 16, etc.). Even towards children they felt no emotion of compassionate regard, such as would express itself in the eye: *chûs*, to feel, more especially to feel with another, *i.e.* to sympathize; here and in Ezek. v. 11 it is ascribed to the eye as the mirror of the soul (compare the Arabic *chasyet el-'ain ala fulânin*, carefulness of eye for a person: Hariri, *Comment.* p. 140). With such inhuman conduct on the part of the foe, the capital of the empire becomes the scene of a terrible conflagration.—Ver. 19. "*And Babel, the ornament of kingdoms, the proud boast of the Chaldeans, becomes like Elohim's overthrowing judgment upon Sodom and Gomorrah.*" The *ornament* of kingdoms (*mamlâcoth*), because it was the centre of many conquered kingdoms, which now avenged themselves upon it (ver. 4) ; the *pride* (cf. ch. xxviii. 1), because it was the primitive dwelling-place of the Chaldeans of the lowlands, that ancient cultivated people, who

[1] See Spiegel's *Eran das Land zwischen dem Indus und Tigris* (1863), p. 308 sqq.

were related to the Chaldean tribes of the Carduchisan mountains in the north-east of Mesopotamia, though not of the same origin, and of totally different manners (see at ch. xxiii. 13). Their present catastrophe resembled that of Sodom and Gomorrah : the two *eths* are accusative ; *mahpēcâh* (καταστροφή) is used like *de'âh* in ch. xi. 9 with a verbal force (τὸ καταστρέψαι, well rendered by the LXX. ὃν τρόπον κατέστρεψεν ὁ Θεός. On the arrangement of the words, see Ges. § 133, 3).

Babel, like the cities of the Pentapolis, had now become a perpetual desert. Vers. 20–22. " *She remains uninhabited for ever, and unoccupied into generation of generations; and not an Arab pitches his tent there, and shepherds do not make their folds there. And there lie beasts of the desert, and horn-owls fill their houses; and ostriches dwell there, and field-devils hop about there. And jackals howl in her castles, and wild dogs in palaces of pleasure; and her time is near to come, and her days will not be prolonged.*" The conclusion is similar to that of the prophecy against Edom, in ch. xxxiv. 16, 17. There the certainty of the prediction, even in its most minute particulars, is firmly declared ; here the nearness of the time of fulfilment. But the fulfilment did not take place so soon as the words of the prophecy might make it appear. According to Herodotus, Cyrus, the leader of the Medo-Persian army, left the city still standing, with its double ring of walls. Darius Hystaspis, who had to conquer Babylon a second time in 518 B.C., had the walls entirely destroyed, with the exception of fifty cubits. Xerxes gave the last thrust to the glory of the temple of Belus. Having been conquered by Seleucus Nicator (312), it declined just in proportion as Seleucia rose. *Babylon*, says Pliny, *ad solitudinem rediit exhausta vicinitate Seleuciæ*. At the time of Strabo (born 60 B.C.) Babylon was a perfect desert; and he applies to it (xvi. 15) the words of the poet, ἐρημία μεγάλη 'στὶν ἡ μεγάλη πόλις. Consequently, in the passage before us the prophecy falls under the law of perspective foreshortening. But all that it foretells has been literally fulfilled. The curse that Babylon would never come to be settled in and inhabited again (a poetical expression, like Jer. xvii. 25, xxxiii. 16), proved itself an effectual one, when Alexander once thought of making Babylon the metropolis of his empire. He was carried off by an early death. Ten thousand workmen were at that time employed for two months in simply clearing away the rubbish of the foundations of the temple of Belus (the Nimrod-tower). "*Not an Arab pitches his tent there*" ('*Arâbi*, from '*Arâbâh*, a steppe, is used here for the first time in the Old Testament, and then again in Jer. iii. 2; *yâhēl*, different from *yâhēl* in ch. xiii. 10 and Job xxxi. 26, is a syncopated form of יַאֲהֵל, *tentorium figet*, according to Ges. § 68, Anm. 2, used instead of the customary יֶאֱהַל): this was simply the natural consequence of the great field of ruins, upon which there was nothing but the most scanty vegetation. But all kinds of beasts of the desert and waste places make their homes there instead. The list commences with *ziyyim* (from *zi*, dryness, or from *ziyi*, an adj. relat. of the noun *zi*), *i.e.* dwellers in the desert; the reference here is not to men, but, as in most other instances, to animals, though it is impossible to determine what are the animals particularly referred to. That *ochim* are horned owls (*Uhus*) is a conjecture of Aurivillius, which decidedly commends itself. On *b'noth ya'ănâh*, see at Job xxxix. 13–18. Wetzstein connects *ya'ănâh* with an Arabic word for desert; it is probably more correct, however, to connect it with the Syriac יַעְנָא, greedy. The feminine plural embraces ostriches of both sexes, just as the '*iyyim* (sing. אִי = אַי, from '*âvâh*, to howl: see Bernstein's *Lex*. on Kirsch's *Chrestom. Syr.* p. 7), *i.e.* jackals, are called *benât âwa* in Arabic, without distinction of sex (*awa* in this appellation is a direct reproduction of the natural voice of the animal, which is called *wâwi* in vulgar Arabic). *Tan* has also been regarded since the time of Pococke and Schnurrer as the name of the jackal; and this is supported by the Syriac and Targum rendering *yaruro* (see Bernstein, p. 220), even more than by the Arabic name of the wolf, *tinân*, which only occurs here and there. אִי, *ibnu âwa*, is the common jackal found in Hither Asia (*Canis aureus vulgaris*), the true type of the whole species, which is divided into at least ten varieties, and belongs to the same genus as dogs and wolves (not foxes). *Tan* may refer to one of these varieties, which derived its name from its distinctive peculiarity as a *long-stretched* animal, whether the extension was in the trunk, the snout, or the tail. The animals mentioned, both quadrupeds (*râbatz*) and birds (*shâcan*), are really found there, on the soil of ancient Babylon. When Kerporter was drawing near to the Nimrod-tower, he saw lions sunning themselves quietly upon its walls, which came down very leisurely when alarmed by the cries of the Arabs. And as Rich heard in Bagdad, the ruins are still regarded as a rendezvous for ghosts: *sâ‘ir*, when contrasted with *‘attūd*, signifies the full-grown shaggy buck-goat; but here *se‘irim* is applied to demons in the shape of goats (as in ch. xxxiv. 14). According to the Scriptures, the desert is the abode of unclean spirits, and such unclean spirits as the popular belief or mythology pictured to itself were *se‘irim*. Virgil, like Isaiah, calls them *saltantes Satyros*. It is remarkable also that Joseph Wolf, the missionary and traveller to *Bochâra*, saw pilgrims of the sect of Yezidis (or devil-worshippers) upon the ruins of Babylon, who performed strange and horrid rites by moonlight, and danced extraordinary dances with singular gestures and sounds. On seeing these ghost-like, howling, moonlight pilgrims, he very naturally recalled to mind the dancing *se‘irim* of prophecy (see Moritz Wagner's *Reise nach Persien und dem Lande der Kurden*, Bd. ii. p. 251). And the nightly howling and yelling of jackals (*‘ânâh* after *rikkēd*, as in 1 Sam. xviii. 6, 7) produces its natural effect upon every traveller there, just as in all the other ruins of the East. These are now the inhabitants of the royal *’arm‘noth*, which the prophet calls *’almʻnoth* with a sarcastic turn, on account of their widowhood and desolation; these are the inhabitants of the palaces of pleasure, the luxurious villas and country-seats, with their hanging gardens. The Apocalypse, in ch. xviii. 2, takes up this prophecy of Isaiah, and applies it to a still existing Babylon, which might have seen itself in the mirror of the Babylon of old.

But it is love to His own people which impels the God of Israel to suspend such a judgment of eternal destruction over Babylon. Ch. xiv. 1, 2. "*For Jehovah will have mercy on Jacob, and will once more choose Israel, and will settle them in their own land: and the foreigner will associate with them, and they will cleave to the house of Jacob. And nations take them, and accompany them to their place; and the house of Israel takes them to itself in the land of Jehovah for servants and maid-servants: and they hold in captivity those who led them away captive; and become lords over their oppressors.*" We have here *in nuce* the comforting substance of ch. xlvi.-lxvi. Babylon falls that Israel may rise. This is effected by the compassion of God.

He chooses Israel once more (*iterum*, as in Job. xiv. 7 for example), and therefore makes a new covenant with it. Then follows their return to Canaan, their own land, Jehovah's land (as in Hos. ix. 3). Proselytes from among the heathen, who have acknowledged the God of the exiles, go along with them, as Ruth did with Naomi. Heathen accompany the exiles to their own place. And now their relative positions are reversed. Those who accompany Israel are now taken possession of by the latter (*hithnachēl*, κληρονομεῖν ἑαυτῷ, like *hithpattēach*, ch. lii. 2, λύεσθαι; cf. p. 94, note, and Ewald, § 124, *b*), as servants and maid-servants; and they (the Israelites) become leaders into captivity of those who led them into captivity (*Lamed* with the participle, as in ch. xi. 9), and they will oppress (*râdâh b'*, as in Ps. xlix. 15) their oppressors. This retribution of like for like is to all appearance quite out of harmony with the New Testament love. But in reality it is no retribution of like for like. For, according to the prophet's meaning, to be ruled by the people of God is the true happiness of the nations, and to allow themselves to be so ruled is their true liberty. At the same time, the form in which the promise is expressed is certainly not that of the New Testament; and it could not possibly have been so, for the simple reason that in Old Testament times, and from an Old Testament point of view, there was no other visible manifestation of the church (*ecclesia*) than in the form of a nation. This national form of the church has been broken up under the New Testament, and will never be restored. Israel, indeed, will be restored as a nation; but the true essence of the church, which is raised above all national distinctions, will never return to those worldly limits which it has broken through. And the fact that the prophecy moves within those limits here may be easily explained, on the ground that it is primarily the deliverance from the Babylonian captivity to which the promise refers. And the prophet himself was unconscious that this captivity would be followed by another.

The song of the redeemed is a song concerning the fall of the king of Babel. Vers. 3, 4*a*. "*And it cometh to pass, on the day that Jehovah giveth thee rest from thy plague, and from thy cares, and from the heavy bondage wherein thou wast made to serve, that thou shalt raise such a song of triumph concerning the king of Babel, and say.*" Instead of the hiphil *hinniach* (to let down) of ver. 1, we have here, as in the original passage, Deut. xxv. 19, the form *hēniach*, which is commonly used in the sense of quieting, or procuring rest. עֶצֶב is trouble which plagues (as עָמָל is trouble which oppresses), and *rōgez* restlessness which wears out with anxious care (Job iii. 26, cf. Ezek. xii. 18). The assimilated *min* before the two words is pronounced *mi*, with a weak reduplication, instead of *mē*, as elsewhere, before ה, ח, and even before ר (1 Sam. xxiii. 28; 2 Sam. xviii. 16). In the relative clause אֲשֶׁר עֻבַּד־בָּךְ, אֲשֶׁר is not the Hebrew *casus adverb.* answering to the Latin ablative *quâ servo te usi sunt;* nor do בָּךְ ... אֲשֶׁר belong to one another in the sense of *quo*, as in Deut. xxi. 3, *quâ (vitulâ)*; but it is regarded as an *acc. obj.* according to Ex. i. 14 and Lev. xxv. 39, *qu'on t'a fait servir*, as in Num. xxxii. 5, *qu'on donne la terre* (Luzzatto). When delivered from such a yoke of bondage, Israel would raise a *mâshâl.* According to its primary and general meaning, *mâshâl* signifies figurative language, and hence poetry generally, more especially that kind of proverbial poetry which loves the emblematical, and, in fact, any artistic composition that is piquant in its character; so that the idea of what is satirical or defiant may easily be associated with it, as in the passage before us.

The words are addressed to the Israel of the future in the Israel of the present, as in ch. xii. 1. The former would then sing, and say as follows. Vers. 4*b*-6. "*How hath the oppressor ceased! the place of torture ceased! Jehovah hath broken the rod of the wicked, the ruler's staff, which smote nations in wrath with strokes without ceasing, subjugated nations wrathfully with hunting that never stays.*" Not one of the early translators ever thought of deriving the *hap. leg. madhelâh* from the Aramæan *dehab* (gold), as Vitringa, Aurivillius, and Rosenmüller have done. The former have all translated the word as if it were *marhēbâh* (haughty, violent treatment), as corrected by J. D. Michaelis, Doederlein, Knobel, and others. But we may arrive at the same result without altering a single letter, if we take דְּאָב as equivalent to דּוּב, דָּיַב, to melt or pine away, whether we go back to the *kal* or to the *hiphil* of the verb, and regard the *Mem* as used in a material or local sense. We understand it, according to *madmenah* (dunghill) in ch. xxv. 10, as denoting the place where they were reduced to pining away, *i.e.* as applied to Babylon as the house of servitude where Israel had been wearied to death. The tyrant's sceptre, mentioned in ver. 5, is the Chaldean world-power regarded as concentrated in the king of Babel (cf. *shēbĕt* in Num. xxiv. 17). This tyrant's sceptre smote nations with incessant blows and hunting: *maccath* is construed with *macceh*, the derivative of the same verb; and *murdâph*, a *hophal* noun (as in ch. viii. 23, xxix. 3), with *rodeh*, which is kindred in meaning. Doederlein's conjecture (*mirdath*), which has been adopted by most modern commentators, is quite unnecessary. Unceasing continuance is expressed first of all with *bilti*, which is used as a preposition, and followed by *sârâh*, a participial noun like *câlâh*, and then with *b'li*, which is construed with the finite verb as in Gen. xxxi. 20, Job xli. 18; for *b'li châsâk* is an attributive clause: with a hunting which did not restrain itself, did not stop, and therefore did not spare. Nor is it only Israel and other subjugated nations that now breathe again. —Vers. 7, 8. *" The whole earth rests, is quiet: they break forth into singing. Even the cypresses rejoice at thee, the cedars of Lebanon: 'Since thou hast gone to sleep, no one will come up to lay the axe upon us.'"* The preterites indicate inchoatively the circumstances into which the whole earth has now entered. The omission of the subject in the case of *pâtz'chu* (they break forth) gives the greatest generality to the jubilant utterances: *pâtzach rinnâh* (*erumpere gaudio*) is an expression that is characteristic of Isaiah alone (*e.g.* ch. xliv. 23, xlix. 13); and it is a distinctive peculiarity of the prophet to bring in the trees of the forest, as living and speaking beings, to share in the universal joy (cf. ch. lv. 12). Jerome supposes the trees to be figuratively employed here for the "chiefs of the nations" (*principes gentium*). But this disposition to allegorize not only destroys the reality of the contents, but the spirit of the poetry also. Cypresses and cedars rejoice because of the treatment which they received from the Chaldean, who made use of the almost imperishable wood of both of them for ornamental buildings, for his siege apparatus, and for his fleets, and even for ordinary ships,—as Alexander, for example, built himself a fleet of cypress-wood, and the Syrian vessels had masts of cedar. Of the old cedars of Lebanon, there are hardly thirty left in the principal spot where they formerly grew. Gardner Wilkinson (1843) and Hooker the botanist (1860) estimated the whole number at about four hundred; and according to the conclusion which the latter drew from the number of concentric rings and other signs, not one of them is more than about five hundred years old.[1]

But whilst it has become so quiet on earth, there is the most violent agitation in the regions below. Ver. 9. "*The kingdom of the dead below is all in uproar on account of thee, to meet thy coming; it stirreth up the shades for thee, all the he-goats of the earth; it raiseth up from their throne-seats all the kings of the nations.*" The notion of Hades, notwithstanding the mythological character which it had assumed, was based upon the double truth, that what a man has been, and the manner in which he has lived on this side the grave, are not obliterated on the other side, but are then really brought to light, and that there is an immaterial self-formation of the soul, in which all that a man has become under certain divinely appointed circumstances, by his own self-determination, is, as it were, reflected in a mirror, and that in a permanent form. This psychical image, to which the dead body bears the same relation as the shattered mould to a cast, is the shade-like corporeality of the inhabitants of Hades, in which they appear essentially though spiritually just as they were on this side the grave. This is the deep root of what the prophet has here expressed in a poetical form; for it is really a *mâshâl* that he has interwoven with his prophecy here. All Hades is overwhelmed with excitement and wonder, now that the king of Babel, that invincible ruler of the world, who, if not unexpected altogether, was not expected so soon, is actually approaching. From עוֹרֵר onwards, *Sheol*, although a feminine, might be the subject; in which case the verb would simply have reverted from the feminine to the radical masculine form. But it is better to regard the subject as neuter; a *nescio quid*, a nameless power. The shades are suddenly siezed with astonishment, more especially the former leaders (leading goats or bell-wethers) of the herds of nations, so that, from sheer amazement, they spring up from their seats.

And how do they greet this lofty new-comer? Ver. 10. "*They all rise up and say to thee, Art thou also made weak like us? art thou become like us?*" This is all that the shades say; what follows does not belong to them. The *pual chullâh* (only used here), "to be made sickly, or powerless," signifies to

[1] See Wilkinson's paper in the *Athenæum* (London, Nov. 1862).

be transposed into the condition of the latter, viz. the *Rephaim* (a word which also occurs in the Phœnician inscriptions, from רָפָה = רָפָא, to be relaxed or weary), since the life of the shades is only a shadow of life (cf. εἴδωλα, ἄκικυς, and possibly also καμόντες in Homer, when used in the sense of those who are dying, exhausted and prostrate with weakness). And in Hades we could not expect anything more than this expression of extreme amazement. For why should they receive their new comrade with contempt or scorn? From ver. 11 onwards, the singers of the *mashal* take up the song again.—Ver. 11. "*Thy pomp is cast down to the region of the dead, the noise of thy harps: maggots are spread under thee, and they that cover thee are worms.*" From the book of Daniel we learn the character of the Babylonian music; it abounded in instruments, some of which were foreign. Maggots and worms (a bitter sarcasm) now take the place of the costly artistic Babylonian rugs, which once formed the pillow and counterpane of the distinguished corpse. יֻצַּע might be a third pers. *hophal* (Ges. § 71); but here, between perfects, it is a third pers. *pual*, like *yullad* in ch. ix. 5. *Rimmâh*, which is preceded by the verb in a masculine and to a certain extent an indifferent form (Ges. § 147, *a*), is a collective name for small worms, in any mass of which the individual is lost in the swarm. The passage is continued with אֵיךְ (on which, as a catchword of the *mashal*, see at ch. i. 21).—Ver. 12. "*How art thou fallen from the sky, thou star of light, sun of the dawn, hurled down to the earth, thou that didst throw down nations from above?*" הֵילֵל is here the morning star (from *hâlal*, to shine, resolved from *hillel*, after the form מֵאֵן, Jer. xiii. 10, סֵעֵף, Ps. cxix. 113, or rather attaching itself as a third class to the forms הֵיכָל, עֵילוֹם: compare the Arabic *sairaf*, exchanger; *saikal*, sword-cleaner). It derives its name in other ancient languages also from its striking brilliancy, and is here called *ben-shachar* (sun of the dawn), just as in the classical mythology it is called son of Eos, from the fact that it rises before the sun, and swims in the morning light as if that were the source of its birth.[1] Lucifer, as a name given to the devil,

---

[1] It is singular, however, that among the Semitic nations the morning star is not personified as a male (*Heôsphoros* or *Phôsphoros*), but as a female (Astarte, see at ch. xvii. 8), and that it is called *Nâghâh*, *Ashtoreth*, *Zuhara*, but never by a name derived from *hâlal*; whilst the moon is re-

was derived from this passage, which the fathers (and lately Stier) interpreted, without any warrant whatever, as relating to the apostasy and punishment of the angelic leaders. The appellation is a perfectly appropriate one for the king of Babel, on account of the early date of the Babylonian culture, which reached back as far as the grey twilight of primeval times, and also because of its predominant astrological character. The additional epithet *chōlēsh 'al-gōyim* is founded upon the idea of the *influxus siderum* :[1] *cholesh* signifies "overthrowing" or laying down (Ex. xvii. 13), and with '*al*, " bringing defeat upon ;" whilst the Talmud (*b. Sabbath* 149*b*) uses it in the sense of *projiciens sortem*, and thus throws light upon the *cholesh* (= *purah*, lot) of the Mishnah. A retrospective glance is now cast at the self-deification of the king of Babylon, in which he was the antitype of the devil and the type of antichrist (Dan. xi. 36 ; 2 Thess. ii. 4), and which had met with its reward.—Vers. 13–15. " *And thou, thou hast said in thy heart, I will ascend into heaven, I will exalt my throne above the stars of God, and sit down on the mount of the assembly of gods in the corner of the north. I will ascend to the heights of the clouds, I will make myself like the Most High. Nevertheless, thou wilt be cast down into the region of the dead, into the corner of the pit.*" An antithetical circumstantial clause commences with *v°attah*, just as in ver. 19, " whilst thou," or " whereas thou." The *har hammōēd* (mount of assembly) cannot be Zion, as is assumed by Schegg and others, who are led astray by the parallel in Ps. xlviii. 3, which has been entirely misunderstood, and has no bearing upon this passage at all. Zion was neither a northern point of the earth, nor was it situated on the north of Jerusalem. The prophet makes the king of Babylon speak according to the general notion of his people, who had not the seat of the Deity in the midst of them, as the Israelites had, but who placed it on the summit of the northern mountains, which were lost in

---

garded as a male deity (*Sin*), and in Arabic *hilâl* signifies the new moon (see p. 145), which might be called *ben-shacar* (son of the dawn), from the fact that, from the time when it passes out of the invisibility of its first phase, it is seen at sunrise, and is as it were born out of the dawn.

[1] In a similar manner, the sun-god (*San*) is called the "conqueror of the king's enemies," " breaker of opposition," etc., on the early Babylonian monuments (see G. Rawlinson, *The Five Great Monarchies*, i. 160).

the clouds, just as the Hindoos place it on the fabulous mountains of *Kailâsa*, which lie towards the north beyond the Himalayas (Lassen, i. 34 sqq.). יַרְכָתַיִם (with an aspirated כ in a loosely closed syllable) are the two sides into which a thing parts, the two legs of an angle, and then the apex at which the legs separate. And so here, יַרְכְּתֵי צָפוֹן (with an unaspirated *Caph* in a triply closed syllable) is the uttermost extremity of the north, from which the northern mountains stretch fork-like into the land, and *yarcethe-bor* the interior of the pit into which its two walls slope, and from which it unfolds or widens. All the foolhardy purposes of the Chaldean are finally comprehended in this, "*I will make myself like the Most High;*" just as the Assyrians, according to Ctesias, and the Persians, according to the *Persæ* of Æschylus, really called their king God, and the Sassanidæ call themselves *bag*, *Theos*, upon coins and inscriptions ('*eddammeh* is *hithpael*, equivalent to '*ethdammeh*, with the usual assimilation of the preformative *Tav:* Ges. § 34, 2, *b*). By the אַךְ in ver. 14, the high-flying pride of the Chaldean is contrasted with his punishment, which hurls him down into the lowest depths. אַךְ, which was originally affirmative, and then restrictive (as *rak* was originally restrictive and then affirmative), passes over here into an adversative, just as in Ps. xlix. 16, Job xiii. 15 (a change seen still more frequently in אָכֵן): *nevertheless* thou wilt be hurled down; nothing but that will occur, and not what you propose. This prophetic *tūrad* is language that neither befits the inhabitants of Hades, who greet his advent, nor the Israel singing the *mashal;* but the words of Israel have imperceptibly passed into words of the prophet, who still sees in the distance, and as something future, what the *mashal* commemorates as already past.

The prophet then continues in the language of prediction. Vers. 16, 17. "*They that see thee look, considering thee, look at thee thoughtfully: Is this the man that set the earth trembling, and kingdoms shaking? that made the world a wilderness, and destroyed its cities, and did not release its prisoners (to their) home?*" The scene is no longer in Hades (Knobel, Umbreit). Those who are speaking thus have no longer the Chaldean before them as a mere shade, but as an unburied corpse that has fallen into corruption. As *tēbēl* is feminine, the suffixes in ver. 17 must refer, according to a *constructio ad sensum*, to the world as changed into a *wilderness* (*midbâr*). *Páthach*, to open, namely locks and fetters; here, with *baithâh*, it is equivalent to releasing or letting go (syn. *shillēach*, Jer. l. 33). By the "prisoners" the Jewish exiles are principally intended; and it was their release that had never entered the mind of the king of Babylon.

The prophet, whose own words now follow the words of the spectators, proceeds to describe the state in which the tyrant lies, and which calls for such serious reflections. Vers. 18, 19. "*All the kings of the nations, they are all interred in honour, every one in his house: but thou art cast away far from thy sepulchre like a shoot hurled away, clothed with slain, with those pierced through with the sword, those that go down to the stones of the pit; like a carcase trodden under feet.*" Every other king was laid out after his death "in his house" (*b'bēthō*), *i.e.* within the limits of his own palace; but the Chaldean lay far away from the sepulchre that was apparently intended for him. The מִן in מִקִּבְרְךָ signifies *procul ab*, as in Num. xv. 24, Prov. xx. 3. He lies there like *nētzer nith'âb*, *i.e.* like a branch torn off from the tree, that has withered and become offensive, or rather (as *nētzer* does not mean a branch, but a shoot) like a side-shoot that has been cut off the tree and thrown away with disgust as ugly, useless, and only a hindrance to the regular growth of the tree (possibly also an excrescence); *nith'âb* (cast away) is a pregnant expression, signifying "cast away with disgust." The place where he lies is the field of battle. A *vaticinium post eventum* would be expressed differently from this, as Luzzatto has correctly observed. For what *Seder 'Olam* says— namely, that Nebuchadnezzar's corpse was taken out of the grave by Evilmerodach, or as Abravanel relates it, by the Medo-Persian conquerors—is merely a conclusion drawn from the passage before us, and would lead us to expect הוּצֵאתָ rather than הָשְׁלַכְתָּ. It is a matter of indifference, so far as the truth of the prophecy is concerned, whether it was fulfilled in the person of Nebuchadnezzar I., or of that second Nebuchadnezzar who gave himself out as a son of Nabonet, and tried to restore the freedom of Babylon. The scene which passes before the mind of the prophet is the field of battle. To clear this they make a hole and throw stones (*abnē-bor*, stones of the pit) on the top, without taking the trouble to shovel in the earth; but the king of Babylon is left lying there, like a carcase that is trampled under foot, and deserves nothing better than to be trampled under foot (*mūbâs*, part. *hoph.* of *būs*, *conculcare*). They do not even think him worth throwing into a hole along with the rest of the corpses.—Ver. 20. *"Thou art not united with them in burial, for thou hast destroyed thy land, murdered thy people: the seed of evil-doers will not be named for ever."* In this way is vengeance taken for the tyrannical manner in which he has oppressed and exhausted his land, making his people the involuntary instruments of his thirst for conquest, and sacrificing them as victims to that thirst. For this reason he does not meet with the same compassion as those who have been compelled to sacrifice their lives in his service. And it is not only all over for ever with him, but it is so with his dynasty also. The prophet, the messenger of the penal justice of God, and the mouthpiece of that Omnipotence which regulates the course of history, commands this.—Ver. 21. *" Prepare a slaughter-house for his sons, because of the iniquity of their fathers! They shall not rise and conquer lands, and fill the face of the earth with cities."* The exhortation is addressed to the Medes, if the prophet had any particular persons in his mind at all. After the nocturnal storming of Babylon by the Medes, the new Babylonian kingdom and royal house which had been established by Nabopolassar vanished entirely from history. The last shoot of the royal family of Nabopolassar was slain as a child of conspirators. The second Nebuchadnezzar deceived the people (as Darius says in the great inscription of Behistan), declaring, " I am Nabukud-rac'ara the son of Nabunita." בַּל (used poetically for אַל, like בְּלִי in ch. xiv. 6 for לֹא) expresses a negative wish (as *pen* does a negative intention) : Let no Babylonian kingdom ever arise again ! Hitzig corrects עָרִים into עִיִּים (heaps of ruins), Ewald into עָרִיצִים (tyrants), Knobel into רֵעִים, and Meier into עֲרָים, which are said to signify conflicts, whilst Maurer will not take עָרִים in the sense of cities, but of enemies. But there is no necessity for this at all. Nimrod, the first founder of a Babylonio-Assyrian kingdom, built cities to strengthen his monarchy. The king of Asshur built cities for the Medes, for the purpose of keeping them better in check. And it is to this building of cities, as a support to despotism, that the prophet here refers.

Thus far the prophet has spoken in the name of God. But the prophecy closes with a word of God Himself, spoken through the prophet.—Vers. 22, 23. "*And I will rise up against them, saith Jehovah of hosts, and root out in Babel name and remnant, sprout and shoot, saith Jehovah. And make it the possession of hedgehogs and marshes of water, and sweep it away with the besom of destruction, saith Jehovah of hosts.*" שֵׁם וּשְׁאָר and נִין וָנֶכֶד are two pairs of alliterative proverbial words, and are used to signify "the whole, without exception" (compare the Arabic expression "*Kiesel und Kies,*" "flint and pebble," in the sense of "altogether:" Nöldecke, *Poesie der alten Araber*, p. 162). Jehovah rises against the descendants of the king of Babylon, and exterminates Babylon utterly, root and branch. The destructive forces, which Babylon has hitherto been able to control by raising artificial defences, are now let loose; and the Euphrates, left without a dam, lays the whole region under water. *Hedgehogs* now take the place of men, and *marshes* the place of palaces. The *kippod* occurs in ch. xxxiv. 11 and Zeph. ii. 14, in the company of *birds;* but according to the derivation of the word and the dialects, it denotes the *hedgehog*, which possesses the power of rolling itself up (LXX. ἔρημον ὥστε κατοικεῖν ἐχίνους), and which, although it can neither fly, nor climb with any peculiar facility, on account of its mode of walking, could easily get upon the knob of a pillar that had been thrown down (Zeph. ii. 14). The concluding threat makes the mode of Babel's origin the omen of its end: the city of טִיט, *i.e.* Babylon, which had been built for the most part of clay or brick-earth, would be strangely swept away. The *pilpel* טִאטֵא (or טָאטָא, as Kimchi conjugates it in *Michlol* 150*ab*, and in accordance with which some codices and early editions read וְטֵאטֵאתִיהָ with double *zere*) belongs to the cognate root which is mentioned at Ps. xlii. 5, with an opening ס, ט, ד (cf. ch. xxvii. 8), and which signifies to drive or thrust away. מַטְאֲטֵא is that with which anything is driven out or swept away, viz. a broom. Jehovah treats Babylon as rubbish, and sweeps it away, destruction (*hashmēd:* an inf. absol. used as a substantive) serving Him as a broom.

There now follows, apparently out of all connection, another prophecy against Asshur. It is introduced here quite abruptly, like a fragment; and it is an enigma how it got here, and what it means here, though not an enigma without solution. This short Assyrian passage reads as follows. Vers. 24-27. "*Jehovah of hosts hath sworn, saying, Surely as I have thought, so shall it come to pass; and as I have purposed, that takes place; to break Asshur to pieces in my land, and upon my mountain will I tread him under foot: then his yoke departs from them, and his burden will depart from their neck. This is the purpose that is purposed over the whole earth; and this the hand that is stretched out over all nations. For Jehovah of hosts hath purposed, and who could bring it to nought? And His hand that is stretched out, who can turn it back?*" It is evidently a totally different judicial catastrophe which is predicted here, inasmuch as the world-power upon which it falls is not called Babel or Chasdim, but Asshur, which cannot possibly be taken as a name for Babylon (Abravanel, Lowth, etc.). Babylon is destroyed by the Medes, whereas Asshur falls to ruin in the mountain-land of Jehovah, which it is seeking to subjugate,—a prediction which was literally fulfilled. And only when this had taken place did a fitting occasion present itself for a prophecy against Babel, the heiress of the ruined Assyrian power. Consequently the two prophecies against Babel and Asshur form a hysteron-proteron as they stand here. The thought which occasioned this arrangement, and which it is intended to set forth, is expressed by Jeremiah in Jer. l. 18, 19, "Behold, I will punish the king of Babylon and his land, as I have punished the king of Assyria." The one event was a pledge of the other. At a time when the prophecy against Assyria had actually been fulfilled, the prophet attached it to the still unfulfilled prophecy against Babylon, to give a pledge of the fulfilment of the latter. This was the pedestal upon which the *Massâh Bâbel* was raised. And it was doubly suited for this, on account of its purely epilogical tone from ver. 26 onwards.

THE ORACLE CONCERNING PHILISTIA.—CHAP. XIV. 28-32.

Among the punishments enumerated in 2 Chron. xxviii. 5-21 as falling upon king Ahaz, we find the following, viz. that the Philistines invaded the low country (*shephelah*) and the south land (*negeb*), took several cities, six of which are mentioned by name, and settled there. This offensive movement of the Philistines against the government of Judæa was probably occasioned either by the oppression of Judah on the part of Syria and Ephraim, or by the permanent crippling of Judah through the Syro-Ephraimitish war. In either case, the fact itself is quite sufficient to throw light upon the threatening prophecy which follows.

This is one of the prophecies the date of which is fixed in ver. 28. "*In the year of the death of king Ahaz the following oracle was uttered.*" "The year of the death of king Ahaz" was (as in ch. vi. 1) the year in which the death of Ahaz was to take place. In that year the Philistines still remained in those possessions, their hold of which was so shameful to Judah, and had not yet met with any humiliating retribution. But this year was the turning-point; for Hezekiah, the successor of Ahaz, not only recovered the cities that they had taken, but thoroughly defeated them in their own land (2 Kings xviii. 8).

It was therefore in a most eventful and decisive year that Isaiah began to prophesy as follows. Ver. 29. "*Rejoice not so fully, O Philistia, that the rod which smote thee is broken to pieces; for out of the serpent's root comes forth a basilisk, and its fruit is a flying dragon.*" Shēbet maccēk, "the rod which smote thee" (not "of him that smote thee," which is not so appropriate), is the Davidic sceptre, which had formerly kept the Philistines in subjection under David and Solomon, and again in more recent times since the reign of Uzziah. This sceptre was now broken to pieces, for the Davidic kingdom had been brought down by the Syro-Epraimitish war, and had not been able to recover itself; and so far as its power over the surrounding nations was concerned, it had completely fallen to pieces. . Philistia was thoroughly filled with joy in consequence, but this joy was all over now. The power from which Philistia had escaped was a common snake (*nâchâsh*), which had been either cut to pieces, or had died out down to the very roots. But out of this root, *i.e.* out of the house of David, which had been reduced to the humble condition of its tribal house, there was coming forth a *zepha'*, a basilisk (*regulus*, as Jerome and other early translators render it: see at ch. xi. 8); and this basilisk, which is dangerous and even fatal in itself, as soon as it had reached maturity, would bring forth a winged dragon as its fruit. The basilisk is Hezekiah, and the flying dragon is the Messiah (this is the explanation given by the Targum); or, what is the same thing, the former is the Davidic government of the immediate future, the latter the Davidic government of the ultimate future. The figure may appear an inappropriate one, because the serpent is a symbol of evil; but it is not a symbol of evil only, but of a curse also, and a curse is the energetic expression of the penal justice of God. And it is as the executor of such a curse in the form of a judgment of God upon Philistia that the Davidic king is here described in a threefold climax as a snake or serpent. The selection of this figure may possibly have also been suggested by Gen. xlix. 17; for the saying of Jacob concerning Dan was fulfilled in Samson, the sworn foe of the Philistines.

The coming Davidic king is *peace* for Israel, but for Philistia *death*. Ver. 30. "*And the poorest of the poor will feed, and needy ones lie down in peace; and I kill thy root through hunger, and he slays thy remnant.*" "The poorest of the poor:" *b˒cōrē dallim* is an intensified expression for *b˒nē dallim*, the latter signifying such as belong to the family of the poor, the former (cf. Job xviii. 13, *mors dirissima*) such as hold the foremost rank in such a family,—a description of Israel, which, although at present deeply, very deeply, repressed and threatened on every side, would then enjoy its land in quietness and peace (Zeph. iii. 12, 13). In this sense וְרָעוּ is used absolutely; and there is no necessity for Hupfeld's conjecture (*Ps.* ii. 258), that we should read בְּכָרַי (in my pastures). Israel rises again, but Philistia perishes even to a root and remnant; and the latter again falls a victim on the one hand to the judgment of God (famine), and on the other to the punishment inflicted by the house of David. The change of persons in ver. 30*b* is no *synallage*; but the subject to *yahărōg* (slays) is the basilisk, the father of the flying dragon. The first strophe of the *massah* terminates here. It consists of eight lines, each of the two Masoretic verses (29, 30) containing four clauses.

The massah consists of two strophes. The first threatens judgment from Judah, and the second—of seven lines—threatens judgment from Asshur. Ver. 31. "*Howl, O gate! cry, O city! O Philistia, thou must melt entirely away; for from the north cometh smoke, and there is no isolated one among his hosts.*" שַׁעַר, which is a masculine everywhere else, is construed here as a feminine, possibly in order that the two imperfects may harmonize; for there is nothing to recommend Luzzatto's suggestion, that שְׁעִיר should be taken as an accusative. The strong gates of the Philistian cities (Ashdod and Gaza), of world-wide renown, and the cities themselves, shall lift up a cry of anguish; and Philistia, which has hitherto been full of joy, shall melt away in the heat of alarm (ch. xiii. 7, *nâmōg,* inf. abs. *niph.;* on the form itself, compare ch. lix. 13): for from the north there comes a singing and burning fire, which proclaims its coming afar off by the smoke which it produces; in other words, an all-destroying army, out of whose ranks not one falls away from weariness or self-will (cf. ch. v. 27), that is to say, an army without a gap, animated throughout with one common desire. (מוֹעֵד, after the form מוֹשָׁב, the mass of people assembled at an appointed place, or *mō'ed,* Josh. viii. 14, 1 Sam. xx. 35, and for an appointed end.)

To understand ver. 32, which follows here, nothing more is needed than a few simple parenthetical thoughts, which naturally suggest themselves. This one desire was the thirst for conquest, and such a desire could not possibly have only the small strip of Philistian coast for its object; but the conquest of this was intended as the means of securing possession of other countries on the right hand and on the left. The question arose, therefore, How would Judah fare with the fire which was rolling towards it from the north? For the very fact that the prophet of Judah was threatening Philistia with this fire, presupposed that Judah itself would not be consumed by it.

And this is just what is expressed in ver. 32 : " *And what answer do the messengers of the nations bring ? That Jehovah hath founded Zion, and that the afflicted of His people are hidden therein.*" " The messengers of the nations " (*mal'acē goi*) : *goi* is to be taken in a distributive sense, and the messengers to be regarded either as individuals who have escaped from the Assyrian army, which was formed of contingents from many nations, or else (as we should expect *pelitē* in that case, instead of *mal'acē*) messengers from the neighbouring nations, who were sent to Jerusalem after the Assyrian army had perished in front of the city, to ascertain how the latter had fared. And they all reply as if with one mouth (*yaaneh*): Zion has stood unshaken, protected by its God ; and the people of this God, the poor and despised congregation of Jehovah (cf. Zech. xi. 7), are, and know that they are, concealed in Zion. The prophecy is intentionally oracular. Prophecy does not adopt the same tone to the nations as to Israel. Its language to the former is dictatorially brief, elevated with strong self-consciousness, expressed in lofty poetic strains, and variously coloured, according to the peculiarity of the nation to which the oracle refers. The following prophecy relating to Moab shows us very clearly, that in the prophet's view the judgment executed by Asshur upon Philistia would prepare the way for the subjugation of Philistia by the sceptre of David. By the wreck of the Assyrian world-power upon Jerusalem, the house of David would recover its old supremacy over the nations round about. And this really was the case. But the fulfilment was not exhaustive. Jeremiah therefore took up the prophecy of his predecessor again at the time of the Chaldean judgment upon the nations (Jer. xlvii.), but only the second strophe. The Messianic element of the first was continued by Zechariah (Zech. ix.).

THE ORACLE CONCERNING MOAB.—CHAP. XV. XVI.

So far as the surrounding nations were concerned, the monarchy of Israel commenced with victory and glory. Saul punished them all severely for their previous offences against Israel (1 Sam. xiv. 47), and the Moabites along with the rest. The latter were completely subdued by David (2 Sam. viii. 2). After the division of the kingdom, the northern kingdom took possession of Moab. The Moabites paid tribute from their flocks to Samaria. But when Ahab died, Mesha the king of Moab refused this tribute (2 Kings i. 1, iii. 4 sqq.). Ahaziah of Israel let this refusal pass. In the meantime, the Moabites formed an alliance with other nations, and invaded Judah. But the allies destroyed one another, and Jehoshaphat celebrated in the valley of Berachah the victory which he had gained without a battle, and which is commemorated in several psalms. And when Jehoram the king of Israel attempted to subjugate Moab again, Jehoshaphat made common cause with him. And the Moabites were defeated; but the fortress, the Moabitish Kir, which was situated upon a steep and lofty chalk rock, remained standing still. The interminable contests of the northern kingdom with the Syrians rendered it quite impossible to maintain either Moab itself, or the land to the east of the Jordan in general. During the reign of Jehu, the latter, in all its length and breadth, even as far south as the Arnon, was taken by the Syrians (2 Kings x. 32, 33). The tribes that were now no longer tributary to the kingdom of Israel oppressed the Israelitish population, and avenged upon the crippled kingdom the loss of their independence. Jeroboam II., as the prophet Jonah had foretold (2 Kings xiv. 25), was the first to reconquer the territory of Israel from Hamath to the Dead Sea. It is not indeed expressly stated that he subjugated Moab again; but as Moabitish bands had disturbed even the country on this side under his predecessor Joash (2 Kings xiii. 20), it may be supposed that he also attempted to keep Moab within bounds. If the Moabites, as is very probable, had extended their territory northwards beyond the Arnon, the war with Moab was inevitable. Moreover, under Jeroboam II. on the one hand, and Uzziah-Jotham on the other, we read nothing about the Moabites rising; but, on the contrary, such notices as those contained in 1 Chron. v. 17 and 2 Chron. xxvi. 10, show that they kept themselves quiet. But the application made by Ahaz to Assyria called up the hostility of Moab and the neighbouring nations again. Tiglath-pileser repeated what the Syrians had done before. He took possession of the northern part of the land on this side, and the whole of the land on the other side, and depopulated them. This furnished an opportunity for the Moabites to re-establish themselves in their original settlements to the north of the Arnon. And this was how it stood at the time when Isaiah prophesied. The calamity which befel them came from the north, and therefore fell chiefly and primarily upon the country to the north of the Arnon, which the Moabites had taken possession of but a short time before, after it had been peopled for a long time by the tribes of Reuben and Gad.

There is no other prophecy in the book of Isaiah in which the heart of the prophet is so painfully affected by what his mind sees, and his mouth is obliged to prophesy. All that he predicts evokes his deepest sympathy, just as if he himself belonged to the unfortunate nation to which he is called to be a messenger of woe. He commences with an utterance of amazement. Ver. 1. " *Oracle concerning Moab! for in a night 'Ar-Moab is laid waste, destroyed; for in a night Kir-Moab is laid waste, destroyed.*" The *ci* (for) is explanatory in both instances, and not simply affirmative, or, as Knobel maintains, recitative, and therefore unmeaning. The prophet justifies the peculiar heading to his prophecy from the horrible vision given him to see, and takes us at once into the very heart of the vision, as in ch. xvii. 1, xxiii. 1. *'Ar Moab* (in which *'Ar* is Moabitish for *'Ir*; cf. Jer. xlix. 3, where we find *'Ai* written instead of *'Ar*, which we should naturally expect) is the name of the capital of Moab (Grecized, *Areopolis*), which was situated to the south of the Arnon, at present a large field of ruins, with a village of the name of *Rabba*. *Kir Moab* (in which Kir is the Moabitish for *Kiryah*) was the chief fortress of Moab, which was situated to the south-east of *Ar*, the present *Kerek*, where there is still a town with a fortification upon a rock, which can be seen from Jerusalem with a telescope on a clear day, and forms so thoroughly one mass with the rock, that in 1834, when Ibrahim Pasha resolved to pull it down, he was obliged to relinquish the project. The identity of *Kir* and *Kerek* is unquestionable, but that of *Ar* and *Rabba* has been disputed; and on the ground of Num. xxii. 36, where it seems to be placed nearer the Arnon, it has been transposed to the ruins on the pasture land at the confluence of the *Lejûm* and *Mujib* (= "the city that is by the river" in Deut. ii. 36 and Josh. xiii. 9, 16: see Com. on Num. xxi. 15),—a conjecture which has this against it, that the name *Areopolis*, which has been formed from *Ar*, is attached to the "*metropolis civitas Ar*," which was called *Rabba* as the metropolis, and of which Jerome relates (on the passage before us), as an event associated with his own childhood, that it was then destroyed by an earthquake (probably in 342). The two names of the cities are used as masculine here, like *Dammesek* in ch. xvii. 1, and *Tzor* in ch. xxiii. 1, though it cannot therefore be said, as at Mic. v. 1, that the *city* stands for the *inhabitants* (Ges. *Lehrgebäude*, p. 469). "*In a night*" (בְּלֵיל absolute, as in ch. xxi. 11, not construct, which would give an illogical assertion, as *shuddad* and *nidmâh* are almost coincident, so far as the sense is concerned) the two pillars of the strength of Moab are overthrown. In the space of a night, and therefore very suddenly (ch. xvii. 14), Moab is destroyed. The prophet repeats twice what it would have been quite sufficient to say once, just as if he had been condemned to keep his eye fixed upon the awful spectacle (on the *asyndeton*, see at ch. xxxiii. 9; and on the *anadiplosis*, ver. 8, ch. viii. 9, xxi. 11, xvii. 12, 13). His first sensation is that of horror.

But just as horror, when once it begins to reflect, is dissolved in tears, the thunder-claps in ver. 1 are followed by universal weeping and lamentation. Vers. 2–4. "*They go up to the temple-house and Dibon, up to the heights to weep: upon Nebo and upon Medebah of Moab there is weeping: on all heads baldness, every beard is mutilated. In the markets of Moab they gird themselves with sackcloth; on the roofs of the land, and in its streets, everything wails, melting into tears. Heshbon cries, and 'Elâle; even to Jahaz they hear their howling; even the armed men of Moab break out into mourning thereat; its soul trembles within it.*" The people (the subject to עָלָה) ascend the mountain with the temple of *Chemosh*, the central sanctuary of the land. This temple is called *hab-baith*, though not that there was a Moabitish town or village with some such name as Bêth-Diblathaim (Jer. xlviii. 22), as Knobel supposes. *Dibon*, which lay above the Arnon (*Wady Mujib*), like all the places mentioned in vers. 2–4, at present a heap of ruins, a short hour to the north of the central Arnon, in the splendid plain of *el-Chura*, had consecrated heights in the neighbourhood (cf. Josh. xiii. 17; Num. xxii. 41), and therefore would turn to them. Moab mourns upon *Nebo* and *Medebah*; יְיֵלִיל, for which we find יְהֵילִיל in ch. lii. 5, is written intentionally for a double preformative, instead of יֵילִיל (compare the similar forms in Job xxiv. 21, Ps. cxxxviii. 6, and Ges. § 70, Anm.). עַל is to be taken in a local sense, as Hendewerk, Drechsler, and Knobel have rendered it. For Nebo was probably a place situated upon a height on the mountain of that name, towards the south-east of Heshbon (the ruins of *Nabo, Nabau*, mentioned in the *Onom.*); and Medebah (still a heap of ruins bearing the same name) stood upon a round hill about two hours to the south-east of Heshbon. According to Jerome, there was an image of Chemosh in Nebo; and among the ruins of Madeba, Seetzen discovered the foundations of a strange temple. There follows here a description of the expressions of pain. Instead of the usual רָאשָׁיו, we read רֹאשָׁיו here. And instead of *gedu'âh* (*abscissæ*), Jeremiah (xlviii. 37) has, according to his usual style, *geru'âh* (*decurtatæ*), with the simple alteration of a single letter.[1] All runs down with weeping (*culloh*, written as in ch. xvi. 7; in ch. ix. 8, 16, we have *cullo* instead). In other cases it is the eyes that are said to run down in tears, streams, or water-brooks; but here, by a still bolder metonymy, the whole man is said to flow down to the ground, as if melting in a stream of tears. *Heshbon* and *Elale* are still visible in their ruins, which lie only half an hour apart upon their separate hills, and are still called by the names *Husban* and *el-Al*. They were both situated upon hills which commanded an extensive prospect. And there the cry of woe created an echo which was audible as far as *Jahaz* (*Jahza*), the city where the king of Heshbon offered battle to Israel in the time of Moses (Deut. ii. 32). The general mourning was so great, that even the armed men, *i.e.* the heroes (Jer. xlviii. 41) of Moab, were seized with despair, and cried out in their anguish (the same figure as in ch. xxxiii. 7). עַל־כֵּן, thereat, namely on account of this universal lamentation. Thus the lamentation was universal, without exception. *Naphsho* (his soul) refers to Moab as a whole nation. The soul of Moab trembles in all the limbs of the national body; יָרֵעָה (forming a play upon the sound with יָרִיעוּ), an Arabic word, and in יְרִיעָה a Hebrew word also, signifies *tremere, huc illuc agitari*,—an explanation which we prefer, with Rosenmüller and Gesenius, to the idea that יָרַע is a secondary verb to רָעַע, *fut.* יֵרַע. לֹ is an ethical dative (as in Ps. cxx. 6 and cxxiii. 4), throwing the action or the pathos inwardly (see *Psychology*, p. 152). The heart of the prophet participates in this pain with which Moab is agitated throughout; for, as Rashi observes, it is just in this that the prophets of Israel were distinguished from heathen prophets, such as Balaam for example, viz. that the calamities which they announced to the nations went to their own heart (compare ch. xxi. 3, 4, with ch. xxii. 4).

The difficult words in which the prophet expresses this sympathy we render as follows: Ver 5*a*. "*My heart, towards Moab it crieth out; its bolts reached to Zoar, the three-year-old*

---

[1] At the same time, the Masora on this passage before us is for *geru'ah* with *Resh*, and we also find this reading in Nissel, Clodius, Jablonsky, and in earlier editions; whilst Sonc. 1486, Ven. 1521, and others, have *yedu'ah*, with *Daleth*.

heifer." The *Lamed* in *l'Moab* is the same both here and in ch. xvi. 11 as in ch. xiv. 8, 9, viz. " turned toward Moab." *Moab*, which was masculine in ver. 4, is feminine here. We may infer from this that בְּרִיחֶהָ עַד־צֹעַר is a statement which concerns Moab as a land. Now, *b'richim* signifies the *bolts* in every other passage in which it occurs; and it is possible to speak of the bolts of a land with just as much propriety as in Lam. ii. 9 and Jer. li. 30 (cf. Jonah ii. 7) of the bolts of a city. And the statement that the bolts of this land went to *Zoar* is also a very appropriate one, for Kir Moab and Zoar formed the southern fortified girdle of the land; and Zoar, on the south-western tongue of land which runs into the Dead Sea, was the uttermost fortress of Moab, looking over towards Judah; and in its depressed situation below the level of the sea it formed, as it were, the opposite pole of Kir Moab, the highest point in the high land itself. Hence we agree with Jerome, who adopts the rendering *vectes ejus usque ad Segor*, whereas all the modern translators have taken the word in the sense of *fugitives*. '*Eglath sh'lishiyyâh*, which Rosenmüller, Knobel, Drechsler, Meier, and others have taken quite unnecessarily as a proper name, is either in apposition to Zoar or to Moab. In the former case it is a distinguishing epithet. An ox of the three years, or more literally of the third year (cf. *m'shullesheth*, Gen. xv. 9), *i.e.* a three-year-old ox, is one that is still in all the freshness and fulness of its strength, and that has not yet been exhausted by the length of time that it has worn the yoke. The application of the term to the Moabitish nation is favoured by Jer. xlvi. 20, where Egypt is called " a very fair heifer" ('*eglâh yephĕh-phiyyâh*), whilst Babylon is called the same in Jer. l. 11 (cf. Hos. iv. 16, x. 11). And in the same way, according to the LXX., Vulg., Targum, and Gesenius, Moab is called *juvenca tertii anni, h. e. indomita jugoque non assueta*, as a nation that was still in the vigour of youth, and if it had hitherto borne the yoke, had always shaken it off again. But the application of it to Zoar is favoured (1) by Jer. xlviii. 34, where this epithet is applied to another Moabitish city; (2) by the accentuation; and (3) by the fact that in the other case we should expect *b'rīchâh* (the three-year-old heifer, *i.e.* Moab, is a fugitive to Zoar: *vid.* Luzzatto). Thus Zoar, the fine, strong, and hitherto unconquered city, is now the destination of the wildest flight before the foe that is coming from the north. A blow has fallen upon Moab, that is more terrible than any that has preceded it.

In a few co-ordinate clauses the prophet now sets before us the several scenes of mourning and desolation. Vers. 5*b*, 6. *"For the mountain slope of Luhith they ascend with weeping; for on the road to Horonayim they lift up a cry of despair. For the waters of Nimrim are waste places from this time forth: for the grass is dried up, the vegetation wasteth away, the green is gone."* The road to *Luhith* (according to the *Onom.* between Ar-Moab and Zoar, and therefore in the centre of Moabitis proper) led up a height, and the road to *Horonaim* (according to Jer. xlviii. 5) down a slope. Weeping, they ran up to the mountain city to hide themselves there (*bo*, as in Ps. xxiv. 3; in Jer. xlviii. 5 it is written incorrectly בְּכִי). Raising loud cries of despair, they stand in front of Horonayim, which lay below, and was more exposed to the enemy. יְעֹעֵרוּ is softened from יְעַרְעֵרוּ (possibly to increase the resemblance to an echo), like כּוֹכָב from כַּבְכָּב. The Septuagint renders it very well, κραυγὴν συντριμμοῦ ἐξαναγεροῦσιν, — an unaccustomed expression of intense and ever renewed cries at the threatening danger of utter destruction, and with the hope of procuring relief and assistance (*sheber*, as in ch. i. 28, xxx. 26). From the farthest south the scene would suddenly be transferred to the extreme north of the territory of Moab, if *Nimrim* were the *Nimra* (*Beth-Nimra*, Talm. *nimrin*) which was situated near to the Jordan in Gilead, and therefore farther north than any of the places previously mentioned, and the ruins of which lie a little to the south of Salt, and are still called *Nimrin*. But the name itself, which is derived from the vicinity of fresh water (Arab. *nemir*, *nemîr*, clear, pure, sound), is one of frequent occurrence; and even to the south of Moabitis proper there is a *Wadi Numere*, and a brook called *Moyet Numere* (two diminutives: " dear little stream of Nimra "), which flows through stony tracks, and which formerly watered the country (Burckhardt, Seetzen, and De Saulcy). In all probability the ruins of *Numere* by the side of this wady are the Nimrim referred to here, and the waters of the brook the " waters of Nimrim " (*me Nimrim*). The waters that flowed fresh from the spring had been filled up with rubbish by the enemy, and would now probably lie waste for ever (a similar expression to that in ch. xvii. 2). He had gone through the land scorching and burning, so that all the vegetation had vanished. On the miniature-like short sentences, see ch. xxix. 20, xxxiii. 8, 9, xxxii. 10; and on לֹא הָיָה ("it is not in existence," or "it has become *not*," *i.e.* annihilated), *vid.* Ezek. xxi. 32.

As Moabitis has thus become a great scene of conflagration, the Moabites cross the border and fly to Idumæa. The reason for this is given in sentences which the prophet again links on to one another with the particle *ci* (for). Vers. 7–9. " *Therefore what has been spared, what has been gained, and their provision, they carry it over the willow-brook. For the scream has gone the round in the territory of Moab; the wailing of Moab resounds to Eglayim, and his wailing to Beër-Elim. For the waters of Dimon are full of blood: for I suspend over Dimon a new calamity, over the escaped of Moab a lion, and over the remnant of the land.*" Yithrâh is what is superfluous or exceeds the present need, and *pekuddâh* (lit. a laying up, *depositio*) that which has been carefully stored; whilst '*âsâh*, as the derivative passage, Jer. xlviii. 36, clearly shows (although the accusative in the whole of ver. 7 is founded upon a different view: see Rashi), is an attributive clause (what has been made, worked out, or gained). All these things they carry across *nachal hâ'arâbim*, *i.e.* not the desert-stream, as Hitzig, Maurer, Ewald, and Knobel suppose, since the plural of '*arâbâh* is '*arâboth*, but either the Arab stream (LXX., Saad.), or the willow-stream, *torrens salicum* (Vulg.). The latter is more suitable to the connection; and among the rivers which flow to the south of the Arnon from the mountains of the Moabitish highlands down to the Dead Sea, there is one which is called *Wadi Sufsaf*, *i.e.* willow-brook (*Tzaphtzâphâh* is the name of a brook in Hebrew also), viz. the northern arm of the *Seil el-Kerek*. This is what we suppose to be intended here, and not the *Wadi el-Ahsa*, although the latter (probably the biblical *Zered*[1]) is the boundary river on the extreme south, and separates Moab from Edom (*Kerek* from *Gebal*: see Ritter, *Erdk.* xv. 1223–4). Wading through the willow-brook, they carry their possessions across, and hurry off to the land of Edom, for their own land

[1] Hence the Targ. II. renders *nachal zered* "the brook of the willows." See Buxtorf, *Lex. chald. s.v. Zerad.*

has become the prey of the foe throughout its whole extent, and within its boundaries the cry of wailing passes from *Eglayim*, on the south-west of Ar, and therefore not far from the southern extremity of the Dead Sea (Ezek. xlvii. 10), as far as *Beer-Elim*, in the north-east of the land towards the desert (Num. xxi. 16-18; עַד must be supplied: Ewald, § 351, *a*), that is to say, if we draw a diagonal through the land, from one end to the other. Even the waters of *Dibon*, which are called *Dimon* here to produce a greater resemblance in sound to *dâm*, blood, and by which we are probably to understand the *Arnon*, as this was only a short distance off (just as in Judg. v. 19 the "waters of Megiddo" are the *Kishon*), are full of blood,[1] so that the enemy must have penetrated into the very heart of the land in his course of devastation and slaughter. But what drives them across the willow-brook is not this alone; it is as if they forebode that what has hitherto occurred is not the worst or the last. Jehovah suspends (*shith*, as in Hos. vi. 11) over Dibon, whose waters are already reddened with blood, *nōsăphōth*, something to be added, *i.e.* a still further judgment, namely *a lion*. The measure of Moab's misfortunes is not yet full: after the northern enemy, a lion will come upon those that have escaped by flight or have been spared at home (on the expression itself, compare ch. x. 20, xxxvii. 32, and other passages). This lion is no other than the basilisk of the prophecy against Philistia, but with this difference, that the basilisk represents one particular Davidic king, whilst the lion is Judah generally, whose emblem was the lion from the time of Jacob's blessing, in Gen. xlix. 9.

But just because this lion is Judah and its government, the summons goes forth to the Moabites, who have fled to Edom, and even to *Sela*, *i.e.* Petra (*Wady Musa*), near Mount Hor in Arabia Petræa, to which it gave its name, to turn for protection to Jerusalem. Ch. xvi. 1. "*Send a land-ruler's tribute of lambs from Sela desert-wards to the mountain of the daughter of Zion.*" This verse is like a long-drawn trumpet-blast. The prophecy against Moab takes the same turn here as in ch. xiv.

---

[1] מָלְאוּ דָם, with *munach* (which also represents the *metheg*) at the first syllable of the verb (compare ver. 4, לוֹ יֶרְעָה, with *mercha*), according to Vened. 1521, and other good editions. This is also grammatically correct.

32, xviii. 7, xix. 16 sqq., xxiii. 18. The judgment first of all produces slavish fear; and this is afterwards refined into loving attachment. Submission to the house of David is Moab's only deliverance. This is what the prophet, weeping with those that weep, calls out to them in such long-drawn, vehement, and urgent tones, even into the farthest hiding-place in which they have concealed themselves, viz. the rocky city of the Edomites. The tribute of lambs which was due to the ruling prince is called briefly *car moshēl-'eretz*. This tribute, which the holders of the pasture-land so rich in flocks have hitherto sent to Samaria (2 Kings iii. 4), they are now to send to Jerusalem, the "mountain of the daughter of Zion" (as in ch. x. 32, compared with ch. xviii. 7), the way to which lay through "*the desert*," *i.e.* first of all in a diagonal direction through the Arabah, which stretched downwards to Ælath.

The advice does not remain without effect, but they embrace it eagerly. Ver. 2. "*And the daughters of Moab will be like birds fluttering about, a scared nest, at the fords of the Arnon.*" "The daughters of Moab," like "the daughters of Judah," for example, in Ps. xlviii. 12, are the inhabitants of the cities and villages of the land of Moab. They were already like birds soaring about (Prov. xxvii. 8), because of their flight from their own land; but here, as we may see from the expression וְהָיָה ... תִּהְיֶינָה, the simile is intended to depict the condition into which they would be thrown by the prophet's advice. The figure (cf. ch. x. 14) as well as the expression (cf. ch. xvii. 2) is thoroughly Isaiah's. It is a state of anxious and timid indecision, resembling the fluttering to and fro of birds, that have been driven away from their nest, and wheel anxiously round and round, without daring to return to their old home. In this way the daughters of Moab, coming out of their hiding-places, whether nearer or more remote, show themselves at the fords of the Arnon, that is to say, on the very soil of their old home, which was situated between the Arnon and Wady el-Ahsa, and which was now devastated by the hand of a foe. מַעְבָּרוֹת לְאַרְנוֹן we should regard as in apposition to *b'noth Moab* (the daughters of Moab), if *ma'bâroth* signified the coast-lands (like *'ebrē* in ch. vii. 20), and not, as it invariably does, the fords. It is locative in its meaning, and is so accentuated.

There they show themselves, on the spot to which their land

once reached before it passed into the possession of Israel,—
there, on its farthest boundary in the direction towards Judah,
which was seated above; and taking heart, address the following
petitions to Zion, or to the Davidic court, on the other side.
Vers. 3, 4*a*. " *Give counsel, form a decision, make thy shadow like
night in the midst of noon; hide the outcasts, do not betray the
wanderers. Let mine outcasts tarry in thee, Moab; be a covert
to it from before the spoiler.*" In their extremity they appeal
to Zion for counsel, and the once proud but now thoroughly
humbled Moabites place the decision of their fate in the hands
of the men of Judah (so according to the *keri*), and stand
before Zion praying most earnestly for shelter and protection.
Their fear of the enemy is so great, that in the light of the
noon-day sun they desire to be covered with the protecting
shade of Zion as with the blackness of night, that they may
not be seen by the foe. The short sentences correspond to the
anxious urgency of the prayer (cf. ch. xxxiii. 8). *Peliláh*
(cf. *peliliyyáh*, ch. xxviii. 7) is the decision of a judge (*pâlil*);
just as in ch. xv. 5 *shelishiyyâh* is the age and standing of
three years. The figure of the shadow is the same as in ch.
xxx. 2, 3, xxxii. 2, etc.; *nōdēd* is the same as in ch. xxi. 14;
niddáchai as in ch. xi. 12; *sēther* as in ch. xxxii. 2, and other
passages; *shōdēd* as in ch. xxxiii. 1; *mippᵉnē* as in ch. xxi. 15.
The whole is word for word Isaiah's. There is no necessity
to read *nidchē* instead of *niddáchai Mo'âb* in ver. 4; still less is
ay a collective termination, as in ch. xx. 4. Nor are the words
to be rendered " my outcasts . . . of Moab," and the expression to be taken as a *syntaxis ornata* (cf. ch. xvii. 6). On the
contrary, such an expression is absolutely impossible here, where
the speaker is alluding to himself. It is better to abide by the
punctuation as we have it, with *niddáchai* (*zakeph*) closing the
first clause of ver. 4*a*, and *Moab* (*tebir*, which is subordinate to
the following *tiphchah*, and with this to *athnach*) opening the
second as an absolute noun. This is the way in which we have
rendered it above: "Moab . . . be a shield to it . . ." (though
without taking *lâmō* as equivalent to *lō*).

The question then arises, By what means has Zion awakened
such reverence and confidence on the part of Moab? This
question is answered in vers. 4*b*, 5 : "*For the extortioner is at an
end, desolation has disappeared, treaders down are away from*

the land. And a throne is established by grace, and there sits thereon in truth in the tent of David one judging, and zealous for right, and practised in righteousness." The imperial world-power, which pressed out both marrow and blood (*mētz*, a noun of the same form as *lētz*, like *mītz* in Prov. xxx. 33, pressure), and devastated and trod down everything (ch. xxix. 20, x. 6, xxxiii. 1, cf. 8), is swept away from the land on this side of the Jordan; Jerusalem is not subject to it now, but has come forth more gloriously out of all her oppressions than ever she did before. And the throne of the kingdom of Judah has not fallen down, but by the manifestation of Jehovah's grace has been newly established. There no longer sits thereon a king who dishonours Him, and endangers His kingdom; but the tent-roof of the fallen and now re-erected hut of David (Amos ix. 11) is spread over a King in whom the truth of the promise of Jehovah is verified, inasmuch as justice and righteousness are realized through all that He does. The Messianic times must therefore have dawned (so the Targum understands it), since grace and truth (*chesed ve'emeth*) and " justice and righteousness" (*mishpât ûtzedâkâh*) are the divino-human signs of those times, and as it were their kindred genii; and who can here fail to recal to mind the words of ch. ix. 6 (cf. xxxiii. 5, 6)? The king depicted here is the same as " the lion out of Judah," threatened against Moab in ch. xv. 9. Only by thus submitting to Him and imploring His grace will it escape the judgment.

But if Moab does this, and the law of the history of Israel, which is that " a remnant shall return," is thus reflected in the history of Moab; ver. 6 cannot possibly contain the answer which Moab receives from Zion, as the more modern commentators assume according to an error that has almost become traditional. On the contrary, the prophecy enters here upon a new stage, commencing with Moab's sin, and depicting the fate of Moab in still more elegiac strains. Ver. 6. " *We have heard of the pride of Moab, the very haughty* (pride), *his haughtiness, and his pride, and his wrath, the falsehood of his speech.*" The future self-humiliation of Moab, which would be the fruit of its sufferings, is here contrasted with the previous self-exaltation, of which these sufferings were the fruit. " *We have heard,*" says the prophet, identifying himself with his people. Boasting pompousness had hitherto been the distinguishing characteristic of Moab in relation to the latter (see ch. xxv. 11). The heaping up of words of the same verbal stem (cf. ch. iii. 1) is here intended to indicate how thoroughly haughty was their haughtiness (cf. Rom. vii. 13, "that sin might become exceeding sinful"), and how completely it had taken possession of Moab. It boasted and was full of rage towards Israel, to which, so far as it retained its consciousness of the truth of Jehovah, the talk of Moab (בַּדָּיו from בַּדַד = בְּרָא, בְּטָא, to talk at random) must necessarily appear as לֹא־כֵן, *not-right, i.e.* at variance with fact. These expressions of opinion had been heard by the people of God, and, as Jeremiah adds in ch. xlviii. 29, 30, by Israel's God as well.

Therefore the delightful land is miserably laid waste. Vers. 7, 8. "*Therefore will Moab wail for Moab, everything will wail: for the grape-cakes of Kir-Hareseth will ye whine, utterly crushed. For the fruit-fields of Heshbon have faded away: the vine of Sibmah, lords of the nations its branches smote down; they reached to Ja'zer, trailed through the desert: its branches spread themselves out wide, crossed over the sea.*" The *Lamed* in *l'Moab* is the same as in ch. xv. 5, and in *la'ashishē*, which follows here. *Kir-Hareseth* (written *Kir-Heres* in ver. 11, and by Jeremiah; compare 2 Kings iii. 25, where the vowel-pointing is apparently false): *Heres* or *Hareseth* may possibly refer to the glazed tiles or grooved stones. As this was the principal fortress of Moab, and according to ch. xv. 1 it had already been destroyed, *'ashishē* appears to mean the "strong foundations,"—namely, as laid bare; in other words, the "ruins" (cf. Jer. l. 15, and *mōsedē* in ch. lviii. 12). But in every other passage in which the word occurs it signifies a kind of cake; and as the devastation of the vines of Moab is made the subject of mourning afterwards, it has the same meaning here as in Hos. iii. 1, namely *raisin-cakes*, or raisins pressed into the form of cakes. Such cakes as these may have been a special article of the export trade of Kir. Jeremiah has altered *'ashishē* into *'anshē* (ch. xlviii. 31), and thus made *men* out of the grapes. *Hágáh* is to be understood in accordance with ch. xxxviii. 14, lix. 11 (viz. of the cooing of the dove); *'ac* (in good texts it is written with *mercha*, not with *makkeph*) according to Deut. xvi. 15. On the construction of the *pluralet. shadmoth*, compare Hab. iii. 17. We have rendered the clause commencing with *baalē goyim* (lords of the nations) with the same amphibolism as we find in the Hebrew. It might mean either "lords of the nations (*domini gentium*) smote down its branches" (viz. those of the vine of *Sibmah*;[1] *hâlam* being used as in ch. xli. 7), or "its branches smote down (*i.e.* intoxicated) lords of the nations" (*dominos gentium*; *hâlam* having the same meaning as in the undisputed prophecy of Isaiah in ch. xxviii. 1). As the prophet enlarges here upon the excellence of the Moabitish wine, the latter is probably intended. The wine of Sibmah was so good, that it was placed upon the tables of monarchs, and so strong that it smote down, *i.e.* inevitably intoxicated, even those who were accustomed to good wines. This Sibmah wine was cultivated, as the prophet says, far and wide in Moab,—northwards as far as *Ja'zer* (between Ramoth, *i.e.* Salt, and Heshbon, now a heap of ruins), eastwards into the desert, and southwards across the Dead Sea,—a hyperbolical expression for close up to its shores. Jeremiah defines *yâm* (the sea) more closely as *yam Ja'zer* (the sea of Jazer; *vid.* Jer. xlviii. 32), so that the hyperbole vanishes. But what sea can the sea of Jazer be? Probably some celebrated large pool, like the pools of Heshbon, in which the waters of the *Wady* (*Nahr*) *Sir*, which takes its rise close by, were collected. Seetzen found some pools still there. The "sea" (*yâm*) in Solomon's temple shows clearly enough that the term *sea* was also commonly applied to artificial basins of a large size; and in Damascus the marble basins of flowing water in the halls of houses are still called *baharât*; and the same term is applied to the public reservoirs in all the streets of the city, which are fed by a network of aqueducts from the river Baradâ. The expression "break through the desert" (*tá'u midbâr*) is also a bold one, probably pointing to the fact that, like the red wines of Hungary at the present time, they were trailing vines, which did not require to be staked, but ran along the ground.

The beauties of nature and fruitfulness of the land, which come into the possession of any nation, are gifts from the riches of divine goodness, remnants of the paradisaical commencement of the history of man, and types of its paradisaical close; and for this very reason they are not matters of in-

[1] In MSS. *Shibmah* is written with *gaya*, in order that the two labials may be distinctly expressed.

difference to the spirit of prophecy. And for the same reason, it is not unworthy of a prophet, who predicts the renovation of nature and the perfecting of it into the beauty of paradise, to weep over such a devastation as that of the Moabitish vineyards which was now passing before his mind (cf. ch. xxxii. 12, 13). Ver. 9. " *Therefore I bemoan the vines of Sibmah with the weeping of Jazer; I flood thee with my tears, O Heshbon and Elealeh, that Hêdad hath fallen upon thy fruit-harvest and upon thy vintage.*" A tetrastich, the Hebrew equivalent, in measure and movement, of a sapphic strophe. The circumstantiality of the vision is here swallowed up again by the sympathy of the prophet; and the prophecy, which is throughout as truly human as it is divine, becomes soft and flowing like an elegy. The prophet mingles his tears with the tears of Jazer. Just as the latter weeps for the devastated vines of *Sibmah*, so does he also weep. The form אֲרַיָּוֶךְ, transposed from אֲרַוֶּךְ=אַרְוָיֵךְ (cf. Ewald, § 253, *a*, where it is explained as being a rare "voluntative" formation), corresponds to the elegiac tone of the whole strophe. *Heshbon* and *Elealeh*, those closely connected cities, with their luxuriant fields (*sh*ᵉ*demoth*, ver. 8), are now lying in ruins; and the prophet waters them with tears, because *hedad* has fallen upon the fruit-harvest and vintage of both the sister cities. In other instances the term *kâtzîr* is applied to the *wheat-harvest;* but here it is used in the same sense as *bâtzîr*, to which it is preferred on account of Isaiah's favourite alliteration, viz. with *kaytz* (compare, for example, the alliteration of *mistor* with *sēther* in ch. iv. 6). That it does not refer to the wheat-harvest here, but to the vintage, which was nearly coincident with the fruit-harvest (which is called *kaytz*, as in ch. xxviii. 4), is evident from the figure suggested in the word *hēdâd*, which was the shout raised by the pressers of the grapes, to give the time for moving their feet when treading out the wine (ver. 10; Jer. xxv. 30). A *hēdâd* of this kind had fallen upon the rich floors of Heshbon-Elealeh, inasmuch as they had been trodden down by enemies, —a *Hedad*, and yet no *Hedad*, as Jeremiah gives it in a beautiful oxymoron (ch. xlviii. 33), *i.e.* no joyous shout of actual grape-treaders.

The prophet, to whose favourite words and favourite figures *Carmel* belongs, both as the name of a place and as the name of a thing, now proceeds with his picture, and is plunged still more deeply into mourning. Vers. 10, 11. "*And joy is taken away, and the rejoicing of the garden-land; and there is no exulting, no shouting in the vineyards: the treader treads out no wine in the presses; I put an end to the Hedad. Therefore my bowels sound for Moab like a harp, and my inside for Kir-Heres.*" It is Jehovah who says "I put an end;" and consequently the words, "My bowels sound like a harp," or, as Jeremiah expresses it (Jer. xlviii. 36), like flutes, might appear to be expressive of the feelings of Jehovah. And the Scriptures do not hesitate to attribute *mē'ayim* (*viscera*) to God (*e.g.* ch. lxiii. 15, Jer. xxxi. 20). But as the prophet is the sympathizing subject throughout the whole of the prophecy, it is better, for the sake of unity, to take the words in this instance also as expressing the prophet's feelings. Just as the hand or plectrum touches the strings of the harp, so that they vibrate with sound; so did the terrible things that he had heard Jehovah say concerning Moab touch the strings of his inward parts, and cause them to resound with notes of pain. By the bowels, or rather entrails (*viscera*), the heart, liver, and kidneys are intended,—the highest organs of the Psyche, and the sounding-board, as it were, of those "hidden sounds" which exist in every man. God conversed with the prophet "in the spirit;" but what passed there took the form of individual impressions in the domain of the soul, in which impressions the bodily organs of the psychical life sympathetically shared. Thus the prophet saw in the spirit the purpose of God concerning Moab, in which he could not and would not make any change; but it threw his soul into all the restlessness of pain.

The ultimate reason for this restlessness is, that Moab does not know the living God. Ver. 12. "*And it will come to pass, when it is seen that Moab is weary with weeping upon the mountain height, and enters into its sanctuary to pray, it will not gain anything.*" נִרְאָה נִלְאָה, a pictorial assonance, such as Isaiah delights in. נִרְאָה is transferred from the Israelitish worship (appearance before God in His temple) to the heathen; syntactically, *si apparuerit*, etc., with *Vav* before the apodosis. It would be with the Moabites as with the priests of Baal in the time of Elijah (1 Kings xviii. 26 sqq.).

The *massa* is now brought to a close, and there follows an

epilogue which fixes the term of the fulfilment of what is not predicted now for the first time, from the standpoint of the anticipated history. Ver. 13. "*This is the word which Jehovah spake long ago concerning Moab. And now Jehovah speaketh thus: In three years, like years of a hireling, the glory of Moab is disgraced, together with all the multitude of the great; a remnant is left, contemptibly small, not great at all.*" The time fixed is the same as in ch. xx. 3. Of working time the hirer remits nothing, and the labourer gives nothing in. The statement as to the time, therefore, is intended to be taken exactly : three years, not more, rather under than over. Then will the old saying of God concerning Moab be fulfilled. Only a remnant, a contemptible remnant, will be left (וּשְׁאָר, cf. וּמְשׁוֹשׂ, ch. viii. 6, in sense equivalent to וְיִשָּׁאֵר); for every history of the nations is but the shadow of the history of Israel.

The *massa* in ch. xv. 1–xvi. 12 was a word that had already gone forth from Jehovah "long ago." This statement may be understood in three different senses. In the *first* place, Isaiah may mean that older prophecies had already foretold essentially the same concerning Moab. But what prophecies? We may get an answer to this question from the prophecies of Jeremiah concerning Moab in Jer. xlviii. Jeremiah there reproduces the *massa Moab* of the book of Isaiah, but interweaves with it reminiscences (1) out of the *mâshal* on Moab in Num. xxi. 27–30; (2) out of Balaam's prophecy concerning Moab in Num. xxiv. 17 ; (3) out of the prophecy of Amos concerning Moab (Amos ii. 1–3). And it might be to these earlier words of prophecy that Isaiah here refers (Hävernick, Drechsler, and others). But this is very improbable, as there is no ring of these earlier passages in the *massa*, such as we should expect if Isaiah had had them in his mind. *Secondly*, Isaiah might mean that ch. xv. 1 sqq. contained the prophecy of an older prophet, which he merely brought to remembrance in order to connect therewith the precise tenor of its fulfilment which had been revealed to him. This is at present the prevailing view. Hitzig, in a special work on the subject (1831), as well as in his Commentary, has endeavoured to prove, on the ground of 2 Kings xiv. 25, that in all probability *Jonah* was the author of the oracle which Isaiah here resumes. And Knobel, Maurer, Gustav Baur, and Thenius agree with him in this ; whilst De

Wette, Ewald, and Umbreit regard it as, at any rate, decidedly non-Messianic. If the conjecture that Jonah was the author could but be better sustained, we should heartily rejoice in this addition to the history of the literature of the Old Testament. But all that we know of Jonah is at variance with such a conjecture. He was a prophet of the type of Elijah and Elisha, in whom the eloquence of a prophet's words was thrown altogether into the shade by the energy of a prophet's deeds. His prophecy concerning the restoration of the kingdom of Israel to its old boundaries, which was fulfilled by the victories of Jeroboam II., we cannot therefore imagine to have been so pictorial or highly poetical as the *massa Moab* (which would only be one part of that prophecy) really is; and the fact that he was angry at the sparing of Nineveh harmonizes very badly with its elegiac softness and its flood of tears. Moreover, it is never intimated that the conquerors to whom Moab was to succumb would belong to the kingdom of Israel; and the hypothesis is completely overthrown by the summons addressed to Moab to send tribute to Jerusalem. But the conclusion itself, that the oracle must have originated with any older prophet whatever, is drawn from very insufficient premises. No doubt it is a thing altogether unparalleled even in Isaiah, that a prophecy should assume so thoroughly the form of a *kinah*, or lamentation; still there are tendencies to this in ch. xxii. 4 (cf. ch. xxi. 3, 4), and Isaiah was an inexhaustible master of language of every character and colour. It is true we do light upon many expressions which cannot be pointed out anywhere else in the book of Isaiah, such as *baalē goyim*, *hedâd*, *y'lâlâh*, *yâra'*, *yithrâh*, *mâhir*, *mētz*, *nosâphoth*, *pekuddâh* (provision, possession); and there is something peculiar in the circular movement of the prophecy, which is carried out to such an extent in the indication of reason and consequence, as well as in the perpetually returning, monotonous connection of the sentences by *ci* (for) and *'al-cēn* (*lâcēn*, therefore), the former of which is repeated twice in ch. xv. 1, three times in ch. xv. 8, 9, and four times in succession in ch. xv. 5, 6. But there is probably no prophecy, especially in ch. xiii.-xxiii., which does not contain expressions that the prophet uses nowhere else; and so far as the conjunctions *ci* and *'al-cēn* (*lâcēn*) are concerned, Isaiah crowds them together in other passages as well, and here almost to monotony, as a natural consequence of the prevailing elegiac tone. Besides, even Ewald can detect the characteristics of Isaiah in ch. xvi. 1-6; and you have only to dissect the whole rhetorically, syntactically, and philologically, with the carefulness of a Caspari, to hear throughout the ring of Isaiah's style. And whoever has retained the impression which he brought with him from the oracle against Philistia, will be constrained to say, that not only the stamp and outward form, but also the spirit and ideas, are thoroughly Isaiah's. Hence the third possible conjecture must be the correct one. *Thirdly*, then, Isaiah may mean that the fate of Moab, which he has just proclaimed, was revealed to him long ago; and the addition made now is, that it will be fulfilled in exactly three years. מֵאָז does not necessarily point to a time antecedent to that of Isaiah himself (compare ch. xliv. 8, xlviii. 3, 5, 7, with 2 Sam. xv. 34). If we assume that what Isaiah predicts down to ch. xvi. 12 was revealed to him in the year that Ahaz died, and that the epilogue reckons from the third or tenth year of Hezekiah, in either case the interval is long enough for the *mê'âz* (from of old). And we decide in favour of this. Unfortunately, we know nothing certain as to the time at which the three years commence. The question whether it was Shalmanassar, Sargon, or Sennacherib who treated the Moabites so harshly, is one that we cannot answer. In Herodotus (ii. 141), Sennacherib is called "king of the Arabians and Assyrians;" and Moab might be included in the Arabians. In any case, after the fulfilment of Isaiah's prophecy in the Assyrian times, there was still a portion left, the fulfilment of which, according to Jer. xlviii., was reserved for the Chaldeans.

THE ORACLE CONCERNING DAMASCUS AND ISRAEL.—
CHAP. XVII.

From the Philistines on the west, and the Moabites on the east, the prophecy relating to the neighbouring nations now turns, without any chronological order, to the people of Damascene Syria on the north. The curse pronounced on them, however, falls upon the kingdom of Israel also, because it has allied itself with heathen Damascus, in opposition to its own brother tribe to the south, as well as to the Davidic government;

and by this unnatural alliance with a *zâr*, or stranger, had become a *zâr* itself. From the period of Hezekiah's reign, to which the *massa Moab* belongs, at least so far as its epilogue is concerned, we are here carried back to the reign of Ahaz, and indeed far beyond " the year that Ahaz died" (ch. xiv. 28), to the very border of the reigns of Jotham and Ahaz,—namely, to the time when the league for the destruction of Judah had only just been concluded. At the time when Isaiah incorporated this oracle in his collection, the threats against the kingdoms of Damascus and Israel had long been fulfilled. Assyria had punished both of them. And Assyria itself had also been punished, as the fourth turn in the oracle indicates. Consequently the oracle stands here as a memorial of the truthfulness of the prophecy; and it answers a further purpose still, viz. to furnish a rich prophetic consolation for the church of all times, when persecuted by the world, and sighing under the oppression of the kingdom of the world.

The first turn: vers. 1–3. " *Behold, Damascus must* (be taken) *away out of the number of the cities, and will be a heap of fallen ruins. The cities of Aroer are forsaken, they are given up to flocks, they lie there without any one scaring them away. And the fortress of Ephraim is abolished, and the kingdom of Damascus; and it happens to those that are left of Aram as to the glory of the sons of Israel, saith Jehovah of hosts." " Behold,"* etc.: *hinnēh* followed by a participle indicates here, as it does everywhere else, something very near at hand. Damascus is removed מֵעִיר (= מֵהְיוֹת עִיר, cf. 1 Kings xv. 13), *i.e.* out of the sphere of existence as a city. It becomes מְעִי, a heap of ruins. The word is used intentionally instead of עִי, to sound as much as possible like מֵעִיר: a mutilated city, so to speak. It is just the same with Israel, which has made itself an appendage of Damascus. The " cities of Aroer" (*gen. appos.* Ges. § 114, 3) represent the land to the east of the Jordan: there the judgment upon Israel (executed by Tiglath-pileser) first began. There were two *Aroers*: an old Amoritish city allotted to the tribe of Reuben, viz. " Aroer on the Arnon" (Deut. ii. 36, iii. 12, etc.); and an old Ammonitish one, allotted to the tribe of Gad, viz. " Aroer before Rabbah" (Rabbath Ammon, Josh. xiii. 25). The ruins of the former are *Arair*, on the lofty northern bank of the *Mugib;* but the situation of the latter has not yet been determined with certainty (see Com. on Josh. xiii. 25). The "cities of Aroer" are these two Aroers, and the rest of the cities similar to it on the east of the Jordan; just as "the Orions" in ch. xiii. 10 are Orion and other similar stars. We meet here again with a significant play upon the sound in the expression *'ārē 'Aro'ēr* (cities of Aroer): the name of Aroer was ominous, and what its name indicated would happen to the cities in its circuit. עָרָה means "to lay bare," to pull down (Jer. li. 58); and עֲרִירִי עָרָר signifies a stark-naked condition, a state of desolation and solitude. After ver. 1 has threatened Damascus in particular, and ver. 2 has done the same to Israel, ver. 3 comprehends them both. Ephraim loses the fortified cities which once served it as defences, and Damascus loses its rank as a kingdom. Those that are left of Aram, who do not fall in the war, become like the proud citizens of the kingdom of Israel, *i.e.* they are carried away into captivity. All this was fulfilled under Tiglath-pileser. The accentuation connects שְׁאָר אֲרָם (the remnant of Aram) with the first half of the verse; but the meaning remains the same, as the subject to יִהְיוּ is in any case the Aramæans.

Second turn: vers. 4–8. "*And it comes to pass in that day, the glory of Jacob wastes away, and the fat of his flesh grows thin. And it will be as when a reaper grasps the stalks of wheat, and his arm mows off the ears; and it will be as with one who gathers together ears in the valley of Rephaim. Yet a gleaning remains from it, as at the olive-beating: two, three berries high up at the top; four, five in its, the fruit tree's, branches, saith Jehovah the God of Israel. At that day will man look up to his Creator, and his eyes will look to the Holy One of Israel. And he will not look to the altars, the work of his hands; and what his fingers have made he will not regard, neither the Astartes nor the sun-gods.*" This second turn does not speak of Damascus, but simply of Israel, and in fact of all Israel, the range of vision widening out from Israel in the more restricted sense, so as to embrace the whole. It will all disappear, with the exception of a small remnant; but the latter will return. Thus "a remnant will return," the law of Israel's history, which is here shown first of all in its threatening aspect, and then in its more promising one. The reputation and prosperity to which the two kingdoms were raised by Jeroboam II, and Uzziah would pass away. Israel was ripe for judgment, like a field of corn for the harvest; and it would be as when a reaper grasps the stalks that have shot up, and cuts off the ears. קָצִיר is not used elliptically for אִישׁ קָצִיר (Gesenius), nor is it a definition of time (Luzzatto), nor an accusative of the object (Knobel), but a noun formed like נָבִיא, פָּלִיל, פָּרִיץ, and used in the sense of reaper (*kōtzēr* in other cases).[1] The figure suggested here is more fully expanded in John iv. and Rev. xiv. Hardly a single one will escape the judgment: just as in the broad plain of Rephaim, which slopes off to the south-west of Jerusalem as far as Bethlehem, where it is covered with rich fields of wheat, the collectors of ears leave only one or two ears lying scattered here and there. Nevertheless a gleaning of Israel ("in it," viz. in Jacob, ver. 4, ch. x. 22) will be left, just as when the branches of the olive tree, which have been already cleared with the hand, are still further shaken with a stick, there still remain a few olives upon the highest branch (two, three; cf. 2 Kings ix. 32), or concealed under the foliage of the branches. "*Its, the fruit tree's, branches:*" this is an elegant expression, as, for example, in Prov. xiv. 13; the carrying over of the ה to the second word is very natural in both passages (see Ges. § 121, *b*). This small remnant will turn with stedfast gaze to the living God, as is becoming in man as such (*hâ'âdâm*), and not regard the idols as worthy of any look at all, at least of any reverential look. As *hammânim* are here images of the sun-god בַּעַל חַמָּן, which is well known from the Phœnician monuments,[2] '*ashērim* (for which we find, though more rarely, '*ashēroth*) apparently signifies images of the moon-goddess. And the combination of "Baal, Asherah, and all the host of heaven" in 2 Kings xxiii. 4, as well as the surname "queen of heaven" in Jer. vii. 18, xliv. 18, 19, appears to require this (Knobel). But the latest researches have proved that '*Ashērâh* is rather the Semitic Aphrodite, and therefore the planet Venus, which was called the "little luck" (*es-sa'd*

---

[1] Instead of *kâtzar* (to cut off, or shorten), they now say *kâratz* in the whole of the land to the east of the Jordan, which gives the idea of sawing off,—a much more suitable one where the Syrian sickle is used.

[2] See Levy, *Phönizisches Wörterbuch* (1864), p. 19; and Otto Strauss on Nahum, p. xxii. ss.

el-as'gar)[1] by the Arabs, in distinction from *Musteri* (Jupiter),[2] or "the great luck." And with this the name ʼ*Asherah* the "lucky" (*i.e.* the source of luck or prosperity) and the similar surname given to the Assyrian *Istar* agree;[3] for ʼ*Asherah* is the very same goddess as ʼ*Ashtoreth*, whose name is thoroughly Arian, and apparently signifies the star (Ved. *stri* = *star;* Zend. *stare;* Neo-Pers. *sitâre*, used chiefly for the morning star), although Rawlinson (without being able to suggest any more acceptable interpretation) speaks of this view as "not worthy of much attention."[4] Thus *Asherim* is used to signify the *bosquets* (shrubberies) or trees dedicated to the Semitic Aphrodite (Deut. xvi. 21; compare the verbs used to signify their removal, גדע, ברת, נתש); but here it probably refers to her statues or images[5] (2 Kings xxi. 7; compare the *miphletzeth* in 1 Kings xv. 13, which is used to denote an obscene exhibition). For these images of the sun-god and of the goddess of the morning star, the remnant of Israel, that has been purified by the smelting furnace of judgment, has no longer any eye. Its looks are exclusively directed to the one true God of man. The promise, which here begins to dawn at the close of the second turn, is hidden again in the third, though only to break forth again in the fourth with double or triple intensity.

Third turn: vers. 9–11. "*In that day will his fortified cities be like the ruins of the forest and of the mountain top, which they cleared before the sons of Israel: and there arises a waste place. For thou hast forgotten the God of thy salvation, and hast not thought of the Rock of thy stronghold, therefore thou plantedst charming plantations, and didst set them with strange*

---

[1] See Krehl, *Religion der vorislamischen Araber* (1863), p. 11.

[2] This was the tutelar deity of Damascus; see *Job*, ii. 446.

[3] "*Ishtar,*" says Rawlinson in his *Five Great Monarchies of the Ancient Eastern World*,—a work which challenges criticism through its dazzling results,—"*Ishtar* is the goddess who rejoices mankind, and her most common epithet is Amra, 'the fortunate' or 'the happy.' But otherwise her epithets are vague and general, insomuch that she is often scarcely distinguishable from Beltis (the wife of Bel-Nimrod)." *Vid.* vol. i. p. 175 (1862).

[4] The planet Venus, according to a Midrash relating to Gen. vi. 1, 2, is ʼ*Istehar* transferred to the sky; and this is the same as *Zuhare* (see Geiger, *Was hat Muhammed*, etc., 1833, pp. 107–109).

[5] The plural *Ashtaroth*, *Hathors*, which occurs upon Assyrian and Egyptian monuments, has a different meaning.

vines. In the day that thou plantedst, thou didst make a fence; and with the morning dawn thou madest thy sowing to blossom: a harvest heap in the day of deep wounds and deadly sorrow of heart." The statement in ver. 3, " The fortress of Ephraim is abolished," is repeated in ver. 9 in a more descriptive manner. The fate of the strongly fortified cities of Ephraim would be the same as that of the old Canaanitish castles, which were still to be discerned in their antiquated remains, either in the depths of forests or high up on the mountains. The word *'azubâh*, which the early translators quite misunderstood, signifies, both here and in ch. vi. 12, desolate places that have gone to ruin. They also misunderstood הַחֹרֶשׁ וְהָאָמִיר. The Septuagint renders it, by a bold conjecture, οἱ Ἀμορραῖοι καὶ οἱ Εὐαῖοι; but this is at once proved to be false by the inversion of the names of the two peoples, which was very properly thought to be necessary. הָאָמִיר undoubtedly signifies the top of a tree, which is quite unsuitable here. But as even this meaning points back to אָמַר, *extollere, efferre* (see at Ps. xciv. 4), it may also mean the mountain-top. The name *hâ'emori* (the Amorites: those who dwell high up in the mountains) proves the possibility of this; and the prophet had this name in his mind, and was guided by it in his choice of a word. The subject of עֲזֻבוּ is self-evident. And the reason why only the ruins in forests and on mountains are mentioned is, that other places, which were situated on the different lines of traffic, merely changed their inhabitants when the land was taken by Israel. The reason why the fate of Ephraim's fortified castles was the same as that of the Amoritish castles, which were then lying in ruins, was that Ephraim, as stated in ver. 10, had turned away from its true rocky stronghold, namely from Jehovah. It was a consequence of this estrangement from God, that Ephraim planted נִטְעֵי נַעֲמָנִים, plantations of the nature of pleasant things, or pleasant plantations (compare on Ps. lxxviii. 49, and Ewald, § 287, *ab*), *i.e.* cultivated all kinds of sensual accompaniments to its worship, in accordance with its heathen propensities; and sowed, or rather (as *zemôrâh* is the layer of a vine) " set," this gardenground, to which the suffix *ennu* refers, with strange grapes, by forming an alliance with a *zâr* (a stranger), namely the king of Damascus. On the very day of the planting, Ephraim fenced it carefully (this is the meaning of the *pilpel, sigsēg* from סוג=שׂוג, not "to raise," as no such verb as שׂוג=שָׂנָה, קָנָא, can be shown to exist), that is to say, he ensured the perpetuity of these sensuous modes of worship as a state religion, with all the shrewdness of a Jeroboam (see Amos vii. 13). And the very next morning he had brought into blossom what he had sown: the foreign layer had shot up like a hot-house plant, *i.e.* the alliance had speedily grown into a hearty agreement, and had already produced one blossom at any rate, viz. the plan of a joint attack upon Judah. But this plantation, which was so flattering and promising for Israel, and which had succeeded so rapidly, and to all appearance so happily, was a harvest heap for the day of the judgment. Nearly all modern expositors have taken *nēd* as the third person (after the form *mēth*, Ges. § 72, Anm. 1), and render it "the harvest flees;" but the third person of נוד would be נָד, like the participle in Gen. iv. 12; whereas the meaning *cumulus* (a heap), which it has elsewhere as a substantive, is quite appropriate, and the statement of the prophet resembles that of the apostle in Rom. ii. 5. The day of the judgment is called "the day of נַחֲלָה" (or, according to another reading, נְחֲלָה), not, however, as equivalent to *nachal*, a stream (Luzzatto, *in giorno di fiumana*), as in Ps. cxxiv. 4 (the tone upon the last syllable proves this), nor in the sense of "in the day of possession," as Rosenmüller and others suppose, since this necessarily gives to נַד the former objectionable and (by the side of קָצִיר) improbable verbal sense; but as the feminine of *nachleh*, written briefly for *maccâh nachlâh* (Jer. xiv. 17), *i.e.* inasmuch as it inflicts grievous and mortal wounds. Ephraim's plantation is a harvest heap for that day (compare *kâtzir*, the harvest of punishment, in Hos. vi. 11 and Jer. li. 33); and the hope set upon this plantation is changed into כְּאֵב אָנוּשׁ, a desperate and incurable heartfelt sorrow (Jer. xxx. 15). The organic connection between vers. 12–14, which follow, and the oracle concerning Damascus and Israel, has also been either entirely misunderstood, or not thoroughly appreciated. The connection is the following: As the prophet sets before himself the manner in which the sin of Ephraim is punished by Asshur, as the latter sweeps over the Holy Land, the promise which already began to dawn in the second turn bursts completely through: the world-power is the instrument of punishment in the hands of Jehovah, but not for ever.

Fourth turn: vers. 12-14. "*Woe to the roaring of many nations: like the roaring of seas they roar; and to the rumbling of nations, like the rumbling of mighty waters they rumble! Nations, like the rumbling of many waters they rumble; and He threatens it: then it flies far away, and is chased like chaff of the mountains before the wind, and like a cloud of dust before the gale. At eventide, behold consternation; and before the morning dawn it is destroyed: this is the portion of our plunderers, and the lot of our robbers.*" It is the destruction of Asshur that the prophet is predicting here (as in ch. xiv. 24-27, xxix. 5-8, etc.), though not of Asshur as Asshur, but of Asshur as the imperial kingdom, which embraced a multitude of nations (ch. xxii. 6, viii. 9, 10, xiv. 26, xxix. 7, 8) all gathered together under the rule of one will, to make a common attack upon the church of God. The connection between this fourth turn and the third is precisely the same as between ch. viii. 9, 10, and ch. viii. 6-8. The exclamation of woe (*hoi*) is an expression of pain, as in ch. x. 1; and this is followed by a proclamation of the judgment of wrath. The description of the rolling wave of nations is as pictorial as the well-known *illi inter sese, etc.*, of the Cyclops in Virgil. "It spreads and stretches out, as if it would never cease to roll, and roar, and surge, and sweep onward in its course" (Drechsler). In the expression "it" (*bo*) in ver. 13a, the many surging nations are kneaded together, as it were, into one mass. It costs God simply a threatening word; and this mass all flies apart (*mimmerchâk* like *mērâchōk*, ch. xxiii. 7), and falls into dust, and whirls about in all directions, like the chaff of threshing-floors in high situations, or like dust whirled up by the storm. The judgment commences in the evening, and rages through the night; and before the morning dawns, the army of nations raised by the imperial power is all destroyed (compare ch. xxix. 7, 8, and the fulfilment in ch. xxxvii. 36). The fact that the oracle concerning Damascus in its fourth stage takes so comprehensive and, so far as Israel is concerned, so promising a form, may be explained on the ground that Syria was the forerunner of Asshur in the attack upon Israel, and that the alliance between Israel and Syria became the occasion of the complications with Asshur. If the substance of the *massâ Dammesek* (the oracle concerning Damascus) had been restricted to the prophecy contained in the name Mahershalal, the element of promise so characteristic of the prophecies against the nations of the world would be entirely wanting. But the shout of triumph, "This is the portion," etc., supplied a terminal point, beyond which the *massa* could not go without the sacrifice of its unity. We are therefore warranted in regarding ch. xviii. as an independent prophecy, notwithstanding its commencement, which apparently forms a continuation of the fourth strophe of ch. xvii.

ETHIOPIA'S SUBMISSION TO JEHOVAH.—CHAP. XVIII.

The notion that ch. xviii. 4-6 contains an account of the judgment of Jehovah upon Ethiopia is quite an untenable one. The prophet is here predicting the destruction of the army of Sennacherib in his usual way, and in accordance with the actual fulfilment (ch. xxxvii. 36). The view which Hofmann has adopted from the Jewish expositors—namely, that the people so strangely described at the commencement and close of the prophecy is the Israelitish nation—is equally untenable. It is Ethiopia. Taking both these facts together, then, the conclusion to which we are brought is, that the prophet is here foretelling the effect that will be produced upon Ethiopia by the judgment which Jehovah is about to inflict upon Asshur. But it is altogether improbable either that the prophecy falls later than the Assyrian expedition against Egypt (as Schegg supposes), or that the Ethiopian ambassadors mentioned here are despatched to Judah to seek for friendship and aid (as Ewald, Knobel, Meier, and Thenius maintain). The expedition was still impending, and that against Judah was the means to this further end. The ambassadors are not sent to Judah, but carry commands with the most stirring despatch to every province under Ethiopian rule. The Ethiopian kingdom is thrown into the greatest excitement in the face of the approaching Assyrian invasion, and the messengers are sent out to raise the militia. At that time both Egypts were governed by the Ethiopian (or twenty-fifth) dynasty, *Sabako* the Ethiopian having made himself master of the country on the Lower Nile.[1] The king of Egypt who was contemporaneous with Sennacherib was the *Tirhaka* of the Old Testament, the *Tarakos* of Manetho,

---

[1] See Brugsch, *Histoire d'Egypte*, i. (1859) 244-246.

and the *Tearkon* of Strabo,—a great conqueror, according to Megasthenes, like Sesostris and Nebuchadnezzar, who had carried his conquests as far as the Pillars of Hercules (Strabo, xv. 1, 6). This explains the strangely sounding description given in vers. 2 and 7 of the Ethiopian people, which had the universal reputation in antiquity of gigantic strength and invincibility. It is impossible to determine the length of time that intervened between the composition of the prophecy and the fourteenth year of Hezekiah's reign, in which the Assyrian army commenced the expedition across Judah to Egypt. The event which the prophecy foretells—namely, that the judgment of Jehovah upon Asshur would be followed by the submission of Ethiopia to Jehovah—was only partially and provisionally fulfilled (2 Chron. xxxii. 23). And there is nothing to surprise us in this, inasmuch as in the prophecies delivered before the destruction of Assyria the latter always presented itself to the mind of the prophet as the kingdom of the world; and consequently the prophecy had also an eschatological feature, which still remained for a future and remote fulfilment.

The prophecy commences with *hoi*, which never signifies *heus*, but always *væ* (woe). Here, however, it differs from ch. xvii. 12, and is an expression of compassion (cf. Isa. lv. 1, Zech. ii. 10) rather than of anger; for the fact that the mighty Ethiopia is oppressed by the still mightier Asshur, is a humiliation which Jehovah has prepared for the former. Vers. 1, 2a: "*Woe to the land of the whirring of wings, which is beyond the rivers of Cush, that sends ambassadors into the sea and in boats of papyrus over the face of the waters.*" The land of *Cush* commences, according to Ezek. xxix. 10 (cf. xxx. 6), where Upper Egypt ends. The *Sevêneh* (*Aswân*), mentioned by Ezekiel, is the boundary-point at which the Nile enters *Mizraim* proper, and which is still a depot for goods coming from the south down the Nile. The *naharê-Cush* (rivers of Cush) are chiefly those that surround the Cushite *Seba* (Gen. x. 7). This is the name given to the present Sennâr, the Meroitic island which is enclosed between the White and Blue Nile (the *Astapos* of Ptolemy, or the present *Bahr el-Abyad*, and the *Astaboras* of Ptolemy, or the present *Bahr el-Azrak*). According to the latest researches, more especially those of Speke, the White Nile, which takes its rise in the Lake of Nyanza, is the chief source of the Nile. The latter, and the Blue Nile, whose confluence (*makran*) with it takes place in lat. 15° 25', are fed by many larger or smaller tributary streams (as well as mountain torrents); the Blue Nile even more than the Nile proper. And this abundance of water in the land to the south of *Sevēnēh*, and still farther south beyond *Seba* (or Meroë), might very well have been known to the prophet as a general fact. The land "beyond the rivers of Cush" is the land bounded by the sources of the Nile, *i.e.* (including Ethiopia itself in the stricter sense of the word) the south land under Ethiopian rule that lay still deeper in the heart of the country, the land of its African auxiliary tribes, whose names (which probably include the later Nubians and Abyssinians), as given in 2 Chron. xii. 3, Nahum iii. 9, Ezek. xxx. 5, Jer. xlvi. 9, suppose a minuteness of information which has not yet been attained by modern research. To this Ethiopia, which is designated by its farthest limits (compare Zeph. iii. 10, where Wolff, in his book of Judith, erroneously supposes Media to be intended as the Asiatic Cush), the prophets give the strange name of *eretz tziltzal cenáphaim*. This has been interpreted as meaning "the land of the wings of an army with clashing arms" by Gesenius and others; but *cenáphaim* does not occur in this sense, like *'agappim* in Ezekiel. Others render it "the land of the noise of waves" (Umbreit); but *cenáphaim* cannot be used of waters except in such a connection as ch. viii. 8. Moreover, *tziltzal* is not a fitting onomatopoetic word either for the clashing of arms or the noise of waves. Others, again, render it "the land of the double shadow" (Grotius, Vitringa, Knobel, and others); but, however appropriate this epithet might be to Ethiopia as a tropical land, it is very hazardous to take the word in a sense which is not sustained by the usage of the language; and the same objection may be brought against Luzzatto's "land of the far-shadowing defence." Schelling has also suggested another objection,—namely, that the shadow thrown even in tropical lands is not a double one, falling northwards and southwards at the same time, and therefore that it cannot be figuratively described as double-winged. *Tziltzal cenáphaim* is the buzzing of the wings of insects, with which Egypt and Ethiopia swarmed on account of the climate and the abundance of water: צִלְצַל, *constr.* צִלְצַל, *tinnitus*, *stridor*, a primary meaning from which the other three meanings of the word—cymbal, harpoon (a whirring dart), and grasshopper[1]—are derived. In ch. vii. 18 the forces of Egypt are called "the fly from the end of the rivers of Egypt." Here Egypt and Ethiopia are called the land of the whirring of wings, inasmuch as the prophet had in his mind, under the designation of swarms of insects, the motley swarms of different people included in this great kingdom that were so fabulously strange to an Asiatic. Within this great kingdom messengers were now passing to and fro upon its great waters in boats of papyrus (on *gōme*, Copt. 'gōme, Talm. *gâmi*, see at Job viii. 11), Greek βαρίδες παπύριναι (βαρίς, from the Egyptian *bari, bali*, a barque). In such vessels as these, and with Egyptian tackle, they went as far as the remote island of Taprobane. The boats were made to clap together (*plicatiles*), so as to be carried past the cataracts (Parthey on *Plutarch. de Iside*, pp. 198-9). And it is to these messengers in their paper boats that the appeal of the prophet is addressed.

He sends them home; and what they are to say to their own people is generalized into an announcement to the whole earth. Vers. 2b, 3. " *Go, swift messengers, to the people stretched out and polished, to the terrible people far away on the other side, to the nation of command upon command and treading down, whose land rivers cut through. All ye possessors of the globe and inhabitants of the earth, when a banner rises on the mountains, look ye; and when they blow the trumpets, hearken!*" We learn from what follows to what it is that the attention of Ethiopia and all the nations of the earth is directed: it is the destruction of Asshur by Jehovah. They are to attend, when they observe the two signals, the banner and the trumpet-blast; these are decisive moments. Because Jehovah was about to deliver the world from the conquering might of Assyria, against which the Ethiopian kingdom was now summoning all the means of self-defence, the prophet sends the messengers home. Their own

---

[1] Schröring supposes *tziltzal* to be the *scarabæus sacer* (Linn.); but it would be much more natural, if any particular animal is intended, to think of the *tzaltzalya*, as it is called in the language of the Gallas, the *tzetze* in the Betschuana language, the most dreaded *diptera* of the interior of Africa, a species of *glossina* which attacks all the larger mammalia (though not men). Vid. Hartmann, *Naturgeschichtlich-medic. Skizze der Nilländer, Abth.* i. p. 205.

people, to which he sends them home, are elaborately described. They are *menusshâk*, stretched out, *i.e.* very tall (LXX. ἔθνος μετέωρον), just as the Sabæans are said to have been in ch. xlv. 14. They are also *mōrât* = *mᵉmorât* (Ges. § 52, Anm. 6), smoothed, *politus, i.e.* either not disfigured by an ugly growth of hair, or else, without any reference to depilation, but rather with reference to the bronze colour of their skin, smooth and shining with healthy freshness. The description which Herodotus gives of the Ethiopians, μέγιστοι καὶ κάλλιστοι ἀνθρώπων πάντων (iii. 20), quite answers to these first two predicates. They are still further described, with reference to the wide extent of their kingdom, which reached to the remotest south, as "the terrible nation מִן־הוּא וָהָלְאָה," *i.e.* from this point, where the prophet meets with the messengers, farther and farther off (compare 1 Sam. xx. 21, 22, but not 1 Sam. xviii. 9, where the expression has a chronological meaning, which would be less suitable here, where everything is so pictorial, and which is also to be rejected, because מִן־הוּא cannot be equivalent to מֵאֲשֶׁר הוּא; cf. Nahum ii. 9). We may see from ch. xxviii. 10, 13, what *kâv* (*kăv*, with connecting accusatives and before *makkeph*), a measuring or levelling line, signifies, when used by the prophet with the reduplication which he employs here: it is a people of "command upon command,"—that is to say, a commanding nation; (according to Ewald, Knobel, and others, *kâv* is equivalent to the Arabic *kûwe*, strength, a nation of double or gigantic strength.) "*A people of treading down*" (*sc.* of others; *mᵉbûsah* is a second genitive to *goi*), *i.e.* one which subdues and tramples down wherever it appears. These are all distinctive predicates—a nation of imposing grandeur, a ruling and conquering nation. The last predicate extols its fertile land. בָּזְאוּ we take not in the sense of *diripere*, or as equivalent to *bâzaz*, like מָאַס, to melt, equivalent to *mâsas*, but in the sense of *findere, i.e.* as equivalent to בָּקַע, like גָּמָא, to sip = גָּמַע. For it is no praise to say that a land is scoured out, or washed away, by rivers. Böttcher, who is wrong in describing this chapter as "perhaps the most difficult in the whole of the Old Testament," very aptly compares with it the expression used by Herodotus (ii. 108), κατετμήθη ἡ Αἴγυπτος. But why this strange elaboration instead of the simple name? There is a divine irony in the fact that a nation so great and glorious, and (though not without reason, considering its natural gifts) so full of self-consciousness, should be thrown into such violent agitation in the prospect of the danger that threatened it, and should be making such strenuous exertions to avert that danger, when Jehovah the God of Israel was about to destroy the threatening power itself in a night, and consequently all the care and trouble of Ethiopia were utterly needless.

The prophet knows for certain that the messengers may go home and announce this act of Jehovah to their own people and to all the world. Vers. 4-6. "*For thus hath Jehovah spoken to me: I will be still, and will observe upon my throne during clear weather in sunshine, during a cloud of dew in the heat of harvest. For before the harvest, when the blossom falls off, and the fruit becomes the ripening grape: then will He cut off the branches with pruning-hooks; and the tendrils He removes, breaks off. They are left altogether to the birds of prey on the mountains, and to the cattle of the land; and the birds of prey summer thereon, and all the cattle of the land will winter thereon.*" The prophecy explains itself here, as is very frequently the case, especially with Isaiah; for the literal words of ver. 6 show us unquestionably what it is that Jehovah will allow to develop itself so prosperously under favourable circumstances, and without any interposition on His part, until He suddenly and violently puts an end to the whole, just as it is approaching perfect maturity. It is the might of Assyria. Jehovah quietly looks on from the heavenly seat of His glorious presence, without disturbing the course of the thing intended. This quietness, however, is not negligence, but, as the hortative expressions show, a well-considered resolution. The two *Caphs* in ver. 4 are not comparative, but indicate the time. He remains quiet whilst there is clear weather with sunshine (עֲלֵי indicating continuance, as in Jer. viii. 18, 1 Sam. xiv. 32), and whilst there is a dew-cloud in the midst of that warmth, which is so favourable for the harvest, by causing the plants that have been thoroughly heated in the day and refreshed at night by the dew, to shoot up and ripen with rapidity and luxuriance. The plant thought of, as ver. 5 clearly shows, is the vine. By *liphnē kātzir* (before the harvest) we are either to understand the period just before the wheat-harvest, which coincides with the flowering of the grape; or, since Isaiah uses *kātzir* for *bātzir* in ch. xvi. 9, the time at the close of the summer, immediately preceding the vintage. Here again the *Caph* indicates the time. When the blossoming is over, so that the flower fades away, and the fruit that has set becomes a ripening grape (*boser*, as in Job xv. 33, not in the sense of *labruscum*, but of *omphax*; and *gâmal*, *maturescere*, as in Num. xvii. 23, *maturare*), He cuts off the branches (*zalzallim*, from *zilzēl*, to swing to and fro; compare the Arabic *dâliye*, a vine-branch, from *dalâ*, to hang long and loose) upon which the nearly ripened grapes are hanging, and removes or nips off [1] the tendrils (*netishoth*, as in Jer. v. 10, from *nâtash*, to stretch far out; *niphal*, to twist about a long way, ch. xvi. 8, compare Jer. xlviii. 32); an intentional asyndeton with a pictorial sound. The words of Jehovah concerning Himself have here passed imperceptibly into words of the prophet concerning Jehovah. The ripening grapes, as ver. 6 now explains, are the Assyrians, who were not far from the summit of their power; the fruit-branches that are cut off and nipped in pieces are their corpses, which are now through both summer and winter the food of swarms of summer birds, as well as of beasts of prey that remain the whole winter through. This is the act of divine judgment, to which the approaching exaltation of the banner, and the approaching blast of trumpets, is to call the attention of the people of Ethiopia.

What effect this act of Jehovah would have upon the Ethiopian kingdom, if it should now take place, is described in ver. 7: *"At that time will there be offered as a homage to Jehovah of hosts a nation stretched out and polished, and from a terrible people, far away on the other side; a nation of command upon command and treading down, whose land rivers cut through, at the place of the name of Jehovah of hosts, the mountain of Zion."* עַם (a people), at the commencement, cannot possibly be equivalent to מֵעַם (from a people). If it were taken in this sense, it would be necessary to make the correction accordingly,

---

[1] הִתֵּז = הִתַּז with a pausal sharpening of the *tzere*, which is lengthened by the tone, from *tâzaz* or *tūz* in post-biblical Hebrew, to knock off, knock to pieces, or weaken (compare *tâshash*). On this change of vowels in pause, see at Gen. xvii. 14; and compare Olshausen, § 91, d. For an example of the post-biblical use of the word, vid. b. *Sanhedrin* 102a. "like two sticks *hammattizōth*," i.e. one of which "hits the other in two" (*hittiz*, apparently from *tūz* or *tiz*, like *hinnīach* from *nuach*).

as Knobel has done; but the important parallels in ch. lxvi. 20 and Zeph. iii. 10 are against this. Consequently *'am* and *goi* (people and nation) must be rendered as subjects; and the מִן in מֵעַם must be taken as partitive. Ethiopia is offered, *i.e.* offers itself, as a free-will offering to Jehovah, impelled irresistibly by the force of the impression made by the mighty act of Jehovah, or, as it is expressed in "the Titan among the Psalms" (Ps. lxviii. 32, probably a Davidic psalm of the time of Hezekiah), "there come kingdoms of splendour out of Egypt; Cush rapidly stretches out its hands to Elohim." In order that the greatness of this spiritual conquest might be fully appreciated, the description of this strangely glorious people is repeated here; and with this poetical rounding, the prophecy itself, which was placed as a kind of overture before the following *massa Mitzraim* when the prophet collected the whole of his prophecies together, is brought to a close.

THE ORACLE CONCERNING EGYPT.—CHAP. XIX.

The three prophecies in ch. xviii. xix. and xx. really form a trilogy. The first (ch. xviii.), which, like ch. i., the introduction to the whole, is without any special heading, treats in language of the sublimest pathos of *Ethiopia*. The second (ch. xix.) treats in a calmer and more descriptive tone of *Egypt*. The third (ch. xx.) treats of both *Egypt* and *Ethiopia* in the style of historic prose. The kingdom to which all three prophecies refer is one and the same, viz. the Egypto-Ethiopian kingdom; but whilst ch. xviii. refers to the ruling nation, ch. xix. treats of the conquered one, and ch. xx. embraces both together. The reason why such particular attention is given to Egypt in the prophecy, is that no nation on earth was so mixed up with the history of the kingdom of God, from the patriarchal times downwards, as Egypt was. And because Israel, as the law plainly enjoined upon it, was never to forget that it had been sheltered for a long time in Egypt, and there had grown into a great nation, and had received many benefits; whenever prophecy has to speak concerning Egypt, it is quite as earnest in its promises as it is in its threats. And thus the *massa* of Isaiah falls into two distinct halves, viz. a threatening one (vers. 1-15), and a promising one (vers. 18-25); whilst between the judgment and the salvation (in vers. 16 and 17) there stands the alarm, forming as it were a connecting bridge between the two. And just in proportion as the coil of punishments is unfolded on the one hand by the prophet, the promise is also unfolded in just as many stages on the other; and moving on in ever new grooves, rises at length to such a height, that it breaks not only through the limits of contemporaneous history, but even through those of the Old Testament itself, and speaks in the spiritual language of the world-embracing love of the New Testament.

The oracle opens with a short introduction, condensing the whole of the substance of the first half into a few weighty words,—an art in which Isaiah peculiarly excelled. In this the name of Egypt, the land without an equal, occurs no less than three times. Ver. 1. "*Behold, Jehovah rideth upon a light cloud, and cometh to Egypt; and the idols of Egypt shake before Him, and the heart of Egypt melteth within it.*" Jehovah rides upon clouds when He is about to reveal Himself in His judicial majesty (Ps. xviii. 11); and in this instance He rides upon a light cloud, because it will take place rapidly. The word *kal* signifies both light and swift, because what is light moves swiftly; and even a light cloud, which is light because it is thin, is comparatively עָב, *i.e.* literally dense, opaque, or obscure. The idols of Egypt shake (נוע, as in ch. vi. 4, vii. 2), because Jehovah comes over them to judgment (cf. Ex. xii. 12; Jer. xlvi. 25; Ezek. xxx. 13): they must shake, for they are to be thrown down; and their shaking for fear is a shaking to their fall (נוע, as in ch. xxiv. 20, xxix. 9). The *Vav apodosis* in וְנָעוּ (*præt. cons.* with the tone upon the last syllable) connects together the cause and effect, as in ch. vi. 7.—In what judgments *the* judgment will be fulfilled, is now declared by the majestic Judge Himself. Vers. 2–4. "*And I spur Egypt against Egypt: and they go to war, every one with his brother, and every one with his neighbour; city against city, kingdom against kingdom. And the spirit of Egypt is emptied out within it: and I swallow up its ready counsel; and they go to the idols to inquire, and to the mutterers, and to the oracle-spirits, and to the soothsayers. And I shut up Egypt in the hand of a hard rule; and a fierce king will reign over them, saith the Lord, Jehovah of hosts.*" Civil war will rage in Egypt (on *sicsēc*, see at ch. ix. 10).

The people once so shrewd are now at their wits' end; their spirit is quite poured out (נְבֻקָה, with the reduplication removed, for נָבְקָה, according to Ges. § 68, Anm. 11,—as, for example, in Gen. xi. 7, Ezek. xli. 7), so that there is nothing left of either intelligence or resolution. Then (and this is also part of the judgment) they turn for help, in counsel and action, where no help is to be found, viz. to their "nothings" of gods, and the manifold demoniacal arts, of which Egypt could boast of being the primary seat. On the names of the practisers of the black art, see ch. viii. 19; *'ittim*, the mutterers, is from *'âtat*, to squeak (used of a camel-saddle, especially when new), or to rumble (used of an empty stomach): see Lane's *Lexicon*. But all this is of no avail: Jehovah gives them up (סִכֵּר, syn. הִסְגִּיר, συγκλείειν) to be ruled over by a hard-hearted and cruel king. The prophecy does not relate to a foreign conqueror, so as to lead us to think of Sargon (Knobel) or Cambyses (Luzzatto), but to a native despot. In comparing the prophecy with the fulfilment, we must bear in mind that ver. 2 relates to the national revolution which broke out in Sais, and resulted in the overthrow of the Ethiopian rule, and to the federal dodekarchy to which the rising of the nation led. "Kingdom against kingdom:" this exactly suits those twelve small kingdoms into which Egypt was split up after the overthrow of the Ethiopian dynasty in the year 695, until *Psammetichus*, the dodekarch of Sais, succeeded in the year 670 in comprehending these twelve states once more under a single monarchy. This very Psammetichus (and the royal house of Psammetichus generally) is the hard ruler, the reckless despot. He succeeded in gaining the battle at Momemphis, by which he established himself in the monarchy, through having first of all strengthened himself with mercenary troops from Ionia, Caria, and Greece. From his time downwards, the true Egyptian character was destroyed by the admixture of foreign elements;[1] and this occasioned the emigration of a large portion of the military caste to Meroe. The Egyptian nation very soon came to feel how oppressive this new dynasty was, when *Necho* (616–597), the son and successor of Psammetichus, renewed

[1] See Leo, *Universalgesch.* i. 152, and what Brugsch says in his *Histoire d'Egypte*, i. 250, with regard to the *brusques changements* that Egypt endured under Psammetichus.

the project of Ramses-Miamun, to construct a Suez canal, and tore away 120,000 of the natives of the land from their homes, sending them to wear out their lives in forced labour of the most wearisome kind. A revolt on the part of the native troops, who had been sent against the rising Cyrene, and driven back into the desert, led to the overthrow of Hophra, the grandson of Necho (570), and put an end to the hateful government of the family of Psammetichus.

The prophet then proceeds to foretell another misfortune which was coming upon Egypt: the Nile dries up, and with this the fertility of the land disappears. Vers. 5-10. "*And the waters will dry up from the sea, and the river is parched and dried. And the arms of the river spread a stench; the channels of Matzor become shallow and parched: reed and rush shrivel up. The meadows by the Nile, on the border of the Nile, and every corn-field of the Nile, dries up, is scattered, and disappears. And the fishermen groan, and all who throw draw-nets into the Nile lament, and they that spread out the net upon the face of the waters languish away. And the workers of fine combed flax are confounded, and the weavers of cotton fabrics. And the pillars of the land are ground to powder; all that work for wages are troubled in mind.*" In ver. 5 the Nile is called *yâm* (a sea), just as Homer calls it *Oceanus*, which, as Diodorus observes, was the name given by the natives to the river (Egypt. *oham*). The White Nile is called *bahr el-abyad* (the White Sea), the Blue Nile *bahr el-azrak*, and the combined waters *bahr en-Nil*, or, in the language of the Besharîn, as here in Isaiah, *yâm*. And in the account of the creation, in Gen. i., *yammim* is the collective name for great seas and rivers. But the Nile itself is more like an inland sea than a river, from the point at which the great bodies of water brought down by the Blue Nile and the White Nile, which rises a few weeks later, flow together; partly on account of its great breadth, and partly also because of its remaining stagnant throughout the dry season. It is not till the tropical rains commence that the swelling river begins to flow more rapidly, and the *yâm* becomes a *nâhâr*. But when, as is here threatened, the Nile sea and Nile river in Upper Egypt sink together and dry up (*nissh'thu*, niphal either of *shâthath* = *nâshattu*, to set, to grow shallow; or more probably from *nâshath*, to dry up, since ch. xli. 17 and Jer. li. 30

warrant the assumption that there was such a verb), the mouths (or *arms*) of the Nile (*nehâroth*), which flow through the Delta, and the many canals (*ye'orim*), by which the benefits of the overflow are conveyed to the Nile valley, are turned into stinking puddles (הֶאֶזְנִיחוּ, a *hiphil*, half substantive half verbal, unparalleled elsewhere,[1] signifying to spread a stench; possibly it may have been used in the place of הִזְנִיחַ, from אָזְנַח or אָזְנָה, stinking, to which a different application was given in ordinary use). In all probability it is not without intention that Isaiah uses the expression *Mâtzor*, inasmuch as he distinguishes *Mâtzor* from *Pathros* (ch. xi. 11), *i.e.* Lower from Upper Egypt (Egyp. *sa-het*, the low land, and *sa-res*, the higher land), the two together being *Mitzrayim*. And *ye'orim* (by the side of *nehâroth*) we are warranted in regarding as the name given of the Nile canals. The canal system in Egypt and the system of irrigation are older than the invasion of the Hyksos (*vid.* Lepsius, in Herzog's *Cyclopædia*). On the other hand, *ye'ōr* in ver. 7 (where it is written three times *plene*, as it is also in ver. 8) is the Egyptian name of the Nile generally (*yaro*).[2] It is repeated emphatically three times, like *Mitzrayim* in ver. 1. Parallel to *mizra'*, but yet different from it, is עָרוֹת, from עָרָה, to be naked or bare, which signifies, like many derivatives of the synonymous word in Arabic, either open spaces, or as here, grassy tracts by the water-side, *i.e.* meadows. Even the meadows, which lie close to the water-side (*pi* = *ora*, as in Ps. cxxxiii. 2, not *ostium*), and all the fields, become so parched, that they blow away like ashes. Then the three leading sources from which Egypt derived its maintenance all fail:— viz. the fishing; the linen manufacture, which supplied dresses for the priests and bandages for mummies; and the cotton manufacture, by which all who were not priests were supplied

---

[1] It is not unparalleled as a *hiph. denom.* (compare הִצְהִיר, oil, יִצְהָר, to press, Job xxiv. 11, Talm. הִתְלִיעַ, to become worm-eaten, and many others of a similar kind); and as a mixed form (possibly a mixture of two readings, as Gesenius and Böttcher suppose, though it is not necessarily so), the language admitted of much that was strange, more especially in the vulgar tongue, which found its way here and there into written composition.

[2] From the fact that *aur* in old Egyptian means the Nile, we may explain the Φρουρῶ ἤτοι Νεῖλος, with which the *Laterculus* of Eratosthenes closes.

with clothes. The Egyptian fishery was very important. In the Berlin Museum there is an Egyptian *micmoreth* with lead attached. The mode of working the flax by means of *serikâh*, *pectinatio* (compare סְרִיק, wool-combs, *Kelim*, 12, 2), is shown on the monuments. In the Berlin Museum there are also Egyptian combs of this description with which the flax was carded. The productions of the Egyptian looms were celebrated in antiquity: *chōrây*, lit. white cloth (*singularet*. with the old termination *ay*), is the general name for cotton fabrics, or the different kinds of byssus that were woven there (compare the βυσσίνων ὀθονίων of the Rosetta inscription). All the castes, from the highest to the lowest, are now thrown into agonies of despair. The *shâthōth* (an epithet that was probably suggested by the thought of *shethi*, a warp, Syr. *'ashti*, to weave, through the natural association of ideas), *i.e.* the "*pillars*" of the land (with a suffix relating to *Mitzrayim*, see at ch. iii. 8, and construed as a masculine as at Ps. xi. 3), were the highest castes, who were the direct supporters of the state edifice; and עֹשֵׂי שָׂכָר cannot mean the citizens engaged in trade, *i.e.* the middle classes, but such of the people as hired themselves to the employers of labour, and therefore lived upon wages and not upon their own property (שָׂכָר is used here as in Prov. xi. 18, and not as equivalent to סֶכֶר, the dammers-up of the water for the purpose of catching the fish, like סִכְרִין, *Kelim*, 23, 5).

The prophet now dwells upon the punishment which falls upon the pillars of the land, and describes it in vers. 11-13: "*The princes of Zoan become mere fools, the wise counsellors of Pharaoh; readiness in counsel is stupified. How can ye say to Pharaoh, I am a son of wise men, a son of kings of the olden time? Where are they then, thy wise men? Let them announce to thee, and know what Jehovah of hosts hath determined concerning Egypt. The princes of Zoan have become fools, the princes of Memphis are deceived; and they have led Egypt astray who are the corner-stone of its castes.*" The two constructives חַכְמֵי יֹעֲצֵי do not stand in a subordinate relation, but in a co-ordinate one (see at Ps. lxxviii. 9 and Job xx. 17; compare also 2 Kings xvii. 13, *keri*), viz. "the wise men, counsellors of Pharaoh,"[1] so that the second noun is the explanatory per-

---

[1] *Pharaoh* does not mean "the king" (equivalent to the Coptic π-ουεο), but according to Brugsch, "great house" (Upper Egyptian *peräa*, Lower

mutative of the first. *Zoan* is the *Tanis* of primeval times (Num. xiii. 22), which was situated on one of the arms through which the Nile flows into the sea (viz. the *ostium Taniticum*), and was the home from which two dynasties sprang. *Noph* (*per aphær.* = *Menoph*, contracted into *Moph* in Hos. ix. 6) is *Memphis*, probably the seat of the Pharaohs in the time of Joseph, and raised by Psammetichus into the metropolis of the whole kingdom. The village of *Mitrahenni* still stands upon its ruins, with the Serapeum to the north-west.[1] Consequently princes of Zoan and Memphis are princes of the chief cities of the land, and of the supposed primeval pedigree; probably priest-princes, since the wisdom of the Egyptian priest was of world-wide renown (Herod. ii. 77, 260), and the oldest kings of Egypt sprang from the priestly caste. Even in the time of Hezekiah, when the military caste had long become the ruling one, the priests once more succeeded in raising one of their own number, namely Sethos, to the throne of Sais. These magnates of Egypt, with their wisdom, would be turned into fools by the history of Egypt of the immediate future; and (this is the meaning of the sarcastic "how can ye say") they would no longer trust themselves to boast of their hereditary priestly wisdom, or their royal descent, when giving counsel to

Egyptian *pher-āo*; *vid. aus dem Orient*, i. 36). Lauth refers in confirmation of this to Horapollo, i. 62, ὄφις καὶ οἶκος μέγας ἐν μέσῳ αὐτοῦ σημαίνει βασιλέα, and explains this Coptic name for a king from that of the Οὐραῖος (βασιλίσκος) upon the head of the king, which was a specifically regal sign.

[1] What the lexicons say with reference to *Zoan* and *Noph* needs rectifying. *Zoan* (old Egyptian *Zane*, with the hieroglyphic of striding legs, Copt. *'Gane*) points back to the radical idea of *pelli* or *fugere*; and according to the latest researches, to which the Turin papyrus No. 112 has led, it is the same as Αὔαρις ("Αβαρις), which is said to mean the house of flight (*Ha-uare*), and was the seat of government under the Hykshōs. But *Memphis* is not equivalent to *Ma-m-ptah*, as Champollion assumed (although this city is unquestionably sometimes called *Ha-ka-ptah*, house of the essential being of Ptah); it is rather equivalent to *Men-nefer* (with the hieroglyphic of the pyramids), place of the good (see Brugsch, *Histoire d'Egypte*, i. 17). In the later language it is called *pa-nuf* or *ma-nuf*, which has the same meaning (Copt. *nufi*, good). Hence *Moph* is the contraction of the name commencing with *ma*, and *Noph* the abbreviation of the name commencing with *ma* or *pa* by the rejection of the local prefix; for we cannot for a moment think of *Nup*, which is the second district of Upper Egypt (Brugsch, *Geogr.* i. 66). *Noph* is undoubtedly Memphis.

Pharaoh. They were the corner-stone of the *shebâtim*, *i.e.* of the castes of Egypt (not of the districts or provinces, νομοί); but instead of supporting and defending their people, it is now very evident that they only led them astray. הִתְעוּ, as the Masora on ver. 15 observes, has no *Vav cop.*

In vers. 14 and 15 this state of confusion is more minutely described: "*Jehovah hath poured a spirit of giddiness into the heart of Egypt, so that they have led Egypt astray in all its doing, as a drunken man wandereth about in his vomit. And there does not occur of Egypt any work, which worked, of head and tail, palm-branch and rush.*" The spirit which God pours out (as is also said elsewhere) is not only a spirit of salvation, but also a spirit of judgment. The judicial, penal result which He produces is here called עִוְעִים, which is formed from עָוֶה (root עוה, to curve), and is either contracted from עִוְעִים, or points back to a supposed singular עִוְעֶה (*vid.* Ewald, § 158, *b*). The suffix in *b'kirbâh* points to Egypt. The divine spirit of judgment makes use of the imaginary wisdom of the priestly caste, and thereby plunges the people, as it were, into the giddiness of intoxication. The prophet employs the *hiphil* הִתְעָה to denote the carefully considered actions of the leaders of the nation, and the *niphal* נִתְעָה to denote the constrained actions of a drunken man, who has lost all self-control. The nation has been so perverted by false counsels and hopes, that it lies there like a drunken man in his own vomit, and gropes and rolls about, without being able to find any way of escape. "*No work that worked,*" *i.e.* that averted trouble (עָשָׂה is as emphatic as in Dan. viii. 24), was successfully carried out by any one, either by the leaders of the nation or by the common people and their flatterers, either by the upper classes or by the mob.

The result of all these plagues, which were coming upon Egypt, would be fear of Jehovah and of the people of Jehovah. Vers. 16, 17. "*In that day will the Egyptians become like women, and tremble and be alarmed at the swinging of the hand of Jehovah of hosts, which He sets in motion against it. And the land of Judah becomes a shuddering for Egypt; as often as they mention this against Egypt, it is alarmed, because of the decree of Jehovah of hosts, that He suspendeth over it.*" The swinging (*tenuphâh*) of the hand (ch. xxx. 32) points back to the foregoing judgments, which have fallen upon Egypt blow after blow. These humiliations make the Egyptians as soft and timid as women (*tert. compar.*, not as in ch. xiii. 7, 8, xxi. 3, 4). And the sacred soil of Judah (*'adâmâh*, as in ch. xiv. 1, 2, xxxii. 13), which Egypt has so often made the scene of war, throws them into giddiness, into agitation at the sight of terrors, whenever it is mentioned (כֹּל אֲשֶׁר, cf. 1 Sam. ii. 13, lit. " whoever," equivalent to " as often as any one," Ewald, § 337, 3, *f*; חֻפָּא is written according to the Aramæan form, with *Aleph* for *He*, like יְרָא in Num. xi. 20, קִרְחָא in Ezek. xxxvii. 31, compare בַּלְּא, Ezek. xxxvi. 5, and similar in form to חֻפָּה in ch. iv. 5).

The author of the plagues is well known to them, their faith in the idols is shaken, and the desire arises in their heart to avert fresh plagues by presents to Jehovah.

At first there is only slavish fear; but there is the beginning of a turn to something better. Ver. 18. "*In that day there will be five cities in the land of Egypt speaking the language of Canaan, and swearing to Jehovah of hosts: 'Ir ha-Heres will one be called.*" Five cities are very few for Egypt, which was completely covered with cities; but this is simply a fragmentary commencement of Egypt's future and complete conversion. The description given of them, as beginning to speak the language of Canaan, *i.e.* the sacred language of the worship of Jehovah (comp. Zeph. iii. 9), and to give themselves up to Jehovah with vows made on oath, is simply a periphrastic announcement of the conversion of the five cities. נִשְׁבַּע לְ (different from נִשְׁבַּע בְּ, ch. lxv. 16, as ch. xlv. 23 clearly shows) signifies to swear to a person, to promise him fidelity, to give one's self up to him. One of these five will be called *'Ir ha-Heres*. As this is evidently intended for a proper name, *lâ'echâth* does not mean *unicuique*, as in Judg. viii. 18 and Ezek. i. 6, but *uni*. It is a customary thing with Isaiah to express the nature of anything under the form of some future name (*vid.* ch. iv. 3, xxxii. 5, lxi. 6, lxii. 4). The name in this instance, therefore, must have a distinctive and promising meaning. But what does *'Ir ha-Heres* mean? The Septuagint has changed it into πόλις ἀσεδέκ, equivalent to *'Ir hazzedek* (city of righteousness), possibly in honour of the temple in the Heliopolitan *nomos*, which was founded under Ptolemæus Philometor about 160 B.C., during the Syrian reign of terror, by Onias IV., son of the high priest Onias III., who emigrated to Egypt.¹ Maurer in his *Lexicon* imagines that he has found the true meaning, when he renders it "city of rescue;" but the progressive advance from the meaning "to pull off" to that of "setting free" cannot be established in the case of the verb *hâras*; in fact, *hâras* does not mean to pull off or pull out, but to pull down. *Heres* cannot have any other meaning in Hebrew than that of "destruction." But as this appears unsuitable, it is more natural to read '*Ir ha-cheres* (which is found in some codices, though in opposition to the Masora²). This is now generally rendered "city of protection" (Rosenmüller, Ewald, Knobel, and Meier), as being equivalent to an Arabic word signifying *divinitus protecta*. But such an appeal to the Arabic is contrary to all Hebrew usage, and is always a very precarious loophole. '*Ir ha-cheres* would mean "city of the sun" (*cheres* as in Job ix. 7 and Judg. xiv. 18), as the Talmud in the leading passage concerning the Onias temple (in *b. Menahoth* 110a) thinks that even the received reading may be understood in accordance with Job ix. 7, and says "it is a description of the sun." "Sun-city" was really the name of one of the most celebrated of the old Egyptian cities, viz. *Heliopolis*, the city of the sun-god *Ra*, which was situated to the north-east of Memphis, and is called *On* in other passages of the Old Testament. Ezekiel (xxx. 17) alters this into *Aven*, for the purpose of branding the idolatry of the city.³ But this alteration of the well-attested text is a mistake; and the true explanation is, that *Ir-haheres* is simply used with a play upon the name *Ir-hacheres*. This is the explanation given by the Targum: "Heliopolis, whose future fate will be destruction." But even if the name is intended to have a distinctive and promising meaning, it is impossible to adopt the explanation given by

---

¹ See Frankel on this Egyptian auxiliary temple, in his *Monatschrift für Geschichte und Wissenschaft des Judenthums*, 1852, p. 273 sqq.; Herzfeld, *Geschichte des Volkes Israel*, iii. 460 sqq., 557 sqq.; and Grätz, *Geschichte der Juden*, iii. 36 sqq.

² But no Greek codex has the reading πόλις ἀχερίς (see Holmes-Parsons' *V. T. Græcum c. var. lect.* t. iv. on this passage), as the Complutensian has emended it after the Vulgate (see the *Vocabularium Hebr.* 37a, belonging to the Complutensian).

³ *Heliopolis* answers to the sacred name *Pe-ra*, house of the sun-god (like *Pe-Ramesses*, house of Ramses), which was a name borne by the city

Luzzatto, "a city restored from the ruins;" for the name points to destruction, not to restoration. Moreover, Heliopolis never has been restored since the time of its destruction, which Strabo dates as far back as the Persian invasion. There is nothing left standing now out of all its monuments but one granite obelisk: they are all either destroyed, or carried away, like the so-called "Cleopatra's Needle," or sunk in the soil of the Nile (Parthey on Plutarch, *de Iside*, p. 162). This destruction cannot be the one intended. But *hâras* is the word commonly used to signify the throwing down of heathen altars (Judg. vi. 25; 1 Kings xviii. 30, xix. 10, 14); and the meaning of the prophecy may be, that the city which had hitherto been *'Ir ha-cheres*, the chief city of the sun-worship, would become the city of the destruction of idolatry, as Jeremiah prophesies in ch. xliii. 13, "Jehovah will break in pieces the obelisks of the sun-temple in the land of Egypt." Hence Herzfeld's interpretation: "*City of demolished Idols*" (p. 561). It is true that in this case *ha-heres* merely announces the breaking up of the old, and does not say what new thing will rise upon the ruins of the old; but the context leaves no doubt as to this new thing, and the one-sided character of the description is to be accounted for from the intentional play upon the actual name of that one city out of the five to which the prophet gives especial prominence. With this interpretation— for which indeed we cannot pretend to find any special confirmation in the actual fulfilment in the history of the church, and, so to speak, the history of missions—the train of thought in the prophet's mind which led to the following groove of promises is a very obvious one.—The allusion to the sun-city, which had become the city of destruction, led to the *mazzeboth*

that was at other times called *On* (old Egyptian *anu*). Cyrill, however, explains even the latter thus, "Ὢν δέ ἐστι κατ' αὐτούς ὁ ἥλιος ("On, according to their interpretation, is the sun"), which is so far true according to Lauth, that *Ain, Oin, Oni*, signifies the eye as an emblem of the sun; and from this, the tenth month, which marks the return of the sun to the equinoctial point, derives its name of *Pa-oni, Pa-one, Pa-uni*. It may possibly be with reference to this that Heliopolis is called *Ain es-sems* in Arabic (see Arnold, *Chrestom. Arab.* p. 56 s.). Edrisi (iii. 3) speaks of this *Ain es-sems* as "the country-seat of Pharaoh, which may God curse;" just as *Ibn el-Faraun* is a common expression of contempt, which the Arabs apply to the Coptic fellahs.

or obelisks (see Jer. xliii. 13), which were standing there on the spot where *Ra* was worshipped. Vers. 19, 20. "*In that day there stands an altar consecrated to Jehovah in the midst of the land of Egypt, and an obelisk near the border of the land consecrated to Jehovah. And a sign and a witness for Jehovah of hosts is this in the land of Egypt: when they cry to Jehovah for oppressors, He will send them a helper and champion, and deliver them.*" This is the passage of Isaiah (not ver. 18) to which Onias IV. appealed, when he sought permission of Ptolemæus Philometor to build a temple of Jehovah in Egypt. He built such a temple in the *nomos* of Heliopolis, 180 stadia (22½ miles) to the north-east of Memphis (Josephus, *Bell.* vii. 10, 3), and on the foundation and soil of the ὀχύρωμα in Leontopolis, which was dedicated to Bubastis (*Ant.* xiii. 3, 1, 2).[1] This temple, which was altogether unlike the temple of Jerusalem in its outward appearance, being built in the form of a castle, and which stood for more than two hundred years (from 160 B.C. to A.D. 71, when it was closed by command of Vespasian), was splendidly furnished and much frequented; but the recognition of it was strongly contested both in Palestine and Egypt. It was really situated "in the midst of the land of Egypt." But it is out of the question to seek in this temple for the fulfilment of the prophecy of Isaiah, from the simple fact that it was by Jews and for Jews that it was erected. And where, in that case, would the obelisk be, which, as Isaiah prophesies, was to stand on the border of Egypt, *i.e.* on the side towards the desert and Canaan? The altar was to be "*a sign*" (*'oth*) that there were worshippers of Jehovah in Egypt; and the obelisk a "*witness*" (*'ēd*) that Jehovah had proved Himself, to Egypt's

---

[1] We are acquainted with two cities called Leontopolis, viz. the capital of the *nomos* called by its name, which was situated between the Busiritic and the Tanitic *nomoi;* and a second between *Herōōn-polis* and *Magdōlon* (see Brugsch, *Geogr.* i. 262). The Leontopolis of Josephus, however, must have been another, or third. It may possibly have derived its name, as Lauth conjectures, from the fact that the goddess *Bast* (from which comes *Boubastos*, House of Bast) was called *Pacht* when regarded in her destructive character (*Todtenbuch*, 164, 12). The meaning of the name is "lioness," and, as her many statues show, she was represented with a lion's head. At the same time, the boundaries of the districts fluctuated, and the Heliopolitan Leontopolis of Josephus may have originally belonged to the Bubastic district.

salvation, to be the God of the gods of Egypt. And now, if they who erected this place of worship and this monument cried to Jehovah, He would show Himself ready to help them; and they would no longer cry in vain, as they had formerly done to their own idols (ver. 3). Consequently it is the approaching conversion of the native Egyptians that is here spoken of. The fact that from the Grecian epoch Judaism became a power in Egypt, is certainly not unconnected with this. But we should be able to trace this connection more closely, if we had any information as to the extent to which Judaism had then spread among the natives, which we do know to have been by no means small. The *therapeutæ* described by Philo, which were spread through all the *nomoi* of Egypt, were of a mixed Egypto-Jewish character (*vid.* Philo, *Opp.* ii. p. 474, ed. Mangey). It was a victory on the part of the religion of Jehovah, that Egypt was covered with Jewish synagogues and coenobia even in the age before Christ. And Alexandria was the place where the law of Jehovah was translated into Greek, and thus made accessible to the heathen world, and where the religion of Jehovah created for itself those forms of language and thought, under which it was to become, as Christianity, the religion of the world. And after the introduction of Christianity into the world, there were more than one *mazzebah* (obelisk) that were met with on the way from Palestine to Egypt, even by the end of the first century, and more than one *mizbeach* (altar) found in the heart of Egypt itself. The importance of Alexandria and of the monasticism and anachoretism of the peninsula of Sinai and also of Egypt, in connection with the history of the spread of Christianity, is very well known.

When Egypt became the prey of Islam in the year 640, there was already to be seen, at all events in the form of a magnificent prelude, the fulfilment of what the prophet foretells in vers. 21, 22: "*And Jehovah makes Himself known to the Egyptians, and the Egyptians know Jehovah in that day; and they serve with slain-offerings and meat-offerings, and vow vows to Jehovah, and pay them. And Jehovah smites Egypt, smiting and healing; and if they return to Jehovah, He suffers Himself to be entreated, and heals them.*" From that small commencement of five cities, and a solitary altar, and one solitary obelisk, it has now come to this: Jehovah extends the knowledge of Himself to the whole of Egypt (נוֹדָע, reflective *se cognoscendum dare*, or neuter *innotescere*), and throughout all Egypt there arises the knowledge of God, which soon shows itself in acts of worship. This worship is represented by the prophet, just as we should expect according to the Old Testament view, as consisting in the offering of bleeding and bloodless, or legal and free-will offerings: וְעָבְדוּ, viz. אֶת־יְהוָֹה, so that עָבַד is construed with a double accusative, as in Ex. x. 26, cf. Gen. xxx. 29; or it may possibly be used directly in the sense of sacrificing, as in the Phœnician, and like עָשָׂה in the *Thorah;* and even if we took it in this sense, it would yield no evidence against Isaiah's authorship (compare ch. xxviii. 21, xxxii. 17). Egypt, though converted, is still sinful; but Jehovah smites it, "smiting and healing" (*nâgoph v^erápho'*, compare 1 Kings xx. 37), so that in the act of smiting the intention of healing prevails; and healing follows the smiting, since the chastisement of Jehovah leads it to repentance. Thus Egypt is now under the same plan of salvation as Israel (*e.g.* Lev. xxvi. 44, Deut. xxxii. 36).

Asshur, as we already know from ch. xviii., is equally humbled; so that now the two great powers, which have hitherto only met as enemies, meet in the worship of Jehovah, which unites them together. Ver. 23. *"In that day a road will run from Egypt to Asshur, and Asshur comes into Egypt, and Egypt to Asshur; and Egypt worships (Jehovah) with Asshur."* אֵת is not a sign of the accusative, for there can be no longer any idea of the subjection of Egypt to Asshur: on the contrary, it is a preposition indicating fellowship; and עָבְדוּ is used in the sense of worship, as in ver. 21. Friendly intercourse is established between Egypt and Assyria by the fact that both nations are now converted to Jehovah. The road of communication runs through Canaan.

Thus is the way prepared for the highest point of all, which the prophet foretells in vers. 24, 25: *"In that day will Israel be the third part to Egypt and Asshur, a blessing in the midst of the earth, since Jehovah of hosts blesseth them thus: Blessed be thou, my people Egypt; and thou Asshur, the work of my hands; and thou Israel, mine inheritance."* Israel is added to the covenant between Egypt and Asshur, so that it becomes a tripartite covenant in which Israel forms the "third part" (*shelīshiyyāh, tertia pars*, like *'asiriyyāh, decima pars*, in ch. vi. 13). Israel has now reached the great end of its calling—to be a blessing in "the midst of the earth" (*b'kereb hā'āretz*, in the whole circuit of the earth), all nations being here represented by Egypt and Assyria. Hitherto it had been only to the disadvantage of Israel to be situated between Egypt and Assyria. The history of the Ephraimitish kingdom, as well as that of Judah, clearly proves this. If Israel relied upon Egypt, it deceived itself, and was deceived; and if it relied on Assyria, it only became the slave of Assyria, and had Egypt for a foe. Thus Israel was in a most painful vice between the two great powers of the earth, the western and the eastern powers. But how will all this be altered now! Egypt and Assyria become one in Jehovah, and Israel the third in the covenant. Israel is no longer the only nation of God, the creation of God, the heir of God; but all this applies to Egypt and Assyria now, as well as to Israel. To give full expression to this, Israel's three titles of honour are mixed together, and each of the three nations receives one of the choice names,—*nachali*, " my inheritance," being reserved for Israel, as pointing back to its earliest history. This essential equalization of the heathen nations and Israel is no degradation to the latter. For although from this time forward there is to be no essential difference between the nations in their relation to God, it is still the God of Israel who obtains this universal recognition, and the nation of Israel that has become, according to the promise, the medium of blessing to the world.

Thus has the second half of the prophecy ascended step by step from salvation to salvation, as the first descended step by step from judgment to judgment. The culminating point in ver. 25 answers to the lowest point in ver. 15. Every step in the ascending half is indicated by the expression " in that day." Six times do we find this sign-post to the future within the limits of vers. 16-25. This expression is almost as characteristic of Isaiah as the corresponding expression, " Behold, the days come" (*hinneh yāmim bā'im*), is of Jeremiah (compare, for example, Isa. vii. 18-25). And it is more particularly in the promising or Messianic portions of the prophecy that it is so favourite an introduction (ch. xi. 10, 11, xii. 1; compare Zech. xii. xiii. xiv.). Nevertheless, the genuineness of vers. 16-25 has recently been called in question, more especially by Hitzig. Sometimes this passage has not been found fanatical enough to have emanated from Isaiah, *i.e.* too free from hatred towards the heathen; whereas, on the other hand, Knobel adduces evidence that the prophet was no fanatic at all. Sometimes it is too fanatical; in reply to which we observe, that there never was a prophet of God in the world who did not appear to a "sound human understanding" to be beside himself, since, even assuming that this human understanding be sound, it is only within the four sides of its own peculiar province that it is so. Again, in vers. 18, 19, a prophecy has been discovered which is too special to be Isaiah's, in opposition to which Knobel proves that it is not so special as is supposed. But it is quite special enough; and this can never astonish any one who can discern in the prophecy a revelation of the future communicated by God, whereas in itself it neither proves nor disproves the authorship of Isaiah. So far as the other arguments adduced against the genuineness are concerned, they have been answered exhaustively by Caspari, in a paper which he contributed on the subject to the *Lutherische Zeitschrift*, 1841, 3. Hävernick, in his *Introduction*, has not been able to do anything better than appropriate the arguments adduced by Caspari. And we will not repeat for a third time what has been said twice already. The two halves of the prophecy are like the two wings of a bird. And it is only through its second half that the prophecy becomes the significant centre of the Ethiopic and Egyptian trilogy. For ch. xix. predicts the saving effect that will be produced upon Egypt by the destruction of Assyria. And ch. xix. 23 sqq. announces what will become of Assyria. Assyria will also pass through judgment to salvation. This eschatological conclusion to ch. xix., in which Egypt and Assyria are raised above themselves into representatives of the two halves of the heathen world, is the golden clasp which connects ch. xix. and xx. We now turn to this third portion of the trilogy, which bears the same relation to ch. xix. as ch. xvi. 13, 14 to ch. xv.-xvi. 12.

SYMBOL OF THE FALL OF EGYPT AND ETHIOPIA, AND ITS
INTERPRETATION.—CHAP. XX.

This section, commencing in the form of historic prose, introduces itself thus: vers. 1, 2a. "*In the year that Tartan came to Ashdod, Sargon the king of Asshur having sent him (and he made war against Ashdod, and captured it)*: *at that time Jehovah spake through Yeshayahu the son of Amoz as follows,*" *i.e.* He communicated the following revelation through the medium of Isaiah (*b'yad,* as in ch. xxxvii. 24, Jer. xxxvii. 2, and many other passages). The revelation itself was attached to a symbolical act. *B'yad* (lit. "by the hand of") refers to what was about to be made known through the prophet by means of the command that was given him; in other words, to ver. 3, and indirectly to ver. 2b. *Tartan* (probably the same man) is met with in 2 Kings xviii. 17 as the chief captain of Sennacherib. No Assyrian king of the name of *Sargon* is mentioned anywhere else in the Old Testament; but it may now be accepted as an established result of the researches which have been made, that Sargon was the successor of Shalmanassar, and that Shalmaneser (Shalman, Hos. x. 14), Sargon, Sennacherib, and Esarhaddon, are the names of the four Assyrian kings who were mixed up with the closing history of the kingdoms of Israel and Judah. It was Longperrier who was the first to establish the identity of the monarch who built the palaces at Khorsabad, which form the northeastern corner of ancient Nineveh, with the Sargon of the Bible. We are now acquainted with a considerable number of brick, harem, votive-tablet, and other inscriptions which bear the name of this king, and contain all kinds of testimony concerning himself.[1] It was he, not Shalmanassar, who took Samaria after a three years' siege; and in the annalistic inscription he boasts of having conquered the city, and removed the house of Omri to Assyria. Oppert is right in calling attention to the fact, that in 2 Kings xviii. 10 the conquest is

---

[1] See Oppert, *Expédition,* i. 328-350, and the picture of Sargon in his war-chariot in Rawlinson's *Five Great Monarchies,* i. 368; compare also p. 304 (prisoners taken by Sargon), p. 352 (the plan of his palace), p. 483 (a glass vessel with his name), and many other engravings in vol. ii.

not attributed to Shalmanassar himself, but to the army. Shalmanassar died in front of Samaria; and Sargon not only put himself at the head of the army, but seized upon the throne, in which he succeeded in establishing himself, after a contest of several years' duration with the legitimate heirs and their party. He was therefore a usurper.[1] Whether his name as it appears on the inscriptions is *Sar-kin* or not, and whether it signifies the king *de facto* as distinguished from the king *de jure*, we will not attempt to determine now.[2] This Sargon, the founder of a new Assyrian dynasty, who reigned from 721–702 (according to Oppert), and for whom there is at all events plenty of room between 721–20 and the commencement of Sennacherib's reign, first of all blockaded Tyre for five years after the fall of Samaria, or rather brought to an end the siege of Tyre which had been begun by Shalmanassar (Jos. *Ant.* ix. 14, 2), though whether it was to a successful end or not is quite uncertain. He then pursued with all the greater energy his plan for following up the conquest of Samaria with the subjugation of Egypt, which was constantly threatening the possessions of Assyria in western Asia, either by instigation or support. The attack upon Ashdod was simply a means to this end. As the Philistines were led to join Egypt, not only by their situation, but probably by kinship of tribe as well, the conquest of Ashdod—a fortress so strong, that, according to Herodotus (ii. 157), Psammetichus besieged it for twenty-nine years — was an indispensable preliminary to the expedition against Egypt. When Alexander the Great marched against Egypt, he had to do the same with Gaza. How long Tartan

---

[1] See Oppert, *Les Inscriptions Assyriennes des Sargonides et les Fastes de Ninive* (Versailles, 1862), and Rawlinson (vol. ii. 406 sqq.), who here agrees with Oppert in all essential points. Consequently there can no longer be any thought of identifying Sargon with Shalmanassar (see Brandis, *Ueber den historischen Gewinn aus der Entzifferung der assyr. Inschriften*, 1856, p. 48 sqq.). Rawlinson himself at first thought they were the same person (*vid. Journal of the Asiatic Society*, xii. 2, 419), until gradually the evidence increased that Sargon and Shalmanassar were the names of two different kings, although no independent inscription of the latter, the actual besieger of Samaria, has yet been found.

[2] Hitzig ventures a derivation of the name from the Zend; and Grotefend compares it with the Chaldee *Sârēk*, Dan. vi. 3 (in his *Abhandlung uber Anlage und Zerstörung der Gebäude von Nimrud*, 1851).

required is not to be gathered from ver. 1. But if he conquered it as quickly as Alexander conquered Gaza,—viz. in five months,—it is impossible to understand why the following prophecy should defer for three years the subjugation of Ethiopia and Egypt. The words, "and fought against Ashdod, and took it," must therefore be taken as anticipatory and parenthetical.

It was not after the conquest of Ashdod, but in the year in which the siege commenced, that Isaiah received the following admonition: 2b. "*Go and loosen the smock-frock from off thy loins, and take off thy shoes from thy feet. And he did so, went stripped and barefooted.*" We see from this that Isaiah was clothed in the same manner as Elijah, who wore a fur coat (2 Kings i. 8, cf. Zech. xiii. 4, Heb. xi. 37), and John the Baptist, who had a garment of camel hair and a leather girdle round it (Matt. iii. 4); for *sak* is a coarse linen or hairy overcoat of a dark colour (Rev. vi. 12, cf. Isa. l. 3), such as was worn by mourners, either next to the skin ('*al-habbâsâr*, 1 Kings xxi. 27, 2 Kings vi. 30, Job xvi. 15) or over the tunic, in either case being fastened by a girdle on account of its want of shape, for which reason the verb *châgar* is the word commonly used to signify the putting on of such a garment, instead of *lâbash*. The use of the word '*ârōm* does not prove that the former was the case in this instance (see, on the contrary, 2 Sam. vi. 20, compared with ver. 14 and John xxi. 7). With the great importance attached to the clothing in the East, where the feelings upon this point are peculiarly sensitive and modest, a person was looked upon as stripped and naked if he had only taken off his upper garment. What Isaiah was directed to do, therefore, was simply opposed to common custom, and not to moral decency. He was to lay aside the dress of a mourner and preacher of repentance, and to have nothing on but his tunic (*cetoneth*); and in this, as well as barefooted, he was to show himself in public. This was the costume of a man who had been robbed and disgraced, or else of a beggar or prisoner of war. The word *cēn* (so) is followed by the inf. abs., which develops the meaning, as in ch. v. 5, lviii. 6, 7.

It is not till Isaiah has carried out the divine instructions, that he learns the reason for this command to strip himself, and the length of time that he is to continue so stripped. Vers.

3, 4: "*And Jehovah said, As my servant Yesha'yahu goeth naked and barefooted, a sign and type for three years long over Egypt and over Ethiopia, so will the king of Asshur carry away the prisoners of Egypt and the exiles of Ethiopia, children and old men, naked and barefooted, and with their seat uncovered—a shame to Egypt.*" The expression "as he goeth" (*ca'asher hâlac*) stands here at the commencement of the symbolical action, but it is introduced as if with a retrospective glance at its duration for three years, unless indeed the preterite *hâlac* stands here, as it frequently does, to express what has already commenced, and is still continuing and customary (compare, for example, Job i. 4 and Ps. i. 1). The strange and unseemly dress of the prophet, whenever he appeared in his official capacity for three whole years, was a prediction of the fall of the Egypto-Ethiopian kingdom, which was to take place at the end of these three years. Egypt and Ethiopia are as closely connected here as Israel and Judah in ch. xi. 12. They were at that time one kingdom, so that the shame of Egypt was the shame of Ethiopia also. *'Ervâh* is a shameful nakedness, and *'ervath Mitzrayim* is in apposition to all that precedes it in ver. 4. *Shēth* is the seat or hinder part, as in 2 Sam. x. 4, from *shâthâh*, to set or seat; it is a substantive form, like בֵּן, עֵץ, עֵד, שֵׂם, with the third radical letter dropt. *Chashŭphay* has the same *ay* as the words in ch. xix. 9, Judg. v. 15, Jer. xxii. 14, which can hardly be regarded as constructive forms, as Ewald, Knobel, and Gesenius suppose (although ךְ— of the construct has arisen from ךַ—), but rather as a singular form with a collective signification. The emendations suggested, viz. *chasŭphē* by Olshausen, and *chasŭphī* with a connecting *i* by Meier, are quite unnecessary.

But if Egypt and Ethiopia are thus shamefully humbled, what kind of impression will this make upon those who rely upon the great power that is supposed to be both unapproachable and invincible? Vers. 5, 6. "*And they cry together, and behold themselves deceived by Ethiopia, to which they looked, and by Egypt, in which they gloried. And the inhabitant of this coast-land saith in that day, Behold, thus it happens to those to whom we looked, whither we fled for help to deliver us from the king of Asshur: and how should we, we escape?*" אִי, which signifies both an island and a coast-land, is used as the name of Philistia in Zeph. ii. 5, and as the name of Phœnicia in ch.

xxiii. 2, 6; and for this reason Knobel and others understand it here as denoting the former with the inclusion of the latter. But as the Assyrians had already attacked both Phœnicians and Philistines at the time when they marched against Egypt, there can be no doubt that Isaiah had chiefly the Judæans in his mind. This was the interpretation given by Jerome ("Judah trusted in the Egyptians, and Egypt will be destroyed"), and it has been adopted by Ewald, Drechsler, Luzzatto, and Meier. The expressions are the same as those in which a little further on we find Isaiah reproving the Egyptian tendencies of Judah's policy. At the same time, by "the inhabitant of this coast-land" we are not to understand Judah exclusively, but the inhabitants of Palestine generally, with whom Judah was mixed up to its shame, because it had denied its character as the nation of Jehovah in a manner so thoroughly opposed to its theocratic standing.

Unfortunately, we know very little concerning the Assyrian campaigns in Egypt. But we may infer from Nahum iii. 8–10, according to which the Egyptian Thebes had fallen (for it is held up before Nineveh as the mirror of its own fate), that after the conquest of Ashdod Egypt was also overcome by Sargon's army. In the grand inscription found in the halls of the palace at Khorsabad, Sargon boasts of a successful battle which he had fought with Pharaoh *Sebech* at Raphia, and in consequence of which the latter became tributary to him. Still further on he relates that he had dethroned the rebellious king of Ashdod, and appointed another in his place, but that the people removed him, and chose another king; after which he marched with his army against Ashdod, and when the king fled from him into Egypt, he besieged Ashdod, and took it. Then follows a difficult and mutilated passage, in which Rawlinson agrees with Oppert in finding an account of the complete subjection of Sebech (Sabako?).[1] Nothing can be built upon this, however; and it must also remain uncertain whether, even if the rest is correctly interpreted, ch. xx. 1 relates to that conquest of Ashdod which was followed by the dethroning of

---

[1] *Five Great Monarchies*, vol. ii. pp. 416-7; compare Oppert, *Sargonides*, pp. 22, 26-7. With regard to one passage of the annals, which contains an account of a successful battle fought at Ra-bek (Heliopolis), see *Journal Asiat.* xii. 462 sqq.; Brandis, p. 51.

the rebellious king and the appointment of another, or to the final conquest by which it became a colonial city of Assyria.[1] This conquest Sargon ascribes to himself in person, so that apparently we must think of that conquest which was carried out by Tartan; and in that case the words, " he fought against it," etc., need not be taken as anticipatory. It is quite sufficient, that the monuments seem to intimate that the conquest of Samaria and Ashdod was followed by the subjugation of the Egypto-Ethiopian kingdom. But inasmuch as Judah, trusting in the reed of Egypt, fell away from Assyria under Hezekiah, and Sennacherib had to make war upon Egypt again, to all appearance the Assyrians never had much cause to congratulate themselves upon their possession of Egypt, and that for reasons which are not difficult to discover. At the time appointed by the prophecy, Egypt came under the Assyrian yoke, from which it was first delivered by Psammetichus; but, as the constant wars between Assyria and Egypt clearly show, it never patiently submitted to that yoke for any length of time. The confidence which Judah placed in Egypt turned out most disastrously for Judah itself, just as Isaiah predicted here. But the catastrophe that occurred in front of Jerusalem did not put an end to Assyria, nor did the campaigns of Sargon and Sennacherib bring Egypt to an end. And, on the other hand, the triumphs of Jehovah and of the prophecy concerning Assyria were not the means of Egypt's conversion. In all these respects the fulfilment showed that there was an element of *human* hope in the prophecy, which made the distant appear to be close at hand. And this element it eliminated. For the fulfilment of a prophecy is divine, but the prophecy itself is both divine and human.

---

[1] Among the pictures from Khorsabad which have been published by Botta, there is a burning fortress that has been taken by storm. Isidor Löwenstern (in his *Essai*, Paris 1845) pronounced it to be Ashdod; but Rödiger regarded the evidence as inconclusive. Nevertheless, Löwenstern was able to claim priority over Rawlinson in several points of deciphering (*Galignani's Messenger*, Feb. 28, 1850). He read in the inscription the king's name, *Sarak*.

THE ORACLE CONCERNING THE DESERT OF THE SEA
(BABYLON).—CHAP. XXI. 1–10.

Ewald pronounces this and other headings to be the glosses of ancient readers (*Proph.* i. 56, 57). Even Vitringa at first attributed it to the collectors, but he afterwards saw that this was inadmissible. In fact, it is hardly possible to understand how the expression "desert of the sea" (*midbar-yâm*) could have been taken from the prophecy itself; for *yâm* cannot signify the south (as though synonymous with *negeb*), but is invariably applied to the west, whilst there is nothing about a *sea* in the prophecy. The heading, therefore, is a peculiar one; and this Knobel admits, though he nevertheless adheres to the opinion that it sprang from a later hand. But why? According to modern critics, the hand by which the whole *massa* was written was certainly quite late enough. From Koppe to Knobel they are almost unanimous in asserting that it emanated from a prophet who lived at the end of the Babylonian captivity. And Meier asserts with dictatorial brevity, that no further proof is needed that Isaiah was not the author. But assuming, what indeed seems impossible to modern critics,— namely, that a prophet's insight into futurity might stretch over hundreds of years,—the *massa* contains within itself and round about itself the strongest proofs of its genuineness. Within itself: for both the thoughts themselves, and the manner in which they are expressed, are so thoroughly Isaiah's, even in the most minute points, that it is impossible to conceive of any prophecy in a form more truly his own. And round about itself: inasmuch as the four massa's (ch. xxi. 1–10, 11–12, 13–17, and xxii.) are so intertwined the one with the other as to form a tetralogy, not only through their emblematical titles (compare ch. xxx. 6) and their visionary bearing, but also in many ways through the contexts themselves. Thus the designation of the prophet as a "watchman" is common to the *first* and *second* massa's; and in the *fourth*, Jerusalem is called the valley of vision, because the watch-tower was there, from which the prophet surveyed the future fate of Babylon, Edom, and Arabia. And just as in the first, Elam and Madai march against Babylon; so in the fourth (ch. xxii. 6) Kir and Elam march against Jerusalem. The form of expression is also strikingly similar in both instances (compare ch. xxii. 6, 7, with ch. xxi. 7). Is it then possible that the first portion of the tetralogy should be spurious, and the other three genuine? We come to the same conclusion in this instance as we did at ch. xiii. 1 sqq.; and that, most truly, neither from a needless apologetical interest, nor from forced traditional prejudice. Just as the *massâ Bâbel* rests upon a prophecy against Asshur, which forms, as it were, a pedestal to it, and cannot be supposed to have been placed there by any one but Isaiah himself; so the *massa midbar-yâm* rests, as it were, upon the pillars of its genuineness, and announces itself *velut de tripode* as Isaiah's. This also applies to the heading. We have already noticed, in connection with ch. xv. 1, how closely the headings fit in to the prophecies themselves. Isaiah is fond of symbolical names (ch. xxix. 1, xxx. 7). And *midbar-yâm* (desert of the sea) is a name of this kind applied to Babylon and the neighbourhood. The continent on which Babylon stood was a *midbâr*, a great plain running to the south into *Arabia deserta;* and so intersected by the Euphrates as well as by marshes and lakes, that it floated, as it were, in the sea. The low-lying land on the Lower Euphrates had been wrested, as it were, from the sea; for before Semiramis constructed the dams, the Euphrates used to overflow the whole just like a sea ($\pi\epsilon\lambda\alpha\gamma i\zeta\epsilon\iota\nu$, Herod. i. 184). Abydenus even says, that at first the whole of it was covered with water, and was called *thalassa* (Euseb. *præp.* ix. 41). We may learn from ch. xiv. 23, why it was that the prophet made use of this symbolical name. The origin and natural features of Babylon are made into ominous prognostics of its ultimate fate. The true interpretation is found in Jeremiah (Jer. li. 13, l. 38), who was acquainted with this oracle.

The power which first brings destruction upon the city of the world, is a hostile army composed of several nations. Vers. 1, 2. "*As storms in the south approach, it comes from the desert, from a terrible land. Hard vision is made known to me: the spoiler spoils, and the devastator devastates. Go up, Elam! Surround, Maday! I put an end to all their sighing.*" "Storms in the south" (compare ch. xxviii. 21, Amos iii. 9) are storms which have their starting-point in the south, and therefore come to Babylon from *Arabia deserta;* and like all winds that come from boundless steppes, they are always violent (Job i. 19, xxxvii. 9 ; see Hos. xiii. 15). It would be natural, therefore, to connect *mimmidbâr* with *lachalōph* (as Knobel and Umbreit do), but the arrangement of the words is opposed to this ; *lachalōph* (" pressing forwards") is used instead of *yachalōph* (see Ges. § 132, Anm. 1, and still more fully on Hab. i. 17). The *conjunctio periphrastica* stands with great force at the close of the comparison, in order that it may express at the same time the violent pressure with which the progress of the storm is connected. It is true that, according to Herod. i. 189, Cyrus came across the Gyndes, so that he descended into the lowlands to Babylonia through Chalonitis and Apolloniatis, by the road described by Isidor v. Charax in his *Itinerarium*,[1] over the Zagros pass through the Zagros-gate (Ptolem. vi. 2) to the upper course of the Gyndes (the present *Diyala*), and then along this river, which he crossed before its junction with the Tigris. But if the Medo-Persian army came in this direction, it could not be regarded as coming " from the desert." If, however, the Median portion of the army followed the course of the Choaspes (*Kerkha*) so as to descend into the lowland of Chuzistan (the route taken by Major Rawlinson with a Guran regiment),[2] and thus approached Babylon from the south-east, it might be regarded in many respects as coming *mimmidbâr* (from the desert), and primarily because the lowland of Chuzistan is a broad open plain—that is to say, a *midbâr*. According to the simile employed of storms in the south, the assumption of the prophecy is really this, that the hostile army is advancing from Chuzistan, or (as geographical exactitude is not to be supposed) from the direction of the desert of *ed-Dahna*, that portion of *Arabia deserta* which bounded the lowland of Chaldea on the south-west. The Medo-Persian land itself is called " a terrible land," because it was situated outside the circle of civilised nations by which the land of Israel was surrounded. After the thematic commencement in ver. 1, which is quite in harmony with Isaiah's

[1] See C. Masson's " Illustration of the route from Seleucia to Apobatana, as given by Isid. of Charax," in the *Asiatic Journal*, xii. 97 sqq.

[2] See Rawlinson's route as described in Ritter's *Erdkunde*, ix. 3 (Westasien), p. 397 sqq.

usual custom, the prophet begins again in ver. 2. *Châzuth* (a vision) has the same meaning here as in ch. xxix. 11 (though not ch. xxviii. 18); and *châzuth kâshâh* is the object of the passive which follows (Ges. § 143, 1, *b*). The prophet calls the look into the future, which is given to him by divine inspiration, hard or heavy (though in the sense of *difficilis*, not *gravis*, *câbēd*), on account of its repulsive, unendurable, and, so to speak, indigestible nature. The prospect is wide-spread plunder and devastation (the expression is the same as in ch. xxxiii. 1, compare ch. xvi. 4, xxiv. 16, *bâgad* denoting faithless or treacherous conduct, then heartless robbery), and the summoning of the nations on the east and north of Babylonia to the conquest of Babylon; for Jehovah is about to put an end (*hishbatti*, as in ch. xvi. 10) to all their sighing (*anchâthâh*, with *He raf.* and the tone upon the last syllable), *i.e.* to all the lamentations forced out of them far and wide by the oppressor.

Here again, as in the case of the prophecy concerning Moab, what the prophet has given to him to see does not pass without exciting his feelings of humanity, but works upon him like a horrible dream. Vers. 3, 4. "*Therefore are my loins full of cramp: pangs have taken hold of me, as the pangs of a travailing woman: I twist myself, so that I do not hear; I am brought down with fear, so that I do not see. My heart beats wildly; horror hath troubled me: the darkness of night that I love, he hath turned for me into quaking.*" The prophet does not describe in detail what he saw; but the violent agitation produced by the impression leads us to conclude how horrible it must have been. *Chalchâlâh* is the contortion produced by cramp, as in Nahum ii. 11; *tzirim* is the word properly applied to the pains of childbirth; *naʿaváh* means to bend, or bow one's self, and is also used to denote a convulsive utterance of pain; *tāʿāh*, which is used in a different sense from Ps. xcv. 10 (compare, however, Ps. xxxviii. 11), denotes a feverish and irregular beating of the pulse. The darkness of evening and night, which the prophet loved so much (*chēshek*, a desire arising from inclination, 1 Kings ix. 1, 19), and always longed for, either that he might give himself up to contemplation, or that he might rest from outward and inward labour, had been changed into quaking by the horrible vision. It is quite impossible to imagine, as Umbreit suggests, that *nesheph chishki* (the darkness of my pleasure) refers to the nocturnal feast during which Babylon was stormed (Herod. i. 191, and Xenophon, *Cyrop.* vii. 23).

On the other hand, what Xenophon so elaborately relates, and what is also in all probability described in Dan. v. 30 (compare Jer. li. 39, 57), is referred to in ver. 5 : " *They cover the table, watch the watch, eat, drink. Rise up, ye princes ! Anoint the shield !*" This is not a scene from the hostile camp, where they are strengthening themselves for an attack upon Babylon : for the express allusion to the covering of the table is intended to create the impression of confident and careless good living ; and the exclamation " anoint the shield" (cf. Jer. li. 11) presupposes that they have first of all to prepare themselves for battle, and therefore that they have been taken by surprise. What the prophet sees, therefore, is a banquet in Babylon. The only thing that does not seem quite to square with this is one of the infinitives with which the picture is so vividly described (Ges. § 131, 4, *b*), namely *tzâphōh hatztzâphith*. Hitzig's explanation, " they spread carpets" (from *tzâphâh, expandere, obducere*, compare the Talmudic *tziphâh, tziphtâh*, a mat, *storea*), commends itself thoroughly ; but it is without any support in biblical usage, so that we prefer to follow the Targum, Peshito, and Vulgate (the Sept. does not give any translation of the words at all), and understand the *hap. leg. tzâphith* as referring to the watch : " they set the watch." They content themselves with this one precautionary measure, and give themselves up with all the greater recklessness to their night's debauch (cf. ch. xxii. 13). The prophet mentions this, because (as Meier acknowledges) it is by the watch that the cry, " Rise up, ye princes," etc., is addressed to the feasters. The shield-leather was generally oiled, to make it shine and protect it from wet, and, more than all, to cause the strokes it might receive to glide off (compare the *laves clypeos* in Virg. *Æn.* vii. 626). The infatuated self-confidence of the chief men of Babylon was proved by the fact that they had to be aroused. They fancied that they were hidden behind the walls and waters of the city, and therefore they had not even got their weapons ready for use.

The prophecy is continued with the conjunction " for" (*ci*).

The tacit link in the train of thought is this: they act thus in Babylon, because the destruction of Babylon is determined. The form in which this thought is embodied is the following: the prophet receives instruction in the vision to set a *m‘tzappeh* upon the watch-tower, who was to look out and see what more took place. Ver. 6. "*For thus said the Lord to me, Go, set a spy; what he seeth, let him declare.*" In other cases it is the prophet himself who stands upon the watch-tower (ver. 11; Hab. ii. 1, 2); but here in the vision a distinction is made between the prophet and the person whom he stations upon the watch-tower (*specula*). The prophet divides himself, as it were, into two persons (compare ch. xviii. 4 for the introduction; and for the expression "go," ch. xx. 2). He now sees through the medium of a spy, just as Zechariah sees by means of the angel speaking in him; with this difference, however, that here the spy is the instrument employed by the prophet, whereas there the prophet is the instrument employed by the angel.

What the man upon the watch-tower sees first of all, is a long, long procession, viz. the hostile army advancing quietly, like a caravan, in serried ranks, and with the most perfect self-reliance. Ver. 7. "*And he saw a procession of cavalry, pairs of horsemen, a procession of asses, a procession of camels; and listened sharply, as sharply as he could listen.*" *Receb*, both here and in ver. 9, signifies neither riding-animals nor war-chariots, but a troop seated upon animals—a procession of riders. In front there was a procession of riders arranged two and two, for Persians and Medes fought either on foot or on horseback (the latter, at any rate, from the time of Cyrus; *vid. Cyrop.* iv. 3); and *párásh* signifies a rider on horseback (in Arabic it is used in distinction from *rákib*, the rider on camels). Then came lines of asses and camels, a large number of which were always taken with the Persian army for different purposes. They not only carried baggage and provisions, but were taken into battle to throw the enemy into confusion. Thus Cyrus gained the victory over the Lydians by means of the great number of his camels (Herod. i. 80), and Darius Hystaspis the victory over the Scythians by means of the number of asses that he employed (Herod. iv. 129). Some of the subject tribes rode upon asses and camels instead of horses: the Arabs rode upon camels in the army of Xerxes, and the Caramanians rode upon asses. What the spy saw was therefore, no doubt, the Persian army. But he only saw and listened. It was indeed "listening, greatness of listening," *i.e.* he stretched his ear to the utmost (*rab* is a substantive, as in ch. lxiii. 7, Ps. cxlv. 7 ; and *hikshib*, according to its radical notion, signifies to stiffen, viz. the ear) ;[1] but he heard nothing, because the long procession was moving with the stillness of death.

At length the procession has vanished; he sees nothing and hears nothing, and is seized with impatience. Ver. 8. "*Then he cried with lion's voice, Upon the watch-tower, O Lord, I stand continually by day, and upon my watch I keep my stand all the nights.*" He loses all his patience, and growls as if he were a lion (compare Rev. x. 3), with the same dull, angry sound, the same long, deep breath out of full lungs, complaining to God that he has to stand so long at his post without seeing anything, except that inexplicable procession that has now vanished away.

But when he is about to speak, his complaint is stifled in his mouth. Ver. 9. "*And, behold, there came a cavalcade of men, pairs of horsemen, and lifted up its voice, and said, Fallen, fallen is Babylon; and all the images of its gods He hath dashed to the ground!*" It is now clear enough where the long procession went to when it disappeared. It entered Babylon, made itself master of the city, and established itself there. And now, after a long interval, there appears a smaller cavalcade, which has to carry the tidings of victory somewhere; and the spy hears them cry out in triumph, "Fallen, fallen is Babylon!" In Rev. xviii. 1, 2, the same words form the shout of triumph raised by the angel, the antitype being more majestic than the type, whilst upon the higher ground of the New Testament everything moves on in spiritual relations, all that is merely national having lost its power. Still even here the spiritual inwardness of the affair is so far expressed, that it is Jehovah who dashes to the ground; and even the heathen conquerors are

---

[1] Böttcher has very correctly compared *kâshab* (*kasuba*) with *kâshâh* (*kasa*), and Fleischer with *sarra* (*tzârar*), which is applied in the *kal* and *hiphil* (*asarra*) to any animal (horse, ass, etc.) when it holds its ears straight and erect to listen to any noise (*sarra udhneihi*, or *udhnahu bi-udhneihi*, or *bi-udhnihi* iv , *asarra bi-udhnihi*, and also absolutely *asarra*, exactly like *kikshib*).

obliged to confess that the fall of Babylon and its *pesilim* (compare Jer. li. 47, 52) is the work of Jehovah Himself. What is here only hinted at from afar—namely, that Cyrus would act as the anointed of Jehovah—is expanded in the second part (ch. xl.-lxvi.) for the consolation of the captives.

The night vision related and recorded by the prophet, a prelude to the revelations contained in ch. xl.-lx., was also intended for the consolation of Israel, which had already much to suffer, when Babylon was still Assyrian, but would have to suffer far more from it when it should become Chaldean. Ver. 10. "*O thou my threshing, and child of my threshing-floor! What I have heard from Jehovah of hosts, the God of Israel, I have declared to you.*" Threshing (*dūsh*) is a figure used to represent *crushing oppression* in ch. xli. 15 and Mic. iv. 12, 13; and *judicial visitation* in Jer. li. 33 (a parallel by which we must not allow ourselves to be misled, as Jeremiah has there given a different turn to Isaiah's figure, as he very frequently does); and again, as in the present instance, *chastising plagues*, in which wrath and good intention are mingled together. Israel, placed as it was under the tyrannical supremacy of the imperial power, is called the *medŭsshâh* (for *medūshah*, *i.e.* the threshing) of Jehovah,—in other words, the corn threshed by Him; also His "child of the threshing-floor," inasmuch as it was laid in the floor, in the bosom as it were of the threshing-place, to come out threshed (and then to become a thresher itself, Mic. iv. 12, 13). This floor, in which Jehovah makes a judicial separation of grains and husks in Israel, was their captivity. Babylon is the instrument of the threshing wrath of God. But love also takes part in the threshing, and restrains the wrath. This is what the prophet has learned in the vision ("I have heard," as in ch. xxviii. 22),—a consolatory figure for the threshing-corn in the floor, *i.e.* for Israel, which was now subject to the power of the world, and had been mowed off its own field and carried captive into Babylonia.

THE ORACLE CONCERNING THE SILENCE OF DEATH (EDOM).—
CHAP. XXI. 11, 12.

This oracle consists of a question, addressed to the prophet from Seir, and of the prophet's reply. Seir is the mountainous country to the south of Palestine, of which Edom took possession after the expulsion of the Horites. Consequently the *Dumah* of the heading cannot be either the *Dûma* of Eastern Hauran (by the side of which we find also a *Tema* and a *Buzan*); or the *Duma* in the high land of Arabia, on the great Nabatæan line of traffic between the northern harbours of the Red Sea and Irak, which bore the cognomen of the rocky (*el-gendel*) or Syrian Duma (Gen. xxv. 14); or the *Duma* mentioned in the *Onom.*, which was seventeen miles from Eleutheropolis (or according to Jerome on this passage, twenty) "*in Daroma hoc est ad australem plagam*," and was probably the same place as the *Duma* in the mountains of Judah,—that is to say, judging from the ruins of *Daume*, to the south-east of Eleutheropolis (see the Com. on Josh. xv. 52), a place out of which Jerome has made " a certain region of Idumæa, near which are the mountains of Seir." The name as it stands here is symbolical, and without any demonstrable topographical application. *Dūmâh* is deep, utter silence, and therefore the land of the dead (Ps. xciv. 17, cxv. 17). The name אדום is turned into an emblem of the future fate of Edom, by the removal of the *a*-sound from the beginning of the word to the end. It becomes a land of deathlike stillness, deathlike sleep, deathlike darkness. Ver. 11. " *A cry comes to me out of Seir: Watchman, how far is it in the night? Watchman, how far in the night?*" Luther translates the participle correctly, " they cry" (*man ruft;* compare the similar use of the participle in ch. xxx. 24, xxxiii. 4). For the rest, however, we have deviated from Luther's excellent translation, for the purpose of giving to some extent the significant change from מִלַּיְלָה and מִלֵּיל. The more winged form of the second question is expressive of heightened, anxious urgency and haste. The wish is to hear that it is very late in the night, and that it will soon be past; *min* is partitive (Saad.), " What part of the night are we at now?" Just as a sick man longs for a sleepless night to come to an end, and is constantly asking what time it is, so do they inquire of the prophet out of Edom, whether the night of tribulation will not be soon over. We are not to understand, however, that messengers were really sent out of Edom to Isaiah; the process was purely a pneumatical one. The prophet stands there in Jerusalem, in the midst of the benighted world of nations, like a sentry upon the watch-tower; he understands the anxious inquiries of the nations afar off, and answers them according to the word of Jehovah, which is the plan and chronological measure of the history of the nations, and the key to its interpretation. What, then, is the prophet's reply? He lets the inquirer "see through a glass darkly."—Ver. 12. "*Watchman says, Morning cometh, and also night. Will ye inquire, inquire! Turn, come!!*" The answer is intentionally and pathetically expressed in an Aramæan form of Hebrew. אָתָא (written even with א at the end, cf. Deut. xxxiii. 2) is the Aramæan word for בּוֹא; and בָּעָה (בְּעָא) the Aramæan word for שָׁאַל, from the primary form of which (בְּעִי) the future tib'áyūn is taken here (as in ch. xxxiii. 7), and the imperative b"áyu (Ges. § 75, Anm. 4). אָתָיוּ, which is here pointed in the Syriac style, אֵתָיוּ, as in ch. lvi. 9, 12, would be similarly traceable to אתי (cf. Ges. § 75, Anm. 4, with § 23, Anm. 2). But what is the meaning? Luther seems to me to have hit upon it: "When the morning comes, it will still be night." But *v'gam* (and also) is not equivalent to "and yet," as Schröring explains it, with a reference to Ewald, § 354, *a*. With the simple connection in the clauses, the meaning cannot possibly be, that a morning is coming, and that it will nevertheless continue night, but that a morning is coming, and at the same time a night, *i.e.* that even if the morning dawns, it will be swallowed up again directly by night. And the history was quite in accordance with such an answer. The Assyrian period of judgment was followed by the Chaldean, and the Chaldean by the Persian, and the Persian by the Grecian, and the Grecian by the Roman. Again and again there was a glimmer of morning dawn for Edom (and what a glimmer in the Herodian age!), but it was swallowed up directly by another night, until Edom became an utter *Dūmâh*, and disappeared from the history of the nations. The prophet does not see to the utmost end of these Edomitish nights, but he has also no consolation for Edom. It is altogether different with Edom from what it is with Israel, the nocturnal portion of whose history has a morning dawn, according to promise, as its irrevocable close. The prophet therefore sends the inquirers home. Would they ask any further questions, they might do so, might turn and come. In *shûbû* (turn back) there lies a significant though ambiguous hint. It is only in the case of their turning, coming, *i.e.*

coming back converted, that the prophet has any consolatory answer for them. So long as they are not so, there is suspended over their future an interminable night, to the prophet as much as to themselves. The way to salvation for every other people is just the same as for Israel,—namely, the way of repentance.

THE ORACLE IN THE EVENING (AGAINST ARABIA).—
CHAP. XXI. 13–17.

The heading מַשָּׂא בַּעְרָב (the ע written according to the best codd. with a simple *sheva*), when pointed as we have it, signifies, according to Zech. ix. 1 (cf. Isa. ix. 7), "oracle against Arabia." But why not *massâ 'Arâb*, since *massâ* is followed by a simple genitive in the other three headings? Or again, is this the only heading in the tetralogy that is not symbolical? We must assume that the *Beth* by which this is distinguished is introduced for the express purpose of rendering it symbolical, and that the prophet pointed it first of all בַּעְרָב, but had at the same time בַּעְרָב in his mind. The earlier translators (LXX., Targum, Syr., Vulg., Ar.) read the second בַּעְרָב like the first, but without any reason. The oracle commences with an evening scene, even without our altering the second בַּעְרָב. And the *massa* has a symbolical title founded upon this evening scene. Just as 'Edom becomes *Dumah*, inasmuch as a night without a morning dawn falls upon the mountain land of Seir, so will בַּעְרָב soon be בַּעְרָב, inasmuch as the sun of Arabia is setting. Evening darkness is settling upon Arabia, and the morning-land is becoming an evening-land. Vers. 13–15 : "*In the wilderness in Arabia ye must pass the night, caravans of the Dedanians. Bring water to meet thirsty ones! The inhabitants of the land of Tema are coming with its bread before the fugitive. For they are flying before swords, before drawn swords, and before a bent bow, and before oppressive war.*" There is all the less ground for making any alteration in בְּיַעַר בַּעְרָב, inasmuch as the second *Beth* (wilderness *in* Arabia for *of* Arabia) is favoured by Isaiah's common usage (ch. xxviii. 21, ix. 2; compare 2 Sam. i. 21, Amos iii. 9). '*Arab*, written with *pathach*, is Arabia (Ezek. xxvii. 21; '*arâb* in pause, Jer. xxv. 24); and *ya'ar* here is the solitary barren desert, as distinguished from the cultivated land with its cities and villages. Wetzstein rejects the meaning *nemus, sylva*, which *ya'ar* has been assumed to have, because it would be rather a promise than a threat to be told that they would have to flee from the steppe into the wood, since a shady tree is the most delicious dream of the Beduins, who not only find shade in the forest, but a constant supply of green pasture, and fuel for their hospitable hearths. He therefore renders it, " Ye will take refuge in the *V'ar* of Arabia," *i.e.* the open steppe will no longer afford you any shelter, so that ye will be obliged to hide yourselves in the *V'ar*. وَعْر, for example, is the name applied to the trachytic rayon of the Syro-Hauranitic volcanoes which is covered with a layer of stones. But as the *V'ar* in this sense is also planted with trees, and furnishes firewood, this epithet must rest upon some peculiar distinction in the radical meaning of the word *ya'ar*, which really does mean a forest in Hebrew, though not necessarily a forest of lofty trees, but also a wilderness overgrown with brushwood and thorn-bushes. The meaning of the passage before us we therefore take to be this: the trading caravans ('*ârchôth*, like *halicoth* in Job vi. 19) of the Dedanians, that mixed tribe of Cushites and Abrahamides dwelling in the neighbourhood of the Edomites (Gen. x. 7, xxv. 3), when on their way from east to west, possibly to Tyre (Ezek. xxvii. 20), would be obliged to encamp in the wilderness, being driven out of the caravan road in consequence of the war that was spreading from north to south. The prophet, whose sympathy mingles with the revelation in this instance also, asks for water for the panting fugitives (הֵתָיוּ, as in Jer. xii. 9, an imperative equivalent to הָאֵתָיוּ = הַאֲתָיוּ; compare 2 Kings ii. 3: there is no necessity to read קַדְּמוּ, as the Targum, Döderlein, and Ewald do). They are driven back with fright towards the south-east as far as Tema, on the border of Negd and the Syrian desert. The Tema referred to is not the trans-Hauranian Têmâ, which is three-quarters of an hour from *Dumah*, although there is a good deal that seems to favour this,[1] but the Tema on the pilgrim road from Damascus to Mecca, between *Tebuk* and *Wadi el-Kora*, which is about the same distance (four days' journey) from both these places, and also from *Chaibar* (it is to be distinguished, however, from *Tihama*, the coast land of Yemen, the antithesis of which is *ne'gd*, the mountain district

[1] See Wetzstein, *ut supra*, p. 202; compare *Job*, ii. 425.

of Yemen[1]). But even here in the land of Tema they do not feel themselves safe. The inhabitants of Tema are obliged to bring them water and bread ("its bread," *lachmo*, referring to *nōdēd*: the bread necessary in order to save them), into the hiding-places in which they have concealed themselves. " How humiliating," as Drechsler well observes, "to be obliged to practise their hospitality, the pride of Arabian customs, in so restricted a manner, and with such unbecoming secrecy!" But it could not possibly be done in any other way, since the weapons of the foe were driving them incessantly before them, and the war itself was rolling incessantly forward like an overwhelming colossus, as the repetition of the word "before" (*mippᵉnē*) no less than four times clearly implies.

Thus does the approaching fate of Arabia present itself in picture before the prophet's eye, whilst it is more distinctly revealed in vers. 16, 17 : "*For thus hath the Lord spoken to me, Within a year, as the years of a hired labourer, it is over with all the glory of Kedar. And the remnant of the number of bows of the heroes of the Kedarenes will be small: for Jehovah, the God of Israel, hath spoken.*" The name *Kedar* is here the collective name of the Arabic tribes generally. In the stricter sense, Kedar, like Nebaioth, which is associated with it, was a nomadic tribe of Ishmaelites, which wandered as far as the Elanitic Gulf. Within the space of a year, measured as exactly as is generally the case where employers and labourers are concerned, Kedar's freedom, military strength, numbers, and wealth (all these together constituting its glory), would all have disappeared. Nothing but a small remnant would be left of the heroic sons of Kedar and their bows. They are numbered here by their bows (in distinction from the numbering by heads), showing that the fighting men are referred to,—a mode of numbering which is customary among the Indian tribes of America, for example.[2] The noun *she'âr* (remnant) is followed by five genitives here (just as *peri* is by four in ch. x. 12); and the predicate יִמְעָטוּ is in the plural because of the copiousness of the subject. The period of the fulfilment of the prophecy keeps us still within the Assyrian era. In Herodotus

[1] See Sprenger, *Post und Reise-routen des Orients*, Heft i. (1864), pp. 118, 119.

[2] See the work of v. Martius on the Indians of Brazil, i. 395, 411, etc.

(2, 141), Sennacherib is actually called "king of Arabians and Assyrians" (compare Josephus, *Ant.* x. 1, 4); and both Sargon and Sennacherib, in their annalistic inscriptions, take credit to themselves for the subjugation of Arabian tribes. But in the Chaldean era Jeremiah predicted the same things against Kedar (ch. xlix.) as against Edom; and Jer. xlix. 30, 31 was evidently written with a retrospective allusion to this oracle of Isaiah. When the period fixed by Isaiah for the fulfilment arrived, a second period grew out of it, and one still more remote, inasmuch as a second empire, viz. the Chaldean, grew out of the Assyrian, and inaugurated a second period of judgment for the nations. After a short glimmer of morning, the night set in a second time upon Edom, and a second time upon Arabia.

THE ORACLE CONCERNING THE VALLEY OF VISION (JERUSALEM).—CHAP. XXII. 1–14.

The *châzûth* concerning Babylon, and the no less visionary prophecies concerning Edom and Arabia, are now followed by a *massâ*, the object of which is "the valley of vision" (*gē' chizzâyōn*) itself. Of course these four prophecies were not composed in the tetralogical form in which they are grouped together here, but were joined together at a later period in a group of this kind on account of their close affinity. The internal arrangement of the group was suggested, not by the date of their composition (they stand rather in the opposite relation to one another), but by the idea of a storm coming from a distance, and bursting at last over Jerusalem; for there can be no doubt that the "valley of vision" is a general name for Jerusalem as a whole, and not the name given to one particular valley of Jerusalem. It is true that the epithet applied to the position of Jerusalem does not seem to be in harmony with this; for, according to Josephus, "the city was built upon two hills, which are opposite to one another and have a valley to divide them asunder, at which valley the corresponding rows of houses on both hills end" (*Wars of the Jews*, v. 4, 1; Whiston). But the epithet is so far allowable, that there are mountains round Jerusalem (Ps. cxxv. 2); and the same city which is on an eminence in relation to the land generally, appears to stand on low ground when contrasted with the mountains in the immediate neighbourhood (πρὸς δὲ τὰ ἐχόμενα ταύτης γηόλοφα χθαμαλίζεται, as Phocas says). According to this twofold aspect, Jerusalem is called the "inhabitant of the valley" in Jer. xxi. 13, and directly afterwards the "rock of the plain;" just as in Jer. xvii. 3 it is called the mountain in the fields, whereas Zephaniah (i. 11) applies the epithet *mactēsh* (the mortar or cauldron) not to all Jerusalem, but to one portion of it (probably the ravine of the Tyropœum). And if we add to this the fact that Isaiah's house was situated in the lower town,—and therefore the standpoint of the epithet is really there,—it is appropriate in other respects still; for the prophet had there the temple-hill and the Mount of Olives, which is three hundred feet higher, on the east, and Mount Zion before him towards the south; so that Jerusalem appeared like a city in a valley in relation to the mountains inside, quite as much as to those outside. But the epithet is intended to be something more than geographical. A valley is a deep, still, solitary place, cut off and shut in by mountains. And thus Jerusalem was an enclosed place, hidden and shut off from the world, which Jehovah had chosen as the place in which to show to His prophets the mysteries of His government of the world. And upon this sacred prophets' city the judgment of Jehovah was about to fall; and the announcement of the judgment upon it is placed among the oracles concerning the nations of the world! We may see from this, that at the time when this prophecy was uttered, the attitude of Jerusalem was so worldly and heathenish, that it called forth this dark, nocturnal threat, which is penetrated by not a single glimmer of promise. But neither the prophecies of the time of Ahaz relating to the Assyrian age of judgment, nor those which were uttered in the midst of the Assyrian calamities, are so destitute of promise and so peremptory as this. The *massa* therefore falls in the intermediate time, probably the time when the people were seized with the mania for liberty, and the way was prepared for their breaking away from Assyria by their hope of an alliance with Egypt (*vid.* Delitzsch-Caspari, *Studien*, ii. 173-4). The prophet exposes the nature and worthlessness of their confidence in vers. 1-3: "*What aileth thee, then, that thou art wholly ascended upon the house-tops? O full of tumult, thou noisy city, shouting castle, thy slain men are not slain with the sword, nor slaughtered in battle. All thy rulers departing together are fettered without bow; all thy captured ones are fettered together, fleeing far away."* From the flat house-tops they all look out together at the approaching army of the foe, longing for battle, and sure of victory (*cullâk* is for *cullēk*, ch. xiv. 29, 31). They have no suspicion of what is threatening them; therefore are they so sure, so contented, and so defiant. תְּשֻׁאוֹת מְלֵאָה is inverted, and stands for מְלֵאַת תְּשֻׁאוֹת, like אֲפֵלָה מְנֻדָּח in ch. viii. 22. עַלִּיזָה is used to denote self-confident rejoicing, as in Zeph. ii. 15. How terribly they deceive themselves! Not even the honour of falling upon the battle-field is allowed them. Their rulers (*kâtzin*, a judge, and then any person of rank) depart one and all out of the city, and are fettered outside " without bow" (*mikkesheth*), *i.e.* without there being any necessity for the bow to be drawn (*min*, as in Job xxi. 9, 2 Sam. i. 22; cf. Ewald, § 217, *b*). All, without exception, of those who are attacked in Jerusalem by the advancing foe (*nimzā'aik*, thy captured ones, as in ch. xiii. 15), fall helplessly into captivity, as they are attempting to flee far away (see at ch. xvii. 13; the *perf. de conatu* answers to the classical *præsens de conatu*). Hence (what is here affirmed indirectly) the city is besieged, and in consequence of the long siege hunger and pestilence destroy the inhabitants, and every one who attempts to get away falls into the hands of the enemy, without venturing to defend himself, on account of his emaciation and exhaustion from hunger. Whilst the prophet thus pictures to himself the fate of Jerusalem and Judah, through their infatuation, he is seized with inconsolable anguish.—Vers. 4, 5. " *Therefore I say, Look away from me, that I may weep bitterly; press me not with consolations for the destruction of the daughter of my people! For a day of noise, and of treading down, and of confusion, cometh from the Lord, Jehovah of hosts, in the valley of vision, breaking down walls; and a cry of woe echoes against the mountains.*" The note struck by Isaiah here is the note of the *kinah* that is continued in the Lamentations of Jeremiah. Jeremiah says *sheber* for *shod* (Lam. iii. 48), and *bath-ammi* (daughter of my people) is varied with *bath-zion* (daughter of Zion) and *bath-yehudah* (daughter of Judah). *Mērēr babbeci* (weep bitterly) is more than *bâcâh mar* (ch. xxxiii. 7): it signifies to give one's self thoroughly up to bitter weeping, to exhaust one's self with weeping. The two similar sounds which occur in ver. 5, in imitation of echoes, can hardly be translated. The day of divine judgment is called a day in which masses of men crowd together with great noise (*mehûmâh*), in which Jerusalem and its inhabitants are trodden down by foes (*mebûsâh*) and are thrown into wild confusion (*mebûcâh*). This is one play upon words. The other makes the crashing of the walls audible, as they are hurled down by the siege-artillery (*mekarkar kir*). *Kirkēr* is not a denom. of *kir*, as Kimchi and Ewald suppose (unwalling walls), but is to be explained in accordance with Num. xxiv. 17, " he undermines," *i.e.* throws down by removing the supports, in other words, " to the very foundations" (*kur*, to dig, hence *karkârâh*, the bottom of a vessel, *Kelim* ii. 2; *kurkoreth*, the bottom of a net, *ib.* xxviii. 10, or of a cask, *Ahaloth* ix. 16). When this takes place, then a cry of woe echoes against the mountain (*shōa'*, like *shūa'*, *sheva'*), *i.e.* strikes against the mountains that surround Jerusalem, and is echoed back again. Knobel understands it as signifying a cry for help addressed to the mountain where Jehovah dwells; but this feature is altogether unsuitable to the God-forgetting worldly state in which Jerusalem is found. It is also to be observed, in opposition to Knobel, that the description does not move on in the same natural and literal way as in a historical narrative. The prophet is not relating, but looking; and in ver. 5 he depicts the day of Jehovah according to both its ultimate intention and its ultimate result.

The advance of the besiegers, which leads to the destruction of the walls, is first described in vers. 6, 7. " *And Elam has taken the quiver, together with chariots with men, horsemen; and Kir has drawn out the shield. And then it comes to pass, that thy choicest valleys are filled with chariots, and the horsemen plant a firm foot towards the gate.*" Of the nations composing the Assyrian army, the two mentioned are *Elam*, the Semitic nation of Susiana (Chuzistan), whose original settlements were the row of valleys between the Zagros chain and the chain of advanced mountains bounding the Assyrian plains on the east, and who were greatly dreaded as bowmen (Ezek. xxxii. 24; Jer. xlix. 35), and *Kir*, the inhabitants of the country of the Cyrus river, which was an Assyrian province, according to

2 Kings xvi. 9 and Amos i. 5, and still retained its dependent position even in the time of the Achæmenides, when Armenia, at any rate, is expressly described in the arrow-headed writings as a Persian province, though a rebellious one. The readiness for battle of this people of Kur, who represent, in combination with Elam, the whole extent of the Assyrian empire from south to north,[1] is attested by their "drawing out the shield" (*ĕrâh mâgēn*), which Cæsar calls *scutis tegimenta detrahere* (*bell. gall.* ii. 21); for the Talmudic meaning *applicare* cannot be thought of for a moment (Buxtorf, *lex. col.* 1664). These nations that fought on foot were accompanied (*beth*, as in 1 Kings x. 2) by chariots filled with men (*receb 'âdâm*), *i.e.* war-chariots (as distinguished from *'agâloth*), and, as is added ἀσυνδέτως, by *pârâshim*, riders (*i.e.* horsemen trained to arms). The historical tense is introduced with וַיְהִי in ver. 7, but in a purely future sense. It is only for the sake of the favourite arrangement of the words that the passage does not proceed with *Vav relat.* מָלְאוּ. "Thy valleys" (*'amâkaik*) are the valleys by which Jerusalem was encircled on the east, the west, and the south, viz. the valley of Kidron on the east; the valley of Gihon on the west; the valley of Rephaim, stretching away from the road to Bethlehem, on the south-west (ch. xvii. 5); the valley of Hinnom, which joins the Tyropæum, and then runs on into a south-eastern angle; and possibly also the valley of Jehoshaphat, which ran on the north-east of the city above the valley of Kidron. These valleys, more especially the finest of them towards the south, are now cut up by the wheels and hoofs of the enemies' chariots and horses; and the enemies' horsemen have already taken a firm position gatewards, ready to ride full speed against the gates at a given signal, and force their way into the city (*shĭth* with a *shoth* to strengthen it, as in Ps. iii. 7; also *sim* in 1 Kings xx. 12, compare 1 Sam. xv. 2).

When Judah, after being for a long time intoxicated with

[1] The name *Gurgistan* (= Georgia) has nothing to do with the river Kur; and it is a suspicious fact that *Kir* has *k* at the commencement, and *i* in the middle, whereas the name of the river which joins the Araxes, and flows into the Caspian sea, is pronounced *Kur*, and is written in Persian with ⊆ (answering to the Armenian and old Persian, in which *Kuru* is equivalent to Κῦρος). Wetzstein considers *Kir* a portion of Mesopotamia.

hope, shall become aware of the extreme danger in which it is standing, it will adopt prudent measures, but without God. Vers. 8–11. "*Then he takes away the covering of Judah, and thou lookest in that day to the store of arms of the forest-house; and ye see the breaches of the city of David, that there are many of them; and ye collect together the waters of the lower pool. And ye number the houses of Jerusalem, and pull down the houses, to fortify the wall. And ye make a basin between the two walls for the waters of the old pool; and ye do not look to Him who made it, neither do ye have regard to Him who fashioned it long ago.*" *Mâsâk* is the curtain or covering which made Judah blind to the threatening danger. Their looks are now directed first of all to the forest-house, built by Solomon upon Zion for the storing and display of valuable arms and utensils (*něshěk*, or rather, according to the Masora on Job xx. 24, and the older editions, *něshěk*), and so called because it rested upon four rows of cedar columns that ran all round (it was in the centre of the fore-court of the royal palace; see Thenius, *das vorexil. Jerusalem*, p. 13). They also noticed in the city of David, the southern and highest portion of the city of Jerusalem, the bad state of the walls, and began to think of repairing them. To this end they numbered the houses of the city, to obtain building materials for strengthening the walls and repairing the breaches, by pulling down such houses as were suitable for the purpose, and could be dispensed with (*vattithtzu*, from *nâthatz*, with the removal of the recompensative reduplication). The lower pool and the old pool, probably the upper, *i.e.* the lower and upper Gihon, were upon the western side of the city, the lower (*Birket es-Sultan*) to the west of Sion, the upper (*Birket el-Mamilla*) farther up to the west of Akra (Robinson, i. 483–486; v. Raumer, *Pal.* pp. 305–6). *Kibbētz* either means to collect in the pool by stopping up the outflow, or to gather together in the reservoirs and wells of the city by means of artificial canals. The latter, however, would most probably be expressed by אָסַף; so that the meaning that most naturally suggests itself is, that they concentrate the water, so as to be able before the siege to provide the city as rapidly as possible with a large supply. The word *sâtham*, which is used in the account of the actual measures adopted by Hezekiah when he was threatened with siege (2 Chron. xxxii. 2–5), is a somewhat different one, and indicates the stopping up, not of the outflow but of the springs, and therefore of the influx. But in all essential points the measures adopted agree with those indicated here in the prophecy. The chronicler closes the account of Hezekiah's reign by still further observing that "Hezekiah also stopped the outflow of the upper Gihon, and carried the water westwards underground to the city of David" (2 Chron. xxxii. 30, explanatory of 2 Kings xx. 20). If the upper Gihon is the same as the upper pool, there was a conduit (*teʻâlâh*), connected with the upper Gihon as early as the time of Ahaz, ch. vii. 3. And Hezekiah's peculiar work consisted in carrying the water of the upper pool "into the city of David." The *mikvâh* between the two walls, which is here prospectively described by Isaiah, is connected with this water supply, which Hezekiah really carried out. There is still a pool of Hezekiah (also called *Birket el-Batrak*, pool of the patriarchs, the *Amygdalon* of Josephus) on the western side of the city, to the east of the Joppa gate. During the rainy season this pool is supplied by the small conduit which runs from the upper pool along the surface of the ground, and then under the wall against or near the Joppa gate. It also lies between two walls, viz. the wall to the north of Zion, and the one which runs to the northeast round the Akra (Robinson, i. 487–489). How it came to pass that Isaiah's words concerning "a basin between the two walls" were so exactly carried out, as though they had furnished a hydraulic plan, we do not know. But we will offer a conjecture at the close of the exposition. It stands here as one of those prudent measures which would be resorted to in Jerusalem in the anticipation of the coming siege; but it would be thought of too late, and in self-reliant alienation from God, with no look directed to Him who had wrought and fashioned that very calamity which they were now seeking to avert by all these precautions, and by whom it had been projected long, long before the actual realization. עֹשֶׂיהָ might be a plural, according to ch. liv. 5; but the parallel יֹצְרָהּ favours the singular (on the form itself, from עָשִׂי = עֹשֶׂה, see ch. xlii. 5, and at ch. v. 12, i. 30). We have here, and at ch. xxxvii. 26, *i.e.* within the first part of the book of Isaiah, the same doctrine of "ideas" that forms so universal a key-note of the second part, the authenticity of which has been denied. That which is realized in time has existed long before as a spiritual pattern, *i.e.* as an idea in God. God shows this to His prophets; and so far as prophecy foretells the future, whenever the event predicted is fulfilled, the prophecy becomes a proof that the event is the work of God, and was long ago the predetermined counsel of God. The whole of the Scripture presupposes this pre-existence of the divine idea before the historical realization, and Isaiah in Israel (like Plato in the heathen world) was the assiduous interpreter of this supposition. Thus, in the case before us, the fate of Jerusalem is said to have been fashioned "long ago" in God. But Jerusalem might have averted its realization, for it was no *decretum absolutum*. If Jerusalem repented, the realization would be arrested.

And so far as it had proceeded already, it was a call from Jehovah to repentance. Vers. 12–14. "*The Lord, Jehovah of hosts, calls in that day to weeping, and to mourning, and to the pulling out of hair, and to girding with sackcloth; and behold joy and gladness, slaughtering of oxen and killing of sheep, eating of flesh and drinking of wine, eating and drinking, for 'to-morrow we die.' And Jehovah of hosts hath revealed in mine ears, Surely this iniquity shall not be expiated for you until ye die, saith the Lord, Jehovah of hosts.*" The first condition of repentance is a feeling of pain produced by the punishments of God. But upon Jerusalem they produce the opposite effect. The more threatening the future, the more insensibly and madly do they give themselves up to the rude, sensual enjoyment of the present. *Shâthoth* is interchanged with *shâthŏ* (which is only another form of שָׁתֹה, as in ch. vi. 9, xxx. 19), to ring with *shâchōt* (compare Hos. x. 4). There are other passages in which we meet with unusual forms introduced for the sake of the play upon the words (*vid.* ch. iv. 6, viii. 6, xvi. 9, and compare Ezek. xliii. 11, and the *keri* of 2 Sam. iii. 25). The words of the rioters themselves, whose conduct is sketched by the *inf. abs.*, which are all governed by *hinnēh*, are simply "for to-morrow we shall die." This does not imply that they feel any pleasure in the thought of death, but indicates a love of life which scoffs at death. Then the unalterable will of the all-commanding God is audibly and distinctly revealed to the prophet. Such scoffing as this, which defies the chastisements of God, will not be expiated in any other way than by the death of the scoffer (*cuppar*, from *câphar, tegere*, means to be covered over, *i.e.* expiated). This is done in the case of sin either by the justice of God, as in the present instance, or by the mercy of God (ch. vi. 7), or by both justice and mercy combined (as in ch. xxvii. 9). In all three cases the expiation is demanded by the divine holiness, which requires a covering between itself and sin, by which sin becomes as though it were not. In this instance the expunging act consists in punishment. The sin of Jerusalem is expiated by the giving up of the sinners themselves to death. The verb *temūthūn* (ye shall die) is written absolutely, and therefore is all the more dreadful. The Targum renders it " till ye die the second (eternal) death" (*mōthâh thinyânâh*).

So far as this prophecy threatened the destruction of Jerusalem by Assyria, it was never actually fulfilled; but the very opposite occurred. Asshur itself met with destruction in front of Jerusalem. But this was by no means opposed to the prophecy; and it was with this conviction that Isaiah, nevertheless, included the prophecy in the collection which he made at a time when the non-fulfilment was perfectly apparent. It stands here in a double capacity. In the first place, it is a memorial of the mercy of God, which withdraws, or at all events modifies, the threatened judgment as soon as repentance intervenes. The falling away from Assyria did take place; but on the part of Hezekiah and many others, who had taken to heart the prophet's announcement, it did so simply as an affair that was surrendered into the hands of the God of Israel, through distrust of either their own strength or Egyptian assistance. Hezekiah carried out the measures of defence described by the prophet; but he did this for the good of Jerusalem, and with totally different feelings from those which the prophet had condemned. These measures of defence probably included the reservoir between the two walls, which the chronicler does not mention till the close of the history of his reign, inasmuch as he follows the thread of the book of Kings, to which his book stands, as it were, in the relation of a commentary, like the *midrash*, from which extracts are made. The king regulated his actions carefully by the prophecy, inasmuch as after the threats had produced repentance, vers. 8-11 still remained as good and wise counsels. In the second place, the oracle stands here as the proclamation of a judgment deferred but not repealed. Even if the danger of destruction which threatened Jerusalem on the part of Assyria had been mercifully caused to pass away, the threatening word of Jehovah had not fallen to the ground. The counsel of God contained in the word of prophecy still remained; and as it was the counsel of the Omniscient, the time would surely come when it would pass out of the sphere of ideality into that of actual fact. It remained hovering over Jerusalem like an eagle, and Jerusalem would eventually become its carrion. We have only to compare the *temŭthŭn* of this passage with the ἀποθανεῖσθε of John viii. 21, to see when the eventual fulfilment took place. Thus the "*massa* of the valley of vision" became a memorial of mercy to Israel when it looked back to its past history; but when it looked into the future, it was still a mirror of wrath.

AGAINST SHEBNA THE STEWARD.—CHAP. XXII. 15–25.

(APPENDIX TO THE TETRALOGY IN CHAP. XXI.–XXII. 14.)

Shebna (שֶׁבְנָא; 2 Kings xviii. 18, 26, שֶׁבְנָה) is officially described as "*over the house*." This was the name given to an office of state of great importance in both kingdoms (1 Kings iv. 6, xviii. 3), in fact the highest office of all, and one so vastly superior to all others (ch. xxxvi. 3, xxxvii. 2), that it was sometimes filled by the heir to the throne (2 Chron. xxvi. 21). It was the post of minister of the household, and resembled the Merovingian office of *major domus* (*maire du palais*). The person "who was over the house" had the whole of the domestic affairs of the sovereign under his superintendence, and was therefore also called the *socēn* or administrator (from *sâcan*, related to *shâcan*, to assist in a friendly, neighbourly manner, or to be generally serviceable: see on Job xxii. 2), as standing nearest to the king. In this post of eminence Shebna had helped to support that proud spirit of self-security and self-indulgent forgetfulness of God, for which the people of Jerusalem had in the foregoing oracle been threatened with death. At the same time, he may also have been a leader of the Egyptian party of magnates, and with this anti-theocratical policy may have been the opponent of Isaiah in advising the king. Hence the general character of ch. xxii. 1–14 now changes into a distinct and special prophecy against this Shebna. The time at which it was fulfilled was the same as that referred to in ch. xxii. 1–14. There was still deep peace, and the great minister of state was driving about with splendid equipages, and engaged in superintending the erection of a family sepulchre. Vers. 15–19. *"Thus spake the Lord, Jehovah of hosts, Go, get thee to that steward there, to Shebna the house-mayor. What hast thou here, and whom hast thou here, that thou hast hewn thyself out a sepulchre here, hewing out his sepulchre high up, digging himself a dwelling in rocks? Behold, Jehovah hurleth thee, hurling with a man's throw, and graspeth thee grasping. Coiling, He coileth thee a coil, a ball into a land far and wide; there shalt thou die, and thither the chariots of thy glory, thou shame of the house of thy lord! And I thrust thee from thy post, and from thy standing-place he pulleth thee down."* לֶךְ־בֹּא, go, take thyself in,—not into the house, however, but into the present halting-place. It is possible, at the same time, that the expression may simply mean "take thyself away," as in Gen. xlv. 17 and Ezek. iii. 4. The preposition אֶל is interchanged with עַל, which more commonly denotes the coming of a stronger man upon a weaker one (1 Sam. xii. 12), and is here used to designate the overwhelming power of the prophet's word. *"That steward there:"* this expression points contemptuously to the position of the minister of the court as one which, however high, was a subordinate one after all. We feel at once, as we read this introduction to the divine address, that insatiable ambition was one of the leading traits in Shebna's character. What Isaiah is to say to Shebna follows somewhat abruptly. The words "and say to him," which are added in the Septuagint, naturally suggest themselves. The question, What hast thou to do here, and whom hast thou to bury here? is put with a glance at Shebna's approaching fate. This building of a sepulchre was quite unnecessary; Shebna himself would never lie there, nor would he be able to bury his relations there. The threefold repetition of the word "here" (*poh*) is of very incisive force: it is not here that he will stay,—here, where he is even now placing himself on a bier, as if it were his home. The participles חֹצְבִי and חֹקְקִי (with *chirek compaginis*: see on Ps. cxiii.) are also part of the address. The third person which is introduced here is syntactically regular, although the second person is used as well (ch. xxiii. 2, 3; Hab. ii. 15). Rock-tombs, *i.e.* a collection of tombs in the form of chambers in the rocks, were indeed to be found to the east of Jerusalem, on the western slope of the Mount of Olives, and in the wall of rock to the west of Jerusalem; but the word *mârom* ("high up"), in connection with the threefold "here" (*poh*), and the contemptuous "that administrator there," warrants us in assuming that *mârom* refers to "the height of the sepulchres of the sons of David" (2 Chron. xxxii. 33), *i.e.* the eastern slope of Zion, where the tombs of the kings were excavated in the rocks. So high did Shebna stand, and so great did he think himself, that he hoped after his death to rest among kings, and by no means down at the bottom. But how he deceived himself! Jehovah would hurl him far away (*tûl*, to be long; *pilpel*, to throw or stretch out to a distance[1]), טַלְטֵלָה גָּבֶר. This is either equivalent to טַלְטֵלָה טַלְטֵלַת גָּבֶר, with a man's throw (Rosenmüller), or גָּבֶר is in apposition to *Jehovah* (Gesenius and Knobel). As *taltêlah* stands too baldly if the latter be adopted, for which reason the vocative rendering "O man," which is found in the Syriac, does not commend itself, and as such an elliptical combination of the absolute with the genitive is by no means unusual (*e.g.* Prov. xxii. 21, Jer. x. 10), we give the preference to the former. Jerome's rendering, "as they carry off a cock," which he obtained from the mouth of his *Hebræus*, cannot be taken into consideration at all; although it has been retained by Schegg (see Geiger, *Lesestücke aus der Mischna*, p. 106). The verb עָטָה does not give a suitable sense as used in Jer. xliii. 12, where it merely signifies to cover one's self, not to wrap up; nor can we obtain one from 1 Sam. xv. 19, xxv. 14, xiv. 32, since the verbal forms which we find there, and which are to be traced to עִיט (from which comes עַיִט, a bird of prey), and not to עטה, signify "to rush upon anything" (when construed with either בְּ or אֶל). It is better, therefore, to take it, as Michaelis, Rosenmüller, Knobel, and others do, in the sense of grasping or laying hold of. On the other hand, *tzânaph*, which is applied in other instances to the twisting of a turban, also

---

[1] In the later form of the language, this verbal stem signifies generally to move onward; hence *tiyyûl*, motion, or a walk, and *metaltelin*, furniture, *i.e.* moveable goods.

signifies to wrap up, make up into a bundle, or coil up. And *caddūr*, like *tzenēphâh*, signifies that into which Shebna would be coiled up; for the *Caph* is not to be taken in a comparative sense, since the use of *caddūr* in the sense of *globus* or *sphæra* is established by the Talmud (see at Job xv. 24), whereas the Arabic *daur* only means *gyrus, periodus*. Shebna is made into a round coil, or ball, which is hurled into a land stretching out on both sides, *i.e.* over the broad surface of Mesopotamia, where he flies on farther and farther, without meeting with any obstacle whatever.[1] He comes thither to die—he who, by his exaggeration and abuse of his position, has not only dishonoured his office, but the Davidic court as well; and thither do his state carriages also come. There can be no doubt that it was by the positive command of Jehovah that Isaiah apostrophized the proud and wealthy Shebna with such boldness and freedom as this. And such freedom was tolerated too. The murder or incarceration of a prophet was a thing of rare occurrence in the kingdom of Judah before the time of Manasseh. In order to pave the way for the institution of another in Shebna's office, the punishment of deposition, which cannot be understood in any other way than as preceding the punishment of banishment, is placed at the close of the first half of the prophecy. The subject in ver. 19*b* is not the king, as Luzzatto supposes, but *Jehovah*, as in ver. 19*a* (compare ch. x. 12).

Jehovah first of all gives him the blow which makes him tremble in his post, and then pulls him completely down from this his lofty station,[2] in order that another worthier man may take his place. Vers. 20–24. *"And it will come to pass in that day, that I call to my servant Eliakim the son of Hilkiah, and invest him with thy coat, and I throw thy sash firmly round him, and place thy government in his hand; and he will become a*

---

[1] Compare the old saying, "The heart of man is an apple driven by a tempest over an open plain."

[2] וּמִמַּעֲמָדְךָ has not only the *metheg* required by the *kametz* on account of the long vowel, and the *metheg* required by the *patach* on account of the following *chateph patach* (the latter of which also takes the place of the *metheg*, as the sign of a subordinate tone), but also a third *metheg* with the *chirek*, which only assists the emphatic pronunciation of the preposition, but which would not stand there at all unless the word had had a disjunctive accent (compare ch. lv. 9, Ps. xviii. 45, Hos. xi. 6).

VOL. I. 2 C

father to the inhabitants of Jerusalem and to the house of Judah. And I place the key of David upon his shoulder: and when he opens, no man shuts; and when he shuts, no man opens. And I fasten him as a plug in a fast place, and he becomes the seat of honour to his father's house. And the whole mass of his father's house hangs upon him, the offshoots and side-shoots, every small vessel, from the vessel of the basins even to every vessel of the pitchers." Eliakim is called the "servant of Jehovah," as one who was already a servant of God in his heart and conduct; the official service is added for the first time here. This title of honour generally embraces both kinds of service (ch. xx. 3). It is quite in accordance with oriental custom, that this transfer of the office is effected by means of investiture (compare 1 Kings xix. 19): *chizzēk*, with a double accusative, viz. that of the person and that of the official girdle, is used here according to its radical signification, in the sense of girding tightly or girding round, putting the girdle round him so as to cause the whole dress to sit firmly, without hanging loose. The word *memshalteká* (thy government) shows how very closely the office forfeited by Shebna was connected with that of the king. This is also proved by the word "father," which is applied in other cases to the king as the father of the land (ch. ix. 5). The "key" signifies the power of the keys; and for this reason it is not given into Eliakim's hand, but placed upon his shoulder (ch. ix. 5). This key was properly handled by the king (Rev. iii. 7), and therefore by the "house-mayor" only in his stead. The power of the keys consisted not only in the supervision of the royal chambers, but also in the decision who was and who was not to be received into the king's service. There is a resemblance, therefore, to the giving of the keys of the kingdom of heaven to Peter under the New Testament. But there the "binding" and "loosing" introduce another figure, though one similar in sense; whereas here, in the "opening" and "shutting," the figure of the key is retained. The comparison of the institution of Eliakim in his office to the fastening of a tent-peg was all the more natural, that *yâthēd* was also used as a general designation for national rulers (Zech. x. 4), who stand in the same relation to the commonwealth as a tent-peg to the tent which it holds firmly and keeps upright. As the tent-peg is rammed into the ground, so that a person could easily sit upon it, the figure is changed, and the tent-peg becomes a seat of honour. As a splendid chair is an ornament to a room, so Eliakim would be an honour to his hitherto undistinguished family. The thought that naturally suggests itself —namely, that the members of the family would sit upon this chair, for the purpose of raising themselves to honour—is expressed by a different figure. Eliakim is once more depicted as a *yâthēd*, but it is as a still higher one this time,—namely, as the rod of a wardrobe, or a peg driven high up into the wall. Upon this rod or peg they hang (*thâlu, i.e.* one hangs, or there hangs) all the *câbōd* of the house of Eliakim, *i.e.* not every one who wished to be honoured and attained to honour in this way (cf. ch. v. 13), but the whole weight of his family (as in ch. viii. 7). This family is then subdivided into its separate parts, and, as we may infer from the juxtaposition of the masculine and feminine nouns, according to its male and female constituents. In צֶאֱצָאִים (offshoots) and צְפִעוֹת ("side-shoots," from יָצָע, to push out; compare יְפִיעַ, dung, with צֵאָה, mire) there is contained the idea of a widely ramifying and undistinguished family connection. The numerous rabble consisted of nothing but vessels of a small kind (*hakkâtân*), at the best of basons (*aggânoth*) like those used by the priests for the blood (Ex. xxiv. 6), or in the house for mixing wine (Song of Sol. vii. 3; Aram. *aggono*, Ar. *iggâne, ingâne*, a washing bason), but chiefly of *nebâlim*, *i.e.* leather bottles or earthenware pitchers (ch. xxx. 14). The whole of this large but hitherto ignoble family of relations would fasten upon Eliakim, and climb through him to honour. Thus all at once the prophecy, which seemed so full of promise to Eliakim, assumes a satirical tone. We get an impression of the favouring of nephews and cousins, and cannot help asking how this could be a suitable prophecy for Shebna to hear.

We will refer to this again. But in the meantime the impression is an irresistible one; and the Targum, Jerome, Hitzig, and others, are therefore right in assuming that Eliakim is the peg which, however glorious its beginning may have been, comes at last to the shameful end described in ver. 25: "*In that day, saith Jehovah of hosts, will the peg that is fastened in a sure place be removed, and be cast down, and fall; and the burden that it bore falls to the ground: for Jehovah hath spoken.*" The prophet could not express in clearer terms the identity of the peg threatened here with Eliakim himself; for how is it conceivable that the prophet could turn all that he has predicated of Eliakim in vers. 23, 24 into predicates of Shebna? What Umbreit says—namely, that common sense must refer ver. 25 to Shebna—is the very reverse of correct. Eliakim himself is also brought down at last by the greatness of his power, on account of the nepotism to which he has given way. His family makes a wrong use of him; and he is more yielding than he ought to be, and makes a wrong use of his office to favour them! He therefore falls, and brings down with him all that hung upon the peg, *i.e.* all his relations, who have brought him to ruin through the rapacity with which they have grasped at prosperity.

Hitzig maintains that vers. 24, 25 form a later addition. But it is much better to assume that the prophet wrote down ch. xxii. 15-25 at one sitting, after the predicted fate of the two great ministers of state, which had been revealed to him at two different times, had been actually fulfilled. We know nothing more about them than this, that in the fourteenth year of Hezekiah it was not Shebna, but Eliakim, " who was over the house " (ch. xxxvi. 3, 22, xxxvii. 2). But Shebna also filled another office of importance, namely that of *sôpher*. Was he really taken prisoner and carried away (a thing which is perfectly conceivable even without an Assyrian captivity of the nation generally)? Or did he anticipate the threatened judgment, and avert it by a penitential self-abasement? To this and other questions we can give no reply. One thing alone is certain,—namely, that the threefold prediction of Shebna's fall, of Eliakim's elevation, and of Eliakim's fall, would not stand where it does, if there were any reason whatever to be ashamed of comparing the prophecy with its fulfilment.

THE ORACLE CONCERNING TYRE.—CHAP. XXIII.

(CONCLUSION OF THE CYCLE OF PROPHECIES RELATING TO THE HEATHEN.)

The second leading type of the pride of heathen power closes the series of prophecies against the nations, as Stier correctly observes, just as Babylon opened it. Babylon was the city of the imperial power of the world; Tyre, the city of the commerce of the world. The former was the centre of the greatest land power; the latter of the greatest maritime power. The former subjugated the nations with an iron arm, and ensured its rule by means of deportation; the latter obtained possession of the treasures of the nations in as peaceable a manner as possible, and secured its advantages by colonies and factories. The Phœnician cities formed at first six or eight independent states, the government of which was in the hands of kings. Of these, Sidon was much older than Tyre. The *thorah* and Homer mention only the former. Tyre did not rise into notoriety till after the time of David. But in the Assyrian era Tyre had gained a kind of supremacy over the rest of the Phœnician states. It stood by the sea, five miles from Sidon; but when hard pressed by enemies it had transferred the true seat of its trade and wealth to a small island, which was three-quarters of a mile farther to the north, and only twelve hundred paces from the mainland. The strait which separated this insular Tyre (Tyrus) from ancient Tyre (*Palætyrus*) was mostly shallow, and its navigable waters near the island had only a draught of about eighteen feet, so that on one or two occasions a siege of insular Tyre was effected by throwing up an embankment of earth,—namely, once by Alexander (the embankment still in existence), and once possibly by Nebuchadnezzar, for Tyre was engaged in conflict with the Chaldean empire as well as the Assyrian. Now which of these two conflicts was it that the prophet had in his mind? Eichhorn, Rosenmüller, Hitzig, and Movers say the Chaldean, and seek in this way to establish the spuriousness of the passage; whereas Gesenius, Maurer, Umbreit, and Knobel say the Assyrian, thinking that this is the only way of sustaining its genuineness. Ewald and Meier say the same; but they pronounce vers. 15–18 an interpolation belonging to the Persian era. De Wette wavers between the genuineness and spuriousness of the whole. In our opinion, however, as in that of Vitringa and those who tread in his footsteps, the question whether the imperial power by which Tyre was threatened was the Assyrian or the Chaldean, is a purely exegetical question, not a critical one.

The prophecy commences by introducing the trading vessels of Phœnicia on their return home, as they hear with alarm the tidings of the fate that has befallen their home. Ver. 1. *"Howl, ye ships of Tarshish; for it is laid waste, so that there is no house, no entrance any more! Out of the land of the Chittæans it is made known to them."* Even upon the open sea they hear of it as a rumour from the ships that they meet. For their voyage is a very long one: they come from the Phœnician colony on the Spanish Bætis, or the Guadalquivir, as it was called from the time of the occupation by the Moors. *"Ships of Tarshish"* are ships that sail to Tartessus (LXX. inaccurately, πλοῖα Καρχηδόνος). It is not improbable that the whole of the Mediterranean may have been called "the sea of Tarshish;" and hence the rendering adopted by the Targum, Jerome, Luther, and others, *naves maris* (see Humboldt, *Kosmos*, ii. 167, 415). These ships are to howl (*hēlīlū* instead of the feminine, as in ch. xxxii. 11) because of the devastation that has taken place (it is easy to surmise that Tyre has been the victim); for the home and harbour, which the sailors were rejoicing at the prospect of being able to enter once more, have both been swept away. Cyprus was the last station on this homeward passage. The *Chittim* (written in the legends of coins and other inscriptions with *Caph* and *Cheth*) are the inhabitants of the Cyprian harbour of *Citium* and its territory. But Epiphanius, the bishop of Salamis in the island of Cyprus, says that Citium was also used as a name for the whole island, or even in a still broader sense. Cyprus, the principal mart of the Phœnicians, was the last landing-place. As soon as they touch the island, the fact which they have only heard of as a rumour upon the open sea, is fully disclosed (*niglâh*), *i.e.* it now becomes a clear undoubted certainty, for they are told of it by eye-witnesses who have made their escape to the island. The prophet now turns to the Phœnicians at home, who have this devastation in prospect.—Vers. 2, 3. *"Be alarmed, ye inhabitants of the coast! Sidonian merchants, sailing over the sea, filled thee once. And the sowing of Sichor came upon great waters, the harvest of the Nile, her store; and she became gain for nations."* The suffixes of מַלְאֲךָ (to fill with wares and riches) and תְּבוּאָה (the bringing in, viz. into barns and granaries) refer to the word אִי, which is used here as a feminine for the name of a country, and denotes the Phœnician coast, including the insular Tyre. *"Sidonian merchants"* are the Phœnicians generally, as in Homer; for the "great Sidon" of antiquity (*Zidon rabbâh*, Josh. xi. 8, xix. 28) was the mother-city of Phœnicia, which so thoroughly stamped its name upon the whole nation, that Tyre is called אם צדנם upon Phœnician coins. The meaning of ver. 3*a* is not that the revenue of Tyre which accrued to it on the great unfruitful sea, was like a Nile-sowing, or an Egyptian harvest (Hitzig, Knobel). Such a simile would be a very beautiful one, but it is a very unlikely one, since the Phœnicians actually did buy up the corn-stores of Egypt, that granary of the ancient world, and housed the cargoes that were brought to them "upon great waters," *i.e.* on the great Mediterranean. *Sichor* is a Hebraic form of *Siris* (the native name of the upper Nile, according to Dionysius Perieg. and Pliny). It signifies the black river (*Melas*, Eust. on Dion. Per. 222), the black slime of which gave such fertility to the land. "*The harvest of the Nile*" is not so much an explanation as an amplification. The valley of the Nile was the field for sowing and reaping, and the Phœnician coast was the barn for this valuable corn; and inasmuch as corn and other articles of trade were purchased and bartered there, it thereby became gain (constr. of *sachar*, Ewald, 213, *a*, used in the same sense as in ver. 18, ch. xlv. 14, and Prov. iii. 14), *i.e.* the means of gain, the source of profit or provision, to whole nations, and even to many such. Others render the word "emporium;" but *sâchâr* cannot have this meaning. Moreover, foreigners did not come to Phœnicia, but the Phœnicians went to them (Luzzatto).

The address to the whole of the coast-land now passes into an address to the ancestral city. Ver. 4. "*Shudder, O Sidon; for the sea speaketh, the fortress of the sea, thus: I have not travailed, nor given birth, nor trained up young men, brought up maidens.*" The sea, or more closely considered, the fortress of the sea, *i.e.* the rock-island on which Neo-tyrus stood with its strong and lofty houses, lifts up its voice in lamentation. Sidon, the ancestress of Canaan, must hear with overwhelming shame how Tyre mourns the loss of her daughters, and complains that, robbed as she has been of her children, she is like a barren woman. For the war to have murdered her young men and maidens, was exactly the same as if she had never given birth to them or brought them up. Who is there that does not recognise in this the language of

Isaiah (compare ch. i. 2)?—Even in Egypt the fate of Phœnicia produces alarm. Ver. 5. "*When the report cometh to Egypt, they tremble at the report from Tzor.*" In the protasis (ver. 5a) *l'mitzraim* (to Egypt) the verb "cometh" is implied; the *Caph* in ver. 5b signifies simultaneousness, as in ch. xviii. 4 and xxx. 19 (Ges. *Thes.* p. 650). The news of the fall of Tyre spreads universal terror in Egypt, because its own prosperity depended upon Tyre, which was the great market for its corn; and when such a bulwark had fallen, a similar fate awaited itself.

The inhabitants of Tyre, who desired to escape from death or transportation, are obliged to take refuge in the colonies, and the farther off the better: not in Cyprus, not in Carthage (as at the time when Alexander attacked the insular Tyre), but in Tartessus itself, the farthest off towards the west, and the hardest to reach. Vers. 6–9. "*Pass ye over to Tarshish; howl, ye inhabitants of the coast! Is this your fate, thou full of rejoicing, whose origin is from the days of the olden time, whom her feet carried far away to settle? Who hath determined such a thing concerning Tzor, the distributor of crowns, whose merchants are princes, whose traders are the chief men of the earth? Jehovah of hosts hath determined it, to desecrate the pomp of every kind of ornament, to dishonour the chief men of the earth, all of them.*" The exclamation "howl ye" (*hēlilu*) implies their right to give themselves up to their pain. In other cases complaint is unmanly, but here it is justifiable (compare ch. xv. 4). In ver. 7a the question arises, whether '*allizâh* is a nominative predicate, as is generally assumed ("Is this, this deserted heap of ruins, your formerly rejoicing city?"), or a vocative. We prefer the latter, because there is nothing astonishing in the omission of the article in this case (ch. xxii. 2; Ewald, 327, *a*); whereas in the former case, although it is certainly admissible (see ch. xxxii. 13), it is very harsh (compare ch. xiv. 16), and the whole expression a very doubtful one to convey the sense of הזאת קריה עליזה אשר לכם. To '*allizâh* there is attached the descriptive, attributive clause: whose origin (*kadmâh*, Ezek. xvi. 55) dates from the days of the olden time; and then a second "whose feet brought her far away (*raglaim* construed as a masculine, as in Jer. xiii. 16, for example) to dwell in a foreign land. This is generally understood as signifying transportation by force into an enemy's country. But Luzzatto very properly objects to this, partly on the ground that יֹבִלוּהָ רַגְלֶיהָ (her feet carried her) is the strongest expression that can be used for voluntary emigration, to which *lâgūr* (to settle) also corresponds; and partly because we miss the antithetical עַתָּה, which we should expect with this interpretation. The reference is to the trading journeys which extended "far away" (whether by land or sea), and to the colonies, *i.e.* the settlements founded in those distant places, that leading characteristic of the Tyro-Phœnician people (this is expressed in the imperfect by *yobiluâh, quam portabant; gūr* is the most appropriate word to apply to such settlements: for *mērâchōk*, see at ch. xvii. 13). Sidon was no doubt older than Tyre, but Tyre was also of primeval antiquity. Strabo speaks of it as the oldest Phœnician city "after Sidon;" Curtius calls it *vetustate originis insignis*; and Josephus reckons the time from the founding of Tyre to the building of Solomon's temple as 240 years (*Ant.* viii. 3, 1; compare Herod. ii. 44). Tyre is called *hamma'atirâh*, not as wearing a crown (*Vulg. quondam coronata*), but as a distributor of crowns (Targum). Either would be suitable as a matter of fact; but the latter answers better to the *hiphil* (as *hikrīn, hiphrīs*, which are expressive of results produced from within outwards, can hardly be brought into comparison). Such colonies as Citium, Tartessus, and at first Carthage, were governed by kings appointed by the mother city, and dependent upon her. Her merchants were princes (compare ch. x. 8), the most honoured of the earth; נִכְבַּדֵּי acquires a superlative meaning from the genitive connection (Ges. § 119, 2). From the fact that the Phœnicians had the commerce of the world in their hands, a merchant was called *cena'ani* or *cena'an* (Hos. xii. 8; from the latter, not from *cin'âni*, the plural *cin'ānim* which we find here is formed), and the merchandise *cin'âh*. The verb *chillēl*, to desecrate or profane, in connection with the "pomp of every kind of ornament," leads us to think more especially of the holy places of both insular and continental Tyre, among which the temple of Melkarth in the new city of the former was the most prominent (according to Arrian, *Anab.* ii. 16, παλαιότατον ὧν μνήμη ἀνθρωπίνη διασώζεται). These glories, which were thought so inviolable, Jehovah will profane. "*To dishonour the chief men:*" *l'hâkēl* (*ad ignominiam deducere*, Vulg.) as in ch. viii. 23.

The consequence of the fall of Tyre is, that the colonies achieve their independence, Tartessus being mentioned by way of example. Ver. 10. "*Overflow thy land like the Nile, O daughter of Tarshish! No girdle restrains thee any longer.*" The girdle (*mēzach*) is the supremacy of Tyre, which has hitherto restrained all independent action on the part of the colony. Now they no longer need to wait in the harbour for the ships of the mother city, no longer to dig in the mines as her tributaries for silver and other metals. The colonial territory is their own freehold now, and they can spread themselves over it like the Nile when it passes beyond its banks and overflows the land. Koppe has already given this as the meaning of ver. 10.

The prophet now proceeds to relate, as it were, to the Phœnicio-Spanish colony, the daughter, *i.e.* the population of Tartessus, what has happened to the mother country. Vers. 11, 12. "*His hand hath He stretched over the sea, thrown kingdoms into trembling; Jehovah hath given commandment concerning Kena'an, to destroy her fortresses. And He said, Thou shalt not rejoice any further, thou disgraced one, virgin daughter of Sidon! Get up to Kittim, go over; there also shalt thou not find rest.*" There is no ground whatever for restricting the "kingdoms" (*mamlâcoth*) to the several small Phœnician states (compare ch. xix. 2). Jehovah, reaching over the sea, has thrown the lands of Hither Asia and Egypto-Ethiopia into a state of the most anxious excitement, and has summoned them as instruments of destruction with regard to Kena'an (אֶל, like עַל in Esther iv. 5). Phœnicia called itself *Kena'an* (Canaan); but this is the only passage in the Old Testament in which the name occurs in this most restricted sense. לִשְׁמִיר, for לְהַשְׁמִיד, as in Num. v. 22, Amos viii. 4. The form מְעֻזֵּנֶיהָ is more rare, but it is not a deformity, as Knobel and others maintain. There are other examples of the same resolution of the reduplication and transposition of the letters (it stands for מְעֻזֶּנֶּיהָ, possibly a Phœnician word; see Hitzig, *Grabschrift*, p. 16, and Levi, *Phœnizische Studien*, p. 17), viz. תָּמְנוּ in Lam. iii. 22 (*vid.* at Ps. lxiv. 7), and קָבְנוֹ in Num. xxiii. 13, at least according to the Jewish grammar (see, however, Ewald, § 250, *b*).[1] "*Virgin*

---

[1] Böttcher derives the form from מָעוֹן, a supposed diminutive; see, however, *Jesurun*, pp. 212–216.

of the daughter of Sidon" (equivalent to "virgin daughter of Sidon," two epexegetical genitives; Ewald, § 289, *c*) is synonymous with *Kena'an*. The name of the ancestral city (compare ch. xxxvii. 22) has here become the name of the whole nation that has sprung from it. Hitherto this nation has been untouched, like a virgin, but now it resembles one ravished and defiled. If now they flee across to Cyprus (*cittiyim* or *cittim*), there will be no rest for them even there, because the colony, emancipated from the Phœnician yoke, will only be too glad to rid herself of the unwelcome guests from the despotic mother country.

The prophet now proceeds to describe the fate of Phœnicia. Vers. 13, 14. "*Behold the Chaldean land: this people that has not been (Asshur—it hath prepared the same for desert beasts)— they set up their siege-towers, destroy the palaces of Kena'an, make it a heap of ruins. Mourn, ye ships of Tarshish: for your fortress is laid waste.*" The general meaning of ver. 13, as the text now runs, is that the Chaldeans have destroyed Kena'an, and in fact Tyre. הֵקִימוּ (they set up) points to the plural idea of "this people," and בַּחוּנָיו (*chethib* בַּחִינָיו) to the singular idea of the same; on the other hand, the feminine suffixes relate to Tyre, "They (the Chaldeans) have laid bare the palaces (*'armenoth*, from *'armoneth*) of Tyre," *i.e.* have thrown them down, or burned them down to their very foundations (עֹרֵר, from עָרַר = עָרָה, Ps. cxxxvii. 7, like עָרְעֵר in Jer. li. 58); it (the Chaldean people) has made her (Tyre) a heap of rubbish. So far the text is clear, and there is no ground for hesitation. But the question arises, whether in the words אַשּׁוּר יְסָדָהּ לְצִיִּים Asshur is the subject or the object. In the former case the prophet points to the land of the Chaldeans, for the purpose of describing the instruments of divine wrath; and having called them "a nation which has not been" (לֹא הָיָה), explains this by saying that Asshur first founded the land which the Chaldeans now inhabit for them, *i.e.* wild hordes (Ps. lxxii. 9); or better still (as *tziyyim* can hardly signify mountain hordes), that Asshur has made it (this nation, עַם fem., as in Jer. viii. 5, Ex. v. 16) into dwellers in steppes (Knobel), which could not be conceived of in any other way than that Asshur settled the Chaldeans, who inhabited the northern mountains, in the present so-called land of Chaldea, and thus made the Chaldeans into a people, *i.e.* a settled, cultivated people, and a people bent on conquest and taking part in the history of the world (according to Knobel, primarily as a component part of the Assyrian army). But this view, which we meet with even in Calvin, is exposed to a grave difficulty. It is by no means improbable, indeed, that the Chaldeans, who were descendants of Nahor, according to Gen. xxii. 22, and therefore of Semitic descent,[1] came down from the mountains which bound Armenia, Media, and Assyria, having been forced out by the primitive migration of the Arians from west to east; although the more modern hypothesis, which represents them as a people of Tatar descent, and as mixing among the Shemites of the countries of the Euphrates and Tigris, has no historical support whatever, the very reverse being the case, according to Gen. x., since Babylon was of non-Semitic or Cushite origin, and therefore the land of Chaldea, as only a portion of Babylonia (Strabo, xvi. 1, 6), was the land of the Shemites. But the idea that the Assyrians brought them down from the mountains into the lowlands, though not under Ninus and Semiramis,[2] as Vitringa supposes, but about the time of Shalmanassar (Ges., Hitzig, Knobel, and others),[3] is pure imagination, and merely an inference drawn from this passage. For this reason I have tried to give a different interpretation to the clause אַשּׁוּר יְסָדָהּ לְצִיִּים in my *Com. on Habakkuk* (p. 22), viz. "Asshur—it has assigned the same to the beasts of the desert." That *Asshur* may be used not only pre-eminently, but directly, for *Nineveh* (like *Kena'an* for *Tzor*), admits of no dispute, since even at the present day the ruins are called الأثور, and this is probably a name applied to Nineveh in the arrow-headed writings also (Layard, *Nineveh and its*

---

[1] *Arpachshad* (Gen. x. 22), probably the ancestor of the oldest Chaldeans, was also Semitic, whether his name is equivalent to *Armachshad* (the Chaldean high-land) or not. *Arrapachitis* rings like *Albagh*, the name of the table-land between the lake of Urmia and that of Van, according to which *shad* was the common Armenian termination for names of places.

[2] The same view is held by Oppert, though he regards the *Casdim* as the primitive Turanian (Tatar) inhabitants of Shinar, and supposes this passage to relate to their subjugation by the Semitic Assyrians.

[3] For an impartial examination of this migration or transplantation hypothesis, which is intimately connected with the Scythian hypothesis, see M. v. Niebuhr's *Geschichte Assurs und Babels seit Phul* (1857, pp. 152-154). Rawlinson (*Monarchies*, i. 71-74) decidedly rejects the latter as at variance with the testimonies of Scripture, of Berosus, and of the monuments.

Remains). The word *tziyyim* is commonly applied to beasts of the wilderness (*e.g.* ch. xiii. 21), and יָסַד לְצִיִּים for שָׂם צִיָּה (used of Nineveh in Zeph. ii. 13, 14) may be explained in accordance with Ps. civ. 8. The form of the parenthetical clause, however, would be like that of the concluding clause of Amos i. 11. But what makes me distrustful even of this view is not a doctrinal ground (Winer, *Real Wörterbuch*, i. 218), but one taken from Isaiah's own prophecy. Isaiah undoubtedly sees a Chaldean empire behind the Assyrian; but this would be the only passage in which he prophesied (and that quite by the way) how the imperial power would pass from the latter to the former. It was the task of Nahum and Zephaniah to draw this connecting line. It is true that this argument is not sufficient to outweigh the objections that can be brought against the other view, which makes the text declare a fact that is never mentioned anywhere else; but it is important nevertheless. For this reason it is possible, indeed, that Ewald's conjecture is a right one, and that the original reading of the text was הֵן אֶרֶץ כְּנַעֲנִים. Read in this manner, the first clause runs thus: "Behold the land of the Canaaneans: this people has come to nothing; Asshur has prepared it (their land) for the beasts of the desert." It is true that לֹא הָיָה generally means not to exist, or not to have been (Ob. 16); but there are also cases in which לֹא is used as a kind of substantive (cf. Jer. xxxiii. 25), and the words mean to become or to have become nothing (Job vi. 21, Ezek. xxi. 32, and possibly also Isa. xv. 6). Such an alteration of the text is not favoured, indeed, by any of the ancient versions. For our own part, we still abide by the explanation we have given in the *Commentary on Habakkuk*, not so much for this reason, as because the seventy years mentioned afterwards are a decisive proof that the prophet had the Chaldeans and not Asshur in view, as the instruments employed in executing the judgment upon Tyre. The prophet points out the Chaldeans,—that nation which (although of primeval antiquity, Jer. v. 15) had not yet shown itself as a conqueror of the world (cf. Hab. i. 6), having been hitherto subject to the Assyrians; but which had now gained the mastery after having first of all destroyed Asshur, *i.e.* Nineveh[1] (namely, with

---

[1] This destruction of Nineveh was really such an one as could be called *yesor l'ziyyim* (a preparation for beasts of the desert), for it has been ever

the Medo-Babylonian army under Nabopolassar, the founder of the Neo-Babylonian empire, in 606 B.C.),—as the destroyers of the palaces of Tyre. With the appeal to the ships of Tarshish to pour out their lamentation, the prophecy returns in ver. 14 to the opening words in ver. 1. According to ver. 4, the fortress here is insular Tyre. As the prophecy thus closes itself by completing the circle, vers. 15–18 might appear to be a later addition. This is no more the case, however, here, than in the last part of ch. xix. Those critics, indeed, who do not acknowledge any special prophecies that are not *vaticinia post eventum*, are obliged to assign vers. 15–18 to the Persian era.

The prophet here foretells the rise of Tyre again at the close of the Chaldean world-wide monarchy. Vers. 15, 16. "*And it will come to pass in that day, that Tzor will be forgotten seventy years, equal to the days of one king; after the end of the seventy years, Tzor will go, according to the song of the harlot. Take the guitar, sweep through the city, O forgotten harlot! Play bravely, sing zealously, that thou mayest be remembered!*" The "*days of a king*" are a fixed and unchangeable period, for which everything is determined by the one sovereign will (as is the case more especially in the East), and is therefore stereotyped. The seventy years are compared to the days of such a king. Seventy is well fitted to be the number used to denote a uniform period of this kind, being equal to 10×7, *i.e.* a compact series of heptads of years (*shabbathoth*). But the number is also historical, prophecy being the power by which the history of the future was "periodized" beforehand in this significant manner. They coincide with the seventy years of Jeremiah (compare 2 Chron. xxxvi. 21), that is to say, with the duration of the Chaldean rule. During this period Tyre continued with its world-wide commerce in a state of involuntary repose. "*Tyre will be forgotten:*" *v'nishcachath* is not a participle (Böttcher), but the *perf. eons.* which is required here, and stands for וְנִשְׁכְּחָה with an original ה fem. (cf. ch. vii. 14, Ps. cxviii. 23). After the seventy years (that is to say, along with the commencement

since a heap of ruins, which the earth gradually swallowed up; so that when Xenophon went past it, he was not even told that these were the ruins of the ancient Ninus. On the later buildings erected upon the ruins, see Marcus v. Niebuhr, p. 203.

of the Persian rule) the harlot is welcomed again. She is like a bayadere or troubadour going through the streets with song and guitar, and bringing her charms into notice again. The prophecy here falls into the tone of a popular song, as in ch. v. 1 and xxvii. 2. It will be with Tyre as with such a musician and dancer as the one described in the popular song.

When it begins again to make love to all the world, it will get rich again from the gain acquired by this worldly intercourse. Ver. 17. "*And it will come to pass at the end of the seventy years: Jehovah will visit Tzor, and she comes again to her hire, and commits prostitution with all the kingdoms of the earth on the broad surface of the globe.*" Such mercantile trading as hers, which is only bent upon earthly advantages, is called *zânâh*, on account of its recognising none of the limits opposed by God, and making itself common to all the world, partly because it is a prostitution of the soul, and partly because from the very earliest times the prostitution of the body was also a common thing in markets and fairs, more especially in those of Phœnicia (as the Phœnicians were worshippers of Astarte). Hence the gain acquired by commerce, which Tyre had now secured again, is called '*ethnân* (Deut. xxiii. 19), with a feminine suffix, according to the Masora without *mappik* (Ewald, § 247, *a*).

This restoration of the trade of Tyre is called a visitation on the part of Jehovah, because, however profane the conduct of Tyre might be, it was nevertheless a holy purpose to which Jehovah rendered it subservient. Ver. 18. "*And her gain and her reward of prostitution will be holy to Jehovah: it is not stored up nor gathered together; but her gain from commerce will be theirs who dwell before Jehovah, to eat to satiety and for stately clothing.*" It is not the conversion of Tyre which is held up to view, but something approaching it. *Sachar* (which does not render it at all necessary to assume a form sâchâr for ver. 3) is used here in connection with '*ethnân*, to denote the occupation itself which yielded the profit. This, and also the profit acquired, would become holy to Jehovah; the latter would not be treasured up and capitalized as it formerly was, but they would give tribute and presents from it to Israel, and thus help to sustain in abundance and clothe in stately dress the nation which dwelt before Jehovah, *i.e.* whose true dwelling-place was in the temple before the presence of God (Ps.

xxvii. 4, lxxxiv. 5; *mecasseh* = that which covers, *i.e.* the covering; *'áthik*, like the Arabic *'atik*, old, noble, honourable). A strange prospect! As Jerome says, "*Hæc secundum historiam necdum facta comperimus.*"

The Assyrians, therefore, were not the predicted instruments of the punishment to be inflicted upon Phœnicia. Nor was Shalmanassar successful in his Phœnician war, as the extract from the chronicle of Menander in the *Antiquities* of Josephus (*Ant.* ix. 14, 2) clearly shows. Elulæus, the king of Tyre, had succeeded in once more subduing the rebellious Cyprians (*Kittaioi*). But with their assistance (if indeed ἐπὶ τούτους πέμψας is to be so interpreted[1]) Shalmanassar made war upon Phœnicia, though a general peace soon put an end to this campaign. Thereupon Sidon, Ace, Palætyrus, and many other cities, fell away from Tyrus (insular Tyre), and placed themselves under Assyrian supremacy. But as the Tyrians would not do this, Shalmanassar renewed the war; and the Phœnicians that were under his sway supplied him with six hundred ships and eight hundred rowers for this purpose. The Tyrians, however, fell upon them with twelve vessels of war, and having scattered the hostile fleet, took about five hundred prisoners. This considerably heightened the distinction of Tyre. And the king of Assyria was obliged to content himself with stationing guards on the river (Leontes), and at the conduits, to cut off the supply of fresh water from the Tyrians. This lasted for five years, during the whole of which time the Tyrians drank from wells that they had sunk themselves. Now, unless we want to lower the prophecy into a mere picture of the imagination, we cannot understand it as pointing to Asshur as the instrument of punishment, for the simple reason that Shalmanassar was obliged to withdraw from the "fortress of the sea" without accomplishing his purpose, and only succeeded in raising it to all the greater honour. But it is a

[1] The view held by Johann Brandis is probably the more correct one, —namely, that Shalmanassar commenced the contest by sending an army over to the island against the Chittæans (ἐπὶ not in the sense of *ad*, to, but of *contra*, against, just as in the expression further on, ἐπ' αὐτοὺς ὑπέστρεψε, *contra eos rediit*), probably to compel them to revolt again from the Tyrians. Rawlinson (*Monarchies*, ii. 405) proposes, as an emendation of the text, ἐπὶ τοῦτον, by which the Cyprian expedition is got rid of altogether.

question whether even Nebuchadnezzar was more successful with insular Tyre. All that Josephus is able to tell us from the Indian and Phœnician stories of Philostratus, is that Nebuchadnezzar besieged Tyre for thirteen years in the reign of Ithobal (*Ant.* x. 11, 1). And from Phœnician sources themselves, he merely relates (*c. Ap.* i. 21) that Nebuchadnezzar besieged Tyre for thirteen years under Ithobal (viz. from the seventh year of his reign onwards). But so much, at any rate, may apparently be gathered from the account of the Tyrian government which follows, viz. that the Persian era was preceded by the subjection of the Tyrians to the Chaldeans, inasmuch as they sent twice to fetch their king from Babylon. When the Chaldeans made themselves masters of the Assyrian empire, Phœnicia (whether with or without insular Tyre, we do not know) was a satrapy of that empire (Josephus, *Ant.* x. 11, 1; *c. Ap.* i. 19, from Berosus), and this relation still continued at the close of the Chaldean rule. So much is certain, however,—and Berosus, in fact, says it expressly,—viz. that Nebuchadnezzar once more subdued Phœnicia when it rose in rebellion; and that when he was called home to Babylon in consequence of the death of his father, he returned with Phœnician prisoners. What we want, however, is a direct account of the conquest of Tyre by the Chaldeans. Neither Josephus nor Jerome could give any such account. And the Old Testament Scriptures appear to state the very opposite,—namely, the failure of Nebuchadnezzar's enterprise. For in the twenty-seventh year after Jehoiachim's captivity (the sixteenth from the destruction of Jerusalem) the following word of the Lord came to Ezekiel (Ezek. xxix. 17, 18): "Son of man, Nebuchadnezzar the king of Babylon has caused his army to perform a long and hard service against Tyre: every head is made bald, and every shoulder peeled; yet neither he nor his army has any wages at Tyre for the hard service which they have performed around the same." It then goes on to announce that Jehovah would give Egypt to Nebuchadnezzar, and that this would be the wages of his army. Gesenius, Winer, Hitzig, and others, infer from this passage, when taken in connection with other non-Israelitish testimonies given by Josephus, which merely speak of a siege, that Nebuchadnezzar did not conquer Tyre; but Hengstenberg (*de rebus Tyriorum*, 1832), Hüvernick (*Ezek.* pp. 427-442), and Drechsler (*Isa.* ii. 166-169) maintain by arguments, which have been passed again and again through the sieve, that this passage presupposes the conquest of Tyre, and merely announces the disproportion between the profit which Nebuchadnezzar derived from it and the effort that it cost him. Jerome (on Ezekiel) gives the same explanation. When the army of Nebuchadnezzar had made insular Tyre accessible by heaping up an embankment with enormous exertions, and they were in a position to make use of their siege artillery, they found that the Tyrians had carried away all their wealth in vessels to the neighbouring islands; " so that when the city was taken, Nebuchadnezzar found nothing to repay him for his labour; and because he had obeyed the will of God in this undertaking, after the Tyrian captivity had lasted a few years, Egypt was given to him" (Jerome). I also regard this as the correct view to take; though without wishing to maintain that the words might not be understood as implying the failure of the siege, quite as readily as the uselessness of the conquest. But on the two following grounds, I am persuaded that they are used here in the latter sense. (1.) In the great trilogy which contains Ezekiel's prophecy against Tyre (Ezek. xxvi.-xxviii.), and in which he more than once introduces thoughts and figures from Isa. xxiii., which he still further amplifies and elaborates (according to the general relation in which he stands to his predecessors, of whom he does not make a species of mosaic, as Jeremiah does, but whom he rather expands, fills up, and paraphrases, as seen more especially in his relation to Zephaniah), he predicts the conquest of insular Tyre by Nebuchadnezzar. He foretells indeed even more than this; but if Tyre had not been at least conquered by Nebuchadnezzar, the prophecy would have fallen completely to the ground, like any merely human hope. Now we candidly confess that, on doctrinal grounds, it is impossible for us to make such an assumption as this. There is indeed an element of human hope in all prophecy, but it does not reach such a point as to be put to shame by the test supplied in Deut. xviii. 21, 22. (2.) If I take a comprehensive survey of the following ancient testimonies: (*a*) that Nebuchadnezzar, when called home in consequence of his father's death, took some Phœnician prisoners with him (Berosus, *ut sup.*); (*b*) that with this fact before us, the statement found in the Phœnician sources, to the effect that the Tyrians fetched two of their rulers from Babylon, viz. Merbal and Eirom, presents a much greater resemblance to 2 Kings xxiv. 12, 14, and Dan. i. 3, than to 1 Kings xii. 2, 3, with which Hitzig compares it; (c) that, according to Josephus (c. *Ap.* i. 20), it was stated "in the archives of the Phœnicians concerning this king Nebuchadnezzar, that he conquered all Syria and Phœnicia;" and (d) that the voluntary submission to the Persians (Herod. iii. 19; Xen. *Cyrop.* i. 1, 4) was not the commencement of servitude, but merely a change of masters;—if, I say, I put all these things together, the conclusion to which I am brought is, that the thirteen years' siege of Tyre by Nebuchadnezzar ended in its capture, possibly through capitulation (as Winer, Movers, and others assume).

The difficulties which present themselves to us when we compare together the prophecies of Isaiah and Ezekiel, are still no doubt very far from being removed; but it is in this way alone that any solution of the difficulty is to be found. For even assuming that Nebuchadnezzar conquered Tyre, he did not destroy it, as the words of the two prophecies would lead us to expect. The real solution of the difficulty has been already given by Hävernick and Drechsler: "The prophet sees the whole enormous mass of destruction which eventually came upon the city, concentrated, as it were, in Nebuchadnezzar's conquest, inasmuch as in the actual historical development it was linked on to that fact like a closely connected chain. The power of Tyre as broken by Nebuchadnezzar is associated in his view with its utter destruction." Even Alexander did not destroy Tyre, when he had conquered it after seven months' enormous exertions. Tyre was still a flourishing commercial city of considerable importance under both the Syrian and the Roman sway. In the time of the Crusades it was still the same; and even the Crusaders, who conquered it in 1125, did not destroy it. It was not till about a century and a half later that the destruction was commenced by the removal of the fortifications on the part of the Saracens. At the present time, all the glory of Tyre is either sunk in the sea or buried beneath the sand,—an inexhaustible mine of building materials for Beirut and other towns upon the coast.

Amidst these vast ruins of the island city, there is nothing standing now but a village of wretched wooden huts. And the island is an island no longer. The embankment which Alexander threw up has grown into a still broader and stronger tongue of earth through the washing up of sand, and now connects the island with the shore,—a standing memorial of divine justice (Strauss, *Sinai und Golgotha*, p. 357). This picture of destruction stands before the prophet's mental eye, and indeed immediately behind the attack of the Chaldeans upon Tyre,—the two thousand years between being so compressed, that the whole appears as a continuous event. This is the well-known law of perspective, by which prophecy is governed throughout. This law cannot have been unknown to the prophets themselves, inasmuch as they needed it to accredit their prophecies even to themselves. Still more was it necessary for future ages, in order that they might not be deceived with regard to the prophecy, that this universally determining law, in which human limitations are left unresolved, and are miraculously intermingled with the eternal view of God, should be clearly known.

But another enigma presents itself. The prophet foretells a revival of Tyre at the end of seventy years, and the passing over of its world-wide commerce into the service of the congregation of Jehovah. We cannot agree with R. O. Gilbert (*Theodulia*, 1855, pp. 273-4) in regarding the seventy years as a sacred number, which precludes all clever human calculation, because the Lord thereby conceals His holy and irresistible decrees. The meaning of the seventy is clear enough: they are, as we saw, the seventy years of the Chaldean rule. And this is also quite enough, if only a prelude to what is predicted here took place in connection with the establishment of the Persian sway. Such a prelude there really was in the fact, that, according to the edict of Cyrus, both Sidonians and Tyrians assisted in the building of the temple at Jerusalem (Ezra iii. 7, cf. i. 4). A second prelude is to be seen in the fact, that at the very commencement of the labours of the apostles there was a Christian church in Tyre, which was visited by the Apostle Paul (Acts xxi. 3, 4), and that this church steadily grew from that time forward. In this way again the trade of Tyre entered the service of the God of revelation.

But it is Christian Tyre which now lies in ruins. One of the most remarkable ruins is the splendid cathedral of Tyre, for which Eusebius of Cæsarea wrote a dedicatory address, and in which Friedrich Barbarossa, who was drowned in the Kalykadnos in the year 1190, is supposed to have been buried. Hitherto, therefore, these have been only preludes to the fulfilment of the prophecy. Its ultimate fulfilment has still to be waited for. But whether the fulfilment will be an ideal one, when not only the kingdoms of the world, but also the trade of the world, shall belong to God and His Christ; or *spiritually*, in the sense in which this word is employed in the Apocalypse, *i.e.* by the true essence of the ancient Tyre reappearing in another city, like that of Babylon in Rome; or *literally*, by the fishing village of *Tzur* actually disappearing again as Tyre rises from its ruins,—it would be impossible for any commentator to say, unless he were himself a prophet.

PART IV.

FINALE OF THE GREAT CATASTROPHE.

CHAP. XXIV.–XXVII.

The cycle of prophecies which commences here has no other parallel in the Old Testament than perhaps Zech. ix.–xiv. Both sections are thoroughly eschatological and apocryphal in their character, and start from apparently sharply defined historical circumstances, which vanish, however, like will-o'-the wisps, as soon as you attempt to follow and seize them; for the simple reason, that the prophet lays hold of their radical idea, carries them out beyond their outward historical form, and uses them as emblems of far-off events of the last days. It is not surprising, therefore, that the majority of modern critics, from the time of Eichhorn and Koppe, have denied the genuineness of these four chapters (xxiv.–xxvii.), notwithstanding the fact that there is nothing in the words themselves that passes beyond the Assyrian times. Rosenmüller did this in the first edition of his *Scholia;* but in the second and third editions he has fallen into another error, chiefly because the prophecy contains nothing which passes beyond the political horizon of Isaiah's own times. Now we cannot accept this test of genuineness; it is just one of the will-o'-the-wisps already referred to. Another consequence of this phenomenon is, that our critical opponents inevitably get entangled in contradictions as soon as they seek for a different historical basis for this cycle of prophecies from that of Isaiah's own times. According to Gesenius, De Wette, Maurer, and Umbreit, the author wrote in Babylonia; according to Eichhorn, Ewald, and Knobel, in Judah. In the opinion of some, he wrote at the close of the captivity; in that of others, immediately after the overthrow of the kingdom of Judah. Hitzig supposes the imperial city, whose destruction is predicted, to be Nineveh; others, for the most part, suppose it to be Babylon. But the prophet only mentions Egypt and Asshur as powers by which Israel is enslaved; and Knobel consequently imagines that he wrote in this figurative manner from fear of the enemies that were still dwelling in Judah. This wavering arises from the fact, that what is apparently historical is simply an eschatological emblem. It is quite impossible to determine whether that which sounds historical belonged to the present or past in relation to the prophet himself. His standing-place was beyond all the history that has passed by, even down to the present day; and everything belonging to this history was merely a figure in the mirror of the last lines. Let it be once established that no human critics can determine *à priori* the measure of divine revelation granted to any prophet, and all possible grounds combine to vindicate Isaiah's authorship of ch. xxiv.-xxvii., as demanded by its place in the book of Isaiah.[1] Appended as they are to ch. xiii.-xxiii. without a distinct heading, they are intended to stand in a relation of steady progress to the oracles concerning the nations; and this relation is sustained by the

---

[1] The genuineness is supported by Rosenmüller, Hensler (*Jesaia neu übersetzt, mit Anm.*), Paulus (*Clavis über Jesaia*), Augusti (*Exeg. Handbuch*), Beckhaus (*über Integrität der proph. Schriften des A. T.* 1796), Kleinert (*über die Echtheit sämmtlicher in d. Buche Jesaia enth. Weissagungen*, 1829), Küper (*Jeremias librorum sacr. interpres atque vindex*, 1837), and Jahn, Hävernick, Keil (in their *Introductions*). In monographs, C. F. L. Arndt (*De loco, c. xxiv.-xxvii., Jesaiæ vindicando et explicando*, 1826), and Ed. Böhl (*Vaticinium Jes. cap. xxiv.-xxvii. commentario illustr.* 1861).

fact that Jeremiah read them in connection with these oracles (compare ch. xxiv. 17, 18, with Jer. xlviii. 43, 44), and that they are full of retrospective allusions, which run out like a hundred threads, though grasped, as it were, in a single hand. Ch. xxiv.–xxvii. stand in the same relation to ch. xiii.–xxiii., as ch. xi. xii. to ch. vii.–x. The particular judgments predicted in the oracle against the nations, all flow into the last judgment as into a sea; and all the salvation which formed the shining edge of the oracles against the nations, is here concentrated in the glory of a mid-day sun. Ch. xxiv.–xxvii. form the *finale* to ch. xiii.–xxiii., and that in a strictly musical sense. What the *finale* should do in a piece of music—namely, gather up the scattered changes into a grand impressive whole—is done here by this closing cycle. But even apart from this, it is full of music and song. The description of the catastrophe in ch. xxiv. is followed by a simple hymnal echo. As the book of Immanuel closes in ch. xii. with a psalm of the redeemed, so have we here a fourfold song of praise. The overthrow of the imperial city is celebrated in a song in ch. xxv. 1–5; another song in ch. xxv. 9 describes how Jehovah reveals himself with His saving presence; another in ch. xxvi. 1–19 celebrates the restoration and resurrection of Israel; and a fourth in ch. xxvii. 2–5 describes the vineyard of the church bringing forth fruit under the protection of Jehovah. And these songs contain every variety, from the most elevated heavenly hymn to the tenderest popular song. It is a grand manifold concert, which is merely introduced, as it were, by the epic opening in ch. xxiv. and the epic close in ch. xxvii. 6 sqq., and in the midst of which the prophecy unfolds itself in a kind of recitative. Moreover, we do not find so much real music anywhere else in the ring of the words. The heaping up of *paronomasia* has been placed among the arguments against the genuineness of these chapters. But we have already shown by many examples, drawn from undisputed prophecies (such as ch. xxii. 5, xvii. 12, 13), that Isaiah is fond of painting for the ear; and the reason why he does it here more than anywhere else, is that ch. xxiv.–xxvii. formed a *finale* that was intended to surpass all that had gone before. The whole of this *finale* is a grand hallelujah to ch. xiii.–xxiii., hymnic in its character, and musical in form, and that to such a degree, that, like ch.

xxv. 6, the prophecy is, as it were, both text and divisions at the same time. There was no other than Isaiah who was so incomparable a master of language. Again, the incomparable depth in the contents of ch. xxiv.-xxvii. does not shake our confidence in his authorship, since the whole book of this Solomon among the prophets is full of what is incomparable. And in addition to much that is peculiar in this cycle of prophecies, which does not astonish us in a prophet so richly endowed, and so characterized by a continual change " from glory to glory," the whole cycle is so thoroughly Isaiah's in its deepest foundation, and in a hundred points of detail, that it is most uncritical to pronounce the whole to be certainly not Isaiah's simply because of these peculiarities. So far as the eschatological and apocalyptical contents, which seem to point to a very late period, are concerned, we would simply call to mind the wealth of eschatological ideas to be found even in Joel, who prophesies of the pouring out of the Spirit, the march of the nations of the world against the church, the signs that precede the last day, the miraculous water of the New Jerusalem. The revelation of all the last things, which the Apocalypse of the New Testament embraces in one grand picture, commenced with Obadiah and Joel; and there is nothing strange in the fact that Isaiah also, in ch. xxiv.-xxvii., should turn away from the immediate external facts of the history of his own time, and pass on to these depths beyond.

THE JUDGMENT UPON THE EARTH.—CHAP. XXIV.

It is thoroughly characteristic of Isaiah, that the commencement of this prophecy, like ch. xix. 1, places us at once in the very midst of the catastrophe, and condenses the contents of the subsequent picture of judgment into a few rapid, vigorous, vivid, and comprehensive clauses (like ch. xv. 1, xvii. 1, xxiii. 1, cf. xxxiii. 1). Vers. 1-3. " *Behold, Jehovah emptieth the earth, and layeth it waste, and marreth its form, and scattereth its inhabitants. And it happeneth, as to the people, so to the priest; as to the servant, so to his master; as to the maid, so to her mistress; as to the buyer, so to the seller; as to the lender, so to the borrower; as to the creditor, so to the debtor. Emptying the earth is emptied, and plundering is plundered: for Jehovah hath spoken this word.*" The question, whether the prophet is speaking of a past or future judgment, which is one of importance to the interpretation of the whole, is answered by the fact that with Isaiah "*hinnēh*" (behold) always refers to something future (ch. iii. 1, xvii. 1, xix. 1, xxx. 27, etc.). And it is only in his case, that we do meet with prophecies commencing so immediately with *hinneh*. Those in Jeremiah which approach this the most nearly (viz. Jer. xlvii. 2, xlix. 35, cf. li. 1, and Ezek. xxix. 3) do indeed commence with *hinnēh*, but not without being preceded by an introductory formula. The opening "behold" corresponds to the confirmatory "for Jehovah hath spoken," which is always employed by Isaiah at the close of statements with regard to the future and occurs chiefly,[1] though not exclusively,[2] in the book of Isaiah, whom we may recognise in the detailed description in ver. 2 (*vid.* ch. ii. 12–16, iii. 2, 3, 18–23, as compared with ch. ix. 13; also with the description of judgment in ch. xix. 2–4, which closes in a similar manner). Thus at the very outset we meet with Isaiah's peculiarities; and Caspari is right in saying that no prophecy could possibly commence with more of the characteristics of Isaiah than the prophecy before us. The play upon words commences at the very outset. *Bâkak* and *bâlak* (compare the Arabic *ballûka*, a blank, naked desert) have the same ring, just as in Nahum ii. 11, cf. 3, and Jer. li. 2. The *niphal* futures are intentionally written like verbs *Pe-Vâv* (*tibbōk* and *tibbōz*, instead of *tibbak* and *tibbaz*), for the purpose of making them rhyme with the infinitive absolutes (cf. ch. xxii. 13). So, again, *cagg'birtâh* is so written instead of *cigbirtâh*, to produce a greater resemblance to the opening syllable of the other words. The form נִשָּׁה is interchanged with נָשָׁא (as in 1 Sam. xxii. 2), or, according to Kimchi's way of writing it, with נֵשָׁא (written with *tzere*), just as in other passages we meet with נָשָׁא along with נָשָׁה, and, judging from نسي, to postpone or credit, the former is the primary form. *Nōsheh* is the creditor, and אֲשֶׁר נָשָׁא בֹו is not the person who has borrowed of him, but, as נָשָׁה invariably signifies to credit (*hiphil*, to give credit), the

---

[1] *Vid.* ch. i. 20, xxi. 17, xxii. 25, xxv. 8, xl. 5, lviii. 14; also compare ch. xix. 4, xvi. 13, and xxxvii. 22.

[2] *Vid.* Ob. 18, Joel iv. 8, Mic. iv. 4, 1 Kings xiv. 11.

person whom he credits (with בְּ *obj.*, like נֹשֶׁה בְּ in ch. ix. 3), not "the person through whom he is נֹשֵׁא" (Hitzig on Jer. xv. 10). Hence, "lender and borrower, creditor and debtor" (or taker of credit). It is a judgment which embraces all, without distinction of rank and condition; and it is a universal one, not merely throughout the whole of the *land* of Israel (as even Drechsler renders הָאָרֶץ), but in all the earth; for as Arndt correctly observes, הָאָרֶץ signifies "the earth" in this passage, including, as in ch. xi. 4, the ethical New Testament idea of "the world" (*kosmos*).

That this is the case is evident from vers. 4–9, where the accursed state into which the earth is brought is more fully described, and the cause thereof is given. Vers. 4–9. "*Smitten down, withered up is the earth; pined away, wasted away is the world; pined away have they, the foremost of the people of the earth. And the earth has become wicked among its inhabitants; for they transgressed revelations, set at nought the ordinance, broke the everlasting covenant. Therefore hath the curse devoured the earth, and they who dwelt in it make expiation: therefore are the inhabitants of the earth withered up, and there are very few mortals left. New wine mourneth, vine is parched, all the merry-hearted groan. The joyous playing of tabrets is silent; the noise of them that rejoice hath ceased; the joyous playing of the guitar is silent. They drink no wine with a song; meth tastes bitter to them that drink it.*" "*The world*" (*tēbēl*) is used here in ver. 4, as in ch. xxvi. 9 (always in the form of a proper name, and without the article), as a parallel to "*the earth*" (*hā'āretz*), with which it alternates throughout this cycle of prophecies. It is used poetically to signify the globe, and that without limitation (even in ch. xiii. 11 and xviii. 3); and therefore "the earth" is also to be understood here in its most comprehensive sense (in a different sense, therefore, from ch. xxxiii. 9, which contains the same play upon sounds). The earth is sunk in mourning, and has become like a faded plant, withered up with heat; the high ones of the people of the earth (*merōm; abstr. pro concr.*, like *cābōd* in ch. v. 13, xxii. 24) are included (עַם is used, as in ch. xlii. 5, xl. 7, to signify humanity, *i.e.* man generally). אֻמְלְלוּ (for the form, see *Job*, i. 328) stands in half pause, which throws the subjective notion that follows into greater prominence. It is the punishment of the inhabitants of the earth, which the earth has to share, because it has shared in the wickedness of those who live upon it: *chânaph* (not related to *tânaph*) signifies to be degenerate, to have decided for what is evil (ch. ix. 16), to be wicked; and in this intransitive sense it is applied to the land, which is said to be affected with the guilt of wicked, reckless conduct, more especially of blood-guiltiness (Ps. cvi. 38, Num. xxxv. 33; compare the transitive use in Jer. iii. 9). The wicked conduct of men, which has caused the earth also to become *chanēphâh*, is described in three short, rapid, involuntarily excited sentences (compare ch. xv. 6, xvi. 4, xxix. 20, xxxiii. 8; also ch. xxiv. 5, i. 4, 6, 8; out of the book of Isaiah, however, we only meet with this in Joel i. 10, and possibly Josh. vii. 11). Understanding "the earth" as we do in a general sense, "the law" cannot signify merely the positive law of Israel. The Gentile world had also a *torâh* or divine teaching within, which contained an abundance of divine directions (*tōrōth*). They also had a law written in their hearts; and it was with the whole human race that God concluded a covenant in the person of Noah, at a time when the nations had none of them come into existence at all. This is the explanation given by even Jewish commentators; nevertheless, we must not forget that Israel was included among the transgressors, and the choice of expression was determined by this. With the expression "therefore" the prophecy moves on from sin to punishment, just as in ch. v. 25 (cf. ver. 24). אָלָה is the curse of God denounced against the transgressors of His law (Dan. ix. 11; compare Jer. xxiii. 10, which is founded upon this, and from which אָבְלָה has been introduced into this passage in some codices and editions). The curse of God devours, for it is fire, and that from within outwards (see ch. i. 31, v. 24, ix. 18, x. 16, 17, xxix. 6, xxx. 27 sqq., xxxiii. 11–14): *chârū* (*milel*, since *pashta* is an *acc. postpos.*),[1] from *chârar*, they are burnt up, *exusti*. With regard to וַיֶּאְשְׁמוּ, it is hardly necessary to observe that it cannot be traced back to אָשֵׁם = יָשֵׁם, שָׁמֵם; and that of the two meanings, *culpam contrahere* and *culpam sustinere*, it has the latter meaning here. We must not overlook the genuine mark of Isaiah here in the description of the vanishing away of men down to

---

[1] In correct texts *chârū* has two *pashtas*, the former indicating the place of the tone.

a small remnant: שְׁאָר (שְׁאָר) is the standing word used to denote this; מִזְעָר (used with regard to number both here and in ch. xvi. 14; and with regard to time in ch. x. 25 and xxix. 17) is exclusively Isaiah's; and אֱנוֹשׁ is used in the same sense as in ch. xxxiii. 8 (cf. ch. xiii. 12). In ver. 7 we are reminded of Joel i. (on the short sentences, see ch. xxix. 20, xvi. 8–10); in vers. 8, 9 any one acquainted with Isaiah's style will recal to mind not only ch. v. 12, 14, but a multitude of other parallels. We content ourselves with pointing to עַלִּיז (which belongs exclusively to Isaiah, and is taken from Isa. xxii. 2 and xxxii. 13 in Zeph. ii. 15, and from Isa. xiii. 3 in Zeph. iii. 11); and for *basshir* (with joyous song) to ch. xxx. 32 (with the beating of drums and playing of guitars), together with ch. xxviii. 7. The picture is elegiac, and dwells so long upon the wine (cf. ch. xvi.), just because wine, both as a natural production and in the form of drink, is the most exhilarating to the heart of all the natural gifts of God (Ps. civ. 15; Judg. ix. 13). All the sources of joy and gladness are destroyed; and even if there is much still left of that which ought to give enjoyment, the taste of the men themselves turns it into bitterness.

The world with its pleasure is judged; the world's city is also judged, in which both the world's power and the world's pleasure were concentrated. Vers. 10–13. " *The city of tohu is broken to pieces; every house is shut up, so that no man can come in. There is lamentation for wine in the fields; all rejoicing has set; the delight of the earth is banished. What is left of the city is wilderness, and the gate was shattered to ruins. For so will it be within the earth, in the midst of the nations; as at the olive-beating, as at the gleaning, when the vintage is over.*" The city of *tohu* (*kiryath tōhu*): this cannot be taken collectively, as Rosenmüller, Arndt, and Drechsler suppose, on account of the annexation of *kiryath* to *tohu*, which is turned into a kind of proper name; nor can we understand it as referring to Jerusalem, as the majority of commentators have done, including even Schegg and Stier (according to ch. xxxii. 13, 14), after we have taken " the earth" (*hā'āretz*) in the sense of *kosmos* (the world). It is rather the central city of the world as estranged from God; and it is here designated according to its end, which end will be *tohu*, as its nature was *tohu*. Its true nature was the breaking up of the harmony of all divine order;

and so its end will be the breaking up of its own standing, and a hurling back, as it were, into the *chaos* of its primeval beginning. With a very similar significance Rome is called *turbida Roma* in Persius (i. 5). The whole is thoroughly Isaiah's, even to the finest points: *tohu* is the same as in ch. xxix. 21; and for the expression מִבּוֹא (so that you cannot enter; namely, on account of the ruins which block up the doorway) compare ch. xxiii. 1, vii. 8, xvii. 1, also v. 9, vi. 11, xxxii. 13. The cry or lamentation for the wine out in the fields (ver. 11; cf. Job v. 10) is the mourning on account of the destruction of the vineyards; the vine, which is one of Isaiah's most favourite symbols, represents in this instance also all the natural sources of joy. In the term '*árbâh* (rejoicing) the relation between joy and light is presupposed; the sun of joy is set (compare Mic. iii. 6). What remains of the city (בָּעִיר is partitive, just as בּוֹ in ch. x. 22) is *shammâh* (desolation), to which the whole city has been brought (compare ch. v. 9, xxxii. 14). The strong gates, which once swarmed with men, are shattered to ruins (*yuccath*, like Mic. i. 7, for *yúcath*, Ges. § 67, Anm. 8; שְׁאִיָּה, ἅπ. λεγ., a predicating noun of sequence, as in ch. xxxvii. 26, "into desolated heaps;" compare ch. vi. 11, etc., and other passages). In the whole circuit of the earth (ch. vi. 12, vii. 22; *há'áretz* is "the earth" here as in ch. x. 23, xix. 24), and in the midst of what was once a crowd of nations (compare Mic. v. 6, 7), there is only a small remnant of men left. This is the leading thought, which runs through the book of Isaiah from beginning to end, and is figuratively depicted here in a miniature of ch. xvii. 4–6. The state of things produced by the catastrophe is compared to the olive-beating, which fetches down what fruit was left at the general picking, and to the gleaning of the grapes after the vintage has been fully gathered in (*cálâh* is used here as in ch. x. 25, xvi. 4, xxi. 16, etc., viz. "to be over," whereas in ch. xxxii. 10 it means to be hopelessly lost, as in ch. xv. 6). There are no more men in the whole of the wide world than there are of olives and grapes after the principal gathering has taken place. The persons saved belong chiefly, though not exclusively, to Israel (John iii. 5). The place where they assemble is the land of promise.

There is now a church there refined by the judgment, and

rejoicing in its apostolic calling to the whole world. Vers. 14, 15. "*They will lift up their voice, and exult; for the majesty of Jehovah they shout from the sea: therefore praise ye Jehovah in the lands of the sun, in the islands of the sea the name of Jehovah the God of Israel.*" The ground and subject of the rejoicing is "the majesty of Jehovah," *i.e.* the fact that Jehovah had shown Himself so majestic in judgment and mercy (ch. xii. 5, 6), and was now so manifest in His glory (ch. ii. 11, 17). Therefore rejoicing was heard "from the sea" (the Mediterranean), by which the abode of the congregation of Jehovah was washed. Turning in that direction, it had the islands and coast lands of the European West in front (*iyyi hayyâm*; the only other passage in which this occurs is ch. xi. 11, cf. Ezek. xxvi. 18), and at its back the lands of the Asiatic East, which are called *'urim*, the lands of light, *i.e.* of the sun-rising. This is the true meaning of *'urim*, as J. Schelling and Drechsler agree; for Döderlein's comparison of the rare Arabic word اوُرٌ *septentrio* is as far removed from the Hebrew usage as that of the Talmud אוֹר אוֹרְתָּא, *vespera*. Hitzig's proposed reading בָּאִיִּים (according to the LXX.) diminishes the substance and destroys the beauty of the appeal, which goes forth both to the east and west, and summons to the praise of the name of Jehovah the God of Israel, עַל־כֵּן, *i.e.* because of His manifested glory. His "name" (cf. ch. xxx. 27) is His nature as revealed and made "nameable" in judgment and mercy.

This appeal is not made in vain. Ver. 16*a*. "*From the border of the earth we hear songs: Praise to the Righteous One!*" It no doubt seems natural enough to understand the term *tzaddîk* (righteous) as referring to Jehovah; but, as Hitzig observes, Jehovah is never called "the Righteous One" in so absolute a manner as this (compare, however, Ps. cxii. 4, where it occurs in connection with other attributes, and Ex. ix. 27, where it stands in an antithetical relation); and in addition to this, Jehovah gives צְבִי (ch. iv. 2, xxviii. 5), whilst כָּבוֹד, and not צְבִי, is ascribed to Him. Hence we must take the word in the same sense as in ch. iii. 10 (cf. Hab. ii. 4). The reference is to the church of righteous men, whose faith has endured the fire of the judgment of wrath. In response to its summons to the praise of Jehovah, they answer it in songs from the border of the earth. The earth is here thought of as a garment spread out; *cenaph* is the point or edge of the garment, the extreme eastern and western ends (compare ch. xi. 12). Thence the church of the future catches the sound of this grateful song as it is echoed from one to the other.

The prophet feels himself, "in spirit," to be a member of this church; but all at once he becomes aware of the sufferings which will have first of all to be overcome, and which he cannot look upon without sharing the suffering himself. Vers. 16–20. "*Then I said, Ruin to me! ruin to me! Woe to me! Robbers rob, and robbing, they rob as robbers. Horror, and pit, and snare, are over thee, O inhabitant of the earth! And it cometh to pass, whoever fleeth from the tidings of horror falleth into the pit; and whoever escapeth out of the pit is caught in the snare: for the trap-doors on high are opened, and the firm foundations of the earth shake. The earth rending, is rent asunder; the earth bursting, is burst in pieces; the earth shaking, tottereth. The earth reeling, reeleth like a drunken man, and swingeth like a hammock; and its burden of sin presseth upon it; and it falleth, and riseth not again.*" The expression "Then I said" (cf. ch. vi. 5) stands here in the same apocalyptic connection as in Rev. vii. 14, for example. He said it at that time in a state of ecstasy; so that when he committed to writing what he had seen, the saying was a thing of the past. The final salvation follows a final judgment; and looking back upon the latter, he bursts out into the exclamation of pain: *râzī-lī*, consumption, passing away, to me (see ch. x. 16, xvii. 4), *i.e.* I must perish (*râzi* is a word of the same form as *kâlī, shânī, 'ânī*; literally, it is a neuter adjective signifying *emaciatum = macies*; Ewald, § 749, *g*). He sees a dreadful, bloodthirsty people preying among both men and stores (compare ch. xxi. 2, xxxiii. 1, for the play upon the word with בגד, root גד, cf. κεύθειν τινά τι, *tecte agere*, *i.e.* from behind, treacherously, like assassins). The exclamation, "Horror, and pit," etc. (which Jeremiah applies in Jer. xlviii. 43, 44, to the destruction of Moab by the Chaldeans), is not an invocation, but simply a deeply agitated utterance of what is inevitable. In the pit and snare there is a comparison implied of men to game, and of the enemy to sportsmen (cf. Jer. xvi. 16, Lam. iv. 19; *yillâcēr*, as in ch. viii. 15, xxviii. 13). The על in עָלֶיךָ is exactly the same as in Judg. xvi. 9 (cf. Isa. xvi. 9). They who should flee as soon as the horrible news arrived (*min*, as in ch. xxxiii. 3) would not escape destruction, but would become victims to one form if not to another (the same thought which we find expressed twice in Amos v. 19, and still more fully in ch. ix. 1–4, as well as in a more dreadfully exalted tone). Observe, however, in how mysterious a background those human instruments of punishment remain, who are suggested by the word *bōgdim* (robbers). The idea that the judgment is a direct act of Jehovah, stands in the foreground and governs the whole. For this reason it is described as a repetition of the flood (for the opened windows or trap-doors of the firmament, which let the great bodies of water above them come down from on high upon the earth, point back to Gen. vii. 11 and viii. 2, cf. Ps. lxxviii. 23); and this indirectly implies its universality. It is also described as an earthquake. "The foundations of the earth" are the internal supports upon which the visible crust of the earth rests. The way in which the earth in its quaking first breaks, then bursts, and then falls, is painted for the ear by the three reflective forms in ver. 19, together with their gerundives, which keep each stage in the process of the catastrophe vividly before the mind. רֹעָה is apparently an error of the pen for רֹעַ, if it is not indeed a *n. actionis* instead of the *inf. absol.* as in Hab. iii. 9. The accentuation, however, regards the *ah* as a toneless addition, and the form therefore as a gerundive (like *kob* in Num. xxiii. 25). The reflective form הִתְרֹעֵעַ is not the *hithpalel* of רוּעַ, *vociferari*, but the *hithpoel* of רָעַע (רָצִין), *frangere*. The threefold play upon the words would be tame, if the words themselves formed an anti-climax; but it is really a *climax ascendens*. The earth first of all receives rents; then gaping wide, it bursts asunder; and finally sways to and fro once more, and falls. It is no longer possible for it to keep upright. Its wickedness presses it down like a burden (ch. i. 4; Ps. xxxviii. 5), so that it now reels for the last time like a drunken man (ch. xxviii. 7, xxix. 9), or a hammock (ch. i. 8), until it falls never to rise again.

But if the old earth passes away in this manner out of the system of the universe, the punishment of God must fall at the same time both upon the princes of heaven and upon the princes of earth (the prophet does not arrange what belongs to the end of all things in a "chronotactic" manner). They are the secrets of two worlds, that are here unveiled to the apocalyptic seer of the Old Testament. Vers. 21-23. "*And it cometh to pass in that day, Jehovah will visit the army of the high place in the high place, and the kings of the earth on the earth. And they are imprisoned, as one imprisons captives in the pit, and shut up in prison; and in the course of many days they are visited. And the moon blushes, and the sun turns pale: for Jehovah of hosts reigns royally upon Mount Zion and in Jerusalem, and before His elders is glory.*" With this doubly expressed antithesis of *mârōm* and *'adâmâh* (cf. xxiii. 17*b*) before us, brought out as it is as sharply as possible, we cannot understand "*the army of the high place*" as referring to certain earthly powers (as the Targum, Luther, Calvin, and Hävernick do). Moreover, the expression itself is also opposed to such an interpretation; for, as ver. 18 clearly shows, in which *mimmârom* is equivalent to *misshâmaim* (cf. ch. xxxiii. 5, xxxvii. 23, xl. 26), צְבָא מָרוֹם is synonymous with צְבָא הַשָּׁמַיִם; and this invariably signifies either the starry host (ch. xl. 26) or the angelic host (1 Kings xxii. 19; Ps. cxlviii. 2), and occasionally the two combined, without any distinction (Neh. ix. 6). As the moon and sun are mentioned, it might be supposed that by the "host on high" we are to understand the angelic host, as Abravanel, Umbreit, and others really do: "the stars, that have been made into idols, the shining kings of the sky, fall from their altars, and the kings of the earth from their thrones." But the very antithesis in the word "kings" (*malchē*) leads us to conjecture that "the host on high" refers to personal powers; and the view referred to founders on the more minute description of the visitation (*pâkad 'al*, as in ch. xxvii. 1, 3, cf. xxvi. 21), "they are imprisoned," etc.; for this must also be referred to the heavenly host. The objection might indeed be urged, that the imprisonment only relates to the kings, and that the visitation of the heavenly host finds its full expression in the shaming of the moon and sun (ver. 23); but the fact that the moon and sun are thrown into the shade by the revelation of the glory of Jehovah, cannot be regarded as a judgment inflicted upon them. Hence the commentators are now pretty well agreed, that "the host on high" signifies here the angelic army. But it is self-evident, that a visitation of the angelic army cannot be merely a relative and partial one. And it is not sufficient to understand the passage as meaning the wicked angels, to the exclusion of the good. Both the context and the parallelism show that the reference must be to a penal visitation in the spiritual world, which stands in the closest connection with the history of man, and in fact with the history of the nations. Consequently the host on high will refer to the angels of the nations and kingdoms; and the prophecy here presupposes what is affirmed in Deut. xxxii. 8 (LXX.), and sustained in the book of Daniel, when it speaks of a *sar* of Persia, Javan, and even the people of Israel. In accordance with this exposition, there is a rabbinical saying, to the effect that " God never destroys a nation without having first of all destroyed its prince," *i.e.* the angel who, by whatever means he first obtained possession of the nation, whether by the will of God or against His will, has exerted an ungodly influence upon it. Just as, according to the scriptural view, both good and evil angels attach themselves to particular men, and an elevated state of mind may sometimes afford a glimpse of this encircling company and this conflict of spirits; so do angels contend for the rule over nations and kingdoms, either to guide them in the way of God or to lead them astray from God; and therefore the judgment upon the nations which the prophet here foretells will be a judgment upon angels also. The kingdom of spirits has its own history running parallel to the destinies of men. What is recorded in Gen. vi. was a seduction of men by angels, and one of later occurrence than the temptation by Satan in paradise; and the seduction of nations and kingdoms by the host of heaven, which is here presupposed by the prophecy of Isaiah, is later than either. Ver. 22*a* announces the preliminary punishment of both angelic and human princes: '*asēphâh* stands in the place of a gerundive, like *taltēlâh* in ch. xxii. 17. The connection of the words '*asēphâh* '*assir* is exactly the same as that of *taltēlâh gâbēr* in ch. xxii. 17: incarceration after the manner of incarcerating prisoners; '*âsaph*, to gather together (ch. x. 14, xxxiii. 4), signifies here to incarcerate, just as in Gen. xlii. 17. Both verbs are construed with '*al*, because the thrusting is from above downwards into the pit and prison ('*al* embraces both *upon* or *over* anything, and *into* it, *e.g.* 1 Sam. xxxi. 4, Job vi. 16; see Hitzig on Nah. iii. 12). We may see from 2 Pet. ii. 4 and Jude 6 how this is to be understood. The reference is to the abyss of Hades, where they are reserved in chains of darkness unto the judgment of the great day. According to this parallel, *yippâkedu* (shall be visited) ought apparently to be understood as denoting a visitation in wrath (like ch. xxix. 6, Ezek. xxxviii. 8; compare *pâkad* followed by an accusative in ch. xxvi. 21, also xxvi. 14, and Ps. lix. 6; *niphkad*, in fact, is never used to signify visitation in mercy), and therefore as referring to the infliction of the final punishment. Hitzig, however, understands it as relating to a visitation of mercy; and in this he is supported by Ewald, Knobel, and Luzzatto. Gesenius, Umbreit, and others, take it to indicate a citation or summons, though without any ground either in usage of speech or actual custom. A comparison of ch. xxiii. 17 in its relation to ch. xxiii. 15[1] favours the second explanation, as being relatively the most correct; but the expression is intentionally left ambiguous. So far as the thing itself is concerned, we have a parallel in Rev. xx. 1-3 and 7-9: they are visited by being set free again, and commencing their old practice once more; but only (as ver. 23 affirms) to lose again directly, before the glorious and triumphant might of Jehovah, the power they have temporarily reacquired. What the apocalyptist of the New Testament describes in detail in Rev. xx. 4, xx. 11 sqq., and xxi., the apocalyptist of the Old Testament sees here condensed into one fact, viz. the enthroning of Jehovah and His people in a new Jerusalem, at which the silvery white moon (*lebânâh*) turns red, and the glowing sun (*chammâh*) turns pale; the two great lights of heaven becoming (according to a Jewish expression) "like a lamp at noonday" in the presence of such glory. Of the many parallels to ver. 23 which we meet with in Isaiah, the most worthy of note are ch. xi. 10 to the concluding clause, "and before His elders is glory" (also ch. iv. 5), and ch. i. 26 (cf. iii. 14), with reference to the use of the word *zekēnim* (elders). Other parallels are ch. xxx. 26, for *chammâh* and *lebânâh*; ch. i. 29, for *châphēr* and *bōsh*; ch. xxxiii. 22, for *mâlak*; ch. x. 12, for "Mount Zion and Jerusalem." We have already spoken at ch. i. 16 of the word *neged*

---

[1] Cf. Targ., Saad., "they will come into remembrance again."

(Arab. *ne'gd*, from *nâgad*, نَجَّد, to be exalted; *vid. opp.* غار, to be pressed down, to sink), as applied to that which stands out prominently and clearly before one's eyes. According to Hofmann (*Schriftbeweis*, i. 320–1), the elders here, like the twenty-four *presbuteroi* of the Apocalypse, are the sacred spirits, forming the council of God, to which He makes known His will concerning the world, before it is executed by His attendant spirits the angels. But as we find counsellors promised to the Israel of the new Jerusalem in ch. i. 26, in contrast with the bad *z^ekēnim* (elders) which it then possessed (ch. iii. 14), such as it had at the glorious commencement of its history; and as the passage before us says essentially the same with regard to the *zekēnim* as we find in ch. iv. 5 with regard to the festal meetings of Israel (*vid.* ch. xxx. 20 and xxxii. 1); and still further, as Rev. xx. 4 (cf. Matt. xix. 28) is a more appropriate parallel to the passage before us than Rev. iv. 4, we may assume with certainty, at least with regard to this passage, and without needing to come to any decision concerning Rev. iv. 4, that the *z^ekēnim* here are not angels, but human elders after God's own heart. These elders, being admitted into the immediate presence of God, and reigning together with Him, have nothing but glory in front of them, and they themselves reflect that glory.

THE FOURFOLD MELODIOUS ECHO.—CHAP. XXV. XXVI.

A. First echo: Salvation of the nations after the fall of the imperial city.—Chap. xxv. 1–8.

There is not merely reflected glory, but reflected sound as well. The melodious echoes commence with ch. xxv. 1 sqq. The prophet, transported to the end of the days, commemorates what he has seen in psalms and songs. These psalms and songs not only repeat what has already been predicted; but, sinking into it, and drawing out of it, they partly expand it themselves, and partly prepare the way for its further extension.

The first echo is ch. xxv. 1–8, or more precisely ch. xxv. 1–5. The prophet, whom we already know as a psalmist from ch. xii., now acts as choral leader of the church of the future, and praises Jehovah for having destroyed the mighty imperial city, and proved Himself a defence and shield against its tyranny towards His oppressed church. Vers. 1-5. "*Jehovah, Thou art my God; I will exalt Thee, I will praise Thy name, that Thou hast wrought wonders, counsels from afar, sincerity, truth. For Thou hast turned it from a city into a heap of stones, the steep castle into a ruin; the palace of the barbarians from being a city, to be rebuilt no more for ever. Therefore a wild people will honour Thee, cities of violent nations fear Thee. For Thou provedst Thyself a stronghold to the lowly, a stronghold to the poor in his distress, as a shelter from the storm of rain, as a shadow from the burning of the sun; for the blast of violent ones was like a storm of rain against a wall. Like the burning of the sun in a parched land, Thou subduest the noise of the barbarians; (like) the burning of the sun through the shadow of a cloud, the triumphal song of violent ones was brought low.*" The introductory clause is to be understood as in Ps. cxviii. 28: Jehovah (*voc.*), my God art Thou. "*Thou hast wrought wonders:*" this is taken from Ex. xv. 11 (as in Ps. lxxvii. 15, lxxviii. 12; like ch. xii. 2, from Ex. xv. 2). The wonders which are now actually wrought are "*counsels from afar*" (*mĕrâchōk*), counsels already adopted afar off, *i.e.* long before, thoughts of God belonging to the olden time; the same ideal view as in ch. xxii. 11, xxxvii. 26 (a parallel which coincides with our passage on every side), and, in fact, throughout the whole of the second part. It is the manifold "counsel" of the Holy One of Israel (ch. v. 19, xiv. 24-27, xix. 12, 17, xxiii. 8, xxviii. 29) which displays its wonders in the events of time. To the verb עָשִׂיתָ we have also a second and third object, viz. אֱמוּנָה אֹמֶן. It is a common custom with Isaiah to place derivatives of the same word side by side, for the purpose of giving the greatest possible emphasis to the idea (ch. iii. 1, xvi. 6). אֱמוּנָה indicates a quality, אֹמֶן an actual fact. What He has executed is the realization of His faithfulness, and the reality of His promises. The imperial city is destroyed. Jehovah, as the first clause which is defined by *tzakeph* affirms, has removed it away from the nature of a city into the condition of a heap of stones. The sentence has its object within itself, and merely gives prominence to the change that has been effected; the *Lamed* is used in the same sense as in ch. xxiii. 13 (cf. xxxvii. 26) · the *min*, as in ch. vii. 8, xvii. 1, xxiii. 1, xxiv. 10.

Mappēlāh, with *kametz* or *tzere* before the tone, is a word that can only be accredited from the book of Isaiah (ch. xvii. 1, xxiii. 13). עִיר, קִרְיָה, and אָמְרוֹ are common parallel words in Isaiah (ch. i. 26, xxii. 2, xxxii. 13, 14); and *zârim*, as in ch. i. 7 and xxix. 5, is the most general epithet for the enemies of the people of God. The fall of the imperial kingdom is followed by the conversion of the heathen; the songs proceed from the mouths of the remotest nations. Ver. 3 runs parallel with Rev. xv. 3, 4. Nations hitherto rude and passionate now submit to Jehovah with decorous reverence, and those that were previously oppressive (*'arītzim*, as in ch. xiii. 11, in form like *pârītzim, shâlīshīm*) with humble fear. The cause of this conversion of the heathen is the one thus briefly indicated in the Apocalypse, " for thy judgments are made manifest" (Rev. xv. 4). דַּל and אֶבְיוֹן (cf. ch. xiv. 30, xxix. 19) are names well known from the Psalms, as applying to the church when oppressed. To this church, in the distress which she had endured (בַּצַּר לוֹ, as in ch. xxvi. 16, lxiii. 9, cf. xxxiii. 2), Jehovah had proved Himself a strong castle (*mâ'ōz*; on the expression, compare ch. xxx. 3), a shelter from storm and a shade from heat (for the figures, compare ch. iv. 6, xxxii. 2, xvi. 3), so that the blast of the tyrants (compare *ruach* in ch. xxx. 28, xxxiii. 11, Ps. lxxvi. 13) was like a wall-storm, *i.e.* a storm striking against a wall (compare ch. ix. 3, a shoulder-stick, *i.e.* a stick which strikes the shoulder), sounding against it and bursting upon it without being able to wash it away (ch. xxviii. 17; Ps. lxii. 4), because it was the wall of a strong castle, and this strong castle was Jehovah Himself. As Jehovah can suddenly subdue the heat of the sun in dryness (*tzâyōn*, abstract for concrete, as in ch. xxxii. 2, equivalent to dry land, ch. xli. 18), and it must give way when He brings up a shady thicket (Jer. iv. 29), namely of clouds (Ex. xix. 9; Ps. xviii. 12), so did He suddenly subdue the thundering (*shâ'on*, as in ch. xvii. 12) of the hordes that stormed against His people; and the song of triumph (*zâmīr*, only met with again in Song of Sol. ii. 12) of the tyrants, which passed over the world like a scorching heat, was soon "brought low" (*'ânâh*, in its neuter radical signification " to bend," related to בָּנָה, as in ch. xxxi. 4).

Thus the first hymnic echo dies away; and the eschatological prophecy, coming back to ch. xxiv. 23, but with deeper prayer-like penetration, proceeds thus in ver. 6: "*And Jehovah of hosts prepares for all nations upon this mountain a feast of fat things, a feast of wines on the lees, of fat things rich in marrow, of wines on the lees thoroughly strained.*" "*This mountain*" is Zion, the seat of God's presence, and the place of His church's worship. The feast is therefore a spiritual one. The figure is taken, as in Ps. xxii. 27 sqq., from the sacrificial meals connected with the *shelâmim* (the peace-offerings). *Sh^emârim m^ezukkâkim* are wines which have been left to stand upon their lees after the first fermentation is over, which have thus thoroughly fermented, and have been kept a long time (from *shâmar*, to keep, *spec.* to allow to ferment), and which are then filtered before drinking (*Gr.* οἶνος σακκίας, i.e. διϋλισμένος or διηθικὸς, from διηθεῖν, *percolare*), hence wine both strong and clear. *Memuchâyīm* might mean *emedullatœ* ("with the marrow taken out;" compare, perhaps, Prov. xxxi. 3), but this could only apply to the bones, not to the fat meat itself; the meaning is therefore "mixed with marrow," made marrowy, *medullosœ*. The thing symbolized in this way is the full enjoyment of blessedness in the perfected kingdom of God. The heathen are not only humbled so that they submit to Jehovah, but they also take part in the blessedness of His church, and are abundantly satisfied with the good things of His house, and made to drink of pleasure as from a river (Ps. xxxvi. 9). The ring of the verse is inimitably pictorial. It is like joyful music to the heavenly feast. The more flexible form מִשְׂחָיִים (from the original, מִשְׂחָי = מִשְׂחָה) is intentionally chosen in the place of מִשְׂחִים. It is as if we heard stringed instruments played with the most rapid movement of the bow.

Although the feast is on earth, it is on an earth which has been transformed into heaven; for the party-wall between God and the world has fallen down: death is no more, and all tears are for ever wiped away. Vers. 7, 8. "*And He casts away upon this mountain the veil that veiled over all peoples, and the covering that covered over all nations. He puts away death for ever; and the Lord Jehovah wipes the tear from every face; and He removes the shame of His people from the whole earth: for Jehovah hath spoken it.*" What Jehovah bestows is followed by what He puts away. The "veil" and "covering" (*massēcâh*, from *nâsac* = *mâsâc*, ch. xxii. 8, from *sâcac*, to weave, twist, and twist over = to cover) are not symbols of mourning and affliction, but of spiritual blindness, like the "veil" upon the heart of Israel mentioned in 2 Cor. iii. 15. The *p'nê hallōt* (cf. Job xli. 5) is the upper side of the veil, the side turned towards you, by which Jehovah takes hold of the veil to lift it up. The second *hallōt* stands for הַלּוֹט (Ges. § 71, Anm. 1), and is written in this form, according to Isaiah's peculiar style (*vid.* ch. iv. 6, vii. 11, viii. 6, xxii. 13), merely for the sake of the sound, like the obscurer *niphal* forms in ch. xxiv. 3. The only difference between the two nouns is this: in *lōt* the leading idea is that of the completeness of the covering, and in *massēcâh* that of its thickness. The removing of the veil, as well as of death, is called בִּלַּע, which we find applied to God in other passages, viz. ch. xix. 3, Ps. xxi. 10, lv. 10. Swallowing up is used elsewhere as equivalent to making a thing disappear, by taking it into one's self; but here, as in many other instances, the notion of receiving into one's self is dropped, and nothing remains but the idea of taking away, unless, indeed, abolishing of death may perhaps be regarded as taking it back into what hell shows to be the *eternal* principle of wrath out of which God called it forth. God will abolish death, so that there shall be no trace left of its former sway. Paul gives a free rendering of this passage in 1 Cor. xv. 54, κατεπόθη ὁ θάνατος εἰς νῖκος (after the Aramæan *n'tzach, vincere*). The Syriac combines both ideas, that of the Targum and that of Paul: *absorpta est mors per victoriam in sempiternum*. But the abolition of death is not in itself the perfection of blessedness. There are sufferings which force out a sigh, even after death has come as a deliverance. But all these sufferings, whose ultimate ground is sin, Jehovah sweeps away. There is something very significant in the use of the expression דִּמְעָה (a tear), which the Apocalypse renders πᾶν δάκρυον (Rev. xxi. 4). Wherever there is a tear on any face whatever, Jehovah wipes it away; and if Jehovah wipes away, this must be done most thoroughly: He removes the cause with the outward symptom, the sin as well as the tear. It is self-evident that this applies to the church triumphant. The world has been judged, and what was salvable has been saved. There is therefore no more shame for the people of God. Over the whole earth there is no further place to be found for this; Jehovah has taken it away. The earth is therefore a holy dwelling-place for blessed men. The new Jerusalem is Jehovah's throne, but the whole earth is Jehovah's glorious kingdom. The prophet is here looking from just the same point of view as Paul in 1 Cor. xv. 28, and John in the last page of the Apocalypse.

B. Second echo: The humiliation of Moab.—Chap. xxv. 9–12.

After this prophetic section, which follows the first melodious echo like an interpolated recitative, the song of praise begins again; but it is soon deflected into the tone of prophecy. The shame of the people of God, mentioned in ver. 8, recalls to mind the special enemies of the church in its immediate neighbourhood, who could not tyrannize over it indeed, like the empire of the world, but who nevertheless scoffed at it and persecuted it. The representative and emblem of these foes are the proud and boasting Moab (ch. xvi. 6; Jer. xlviii. 29). All such attempts as that of Knobel to turn this into history are but so much lost trouble. Moab is a mystic name. It is the prediction of the humiliation of Moab in this spiritual sense, for which the second echo opens the way by celebrating Jehovah's appearing. Jehovah is now in His manifested presence the conqueror of death, the drier of tears, the saviour of the honour of His oppressed church. Ver. 9. "*And they say in that day, Behold our God, for whom we waited to help us: this is Jehovah, for whom we waited; let us be glad and rejoice in His salvation.*" The undefined but self-evident subject to *v'âmar* ("they say") is the church of the last days. "Behold:" *hinnēh* and *zeh* belong to one another, as in ch. xxi. 9. The *waiting* may be understood as implying a retrospective glance at all the remote past, even as far back as Jacob's saying, "I wait for Thy salvation, O Jehovah" (Gen. xlix. 18). The appeal, "Let us be glad," etc., has passed over into the grand *hodu* of Ps. cxviii. 24.

In the land of promise there is rejoicing, but on the other side of the Jordan there is fear of ruin. Two contrasted pictures are placed here side by side. The Jordan is the same as the "great gulf" in the parable of the rich man. Upon Zion Jehovah descends in mercy, but upon the highlands of Moab in His wrath. Vers. 10–12. "*For the hand of Jehovah will sink down upon this mountain, and Moab is trodden down there where it is, as straw is trodden down in the water of the dung-pit. And he spreadeth out his hands in the pool therein, as the swimmer spreadeth them out to swim; but Jehovah forceth down the pride of Moab in spite of the artifices of his hands. Yea, thy steep, towering walls He bows down, forces under, and casts earthwards into dust.*" Jehovah brings down His hand upon Zion (nûach, as in ch. vii. 2, xi. 1), not only to shelter, but also to avenge. Israel, that has been despised, He now makes glorious, and for contemptuous Moab He prepares a shameful end. In the place where it now is (תַּחְתָּיו, as in 2 Sam. vii. 10, Hab. iii. 16, "in its own place," its own land) it is threshed down, stamped or trodden down, as straw is trodden down into a dung-pit to turn it into manure: *hiddûsh*, the *inf. constr.*, with the vowel sound *u*, possibly to distinguish it from the inf. absol. *hiddosh* (Ewald, § 240, *b*). Instead of בְּמוֹ (as in ch. xliii. 2), the *chethib* has בְּמֵי (cf. Job ix. 30); and this is probably the more correct reading, since *madmēnâh*, by itself, means the dunghill, and not the tank of dung water. At the same time, it is quite possible that *b'mo* is intended as a play upon the name *Moab*, just as the word *madmēnâh* may possibly have been chosen with a play upon the Moabitish *Madmēn* (Jer. xlviii. 2). In ver. 11 Jehovah would be the subject, if *b'kirbo* (in the midst of it) referred back to Moab; but although the figure of Jehovah pressing down the pride of Moab, by spreading out His hands within it like a swimmer, might produce the impression of boldness and dignity in a different connection, yet here, where Moab has just been described as forced down into the manure-pit, the comparison of Jehovah to a swimmer would be a very offensive one. The swimmer is Moab itself, as Gesenius, Hitzig, Knobel, and in fact the majority of commentators suppose. "*In the midst of it:*" *b'kirbo* points back in a neuter sense to the place into which Moab had been violently plunged, and which was so little adapted for swimming. A man cannot swim in a manure pond; but Moab attempts it, though without success, for Jehovah presses down the pride of Moab in spite of its artifices (עִם, as in Neh. v. 18; אָרְבּוֹת, written with *dagesh* according to the majority of MSS., from אָרְבָּה, like the Arabic *urbe, irbe*, cleverness, wit, sharpness), *i.e.* the skilful and cunning movement of its hands. Saad. gives it correctly, as *muchâtale*, wiles and stratagems; Hitzig also renders it "machinations," *i.e.* twistings and turnings, which Moab makes with its arms, for the purpose of keeping itself up in the water. What ver. 11 affirms in figure, ver. 12 illustrates without any figure. If the reading were מִשְׂגַּב חוֹמוֹת סִבְצָרֶךָ, the reference would be to Kir-Moab (ch. xv. 1, xvi. 7). But as the text stands, we are evidently to understand by it the strong and lofty walls of the cities of Moab in general.

C. *Third echo : Israel brought back, or raised from the dead.—*Chap. xxvi.

Thus the second hymnic echo has its confirmation in a prophecy against Moab, on the basis of which a third hymnic echo now arises. Whilst on the other side, in the land of Moab, the people are trodden down, and its lofty castles demolished, the people in the land of Judah can boast of an impregnable city. Ver. 1. "*In that day will this song be sung in the land of Judah: A city of defence is ours; salvation He sets for walls and bulwark.*" According to the punctuation, this ought to be rendered, "A city is a shelter for us;" but עִיר עֹז seem rather to be connected, according to Prov. xvii. 19, "a city of strong, *i.e.* of impregnable offence and defence." The subject of יָשִׁית is Jehovah. The future indicates what He is constantly doing, and ever doing afresh; for the walls and bulwarks of Jerusalem (*chēl*, as in Lam. ii. 8, the small outside wall which encloses all the fortifications) are not dead stone, but *yeshuâh*, ever living and never exhausted *salvation* (ch. lx. 18). In just the same sense Jehovah is called elsewhere the wall of Jerusalem, and even a wall of fire in Zech. ii. 9,—parallels which show that *yeshuâh* is intended to be taken as the accusative of the object, and not as the accusative of the predicate, according to ch. v. 6, Ps. xxi. 7, lxxxiv. 7, Jer. xxii. 6 (Luzzatto).

In ver. 1 this city is thought of as still empty: for, like paradise, in which man was placed, it is first of all a creation of God; and hence the exclamation in ver. 2: "*Open ye the gates, that a righteous people may enter, one keeping truthfulness.*" The cry is a heavenly one; and those who open, if indeed we are at liberty to inquire who they are, must be angels. We recal to mind Ps. xxiv., but the scene is a different one. The author of Ps. cxviii. has given individuality to this passage in vers. 19, 20. *Goi tzaddik* (a righteous nation) is the church of the righteous, as in ch. xxiv. 16. *Goi* (nation) is used here, as in ver. 15 and ch. ix. 2 (cf. p. 80), with reference to Israel, which has now by grace become a righteous nation, and has been established in covenant truth towards God, who keepeth truth (*'emunim*, from *'ēmūn*, Ps. xxxi. 24).

The relation of Israel and Jehovah to one another is now a permanent one. Ver. 3. "*Thou keepest the firmly-established mind in peace, peace; for his confidence rests on Thee.*" A gnome (borrowed in Ps. cxii. 7, 8), but in a lyrical connection, and with a distinct reference to the church of the last days. There is no necessity to take יֵצֶר סָמוּךְ as standing for סְמוּךְ יֵצֶר, as Knobel does. The state of mind is mentioned here as designating the person possessing it, according to his inmost nature. יֵצֶר (the mind) is the whole attitude and habit of a man as inwardly constituted, *i.e.* as a being capable of thought and will. סָמוּךְ is the same, regarded as having a firm hold in itself, and this it has whenever it has a firm hold on God (ch. x. 20). This is the mind of the new Israel, and Jehovah keeps it, *shâlom, shâlom* (peace, peace; accusative predicates, used in the place of a consequential clause), *i.e.* so that deep and constant peace abides therein (Phil. iv. 7). Such a mind is thus kept by Jehovah, because its trust is placed in Jehovah. בָּטוּחַ refers to יֵצֶר, according to Ewald, § 149, *d*, and is therefore equivalent to בָּטוּחַ הוּא (cf. Ps. vii. 10, lv. 20), the passive participle, like the Latin *confisus, fretus*. To hang on God, or to be thoroughly devoted to Him, secures both stability and peace.

A cry goes forth again, as if from heaven, exhorting Israel to continue in this mind. Ver. 4. "*Hang confidently on Jehovah for ever: for in Jah, Jehovah, is an everlasting rock.*" The combination *Jah Jehovah* is only met with here and in ch. xii. 2. It is the proper name of God the Redeemer in the most emphatic form. The *Beth essentiæ* frequently stands before the predicate (Ges. § 151, 3); here, however, it stands before the subject, as in Ps. lxviii. 5, lv. 19. In Jah Jehovah (*munach, tzakeph*) there is an everlasting rock, *i.e.* He is essentially such a rock (compare Deut. xxxii. 4, like Ex. xv. 2 for ch. xii. 2).

He has already proved Himself to be such a rock, on which everything breaks that would attack the faithful whom He surrounds. Vers. 5, 6. "*For He hath bent down them that dwell on high; the towering castle, He tore it down, tore it down to the earth, cast it into dust. The foot treads it to pieces, feet of the poor, steps of the lowly.*" Passing beyond the fall of Moab, the fall of the imperial city is celebrated, to which Moab was only an annex (ch. xxv. 1, 2, xxiv. 10-12). The futures are determined by the preterite; and the *anadiplosis*, which in other instances (*e.g.* ch. xxv. 1, cf. Ps. cxviii. 11) links together derivatives or variations of form, is satisfied in this instance with changing the forms of the suffix. The second thought of ver. 6 is a more emphatic repetition of the first: it is trodden down; the oppression of those who have been hitherto oppressed is trodden down.

The righteous, who go astray according to the judgment of the world, thus arrive at a goal from which their way appears in a very different light. Ver. 7. "*The path that the righteous man takes is smoothness; Thou makest the course of the righteous smooth.*" יָשָׁר is an accusative predicate: Thou rollest it, *i.e.* Thou smoothest it, so that it is just as if it had been bevelled with a rule, and leads quite straight (on the derivative *peles*, a level, see at Job xxxvii. 16) and without interruption to the desired end. The song has here fallen into the language of a *mashal* of Solomon (*vid.* Prov. iv. 26, v. 6, 21). It pauses here to reflect, as if at the close of a strophe.

It then commences again in a lyrical tone in vers. 8 and 9: "*We have also waited for Thee, that Thou shouldest come in the path of Thy judgments; the desire of the soul went after Thy name, and after Thy remembrance. With my soul I desired Thee in the night; yea, with my spirit deep within me, I longed to have Thee here: for when Thy judgments strike the earth, the inhabitants of the earth learn righteousness.*" In the opinion of Hitzig, Knobel, Drechsler, and others, the prophet here comes back from the ideal to the actual present. But this is not the case. The church of the last days, looking back to the past, declares with what longing it has waited for that manifestation of the righteousness of God which has now taken place. "The path of Thy judgments:" *'orach mishpâtēkâ* belongs to the *te; venientem* (or *venturum*) being understood. The clause follows the poetical construction בּוֹא אֹרַח, after the analogy of הָלַךְ דֶּרֶךְ. They longed for God to come as a Redeemer in the way of His judgments. The "name" and "remembrance" are the nature of God, that has become nameable and memorable through self-assertion and self-manifestation (Ex. iii. 15). They desired that God should present Himself again to the consciousness and memory of man, by such an act as should break through His concealment and silence. The prophet says this more especially of himself; for he feels himself "in spirit" to be a member of the perfected church. "My soul" and "my spirit" are accusatives giving a more precise definition (Ewald, § 281, c). "*The night*" is the night of affliction, as in ch. xxi. 11. In connection with this, the word *shichēr* (lit. to dig for a thing, to seek it eagerly) is employed here, with a play upon *shachar*. The dawning of the morning after a night of suffering was the object for which he longed, *naphshi* (my soul), *i.e.* with his entire personality (*Psychol.* p. 202), and *ruchi b'kirbi* (my spirit within me), *i.e.* with the spirit of his mind, πνεῦμα τοῦ νοός (*Psychol.* p. 183). And why? Because, as often as God manifested Himself in judgment, this brought men to the knowledge, and possibly also to the recognition, of what was right (cf. Ps. ix. 17). "*Will learn:*" *lâmdu* is a *præt. gnomicum*, giving the result of much practical experience.

Here again the *shir* has struck the note of a *mâshâl*. And proceeding in this tone, it pauses here once more to reflect as at the close of a strophe. Ver. 10. "*If favour is shown to the wicked man, he does not learn righteousness; in the most upright land he acts wickedly, and has no eye for the majesty of Jehovah.*" יֻחַן רָשָׁע is a hypothetical clause, which is left to be indicated by the emphasis, like Neh. i. 8 (Ewald, § 357, *b*): granting that favour (*chēn* = " goodness," Rom. ii. 4) is constantly shown to the wicked man. "*The most upright land:*" '*eretz necochoth* is a land in which everything is right, and all goes honourably. A worthless man, supposing he were in such a land, would still act knavishly; and of the majesty of Jehovah, showing itself in passing punishments of sin, though still sparing him, he would have no perception whatever. The prophet utters this with a painful feeling of indignation; the word *bal* indicating denial with emotion.

The situation still remains essentially the same in vers. 11-13: "*Jehovah, Thy hand has been exalted, but they did not see: they will see the zeal for a people, being put to shame; yea, fire will devour Thine adversaries. Jehovah, Thou wilt establish peace for us: for Thou hast accomplished all our work for us. Jehovah our God, lords besides Thee had enslaved us; but through Thee we praise Thy name.*" Here are three forms of address beginning with Jehovah, and rising in the third to " Jehovah our God." The standpoint of the first is the time before the judgment; the standpoint of the other two is in the midst of the redemption that has been effected through judgment. Hence what the prophet states in ver. 11 will be a general truth, which has now received its most splendid confirmation through the overthrow of the empire. The complaint of the prophet here is the same as in ch. liii. 1. We may also compare Ex. xiv. 8, not Ps. x. 5; (*rûm* does not mean to remain beyond and unrecognised, but to prove one's self to be high.) The hand of Jehovah had already shown itself to be highly exalted (*râmâh*, 3 *pr.*), by manifesting itself in the history of the nations, by sheltering His congregation, and preparing the way for its exaltation in the midst of its humiliation; but as they had no eye for this hand, they would be made to feel it upon themselves as the avenger of His nation. The "zeal for a people," when reduced from this ideal expression into a concrete one, is the zeal of Jehovah of hosts (ch. ix. 6, xxxvii. 32) for His own nation (as in ch. xlix. 8). *Kin'ath 'âm* (zeal for a people) is the object to *yechezû* (they shall see); *v'yēbōshū* (and be put to shame) being a parenthetical interpolation, which does not interfere with this connection. "*Thou wilt establish peace*" (*tishpōt shâlom*, ver. 12) expresses the certain hope of a future and imperturbable state of peace (*pones, stabilies*); and this hope is founded upon the fact, that all which the church has hitherto accomplished (*ma'aseh*, the acting out of its calling, as in Ps. xc. 17, see at ch. v. 12) has not been its own work, but the work of Jehovah *for it*. And the deliverance just obtained from the yoke of the imperial power is the work of Jehovah also. The meaning of the complaint, " other lords beside Thee had enslaved us," is just the same as that in ch. lxiii. 18; but there the standpoint is in the midst of the thing complained of, whereas here it is beyond it. Jehovah is Israel's King. He seemed indeed to have lost His rule, since the masters of the world had done as they liked with Israel. But it was very different now, and it was only through Jehovah ("through Thee") that Israel could now once more gratefully celebrate Jehovah's name.

The tyrants who usurped the rule over Israel have now utterly disappeared. Ver. 14. "*Dead men live not again, shades do not rise again: so hast Thou visited and destroyed them, and caused all their memory to perish.*" The meaning is not that Jehovah had put them to death because there was no resurrection at all after death; for, as we shall see further on, the prophet was acquainted with such a resurrection. In *mēthim* (dead men) and *rephā'im* (shades) he had directly in mind the oppressors of Israel, who had been thrust down into the region of the shades (like the king of Babylon in ch. xiv.), so that there was no possibility of their being raised up or setting themselves up again. The לָכֵן is not argumentative (which would be very freezing in this highly lyrical connection), but introduces what must have occurred *eo ipso* when the other had taken place (it corresponds to the Greek ἄρα, and is used here in the same way as in ch. lxi. 7, Jer. v. 2, ii. 33, Zech. xi. 7, Job xxxiv. 25, xlii. 3). They had fallen irrevocably into Sheol (Ps. xlix. 15), and consequently God had swept them away, so that not even their name was perpetuated.

Israel, when it has such cause as this for praising Jehovah, will have become a numerous people once more. Ver. 15. "*Thou hast added to the nation, O Jehovah, hast added to the nation; glorified Thyself; moved out all the borders of the land.*" The verb יָסַף, which is construed in other cases with עַל, אֶל, here with לְ, carries its object within itself: to add, *i.e.* to give an increase. The allusion is to the same thing as that which caused the prophet to rejoice in ch. ix. 2 (compare ch. xlix. 19, 20, liv. 1 sqq., Mic. ii. 12, iv. 7, Obad. 19, 20, and many other passages; and for *richaktâ*, more especially Mic. vii. 11). Just as ver. 13 recals the bondage in Egypt, and ver. 14 the destruction of Pharaoh in the Red Sea, so ver. 16 recals the numerical strength of the nation, and the extent of the country in the time of David and Solomon. At the same time, we cannot say that the prophet intended to recal these to mind. The antitypical relation, in which the last times stand to these events and circumstances of the past, is a fact in sacred history, though not particularly referred to here.

The *tephillâh* now returns to the retrospective glance already cast in vers. 8, 9 into that night of affliction, which preceded the redemption that had come. Vers. 16–18. "*Jehovah, in trouble they missed Thee, poured out light supplication when Thy chastisement came upon them. As a woman with child, who draws near to her delivery, writhes and cries out in her pangs, so were we in Thy sight, O Jehovah. We went with child, we writhed; it was as if we brought forth wind. We brought no deliverance to the land, and the inhabitants of the world did not come to the light.*" The substantive circumstantial clause in the parallel line, מוּסָרְךָ לָמוֹ, *castigatione tua eos affligente* (לְ as in ver. 9), corresponds to בַּצַּר; and צָקוּן לַחַשׁ, a preterite (צוּק = יָצַק, Job xxviii. 2, xxix. 6, to be poured out and melt away) with *Nun paragogic* (which is only met with again in Deut. viii. 3, 16, the *yekôshûn* in Isa. xxix. 21 being, according to the syntax, the future of *kôsh*), answers to *pâkad*, which is used here as in ch. xxxiv. 16, 1 Sam. xx. 6, xxv. 15, in the sense of *lustrando desiderare*. *Lachash* is a quiet, whispering prayer (like the whispering of forms of incantation in ch. iii. 3); sorrow renders speechless in the long run; and a consciousness of sin crushes so completely, that a man does not dare to address God aloud (ch. xxix. 4). Pregnancy and pangs are symbols of a state of expectation strained to the utmost, the object of which appears all the closer the more the pains increase. Often, says the perfected church, as it looks back upon its past history, often did we regard the coming of salvation as certain; but again and again were our hopes deceived. The first כְּמוֹ is equivalent to כְּ, "*as* a woman with child," etc. (see at ch. viii. 23); the second is equivalent to כַּאֲשֶׁר, "as it were, we brought forth wind." This is not an inverted expression, signifying we brought forth as it were wind; but כְּמוֹ governs the whole sentence in the sense of "(it was) *as if.*" The issue of all their painful toil was like the result of a false pregnancy (*empneumatosis*), a delivery of wind. This state of things also proceeded from Jehovah, as the expression "before Thee" implies. It was a consequence of the sins of Israel, and of a continued want of true susceptibility to the blessings of salvation. Side by side with their disappointed hope, ver. 18 places the ineffectual character of their own efforts. Israel's own doings,—no, they could never make the land into יְשׁוּעֹת (*i.e.*

bring it into a state of complete salvation); and (so might the final clause be understood) they waited in vain for the judgment of Jehovah upon the sinful world that was at enmity against them, or they made ineffectual efforts to overcome it. This explanation is favoured by the fact, that throughout the whole of this cycle of prophecies *yōshbē tēbēl* does not mean the inhabitants of the holy land, but of the globe at large in the sense of "the world" (ver. 21, ch. xxiv. 5, 6). Again, the relation of יִפֹּלוּ to the תַּפִּיל in ver. 19, and the figure previously employed of the pains of child-birth, speak most strongly in favour of the conclusion, that *náphal* is here used for the falling of the fruit of the womb (cf. Wisd. vii. 3, *Il.* xix. 110, καταπεσεῖν and πεσεῖν). And *yōshbē tēbēl* (the inhabitants of the world) fits in with this sense (viz. that the expected increase of the population never came), from the fact that in this instance the reference is not to *the* inhabitants of the earth; but the words signify inhabitants generally, or, as we should say, young, new-born "mortals." The punishment of the land under the weight of the empire still continued, and a new generation did not come to the light of day to populate the desolate land (cf. *Psychol.* p. 414).

But now all this had taken place. Instead of singing what has occurred, the *tephillah* places itself in the midst of the occurrence itself. Ver. 19. " *Thy dead will live, my corpses rise again. Awake and rejoice, ye that lie in the dust! For thy dew is dew of the lights, and the earth will bring shades to the day.*" The prophet speaks thus out of the heart of the church of the last times. In consequence of the long-continued sufferings and chastisements, it has been melted down to a very small remnant; and many of those whom it could once truly reckon as its own, are now lying as corpses in the dust of the grave. The church, filled with hope which will not be put to shame, now calls to itself, "Thy dead will live" (יְחִיוּ מֵתֶיךָ, *reviviscent*, as in תְּחִיַּת הַמֵּתִים, the resurrection of the dead), and consoles itself with the working of divine grace and power, which is even now setting itself in motion: "my corpses will rise again" (נְבֵלָתִי יְקוּמוּן, *nebēlah*: a word without a plural, but frequently used in a plural sense, as in ch. v. 25, and therefore connected with יְקוּמוּן, equivalent to תָּקֹמְנָה: here before a light suffix, with the *ē* retained, which is lost in other cases). It also cries out, in full assurance of the purpose of God, the believing word of command over the burial-ground of the dead, "Wake up and rejoice, ye that sleep in the dust," and then justifies to itself this believing word of command by looking up to Jehovah, and confessing, "Thy dew is dew born out of (supernatural) lights," as the dew of nature is born out of the womb of the morning dawn (Ps. cx. 3). Others render it "dew upon herbs," taking אוֹרוֹת as equivalent to יְרָקוֹת, as in 2 Kings iv. 39. We take it as from אוֹרָה (Ps. cxxxix. 12), in the sense of אוֹר הַחַיִּים. The plural implies that there is a perfect fulness of the lights of life in God ("the Father of lights," Jas. i. 17). Out of these there is born the gentle dew, which gives new life to the bones that have been sown in the ground (Ps. cxli. 7),—a figure full of mystery, which is quite needlessly wiped away by Hofmann's explanation, viz. that it is equivalent to *tal hōrōth*, "dew of thorough saturating." Luther, who renders it, "Thy dew is a dew of the green field," stands alone among the earlier translators. The Targum, Syriac, Vulgate, and Saad. all render it, "Thy dew is light dew;" and with the uniform connection in which the Scriptures place '*or* (light) and *chayyīm* (life), this rendering is natural enough. We now translate still further, " and the earth (*vá'áretz*, as in ch. lxv. 17, Prov. xxv. 3, whereas וְאֶרֶץ is almost always in the construct state) will bring shades to the day" (*hippil*, as a causative of *náphal*, ver. 18), *i.e.* bring forth again the dead that have sunken into it (like Luther's rendering, "and the land will cast out the dead"—the rendering of our English version also: TR.). The dew from the glory of God falls like a heavenly seed into the bosom of the earth; and in consequence of this, the earth gives out from itself the shades which have hitherto been held fast beneath the ground, so that they appear alive again on the surface of the earth. Those who understand ver. 18 as relating to the earnestly descried overthrow of the lords of the world, interpret this passage accordingly, as meaning either, " and thou castest down shades to the earth" (אֶרֶץ, *acc. loci*, = עַד־אֶרֶץ, ver. 5, לָאָרֶץ, ch. xxv. 12), or, "and the earth causeth shades to fall," *i.e.* to fall into itself. This is Rosenmüller's explanation (*terra per prosopopœiam, ut supra* xxiv. 20, *inducta, deturbare in orcum sistitur impios, eo ipso manes eos reddens*). But although *rephaim*, when so interpreted, agrees with ver.

14, where this name is given to the oppressors of the people of God, it would be out of place here, where it would necessarily mean, "those who are just becoming shades." But, what is of greater importance still, if this concluding clause is understood as applying to the overthrow of the oppressors, it does not give any natural sequence to the words, "dew of the lights is thy dew;" whereas, according to our interpretation, it seals the faith, hope, and prayer of the church for what is to follow. When compared with the New Testament Apocalypse, it is "the first resurrection" which is here predicted by Isaiah. The confessors of Jehovah are awakened in their graves to form one glorious church with those who are still in the body. In the case of Ezekiel also (Ez. xxxvii. 1–14), the resurrection of the dead which he beholds is something more than a figurative representation of the people that were buried in captivity. The church of the period of glory on this side is a church of those who have been miraculously saved and wakened up from the dead. Their persecutors lie at their feet beneath the ground.

The judgment upon them is not mentioned, indeed, till after the completion of the church through those of its members that have died, although it must have actually preceded the latter. Thus the standpoint of the prophecy is incessantly oscillating backwards and forwards in these four chapters (xxiv.–xxvii.). This explains the exhortation in the next verses, and the reason assigned. Vers. 20, 21. "*Go in, my people, into thy chambers, and shut the door behind thee; hide thyself a little moment, till the judgment of wrath passes by. For, behold, Jehovah goeth out from His place to visit the iniquity of the inhabitants of the earth upon them; and the earth discloses the blood that it has sucked up, and no more covers her slain.*" The *shīr* is now at an end. The prophet speaks once more as a prophet. Whilst the judgment of wrath (*za'am*) is going forth, and until it shall have passed by (on the *fut. exact.*, see ch. x. 12, iv. 4; and on the fact itself, *acharith hazza'am*, Dan. viii. 19), the people of God are to continue in the solitude of prayer (Matt. vi. 6, cf. Ps. xxvii. 5, xxxi. 21). They can do so, for the judgment by which they get rid of their foes is the act of Jehovah alone; and they are to do so because only he who is hidden in God by prayer can escape the wrath. The judgment only lasts a little while (ch. x. 24, 25, liv. 7, 8, cf. Ps. xxx. 6), a short time which is shortened for the elect's sake. Instead of the dual דְּלָתֶיךָ (as the house-door is called, though not the chamber-door), the word is pointed דְּלָתְךָ (from דְּלָה = דֶּלֶת), just as the prophet intentionally chooses the feminine חֲבִי instead of חֲבֵה. The nation is thought of as feminine in this particular instance (cf. ch. liv. 7, 8); because Jehovah, its avenger and protector, is acting on its behalf, whilst in a purely passive attitude it hides itself in Him. Just as Noah, behind whom Jehovah shut the door of the ark, was hidden in the ark whilst the water-floods of the judgment poured down without, so should the church be shut off from the world without in its life of prayer, because a judgment of Jehovah was at hand. "He goeth out of His place" (verbatim the same as in Mic. i. 3), *i.e.* not out of His own divine life, as it rests within Himself, but out of the sphere of the manifested glory in which He presents Himself to the spirits. He goeth forth thence equipped for judgment, to visit the iniquity of the inhabitant of the earth upon him (the singular used collectively), and more especially their blood-guiltiness. The prohibition of murder was given to the sons of Noah, and therefore was one of the stipulations of "the covenant of old" (ch. xxiv. 5). The earth supplies two witnesses: (1) the innocent blood which has been violently shed (on *dâmim*, see ch. i. 15), which she has had to suck up, and which is now exposed, and cries for vengeance; and (2) the persons themselves who have been murdered in their innocence, and who are slumbering within her. Streams of blood come to light and bear testimony, and martyrs arise to bear witness against their murderers.

Upon whom the judgment of Jehovah particularly falls, is described in figurative and enigmatical words in ch. xxvii. 1: "*In that day will Jehovah visit with His sword, with the hard, and the great, and the strong, leviathan the fleet serpent, and leviathan the twisted serpent, and slay the dragon in the sea.*" No doubt the three animals are emblems of three imperial powers. The assertion that there are no more three animals than there are three swords, is a mistake. If the preposition were repeated in the case of the swords, as it is in the case of the animals, we should have to understand the passage as referring to three swords as well as three animals. But this is not the case. We have therefore to inquire what the three world-powers are; and this question is quite a justifiable one: for we have no reason to rest satisfied with the opinion held by Drechsler, that the three emblems are symbols of ungodly powers in general, of every kind and every sphere, unless the question itself is absolutely unanswerable. Now the *tannin* (the stretched-out aquatic animal) is the standing emblem of Egypt (ch. li. 9; Ps. lxxiv. 13; Ezek. xxix. 3, xxxii. 2). And as the Euphrates-land and Asshur are mentioned in vers. 12, 13 in connection with Egypt, it is immediately probable that the other two animals signify the kingdom of the Tigris, *i.e.* Assyria, with its capital Nineveh which stood on the Tigris, and the kingdom of the Euphrates, *i.e.* Chaldea, with its capital Babylon which stood upon the Euphrates. Moreover, the application of the same epithet Leviathan to both the kingdoms, with simply a difference in the attributes, is suggestive of two kingdoms that were related to each other. We must not be misled by the fact that *náchâsh bâriach* is a constellation in Job xxvi. 13; we have no *lammarôm* (on high) here, as in ch. xxiv. 21, and therefore are evidently still upon the surface of the globe. The epithet employed was primarily suggested by the situation of the two cities. Nineveh was on the Tigris, which was called *Chiddekel*,[1] on account of the swiftness of its course and its terrible rapids; hence Asshur is compared to a serpent moving along in a rapid, impetuous, long, extended course (*bâriach*, as in ch. xliii. 14, is equivalent to *barriach*, a noun of the same form as עָלִיץ, and a different word from *b'riach*, a bolt, ch. xv. 5). Babylon, on the other hand, is compared to a twisted serpent, *i.e.* to one twisting about in serpentine curves, because it was situated on the very winding Euphrates, the windings of which are especially labyrinthine in the immediate vicinity of Babylon. The river did indeed flow straight away at one time, but by artificial cuttings it was made so serpentine that it passed the same place, viz. Arderikka, no less than three times; and according to the

---

[1] In point of fact, not only does تير signify both an arrow and the Tigris, according to the Neo-Persian lexicons, but the old explanation "Tigris, swift as a dart, since the Medes call the Tigris *tozeuma*" (the shot or shot arrow; Eustath. on Dion Perieg. v. 984), is confirmed by the Zendic *tighri*, which has been proved to be used in the sense of arrow or shot (*Yesht* 8, 6, *yatha tighris mainyavaçâo*), *i.e.* like a heavenly arrow.

declaration of Herodotus in his own time, when any one sailed down the river, he had to pass it three times in three days (Ritter, x. p. 8). The real meaning of the emblem, however, is no more exhausted by this allusion to the geographical situation, than it was in the case of "the desert of the sea" (ch. xxi. 1). The attribute of winding is also a symbol of the longer duration of one empire than of the other, and of the more numerous complications into which Israel would be drawn by it. The world-power on the Tigris fires with rapidity upon Israel, so that the fate of Israel is very quickly decided. But the world-power on the Euphrates advances by many windings, and encircles its prey in many folds. And these windings are all the more numerous, because in the prophet's view Babylon is the final form assumed by the empire of the world, and therefore Israel remains encircled by this serpent until the last days. The judgment upon Asshur, Babylon, and Egypt, is the judgment upon the world-powers universally.

D. *The fourth echo: The fruit-bearing vineyard under the protection of Jehovah.*—Chap. xxvii. 2–6.

The prophecy here passes for the fourth time into the tone of a song. The church recognises itself in the judgments upon the world, as Jehovah's well-protected and beloved vineyard. Vers. 2–5. " *In that day*

A merry vineyard—sing it!
I, Jehovah, its keeper,
Every moment I water it.
That nothing may come near it,
I watch it night and day.
Wrath have I none;
O, had I thorns, thistles before me!
I would make up to them in battle,
Burn them all together.
Men would then have to grasp at my protection,
Make peace with me,
Make peace with me."

Instead of introducing the song with, "In that day shall this song be sung," or some such introduction, the prophecy passes at once into the song. It consists in a descending scale of strophes, consisting of one of five lines (vers. 2, 3), one of four lines (ver. 4), and one of three lines (ver. 5). The thema is placed at the beginning, in the absolute case: *cerem chemer.* This may signify a vineyard of fiery or good wine (compare *cerem zaith* in Judg. xv. 5); but it is possible that the reading should be *cerem chemed,* as in ch. xxxii. 12, as the LXX., Targum, and most modern commentators assume. עָנָה לְ signifies, according to Num. xxi. 17, Ps. cxlvii. 7 (cf. Ex. xxxii. 18, Ps. lxxxviii. 1), to strike up a song with reference to anything, —an onomatopoetic word (different from עָנָה, to begin, literally to meet, see p. 156). *Cerem* (the vineyard) is a feminine here, like בְּאֵר, the well, in the song of the well in Num. xxi. 17, 18, and just as Israel, of which the vineyard here is a symbol (ch. iii. 14, v. 1 sqq.), is sometimes regarded as masculine, and at other times as feminine (ch. xxvi. 20). Jehovah Himself is introduced as speaking. He is the keeper of the vineyard, who waters it every moment when there is any necessity (*lirgā'im,* like *labb^ekârim* in ch. xxxiii. 2, every morning), and watches it by night as well as by day, that nothing may visit it. פָּקַד עַל (to visit upon) is used in other cases to signify the infliction of punishment; here it denotes visitation by some kind of misfortune. Because it was the church purified through afflictions, the feelings of Jehovah towards it were pure love, without any admixture of the burning of anger (*ch^emâh*). This is reserved for all who dare to do injury to this vineyard. Jehovah challenges these, and says, Who is there, then, that gives me thorns, thistles! (יִתֵּן לִי = יִתְּנֵנִי, as in Jer. ix. 1, cf. Josh. xv. 19.) The *asyndeton,* instead of שָׁמִיר וָשַׁיִת, which is customary elsewhere, corresponds to the excitement of the exalted defender. If He had thorns, thistles before Him, He would break forth upon them in war, *i.e.* make war upon them (*bâh,* neuter, upon such a mass of bush), and set it all on fire (הִצִּית = הִצִּיה). The arrangement of the strophes requires that we should connect בַּמִּלְחָמָה with אֶפְשָׂעָה (var. אֶפְשְׂעָה), though this is at variance with the accents. We may see very clearly, even by the choice of the expression *bammilchâmâh,* that thorns and thistles are a figurative representation of the enemies of the church (2 Sam. xxiii. 6, 7). And in this sense the song concludes in ver. 5: only by yielding themselves to mercy will they find mercy. אִם with a voluntative following, "unless," as in Lev. xxvi. 41. "*Take hold of:*" *hechĕzik b'*, as in 1 Kings i. 50, of Adonijah, who lays hold of the horns of the altar. "*Make peace with:*" *'âsâh shâlōm l'*, as in Josh. ix. 15. The song closes here. What the church here utters, is the consciousness of the gracious protection of its God, as confirmed in her by the most recent events.

The prophet now adds to the song of the vineyard, by way of explanation,—Ver. 6. "*In future will Jacob strike roots, Israel blossom and bud, and fill the surface of the globe with fruits.*" We may see from הַבָּאִים (*acc. temp.* as in Eccles. ii. 16, equivalent in meaning to "Behold, the days come," Jer. vii. 32, etc.), that the true language of prophecy commences again here. For the active וּמָלְאוּ, compare Jer. xix. 4, Ezek. viii. 17, etc. The prophet here says, in a figure, just the same as the apostle in Rom. xi. 12, viz. that Israel, when restored once more to favour as a nation, will become "the riches of the Gentiles."

JEHOVAH'S CHASTISING AND SAVING COURSE TOWARDS ISRAEL.—CHAP. XXVII. 7–13.

The prophet does not return even now to his own actual times; but, with the certainty that Israel will not be exalted until it has been deeply humbled on account of its sins, he places himself in the midst of this state of punishment. And there, in the face of the glorious future which awaited Israel, the fact shines out brightly before his eyes, that the punishment which God inflicts upon Israel is a very different thing from that inflicted upon the world. Vers. 7, 8. "*Hath He smitten it like the smiting of its smiter, or is it slain like the slaying of those slain by Him? Thou punishedst it with measures, when thou didst thrust it away, sifting with violent breath in the day of the east wind.*" "*Its smiter*" (*maccēhū*) is the imperial power by which Israel had been attacked (ch. x. 20); and "those slain by Him" (הֲרֻגָיו) are the slain of the empire who had fallen under the strokes of Jehovah. The former smote unmercifully, and its slain ones now lay without hope (ch. xxvi. 14). Jehovah smites differently, and it is very different with the church, which has succumbed in the persons of its righteous members. For the double play upon words, see ch. xxiv. 16,

xxii. 18, x. 16. When Jehovah put Israel away (as if by means of a "bill of divorcement," ch. l. 1), He strove against it (ch. xlix. 25), *i.e.* punished it, "*in measure,*" *i.e.* determining the measure very exactly, that it might not exceed the enduring power of Israel, nor endanger the existence of Israel as a nation (cf. *b^emishpât* in Jer. x. 24, xxx. 11, xlvi. 28). On the other hand, Hitzig, Ewald, and Knobel read בְּסַאסְאָה, from a word סַאסְא,[1] related to יָעַע, or even סָאטָא, "when thou didst disturb (or drive forth);" but the traditional text does not indicate any various reading with ה *mappic.*, and the ancient versions and expositors all take the word as a reduplication of סְאָה, which stands here as the third of an ephah to denote a moderately large measure. The clause *hâgâh b^erûchô* is probably regarded as an elliptical relative clause, in which case the transition to the third person can be best explained: "thou, who siftedst with violent breath." *Hâgâh*, which only occurs again in Prov. xxv. 4, signifies to separate, *e.g.* the dross from silver (ch. i. 25). Jehovah sifted Israel (compare the figure of the threshing-floor in ch. xxi. 10), at the time when, by suspending captivity over it, He blew as violently upon it as if the east wind had raged (*vid. Job,* ii. 77). But He only sifted, He did not destroy.

He was angry, but not without love; He punished, but only to be able to pardon again. Ver. 9. "*Therefore will the guilt of Jacob be purged thus; and this is all the fruit of the removal of his sin: when He maketh all altar-stones like chalkstones that are broken in pieces, Astarte images and sun-pillars do not rise up again.*" With the word "therefore" (*lâcēn*) a conclusion is drawn from the expression "by measure." God punished Israel "by measure;" His punishment is a way to salvation: therefore it ceases as soon as its purpose is secured; and so would it cease now, if Israel would thoroughly renounce its sin, and, above all, the sin of all sins, namely idolatry. "Thus" (by this) refers to the בְּשׂוּמוֹ which follows; "by this," namely the breaking to pieces of the altars and images of the moon goddess; or possibly, to speak more correctly, the goddess of the morning-star, and those of the sun-god as well (see ch.

---

[1] Böttcher refers to a Talmudic word, הסיא (to remove), but this is to be pronounced הָפִיא (= הֵפִיעַ), and is, moreover, very uncertain.

xvii. 8). By the fact that Israel put away the fundamental cause of all mischief, viz. idolatry, the guilt for which it had yet to make atonement would be covered, made good, or wiped away (on *cuppar*, see at ch. xxii. 14). The parenthesis (cf. ch. xxvi. 11*b*) affirms that this very consequence would be all the fruit (*cŏl-peri*) desired by Jehovah of the removal of the sin of Israel, which the chastisement was intended to effect.

The prophet said this from out of the midst of the state of punishment, and was therefore able still further to confirm the fact, that the punishment would cease with the sin, by the punishment which followed the sin. Vers. 10, 11. "*For the strong city is solitary, a dwelling given up and forsaken like the steppe: there calves feed, and there they lie down, and eat off its branches. When its branches become withered, they are broken: women come, make fires with them; for it is not a people of intelligence: therefore its Creator has no pity upon it, and its Former does not pardon it.*" The nation without any intelligence (ch. i. 3), of which Jehovah was the Creator and Former (ch. xxii. 11), is Israel; and therefore the fortress that has been destroyed is the city of Jerusalem. The standpoint of the prophet must therefore be beyond the destruction of Jerusalem, and in the midst of the captivity. If this appears strange for Isaiah, nearly every separate word in these two verses rises up as a witness that it is Isaiah, and no other, who is speaking here (compare, as more general proofs, ch. xxxii. 13, 14, and v. 17; and as more specific exemplifications, ch. xvi. 2, 9, xi. 7, etc.). The suffix in "*her* branches" refers to the city, whose ruins were overgrown with bushes. Synonymous with סְעִפִּים, branches (always written with *dagesh* in distinction from סְעָפִים, clefts, ch. ii. 21), is *kâtzir*, cuttings, equivalent to shoots that can be easily cut off. It was a mistake on the part of the early translators to take *kâtzir* in the sense of "harvest" (Vulg., Symm., Saad., though not the LXX. or Luther). As *kâtzir* is a collective term here, signifying the whole mass of branches, the predicate can be written in the plural, *tisshâbarnâh*, which is not to be explained as a singular form, as in ch. xxviii. 3. אוֹתָהּ, in the neuter sense, points back to this: women light it (הֵאִיר, as in Mal. i. 10), *i.e.* make with it a lighting flame (אוֹר) and a warming fire (אוּר, ch. xliv. 16). So desolate does Jerusalem lie, that in the very spot which once swarmed with men a calf now quietly eats the green foliage of the bushes that grow between the ruins; and in the place whence hostile armies had formerly been compelled to withdraw without accomplishing their purpose, women now come and supply themselves with wood without the slightest opposition.

But when Israel repents, the mercy of Jehovah will change all this. Vers. 12, 13. "*And it will come to pass on that day, Jehovah will appoint a beating of corn from the water-flood of the Euphrates to the brook of Egypt, and ye will be gathered together one by one, O sons of Israel. And it will come to pass in that day, a great trumpet will be blown, and the lost ones in the land of Asshur come, and the outcasts in the land of Egypt, and cast themselves down before Jehovah on the holy mountain in Jerusalem.*" I regard every exposition of ver. 12 which supposes it to refer to the return of the captives as altogether false. The Euphrates and the brook of Egypt, *i.e.* the *Wady el-Arish*, were the north-eastern and south-western boundaries of the land of Israel, according to the original promise (Gen. xv. 18 ; 1 Kings viii. 65), and it is not stated that Jehovah will beat on the outside of these boundaries, but within them. Hence Gesenius is upon a more correct track, when he explains it as meaning that " the kingdom will be peopled again in its greatest promised extent, and that as rapidly and numerously as if men had fallen like olives from the trees." No doubt the word *chábat* is applied to the beating down of olives in Deut. xxiv. 20 ; but this figure is inapplicable here, as olives must already exist before they can be knocked down, whereas the land of Israel is to be thought of as desolate. What one expects is, that Jehovah will cause the dead to live within the whole of the broad expanse of the promised land (according to the promise in ch. xxvi. 19, 21). And the figure answers this expectation most clearly and most gloriously. *Chábat* was the word commonly applied to the knocking out of fruits with husks, which were too tender and valuable to be threshed. Such fruits, as the prophet himself affirms in ch. xxviii. 27, were knocked out carefully with a stick, and would have been injured by the violence of ordinary threshing. And the great field of dead that stretched from the Euphrates to the Rhinokoloura,[1] re-

---

[1] *Rhinokoloura* (or *Rhinokoroura*). for the origin of this name of the Wady el-Arish, see Strabo, xvi. 2, 31.

sembled a floor covered over with such tender, costly fruit. There true Israelites and apostate Israelites lay mixed together. But Jehovah would separate them. He would institute a beating, so that the true members of the church would come to the light of day, being separated from the false like grains sifted from their husks. "Thy dead will live;" it is to this that the prophet returns. And this view is supported by the choice of the word *shibboleth*, which combines in itself the meanings of "flood" (Ps. lxix. 3, 16) and "ear" (*sc.* of corn). This word gives a fine dilogy (compare the dilogy in ch. xix. 18 and Hab. ii. 7). From the "*ear*" of the Euphrates down to the Peninsula of Sinai, Jehovah would knock—a great heap of ears, the grains of which were to be gathered together "one by one," *i.e.* singly (in the most careful manner possible; Greek, καθεῖς, καθ' ἕνα). To this risen church there would be added the still living *diaspora*, gathered together by the signal of God (compare ch. xviii. 3, xi. 12). Asshur and Egypt are named as lands of banishment. They represent all the lands of exile, as in ch. xix. 23–25 (compare ch. xi. 11). The two names are emblematical, and therefore not to be used as proofs that the prophecy is within the range of Isaiah's horizon. Nor is there any necessity for this. It is just as certain that the cycle of prophecy in ch. xxiv.–xxvii. belongs to Isaiah, and not to any other prophet, as it is that there are not two men to be found in the world with faces exactly alike.

END OF VOL. I.

www.ingramcontent.com/pod-product-compliance
Lightning Source LLC
Chambersburg PA
CBHW022109300426
44117CB00007B/648